Studies in Classification, Data Analysis, and Knowledge Organization

T0142915

Springer

Berlin
Heidelberg
New York
Hong Kong
London
Milan
Paris
Tokyo

Titles in the Series

H.-H. Bock and P. Ihm (Eds.)
Classification, Data Analysis,
and Knowledge Organization. 1991
(out of print)

M. Schader (Ed.)
Analyzing and Modeling Data
and Knowledge. 1992

O. Opitz, B. Lausen, and R. Klar (Eds.)
Information and Classification. 1993
(out of print)

H.-H. Bock, W. Lenski,
and M. M. Richter (Eds.)
Information Systems and Data
Analysis. 1994 (out of print)

E. Diday, Y. Lechevallier, M. Schader,
P. Bertrand, and B. Burtschy (Eds.)
New Approaches in Classification and
Data Analysis. 1994
(out of print)

W. Gaul and D. Pfeifer (Eds.)
From Data to Knowledge. 1995

H.-H. Bock and W. Polasek (Eds.)
Data Analysis and Information
Systems. 1996

E. Diday, Y. Lechevallier
and O. Opitz (Eds.)
Ordinal and Symbolic Data Analysis.
1996

R. Klar and O. Opitz (Eds.)
Classification and Knowledge
Organization. 1997

C. Hayashi, N. Ohsumi, K. Yajima,
Y. Tanaka, H.-H. Bock, and Y. Baba
(Eds.)
Data Science, Classification,
and Related Methods. 1998

I. Balderjahn, R. Mathar,
and M. Schader (Eds.)
Classification, Data Analysis,
and Data Highways. 1998

A. Rizzi, M. Vichi, and H.-H. Bock
(Eds.)
Advances in Data Science
and Classification. 1998

M. Vichi and O. Opitz (Eds.)
Classification and Data Analysis. 1999

W. Gaul and H. Locarek-Junge (Eds.)
Classification in the Information Age.
1999

H.-H. Bock and E. Diday (Eds.)
Analysis of Symbolic Data. 2000

H. A. L. Kiers, J.-P. Rasson,
P. J. F. Groenen, and M. Schader (Eds.)
Data Analysis, Classification,
and Related Methods. 2000

W. Gaul, O. Opitz and M. Schader
(Eds.)
Data Analysis. 2000

R. Decker and W. Gaul
Classification and Information
Processing at the Turn of the
Millenium. 2000

S. Borra, R. Rocci, M. Vichi,
and M. Schader (Eds.)
Advances in Classification
and Data Analysis. 2001

W. Gaul and G. Ritter (Eds.)
Classification, Automation,
and New Media. 2002

K. Jajuga, A. Sokołowski,
and H.-H. Bock (Eds.)
Classification, Clustering and Data
Analysis. 2002

M. Schwaiger, O. Opitz (Eds.)
Exploratory Data Analysis
in Empirical Research. 2003

Martin Schader · Wolfgang Gaul
Maurizio Vichi
Editors

Between Data Science and Applied Data Analysis

Proceedings of the 26th Annual Conference
of the Gesellschaft für Klassifikation e.V.,
University of Mannheim, July 22–24, 2002

With 167 Figures and 108 Tables

 Springer

Prof. Dr. Martin Schader
Department of Information Systems
University of Mannheim
Schloss
68131 Mannheim
Germany
martin.schader@uni-mannheim.de

Prof. Dr. Wolfgang Gaul
Institute of Decision Theory
University of Karlsruhe
Kaiserstr. 12
76128 Karlsruhe
Germany
wolfgang.gaul@wiwi.uni-karlsruhe.de

Prof. Maurizio Vichi
Department of Statistics
University of Rome
Piazzale Aldo Moro
00185 Rome
Italy
maurizio.vichi@uniroma1.it

ISSN 1431-8814
ISBN 3-540-40354-X Springer-Verlag Berlin Heidelberg New York

Cataloging-in-Publication Data applied for
A catalog record for this book is available from the Library of Congress.
Bibliographic information published by Die Deutsche Bibliothek
Die Deutsche Bibliothek lists this publication in the Deutsche Nationalbibliografie; detailed biblio-
graphic data is available in the Internet at <http://dnb.ddb.de>.

Springer-Verlag Berlin Heidelberg New York
a member of BertelsmannSpringer Science+Business Media GmbH

http://www.springer.de

© Springer-Verlag Berlin · Heidelberg 2003
Printed in Germany

Softcover-Design: Erich Kirchner, Heidelberg

SPIN 10902882   43/3130/DK – 5 4 3 2 1 0 – Printed on acid-free paper

Preface

This volume contains revised versions of selected papers presented during the 26th Annual Conference of the Gesellschaft für Klassifikation GfKl, the German Classification Society. The conference was held at the University of Mannheim, Germany, in July 2002. Martin Schader was the local organizer, Wolfgang Gaul chaired the program committee, and Maurizio Vichi and his colleagues in CLADAG, the Classsification and Data Analysis Group of the Societ Italiana di Statistica, provided strong support during all phases of the conference.

The scientific program of the conference included 137 contributed papers. Moreover, it was possible to recruit eighteen notable and internationally renowned invited speakers for plenary and semi-plenary talks on their current research works regarding the conference topic Between Data Science and Everyday Web Practice or, respectively, on the GfKl members' general fields of interest: "Classification, data analysis, and their application." Thus, the conference, which was traditionally designed as an interdisciplinary event, again provided a large number of scientists and experts from home and abroad with an attractive forum for discussions and the mutual exchange of knowledge.

Besides on traditional subjects, the talks in the different sections focused on topics like Methods of Data Analysis for Finance, Capital Market and Risk Management, Marketing and Market Research, Data and Web Mining, as well as New Media and Recommender Systems.
This suggested the presentation of the papers of the volume in the following six chapters:

- Clustering and Discrimination
- Data Analysis and Statistics
- Data Mining, Information Processing, and Automation
- Finance, Marketing, and Management Science
- Biology, Archaeology, and Medicine

The conference owed much to its sponsors

- AbsolventUM GmbH
- Audi AG
- Deutsche Forschungsgemeinschaft
- Fakultät für Betriebswirtschaftslehre, Universität Mannheim
- Gesellschaft für Klassifikation e.V.
- j&m Management Consulting AG
- Lehrstuhl für Wirtschaftsinformatik III, Universität Mannheim
- Prechel-Stiftung e.V.

- SAS Institute Inc.
- Springer-Verlag
- Universität Mannheim

who helped in many ways. Their generous support is gratefully acknowledged.

Additionally, we wish to express our gratitude towards the authors of the papers in the present volume, not only for their contributions, but also for their diligence and timely production of the final versions of their papers. Furthermore, we thank the reviewers for their careful reviews of the originally submitted papers, and in this way, for their support in selecting the best papers in this publication. We also would like to emphasize the excellent work of the GfKl-2002 team that managed the organization of the conference and helped to prepare the final program as well as this volume. In this context, special thanks are given to Ingo Bayer, Martina Hey, Axel Korthaus, Ingo Ott, Nils Schumacher, and Christoph Stritzke.

Finally, we want to thank Dr. Martina Bihn of Springer-Verlag, Heidelberg, for her support and dedication to the production of this volume.

Mannheim, Karlsruhe, and Rome, April 2003

Martin Schader
Wolfgang Gaul
Maurizio Vichi

Contents

Part I. Clustering and Discrimination

Robust Classification Through the Forward Search 3
Anthony Atkinson, Andrea Cerioli, Marco Riani

Fitting and Smoothing Properties of Length Constrained
Smoothers Applied to Time Series 13
Estela Bee Dagum, Alessandra Luati

Interaction Terms in Non-linear PLS via Additive Spline
Transformation 22
Jean-François Durand, Rosaria Lombardo

Discriminant Analysis With Categorical Variables: A Biplot
Based Approach 30
Sugnet Gardner, Niël le Roux

Efficient Density Clustering Using Basin Spanning Trees 39
Sören Hader, Fred A. Hamprecht

Some Issues on Clustering of Functional Data 49
Salvatore Ingrassia, Andrea Cerioli, Aldo Corbellini

Scalable Clustering of High Dimensional Data 57
David Littau, Daniel Boley

Methods to Combine Classification Trees 65
Rossella Miglio, Gabriele Soffritti

Core-Based Clustering Techniques 74
Hans-Joachim Mucha, Hans-Georg Bartel, Jens Dolata

Combining Regression Trees and Radial Basis Function
Networks in Longitudinal Data Modelling 83
Marilena Pillati, Daniela G. Calò, Giuliano Galimberti

Implementing a new Method for Discriminant Analysis
When Group Covariance Matrices are Nearly Singular 92
Britta Pouwels, Winfried Theis, Christian Röver

Two Approaches for Discriminant Partial Least Squares 100
Robert Sabatier, Myrtille Vivien, Pietro Amenta

Improving the Classification Performance of a Discriminant
Rule by Dealing With Data Cases Having a Substantial
Influence on Variable Selection 109
Sarel Steel, Nelmarie Louw

Classification and Clustering of Vocal Performances 118
Claus Weihs, Uwe Ligges, Jörg Güttner, Petra Hasse-Becker,
Sonja Berghoff

Cluster- and Discriminant Analysis With Both Metric and
Categorial Data 127
Michael Wodny, Bernd Jäger, Karl-Ernst Biebler

Part II. Data Analysis and Statistics

Multivariate Mixture Models Estimation: A Genetic
Algorithm Approach.. 133
Roberto Baragona, Francesco Battaglia

Two-Way Clustering for Contingency Tables: Maximizing
a Dependence Measure 143
Hans-Hermann Bock

Localised Mixtures of Experts for Mixture of Regressions 155
Guillaume Bouchard

A Bayesian Approach for the Estimation of the Covariance
Structure of Separable Spatio-Temporal Stochastic Processes . 165
Silvia Bozza, Anthony O'Hagan

An Algorithm for the HICLAS-R Model...................... 173
Eva Ceulemans, Iven Van Mechelen

Some Applications of Time-Varying Coefficient Models to
Count Data... 182
Monica Chiogna, Carlo Gaetan

On Ziggurats and Dendrograms.............................. 191
Frank Critchley

A Dimensionality Reduction Method Based on Simple Linear
Regressions 201
Luigi D'Ambra, Pietro Amenta, Rosaria Lombardo

Evolutionary Strategies to Avoid Local Mimima
in Multidimensional Scaling 209
Stefan Etschberger, Andreas Hilbert

Principal Component Analysis of Boolean Symbolic Objects .. 218
Paolo Giordani

Multivariate Analysis for Variables of Arbitrary Information
Level 226
Jürgen Hansohm

How Wrong Models Become Useful - and Correct Models
Become Dangerous 235
Christian Hennig

Visualizing Symbolic Data by Closed Shapes 244
Antonio Irpino, Carlo Lauro, Rosanna Verde

LBGU-EM Algorithm for Mixture Density Estimation........ 252
Bambang Heru Iswanto, Bernd Fritzke

Change-Points in Bernoulli Trials With Dependence 261
Joachim Krauth

Two-Mode Clustering Methods: Compare and Contrast 270
Sabine Krolak-Schwerdt

Sensitivity of Graphical Modeling Against Contamination 279
Sonja Kuhnt, Claudia Becker

New Graphical Symbolic Objects Representations in Parallel
Coordinates 288
Carlo N. Lauro, Francesco Palumbo, Alfonso Iodice D'Enza

A Hierarchical Classes Approach to Discriminant Analysis.... 296
Luigi Lombardi, Eva Ceulemans, Iven Van Mechelen

Prediction Optimal Data Analysis by Means of Stochastic
Search 305
Karsten Luebke, Claus Weihs

System Error Variance Tuning in State-Space Models 313
Pietro Mantovan, Andrea Pastore

Corrado Gini and Multivariate Statistical Analysis: The (so
far) Missing Link 321
Paola Monari, Angela Montanari

On Correspondence Analysis of Incomplete Orderings 329
Kalev Pärna

Some Statistical Issues in Microarray Data Analysis 337
Stéphane Robin

Background of the Variability in Past Human Populations:
Selected Methodological Issues 348
Arkadiusz Sołtysiak

Spatial Prediction With Space-Time Models 358
Stefano F. Tonellato

**Part III. Data Mining, Information Processing,
and Automation**

Neural Budget Networks of Sensorial Data 369
Massimo Aria, Ab Mooijaart, Roberta Siciliano

Evolutionary Model Selection in Bayesian Neural Networks .. 378
Silvia Bozza, Pietro Mantovan, Rosa A. Schiavo

Extreme Datamining 387
*Valérie C. Chavez-Demoulin, Stephen A. Jarvis, Rafael Perera,
Armin S.A. Roehrl, Stefan W. Schmiedl, M.P. Sondergaard*

Information Filtering Based on Modal Symbolic Objects...... 395
Francisco de A. T. de Carvalho, Byron L. D. Bezerra

Analyzing Learner Behavior and Performance 405
Karsten Friesen, Hans Schmitz

An Integration Strategy for Distributed Recommender
Services in Legacy Library Systems 412
*Andreas Geyer-Schulz, Michael Hahsler, Andreas Neumann, Anke
Thede*

Comparing Simple Association-Rules and Repeat-Buying Based
Recommender Systems in a B2B Environment 421
Andreas Geyer-Schulz, Michael Hahsler, Anke Thede

Students' Preferences Related to Web Based E-Learning:
Results of a Survey 430
Marc Göcks, Daniel Baier

MURBANDY: The (so far) Missing Link: User-Friendly
Retrieval and Visualization of Geographic Information 438
*Bernd Hermes, Maximilian Stempfhuber, Luca Demicheli, Carlo
Lavalle*

ASCAID: Using an Asymmetric Correlation Measure for
Automatic Interaction Detection 447
Andreas Hilbert

Discriminative Clustering: Vector Quantization in Learning
Metrics 456
Samuel Kaski, Janne Sinkkonen

Neural Network Hybrid Learning: Genetic Algorithms &
Levenberg-Marquardt 464
Ricardo B. C. Prudêncio, Teresa B. Ludermir

Syntagmatic and Paradigmatic Associations in Information
Retrieval 473
Reinhard Rapp

Finding the Most Useful Clusters: Clustering and the
Usefulness Metric 483
Caroline St. Clair

Internet Thesaurus - Extracting Relevant Terms from WWW
Pages using Weighted Threshold Function over a Cross-Reference
Matrix 492
Raz Tamir

Reflections on a Supervised Approach to Independent
Component Analysis 501
Cinzia Viroli

Simulated Annealing and Tabu Search for Optimization of
Neural Networks 510
Akio Yamazaki, Teresa B. Ludermir, Marcilio C. P. de Souto

Part IV. Finance, Marketing, and Management Science

Decentralizing Risk Management in the Case of Quadratic
Hedging 521
*Julia Bondarenko, Nicole Branger, Angelika Esser, Christian
Schlag*

Multimedia Stimulus Presentation Methods for Conjoint
Studies in Marketing Research 530
Michael Brusch, Daniel Baier

Forecasting the Customer Development of a Publishing
Company with Decision Trees 538
Andreas Hilbert, Alexander Spatz

Estimation of Default Probabilities in a Single-Factor Model .. 546
Steffi Höse, Stefan Huschens

Simultaneous Confidence Intervals for Default Probabilities... 555
Steffi Höse, Stefan Huschens

Model-Based Clustering With Hidden Markov Models
and its Application to Financial Time-Series Data 561
*Bernhard Knab, Alexander Schliep, Barthel Steckemetz, Bernd
Wichern*

Classification of Multivariate Data With Missing Values
Using Expected Discriminant Scores 570
Wolfgang Kossa

Assessment of the Polish Manufacturing Sector
Attractiveness: An End-User Approach 578
Dorota Kwiatkowska-Ciotucha, Józef Dziechciarz

Developing a Layout of a Supermarket Through Asymmetric
Multidimensional Scaling and Cluster Analysis of Purchase
Data.. 587
Akinori Okada, Tadashi Imaizumi

Market Segmentation Method From the Bayesian Viewpoint . 595
Kazuo Shigemasu, Takuya Ohmori, Takahiro Hoshino

Support Vector Machines for Credit Scoring: Comparing to
and Combining With Some Traditional Classification Methods 604
Ralf Stecking, Klaus B. Schebesch

Part V. Biology, Archaeology, and Medicine

Classification of Amino-Acid Sequences Using State-Space
Models 615
Marcus Brunnert, Tillmann Krahnke, Wolfgang Urfer

Quantitative Study of Images in Archaeology: I. Textual
Coding 624
Sergio Camiz, Elena Rova

Quantitative Study of Images in Archaeology: II. Symbolic
Coding 633
Sergio Camiz, Elena Rova, Vanda Tulli

Power Functions in Multiple Sampling Plans Using DNA
Computation 643
*Carles Capdevila, M. Angels Colomer, Josep Conde, Josep Miret,
Alba Zaragoza*

Methodological Issues in the Baffling Relationship Between Hepatitis C Virus and Non Hodgkin's Lymphomas .. 652
Stefano De Cantis, Daria Mendola, Emilio Iannitto

Class Discovery in Gene Expression Data: Characterizing Splits by Support Vector Machines................................ 662
Florian Markowetz, Anja von Heydebreck

Efficient Clustering Methods for Tumor Classification With Microarrays 670
Jörg Rahnenführer

A Method to Classify Microarray Data 680
Marco Scarnó, Donatella Sforzini, Alessandra Ulivieri, Sergio Nasi

Index 689

Part I

Clustering and Discrimination

Robust Classification Through the Forward Search

Anthony Atkinson[1], Andrea Cerioli[2], and Marco Riani[2]

[1] Department of Statistics, London School of Economics,
London WC2A 2AE, UK
[2] Dipartimento di Economia, Sezione di Statistica e Informatica,
Università di Parma, Via J. Kennedy 6, 43100 Parma, Italy

Abstract. The forward search is a powerful robust method for identifying the structure of data and for determining the classification of each unit and its effect on the classification of other units. We use plots of the Mahalanobis distances of the individual observations during the search to obtain our classification. Normality of the data is important, so we present a multivariate form of the Box-Cox family of transformations, of course combined with the forward search.

1   Introduction

This paper summarises joint research on the forward search, a powerful general method for detecting unidentified subsets and multiple masked outliers and for determining their effect on models fitted to the data. Atkinson and Riani (2000) describe its use in linear and nonlinear regression, response transformation and in generalized linear models. These examples are here extended to include the difficult problems of classification and cluster analysis. They are described more fully in the forthcoming book by Atkinson, Riani and Cerioli (2003).

In most examples we fit one multivariate normal distribution to the data, which is sufficient, in combination with the forward search, to reveal the structure. The first example, with two clusters, is analysed in §2, using the methods of the forward search described in §3. Unlike standard robust methods, the forward search reveals the presence of the clusters. Section 4 is an analysis of measurements of Swiss heads. In §5 we calibrate our method with an example with three clusters. Analyses of two further examples are outlined in §6. The final sections discuss the importance of transformations in model-based multivariate data analysis.

2   The 60:80 data and failure of the minimum covariance determinant

Figure 1 of Atkinson (2002) shows a scatterplot of 140 data points, 80 from a rather diffuse group and 60 from a tight cluster. The pattern is obvious to the unaided eye. The purpose of classification is to detect such groups, usually when the number of groups is unknown. This can be a difficult task for high dimensional data. But it would not seem to be particularly challenging when there are just two dimensions. However, when we fit a single model to these data, neither standard classical methods nor very robust diagnostic methods unambiguously show that there are two different groups of observations.

The main diagnostic tools that we use are various plots of Mahalanobis distances. The squared distances for the sample are defined as

$$d_i^2 = \{y_i - \hat{\mu}\}^T \hat{\Sigma}^{-1} \{y_i - \hat{\mu}\}, \tag{1}$$

where $\hat{\mu}$ and $\hat{\Sigma}$ are estimates of the mean and covariance matrix of the n observations.

Figure 2(a) of Atkinson (2002) shows a QQ plot of the Mahalanobis distances from the fit to all the data. This plot fails to give any indication of the existence of two clusters of observations. The same is true of the plot of the distances from a very robust fit in his Figure 2(b) using parameter estimates from the "fast" algorithm of Rousseeuw and Van Driessen (1999).

The evidence from this example is that both standard and very robust methods can fail to indicate the presence of clusters in data. We now look at diagnostics based on the forward search which do reveal the existence of groups.

3   The forward search

The parameters μ and Σ are estimated by maximum likelihood applied to a subset of m observations to give the estimates $\hat{\mu}(m)$ and $\hat{\Sigma}(m)$. From this subset we obtain n squared Mahalanobis distances

$$d_i^2(m) = \{y_i - \hat{\mu}(m)\}^T \hat{\Sigma}^{-1}(m) \{y_i - \hat{\mu}(m)\}. \tag{2}$$

We start the search with a small subset of m_0 observations, chosen from the robust bivariate boxplots of Zani, Riani and Corbellini (1998) to exclude outlying observations in any two-dimensional plot of the data. The content of the contours is adjusted to give an initial subset of the required size. The search is not sensitive to the exact choice of this subset.

When m observations are used in fitting, the optimum subset $S^*(m)$ yields n squared distances $d_i^2(m^*)$. We order these squared distances and take the observations corresponding to the $m+1$ smallest as the new subset $S^*(m+1)$. Usually this process augments the subset by one observation, but sometimes two or more observations enter as one or more leave. Due to the form of the search, outliers, if any, tend to enter as m approaches n.

In our examples we look at forward plots of the distances $d_i(m^*)$. These distances tend to decrease as n increases. If interest is in the latter part of the search we may also look at **scaled** distances

$$d_i(m^*) \times \left(|\hat{\Sigma}(m^*)| / |\hat{\Sigma}(n)| \right)^{1/2p}, \tag{3}$$

where p is the dimension of the observations y and $\hat{\Sigma}(n)$ is the estimate of Σ at the end of the search.

Such a rescaling increases emphasis on the later parts of forward plots. Thus, for detecting initial clusters, the original distances may be better, whereas for a confirmatory analysis, where we are interested in the possible presence of outliers or undetected small clusters, we might prefer scaled distances.

In the confirmatory part of our analysis we run a forward search fitting an individual model for each cluster. For all unassigned observations we calculate the distance from each cluster centre. Observations are included in the subset of the cluster to which they are nearest and the distances to all cluster centres are monitored.

Unfortunately we may be comparing Mahalanobis distances for compact and dispersed clusters. A forward allocation can then lead to a dispersed group "invading" a compact group with a wrong allocation of several observations. We therefore introduce standardized distances, adjusted for the variance of the individual cluster. The customary squared Mahalanobis distance for the ith observation from the gth group at step m is

$$d_{gi}^2(m) = \{y_{gi} - \hat{\mu}_g(m)\}^T \hat{\Sigma}_g^{-1}(m)\{y_{gi} - \hat{\mu}_g(m)\}, \qquad (4)$$

where μ and Σ are estimated for each group. The **standardized** distance is

$$d_{gi}(m) = d_{gi}(m)|\hat{\Sigma}_{gm}|^{1/2p}, \qquad (5)$$

in which the effect of differing variances between groups has been completely eliminated. These distances will produce measures close to Euclidean distance, with the consequence that compact clusters may tend to "invade" dispersed ones, the reverse of the behaviour with the usual Mahalanobis distance. We therefore need to look at plots of both distances.

4   Swiss heads

As a first example of the use of forward plots we start with data which seem to have a single multivariate normal distribution. The data, given by Flury and Riedwyl (1988, p.218), are six readings on the dimensions of the heads of 200 twenty year old Swiss soldiers. The forward plot of scaled distances in Figure 1(a) shows little structure. The rising diagonal white band separates those units which are in the subset from those that are not. At the end of the search there seem to be two outliers, observations 104 and 111.

A plot of unscaled distances is in Figure 1(b). As we would expect, these are initially larger and decrease more rapidly with m than the scaled distances in Figure 1(a), although the general shape is similar. In the figure we highlight the evolution of the distances for units 104 and 111. These are the largest at the end of the search, but rank much lower on size earlier in the search. This atypical behaviour during the search is a useful way of detecting outliers or units that have been classified into an incorrect group.

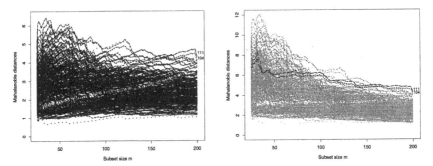

Fig. 1. Swiss Heads: forward plots of Mahalanobis distances, (a) scaled distances and (b) unscaled distances with trajectories for units 104 and 11 highlighted

5   Three clusters, two outliers

We continue to consider analyses of simulated data sets in order to understand the properties of the forward search and to train our eyes to the interpretation of the plots.

The data are an extension of the 60:80 data of §2 to include a third cluster and two outliers. The sizes of the groups are 60, 80, 18 and 2. This example shows how extra information can be obtained by using several forward searches with different starting points. Our first search starts with $m_0 = 28$, the observations being chosen by the method of bivariate boxplots. The forward plot of unscaled Mahalanobis distances in Figure 2(a) is particularly clear up to $m = 60$: the second group of 80 observations is well separated from the first, the distances of the compact group of 18 are evident at the top of the plot and the two outliers follow an independent path. Once the second group starts to enter at $m = 61$ the smaller distances are not so readily interpreted, although the group of 18 remains distinct. The two outliers re-emerge at the very end of the plot.

We do not have to plot all the Mahalanobis distances. Figure 2(b) is a forward plot of the minimum Mahalanobis distances amongst units not in the subset. This clearly shows the end of the first cluster through the sharp spike at $m = 60$. At this point the next observation to enter the subset is far from the tight cluster which has been found. The second spike at $m = 142(= 60+80+2)$ is a rather less clear indication of the second group; the spike at the end of the plot clearly shows the presence of the two outliers.

To illustrate the effect of the starting point of the search we now begin with 20 observations from the cluster of 80 indicated in Figure 2(a). The forward plot of scaled Mahalanobis distances is in Figure 3. It is amazingly informative. The first part of the plot, up to $m = 80$ seems to show two groups and two outliers. Something is clearly wrong with fitting a single model around $m = 100$: there are perhaps two clusters, of different sizes than before. The

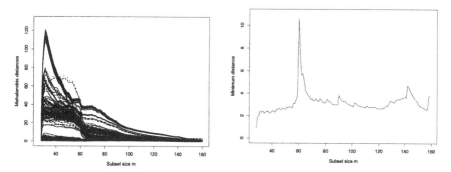

Fig. 2. Three clusters, two outliers: forward plot of Mahalanobis distances $m_0 = 28$; (a) unscaled distances and (b) minimum Mahalanobis distances amongst units not in the subset

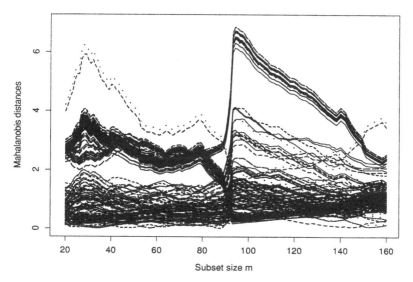

Fig. 3. Three clusters, two outliers: forward plot of scaled Mahalanobis distances from the forced start. All the structure is revealed

transition between these two parts of the plot is fascinating. Above $m = 80$ the seemingly larger cluster splits into two parts. One becomes the group of 18 outliers in the latter part of the plot. The other becomes the group of 60 with the smallest distances in the latter part of the plot. Thus the plot reveals the three groups and two outliers, which reappear at the end of the search. This one plot shows all the structure that we have built into the data. The indication is that we may need to run more than one forward search, constraining the starting point by the information that we have obtained from earlier searches.

6   Swiss banknotes and diabetes

The structure of the data in the previous example was made very clear partly because the clusters were well defined. In some real examples this is so, in others not. We look very briefly at one of each kind.

As a second non-simulated example we take readings on six dimensions of 200 Swiss bank notes, 100 of which may be genuine and 100 forged. All notes have been withdrawn from circulation, so some of the notes in either group may have been misclassified. Also, the forged notes may not form a homogeneous group, since there may be more than one forger at work. The data, and a reproduction of the bank note, are given by Flury and Riedwyl (1988, p.4-8).

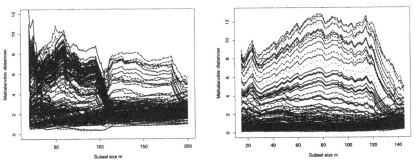

Fig. 4. Forwards plots of scaled Mahalanobis distances: (a) Swiss banknote data. Three groups are evident; (b) diabetes data. The three groups overlap

Figure 4(a) shows the scaled Mahalanobis distances from a forward search starting with 20 observations on notes believed genuine. In the first part of the search, up to $m = 93$, the observations seem to fall into two groups. One has small distances and is composed of observations within or shortly to join the subset. Above these there are some outliers and then, higher still, a concentrated band of outliers, all of which are behaving similarly. Around $m = 100$ there is a clear change as units believed to be forgeries join the subset. The pattern is then stable until around $m = 185$, when the effect of a third, unsuspected, group becomes apparent.

This example is similar to that of §5 in that a forward plot of scaled Mahalanobis distances is enough to reveal the structure of the data. The data can then be split into notes believed genuine and those that are thought to be forgeries, both of which are then analysed separately. Fuller details of this analysis are in Atkinson (2002).

Our third example is of 145 observations on diabetes patients, which have been used in the statistical literature as a difficult example of cluster analysis. A discussion is given, for example, by Fraley and Raftery (1998). There are three measurements on each patient The observations were classified into three clusters by doctors, but we ignore this information in our analysis. The scatterplot matrix of the data shows no obvious breaks between clusters, so that we can expect our plots to yield less sharp answers than those for the previous examples. The forward plot of Mahalanobis distances in Figure 4(b) has some strange features. There is a shortage of very small distances and overall the distances arguably fall into three groups: there is a gap between the largest distances and the rest around $m = 70$, these largest distances being rather uniformly distributed. Around $m = 45$ it looks as if there is a gap between the smallest distances and those which are somewhat larger, which again have a rather uniform distribution. These impressions are confirmed by a QQ plot of Mahalanobis distances.

Further analysis is described by Atkinson (2002). This includes separate analysis of each tentative group combined with the monitoring of distances for individual units as in Figure 1(b) from a variety of starting points. The final confirmatory stage is to classify the few remaining units about which we are still uncertain, using standardised distances as well as unstandardised ones. Not all units can be unambiguously classified, but the classification suggested appears to be an improvement on the original one provided by the doctors.

7 Finding a transformation with the forward search

Transformations of the data can be used to help satisfy the assumptions of multivariate normality. We have found that extension of the Box and Cox (1964) family to multivariate responses often leads to a significant increase in normality, and so to a simplified analysis of the data. We let y_{ij} be the i-th observation on response j; $j = 1, \ldots, p$. The normalized transformation of y_{ij} is

$$z_{ij}(\lambda_j) = \frac{y_{ij}^{\lambda_j} - 1}{\lambda_j G_j^{\lambda_j - 1}} \qquad (\lambda \neq 0) \tag{6}$$

$$= G_j \log y_{ij} \qquad (\lambda = 0) \tag{7}$$

where G_j is the geometric mean of the j-th variable. The value $\lambda_j = 1$ corresponds to no transformation of any of the responses. If the transformed observations are normally distributed with mean $\mu(\lambda)$ and covariance matrix $\Sigma(\lambda)$, the loglikelihood of the observations is given by:

$$l(\lambda) = -\frac{n}{2} \log 2\pi |\Sigma(\lambda)| - \frac{1}{2} \sum_{i=1}^{n} \{z_i - \mu(\lambda)\}^T \Sigma^{-1}(\lambda) \{z_i - \mu(\lambda)\}, \tag{8}$$

where $z_i = (z_{i1}, \ldots z_{ip})^T$ is the $p \times 1$ vector which denotes the transformed data for unit i. Substituting the maximum likelihood estimates $\hat{\mu}(\lambda)$ and $\hat{\Sigma}(\lambda)$ in equation (8), the maximized log likelihood can be written as:

$$l(\lambda) = \text{constant} - n/2 \log|\hat{\Sigma}(\lambda)|. \tag{9}$$

To test the hypothesis $\lambda = \lambda_0$, the likelihood ratio test

$$T_{LR} = n \log\{|\hat{\Sigma}(\lambda_0)|/|\hat{\Sigma}(\hat{\lambda})|\} \tag{10}$$

can be compared with the χ^2 distribution on p degrees of freedom. In equation (10) the maximum likelihood estimate $\hat{\lambda}$ is found by numerical search.

Atkinson and Riani (2000, Chapter 4) use the forward search to find satisfactory transformations for a single variable, if such exist, and the observations that are influential in their choice. For multivariate transformations Riani and Atkinson (2001) monitor a sequence of forward plots of test statistics (10) and parameter estimates to obtain transformations which described most of the data, with the outliers entering at the end of the searches.

8   Horse mussels

In our final example, the effect of the outliers is masked unless the search uses a suitable transformation. We therefore have to use a series of searches, the parameter values for the transformation in successive searches being guided by the results of previous searches.

The data, introduced by Cook and Weisberg (1994, p.161), are five measurements on each of 82 horse mussels from New Zealand. Some pairwise scatterplots of the data are decidedly curved, indicating that there is plenty for a transformation to do in achieving normality. We see whether multivariate normality can be obtained by joint transformation of all five variables. We start with a forward search with untransformed data. Figure 5(a) is the forward plot of the resulting estimates of λ. The estimates all trend down at the end of the search, indicating the continuing introduction of units which are further and further from the untransformed multivariate normal model. The general shape of the curves towards the end of the search suggests we might try $\lambda = (1, 0.5, 1, 0, 1/3)^T$. The forward search shows that this transformation is almost acceptable for all the data. However it is not acceptable at some earlier stages in the search. The behaviour of the estimates suggests we try $\lambda = (0.5, 0, 0.5, 0, 0)^T$, a stronger transformation than before.

This transformation does very well. The likelihood ratio test shows that it is supported by all the data except the outliers, which enter at the end of the search. The forward plot of the parameter estimates in Figure 5(b) shows that, until $m = 79$, three of the parameter estimates are stable around zero and two around 0.5. Use of fan plots confirms these individual values of λ. We now compare the data after the transformation $\lambda = (0.5, 0, 0.5, 0, 0)^T$ with that without transformation. One feature is that the transformation has

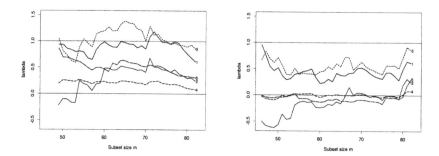

Fig. 5. Horse mussels: forward plots of the five elements of the estimate $\hat{\lambda}$. (a) search on untransformed data suggesting that at least three variables should be transformed; (b) search with $\lambda_R = (0.5, 0, 0.5, 0, 0)^T$. The estimates are stable until the outliers enter at the end of the search

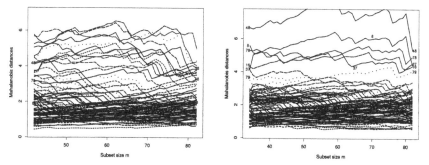

Fig. 6. Horse mussels; untransformed data. Forward plot of scaled Mahalanobis distances, showing many outliers. Horse mussels; transformed data, $\lambda = (0.5, 0, 0.5, 0, 0)^T$. Forward plot of scaled Mahalanobis distances, showing six well-separated outliers

separated the outliers from the bulk of the data as is seen by a comparison of forward plots of scaled Mahalanobis distances. Figure 6(a) shows that for the untransformed data, there is a large number of outliers without any apparent structure, which do not reduce in number as the search progresses. But, after transformation, Figure 6(b), there is a much clearer group of six outliers, two of which are particularly remote.

This is a canonical example of our approach to finding a multivariate transformation in the potential presence of outliers and influential observations. Riani and Atkinson (2001) use the same procedure to find transformations for discriminant analysis where a different multivariate normal distribution is fitted to each population to be classified.

A .pdf version of Atkinson (2002) can be found at `http://stat.econ.unipr` `it/sis2002`

References

ATKINSON, A. C. (2002): Robust Diagnostics for Multivariate Analysis and Classification Problems: *Società Italiana di Statistica. Atti della XLI Riunione Scientifica: Sessioni Plenarie & Specializzate.* Padova, CLEUP, 283–294.

ATKINSON, A.C. and RIANI, M. (2000): *Robust Diagnostic Regression Analysis.* Springer-Verlag, New York.

ATKINSON, A.C., RIANI, M. and CERIOLI, A. (2003): *Robust Diagnostic Multivariate Data Analysis.* Springer-Verlag, New York (in preparation).

BOX, G. E. P. and COX, D. R. (1964): An Analysis of Transformations (with Discussion). *Journal of the Royal Statistical Society Series B, 26,* 211–246.

COOK, R. D. and WEISBERG, S. (1994): *An Introduction to Regression Graphics.* Wiley, New York.

FLURY, B. and RIEDWYL, H. (1988): *Multivariate Statistics: A Practical Approach.* Chapman and Hall, London.

FRALEY, C. and RAFTERY, A. E. (1998): How Many Clusters? Which Clustering Method? – Answers via Model-based Cluster Analysis. *Computer Journal, 41,* 578–588.

RIANI, M. and ATKINSON, A C. (2001): A Unified Approach to Outliers, Influence and Transformations in Discriminant Analysis. *Journal of Computational and Graphical Statistics, 10,* 513-544.

ROUSSEEUW, P. J. and VAN DRIESSEN, K. (1999): A Fast Algorithm for the Minimum Covariance Determinant Estimator. *Technometrics, 41,* 212–223.

ZANI, S., RIANI, M., and CORBELLINI, A. (1998): Robust Bivariate Boxplots and Multiple Outlier Detection. *Computational Statistics and Data Analysis, 28,* 257–270.

Fitting and Smoothing Properties of Length Constrained Smoothers Applied to Time Series

Estela Bee Dagum and Alessandra Luati

Department of Statistics,
University of Bologna, Italy

Abstract. We study the fitting and smoothing properties of several non parametric smoothers restricted to be all of the same length for the trend-cycle (signal) estimation of time series. The fitting property is evaluated in terms of the mean square error (MSE), and that of smoothing in terms of the sum of squares of the third differences of the predicted values. These properties are studied for each symmetric (applied to central observations) and asymmetric (for the most recent data point) smoother. The analysis is done on the basis of the results obtained on a large sample of simulated and real-life time series (adjusted for seasonality) characterized by different degrees of signal-to-noise ratio.

1 Introduction

Non parametric estimators have often been applied to smooth noisy data. Henderson (1916) and Macaulay (1931) are some of the earliest classical references. These authors were very much concerned with linear estimators, Henderson being the first to show that the smoothing power of a linear filter depends on the shape of its weighting system. The Henderson smoothing filters, based on summation formulae mainly used by actuaries, are often applied for trend estimation in time series decomposition.

Similarly to the Henderson filters, graduation theory is the basis of the original work on smoothing spline functions. Whittaker (1923) proposed a graduation method that basically consisted of a trade-off between fitting and smoothing. The theoretical properties and the empirical performance of the cubic smoothing spline related to the Henderson filters have been analyzed by Dagum and Capitanio (1998).

Other widely applied smoothers belong to two classes of weight generating functions, local polynomials and probability distributions. Local polynomial fitting has a long history in the smoothing of time series. Cleveland (1979) developed a locally weighted regression smoother known in the current literature as loess and originally called lowess (LOcally WEighted Scatterplot Smoother). Further contributions can be found in Lejeune (1985), Cleveland et al. (1990), Fan (1993), and Dagum and Luati (2000).

On the other hand, kernel estimators are mainly used in probability density estimation for it is known that if a kernel function is continuous and differentiable, the corresponding output inherits the same properties (see among several others, Priestley and Chao, 1972; Nadaraya, 1964; Gasser, Muller and Mammitzsch, 1985; Hastie and Tibshirani, 1990; Wand and Jones, 1995). Recently, De Gooijer and Zerom (2000) studied the forecasting performance of some kernel estimators for financial data and Dagum and Luati (2001) investigated the impact that fixing both the smoothing parameters and the length of the bandwidth have on the smoothing properties of kernel-based methods.

The statistical properties of the above smoothers have been thoroughly studied for optimally selected smoothing parameters, where optimality is defined in terms of minimizing a given loss function, usually, the mean square error or the prediction risk.

In general, when the smoothing parameters are estimated by data-driven automated procedures, the span of the smoother tends to be large and, thus, a large number of end points can be estimated only with asymmetric weights. These latter have the undesirable property of introducing revisions in the more recently estimated values as new observations are added as well as phaseshifts in cyclical turning points. To avoid these shortcomings, we constrain all the smoothers to be of the fixed length of 13 terms, in agreement with the classical Henderson filter widely applied for trend-cycle estimation. In this manner, all the smoothers become linear and do not depend on the data they will be applied on. However, the imposed constraint affects their optimal properties of fitting and smoothing, as shown theoretically by Dagum and Luati (2002a, 2002b).

The main purpose of this study is to evaluate the fitting and smoothing properties of various constrained smoothers applied to a large sample of simulated and real-life data with different degrees of variability. Our benchmark is the classical 13-term Henderson filter (H13). The smoothers considered are second order kernels and higher order estimators. We discuss, within the first class, the locally weighted regression smoother (loess) of degree 1 (L1) and the Gaussian kernel (GK); and, in the second class, the cubic smoothing spline (CSS), the loess of degree 2 (L2) and the Henderson smoothing linear filter (H13). For each of them, we applied the symmetric and asymmetric (end point) 13-term filters to a wide sample of simulated and real life series characterized by different degrees of noise. We studied their fitting and smoothing properties by means of the mean square error and the sum of squares of the third order differences of the estimated series, respectively.

Section 2 introduces briefly the constrained smoothers analyzed. Section 3 gives the fitting and smoothing measures to be used for a comparative analysis. Section 4 presents the empirical analysis and, finally, section 5 gives the conclusions.

2   Length constrained non parametric smoothers

In time series analysis, it is often assumed that a time series $\{y_t\}_{t=1,...,N}$, $N < \infty$, is decomposed as the sum of a signal, $g(t)$, plus an erratic component, u_t, that is, $y_t = g(t) + u_t$, where $g(t)$ can be either deterministic or stochastic and u_t usually follows a stationary stochastic process with zero mean and constant variance σ_u^2. The most common assumption for u_t is that of a white noise but, more generally, it can be assumed that it follows an Autoregressive Moving Average $(ARMA)$ process.

The signal $g(t)$ can be estimated through a smoothing function $\widehat{g}_\eta(t)$, where η is a smoothing parameter that determines the degree of smoothness of the estimated values.

For fixed values of the smoothing parameter, $\eta = \eta_0$, any estimator $\widehat{g}_{\eta_0}(t)$ becomes linear and estimation of $g(t)$ results from applying, in a moving manner, a finite number of weights to the observations, such that, for $m < t \leq N - m$, that is, $\widehat{g}_{\eta_0}(t) = \sum_{j=-m}^{m} w_j y_{t+j}$, where the length of the symmetric filter, $2m + 1$, is determined by η_0. Hence, $\widehat{g}_{\eta_0}(t)$ can be interpreted equivalently as: (a) a non parametric estimator of $g(t)$ and (b) a smooth estimate of the value y_t, say $\widehat{y}_t$, resulting from a $2m + 1$-term symmetric moving average of neighboring observations. For the first and last m observations only asymmetric filters can be used, such that, e.g., the last observation $\widehat{y}_N$ is estimated by $\widehat{g}(N) = \sum_{j=-m}^{0} w_j y_{N+j}$.

We calculated the symmetric and asymmetric weights of the constrained smoothers based on the following formulae (refer to Dagum and Luati, 2000, for more details).

For the loess of degree d, the vector of weights to be applied to the 13 observations neighboring and including each y_j in order to produce the estimated $\widehat{y}_j$ is calculated by

$$\mathbf{S}_j = \mathbf{t}_j^T \left(\mathbf{T}_j^T \mathbf{W}_j \mathbf{T}_j \right)^{-1} \mathbf{T}_j^T \mathbf{W}_j$$

where $\mathbf{t}_j^T = \left[1 \; t_j \; \ldots \; t_j^d \right]$, $\mathbf{T}_j$ is a $13 \times (d+1)$ matrix of t_ks belonging to each 13-term neighborhood $N(t_j)$ of t_j, and $\mathbf{W}_j$ is the 13×13 diagonal matrix of weights $w_k(t_j) = W \left(\dfrac{|t_j - t_k|}{\max\limits_{t_k \in N(t_j)} |t_j - t_k|} \right)$ based on the tricube weighting function $W(x) = \left(1 - |x|^3 \right)^3 \mathbb{I}_{\{[0,1[\}}(x)$.

The weights of the Gaussian kernel are obtained by

$$w_{hj} = \frac{K \left(\frac{t_h^* - t_j}{b} \right)}{\sum_{i=1}^{N} K \left(\frac{t_h^* - t_i}{b} \right)}$$

where $K \left(\frac{t_h^* - t_j}{b} \right) = \frac{1}{\sqrt{2\pi}} \exp \left\{ -\frac{1}{2} \left(\frac{t_h^* - t_j}{b} \right)^2 \right\}$ and b is the smoothing parameter which determines the filter span and denotes the standard deviation of the Gaussian distribution function. For an approximation of the weights to three decimal points, the span is equal to $6b + 1$ or equivalently to $6\sigma + 1$ and therefore we have chosen $b = 2$.

The weights of the cubic smoothing spline constitute the rows of the matrix

$$\mathbf{S}_{\lambda_0} = \left[\mathbf{I}_N - \mathbf{D}^T \left(\frac{1}{\lambda_0}\mathbf{B}+\mathbf{DD}^T\right)^{-1} \mathbf{D}\right]$$

where λ_0 is the (fixed) smoothing parameter, here equal to 0.2, $\mathbf{I}_N$ is the $N \times N$ identity matrix, $\mathbf{B}$ and $\mathbf{D}$ are respectively $(N-2) \times (N-2)$ and $(N-2) \times N$ matrices whose elements depend on the distance between the target points t_j and can be easily calculated setting $t_j = j, j = 1, \ldots, N$.

The Henderson symmetric weights are obtained from the general formula for a filter of length $2k - 3$,

$$w_j = \frac{315 \left[(k-1)^2 - j^2\right] (k^2 - j^2) \left[(k+1)^2 - j^2\right] (3k^2 - 16 - 11j^2)}{8k (k^2 - 1) (4k^2 - 1) (4k^2 - 9) (4k^2 - 25)}$$

by making $k = 8$ for $j = 1, \ldots, 13$.

The Henderson asymmetric weights, available in software like $CensusX11$, $X11ARIMA$ and $X12ARIMA$, are based on the minimization of the mean squared revision between the final estimates (obtained by the application of the symmetric filter) and the preliminary estimates (obtained by the application of an asymmetric filter) subject to the constraint that the sum of the weights is equal to one (see Dagum and Luati, 2002b, and references therein).

The weights up to three decimals (for space reasons) are shown in tables 1 and 2 below.

L1	0.006	0.032	0.066	0.097	0.115	0.122	**0.123**
L2	-0.015	-0.036	-0.004	0.074	0.157	0.210	**0.227**
CSS	0.001	-0.001	-0.010	-0.023	0.022	0.250	**0.522**
GK	0.001	0.007	0.023	0.060	0.121	0.183	**0.210**
H13	-0.019	-0.028	0.000	0.066	0.147	0.214	**0.240**

Table 1. Symmetric weights of 13-term length constrained smoothers (central weight in bold).

L1	-0.018	0.030	0.085	0.142	0.199	0.254	**0.308**
L2	-0.099	-0.085	-0.029	0.067	0.201	0.371	**0.574**
CSS	0.002	0.002	-0.008	-0.037	-0.038	0.201	**0.879**
GK	0.002	0.011	0.038	0.100	0.199	0.302	**0.347**
H13	-0.092	-0.058	0.012	0.120	0.244	0.353	**0.421**

Table 2. Asymmetric weights of 13-term length constrained smoothers (last point weight in bold).

It is apparent that L1 and GK are second order kernels for they satisfy the conditions $\sum_{j=-m}^{m} w_j = 1$, $\sum_{j=-m}^{m} jw_j = 0$ and $\sum_{j=-m}^{m} j^2 w_j \neq 0$, whereas the remaining are higher order estimators. In fact, besides the conditions of adding up to unity and of symmetry, these latter satisfy $\sum\limits_{j=-m}^{m} j^p w_j \neq 0$ for some even $p > 2$.

Next, we give the measures of fitting and smoothing used for the comparative analysis with real and simulated data.

3 Fitting and smoothing properties

As a **measure of fitting**, we use the mean square error given by

$$MSE = \frac{1}{N} \sum_{t=1}^{N} (\widehat{y}_t - y_t)^2$$

where y_t denotes the original observations and $\widehat{y}_t$ the predicted values.

As a **measure of smoothing**, we use the sum of the squares of the third order differences of the predicted values

$$Q = \sum_{t=4}^{N} \left(\Delta^3 \widehat{y}_t\right)^2$$

where $\Delta = 1 - B$ is the ordinary difference operator. The smaller Q, the closer $\Delta^3 \widehat{y}_t$ is to zero and the closer the estimated curve $\widehat{y}_t$ is to a second order polynomial in t.

In general, the smaller the MSE of an estimator, the higher is its corresponding smoothness value. This is essentially due to the fact that Q does not depend on the bias and variance of the estimated series but on the amount of noise present. In fact, the gain function of the filter Δ^3 suppresses the power corresponding to the frequency band $0 \leq \omega \leq 0.06$, usually attributed to the signal, and amplifies the power of the remainder, attributed to the noise. Hence, if a smoother leaves a lot of noise in the estimated $\widehat{y}_t$, it also produces a high value of Q. On the other hand, a filter which removes all the noise, even if at the expenses of the signal, gives a small value of Q. For these reasons it is important to consider the two measures of fitting and smoothing simultaneously.

According to these criteria, the estimator to be preferred is the one which gives the 'best compromise' between the values of the MSE and Q.

Since our benchmark is H13, the best compromise for symmetric filters is here defined as the one producing a smoothing measure greater than H13 (in our tables this means values of Q smaller than one) without increasing the MSE by more of 10%. It should be noted that these conditions favor the smoothing property of each estimator with a small loss in the goodness of fit. Since the asymmetric filters are always of shorter length than their corresponding symmetric ones, both the Q values and the MSE tend to be smaller. Consequently, we define as best compromise for the asymmetric filters, the estimator that, among those giving standardized Q values smaller than one, produces the minimum MSE. It should be noted here that, for asymmetric filters, the conditions for best compromise favor MSE since, as well known, short filters are usually applied to obtain appropriate fitted values. On the other hand, long filters are preferred for smoothing.

4   An empirical analysis

The symmetric and asymmetric weights reported in tables 1 and 2 have been implemented with the software MATLAB and, then, applied to each series of the data set. The latter is composed of 100 simulated and real-life time series characterized by different degrees of noise. Twenty simulated series are obtained with an unobserved component structural model where the trend follows a random walk without drift, plus a linear combination of sines and cosines for the business cycle; and the irregulars are assumed to be Gaussian white noise. The remaining 80 real life series are monthly seasonally adjusted socio-economic data. Results are shown for real and simulated series, and for three Canadian leading indicators discussed in Dagum (1996).

Symmetric	Real	series	Asymmetric	Real	series
	MSE	Q		MSE	Q
L1	1.47	0.18	**L1**	0.86	0.53
GK	1.06	0.57	**GK**	0.73	0.57
L2	1.05	1.34	**L2**	1.35	2.25
H13	1	1	**H13**	1	1
CSS	0.42	53.54	**CSS**	1.14	7.57

Table 3. Fitting and smoothing measures for symmetric and asymmetric smoothers applied to a set of real time series characterized by various degrees of variability (mean values, standardized by H13).

Table 3 illustrates the values of MSE and Q when symmetric and asymmetric filters are applied to real time series. All the values given there as well as in all the following tables are standardized by those of H13 to facilitate the smoothers comparison. Table 4 gives the values for simulated time series with small and high level of noise, and table 5 illustrates the impact of the filters on three Canadian leading indicators. These are New Order for Durable Goods (NODG), Average Workweek in Manufacturing (AWM), House Spending Index (HSI), characterized by low, medium and high signal to noise ratio, respectively. Concerning the **symmetric filters**, table 3 shows the standardized values of MSE and Q calculated on a set of real time series. The minimum MSE is that of CSS whereas the maximum is that of L1. Conversely, symmetric CSS and L1 show the greatest and smallest standardized values of Q, respectively. The MSE values of the remaining filters are close to one-another whereas the values of Q are more variable, giving GK the smallest, followed by H13 and L2.

Symmetric	Simulated **small noise** MSE	Q	Simulated **high noise** MSE	Q
L1	1.25	0.14	1.96	0.12
GK	1	0.59	1.19	0.56
L2	1	1.50	1.04	1.19
H13	1	1	1	1
CSS	0.58	77.68	0.35	28.62
Asymmetric				
L1	0.85	0.54	0.88	0.52
GK	0.77	0.61	0.75	0.63
L2	1.21	2.25	1.5	2.17
H13	1	1	1	1
CSS	1.13	8.43	1.13	7.80

Table 4. Fitting and smoothing measures for symmetric and asymmetric smoothers applied to a set of simulated series characterized by small and high variability (mean values, standardized by H13).

Symmetric	Series: **NODG** MSE	Q	Series: **AWM** MSE	Q	Series: **HSI** MSE	Q
L1	1.41	0.10	1	0.00	2.17	0.09
GK	1.09	0.46	1	0.5	1.25	0.52
L2	1.02	1.27	1	1.5	1.08	1.12
H13	1	1	1	1	1	1
CSS	0.54	52.04	0	46	0.33	20.96
Asymmetric						
L1	0.86	0.55	0.89	0.55	0.82	0.50
GK	0.74	0.62	0.78	0.65	0.73	0.61
L2	1.34	2.28	1.44	2.28	1.28	2.11
H13	1	1	1	1	1	1
CSS	1.10	8.76	1.22	8.83	1.03	7.38

Table 5. Fitting and smoothing measures for symmetric and asymmetric smoothers applied to three Canadian leading indicators characterized by small, medium and high signal-to-noise ratio (values standardized by H13).

The same smoothers ranking, where second order estimators are favored for smoothing whereas higher order estimators are better for fitting, is maintained when considering simulated series with small noise (see table 4). Similar conclusions can be drawn from the series NODG in table 5.

Same results are obtained when the level of noise increases as also shown in table 4 and by AWM and HSI of table 5, but the differences in MSE

values tend to be larger. The fitting performance of second order estimators seems to decrease when the level of noise increases without major variations in their smoothing properties.

The symmetric filter that systematically gives the best compromise between fitting and smoothing is GK followed by H13. CSS gives the best fit and L1 the greatest smoothness.

Except for the CSS, the standardized Q produced by the **asymmetric filters** are much higher than those derived from the corresponding symmetric filters. The reason lies in the fact that asymmetric filters are of much shorter span than the symmetric ones and, thus, will smooth less. Concerning the MSE, the second order kernels give a better fit but the remaining smoothers have larger values than the respective symmetric ones. In fact, tables 3 and 4b show that GK and L1 have the smallest values for both MSE and Q, followed by H13. The asymmetric CSS looses its good fitting performance and remains the worst for smoothing.

5   Conclusions

We analyzed the fitting and smoothing properties of several nonparametric smoothers restricted to be of a fixed 13-term length for the trend-cycle (signal) estimation of time series.

The symmetric GK and the H13 filters gave the best compromise between fitting and smoothing. In general, for symmetric filters, second order kernels were the best for smoothing, whereas higher order showed a better fitting performance. On the contrary, the constraint on the span to 13 terms destroyed the optimal smoothing properties of the CSS, that almost perfectly fitted the input series but passed a large amount of noise, for both symmetric and asymmetric filters.

The results were different for the fixed-length asymmetric (last point) filters, where GK and L1 turned out to be the best for both fitting and smoothing, being H13 in the third position.

In summary, for symmetric filters, the constrained GK showed the best compromise for fitting and smoothing followed by H13. L1 seemed to oversmooth giving the largest MSE value and the opposite was observed for CSS.

For the asymmetric (last point) filter, GK and L1 gave the best results, followed by H13. The noise levels did not affect the smoothers ranking.

References

CLEVELAND W.S. (1979): Robust Locally Weighted Regression and Smoothing Scatterplots, *JASA*, 74, pp. 829-836.

CLEVELAND R., CLEVELAND W.S., MCRAE J.E. and TERPERNNING I. (1990): STL: A Seasonal-Trend Decomposition Procedure Based on Loess. *Journal of Official Statistics*, 6, pp.3-33.

DAGUM. E. B. (1996): A New Method to Reduce Unwanted Ripples and Revisons in Trend-cycle Estimates from X11ARIMA, *Survey Methodology*, 22, n.1, 77-83.

DAGUM E.B. and CAPITANIO A. (1998): Smoothing Methods for Short-Term Trend Analysis: Cubic Splines and Henderson Filters, *Statistica*, anno LVIII, n. 1, pp. 5-24.

DAGUM E. B. and LUATI A. (2000): Predictive Performance of Some Linear and Nonlinear Smoothers for Noisy Data. *Statistica*, anno LX, 4, pp. 635-654.

DAGUM E. B. and LUATI A. (2001): A Study of the Asymmetric and Symmetric Weights of Kernel Smoothers and their Spectral Properties. *Estadistica, Journal of the Interamerican Statistical Institute*, vol. 53, 160-161, pp. 215-258.

DAGUM E.B. and LUATI A. (2002a): Smoothing Seasonally Adjusted Time Series, *Proc. of the Bus. and Econ. Stat. Sec. of the A.S.A* (forthcoming).

DAGUM E.B. and LUATI A. (2002b): Global and Local Statistical Properties of Fixed-Length Nonparametric Smoothers, *Statistical Methods and Applications* (forthcoming).

DE GOOIJER J.G. and ZEROM D. (2000): Kernel-Based Multistep-Ahead Predictions of the U.S. Short-Term Interest Rate, *Journal of Forecasting*, 19, pp. 335-353.

FAN J. (1993): Local Linear Regression Smoothers and their Minimax Efficiencies, *Annals of Statistics*, 21, pp. 196-216.

GASSER T. MULLER H.G. and MAMMITZSCH V. (1985): Kernels for Nonparametric Curve Estimation, *Journal of the Royal Statistical Society B*, 47, pp. 238-252.

HASTIE T.J. and TIBSHIRANI R.J. (1990): *Generalized Additive Models*, Chapman and Hall, London.

HENDERSON R. (1916): Note on Graduation by Adjusted Average. *Transaction of the Actuarial Society of America*, 17, pp. 43-48.

LEJEUNE M. (1985): Estimation Non-paramétrique par Noyaux: Régressions Polynomial Mobile, *Revue Statistique Appliquée*, 33, pp. 43-67.

MACAULAY F.R. (1931) *The Smoothing of Time Series*. NBER, New York.

NADARAYA E.A. (1964): On Estimating Regression, *Theory of Probability and Applications*, 9, pp. 141-142.

PRIESTLEY M.B. and CHAO M.T. (1972): Non-Parametric Function Fitting, *Journal of the Royal Statistical Society B*, 4, pp. 385-392.

WAND M.P. and JONES M.C. (1995): *Kernel Smoothing*. Monographs on Statistics and Applied Probability, 60, Chapman&Hall.

WHITTAKER E.T. (1923): On a New Method of Graduation. *Proceedings of the Edinburgh Mathematical Association*, 78, pp. 81-89.

Acknowledgment: Financing from MURST is gratefully acknowledged.

Interaction Terms in Non-linear PLS via Additive Spline Transformation

Jean-François Durand[1] and Rosaria Lombardo[2]

[1] Laboratoire de Probabilités et Statistique,
University of Montpelier II, France
E-Mail: jfd@helios.ensam.inra.fr
[2] Department of Accounting and Quantitative Methods,
II University of Naples, Italy
E-Mail: rosaria.lombardo@unina2.it

Abstract. This paper aims to extend the non-linear additive Partial Least Squares model via Spline transformation (PLSS,Durand 2001) to the detection and introduction of significant interaction terms as linear manifolds of multivariately transformed variables (Lombardo & van Rijckevorsel 2000).

1 Introduction

In a typical Partial Least Squares regression (Wold 1966, Tenenhaus 1998) one assumes that there exists an underlying linear relationship between the response and predictor variables. Sometimes there is reason to doubt this assumption and a non-linear transformation of the variables might be useful to reveal the model underlying the data, producing a linear relationship among the transformed variables. This paper introduces a generalization of PLSS, the non-linear additive Partial Least Squares model via spline transformation (Durand 2001) by the inclusion of variable interactions. Additive splines for PLS regression are based on the transformation of each predictor by B-spline functions. In this paper, the additive model involves both univariate and multivariate B-spline transformations. The use of interaction terms in this new version of PLSS means looking for functions of two or more variables which help to understand a complex and or noisy relationship. The interaction degree depends on the number of variables involved in the analysis. In this first exercise in order not to heavy the computational burden of the procedure, we focus on the bivariate interactions. The usual strategy to select the optimal interaction terms (MARS, Friedman 1991) implies a forward and a backward phase: to let the forward phase produce a complete number of predictors and then have the backward one trim the model back to an appropriate size. In the PLS component based regression context, taking into account the whole set of main effects and interactions terms can theoretically be envisaged. However, the price to be payed by PLSS for interactions through tensor products of B-spline functions which is tantamount to expending the column dimension of the new design matrix, is excessive when the method is applied on typical PLS number of predictors. A selection of interaction candidates is proposed that is based on a criterion depending on both goodness-of-fit and goodness-of-prediction.

Piecewise polynomials or splines extend the advantages of polynomials to include flexibility and local effect of parameter changes. Due to local B-spline basis functions, the PLSS model is resistant to the presence of extreme values of the predictors. Note that locating knots in empty regions is well accepted by PLSS since regressions are made on uncorrelated components that are linear compromises of centered univariate and multivariate B-spline functions.

In the second section we briefly reviewed PLSS, while the detection and importance of interaction terms is illustrated in section 3. The details of the computational procedure are presented in section 4. In the last section a real example illustrates the capabilities of PLS on a sensory data set in the presence of outliers and non-linear interactions.

2 Modelling main effects by Partial Least Squares through Splines

Let $\mathbf{Y} = [Y^1|..|Y^q]$ be the quantitative or categorical $n \times q$ response matrix and $\mathbf{X} = [X^1|..|X^p]$ the $n \times p$ observation matrix of the predictors on the same n statistical units. Various articles have been presented in literature to generalize PLS in the non-linear framework, most of them replace the standard regression with non linear functions (Wold, Kettaneh-Wold, Skagerberg 1989, Durand & Sabatier 1997). In this paper we enhance a recently devised non-linear additive model for PLS via B-spline transformations that is called PLSS (Durand 2001), so introducing a non parametric character in the PLS regression. In short, PLSS is defined as the usual linear PLS regression of $\mathbf{Y}$ onto the space spanned by the centered coding matrix $\mathbf{B} = [\mathbf{B}^1|..|\mathbf{B}^p]$ ($n \times r$ matrix), whose columns are constructed by transforming the predictors through B-spline basis functions (De Boor 1978)

$$PLSS(\mathbf{X}, \mathbf{Y}) = PLS(\mathbf{B}, \ \mathbf{Y}) .$$

Notice that Principal Component Analysis (PCA) can be seen as a "self-PLS" regression of $\mathbf{X}$ onto itself. Then, in the same way as a particular property, comparing PLSS with Non-Linear Principal Component Analysis (NLPCA, Gifi 1990), we can say that NLPCA can be considered as a "self-PLS" of the coding matrix $\mathbf{B}$ onto itself

$$PLSS(\mathbf{X}, \mathbf{Y} = \mathbf{B}) = PLS(\mathbf{B}, \mathbf{Y} = \mathbf{B}) = PCA(\mathbf{B}) = NLPCA(\mathbf{X}) .$$

In the multivariate context, the column dimension of the column centered coding matrix $\mathbf{B}$ is the sum $r = \sum_{j=1}^{p} r_j$, where r_j, the column dimension of the block $\mathbf{B}^j$, is given by $r_j = d_j + K_j$ if d_j denotes the degree of the local polynomial and K_j the number of interior knots. Using B-spline functions, we can simultaneously treat variables of different nature (qualitative and quantitative) and at the same time we warrant against the presence of extreme values of the predictors since B-spline functions have a local support. A multi-response additive spline model is a fit of the form

$$\hat{Y}_A^i = \sum_{j=1}^{p} s_A^{i,j}(X^j) = \sum_{j=1}^{p} \mathbf{B}^j \hat{\beta}_A^{i,j} \quad \text{(for} \quad i = 1, .., q\text{)}$$

where the spline function $s_A^{i,j}$ measures the additive influence of the predictor X^j on the response Y^i and depends on the number A of the carried out components. This is an univariate spline function summing over all single variable basis functions involving only x_j. When the number A is equal to the rank of $\mathbf{B}$, then PLSS is identical to the usual Least-Squares Splines estimator, see Durand (2000). The risk of overfitting related to an increasing column dimension for the new design matrix $\mathbf{B}$ is well supported by PLSS which inherits the advantages of the standard PLS method.

The non-linear additive influence of the predictors on the ith response is interpreted by looking at the most significant coordinate function plots $(x^j, s_A^{i,j}(x^j))$. In practice, the selection of predictors can be reached by means of different strategies (Durand 2000): ordering in decreasing order the range of $s_A^{i,j}(X^j)$ for $j = 1, \ldots, p$, or grouping the predictors with the same coordinate shape.

The building-model stage consists of finding a balance between "goodness" (of fit and prediction) and "thriftiness" (of dimension for both the number A of PLSS components and r the total dimension). In order to evaluate the goodness-of-fit, we look at the criterion $R^2(A)$, that is the proportion of the total $\mathbf{Y}$ variance accounted for by the PLSS components $t^1, .., t^A$:

$$R^2(A) = \frac{1}{q} \sum_{i=1}^{q} R^2(Y^i, span(t^1, .., t^A))$$

which is an increasing function of A. In the same way the construction of the $PRESS^i(A)$ criterion, identical to that of the usual PLS regression, is computed for each response, while the total $PRESS(A) = \sum_{i=1}^{q} PRESS^i(A)$ is a function of A expected to be firstly decreasing. In conclusion to avoid overfitting problems, we look for parsimonious models with the best values of both $R^2(A)$ and $PRESS(A)$ criteria.

3   Interaction terms in non-linear Partial Least Squares

The problem to replace complex and/or noisy relationships between variables in order to reveal the model underlying the data is a vast topic in literature. To generalize PLS, Hoskuldsson (1988) discussed a model with quadratic and interaction terms in the original variables. In the present paper we propose to include interaction terms not involving the original variables but the non-linearly transformed ones. Suppose we have three chemical substances, two of them react into a new polluting hazardous substance correlated to the third one. The coordinate-wise product of two of the variables is correlated, our problem is to identify the best interaction terms out of all possible interactions, avoiding multicollinearity problems.

The higher order interactions in non-linear PLS allow to detect dependencies i.e. interactions among variables, using multivariate transformations. The use of interaction terms means looking for functions of two or more variables. The order number of interaction depends on the number of variables involved in the analysis. In this paper the adopted functions are bivariate splines, which are tensor products of B-spline univariate functions.

In order to investigate more complex interrelationships, the PLSS fit is casted in the following ANOVA decomposition which is the sum of the main effects and the accepted bivariate interactions

$$\hat{Y}_A^i = \sum_{j=1}^p s_A^{i,j}(X^j) + \sum_{(j,j') \in \mathcal{I}} s_A^{i,jj'}(X^j, X^{j'}) \tag{1}$$

where $\mathcal{I}$ is the set of the accepted couples of interactions. A bivariate ANOVA interaction $s_A^{i,jj'}(X^j, X^{j'})$ is a linear compromise of $\mathbf{B}^{jj'}$, the $n \times (r_j r_{j'})$ centered matrix of the tensor product of columns in both $\mathbf{B}^j$ and $\mathbf{B}^{j'}$, respectively. It represents the joint bivariate contribution of X^j and $X^{j'}$ to the model. This model is obtained by the PLS regression of the standardized responses Y on centered spline transformations $\mathbf{B} = [\mathbf{B}^1 \dots \mathbf{B}^p | \dots \mathbf{B}^{jj'} \dots]$. The computational cost is clearly related to the increase of the column dimension for the new design matrix $\mathbf{B}$, which depends on the dimension of the spline space for the predictors and on the detected interactions.

The tuning parameters of the model are now: 1) the degree, number and location knots, 2) the number of components, 3) the interactions accepted by the building-model stage.

Let us firstly detail the first phase of the selection based on the individual evaluation of all possible bivariate interactions. When A is fixed, the criterion for accepting one candidate interaction is based on the gain in fit and prediction compared to that from the model with only the main effects. Denoting "m", and "m+i", the models including respectively the main effects and the main effects plus one interaction, then, the criterion used to evaluate that interaction, i, is defined by

$$CRIT(A) = \frac{R_{m+i}^2(A) - R_m^2(A)}{R_m^2(A)} + \frac{PRESS_m(A) - PRESS_{m+i}(A)}{PRESS_m(A)}$$

Note that the second term in the sum is generally larger than the first when $R_m^2(A)$ is close to one, that is when the main effects fit is good. One interaction is accepted if $CRIT > 0$, thus providing a natural selection procedure to decide on how many candidate interactions, among all the $(p-1)p/2$

possible ones, are accepted. Then, the selected interactions are decreasingly ordered to add them step-by-step to the main effects model.

4   The building-model stage

In this section we illustrate the main aspects of the computational procedure used to compute and select the best interaction terms in the non-linear model.

0 Preliminary phase: the main effects model.
Decide on the spline parameters as well as on A for the main effects model (m): denote $PRESS_m(A)$ and $R_m^2(A)$.
1 Phase 1: individual evaluation of candidate interactions.
Each interaction i is separately added to the main effects. Eliminate interactions such that $CRIT(A) < 0$. Then, order decreasingly the accepted candidate interactions.
2 Phase 2: stepwise forward building-model stage.
Set $PRESS_0 = PRESS_m(A)$, $i = 0$ and index by i the partial current model. Repeat the procedure: add to the model i the accepted interaction candidate $i + 1$ only if the corresponding optimal PRESS fulfils the condition $PRESS \leq PRESS_i$.

5   Application: the orange juice data

The example from sensometrics herein outlined, is discussed in Durand (2001). The real data set consists of 10 explanatory variables illustrating the mineralogical properties of 24 orange juices and one sensory response. For confidentiality, the 24 orange juices have been named by the capital letters "A",..,"X". We assume that they all have identical quantity of fruit and same glucid content. The predictors are given by eight mineralogical characters SiO_2, Na, K, Ca, Mg, Cl, SO_4, HCO_3 and their sum Sum, plus the conductivity $COND$. The response is given by the sensory variable $HEAVY$, whose protocol of measurements is not revealed for confidentiality. The a priori knowledge of this sensory data permits to select the degree 2 and locate knots for each variable at the points specified in Table 1.

COND	SiO_2	Na	K	Ca	Mg	Cl	SO_4	HCO_3	Sum
400	10	10	2.5	160	40	4	400	100	600
1600	20	40	5	400	110	11	1700	300	2600
	40				30		500		

Table 1. Selected knots for the predictors

Figure 1 displays the comparison of PRESS values between the main effects model and the final model with interactions, both computed with 2 dimensions. The respective R^2 (from 0.917 to 0.93) measures the gain in

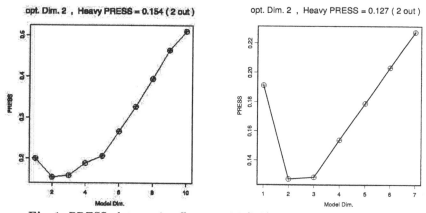

Fig. 1. PRESS plots: main effects model (left), interactions model (right)

goodness-of-fit when the interaction terms are included as predictors into the model.

Figure 2, left-side, displays the phase 1 individual evaluation and selection of the 45 possible interactions. The right-side of this figure shows the PRESS values of the successive steps in the phase 2 building-model-stage. The final model includes 10 interactions added to the 10 main effects.

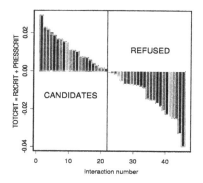
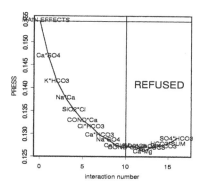

Fig. 2. Phase 1 (left) and phase 2 (right) of the building-model stage

In Figure 3, univariate and bivariate ANOVA functions have been ordered according to their decreasing additive influence on the response $HEAVY$: the graphs are ordered from left to right and up to down according to the range of the transformed variables. Vertical in the main effects plots indicate the location of the knots. We notice that the most influent interaction $Ca * SO_4$ belongs to the group of the five largest predictors. Furthermore, one can see that extreme values of the predictors (for example, orange juice P in the variables SO_4, Ca, Sum) do not perturb the coordinate functions due to the location of knots.

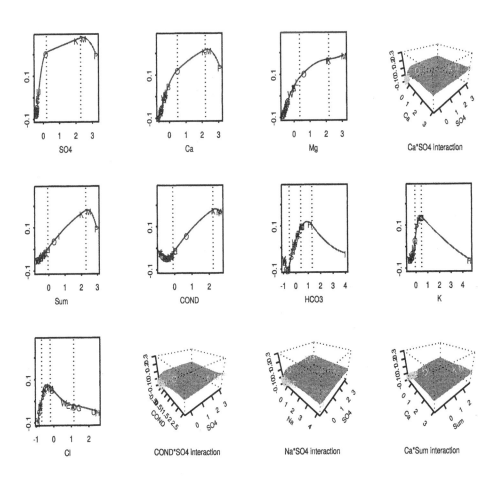

Fig. 3. Figure 3: ANOVA functions of main influence on HEAVY (2 dimensions).

6   Conclusion

PLSS with interactions is a straightforward extension of *PLSS* (Durand 2000, 2001), it inherits from *PLSS* the robustness against the presence of extreme values of predictors and from *PLS* the traditional robustness against both scarcity of data and multicollinearity of the variables. This method does not automatically estimate the optimal transformations of univariate and bivariate predictors, but exploring different sets of tuning spline parameters, it allows users to experiment with a wide range of PLS tools, from linearity to non-linearity, through local polynomial models with interactions.

References

DE BOOR C. (1978) *A Practical Guide to Splines*, Springer-Verlag,Berlin, 1978.

DURAND J.F. (2000) La Régression Partial Least Squares Spline, PLSS, guide d'utilisation sous S-plus. *Rapport de Recherche 00-06, Groupe de Biostatistique et d'Analyse des Systèmes ENSAM-INRA-UM II.*

DURAND J.F. (2001) Local Polynomial additive regression through PLS and Splines: PLSS. *In Chemometrics & Intelligent Laboratory Systems, 58, 235-246.*

DURAND J.F. and SABATIER R. (1997) Additive Splines for Partial Least Squares Regression. *In Journal of the American Statistical Association, vol.92, n.440.*

FRIEDMAN, J. (1991) Multivariate Adaptive Regression Splines. *The Annals of Statistics, 19,1:1-141.*

GIFI, A.(1990) *Non-linear Multivariate Analysis*, Chichester: Wiley.

HOSKULDSSON P. (1988) PLS Regression Methods. *Journal of Chemometrics, 2,211-228.*

LOMBARDO, R. RIJCKEVORSEL, J.VAN (2000): Interaction Terms in Homogeneity Analysis: Higher order non-linear Multiple Correspondence Analysis. *In "Studies in Classification, Data Analysis and knowledge Organization"* Springer.

TENENHAUS, M. (1998): *La Régression PLS, Théorie et Pratique.* Editions Technip, Paris.

WOLD, H. (1966): Estimation of principal components and related models by iterative least squares. *In Multivariate Analysis, (Eds.) P.R. Krishnaiah, New York: Academic Press, 391-420.*

WOLD, H. (1992): Non Linear Partial Least Squares Modeling II. Spline Inner Relation. *In Chemometrics and Intelligent laboratory Systems, 14, 71-84.*

WOLD, S., KETTANEH-WOLD, H., Skagerberg B.(1989): Non Linear Partial Least Squares Modeling. *In Chemometrics & Intelligent Laboratory Systems, 7,53-65.*

Discriminant Analysis With Categorical Variables: A Biplot Based Approach

Sugnet Gardner and Niël le Roux

Department of Statistics and Actuarial Science,
University of Stellenbosch, Stellenbosch, South Africa

Abstract. Gower and Hand (1996) provide a new perspective on the traditional biplot of Gabriel (1971) by viewing biplots as multivariate analogues of ordinary scatterplots. It is demonstrated by Gardner (2001) that extending biplot methodology to discriminant analysis is not only extremely useful for visual displays to accompany discriminant analysis but how the process of classification can be performed using biplot methodology. In particular, a method developed for the inclusion of categorical predictors is discussed. Specific attention is devoted to what is termed a 'reversal' when dealing with two binary (categorical) predictor variables. A proposal using biplot methodology is made for dealing with this problem.

1 Introduction to biplot methodology

The biplot was introduced by Gabriel (1971) as a graphical display consisting of a vector for each row and a vector for each column of a matrix of rank two. In this display any element of the matrix is represented by the inner product of the vectors corresponding to its row and column. The biplot can be related to principal component analysis (PCA) and involves the rank two approximation of the data matrix via the singular value decomposition. Although the traditional Gabriel biplot can be used - and is widely applied in practice - as a graphical aid in the important field of classification, the new philosophy of Gower and Hand (1996) have much to offer when applying biplot methodology in discriminant analysis and related classification procedures. According to this philosophy, biplots are regarded as the multivariate analogues of scatterplots allowing for visual appraisal of the structure of the data in a few dimensions. Biplot axes are used to relate the plotted points to the original variables, as is the case in ordinary scatterplots. Gower and Hand (1996, p.1) comment that scatterplots "are not only easy to produce, but they also have the merit of being straightforward to interpret, requiring very little, if any, formal training". By extending the scatterplot principles to multivariate displays the resulting biplots ease interpretation and are accessible to non-statistical audiences.

The Gower and Hand philosophy allows well-known methods such as PCA and canonical variate analysis (CVA), as well as some newer and less well-known methods to be integrated into a unified presentation. The concept of inter-sample distance is central to all these methods of multidimensional scaling and is the unifying concept. The PCA biplot is based on Pythagorean distance, also known as Euclidean distance. Apart from PCA, the CVA biplot based on Mahalanobis distance can be constructed in a similar fashion.

A generalisation based on principal co-ordinate analysis (PCO) using any Euclidean embeddable distance leads to the non-linear biplot. An even further generalisation provides for categorical variables, resulting in the generalised biplot.

The principal axes obtained from the eigenvector solution for PCA, CVA or PCO are used only as scaffolding for plotting in the biplot. Instead of plotting these principal axes, biplot axes are fitted, one for each variable. These non-perpendicular axes can be calibrated according to the original units of measurement of the variables. Gower and Hand (1996) use the terms *interpolation* for superimposing a (new) observation on the biplot display and *prediction* for the inverse action of inferring the values of the original variables for a point in the biplot display. Two sets of biplot axes can thus be defined - interpolation axes and prediction axes, for use with the respective operations. It can be shown that in most cases the two sets of axes do not correspond, or if they do, they are fitted with differently scaled markers. Gardner (2001) proposes showing only prediction axes on biplots since it is intuitive to use axes for prediction and interpolation can be easily performed using a suitable computer programme.

2   Discriminant analysis in terms of biplot methodology

Gardner (2001) introduces several extensions of biplot methodology to discriminant analysis. The simplest application of biplot methodology in discriminant analysis follows from using the CVA biplot as a graphical representation of linear discriminant analysis (LDA). The Mahalanobis distances between class means in the original space is transformed to Pythagorean distance in the canonical space. Since the last $J - 1$ components ($J =$ number of classes) of the class means are all equal (*cf.* Flury, 1997), the dimension of the canonical space is $K = min(p, J - 1)$ with p the number of predictor variables. In a three class problem, the two dimensional CVA biplot is an exact graphical representation of the LDA problem. If more than three classes are present, the biplot is the "best" two dimensional display of the multi-dimensional problem.

Gardner (2001) interpolates the sample points onto the biplot of class means, obtaining a visual description of class separation or overlap. Since both the PCA and CVA biplots are special cases of the non-linear biplot based on Pythagorean distance and Mahalanobis distance respectively, the non-linear biplot can also be used for performing LDA. A CVA biplot is obtained by applying the non-linear biplot method to the Mahalanobis inter-sample distance matrix. In the biplot space, Pythagorean distance is used to classify a (new) sample to the nearest class mean. The classification regions can be indicated on the biplot by appropriately colouring each point according to the nearest class mean. If K ¿ 2, the LDA classification can be done in the full canonical space. Approximate classification regions can be indicated on the biplot according to the algorithm of Gower and Hand (1996) for indicating so-called category level points. Since the classification regions in the biplot space is a slice through the full canonical space it might not intersect with all the classification regions. Therefore all the classes might not appear in the biplot classification region diagram. Apart from supplying a visual representation of the classification of observations, the advantage of using biplot methodology is the reduction in dimension achieved. Hastie, Tibshirani and Buja (1994) remark that the reduced space can be more stable and therefore the dimension reduction could yield better classification performance. An alternative to the above classification scheme is therefore to classify a (new) observation to the nearest approximated canonical mean in the biplot space. Since all the canonical means are represented in the biplot, each class will have an associated classification region. Although it cannot be graphically represented, formulating LDA in terms of biplot methodology yields a series of possible classification schemes, one in each of the dimensions $2, 3, \ldots, K$.

A non-linear biplot based on a Pythagorean inter-sample distance matrix results in a PCA biplot. Approximate classification regions can therefore also be constructed in the PCA biplot, with classification to the nearest class mean in terms of Mahalanobis distance. Although the alternative classification with a CVA biplot can be used, the PCA classification allows for generalisation to other discrimination procedures.

One of the assumptions of LDA is equal within class covariance matrices. If this assumption is violated, quadratic discriminant analysis (QDA) can be considered. Where equal covariance matrices allowed for a common within class covariance matrix to be associated with the Mahalanobis distance between class means, each individual class's covariance matrix must be used in QDA. In a PCA biplot QDA classification regions can therefore be constructed by, for each point in the biplot space, calculating the Mahalanobis distance to the class means, using that mean's associated within class covariance matrix, and classifying the point to the 'nearest' class mean. However, finding a biplot space where the distances between class means are in terms of Pythagorean distance is much more intuitive. Such a QDA biplot can be derived as follows: Instead of finding the eigenvectors maximising the common within class to between class variance ratio, J such ratios must be maximised simultaneously. This can be formulated in terms of simultaneously diagonalising J positive definite matrices. Graybill (1983) proves that such a solution exists if and only if all J matrices are pairwise commutative. Since this is generally not the case, the FG-algorithm of Flury and Gautschi (1986, in Flury, Nel and Pienaar, 1994) is used to simultaneously bring the J matrices as close to diagonality as possible. The resulting matrix then forms the scaffolding for the QDA biplot.

Flury, Boukai and Flury (1997) remark that linear discrimination sometimes outperforms quadratic discrimination even when the assumption of equal covariance matrices is violated (cf. also McLachlan, 1992). This can be attributed to the large number of parameters that has to be estimated in QDA, resulting in over-parameterisation inducing a loss of power. In order to find a solution less rigid than LDA, but estimating fewer parameters than QDA Hastie, Tibshirani and Buja (1994) generalise LDA by using the relationship between LDA and multivariate regression and replacing the multivariate regression by a non-parametric multivariate regression procedure. They term the resulting discrimination procedure flexible discriminant analysis (FDA). Essentially the observations are transformed to a 'canonical space' where the transformation involves the fitted values from a non-parametric multivariate regression procedure such as MARS or BRUTO. These procedures have the additional advantage of providing criteria for the automatic selection of variables. Calculating the Pythagorean distance between the transformed samples, an inter-sample distance matrix is obtained to be used as input for the non-linear biplot method. The resulting biplot is termed an FDA biplot and since the distances between class means in this biplot space are Pythagorean, classification regions can easily be constructed, similar to a CVA biplot.

An alternative model of reducing the number of QDA parameters that has to be estimated, is proposed by Flury, Boukai and Flury (1997) termed the discrimination subspace model (DSM). This is accomplished by assuming that all differences between two p-variate normal populations occur in a subspace of dimension $q < p$. A transformation from the p-dimensional to a q-dimensional subspace is found and QDA performed in the q-dimensional subspace. A DSM biplot is therefore easily obtained by calculating distances in the transformed subspace according to one of the QDA biplot methods - either constructing a PCA biplot of the transformed observations in the q-dimensional subspace with QDA classification regions, or constructing a QDA biplot of the transformed observation in the q-dimensional subspace and Pythagorean classification regions.

3   Discriminant analysis with categorical predictor variables

In this paper the focus is on discriminant analysis with categorical predictor variables and in particular the ease of dealing with these categorical predictors by formulating discriminant analysis in terms of biplot methodology. Furthermore, since it is known that categorical predictors can cause problems in certain discrimination situations, in particular where so-called reversals are present, it will be shown that by using biplot methodology these problems can be overcome efficiently.

The generalised biplot defined by Gower and Hand (1996) allows for the calculation of distances between samples with continuous and categorical measurements and plugging this distance matrix into the non-linear biplot method. In the construction of the generalised biplot the only assumption to be made is that the inter-sample distances are additive Euclidean embeddable distance measures. Due to the assumption of additive distance it can be assumed without loss of generality that the variables are ordered such that the first $p_{(1)}$ are continuous and the remaining $p_{(2)}$ are categorical with $p_{(1)} + p_{(2)} = p$ leading to an inter-sample distance matrix D consisting of two parts *i.e.*

$$D = \sum_{k=1}^{p_{(1)}} D_k + \sum_{k=p_{(1)}+1}^{p} D_k = D_{(1)} + D_{(2)}.$$

In this paper the matrix $D_{(1)}$ is calculated using Pythagorean distance in the case of the $p_{(1)}$ continuous variables while the extended matching coefficient (EMC) discussed in detail by Gower (1992), is used for the categorical predictors to obtain $D_{(2)}$.

Once the distance matrix has been obtained, the non-linear biplot method which can be regarded as a PCO analysis, is performed. Although it cannot be plotted for $r > 2$, including all r principal co-ordinates, no loss of information is incurred. The generalised r-dimensional biplot is in essence a transformation to r continuous pseudo-variables. These pseudo-variables can then be used in any of the biplot techniques discussed in section 2.

4   Reversal

In the discussion of McLachlan (1992) on the performance of LDA with categorical predictor variables it is concluded that LDA is quite robust for departures from normality if the true log ratio of the class-conditional densities is an (approximately) linear function of the predictor variables. Krzanowski (1977) gives a detailed discussion on the performance of LDA with categorical or mixed predictor variables. In particular, Krzanowski points out that LDA will behave poorly in a two class situation with two binary predictor variables where the values (0, 0) and (1, 1) are more frequently associated with the one class and the values (0, 1) and (1, 0) with the other. Since the true log ratio of the class-conditional densities does not increase monotonically with the number of positive predictor variables, it is said to undergo a *reversal*.

Both McLachlan and Krzanowski base their discussions on the simulation results of Moore (1973). Moore's results clarified why Gilbert (1968), referred to by Krzanowski (1977), McLachlan (1992) and Moore (1973), found that LDA performed well in a two class discrimination problem with only binary predictor variables. There was no reversal in Gilbert's simulation studies. An example of a reversal in real data is given by Yerushalmy, Van den Berg, Erhardt and Jacobziner (1965). Birth weight and length of gestation period were used to indicate immaturity in newborn babies. Babies were classified as normal for the combinations low birth weight and short gestation period or high birth weight and long gestation period. Abnormal babies were associated with the remaining combinations of long gestation but low birth weight or short gestation with high birth weight.

In the above example the two predictor variables are positively correlated for normal babies, but negatively correlated for abnormal babies. Therefore the assumption of equal within class covariance matrices needed for LDA is not satisfied. McLachlan mentions further that Dillon and Goldstein (1978) demonstrated that reversals can occur even in situations where the within class covariance matrices are equal. If the within class covariance matrices differ, QDA could be applied. It was already mentioned in section 2 that LDA sometimes outperforms QDA even when the assumptions for LDA are not satisfied due to the large number of parameters that has to be estimated for QDA. Moore (1973) further concludes that the use of QDA with binary variables is not recommended since it rarely performs as well as LDA.

To investigate the performance of discrimination formulated in terms of biplot methodology a simulation study similar to that of Moore (1973) is performed. Moore used the second-order approximation to the Bahadur reparameterisation of the multinomial distribution (*cf.* Bahadur, 1961). To simulate an example similar to that of Yerushalmy, *et al.* (1965) the parameters were chosen as follows:

Class 1	Class 2
$p_{11} = 0.5$	$p_{12} = 0.5$
$p_{21} = 0.5$	$p_{22} = 0.5$
$r_1(12) = 0.8$	$r_2(12) = -0.8$

A random sample of size 100 with 50 observations from each of the classes was simulated from the above distributions, respectively. Class 1 is associated with the response patterns (0, 0) and (1, 1) while class 2 is associated with (1, 0) and (0, 1). It can be expected that those observations which fall into one class but have a response pattern associated with the other class will be misclassified by an efficient classification technique. In this sample there were 14 of these observations, therefore an apparent error rate (APER) of 0.14 will be considered excellent.

The two binary variables were used as input for the generalised biplot method as categorical variables (no continuous variable was present). The generalised biplot with the ordination is given in Figure 1. Since only four distinct response vectors are possible, the values were jittered to display the different samples. In the biplot it can be seen that the left hand and right hand values are predominantly associated with class 1 while the top and bottom values are predominantly associated with class 2. The ordination resulting from the generalised biplot method provides two continuous pseudo-variables which are in turn used as input to the non-linear biplot classification method. Using the Mahalanobis distance metric with common within class covariance matrix a CVA biplot with LDA classification regions was obtained as shown in Figure 2(a). Since there are only two classes only the first dimension is relevant for classification. The one-dimensional biplot therefore falls onto the horisontal line in Figure 2(a). Since only four distinct response vectors are possible the pseudo-variable matrix has only four different rows. The samples in the biplot are spread vertically to see the individual observations.

It is evident from the biplot that no clear separation exists between the two classes. An APER of 0.41 confirms the inability of LDA to discriminate be-

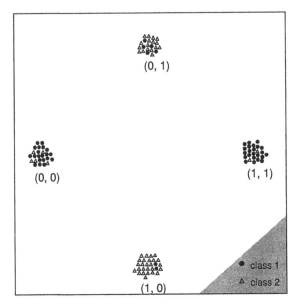

Fig. 1. Generalised biplot of simulation data

tween the two classes. This is in agreement with the conclusion of Krzanowski (1977) that LDA behaves poorly in this situation. Since Moore (1973) showed that the use of QDA with binary variables is not recommended an alternative classification procedure is needed. FDA is such a candidate where the linearity restriction is relaxed allowing for the more flexible non-parametric methods of MARS or BRUTO to be applied. For this example the APER obtained for both MARS and BRUTO is an excellent 0.11. However, it must be borne in mind that this error rate is optimistically biased (Lachenbruch and Mickey, 1968; McLachlan, 1992). The biplot for FDA (BRUTO) is given in Figure 2(b). Since the FDA (MARS) and FDA (BRUTO) biplots are identical, only the FDA (BRUTO) biplot is given. The FDA procedure includes non-linear terms of the pseudo-variable matrix resulting in five different values in the FDA biplot for both MARS and BRUTO.

5 Conclusion

These findings demonstrate an important advantage of formulating discriminant analysis in terms of biplot methodology. LDA classification can be represented by a CVA biplot. The rigid constraints of linearity of LDA can be generalised to the more flexible method of FDA. By defining a suitable distance metric any of these discrimination procedures can be applied with ease by a non-linear biplot classification method. Categorical variables can be included in the discrimination process by obtaining an ordination with the generalised biplot method. Once this ordination is obtained, the prob-

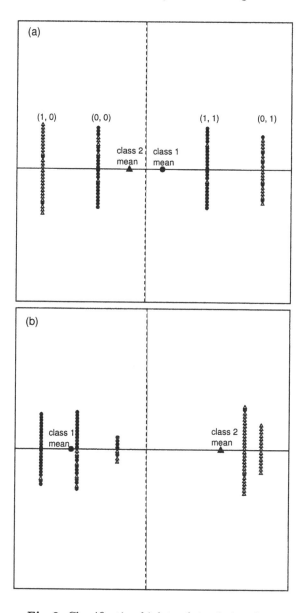

Fig. 2. Classification biplots of simulation data

lem of LDA classification in the presence of a reversal can be resolved with ease by simply changing the distance metric applied in the non-linear biplot classification procedure.

References

BAHADUR, R.R. (1961): A representation of the joint distribution of responses to n dichotomous items. In: H.Solomon (Ed.): *Studies in item analysis and prediction.* Stanford University Press, Stanford, California, 158–168.

DILLON, W.R. and GOLDSTEIN, M. (1978): On the performance of some multinomial classification rules. *Journal of the American Statistical Association, 73, 305–313.*

FLURY, B. (1997): *A first course in multivariate statistics.* Springer-Verlag, New York.

FLURY, B.D., NEL, D.G. and PIENAAR, I. (1995): Simultaneous detection in shift in means and variances. *Journal of the American Statistical Association, 90, 1474–1481.*

FLURY, L., BOUKAI, B. and FLURY, B.D. (1997): The discrimination subspace model. *Journal of the American Statistical Association, 92, 758–766.*

GABRIEL, K.R. (1971): The biplot graphical display of matrices with application to principal component analysis. *Biometrika, 58, 453–467.*

GARDNER, S. (2001): Extensions of biplot methodology to discriminant analysis with applications of non-parametric principal components. Unpublished PhD thesis. University of Stellenbosch, Stellenbosch.

GILBERT, E.S. (1968): On discrimination using qualitative variables. *Journal of the American Statistical Association, 63, 1399–1418.*

GOWER, J.C. (1992): Generalized biplots. *Biometrika, 79, 475–493.*

GOWER, J.C. and HAND,D.J. (1996): *Biplots.* Chapman & Hall, London.

GRAYBILL, F.A. (1983): *Matrices with applications in statistics.* 2nd edition. Wadsworth, Belmont, California.

HASTIE, T., TIBSHIRANI, R. and BUJA, A. (1994): Flexible discriminant analysis by optimal scoring. *Journal of the American Statistical Association, 89, 1255–1270.*

KRZANOWSKI, W.J. (1977): The performance of Fisher's linear discriminant function under non-optimal conditions. *Technometrics, 19, 191–200.*

LACHENBRUCH, P.A. and MICKEY, M.R. (1968): Estimation of error rates in discriminant analysis. *Technometrics, 10, 1–11.*

McLACHLAN, G.J.(1992): *Discriminant analysis and statistical pattern recognition.* John Wiley, New York.

MOORE, D.H. (1973): Evaluation of five discrimination procedures for binary variables. *Journal of the American Statistical Association, 68, 399–404.*

YERUSHALMY, J., VAN DEN BERG, B.J., ERHARDT, C.L. and JACOBZINER, H. (1965): Birth weight and gestation as indices of "immaturity". *American Journal of Diseases of Children, 109, 43–57.*

Efficient Density Clustering
Using Basin Spanning Trees

Sören Hader[1] and Fred A. Hamprecht[2]

[1] Robert Bosch GmbH, FV/PLF2, Postfach 30 02 40
D-70442 Stuttgart, Germany
[2] Interdisziplinäres Zentrum für Wissenschaftliches Rechnen (IWR),
Universität Heidelberg, D-69120 Heidelberg, Germany

Abstract. We present a method to cluster multivariate data according to their density (or any other target function): all observations lying within one "basin" or sitting on the slopes of one "mountain" are assigned to one cluster. The method exploits a neighborhood structure given by the Delaunay triangulation or a k-nearest neighbor graph, and each cluster is given in terms of a *basin spanning tree*. The root of each basin spanning tree corresponds to a local density maximum, and the trees can be used for simplified representation and visualization of the observations. We compare the accuracy and speed of different approximations, apply the method to real-world data sets and compare its computational complexity to published algorithms.

1 Introduction

Unsupervised learning techniques seek to identify patterns in a given data set. We restrict ourselves to data that can be represented as a set of points in Euclidean space, with each object being represented by a single point.

Most clustering methods seek to maximize some measure of intra-group compactness or inter-group distance. We propose a computationally efficient method to cluster a set of points according to a specific measure of group compactness, namely according to their density (for a short history of density clustering, see Bock (1974), Kowalewski (1995), Ester et al. (1996)).

1.1 Clustering by local maxima

We first present an operational definition of clustering by local maxima.

Consider a set of points in D-dimensional Euclidean space $\mathbb{R}^D$ and an additional arbitrary continuous function[1] $f : \mathbb{R}^D \mapsto \mathbb{R}$.

Each point in the data set has an associated steepest-ascent trajectory which originates at the datum and ends in one of the local maxima. All

---

[1] More precisely, we have to assume that the first derivative is continuous everywhere and that the function has no ridges, i.e., the curvature may only become zero at single points.

those points whose steepest-ascent trajectories[2] converge to the same local maximum form one cluster.

A data set can be clustered according to any user-supplied function f as defined above. In the following, we shall assume that f is an estimate of the data density and refer to "density clustering" when we group data according to its local maxima. A density estimate with favorable properties is the kernel density estimate of the data set (Silverman (1986), Scott (1992)); the basic idea is to center a "bump" or kernel $K(x)$ on each of the N data points X_i and to sum over all these to obtain an estimate of the density of points in space, $\hat{f}(x) = (Nh^D)^{-1} \cdot \sum_{i=1}^{N} K\left((x - X_i)/h\right)$. There is, of course, some choice in the shape of the kernel K and, more importantly, in its width h. By linearity, the density estimate inherits all regularity properties of the kernel K and it turns out that the choice ofreviodPapers the kernel width h is by far more important than the shape (Silverman, 1986).

If the width h is very small, the resulting density estimate will have as many local maxima as there are distinct data points; if h is very large, the resulting estimate will have the same shape as the kernel used, see Fig. 1.

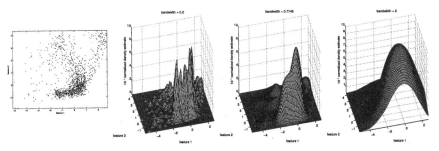

Fig. 1. Bivariate data from a multimodal imaging experiment with kernel density estimates using different widths of the Epanechnikov kernel (Silverman (1986)). The wider the kernel, the smoother the resultant density estimate and the smaller the number of local maxima.

1.2   Previous work on density clustering

A naive implementation of the operational definition above is costly: the exact steepest ascent trajectories can be approximated with a series of steps of finite size in the direction of the gradient. The cost of each gradient evaluation is $\mathcal{O}(N)$, it needs to be performed multiple times until a local maximum is reached and the procedure is repeated for each individual datum. Assuming,

---

[2] In a physical analogy, steepest-descent trajectories are obtained by letting mass points roll downhill on the surface given by f under infinite friction conditions. This procedure would lead to a clustering by local minima, whereas steepest-ascent trajectories yield a clustering by local maxima.

for simplicity, that each datum reaches a local maximum after t steps, a total of $N \cdot t$ density gradient estimates is required, each of which is $\mathcal{O}(N)$. One way forward is to choose the step sizes wisely (as long as possible, as short as necessary) to minimize t. This is the route explored by Kowalewski (1995).

Cheng (1995) proves that an iterative "mean-shift process" corresponds to density clustering according to a kernel density estimate with a kernel that is dual to the one used in the shifting process. This procedure moves all points simultaneously, but it also requires a total of $N \cdot t$ density evaluations at single points, each of which is $\mathcal{O}(N)$.

An obvious speed-up is to reduce the amount of data at the cost of accuracy of the density estimate (Domeniconi and Gunopulos, 2001).

Since many kernels have finite support (such as Epanechnikov or biweight) or decay quickly with distance (such as the Gaussian), the kernel density estimation can be speeded up by partitioning the space as in DENCLUE (Hinneburg and Keim, 1998) or using range search machinery.

2 Basin spanning trees

The aim of this contribution is to obtain a density clustering with just one evaluation of the density and (and possibly the gradient) at each datum, at the expense of a more extensive pre-processing.

We propose the following heuristic approximation to exact density clustering:

- Firstly, find the topological neighbors for each point in the data set. Various definitions can be used, such as the k-nearest neighbors or the Delaunay triangulation. The latter definition is particularly suitable for our application (see section 2.1).
- Secondly, compute the density estimate (or evaluate the function f, and possibly its gradient) at each point.
- Thirdly, do for each data point: among those of its neighbors that have a density higher than the point itself, find the one that offers the steepest increase in density[3]. Create a "link" or, in terms of graph theory, a "directed edge" to that neighbor. If none of the neighbors have a higher density, the point corresponds to a local density maximum and becomes the root of a tree (see section 2.2).
- Lastly, the cluster membership of each datum can be established by following the edges until a point with known membership or a tree root is reached.

The resultant graph is a collection of trees, with each tree having a root close to a local maximum of f. Its leaves extend to the boundaries beyond which the next local maximum "attracts" the data; we denote these graphs "basin spanning trees" (Hamprecht et al., 2001). The procedure is illustrated in Fig. 2. Details of the mentioned steps are discussed in the following sections.

---

[3] Refinements of this step are discussed in section 2.2.

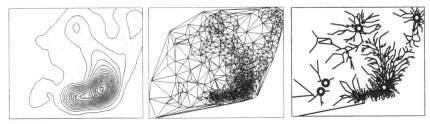

Fig. 2. Left: data from Fig. 1 with density estimated using the Epanechnikov kernel of width 0.775; middle: topological neighborhood as given by Delaunay triangulation; right: basin spanning trees corresponding to local density maxima; tree roots corresponding to local density maxima are marked by circles.

2.1   Topological neighborhood

The entire procedure hinges on a reasonable definition of topological neighborhood. If a complete graph[4] was used and if the density estimate features high, narrow maxima, then many points would be connected directly to such maxima, even across density valleys, i.e., across proper density boundaries. In addition, a large number of topological neighbors slows down the procedure.

The Delaunay triangulation returns a set of simplices such that no data points are contained in any circumspheres of these simplices. Roughly speaking, the resultant triangulation finds the closest neighbors in the different spatial directions. The computational complexity is $\mathcal{O}\left(N^{D/2}\right)$ which renders the procedure unattractive for dimensions greater than four.

In higher dimensions, using the k nearest neighbors becomes computationally more efficient. Also, the distances computed to find the nearest neighbors can be reused in the density estimation. The problem is that when the parameter k is chosen too small, "holes" in the triangulation result that prevent a proper density clustering, see Fig. 3. If k is chosen too large, the problem discussed in section 4.1 arises. Another drawback is that a further user-adjustable parameter is introduced.

2.2   Topography

Besides the topological neighborhood, it is the topography of the density estimate that determines whether or not two points will be part of the same cluster.

Strictly speaking, the density along an edge of a basin spanning tree should never fall below the density at the starting point. This condition can only be verified by sampling along a putative edge, which is computationally prohibitive. The fastest approximation is to consider only the starting and end points of an edge and thus approximate the underlying density linearly.

---

[4] A graph in which each point is connected to every other.

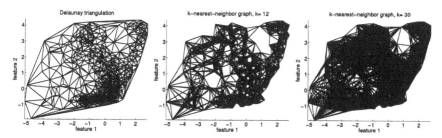

Fig. 3. Topological neighborhoods as defined through the Delaunay triangulation (left) and k nearest neighbors (middle, right); choosing k too small leads to holes in the triangulation, choosing k too large connects points that are not topological neighbors.

A more exact approximation will also consider the gradient of the density at the starting point: if the derivative of the density along the putative edge does not indicate a positive slope, then the density along that edge must necessarily fall below the density of the starting point and the edge is not admissible. In other words, in this improved approximation, all topological neighbors in the half-space defined by a locally negative slope can be discarded without further investigation.

2.3   Algorithmic details

We wish to use all available data. Once the distance between points X_i and X_j has been evaluated, there contribution to each other's density can be added to both. The same distance is used for evaluation of the gradient, if applicable (see section 2.2).

Also, the number of clusters is determined by the bandwidth of the kernel K. An exploratory phase will typically require experimenting with this width which should be equally distributed on a logarithmic scale. The densities (and gradients) for these different widths should be constructed in one run with a single evaluation of all distances.

Range searches can be performed using a kD-tree. Building a tree costs $\mathcal{O}(N\log(N))$, a single query costs $\mathcal{O}(\log(N))$. We have, instead, used an algorithm exploiting the triangle inequality as implemented in the TSTOOL toolbox (Merkwirth et al., 2000).

Finally, the computational cost depends on the kernel K and the Epanechnikov kernel is favorable in this respect.

3   Results

The algorithm is illustrated using a real-world data set from a multimodal imaging experiment.

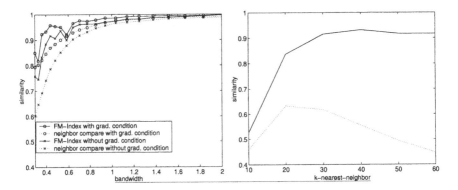

Fig. 4. Left: this plot compares the density clusters obtained when sampling along putative edges (the expensive "gold standard") vs. computing density differences only, and sampling along putative edges vs. calculating the gradient at the starting point, see section 2.2. The FM-index (solid line, Fowlkes and Mallows (1983)) gives the average probability that a pair of points is in the same cluster for the different approximations and is a measure of the similarity of the resulting clusters. The dashed line gives the percentage of identical edges in the different sets clusters. As expected, computing the gradient at the starting point leads to better performance at a moderate cost. Both similarity measures deviate significantly from unity when the kernel width is chosen too narrow, resulting in a rough density estimate with (too) many local maxima. Right: this plot compares the density clusters obtained for the same kernel width when defining topological neighborhood by means of the Delaunay triangulation or k nearest neighbors, respectively, see section 2.1. The solid and dashed lines again give the FM-index and percentage of basin spanning tree edges conserved. For this particular data set, the final cluster memberships are identical to around 90% when the number of nearest neighbors is chosen large enough.

The original data consists of four different images of the same region, each image emphasizing a different characteristic. Each pixel is thus represented by a point in four-dimensional "contrast space". After a robust scaling of the different dynamic ranges, the ∼ 21000 pixels were clustered according to a kernel density estimate in contrast space.

For the same data set, Fig. 4 illustrates the discrepancy that results between clusterings when different variants of the algorithm are used.

Fig. 5 shows a basin spanning tree that has been derived based on a four-dimensional density estimate and Delaunay triangulation and then projected down to the first three principal components. Such plots allow for the detailed analysis of individual clusters.

3.1   Computational cost

The algorithm has been implemented in Matlab and executed on a Pentium III with 1.2 GHz. Execution times are given in table 1 where gradient eval-

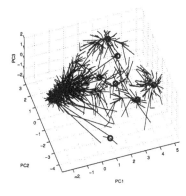

Fig. 5. Basin spanning trees for a part of the multimodal imaging data that have
been computed in four dimensions and projected onto the first three principal components. Using a four-dimensional density estimate retains distinct clusters that
merge when projecting down to three dimensions. The shape of individual clusters
can be analyzed in the spirit of Godtliebsen et al. (2002).

	Estimation of dens. and gradient values		
	D=2	D=3	D=4
N=1305	5.7	6.4	6.2
N=5226	45.5	55.6	67.1
N=20907	621.8	812.8	1096.0

	Delaunay triangulation			Conversion of triang. to connect. matrix			Building of basin spanning trees			Assignment of class memberships		
	D=2	D=3	D=4	D=2	D=3	D=4	D=2	D=3	D=4	D=2	D=3	D=4
N=1305	0.2	0.8	2.8	0.1	0.2	0.7	0.4	0.4	0.4	0.2	0.2	0.2
N=5226	0.7	2.6	12.7	0.3	0.6	3.4	1.5	1.5	1.7	0.6	0.6	0.9
N=20907	3.7	10.8	65.7	1.3	2.5	63.8	6.6	5.8	12.4	2.3	2.1	3.4

Table 1. Execution time in seconds on a Pentium III 1.2 GHz for data sets of
various sizes N and dimensionalities D. The single density estimation using the
Epanechnikov kernel (with no speed-ups by range search, etc.) takes much longer
than the other steps, indicating that density clustering by basin spanning trees is
much faster than an iterative hill-climbing approach.

uation at the starting point (see section 2.2) has been used. The Delaunay
triangulation has been performed with Qhull which now ships with Matlab
(Barber et al., 1996).

4 Discussion

In the example provided, the time for a single density estimation at all points
outweighs the time required for building and querying a basin spanning tree

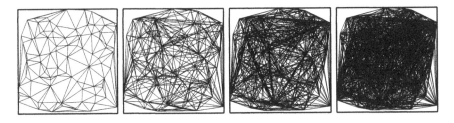

Fig. 6. Curse of dimensionality: how the Delaunay triangulation of 100 points in the unit square (left) is affected by 1% noise in the third, third and fourth, and third-to-fifth dimension.

(see table 1) so that the proposed procedure is significantly faster than an iterative steepest-ascent procedure which requires multiple density estimations.

In summary, density clustering is now a computationally viable option and should be considered as an alternative, especially in applications in which the density of points has an interpretation, such as in computer simulations of systems in thermodynamic equilibrium, in which all thermodynamic quantities of interest can be derived from the density (Hamprecht et al., 2001).

4.1   Curse of dimensionality

The applicability of density clustering to high-dimensional data is limited by several factors. On one hand, the number of points required for a reliable density estimate grows exponentially with the number of dimensions (Scott, 1992). This affects, of course, all methods of density clustering. The approach presented here also suffers from the fact that topological neighborhoods are not well preserved if the number of points does not grow fast enough with dimension, consider Fig. 6 for illustration. As a consequence, basin spanning trees should be constructed after appropriate dimension reduction or on a neighborhood topology of low local dimension.

5   Outlook

A further limitation is that density clustering as defined in the introduction will interpret an extended cluster as a "mountain range" with multiple local maxima and a correspondingly high number of clusters. If two clusters separated by a high-density saddle point should be interpreted as a single cluster (Hinneburg and Keim, 1998), an efficient computation in the framework of basin spanning trees is possible: it is sufficient to truncate basin spanning trees at the desired density level and check which of the resultant stumps are connected in the topological neighborhood graph. Efficient algorithms that check for the connectedness of subgraphs can be exploited.

The number of clusters is determined by the kernel width, and this is a user-adjustable parameter. In model-based clustering (e.g. Wehrens et al., 2001), the number of clusters can be estimated objectively. Also, if a mixture of, for instance, Gaussians, is abused as a density estimate and parametrized using expectation maximization (EM-algorithm), the computational complexity becomes linear in N. If, in addition, the number of mixture components is small, an iterative steepest ascent procedure can become computationally competitive, though it does not offer the visualization possibilities of a basin spanning tree.

References

BARBER, C. B., DOBKIN, D. P., and HUHDANPAA, H. (1996): The quick-hull algorithm for convex hulls. *ACM Trans. Math. Soft.*, 22(4):469–483. http://www.geom.umn.edu/locate/qhull.

BOCK, H.H. (1974): *Automatische Klassifikation.* Vandenhoeck & Ruprecht, Göttingen.

CHENG, Y. (1995): Mean shift, mode seeking, and clustering. *IEEE Transactions on Pattern Analysis and Machine Intelligence*, 17:790–799.

DOMENICONI, C. and GUNOPULOS, D. (2001): An efficient approach for approximating multi-dimensional range queries and nearest neighbor classification in large datasets. In *Proc. 18th International Conf. on Machine Learning*, pages 98–105, San Francisco. Morgan Kaufmann.

FOWLKES, E. B. and MALLOWS, C. L. (1983): A method for comparing two hierarchical clusterings. *Journal of the American Statistical Association*, 78:553–569.

ESTER, M., KRIEGEL, H.-P., SANDER, J. and XIAOWEI XU (1996): A density-based algorithm for discovering clusters in large spatial databases with noise. In *Proc. 2nd Int. Conf. on Knowledge Discovery and Data Mining (KDD 96)*, pages 226–231, Portland. AAAI Press.

GODTLIEBSEN, F., MARRON, J. S., and CHAUD (2002): Significance in scale space for bivariate density estimation. *Journal of Computational and Graphical Statistics*, 11:1–21.

HAMPRECHT, F. A., PETER, C., DAURA, X., THIEL, W., and VAN GUN-STEREN, W. F. (2001): A strategy for analysis of (molecular) equilibrium simulations: configuration space density estimation, clustering and visualization. *J. Chem. Phys.*, 114:2079–2089.

HINNEBURG, A. and KEIM, D. A. (1998): An efficient approach to clustering in multimedia databases with noise. In *Proc. 4th Int. Conf. on Knowledge Discovery and Data Mining (KDD 98)*, pages 58–65, New York. AAAI Press.

KOWALEWSKI, F. (1995): A gradient procedure for determining clusters of relatively high point density. *Pattern Recognition*, 28:1973–1984.

MERKWIRTH, C., PARLITZ, U., and LAUTERBORN, W. (2000): Fast exact and approximate nearest neighbor searching for nonlinear signal processing. *Physical Review E*, 62:2089–2097.

SCOTT, D. W. (1992): *Multivariate Density Estimation.* Wiley, New York.

SILVERMAN, B. W. (1986): *Density Estimation for Statistics and Data Analysis.* Monographs on Statistics and Applied Probability. Chapman & Hall.

WEHRENS, R., SIMONETTI, A. W., and BUYDENS, L. M. C. (2001): Mixture modelling of medical magnetic resonance data. *Journal of Chemometrics*, 16:1–10.

Some Issues on Clustering of Functional Data

Salvatore Ingrassia[1], Andrea Cerioli[2], and Aldo Corbellini[2]

[1] Dipartimento di Economia e Statistica, Università della Calabria
87036 Arcavacata di Rende (CS), Italy
[2] Dipartimento di Economia, Università di Parma
Via J. F. Kennedy, 6 – 43100 Parma, Italy

Abstract. In this paper we address the problem of clustering when for each unit the available response is a smooth function. We propose a novel approach based on a landmark description which takes into account the *shape* of each function and suggest also a graph-like representation which can help in the classification process. The method is illustrated using a real data set based on precipitation records.

1 Introduction

Let $\{\omega_1, \ldots, \omega_N\}$ be a set of N units and $\mathbf{y}_i = (y_i(t_1), \ldots, y_i(t_K))$ be a sample of measurements of some variable Y taken at K times $t_1, \ldots, t_K \in \mathcal{T} = [a, b]$ in the i-th unit ω_i, $(i = 1, \ldots, N)$. Throughout this paper we shall assume that some smooth function $x_i(t)$, computable for each $t \in \mathcal{T}$, lies behind $\mathbf{y}_i$. We distinguish two cases according to the data $\mathbf{y}_i$ are assumed to be errorless or not. In the first case the function $x_i(t)$ should satisfy the constraints:

$$x_i(t_j) = y_i(t_j) \qquad j = 1, \ldots, K .$$

In the second case, when some observational error is assumed to be present in the the raw data, the conversion from $\mathbf{y}_i$ to the function $x_i(t)$ may involve some smoothing procedure and in modeling terms we write:

$$y_i(t_j) = x_i(t_j) + \epsilon_j \qquad j = 1, \ldots, K$$

where the error or otherwise exogenous term ϵ_j contributes a roughness to the raw data. The standard assumption requires that the ϵ_j's are i.i.d. with zero mean and common finite variance. In the rest of this paper we shall concentrate on the second case.

The data $\mathbf{y}_i$ $(i = 1, \ldots, N)$ are regarded as *functional*. The motivation is that we consider $\mathbf{y}_i$ as a single entity rather than merely a sequence of individual observations; indeed the term functional refers to the intrinsic structure of the data rather than to their explicit form. The function $x_i(t)$ is called the *true functional form* of $\mathbf{y}_i$, and the set $\mathcal{X}_\mathcal{T} = \{x_1(t), \ldots, x_N(t)\}_{t \in \mathcal{T}}$ is called *functional dataset*, see Ramsay and Silverman (1997).

Even though functional data analysis (FDA) deals with temporal data, its scopes and objectives are quite different from those of time series analysis. While in time series analysis the focus is mainly on modeling data or predicting future observations, the techniques developed in FDA are essentially exploratory, since the emphasis is here on trajectories and their shapes. More-over, also the difficult case (from the time series perspective) of unequally-spaced observations with several missing values is easily dealt with in FDA.

Discrimination and clustering have been approached quite recently in the FDA literature. In this field common measures of similarity include the usual L_1 and L_2 distances. However, such distances often prove to be inadequate since they do not take curve shapes into account. In order to compare shapes, Heckman and Zamar (2000) proposed a measure of similarity based on a quantity called *rank correlation between two functions*. In this paper we pro-pose another approach based on a symbolic description of shapes, following some ideas proposed in Azencott and Ingrassia (1998).

The paper is organized as follows. In the next section we summarize some distance measures between functional data; in Section 3 we present our sym-bolic description and some related results; in Section 4 we propose a case study based on real data; finally in Section 5 we give the conclusions and some ideas for further research.

2 Some distances between functional data

Let $C^0(\mathcal{T})$ be the set of all continuous functions defined in $\mathcal{T}$ and $C^k(\mathcal{T})$, $k = 1, 2, \ldots$, be the subsets of $C^0(\mathcal{T})$ consisting of functions with continuous derivatives up to order k in $\mathcal{T}$. The set $C^k(\mathcal{T})$ is a linear space. In the follow-ing we shall denote by $\mathcal{X}$ a generic functional space. Common measures of similarity on $\mathcal{X} \times \mathcal{X}$ include the usual L_p distances in the functional spaces.

However, it has been remarked that such distances do not adequately measure what our eye sees, see e.g. Marron and Tsybakov (1995). For this reason a quite different approach has been proposed by Heckman & Zamar (2000) who compare the shapes of two curves in terms of a monotonic trasfor-mation. Two curves x, y defined on the unit interval are said to have the same shape if there exists a strictly increasing function g such that $x(t) = g[y(t)]$ for all $t \in [0, 1]$, that is the plot of y versus t is the same of x versus t after a deformation of the vertical axis. Afterwards they associate a rank function to each curve $x(t)$ as follows.

Let $x \in C^0(\mathcal{T})$ and μ be a probability measure on $[0, 1]$. The rank of $x(t)$ among all $x(s)$'s, relative to μ, is defined as:

$$r_x(t) := \mu\{s : x(s) < x(t)\} + \frac{1}{2}\mu\{x : x(s) = x(t)\} \qquad (1)$$

which extends the usual definition of rank. Two functions $x, y \in C^0(\mathcal{T})$ are said to be μ-similar if there exists a set A with $\mu(A) = 1$ and a function g stricly increasing on $y(A)$ such that $x(t) = g[y(t)]$ for all $t \in A$.

In the next section we shall introduce a (wider) definition of similarity between curves based on their symbolic description.

3 The *landmark description* for functional data

Assume the functional space $\mathcal{X} = C^1(\mathcal{T})$ of the functions $x(\cdot)$ with continuous first derivative in $\mathcal{T}$. In this section we introduce a symbolic description of x which is based on the sequence of the extremal points of x, i.e. on its *vertices*; it will be called the *landmark description* of x and denoted by $L(x)$. The number of vertices of x will be denoted by $|L(x)|$. Assume that x has k vertices, that is $|L(x)| = k$, then $L(x) = (l_1, \ldots, l_k)$, where:

$$l_i := \begin{cases} +1 & \text{if the } i\text{-th vertex is a local maximum of } x \\ -1 & \text{if the } i\text{-th vertex is a local minimum of } x. \end{cases}$$

For example $L(x) = (+1, -1, +1)$ means that the datum x has, in order, a maximum, a minimum and another maximum in $\mathcal{T}$. If the function $x(t)$ is monotone, then we set $L(x) = \emptyset$ and $|L(x)| = 0$.

We remark that if two functional data x_1 and x_2 are μ-similar (according to the definition of Heckman & Zamar (2000)), then they have the same landmark description; the converse in general is not true.

This landmark description induces also some equivalence classes on $\mathcal{X}$ and a dissimilarity measure on $\mathcal{X} \times \mathcal{X}$. Preliminarly, we remark that given $x_i, x_j \in \mathcal{X}$, with $x_i = x_j$, then $L(x_i) = L(x_j)$; on the contrary it may result $L(x_i) = L(x_j)$ even if $x_i \neq x_j$. This leads to the concept of L-equivalence.

Definition 1. Two functional data $x_i, x_j \in \mathcal{X}$ are called *L-equivalent* if $L(x_i) = L(x_j)$.

Given two functional data $x_i, x_j \in \mathcal{X}$, we shall denote by $|L(x_i) \cap L(x_j)|$ the length of the largest subsequence shared by $L(x_i)$ and $L(x_j)$. For example, if $L(x_i) = (+1, -1, +1)$ and $L(x_j) = (-1, +1, -1)$, then we have $|L(x_i) \cap L(x_j)| = 2$ because $L(x_i)$ and $L(x_j)$ share the subsequences $(-1, +1)$ and $(+1, -1)$ having both two elements. In particular it results:

$$|L(x_i) \cap L(x_j)| = \begin{cases} 0 & \text{if either } L(x_i) = \emptyset \text{ or } L(x_j) = \emptyset \\ |L(x_i)| & \text{if } x_i = x_j \\ |L(x_i)| - 1 & \text{if } x_i \neq x_j \text{ and } L(x_i) = L(x_j) \\ \min\{|L(x_i)|, |L(x_j)|\} & \text{otherwise, i.e. if } L(x_i) \neq L(x_j). \end{cases} \quad (2)$$

Let us introduce the following dissimilarity measure on $\mathcal{X} \times \mathcal{X}$:

$$d_L(x_i, x_j) := |L(x_i)| + |L(x_j)| - 2|L(x_i) \cap L(x_j)|. \quad (3)$$

According to the relations (2), it results $d_L(x_i, x_i) = 0$ since $|L(x_i)| + |L(x_i)| - 2|L(x_i)| = 0$. Moreover d_L is symmetric since $|L(x_i) \cap L(x_j)| = |L(x_j) \cap L(x_i)|$. Thus measure (3) specializes:

$$d_L(x_i, x_j) = \begin{cases} |L(x_j)| & \text{if } |L(x_i)| = 0 \quad (\text{resp. } |L(x_i)| \text{ if } |L(x_j)| = 0) \\ 2 & \text{if } x_i \neq x_j \text{ and } |L(x_i)| = |L(x_j)| \geq 1 \\ |L(x_i)| + |L(x_j)| - 2\min\{|L(x_i)|, |L(x_j)|\} & \text{if } L(x_i) \neq L(x_j). \end{cases} \quad (4)$$

Below we give some examples:

$L(x_i)$	$L(x_j)$	$\|L(x_i)\|$	$\|L(x_j)\|$	$\|L(x_i) \cap L(x_j)\|$	$d_L(x_i, x_j)$
$\emptyset$	$(-1, +1)$	0	2	0	2
$(+1)$	(-1)	1	1	0	2
$(+1, -1)$	$(+1, -1, +1)$	2	3	2	1
$(-1, +1, -1)$	$(+1, -1, +1)$	3	3	2	2
$(+1, -1)$	$(-1, +1, -1, +1)$	2	4	2	2
(-1)	$(+1, -1, +1, -1)$	1	4	1	3

Finally we prove that d_L satisfies the triangle inequality.

Proposition 1. For any $x_i, x_j, x_k \in \mathcal{X}$ it results:

$$d_L(x_i, x_j) \le d_L(x_i, x_k) + d_L(x_k, x_j) . \tag{5}$$

Proof. If either $x_i = x_j$ or $x_i = x_k$ (or $x_j = x_k$) the proof is trivial; again if either $L(x_i) = \emptyset$ or $L(x_j) = \emptyset$ the proof is trivial. So in the rest of the proof we shall assume $x_i \ne x_j$, $x_i \ne x_k$, $x_k \ne x_j$, $|L(x_i)| \ge 1$ and $|L(x_j)| \ge 1$. We have to distinguish some subcases:

   i) $|L(x_k)| < |L(x_i)| = |L(x_j)|$;
   ii) $|L(x_i)| = |L(x_j)| < |L(x_k)|$;
  iii) $|L(x_k)| = |L(x_i)| < |L(x_j)|$;
  iv) $|L(x_i)| < |L(x_j)| = |L(x_k)|$;
   v) $|L(x_k)| < |L(x_i)| < |L(x_j)|$;
  vi) $|L(x_i)| < |L(x_k)| < |L(x_j)|$;
 vii) $|L(x_i)| < |L(x_j)| < |L(x_k)|$.

i) $\underline{|L(x_k)| < |L(x_i)| = |L(x_j)|}$, i.e. $|L(x_i)| - |L(x_k)| \ge 1$. Relation (4) yields:

$$d_L(x_i, x_j) = 2$$
$$\begin{aligned} d_L(x_i, x_k) + d_L(x_k, x_j) &= |L(x_i)| + |L(x_k)| - 2|L(x_k)| \\ &\quad + |L(x_j)| + |L(x_k)| - 2|L(x_k)| \\ &= 2(|L(x_i)| - |L(x_k)|) \ge 2 = d_L(x_i, x_j) \end{aligned}$$

so that inequality (5) is here satisfied.

ii) $\underline{|L(x_i)| = |L(x_j)| < |L(x_k)|}$, i.e. $|L(x_k)| - |L(x_i)| \ge 1$. In this case again it results $d_L(x_i, x_j) = 2$ and the proof follows along the same lines of the previous case.

iii) $\underline{|L(x_k)| = |L(x_i)| < |L(x_j)|}$. Here $\min\{|L(x_i)|, |L(x_j)|\} = |L(x_i)|$ and thus:

$$d_L(x_i, x_j) = |L(x_i)| + |L(x_j)| - 2|L(x_i)| = |L(x_j)| - |L(x_i)|$$

so that, as $|L(x_k)| = |L(x_i)|$, we get:

$$\begin{aligned} d_L(x_i, x_k) + d_L(x_k, x_j) &= 2 + |L(x_k)| + |L(x_j)| - 2|L(x_k)| \\ &= 2 + |L(x_j)| - |L(x_i)| \ge d_L(x_i, x_j) . \end{aligned}$$

iv) $|L(x_i)| < |L(x_j)| = |L(x_k)|$. The proof goes as in the previous case.

v) $|L(x_k)| < |L(x_i)| < |L(x_j)|$. In this case we have $d_L(x_i, x_j) = |L(x_i)| + |L(x_j)| - 2|L(x_i)| = |L(x_j)| - |L(x_i)|$ and thus:

$$
\begin{aligned}
d_L(x_i, x_k) + d_L(x_k, x_j) &= |L(x_k)| + |L(x_i)| - 2|L(x_k)| \\
&\quad + |L(x_j)| + |L(x_k)| - 2|L(x_k)| \\
&= |L(x_j)| + |L(x_i)| - 2|L(x_k)| \\
&> |L(x_j)| + |L(x_i)| - 2|L(x_i)| \\
&= |L(x_j)| - |L(x_i)| = d_L(x_i, x_j) .
\end{aligned}
$$

vi) $|L(x_i)| < |L(x_k)| < |L(x_j)|$. In this case again $d_L(x_i, x_j) = |L(x_j)| - |L(x_i)|$ and then we get:

$$
\begin{aligned}
d_L(x_i, x_k) + d_L(x_k, x_j) &= |L(x_k)| + |L(x_i)| - 2|L(x_i)| \\
&\quad + |L(x_j)| + |L(x_k)| - 2|L(x_k)| \\
&= |L(x_j)| - |L(x_i)| = d_L(x_i, x_j) .
\end{aligned}
$$

vii) $|L(x_i)| < |L(x_j)| < |L(x_k)|$. Also in this case we have $d_L(x_i, x_j) = |L(x_j)| - |L(x_i)|$. Here we have:

$$
\begin{aligned}
d_L(x_i, x_k) + d_L(x_k, x_j) &= |L(x_k)| + |L(x_i)| - 2|L(x_i)| \\
&\quad + |L(x_j)| + |L(x_k)| - 2|L(x_j)| \\
&= |L(x_k)| - |L(x_i)| + |L(x_k)| - |L(x_j)|
\end{aligned}
$$

The hypotheses imply that $|L(x_k)| > |L(x_j)|$ so we get:

$$
\begin{aligned}
d_L(x_i, x_k) + d_L(x_k, x_j) &> |L(x_j)| - |L(x_i)| + |L(x_j)| - |L(x_j)| \\
&= |L(x_j)| - |L(x_i)| = d_L(x_i, x_j).
\end{aligned}
$$

This completes the proof. ∎

Once we have established the triangle inequality for d_L, it can be regarded as a distance measure between L-equivalence classes.

The equivalence classes on $\mathcal{X}$ induced by the landmark description can be graphically represented by a *landmark description graph*, displayed in Figure 1, where the vertices are the equivalence classes and the edges link pairs of vertices at distance equal to 1. Moreover, the diameter of the circles representing the vertices is proportional to the number of data in the corresponding class. Obviously, if some class is empty then there is neither the corresponding vertex nor the related edges in the graph (see Figure 2 in the next section).

For example, the neighbourhood of $(-1, +1)$ is $\{(-1), (+1), (+1, -1, +1), (-1, +1, -1)\}$ and the neighbourhood of $(-1, +1, -1)$ is $\{(-1, +1), (+1, -1), (-1, +1, -1, +1), (+1, -1, +1, -1)\}$. This clarifies why the sequences such that $x_i \neq x_j$ but $L(x_i) = L(x_j)$ are at distance equal to 2. In this graph, the

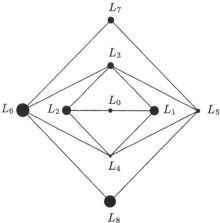

Fig. 1. Example of landmark description graph, where: L_0 : $\emptyset$ (two data), L_1 : $(+1)$ (four data), L_2 : (-1) (four data), L_3 : $(+1, -1)$ (three data), L_4 : $(-1, +1)$ (one datum), L_5 : $(+1, -1, +1)$ (two data), L_6 : $(-1, +1, -1)$ (six data), L_7 : $(+1, -1, +1, -1)$ (three data), L_8 : $(-1, +1, -1, +1)$ (five data).

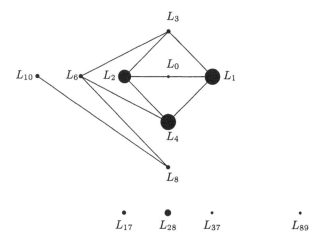

Fig. 2. Landmark description graph of the Canadian precipitation dataset.

vertices put at the top or on the right (at the bottom or on the left) correspond to sequences starting with a maximum, i.e. with a $+1$ (a minimum, i.e. with a -1). Moving from left to right or from the bottom to the top corresponds to add a maximum, i.e. a $+1$ in the sequence; on the contrary we add a minimum (-1) when we move from right to left or from the top to the bottom of the graph.

4   A case study: The Canadian precipitation dataset

The proposed approach is here synthetically illustrated using the Canadian weather dataset (available from the web site www.psych.mcgill.ca), consisting of average daily precipitation in millimetres for 35 Canadian weather stations averaged over the years since 1961 to 1994. Thus we have a 35×365 data matrix. According to our landmark descriptions, we obtain the following L-equivalence classes which are graphically represented in Figure 2. Of course, the four vertices at the bottom of the graph in Figure 2 represent as many isolated classes.

L_0 : {London}

L_1 : {Churchill, Montreal, Ottawa, Resolute, Sherbrooke, Toronto, Winnipeg}

L_2 : {Charlottetown, Fredericton, Halifax, Saint John, Sydney, Yarmouth}

L_3 : {Prince Albert, Regina},

L_4 : {Bagottville, Dawson, Quebec, Thunder Bay, Victoria, Yellowknife, Iqaluit},

L_6 : {Arvida, Whitehorse},

L_8 : {The Pass, Prince George},

L_{10} : {Calgary},

L_{17} : {Schefferville, Uranium City},

L_{28} : {Vancouver, Edmonton, Inuvik},

L_{37} : {Kamloops},

L_{89} : {Prince Rupert},

We remark that the obtained classes depend only on the variability of precipitations regardless of the season when they actually occur. For example, the classes L_0, L_1 and L_2 present slowly varying precipitations, while L_{28}, L_{37} and L_{89} are characterized by a quite high variability in rainfalls. It is worth noting that such groups (and distances) reflect quite often geographical proximities: for example the cities in L_2 are on the Atlantic coast; many of the cities in L_0 and L_1 are near the Lakes Ontario and Erie (the other ones are also close to some lake or to the sea: Churchill is on the Bay of Hudson, Winnipeg is on the Lake Winnipeg, Resolute is placed on a small island in the North on the country); the cities in the classes L_{28}, L_{37} and L_{89} are on the Pacific coast (except Inuvik placed in the North-West close to the Beaufort Sea).

5   Concluding remarks

The obtained clustering is coherent with the proposed analysis based on the sequence of maxima and minima (regardless neither of their seasonality nor of their numerical values). An obvious criticism is that some small variations in shape might be considered as a sequence of vertices rather than random perturbations. This explains, for example, why Victoria and Vancouver have quite different landmark descriptions (respectively L_4 and L_{28}) even if they are quite close from a geographical point of view. This aspect depends also on the adopted smoothing procedure and it will be refined later on.

The present approach must be considered only as the first step in the context of a larger project taking into account also other relevant aspects of functional data, like the seasonality and the function values at the vertices. For this purpose, in Cerioli *et al.* (2002) we propose a *structured landmark description* coming from a partition of the interval $[a, b]$ into a fixed number of 2^m subintervals. Then we consider landmark descriptions and curve slopes within each subinterval. Our full approach will also involve a combination of both shape dissimilarity and metric distances, in order to summarize such features. In this context the analysis of symbolic data provides many interesting ideas, see De Carvalho (1994), Gordon (1999) and Esposito *et al.* (2000).

References

AZENCOTT R. and INGRASSIA S. (1998): Learning planar shapes and neural nets complexity, *Tech. Rep. 9822, CMLA at École Normale Supérieure de Cachan.*

CERIOLI A., INGRASSIA S. and CORBELLINI A. (2002): Symbolic descriptions for clustering of functional data, in preparation.

DE CARVALHO, F. A. T. (1994): Proximity coefficients between boolean symbolic objects. In: E. Diday et al. (Eds.): *New Approaches in Classification and Data Analysis, Springer, Berlin, 387-394.*

ESPOSITO F., MALERBA D. and TAMMA V. (2000): Dissimilarity Measures for symbolic objects, in *Analysis of Symbolic Data, Bock H.-H. and Diday E. (Eds.), Springer-Verlag, Berlin, 165-185.*

GORDON A.D (1999): *Classification,* Chapman & Hall, London, 2nd Edition.

HECKMAN N. and ZAMAR R. (2000): Comparing the shapes of regression functions, *Biometrika, 87, 135-144.*

MARRON J.S. and TSYBAKOV A.B. (1995) Visual error criteria for qualitative smoothing, *Journal of the American Statistical Association, 90, 499-507.*

RAMSAY J.O. and SILVERMAN B.W. (1997): *Functional Data Analysis,* Springer-Verlag, New York.

Scalable Clustering of High Dimensional Data

David Littau and Daniel Boley

Department of Computer Science and Engineering,
University of Minnesota,
Minneapolis, MN 55455 USA
{littau,boley}@cs.umn.edu

Abstract. Existing data collections can be large in both number of samples and in number of attributes per sample. In either case, we have found that many advanced techniques in numerical linear algebra can be used to design efficient algorithms for clustering and exploring these datasets. We illustrate this point with the method of Principal Direction Divisive Partitioning, a scalable unsupervised clustering algorithm which has been found to give high quality clusters. We show how the scalability to large sizes is achieved using those advanced linear algebra techniques. These techniques also lead to an alternate representation of the dataset which is close enough to the original for the purposes of clustering while occupying a much smaller memory footprint.

1   Introduction

Large and/or high dimension data sets present a challenge for clustering algorithms in terms of scalability, speed of execution, and limitations in available memory. When a clustering algorithm doesn't scale well, the usual solution is to either adapt the method so it will scale better (Cutting et. al. (1992), Guha et. al. (1998)), or to sub-sample the original data and use the sub-sample to get a clustering of the entire data set. Solutions responding to a lack of available memory usually involve constructing representations of the original data, such that a single vector represents many original data items (e.g. Cutting et. al. (1992), Bradley et. al. (1998), Zhang et. al. (1997)). These representatives are used to produce a clustering of the original data.

We propose two alternatives to solve the speed and memory issues. To address the issues of scalability and speed, we present Principal Direction Divisive Partitioning (PDDP)(Boley, 1998). PDDP is an unsupervised, divisive algorithm which uses the principal direction of the data in a given cluster to determine how to split that cluster. The method used to find the principal direction can be fast since a high degree of accuracy is not required. PDDP scales linearly with the dimension of the data items and the number of samples in the data set.

When there is insufficient memory to contain the entire data set, our solution is to construct a low-memory representation of the data. Each original data item is uniquely represented using a least-squares approximation to a small number of basis vectors. The basis vectors for each data item are chosen from a larger set of basis vectors which are inexpensive to obtain. The low-memory representation of the data is then clustered using PDDP. We term this method Piecemeal PDDP (PMPDDP) since the low-memory representations are constructed in a piecemeal fashion using disjoint subsets of the original data set.

The clustering methods we present produce good clusterings in a reasonable amount of time. We offer them as alternative solutions to clustering large and/or high dimension data sets.

2 PDDP

PDDP is an unsupervised divisive clustering algorithm. The values of the data attributes are used to determine the clustering, and there is no prior knowledge of class membership of the data items. PDDP constructs a hierarchical binary tree by recursively splitting clusters. The process starts with the root cluster, which contains all the data samples. The root cluster is split by finding the principal direction $\mathbf{u}$ of the cluster around the centroid and projecting all the data in the cluster onto $\mathbf{u}$. All data on one side of the mean $\mathbf{w}$ of the cluster are placed in one child cluster, and the rest are placed in the other child cluster. The leaf cluster with the largest scatter is split next, and the process continues until some stopping criterion is met. The leaf nodes of the PDDP tree define the clustering of the data set. An example of a two-dimensional split is shown in Figure 1.

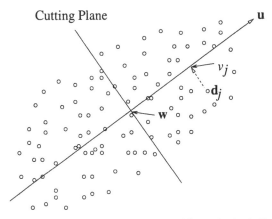

Fig. 1. A PDDP split in two-dimensional space. The principal direction $\mathbf{u}$ of the data is computed, and the data points $\mathbf{d}_i$ in the cluster are projected onto $\mathbf{u}$, defining the points v_i. All v_i greater than the mean $\mathbf{w}$ are placed in one new cluster, and the rest of the points are placed in the other new cluster.

The cost of splitting a cluster is dominated by the cost of computing the principal direction, or leading singular vector, of the data in the cluster. The principal direction of the data is computed using the iterative method proposed by Lanczos. The primary expense in Lanczos' method is the computation of a matrix-vector product. Therefore, the cost to split a root cluster which has m data samples with n attributes per sample and fill fraction γ is:

$$c_1 m \gamma n, \tag{1}$$

where c_1 represents the number of iterations to convergence. If we assume for the sake of this analysis that the clusters resulting from splitting the root cluster have the same cardinality, then the cost of splitting the next two clusters will be $c_1 \frac{m}{2} \gamma n + c_1 \frac{m}{2} \gamma n$, which is the same cost as in (1). If we assume a perfectly balanced binary tree in which the number of leaf clusters is a power of 2, then producing the entire PDDP tree costs:

$$c_1 m \gamma n \log_2(k_f), \tag{2}$$

where k_f is the number of leaf clusters in the PDDP tree. PDDP is scalable in the sense that the cost of clustering is linear in the number of samples and the number of attributes, and logarithmic in the number of clusters.

The results for PDDP clustering of various document data sets is shown in Figure 2. The results indicate that PDDP is linear in the number of words and in the number of documents. This agrees with the complexity analysis.

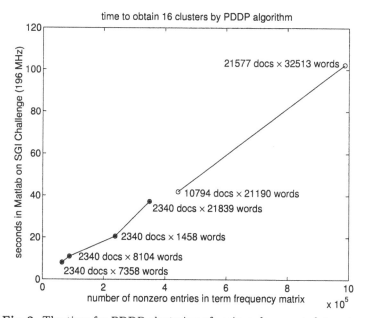

Fig. 2. The time for PDDP clustering of various document data sets.

3 PMPDDP

PDDP requires the data set be small enough to fit into memory for efficient computation, since the data are scanned many times during the iterative process used to obtain the rank 1 SVD. There are many large data sets which will not fit into the memory of most workstations, and therefore cannot be clustered quickly using PDDP. PMPDDP resolves this problem by creating a low-memory representation of the original data set that will fit into memory, and then clusters the representation using PDDP.

To construct the low-memory representation, the data set is divided into k_s disjoint samples called *sections*. For each section, PDDP is used to compute k_c clusters. The centers of these clusters form the basis of the representation for that section. For each data item in a section, the k_z closest centers in the basis are used to compute a least-squares approximation to that data item. Once the low-memory representation for each section has been computed, the results are assembled into a two-matrix system. The construction of the low-memory representation is shown in Figure 3, and the associated parameters are summarized in Table 1. Since the low-memory representations for each section of data are computed independently, they can be computed in parallel.

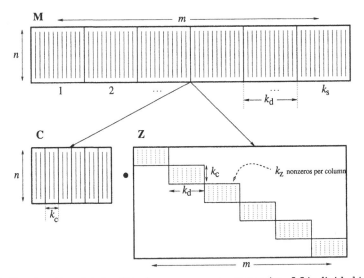

Fig. 3. Construction details of the low-memory representation. M is divided into k_s sections, and the low-memory representation of each section is computed without referring to any other section. Each section is associated with a subdivision of C and Z. The columns of a subdivision of C are the cluster centers resulting from a clustering of the associated section. A column of a subdivision of Z is computed with a least-squares approximation to the corresponding column of M, using the k_z closest centers from the associated subdivision of C.

parameter	description
m	total number of data items
n	number of attributes per data item
γ	fill fraction for the attributes
k_s	number of sections
k_d	number of data items per section
k_c	number of centers per section
k_z	number of centers approximating each data item
k_f	number of final clusters

Table 1. Definition of the parameters used in PMPDDP (see Figure 3).

This low-memory representation is similar to the concept decomposition (Dhillon and Modha (2001)), except that the concept decomposition does not enforce a sparsity condition and was designed to process the entire data set at once. The sparse representation in Zhang et. al. (2002) is based on the SVD, and therefore attempts to generate orthogonal basis vectors. Both of these other methods were designed in the context of performing Latent Semantic Indexing (LSI)(Berry et. al. (1995)), while our method was designed specifically to be an aid when clustering large data sets.

PDDP has a unique advantage when clustering this low-memory representation. Unlike traditional clustering algorithms, PDDP does not compute a pairwise similarity or a distance between every data sample and every other data sample. The sample vectors represented by **CZ** never have to be re-generated during the clustering process. Doing so, in fact, would destroy any of the memory savings gained from forming the low-memory representation.

If this representation is to save memory, k_z must be smaller than the number of attributes n. The resulting least-squares problem is under-determined. If the k_z basis vectors are linearly independent, we use the normal equations with the Cholesky decomposition to solve the least-squares problem. Otherwise, we use the SVD to get the least-squares approximation of the data item. Even though there has been no attempt to create orthogonal basis vectors, in the majority of cases the normal equations give a satisfactory approximation.

We break down the cost of computing a PMPDDP clustering as being the cost of computing the low-memory representation of the data and the cost of clustering the low-memory representation. Constructing the low-memory representation for each section of data requires:(1) clustering the data in the section, (2) extracting the cluster centers to use as a basis, (3) finding the basis vectors closest to each data item, and (4) computing a least-squares approximation for each data item. We present the cost for computing the low-memory representation of a given section, after which we will show the cost of clustering the low-memory representation of the entire data set.

The cost of computing a clustering for each section of data is:

$$c_1 k_d \gamma n \log_2(k_c), \qquad (3)$$

which is the cost of a PDDP clustering of the section with the appropriate parameters inserted. The centers of the clusters are extracted at negligible expense. The cost of finding the centers closest to each data item is:

$$k_d(\gamma n k_c + k_z k_c), \qquad (4)$$

where $\gamma n k_c$ is the cost of finding the distance from a given data item to every center in the basis, and $k_z k_c$ is the cost of finding the k_z centers closest to that data item. Once the k_z centers are chosen, then the least-squares approximation to the data item using the normal equations costs:

$$k_d(k_z^2 n + \frac{1}{3}k_z^3) \qquad (5)$$

for all the data items in a given section. This cost is the same for each section of data, since the assumption is that k_d, k_c, and k_z are the same for each section. To get the cost over all sections, replace k_d in the above formulas with m.

At this point, we have a low-memory representation of the original data set. Recall that the majority of the cost of PDDP is in forming a matrix-vector product in the Lanczos SVD solver. Replacing the original data matrix $\mathbf{M}$ with the factored form $\mathbf{CZ}$ means that the matrix-vector product will be replaced with a matrix-matrix-vector product.

To form the product $\mathbf{CZv}$ for some $\mathbf{v}$, it is much more efficient to group it as $\mathbf{C(Zv)}$ than $(\mathbf{CZ})\mathbf{v}$. The cost of computing a matrix-vector product associated with $\mathbf{C}$ is $c_2 k_s k_c n$, and the cost of computing the matrix-vector product associated with $\mathbf{Z}$ is $c_2 k_z \tilde{m}$, where $\tilde{m}$ is the number of data items in the cluster. The assumption is that since $\mathbf{Z}$ is sparse, only the non-zeroes will participate in the product. To produce a completely balanced binary tree, the cost of clustering $\mathbf{CZ}$ is:

$$c_2(k_f - 1)k_s k_c n + c_2 \log_2(k_f) k_z m. \qquad (6)$$

The total cost of the matrix-vector product associated with $\mathbf{C}$ differs from previous results since all the columns of $\mathbf{C}$ are involved in every iteration for every cluster at every level, while the columns of $\mathbf{Z}$ are dispersed across all the clusters in a given level of the tree.

The scatter values for a PMPDDP clustering of four data sets with varying k_z are shown in Figure 4. The experiment parameters are summarized in Table 2. The values in Figure 4 are normalized with respect to a PDDP clustering using the same k_f. The results indicate that within the context of clustering using PDDP, it is possible to get a more accurate clustering by using more than one vector to approximate each data item.

4   Conclusion

Clustering large, high-dimension data sets can be expensive if the clustering algorithm is not scalable. In this work, we presented a clustering algorithm,

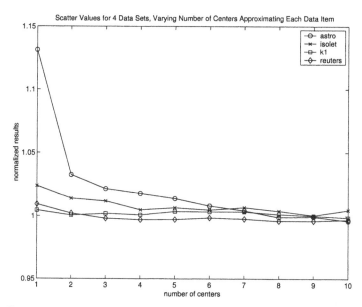

Fig. 4. Scatter values for four data sets with an increasing number of centers k_z approximating each data item. The results are normalized with respect to a PDDP clustering of the entire data set at once with the same number of final clusters k_f.

dataset		astro	isolet	k1	reuters
number of samples	m	212089	7997	2340	9494
number of attributes per sample	n	26	617	21839	19968
sparsity (percentage nonzeroes)		dense	dense	0.68%	0.20%
number of sections	k_s	10	5	5	5
number of centers per section	k_c	1000	150	50	100
number of centers in final clustering k_f		2000	150	50	100

Table 2. Datasets and parameter values used for PMPDDP experiments. The astro data is from the Minnesota Automated Plate Scan (APS) (Pennington et. al. (1993)), the isolet data is from Murphy and Aha (1994), the k1 document data is from Boley et. al. (1999), and the reuters data is the standard reuters data set (Lewis (1997)) selecting the items which had only one topic assigned to them.

PDDP, which is fast and scalable. We showed that for the document data sets examined, PDDP is linear in the number of data items and the number of attributes. This agrees with the complexity analysis of PDDP.

For situations in which there isn't enough memory to contain the data set, we presented a method to construct a low-memory representation of the data which can be clustered efficiently using PDDP. We call the combination of producing the low-memory representation and clustering it PMPDDP. The low-memory representation is different from those presented in other clustering methods (e.g. Zhang et. al. (1997) and Bradley et. al. (1998)) in that each original data item has a unique representation, and each data item can be approximated using more than one basis vector. In the context of PDDP clustering, using more than one basis vector to approximate each data item resulted in a better quality clustering.

References

BERRY, M.W. and DUMAIS, S.T. and O'BRIEN, G.W. (1995): Using Linear Algebra for Intelligent Information Retrieval. *SIAM Review, 37, 573-595.*

BOLEY, D.L. (1998): Principal Direction Divisive Partitioning. *Data Mining and Knowledge Discovery, 2, 325-344.*

BOLEY, D.L. and GINI, M. and GROSS, R. and HAN, E-H and HASTINGS, K. and KARYPIS, G. and KUMAR, V. and MOBASHER, B. and MOORE, J. (1999): Document Categorization and Query Generation on the World Wide Web using WebACE. *AI Review, 13, 5-6, 365-391*

BRADLEY, P.S. and FAYYAD, U.M. and REINA, C. (1998): Scaling Clustering Algorithms to Large Databases. In: *Knowledge Discovery and Data Mining.* 9-15.

CUTTING, D.R. and PEDERSEN, J.O. and KARGER, D. and TUKEY, J.W. (1992): Scatter/Gather: A Cluster-Based Approach to Browsing Large Document Collections. In: *Proc. of the Fifteenth Annual International ACM SIGIR Con. on Res. and Dev. in Information Retrieval.* 318-329.

DHILLON, I.S. and MODHA, D.S. (2001): Concept Decomposition for Large Sparse Text Data Using Clustering. *Machine Learning, 42, 1, 143-175.*

GUHA, S. and RASTOGI, R. and SHIM, K. (1998): CURE: An Efficient Clustering Algorithm for Large Data Bases. In: *Proc. of 1998 ACM-SIGMOD Int. Conf. on Management of Data.* 73-84.

LEWIS, D. (1997): Reuters-21578.

MURPHY, P.M. and AHA, D.W. (1994): UCI Repository of Machine Learning Databases.

PENNINGTON, R.L. and HUMPHREYS, R.M. and ODEWAHN, S.C. and ZU-MACH, W. and THURMES, P.M. (1993): The Automated Plate Scanner Catalog of the Palomar Sky Survey – Scanning Parameters and Procedures. *P. A. S. P., 105, 521ff.*

ZHANG, T. and RAMAKRISHNAN, R. and LIVNY, M. (1997): BIRCH: A New Data Clustering Algorithm and Its Applications. *Data Mining and Knowledge Discovery, 1, 2 141-182.*

ZHANG, Z. and ZHA, H. and SIMON, H. (2002): Low-Rank Approximation with Sparse Factors i: Basic Algorithms and Error Analysis. *SIAM J. Matrix Anal., 23, 706-727.*

Acknowledgments: This research was partially supported by NSF grant IIS-9811229. The authors gratefully acknowledge the invitation of Profs. Hans-Hermann Bock, Wolfgang Gaul, and Martin Schader to present this work at the 2002 annual meeting of the German Classification Society.

Methods to Combine Classification Trees

Rossella Miglio and Gabriele Soffritti

Dipartimento di Scienze Statistiche
Università di Bologna, I-40126 Bologna, Italy

Abstract. In this paper some methods to combine classification trees are described; then a new method based on a proximity measure is proposed that simultaneously takes into account structural and predictive differences between trees; it allows to summarize the information contained in different trees constructed by means of cross-validation or bootstrap samples, or obtained from independent data sets having the same predictors and class variables. An example of application of the proposed procedure to a real data set is then illustrated and discussed.

1 Introduction

Generally speaking, the consensus problem consists of aggregating several objects into a unique object of the same type (Léclerc (1998)). This problem has been the subject of some research in the classification literature and the obtained results are particularly applicable to the comparison of partitions, dendrograms, n-trees, ordered trees, and phylogenetic trees. In 1988 an issue of the Journal of Classification was completely devoted to methodologies for the comparison and consensus of classifications; more recently, Léclerc (1998) presented a survey of the literature on the consensus of classification trees, based on a corpus of about ninety papers.

Starting from a set of classifications obtained from the analysis of a data set, the purpose of the different methods proposed in literature has been either to recover an hypothetical "true" classification, or to find a classification summarizing at best the given set of classifications. There are three (possibly overlapping) approaches to obtain consensus classifications (Barthélemy, Léclerc, and Monjardet (1986)): (*i*) optimization, where a loss function has to be minimized; (*ii*) constructive, when purely combinatorial methods are proposed involving heuristic algorithms with interesting properties; (*iii*) axiomatic, where particular properties of consensus procedures are formulated, and methods satisfying these properties are defined.

Some methodologies have been proposed also to identify a consensus of a set of binary trees. It is well known that classification trees represent non parametric classifiers that exploit the local relationship between the class variable and the predictors. They allow an automatic feature selection and a hierarchical representation of the measurement space. A typical segmentation procedure repeatedly splits the predictor space generally in two disjoint regions according to a local optimization criterion; in order to control the effective complexity of the model, a pruning procedure follows the growing step (Breiman et al. (1984)). A binary tree is the representation of such a sequence of binary partitions.

Given an observed set of binary trees $T = \{T_i, i = 1, \ldots, m\}$, which can be obtained, for instance, by means of m cross-validation or bootstrap samples, or from m independent data sets containing the same predictor and class variables, a first way to obtain a consensus tree is to combine those parts of the observed trees about which there is general agreement. Starting with the root node labelled $k = 1$, the node k, $k \geq 1$, of the consensus tree can be splitted on the variable that occurred most frequently at node k among the set of observed trees. If the most frequent event at node k is not to split, then the consensus tree will not split at k. If two or more variables tie for the most frequent split, then one solution is to pick a tied variable at random or, alternatively, ties can be broken by conditioning on previous splitting variables in the path (Shannon and Banks (1999)).

A different way to obtain a consensus tree is to grow a structure which results similar as much as possible to the elements of T according to specific proximity measures. Two consensus methods which follow this proximity-based approach are described in Section 2; in the first one a distance metric between trees is used (Shannon and Banks (1999)), while in the second a similarity measure (Miglio (1996)); however both measures are not completely satisfactory. In Section 3 a new consensus method is thus defined; it is based on a dissimilarity measure which has been recently proposed to overcome the limitations of the previous ones (Miglio and Soffritti (2001)). Section 4 reports the results of an application to a real data example and concluding remarks.

2   Two proximity-based consensus methods

2.1   Shannon and banks' consensus method

The consensus method proposed by Shannon and Banks (1999) was motivated by the availability of independent data sets having the same predictors and class variables. They defined a probability distribution for an equivalence class G of classification trees (that is, those that ignore the value of the cutpoints but retain tree structure). Their distribution is parametrized by a tree $g*$, representing the central tree structure, and a precision or concentration coefficient $\tau \geq 0$, representing the variability around this central tree:

$$P(g) = c(g*, \tau) \exp[-\tau d(g, g*)], \tag{1}$$

where g denotes a generic tree belonging to G, $c(g*, \tau)$ is the normalizing constant, and $d(g, g*)$ is an arbitrary metric on G. Intuitively $g*$ can be seen as the 'mean' and τ as a measure of precision (the inverse of dispersion) of the distribution; these unknown parameters are estimated from a random sample of m observed trees by the maximum likelihood. The estimate of $g*$ will be the consensus tree for the observed set of binary trees. Since the maximum likelihood equations are hard to solve, numerical approximated solutions have to be determined. Shannon and Banks implemented an ascent search algorithm which obtains the maximum likelihood estimate of the central tree by an iterative process starting at each of the observed trees. The search for the maximum likelihood estimation is based on trees generated by randomly adding one split to a terminal node or deleting one terminal node from each candidate tree (for more details on their numerical search algorithm, see Shannon and Banks (1999), p. 735).

Since the method requires the specification of a metric on G, the authors defined a distance metric $d(T_i, T_j)$ between trees T_i, T_j which measures the amount of rearrangement needed to change one of the trees so that its structure is identical to the other. Specifically, the distance between trees T_i and T_j is defined by Shannon and Banks as

$$d(T_i, T_j) = \sum_r \alpha_r |S_{ijr}|, \qquad (2)$$

where S_{ijr} denotes the set composed by discrepant r-paths (paths of length r found in only one of the two trees), and $\alpha_r = \alpha(r)$ is a weight function that depends only on r. The weight function can be selected to penalize structural differences between trees based on where these occur. For example, a constant weight function ($\alpha_r = 1$) does not distinguish between differences occurring early or late in the trees, while the function $\alpha_r = 1/r$ penalizes early discrepancies more heavily than those occurring later in the tree.

As discussed in Miglio and Soffritti (2001), this measure has some limitations. In fact, the value of $d(T_i, T_j)$ cannot be easily interpreted on its own to describe the intensity of the distance (for instance to compare the distance between different pairs of trees) since it is highly dependent on the number of paths present in T_i and T_j and on the lengths of each of them. To overcome this limitation, the value of $d(T_i, T_j)$ should be divided by a normalizing factor (for details, see Miglio and Soffritti (2001)). Furthermore, this distance considers only tree topology, and takes into explicit consideration neither the partitions of the units nor the predictions associated to each observed tree.

2.2 Miglio's consensus method

This second consensus method was defined by Miglio in order to grow a simple and stable structure which summarizes the information contained in different trees constructed by means of cross-validation samples. It is based on the similarity measure between trees which Miglio (1996) obtained by suitably modifying the one introduced by Fowlkes and Mallows (1983) for the comparison of two hierarchical clusterings.

Let H and K be the number of leaves of T_i and T_j respectively; we may label from one to H the leaves of T_i and from one to K the leaves of T_j and form the matrix

$$M = [m_{hk}] \, h = 1, \ldots, H, \, k = 1, \ldots, K,$$

where m_{hk} is the number of objects which belong both to the h-th leaf of T_i and to the k-th leaf of T_j. Furthermore, let $c_{hk} = 1$ if the h-th leaf of T_i has the same class label as the k-th leaf of T_j, and $c_{hk} = 0$ otherwise. The similarity measure between trees T_i and T_j is then defined as follows (Miglio (1996)):

$$B\left(T_i, T_j\right) = \frac{\sum_{h=1}^{H} \sum_{k=1}^{K} m_{hk}^2 c_{hk} - \sum_{h=1}^{H} \sum_{k=1}^{K} m_{hk} c_{hk}}{\sqrt{P_i Q_j}}, \tag{3}$$

where the numerator counts the pairs of objects which are classified together in both partitions and that are also assigned to the same class; the denominator is a normalizing factor which compels the measure to lie between 0 and 1, computed as follows:

$$m_{h0} = \sum_{k=1}^{K} m_{hk}; \; m_{0k} = \sum_{h=1}^{H} m_{hk}; \; P_i = \sum_{h=1}^{H} m_{h0}^2 - n; \; Q_j = \sum_{k=1}^{K} m_{0k}^2 - n.$$

Miglio (1996) used this measure to define a method to grow a consensus tree T_c; it is based on the following consensus measure:

$$CVCON = \frac{1}{m} \sum_{i=1}^{m} B(T_i, T_c), \tag{4}$$

where $B(T_i, T_c)$ is the similarity measure defined in equation (3) computed between the consensus tree and a generic observed tree. Then, she proposed an algorithm which grows a structure T_c with the highest consensus measure. At the first step of this algorithm all the split defining questions involved in the given trees are set as possible splits of the consensus tree. At the second step an iterative growing procedure is performed. First, it evaluates each of the binary splits specified at the previous step as split defining questions for the root node. The best split will be the one producing a tree with the highest consensus measure. If different splits have the same associated consensus measure, the choice among them can be made on the basis of different criteria, for example the one with the highest frequency of occurrence in the given trees. After having selected the first split, the tree growing procedure will continue with the iterative selection of the other splits, until the consensus measure increases or other stop conditions are satisfied (e.g., the number of units reaching each leaf is small or the leaf is homogeneous enough). Measures (3) and (4) take into account the partitions and the predictive powers of the trees but don't explicitly consider the predictors used at each split. Therefore also this second consensus method seems to be not completely satisfactory.

3   A new proximity-based consensus method

The new consensus method we propose is based on a dissimilarity measure which takes into account not only both the partitions and the predictive powers of the trees but also the predictors used at each split. We briefly recall this measure, then we describe the consensus method.

3.1   A dissimilarity measure based on topology, partition and prediction

The dissimilarity measure proposed by Miglio and Soffritti (2001) is defined as follows:

$$\delta\left(T_i, T_j\right) = \sum_{h=1}^{H} \alpha_{ih}(1 - s_{ih})\frac{m_{h0}}{n} + \sum_{k=1}^{K} \alpha_{jk}(1 - s_{jk})\frac{m_{0k}}{n}, \tag{5}$$

where m_{h0} and m_{0k} denote the number of units which belong to the h-th leaf of T_i and to the k-th leaf of T_j, respectively; s_{ih} and s_{jk} are similarity coefficients whose values synthesize the similarities s_{hk} between the H leaves of T_i and the K leaves of T_j, computed as follows:

$$s_{hk} = \frac{m_{hk}c_{hk}}{\sqrt{m_{h0}m_{0k}}}, \quad h = 1, \ldots, H, \ k = 1, \ldots, K; \tag{6}$$

s_{hk} is equal to 0 when $m_{hk} = 0$ and/or $c_{hk} = 0$, and equal to 1 when $c_{hk} = 1$ and both the h-th leaf of T_i and the k-th leaf of T_j have exactly the same objects, that therefore are assigned to the same class. When T_i and T_j are equal, each leaf of T_i will result maximally similar to a particular leaf of T_j, and minimally similar to any other. For this reason, a suitable way of synthesizing the similarities s_{hk} seems to be choosing the maximum:

$$s_{ih} = \max\{s_{hk}, \ k = 1, \ldots, K\}, \tag{7}$$

$$s_{jk} = \max\{s_{hk}, \ h = 1, \ldots, H\}. \tag{8}$$

The coefficients α_{ih} and α_{jk} are dissimilarity measures: the first is computed between the h-th leaf of T_i and that particular leaf of T_j identified by the criterion (7), while the second between the k-th leaf of T_j and that particular leaf of T_i identified by the criterion (8). If the paths associated to these pairs of leaves are identical, α_{ih} (α_{jk}) is set equal to 0. On the contrary, α_{ih} (α_{jk}) has to be set greater than 0 on the basis of the values of q and p, which denote the length of the longest path and the level where the two paths differ from each other, respectively. Specifically, α_{ih} (α_{jk}) can be set equal to $q - p + 1$ when it is useless to distinguish between differences occurring early or late in the paths, or equal to $\sum_{l=p}^{q} \frac{1}{l}$ when early discrepancies have to be penalized. Furthermore, the introduction of the relative frequency of each leaf weights the discrepancies proportionally to the number of their observations.

The maximum value of $\delta(T_i, T_j)$ can be reached when the difference between the structures of T_i and T_j is maximum and the similarity between their predictive powers is zero. The normalizing factor for $\delta(T_i, T_j)$ is thus equal to

$$\max \delta\left(T_i, T_j\right) = \sum_{h=1}^{H} \alpha_{ih}\frac{m_{h0}}{n} + \sum_{k=1}^{K} \alpha_{jk}\frac{m_{0k}}{n}, \tag{9}$$

where α_{ih} is set equal to q_{ih} (the length of the path from the root node to the h-th leaf of T_i) when a set of constant weights is considered, and equal to $\sum_{l=1}^{q_{ih}} \frac{1}{l}$ otherwise; α_{jk} is defined in an analogous way. The normalized version of the proposed dissimilarity is thus:

$$\Delta(T_i, T_j) = \frac{\delta(T_i, T_j)}{\max \delta(T_i, T_j)}. \tag{10}$$

The proposed measure, normalized and obtained by using a set of constant weights, can be interpreted as the overall length of discrepant paths out of the overall length of all the paths present in the trees, where the lengths of discrepant paths are measured taking into account also the dissimilarity between the predictive powers of the trees. This is the measure used in the following section to define an objective criterion whose optimization allows to identify a consensus tree.

3.2   A new procedure to combine classification trees

The aim of the procedure described in this section is to identify a tree T_c which summarizes as much as possible the information contained in the observed set of trees $T = \{T_i, i = 1, \ldots, m\}$. This purpose can be pursued searching for the tree T_c which minimizes the following objective function:

$$V(T_c) = \sum_{i=1}^{m} W_i \Delta(T_c, T_i), \tag{11}$$

where the W_i $(i = 1, \ldots, m)$ are researcher-supplied, nonnegative weights such that $\sum_{i=1}^{m} W_i = 1$, and $\Delta(T_c, T_i)$ is the dissimilarity computed following equation (10) between the consensus tree and a generic tree of T. A possible way to choose W_i is to use an inverse function of the error rate of T_i.

Since the minimization of $V(T_c)$ is computationally intensive, we propose to obtain T_c through an algorithm that restricts the search to the trees belonging to T and to those that can be obtained by deleting nodes from the trees of T. Specifically, the algorithm is composed of three main steps.

i) For each tree $T_i \in T$, the sub-trees obtained considering only the paths of length r (starting with $r = 1$) and the corresponding leaves are identified; let $T^r = \{T_j^r, j = 1, \ldots, z_r\}$ be the set of trees obtained in this way.
ii) For each tree $T_j^r \in T^r$, $V(T_j^r)$ is computed, where:

$$V(T_j^r) = \sum_{i=1}^{m} W_i \Delta(T_j^r, T_i) \tag{12}$$

is the weighted sum of the dissimilarities between the generic sub-tree of length r, T_j^r, and the trees of T.

iii) The tree of T^r for which the value of $V(T_j^r)$ results minimum is selected; this tree is T_c^r, the consensus tree of length r; r is set equal to $r + 1$; if this value is not greater than r_{max}, the length of the longest path present in trees of T, then the algorithm will return to step 1; otherwise it will stop.

The output of this algorithm is a sequence of consensus trees and of values of the objective function $\{T_c^r, V(T_c^r); r = 1, \ldots, r_{max}\}$. The value of $V(T_c^r)$ indicates the dissimilarity between T_c^r and the observed set of trees T; the tree T_c^r with the minimum value of $V(T_c^r)$ will be the consensus tree T_c.

The number of trees considered in this restricted search depends on m and r_{max}, so the solution identified by the algorithm will be optimal only if the number of observed trees is high and/or their paths are long. Otherwise the algorithm should be modified to extend the search to more trees; for instance, similarly to the algorithm proposed by Miglio, all the split defining questions involved in the m trees of T can be considered as possible splits for the identification of T_c.

4   Experimental results and concluding remarks

In this section we analyze the performance of the proposed algorithm studying a real classification problem, where the objective is to correctly identify benign from malignant breast tumors (Mangasarian and Wolberg (1990)). It is a two-class problem. Each of the 699 instances consists of 9 cell attributes each of which is measured on a 1-10 scale plus the class variable. The class labels 1 and 2 denote benign and malignant breast tumors, respectively; high predictor values correspond to worse health conditions. The Wisconsin Breast Cancer Database is in the UCI repository of machine learning databases (*ftp.ics.uci.edu/pub/machine-learning-databases*) and was obtained from the University of Wisconsin Hospitals. We generated $m = 60$ training sets of 600 observations, bootstrapping a reduced data set (we considered only 683 observations without missing values), while the whole data set has been considered as a test set. The $m = 60$ trees were fit using a procedure like CART (Breiman et al., 1984) implemented in GAUSS, with the Gini criterion for splitting and using the test set for pruning.

The 60 trees can be divided in 4 groups on the basis of the length p of the longest path present in each tree; Table 1 shows the number of trees for each group and some descriptive measures of the dissimilarity values between pairs of trees computed within each group and using a set of constant weights. From the comparison of each measure among the four groups it can be seen that both the average and the variability of the dissimilarities increase with p.

The algorithm described in Section 3.2 has been applied giving the trees the same weight $(W_i = 1/m$, for $i = 1, \ldots, m)$; the results are summarized in Table 2. The tree T_c^r with the minimum value of $V(T_c^r)$ is T_{34}^2 (see Figure

p	Nr. of trees	Minimum	Median	Maximum	Mean	St. dev.
2	29	0.000	0.119	0.166	0.100	0.048
3	19	0.000	0.148	0.295	0.142	0.068
4	7	0.018	0.226	0.380	0.213	0.092
5	5	0.033	0.229	0.350	0.213	0.119

Table 1. Some descriptive measures of the dissimilarity values computed within groups of trees having the same length p of the longest path (p=2, 3, 4, 5).

r	T_c^r	$V(T_c^r)$	Error rate × 100 (test set)
1	17 trees from T^1 all identical	0.1267	7.03
2	T_{34}^2	0.0978	4.25
3	T_{13}	0.1125	4.54
4	T_{34}	0.1305	3.07
5	T_{37}	0.2035	4.39

Table 2. Consensus trees T_c^r identified by the proposed algorithm in the example.

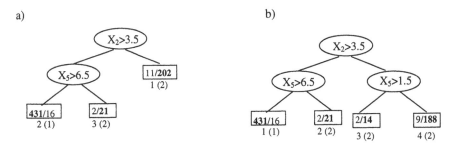

Fig. 1. Consensus trees identified by the two algorithms in the example.

1a): it has the minimum mean dissimilarity with respect to the trees of T among the ones considered by the proposed algorithm; so it will be chosen as the consensus tree T_c for the observed set of trees T. From the comparison among the error rates (computed on the test set) it can be seen that T_{34}^2 is not the tree with the minimum error rate, but its accuracy is similar to T_{34}, the consensus tree with the minimum error rate.

The same set of trees has been analyzed also through Miglio's algorithm but using measure (10) instead of (3). The consensus tree identified in this way is equal to the one previously obtained but with one more split on the right leaf (see Figure 1b); with respect to that tree, this one has a very similar value (0.094) of the consensus measure (11), and the same error rate computed on the test set.

In this example the consensus trees identified by the described algorithms are quite similar, but in general they can have very different structures. The algorithm described in Section 3.2 is preferable when we want to determine a consensus tree identical to one of the observed trees. On the contrary, the consensus tree identified by Miglio's algorithm can be different from every analyzed tree. Moreover, as in the illustrated example, this second algorithm can derive a tree where two descendent nodes belong to the same class; restrictions suitable to avoid such situations should be introduced, particularly in the leaves of the consensus tree.

The obtained results seem to be promising, but more data sets should be analyzed to obtain a wider evaluation of the performances of both algorithms; in particular, more specific studies should be addressed to the identification of situations where the algorithms determine different consensus trees.

References

BARTHELEMY, J.P., LECLERC, B. and MONJARDET, B. (1986): On the Use of Ordered Sets in Problems of Comparison and Consensus of Classifications. *Journal of Classification*, 3, 187–224.

BREIMAN, L., FRIEDMAN, J.H., OLSHEN, R.A. and STONE, C.J. (1984): *Classification and Regression Trees*. Wadsworth, Belmont, California.

CHIPMAN, H.A., GEORGE, E.I. and McCULLOCH, R.E. (2001): Managing Multiple Models. In: T. Jaakola and T. Richardson (Eds.): *Artificial Intelligence and Statistics 2001*. ProBook, Denver, 11–18.

LECLERC, B. (1998): Consensus of Classifications: the Case of Trees. In: A. Rizzi, M. Vichi and H.-H. Bock. (Eds.): *Advances in Data Science and Classification*. Springer, Berlin, 81–90.

MANGASARIAN, O.L. and WOLBERG, W.H. (1990): Cancer Diagnosis via Linear Programming. *SIAM News*, 23, 1–18.

MIGLIO, R. (1996): *Metodi di Partizione Ricorsiva nell'Analisi Discriminante*. Dipartimento di Scienze Statistiche, Bologna.

MIGLIO, R. and SOFFRITTI, G. (2001): The Comparison between Classification Trees through Proximity Measures. Submitted for publication.

SHANNON, W. D. and BANKS, D. (1999): Combining Classification Trees Using MLE. *Statistics in Medicine*, 18, 727–740.

Core-Based Clustering Techniques

Hans-Joachim Mucha[1], Hans-Georg Bartel[2], and Jens Dolata[3]

[1] Weierstraß-Institut für Angewandte Analysis und Stochastik,
   D-10117 Berlin, Germany
[2] Institut für Chemie,
   Humboldt-Universität zu Berlin, D-12489 Berlin, Germany
[3] Landesamt für Denkmalpflege Rheinland-Pfalz,
   D-55116 Mainz, Germany

Abstract. Starting from model-based clustering simple techniques based on cores are proposed. A core is a dense region in the high-dimensional space that, for example, can be represented by its most typical observation, by its centroid or, more generally, by assigning weight functions to the observations. Well-known cluster analysis techniques like the partitional *K-Means* or the hierarchical *Ward* are useful for discovering partitions or hierarchies in the underlying data. Here these methods are generalised in two ways, firstly by using weighted observations and secondly by allowing different volumes of clusters. Then a more general *K-Means* approach based on pair-wise distances is recommended. Simulation studies are carried out in order to compare the new clustering techniques with the well-known ones. Moreover, a successful application is presented. Here the task is to discover clusters with quite different number of observations in a high-dimensional space.

1 Introduction

Cluster analysis aims at finding interesting partitions or hierarchies directly from the data without using any background knowledge. Here a partition $P(I,K)$ is an exhaustive subdivision of the set of I objects (observations) into K non-empty clusters (subsets, groups) C_k that are pair-wise disjoint. On the other hand a hierarchy is a sequence of nested partitions. There are model-based as well as heuristic clustering techniques. At most one will set up new hypotheses about the data. At least clustering should result in practical useful partitions or hierarchies. More details and many more references can be found, for example, in the monographs of Späth (1985), Jain and Dubes (1988), Kaufman and Rousseeuw (1990), Mucha (1992), and Gordon (1999). Concerning model-based clustering the papers of Banfield and Raftery (1993), Fraley (1998) as well as Fraley and Raftery (2002) are a good introduction.

Two simple models will be considered here in a generalised form using weighted observations. They lead to the sum of squares and logarithmic sum of squares criterion. Both criteria can be formulated in an equivalent fashion using pair-wise distances between observations. The principle of weighting of observations is a key idea for handling cores and outliers. In the case of outliers one has to downweight them in order to reduce their influence. A first important attempt at downweighting of the observations goes back to Hampel (1968). Based on the theory of median absolute deviation (MAD) clear outliers in single coordinates can be downweighted and rejected. Below only a simple multivariate empirical approach of downweighting will be investigated.

2   Model-based clustering

Generally, the population of interest consists of K different subpopulations (clusters) with densities $f_k(\mathbf{x}; \theta)$, $k = 1, 2, ..., K$, for some unknown vector of parameters θ. Here $\mathbf{x}$ is a J-dimensional observation. Let $\gamma = (\gamma_1, ..., \gamma_I)$ be a set of identifying labels so that $\gamma_i = k$ if $\mathbf{x}_i$ comes from the k-th cluster. In the classification likelihood approach, the identifying labels are chosen so as to maximize the likelihood $L(\mathbf{x}; \theta, \gamma) = \prod_{i=1}^{I} f_{\gamma_i}(\mathbf{x}; \theta)$. Mardia et al. (1979) described in detail the classification likelihood approach to model-based Gaussian clustering. The alternative is the mixture likelihood approach, which is recently favoured by Fraley and Raftery (2002). One reason for this is that outliers and noisy data can be handled more easily within a mixture context.

Here the focus is only on classification likelihood approach and especially on two special assumptions about the covariance structure in the Gaussian model (for further reading see, for example, Banfield and Raftery (1993)). One has to pay a price that is fulfilling these restrictive assumptions. On the other side one can model clusters without a lower limit on the number of observations. Let $\mathbf{X}$ be the $(I \times J)$-data matrix under investigation consisting of I observations (objects) and J variables. When the covariance matrix is constrained to be diagonal and uniform across all groups, the well-known sum of squares criterion

$$V_K = \sum_{k=1}^{K} tr(\mathbf{W}_k), \tag{1}$$

has to be minimized. Herein $\mathbf{W}_k = \sum_{i \in C_k}(\mathbf{x}_i - \bar{\mathbf{x}}_k)(\mathbf{x}_i - \bar{\mathbf{x}}_k)^T$ is the sample cross-product matrix for the k-th cluster C_k, and $\bar{\mathbf{x}}_k$ is the usual maximum likelihood estimate of expectation values in cluster C_k. Criterion (1) can be written in the following equivalent form without explicit specification of cluster centres (centroids) $\bar{\mathbf{x}}_k$

$$V_K = \sum_{k=1}^{K} 1/n_k \sum_{i \in C_k} \sum_{l \in C_k, l>i} d_{il}, \tag{2}$$

where d_{il} is the pair-wise squared Euclidean distance between two observations i and l: $d(\mathbf{x}_i, \mathbf{x}_l) = (\mathbf{x}_i - \mathbf{x}_l)^T(\mathbf{x}_i - \mathbf{x}_l) = \|\mathbf{x}_i - \mathbf{x}_l\|^2$. Furthermore, n_k is the cardinality of cluster C_k. There are at least two well-known clustering techniques for minimizing the sum of squares criterion: the partitional K-Means (MacQueen (1967), Bock (1974), Mucha (1992)) minimizes criterion (1) for a single partition $P(I,K)$ by exchanging observations between clusters, and the hierarchical *Ward* (Ward (1963), Mucha (1992)) minimizing (2) in a stepwise manner by agglomerative hierarchical clustering.

When the covariance matrix of each cluster is constrained to be diagonal, but allowed to vary between groups, the logarithmic sum of squares criterion

$$U_K = \sum_{k=1}^{K} n_k \log tr(\mathbf{W}_k/n_k), \tag{3}$$

has to be minimized. Again the following equivalent formulation can be derived:

$$U_K = \sum_{k=1}^{K} n_k \log(\sum_{i \in C_k} \sum_{l \in C_k, l > i} \frac{1}{n_k^2} d_{il}). \tag{4}$$

3   Model-based clustering using weighted observations

Usually, all observations have the same weight. The principle of weighting the observations is a key idea for handling cores and outliers. In the case of outliers one has to downweight them in some way in order to reduce their influence. Here a quite simple weight function having only two stages is used in the simulations below. The above given formulae (2) can be generalized by using positive weights of observations to

$$V_K = \sum_{k=1}^{K} v(C_k) = \sum_{k=1}^{K} \frac{1}{M_k} \sum_{i \in C_k} m_i \sum_{l \in C_k, l > i} m_l d_{il}, \tag{5}$$

where $M_k = \sum_{i \in C_k} m_i$ and m_i denote the mass of cluster C_k and the mass of observation i, respectively. Furthermore, $v(C_k)$ denotes the within-cluster variance of cluster k. Concerning the *K-Means* algorithm based on exchanging observations between clusters in order to minimize (5) the following condition of exchange of an observation i from cluster k into cluster g has to be fulfilled

$$v(C_k \backslash \{i\}) + v(C_g \cup \{i\}) < v(C_k) + v(C_g),$$

where

$$v(C_k \backslash \{i\}) = \frac{1}{M_k - m_i}(\sum_{l \in C_k} \sum_{h \in C_k, h > l} m_l m_h d_{lh} - \sum_{h \in C_k} m_i m_h d_{ih})$$

and

$$v(C_g \cup \{i\}) = \frac{1}{M_g + m_i}(\sum_{l \in C_g} \sum_{h \in C_g, h > l} m_l m_h d_{lh} + \sum_{h \in C_g} m_i m_h d_{ih}).$$

Considering formulae (4) the generalized logarithmic sum of squares criterion can be derived as follows:

$$U_K = \sum_{k=1}^{K} M_k \log(\sum_{i \in C_k} \sum_{l \in C_k, l > i} \frac{m_i m_l}{M_k^2} d_{il}). \tag{6}$$

According to this logarithmic sum of squares criterion the partitional *K-Means*-like clustering algorithm is denoted here *Log-K-Means* and the hierarchical *Ward*-like agglomerative method is denoted *LogWard*. Concerning the hierarchical algorithms there are special treatments of observations with low weights in use (see, for example, section 6 below). As long as only one observation out of all is downweighted to quasi-zero (see Gordon and De Cata (1988)) there are no special treatments necessary. These more general algorithms, as the original *K-Means* and *Ward*, are part of our prototype-software ClusCorr98 using the Excel spreadsheet environment and its data base connectivity. ClusCorr98 contains a set of statistical tools for data exploration with emphasis on (adaptive) clustering and multivariate graphical visualizations. The programming language is Visual Basic for Applications (VBA). By the way, *K-Means* and *Log-K-Means* based on pair-wise distances are also more general because they never require an $(I \times J)$-data matrix $\mathbf{X}$.

4   Core-based clustering

There are at least two reasons for dealing with weighted observations. Firstly, a huge amount of data has to be clustered efficiently. Secondly, the problem of outliers in high-dimensional spaces has to be solved in an at least pragmatic way. Concerning these tasks there are, for example, some interesting proposals from Zhang et al. (1996) and Guha et al. (1998). The first one, called BIRCH (Balanced Iterative Reducing and Clustering using Hierarchies), performs preclustering and then uses a centroid-based hierarchical clustering algorithm. The second one, called CURE (Clustering Using REpresentatives), identifies clusters having non-spherical shapes and wide variances in size. CURE seems to be more robust against outliers than BIRCH.

Here only the sum of squares and the logarithmic sum of squares clustering based on cores is proposed, respectively. Generally, a core is a compact dense region in the high-dimensional space that, for example, can be represented by its most typical observation, its centroid or, more generally, by assigning weight functions to the observations. There are many ways to deal with cores. Two of them, which are considered here only, use the computationally fast *K-Means* as a preclustering step in order to get so-called micro-clusters that form afterwards cores by applying an appropriate threshold value for minimum size of cores. For one of them performance and stability of partitional clustering based on weighted observations are investigated in a simulation study. For the other one a successful application of hierarchical clustering based on representatives of cores is given.

5   Simulation studies

Two simple examples of two class data will be considered here. The aim is to investigate performance and stability of the new clustering techniques compared with the well-known ones. The number of variables J is always equals

20. Generally for each of the examples, there are drawn 200 artificially generated Gaussian samples of size $I = 300$ with equal class probabilities. They are analysed in a parallel fashion by traditional and core-based partitional cluster analysis methods. The following simple algorithm has been applied in the case of the latter ones:

   $i)$ Preclustering of all $I = 300$ observations by *K-Means* into $L = 50$ micro-clusters A_l,
  $ii)$ Setting up the set of cores $\{B_1, B_2, ..., B_Q\} = \{A_l : \#A_l \geq t, l = 1, ..., L\}$, where t is a threshold for the minimum cardinality of a core. Here in the simulation studies below, for example, $t = 2$ is used.
 $iii)$ Model-based clustering (*K-Means*: sum of squares criterion (5), and *Log-K-Means*: logarithmic sum of squares criterion (6)) into $K = 2$ clusters with taking into account the weights

$$m_i = \begin{cases} 1 \text{ if } \mathbf{x}_i \in B_q, q = 1, 2, ..., Q \\ \varepsilon \text{ otherwise} \end{cases}$$

Herein $\varepsilon \geq 0$ is usually nearly 0 (quasi-zero). That is, observations out of cores are downweighted (or can be even discarded by setting $\varepsilon = 0$).

Indeed, $\varepsilon = 0$ is leading to a hard rejection of outlying observations. Because of computational simplicity ε is chosen to be a quite small positive value ($\varepsilon = 1.E - 15$) in order to assign the outlying observations to their nearest distance cluster. However, these outliers don't affect the clustering result. The misclassification rate measures the performance of the clustering methods. In practical applications however, where usually nothing about the supposed classes are known beforehand, other measures for performance and stability of clustering methods have to be used (Rand (1971), Hubert and Arabie (1985), and Mucha (1992, 1995)).

Example *RingNorm* (after Breiman (1996))

Class 1 is multivariate normal with mean zero and covariance matrix 4 times the identity. Class 2 has unit covariance matrix and mean $(a, a, ..., a)$ with $a = (1/J)^{1/2}$. The appropriate clustering method for this kind of data is *Log-K-Means*, which minimizes criterion (3). Clustering of this kind of data is a hard problem for *K-Means*. The upper part of Figure 1 shows both the most important numerical results concerning the misclassification rate (in percents) and a corresponding graphical representation of these univariate statistics. The reading here is as follows. The axis at the left hand side and the bars in the graphic are assigned to the standard deviation of errors, whereas the axis at the right hand side and the box-whisker-plots are linked to all other statistics. One can see that the core-based clustering methods *K-MeansCore* and *Log-K-MeansCore* perform similar as the traditional ones.

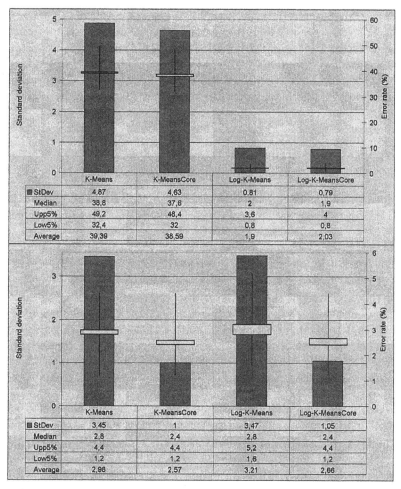

Fig. 1. Summary of simulation results of clustering (a) the *RingNorm*-data (top of the figure) and (b) the *TwoNorm*-data (bottom).

Example *TwoNorm*

This two class data is also taken from Breiman (1996), but it is slightly changed. Each class is drawn from a multivariate normal distribution with unit covariance matrix. Class 1 has mean $(a, a, ..., a)$ and class 2 has mean $(-a, -a, ..., -a)$ with $a = (2/J)^{1/2}$. In order to investigate the influence of outliers modifications of the original *TwoNorm* data model are made. One out of the 150 observations of each class is randomly generated with 4 times standard deviation. As a consequence there is a high probability that the data contains at least one outlier. The most appropriate clustering method is *K-Means*. For this kind of data however, the more general *Log-K-Means* is also a suitable technique. It performs like *K-Means* here. The lower part of Figure 1 shows the simulation results. The reading is like as the one of the upper part of Figure 1. The core-based clustering methods perform slightly better (0.5% in average error rate) than the traditional ones, but much more important is that the standard deviation of error rates as a measure of stability decreases to less than a third of the one of the traditional methods. The reason for this may be that the influence of the outliers is taken away by core-based clustering.

6   Application in archaeometry

The following looks like an application of a simple BIRCH proposal (Zhang et al. (1996)). Indeed, hierarchical clustering based on representatives of only some few cores can enable a "good" hierarchical cluster analysis of a huge amount of observations and can lead additionally to benefits. For example, the well known *Single Linkage* method (or *minimum spanning tree*, see Gordon (1999)) becomes resistive against outliers and bridges building long chains.

In this application, the task is to discover clusters with quite different number of observations in a high-dimensional space. Simple Gaussian models are able to detect small clusters with number of elements much smaller than the number of variables. The data set under consideration consists of 613 Roman tiles. X-Ray Fluorescence Analysis (RFA) measured their chemical composition. In a data preprocessing step, each of the 19 original variables z is standardised to an average 1 (via $z_i/\overline{z}$, where $\overline{z}$ is the original average). Here, one of the main difficulties is that clusters with quite different volumes and cardinality have to be detected (Mucha et al. (2002)).

Firstly, a preclustering of all observations by *K-Means* into $L = 100$ micro-clusters is carried out. Then the cores are obtained by setting up the set of cores, where the threshold $t = 5$ (minimum cardinality of a core) is chosen. This is done due to the consideration that clusters with at least five members are interesting from the archaeological point of view. The centroids of the resulting cores representing 479 observations out of 613 are the input for hierarchical clustering by *LogWard* minimizing criterion (6). Here the weight of the representative m_i of the core i is the cardinality of the core. The remaining 134 observations coming from sparse regions are assigned to the final clusters by minimum distance afterwards.

Figure 2 shows the principal components plot of 44 cores into 8 final clusters. The size of each core (bubble) is proportional to $tr(\mathbf{W}_q)$, the track of the cross-product matrix of core q. The number of clusters is chosen by the elbow criterion. It was found that the small cluster consisting of 7 observations only (near the bottom and the second axis) could be confirmed (Mucha et al. (2002)). Moreover, there occurs a new aspect for further archaeological and statistical investigations: Frankfurt-Nied at the upper right hand corner of Figure 2 is clearly divided into at least two parts.

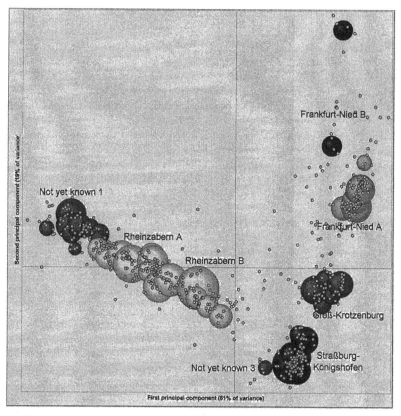

Fig. 2. Principal components plot of the final 8 clusters found by core-based clustering (data: Roman tiles). The observations are projected additionally.

7   Conclusions

The principle of weighting of observations is a key idea for handling cores and outliers. Often the stability of clustering methods like *K-Means* or *Log-K-Means* can be improved. However, the problem of choosing appropriate thresholds for establishing cores remains under investigation. Even for a fixed and arbitrary threshold $t = 2$, the simulation results (lower part of Figure 1 especially) are promising. The threshold value $t = 1$ followed by *Ward's* method based on centroids of L cores give exactly the same clustering result as *Ward's* clustering of the original (huge) data matrix on the understanding that the latter one comes at one stage (partition) of the amalgamation process exactly over the partition of cores $P(I, L)$. Moreover, the chosen number of micro-clusters as well as the preclustering method itself affect the result of core-based clustering.

References

BANFIELD, J.D. and RAFTERY, A.E. (1993): Model-Based Gaussian and Non-Gaussian Clustering. *Biometrics, 49, 803–821.*

BREIMAN, L. (1996): Bias, Variance, and Arcing Classifiers. *Technical Report, 460.* Statistical Department, University of California, Berkeley.

FRALEY C. (1998): Algorithms for Model-Based Gaussian Hierarchical Clustering. *Siam J. Sci. Comput., 20, No. 1, 270–281.*

FRALEY, C. and RAFTERY, A.E. (2002): Model-based Clustering, Discriminant Analysis, and Density Estimation. *JASA, 97, No. 458, 611–631.*

GORDON, A. D. (1999): *Classification.* Chapman & Hall/CRC, London.

GORDON, A. D. and DE CATA, A. (1988): Stability and Influence in Sum of Squares Clustering. *Metron, 46, 347–360.*

GUHA, S., RASTOGI, R., and SHIM, K. (1998): CURE: An Efficient Clustering Algorithm for Large Databases. In: *Proc. SIGMOD.* ACM, Seattle, 73–84.

HAMPLEL, F. (1968): *Contributions to the Theory of Robust Estimation.* Ph.D. thesis, University of California, Berkeley.

HUBERT, L.J. and ARABIE, P. (1985): Comparing Partitions. *Journal of Classification, 2, 193–218.*

JAIN, A.K. and DUBES, R.C. (1988): *Algorithms for Clustering Data.* Prentice Hall, New Jersey.

KAUFMAN, L. and ROUSSEEUW, P.J. (1990): *Finding Groups in Data.* Wiley, New York.

MACQUEEN, J.B. (1967): Some Methods for Classification and Analysis of Multivariate Observations. In: L. Lecam and J. Neyman (Eds.): *Proc. 5th Berkeley Symp. Math. Statist. Prob., Vol. 1.* Univ. California Press, Berkeley, 281–297.

MARDIA, K.V., KENT, J.T., and BIBBY, J.M. (1979): *Multivariate Analysis.* Academic Press, London.

MUCHA, H.-J. (1992): *Clusteranalyse mit Mikrocomputern.* Akademie Verlag, Berlin.

MUCHA, H.-J. (1995). XClust: Clustering in an Interactive Way. In: W. Härdle, S. Klinke, and B.A. Turlach (Eds.): *XploRe: An Interactive Statistical Computing Environment.* Springer, New York, 141–168.

MUCHA, H.-J., BARTEL, H.-G., and DOLATA, J. (2002): Exploring Roman Brick and Tile by Cluster Analysis with Validation of Results. In: W. Gaul and G. Ritter (Eds.): *Classification, Automation, and New Media.* Springer, Heidelberg, 471–478.

RAND, W.M. (1971): Objective Criteria for the Evaluation of Clustering Methods. *JASA, 66, 846–850.*

SPÄTH, H. (1985): *Cluster Dissection and Analysis.* Ellis Horwood, Chichester.

WARD, J.H. (1963): Hierarchical Grouping Methods to Optimise an Objective Function. *JASA, 58, 235–244.*

ZHANG, T., RAMAKRISHNAN, R., and LIVNY, M. (1996): Birch: An efficient clustering method for very large databases. In: *Proc. SIGMOD.* ACM Press, Montreal, 103–114.

Combining Regression Trees and Radial Basis Function Networks in Longitudinal Data Modelling

Marilena Pillati, Daniela G. Calò, and Giuliano Galimberti

Dipartimento di Scienze statistiche
Università di Bologna, I-40126 Bologna, Italy

Abstract. Starting from the results obtained by recursive partitioning methods, radial basis function networks for longitudinal data are derived. The aim of this work is to show how the joint use of the two methods allows to overcome some drawbacks that they show when they are used separately. More precisely, this strategy allows not only to obtain a smooth nonparametric estimate of the regression surface, but also to automatically determine the model complexity and to perform a covariate selection. The performances of the proposed strategy are evaluated on simulated data sets.

1 Introduction

When dealing with longitudinal data with time-dependent covariates we have to treat measurements that are taken on n units over q occasions. In this paper we will assume that all the units have the same number of occasions q. For unit i ($i = 1, \ldots, n$) at occasion j ($j = 1, \ldots, q$), $x_{k,ij}$ and y_{ij} are the measurement of the k-th covariate X_k ($k = 1, \ldots, p$) and the observed value of the response variable Y respectively.

The problem of interest is to model the relationship of Y to time t and the p-dimensional vector of covariates

$$y_{ij} = g\left(t_{ij}, x_{1,ij}, \ldots, x_{p,ij}\right) + e_{ij}, \tag{1}$$

where g is an unknown function and e_{ij} is the error term, with zero mean. Model (1) differs from a usual regression model as the error term e_{ij} ($j = 1, \ldots, q$) has an autocorrelation structure, represented by a $q \times q$ matrix $\boldsymbol{\Sigma}_i$, within the same unit i. In this paper we will assume that $\boldsymbol{\Sigma}_i$ may be somehow estimated and that it may be inverted.

The aim of this paper is to propose an approximation f of the unknown function g, which takes the form of a linear basis function expansion

$$f\left(t_{ij}, x_{1,ij}, \ldots, x_{p,ij}\right) = f\left(\mathbf{x}_{ij}\right) = \sum_{m=1}^{M} a_m b_m\left(\mathbf{x}_{ij}\right), \tag{2}$$

where each of the b_m is a flexible function defined on the covariate space (including time) and the term "linear" refers to the action of the parameters $\{a_m\}_{m=1}^{M}$. This class of approximating functions covers a variety of methods, according to the particular form of b_m. The proposed method is a combination of two particular elements of this class: recursive partitioning techniques and radial basis function networks.

As it will be shown in Section 2, the problem of longitudinal data modelling in presence of time-dependent covariates has already been addressed through recursive partitioning methods by Galimberti and Montanari (2002), who proposed a generalization of the classification and regression tree (CART) approach (Brieman *et al.* (1984)). One of the major disadvantages of this kind of techniques is the lack of continuity of the estimates. After a brief introduction to radial basis function networks (Section 3), Section 4 describes the joint use of these two approaches to estimate the unknown regression surface g. This new method allows not only to derive a smooth estimate for g (so as to overcome the discontinuity problem of regression trees), but also to automatically determine the radial basis function network complexity and to perform a covariate selection. The results of a simulation study (Section 5) show the improvement achieved by the proposed method with respect both to regression trees and to radial basis function networks.

2   Regression trees for longitudinal data with time-dependent covariates

In binary trees, each b_m $(m = 1, \ldots, M)$ in (2) takes the form

$$b_m (\mathbf{x}_{ij}) = I (\mathbf{x}_{ij} \in R_m), \tag{3}$$

where $I(\cdot)$ is the indicator function and $\{R_m\}_{m=1}^{M}$ represents a partition of the covariate space (including time) whose elements (also called terminal nodes or leaves), for real valued covariates, usually take the form of hyper-rectangular axis oriented sets. Recursive partitioning methods allow not only to determine the $\{a_m\}$ values that best fit the data, but also to derive a good set of basis functions (that is, a good partition of the covariate space) by a stepwise procedure that repeatedly splits a region (parent node) of the covariate space into two subregions (daughter nodes).

Following the CART approach of Brieman *et al.* (1984), tree-based procedures can be characterized by the definition of *i*) a set of questions, also called splits, regarding the covariates in order to partition the covariate space, *ii*) a split function that, at each step, leads to the best split, *iii*) how to determine the optimal value for M, which in CART is accomplished by what is called tree pruning.

One of the major advantages of these techniques is their ability in detecting relevant covariates. Furthermore, they are able to explore local relations between the dependent variable and the predictors. This feature is particularly important because the relevance of each covariate may vary in different regions of the covariate space.

In 1992 Segal proposed an extension of the CART methodology able to take into account the particular features of longitudinal data. This proposal, however, does not seem completely satisfactory in presence of time-dependent covariates. In order to overcome this difficulty, Galimberti and Montanari (2002) formulated an alternative tree-based regression strategy. They consider a different notion of split, allowing a unit not to belong to a given element of the covariate space partition for all occasions. Furthermore, they generalize the split function, which is often based on the decrease in the residual sum of squares, allowing for correlated errors. The generalized split function $\Phi(s, h)$ that, at each step, can be evaluated for any split s of any node h may be expressed as

$$\Phi(s, h) = \left[\mathbf{y} - \hat{f}_h(\mathbf{X})\right]' \mathbf{S}^{-1} \left[\mathbf{y} - \hat{f}_h(\mathbf{X})\right] +$$
$$- \left[\mathbf{y} - \hat{f}_{r,l}(\mathbf{X})\right]' \mathbf{S}^{-1} \left[\mathbf{y} - \hat{f}_{r,l}(\mathbf{X})\right], \qquad (4)$$

where $\mathbf{y}$ is the $nq \times 1$ vector whose entries are the Y values for each unit at each occasion, $\mathbf{X}$ is a $nq \times (p+1)$ matrix containing the covariate (including time) observed values, $\hat{f}_h(\mathbf{X}) = B_h(\mathbf{X})\hat{\mathbf{a}}_h$ and $\hat{f}_{r,l}(\mathbf{X}) = B_{r,l}(\mathbf{X})\hat{\mathbf{a}}_{r,l}$ are $nq \times 1$ vectors containing the estimates for f before and after performing split s on node h, respectively. $B_h(\mathbf{X})$ is the matrix whose columns represent the indicator variables denoting node membership when node h is not splitted and $\hat{\mathbf{a}}_h$ is the generalized least squares estimate of the corresponding regression coefficient vector

$$\hat{\mathbf{a}}_h = [B_h(\mathbf{X})' \mathbf{S}^{-1} B_h(\mathbf{X})]^{-1} B_h(\mathbf{X})' \mathbf{S}^{-1} \mathbf{y}; \qquad (5)$$

$B_{r,l}(\mathbf{X})$ and $\hat{\mathbf{a}}_{r,l}$ are the corresponding quantities once the node h is splitted into the right and left nodes r and l. $\mathbf{S} = \mathbf{I}_n \otimes \hat{\mathbf{\Sigma}}_i$ is a block diagonal matrix whose non-zero entries are suitable estimates of $\mathbf{\Sigma}_i$, for all i. Of course the role of the inverse of $\mathbf{S}$ here is to weight the differences between the observed values and the fitted model taking into account the correlation structure. When $\mathbf{S}$ is the identity matrix, (4) reduces to the CART split function, so that ordinary least squares regression trees are fitted.

The tree-based procedure leads to an approximation of the function g which is given by

$$\hat{f}(\mathbf{X}) = \sum_{m=1}^{M} \hat{a}_m b_m(\mathbf{X}) = B(\mathbf{X})\hat{\mathbf{a}}, \qquad (6)$$

where the indicator variable matrix $B(\mathbf{X})$ and the estimated coefficient vector $\hat{\mathbf{a}}$ refer to the optimal partition. The piecewise-constant nature of approximations based on recursive partitioning methods limits their accuracy on smooth target functions, especially near the region boundaries. A smooth estimate of g could be obtained by exploiting the optimal partition in M elements to construct a radial basis function network.

3   Radial basis function networks for longitudinal data

Radial basis function (hereafter RBF) networks can be obtained from (2) by considering radially symmetric basis functions (see Bishop (1995) and Ripley (1996) for more details).

Gaussian RBF networks approximate the unknown function g in (1) by a linear expansion of the form

$$f(\mathbf{x}_{ij}) = \sum_{m=1}^{M} a_m b_m^*(\mathbf{x}_{ij}) = \sum_{m=1}^{M} a_m \exp\left(-\frac{1}{2\sigma_m^2}\|\mathbf{x}_{ij} - \boldsymbol{\mu}_m\|^2\right), \quad (7)$$

where each basis function depends on a location parameter $\boldsymbol{\mu}_m$, a scale parameter $\sigma_m > 0$ and $\|\cdot\|$ denotes the Euclidean norm: the larger is the distance between $\mathbf{x}_{ij}$ and $\boldsymbol{\mu}_m$, the smaller is the value of the basis function $b_m^*(\mathbf{x}_{ij})$. A constant term a_0 can be added.

There are several approaches to estimating the parameters $\{a_m, \boldsymbol{\mu}_m, \sigma_m\}$, $m = 1, \ldots, M$, but most of them consider the value of M as fixed a priori. As an alternative to nonlinear least squares to jointly estimate all the parameters, a simpler two-step strategy consists of estimating the $\{\boldsymbol{\mu}_m, \sigma_m\}$ separately from the $\{a_m\}$. In particular, given the former, the estimation of the latter is a simple least squares problem. Its solution is given by

$$\hat{\mathbf{a}} = [B^*(\mathbf{X})'B^*(\mathbf{X})]^{-1}B^*(\mathbf{X})'\mathbf{y}, \quad (8)$$

where

$$B^*(\mathbf{X}) = [b_1^*(\mathbf{X}), \ldots, b_M^*(\mathbf{X})]. \quad (9)$$

For unit i at occasion j, the corresponding entry in each $nq \times 1$ vector $b_m^*(\mathbf{X})$ is equal to $b_m^*(\mathbf{x}_{ij})$ in (7).

However, when using RBF networks in regression modelling with longitudinal data the correlation structure of the error terms e_i, $i = 1, \ldots, n$, must be taken into account. In analogy with the solution adopted in other parametric and nonparametric regression techniques (see Section 2), this can be achieved by means of a generalized least squares criterion to estimating $\{a_m\}$:

$$\hat{\mathbf{a}} = [B^*(\mathbf{X})'\mathbf{S}^{-1}B^*(\mathbf{X})]^{-1}B^*(\mathbf{X})'\mathbf{S}^{-1}\mathbf{y}. \quad (10)$$

When a two-step approach is employed, often the radial basis function parameters $\{\boldsymbol{\mu}_m, \sigma_m\}$ are estimated in an unsupervised way, exploiting only the information on the covariates. The theoretical foundations of unsupervised estimate solutions may be found in Poggio and Girosi (1990), who showed that a gradient descent approach used to update the basis function centers actually "... makes the centers move toward the majority of the data, to find the position of the clusters". This is why the use of several clustering techniques has been proposed.

One of the most important and broadly accepted contributions on this topic is due to Moody and Darken (1989). They use K-means clustering to determine a partition of the training data and they propose to estimate $\{\mu_m\}$ through the cluster centroids, each cluster being represented by one basis function, even if the presence of outliers can strongly affect the performance of RBF parameter estimates based on the K-means method (Pillati and Calò (2001)).

As far as the smoothing parameters $\{\sigma_m\}$ are concerned, one broadly used solution is to derive them from the average distance of each basis center to its L-nearest neighbors, with L typically small (see Bishop (1995) for a review).

When a two-step procedure is considered, the estimates of $\{\mu_m, \sigma_m\}$ depend only on the matrix $\mathbf{X}$. The obvious drawback of this approach is that these estimates do not take the information on the target variable Y into account. Thus, there is no way to distinguish relevant variables from irrelevant ones, whose presence can distort a metric such as the one defined by the Gaussian basis function.

The joint use of RBF networks and regression trees, described in the following section, allows also to overcome this problem.

4   Tree-based radial basis function networks for longitudinal data with time-dependent covariates

As shown in the previous sections, regression trees and RBF networks can be represented in the common framework of linear basis function expansions. Furthermore, due to the particular form of the corresponding basis functions, they share the ability of exploring the local relations between the dependent variable and the predictors. For these reasons several authors proposed to combine these two techniques to solve classification problems (see, among the others, Kubat (1998), Miglio and Pillati (2000)).

In this section we show how this idea can be exploited also in the context of longitudinal data modelling. The basic idea of the proposal is to construct a regression tree as sketched in Section 2 and then to associate a Gaussian radial basis function to each element of the induced partition of the covariate space (including time). This strategy allows not only to obtain a smooth estimate for g, but also to automatically determine the RBF network complexity (i.e. the value of M in (7)), to let the RBF parameter estimates depend on Y and to perform a covariate selection.

Instead of using an unsupervised clustering technique to find the parameters $\{\mu_m\}$, the basis functions are located on the centroids of the regions selected by the regression tree. This leads to RBF location parameter estimates that can be expressed as

$$\hat{\mu}'_m = [b_m(\mathbf{X})'b_m(\mathbf{X})]^{-1}b_m(\mathbf{X})'\mathbf{X}, \tag{11}$$

where b_m $(m = 1, \ldots, M)$ denotes the m-th indicator basis function of the optimal (generalized least squares) regression tree. Note that each b_m is a column of matrix $B(\mathbf{X})$ in (6).

Once the M location parameters are obtained, the L-nearest neighbor heuristic can be used to determine the $\hat{\sigma}_m$ $(m = 1, \ldots, M)$.

This proposal allows the estimates of the parameters $\{\mu_m, \sigma_m\}$ to depend on the target variable Y, as the optimal partition of the covariate space (*i.e.* the matrix $B(\mathbf{X})$) is associated to the regression tree with M terminal nodes which minimizes the residual sum of squares of the dependent variable.

In order to reduce the sensibility of the radial basis functions to the presence of irrelevant predictors, we propose to compute the Euclidean distance in (7) only with respect to the covariates that, according to the optimal regression tree, play the main role in explaining the dependent variable. This can be done by introducing a $(p + 1) \times (p + 1)$ indicator diagonal matrix $\mathbf{D}$, whose non-zero entries are associated to the covariates (including time) involved in the splits performed to build the optimal regression tree. Thus, each basis function in (7) takes now the form

$$b_m^* (\mathbf{x}_{ij}) = \exp\left(-\frac{1}{2\hat{\sigma}_m^2}\|\mathbf{x}_{ij} - \hat{\boldsymbol{\mu}}_m\|_{\mathbf{D}}^2\right), \tag{12}$$

with

$$\|\mathbf{x}_{ij} - \hat{\boldsymbol{\mu}}_m\|_{\mathbf{D}}^2 = (\mathbf{x}_{ij} - \hat{\boldsymbol{\mu}}_m)' \, \mathbf{D} \, (\mathbf{x}_{ij} - \hat{\boldsymbol{\mu}}_m) \,. \tag{13}$$

These new basis functions are then used to compute the entries of matrix $B^*(\mathbf{X})$ defined in (9). Finally, the tree-based RBF network leads to a nonparametric estimate of g given by

$$\hat{f}(\mathbf{X}) = B^*(\mathbf{X})\hat{\mathbf{a}}, \tag{14}$$

where the vector $\hat{\mathbf{a}}$ is obtained according to a generalized least squares criterion as in (10), so that the correlation structure of the error terms is taken into account.

A further enhancement of the proposed method consists in letting the matrix $\mathbf{D}$ be different for each basis function. In this case, the non-zero entries of the m-th matrix $\mathbf{D}_m$ correspond only to the covariates involved in the splits which define the path to the m-th terminal node of the optimal tree. This may improve the performance of the RBF network when the relevance of each covariate varies heavily in different parts of the covariate space.

5   A simulation study

Regression trees, tree-based RBF networks and RBF networks based on a K-means clustering algorithm[1] were compared on simulated data sets. The instructions to generate the simulated samples and to perform the analysis were implemented in GAUSS.

---

[1] A number of basis functions varying from 4 to 20 was considered. For each setting, only the performances of the best and the worst network are presented.

The variables involved in this simulation are time t, which takes the integer values from 1 to q, response Y and two time-dependent covariates X_1 and X_2 which, for each occasion, are uniformly distributed on $[0, 10]$ and $[-5, 5]$, respectively. The number n of units and the number of occasions q in each of the 50 training samples were set equal to 50 and 4 respectively. The observations for y_{ij} are obtained from model (1), where

$$g\left(\mathbf{x}_{ij}\right) = 0.8 \sin\left(x_{1,ij}/4\right) \sin\left(x_{2,ij}/2\right) + 0.4 t_{ij} \qquad (15)$$

For each unit i, the error term e_i was generated from a 4-dimensional normal distribution with covariance matrix that has 1 along the diagonal and a constant non zero value θ in the off-diagonal. The correlation structure was assumed known. Several situations were considered according to the inclusion of a different number of standard normally distributed time-dependent and time-independent noise covariates.

For each of the considered methods, the estimated function $\hat{f}_{T,l}$ obtained from the l-th training sample ($l = 1, \ldots, 50$) was used to predict the values of g_T in an independent test set T of 100 units observed in 4 occasions. In order to compare their performances, the following quantity

$$R_T(l) = \sum_{i=1}^{100} \sum_{j=1}^{4} \left[g_T\left(\mathbf{x}_{ij}\right) - \hat{f}_{T,l}\left(\mathbf{x}_{ij}\right) \right]^2 \qquad (16)$$

has been considered. The distributions of $R_T(l)$ are summarized in Table 1 and 2 by means of the average values and standard deviations (in brackets). For each of the considered methods, the (mean) number of basis functions $\bar{M}$ is also reported. These results refer to a value of $\theta = 0.8$.

Without noise covariates, the regression trees show the worst accuracy (see first two columns of Table 1), while the performances of TREE-RBF networks and the best K-MEANS-RBF networks are comparable. However, it is worth noting that TREE-RBF networks are, on average, less complex than K-MEANS-RBF ones. On the contrary, as the number of noise covariates increases, the behavior of K-MEANS-RBF networks heavily worsens, particularly when the noise covariates are time-independent (compare columns 3 and 5 with columns 7 and 9 in Table 1). Regression trees do not show this worsening, given their ability in selecting the relevant covariates. TREE-RBF networks seem to take advantage of this property, showing stable performances also with a large number of noise covariates.

The role of generalized least squares in dealing with longitudinal data is highlighted in Table 2. As it can be seen, when the autocorrelation structure is not taken into account (and ordinary least squares are used), the covariate selection ability of regression trees is lost, particularly in presence of time-independent covariates. This clearly affects the performances of TREE-RBF networks, which become comparable with the ones of K-MEANS-RBF networks.

	0		*Time-independent noise covariates*				*Time-dependent noise covariates*			
			3		6		3		6	
	$\bar{R}_T$	$\bar{M}$	$\bar{R}_T$	$\bar{M}$	$\bar{R}_T$	$\bar{M}$	$\bar{R}_T$	$\bar{M}$	$\bar{R}_T$	$\bar{M}$
TREE	47.66	7.68	51.29	8.76	54.86	9.18	52.62	8.86	57.31	9.58
	(16.72)		(18.01)		(19.68)		(18.90)		(17.33)	
TREE-RBF	22.86	7.68	25.72	8.76	30.67	9.18	23.16	8.86	25.62	9.58
	(13.70)		(14.91)		(21.74)		(14.35)		(13.72)	
K-M RBF	19.05	12	44.64	12	78.76	10	26.29	14	32.03	16
(best)	(13.55)		(20.46)		(28.97)		(14.22)		(14.96)	
K-M RBF	50.52	4	86.94	4	183.07	4	83.40	4	96.08	4
(worst)	(29.68)		(30.13)		(88.94)		(28.15)		(23.84)	

Table 1. Summary results for the estimated functions obtained by GENERALIZED LEAST SQUARES: average values and standard deviations (in brackets) for R_T and average number of basis functions.

	0		*Time-independent noise covariates*				*Time-dependent noise covariates*			
			3		6		3		6	
	$\bar{R}_T$	$\bar{M}$	$\bar{R}_T$	$\bar{M}$	$\bar{R}_T$	$\bar{M}$	$\bar{R}_T$	$\bar{M}$	$\bar{R}_T$	$\bar{M}$
TREE	79.75	5.24	142.62	7.52	187.28	9.14	101.72	7.18	121.09	8.26
	(34.08)		(62.96)		(83.91)		(37.46)		(36.43)	
TREE-RBF	36.49	5.24	58.90	7.52	81.29	9.14	40.37	7.18	42.60	8.26
	(20.04)		(30.19)		(48.35)		(20.82)		(21.79)	
K-M RBF	32.97	8	60.71	7	78.73	9	44.64	12	51.95	12
(best)	(18.81)		(26.72)		(31.33)		(20.46)		(22.96)	
K-M RBF	58.77	20	88.83	4	108.40	20	86.94	4	99.04	4
(worst)	(32.18)		(31.84)		(46.45)		(30.13)		(26.86)	

Table 2. Summary results for the estimated functions obtained by ORDINARY LEAST SQUARES: average values and standard deviations (in brackets) for R_T and average number of basis functions.

Other values of θ were considered, but the results are not shown. However, it is worth mentioning that the use of ordinary least squares gives results more similar to the ones obtained by generalized least squares, when θ tends to zero.

6 Concluding remarks and open issues

On the basis of the results obtained on simulated data, it seems possible to conclude that the proposed method represents a useful tool for the analysis of longitudinal data with time-dependent covariates.

This strategy allows not only to obtain a smooth estimate for the unknown target function (so as to overcome the discontinuous nature of the tree-based solution), but also to automatically determine the RBF network complexity (that is, the value of M in (7)) and to perform covariate selection (by the introduction of the matrix $\mathbf{D}$ in (13)).

Tree-based RBF networks outperform the two component methods, when used separately, in most of the considered settings. In fact, the K-means RBF solution can be superior to regression trees from an accuracy point of view, but, unlike regression trees, is affected by the presence of noise covariates and is not completely satisfactory as far as interpretation is concerned. Tree-based RBF networks seem to share regression tree robustness against noise covariates and RBF network accuracy.

It is worth mentioning that an alternative method to obtain smooth non-parametric estimates of g in (1) is presented in Zhang (1997), where an extension of multivariate adaptive regression splines is introduced. This strategy, however, does not share the local adaptivity of regression trees and RBF networks, which is one of the most attracting properties of these latter methods. Nevertheless, a comparison between their performances could be interesting.

References

BISHOP, C. M. (1995): *Neural Networks for Pattern Recognition*. Clarendon Press, Oxford.

BREIMAN, L., FRIEDMAN, J. H., OLSHEN, R. A. and STONE, C. J. (1984): *Classification and Regression Trees*. Wadsworth, Belmont.

GALIMBERTI, G. and MONTANARI, A. (2002): Regression Trees for Longitudinal Data with Time-Dependent Covariates. In: K. Jajuga, A. Sokolowsky and H.-H. Bock (Eds.): *Classification, Clustering and Data Analysis*. Springer, Heidelberg, 391–398.

KUBAT, M. (1998): Decision Trees Can Initialize Radial-Basis-Function Networks. *IEEE Transactions on Neural Networks*, 9, 813–821.

MOODY, J. and DARKEN, C. J. (1989): Fast learning in Network of Locally-Tuned Processing Units. *Neural Computation*, 1, 281–297.

PILLATI, M. and CALÒ, D. G. (2001): A Robust Clustering Procedure for Centre Location in RBF Networks. In: C. Provasi (Ed.): *Modelli complessi e metodi computazionali intensivi per la stima e la previsione*. Cluep Editrice, Padova, 373–378.

PILLATI, M. and MIGLIO, R. (2000): Radial Basis Function Networks and Decision Trees in the Determination of a Classifier. In: H. A. L. Kiers, J.-P. Rasson, P. J. F. Groenen and M. Schader (Eds.): *Data Analysis, Classification and Related Methods*. Springer, Heidelberg, 211–216.

POGGIO, T. and GIROSI F. (1990): Networks for Approximation and Learning. *Proceedings of the IEEE*, 78, 1481–1497.

RIPLEY, B. D. (1996): *Pattern Recognition and Neural Networks*. Cambridge University Press, Cambridge.

SEGAL, M. R. (1992): Tree-Structured Methods for Longitudinal Data. *Journal of the American Statistical Association*, 87, 407–418.

ZHANG, H. (1997): Multivariate Adaptive Splines for the Analysis of Longitudinal Data. *Journal of Computational and Graphical Statistics*, 6, 79–91.

Implementing a new Method for Discriminant Analysis When Group Covariance Matrices are Nearly Singular

Britta Pouwels[1], Winfried Theis[2], and Christian Röver[2]

[1] Universitäts- und Landesbibliothek Münster,
D-48143 Münster, Germany
[2] Sonderforschungsbereich 475, Fachbereich Statistik,
Universität Dortmund, D-44221 Dortmund, Germany

Abstract. We consider a unified description of classification rules for nearly singular covariance matrices. When the covariance matrices of the groups or the pooled covariance matrix become nearly singular, bayesian classification rules become seriously unstable. Several procedures have been proposed to tackle this problem, e.g. SIMCA, and Regularized Discriminant Analysis. Næs and Indahl (1998) discovered common properties for all of these procedures and proposed a unified classifier that incorporates the functionality of them all. Since the unified approach needs many parameters, they also proposed an alternative classifier with fewer parameters. We implemented both classifiers and compared them in a simulation study to the procedures RDA, LDA, and QDA. To enhance the comparability of our results we based the simulation study on the study of Friedman (1989).

In the implementation, we used a combination of the Nelder-Mead Simplex-algorithm and Simulated Annealing (Bohachevsky et al. (1986)) to optimize the classification error directly.

1 Introduction

The classical approaches to discriminant analysis are based on estimates of the inverse covariance matrices for each group (Quadratic Discriminant Analysis, QDA) or on a common inverse covariance matrix (Linear Discriminant Analysis, LDA). The estimates of the covariance matrix can become badly conditioned for several reasons. First of all the explanatory variables may be multicollinear. Another situation encountered is an insufficient number of observations per group, which leads to a similar problem. Since these problems are encountered in many studies, a wide variety of methods has been developed to tackle this problem. There are mainly two typical approaches: On the one hand dimension reduction techniques like Principal Component Analysis (PCA), Partial Least Squares (PLS) or Minimal Error Rate Classifiers (MEC) (Röhl et al. (2002)) are applied. On the other hand there are methods which preserve the dimensionality but manipulate the covariance matrix estimates, like MCA, SIMCA, DASCO or Regularized Discriminant Analysis (RDA) (please refer to Næs and Indahl (1998) for these methods). Næs and Indahl (1998) recognized that the latter methods could be described in a unified way.

In this paper we consider first the unified description of Næs and Indahl in section 2. Next we explain our approach for an implementation of the method (section 3). We tested our algorithm in an extensive simulation study and compared it to RDA, and the classical LDA and QDA (sections 4 and 5). Finally we conclude with some comments and suggestions for further research.

2   Unified description

Næs and Indahl recognized three "conceptual dimensions" in which the different methods for manipulating the covariance matrix can be organized.

i) They either delete or shrink the variation in certain eigenvector directions: in most cases these correspond to the small eigenvalues.
ii) The shrinking of the covariance matrices either towards a pooled covariance matrix Σ or towards identity.
iii) The shrinking in (2) is done with the full d-dimensional covariance matrix or with a restricted version defined by eigenvalues of the original empirical matrix.

We reformulated these "dimensions" in the following way, because in this way they seemed to be clearer to us:

i) Manipulation of singular eigenvalues λ_k ; $k = 1, \dots, d$.
ii) The shrinking of the group-specific covariance matrices S_j , $j = 1, \dots, G$, towards the pooled covariance matrix S_p
iii) The shrinking of the covariance matrices S_j , $j = 1, \dots, G$, towards the identitiy matrix I_d

The first dimension yields the opportunity to replace some eigenvalues by values which result in more stable inverses or reduce the typical bias in eigenvalue-estimates. The aforementioned bias corresponds to the fact that small eigenvalues are underestimated and large eigenvalues are overestimated.

The second dimension focuses on stabilizing the estimate by moving towards an estimator which comprises more knowledge from the data, and is therefore more stable.

Finally the third dimension tries to solve the multicollinearity problem by reducing the influence of covariances between the explanatory variables.

Formula 1 gives the complete form of the covariance estimator which includes all regularisation possibilities.

$$\hat{\Sigma}_U^j = c_j \left[\delta(U_1^j U_2^j) \begin{pmatrix} m\Lambda_1^j + \alpha_j I_K & 0 \\ 0 & (\alpha_j + \beta_j) I_{d-K} \end{pmatrix} (U_1^j U_2^j)^T + (1 - \delta) S_p \right] \tag{1}$$

where $(U_1^j U_2^j)$ is a partition of the $d \times d$ eigenvector matrix of the j-th group covariance matrix, with U_1^j corresponding to the large eigenvalues in the K-dimensional diagonal matrix Λ_1^j and U_2^j corresponding to the small eigenvalues. The other parameters correspond to the different regularisations in the following way:

- $K \in \{0, \ldots, d\}$ is the dimension of the space of high variability.
- $\delta \in [0, 1]$ models the shrinking towards the pooled covariance matrix.
- $\alpha_j \in [0, \infty)$ models the shrinking towards the identity matrix.
- m manipulates the large eigenvalues similarly for all groups.
- $\beta_j \in [0, \infty)$ is the replacement for the small eigenvalues.
- $c_j \in [0, \infty)$ is an additional scaling factor.

Thus all mentioned directions of regularisation can be achieved with this estimator. A great problem are the additional $3 + 2G$ parameters which have to be derived from the data to use this estimator. When a covariance estimate for LDA is to be regularized, the pooled covariance matrix is used instead of the group covariance matrices. Thus the group indices j and parameter δ are omitted in formula 1, and the eigenvalue-decomposition is applied directly to the pooled covariance matrix.

To avoid the large number of parameters of the unified approach, Næs and Indahl proposed an alternative estimator which is reduced by the parameters c_j, α_j and the group-specific choice of β:

$$\hat{\Sigma}_A^j = \delta(U_1^j U_2^j) \begin{pmatrix} m\Lambda_1^j & 0 \\ 0 & \beta I_{d-K} \end{pmatrix} (U_1^j U_2^j)^T + (1 - \delta)S_p \qquad (2)$$

This parameter reduction leads mainly to the loss of the possibility of regularization in the third of our dimensions, the shrinking towards the identity matrix. Furthermore the group-specific manipulation of the small eigenvalues is lost.

In our simulations (see section 4) we compare these two approaches which will be called **U**nified **R**egularized **C**lassification method (URC), or **A**lternative **R**egularized **C**lassification method (ARC), resp., to standard LDA and QDA, and as a further competitor we chose Regularized Discriminant Analysis (Friedman (1989)), since RDA especially shrinks towards the identity matrix and so it is of great interest to compare the performance of the alternative estimator to RDA. RDA regularizes in dimensions 2 and 3 and actually has two paramters δ, γ steering the shrinkage. The first step is the shrinkage towards the pooled covariance matrix:

$$\hat{\Sigma}_j(\delta) = \delta S_j + (1 - \delta)S_p,$$

and the second step is towards a weighted identity matrix:

$$\hat{\Sigma}_j(\delta, \gamma) = (1 - \gamma)\hat{\Sigma}_j(\delta) + \frac{\gamma}{d}tr(\hat{\Sigma}_j(\delta))I_d, \; j = 1, \ldots, G$$

The unified estimate equals the RDA estimate, if

$$K = d, \; c_j = 1 - \gamma, \; m = 1, \; \alpha_j = \frac{\gamma tr(\delta S_j + (1 - \delta)S_p)}{d(1 - \gamma)\delta}.$$

Before the simulation study will be described, we point out some important issues about the implementation.

3 Algorithm

Since there is no analytical way to estimate the regularization parameters, an optimization has to be performed. We chose as objective for this optimization the minimization of a prediction error rate, which is calculated by splitting the observations into equally sized training and test sets four times and predicting the classes of the test data. As optimization algorithm we chose the Nelder-Mead-Simplex Algorithm which is able to cope with a higher dimensional search space and does not need derivatives or other information of the functional form of the objective. We also tested a combination of Nelder-Mead with Simulated Annealing to overcome possible local minima. The standard version of this algorithm makes the assumption of an unrestricted parameter space, which is not true in our case. So the different restrictions on the parameters had to be implemented to ensure the selection of valid parameter values. Furthermore the parameter K is an integer which has to be optimized separately or appropriately included in the optimization process.

The restrictions are implemented by testing the validity for each new parameter vector. If one parameter is outside its respective boundaries, it is set to the nearer bound of the parameter space. For example, if δ, which stands for the convex combination of the group covariance with the pooled covariance, becomes greater than 1 by expansion of the simplex, it is set to 1.

The greatest difficulty was the inclusion of the parameter K into the optimization. The first approach was to select a range of interest for K and optimize for each K and then select the set of parameters with the best estimated error rate. But this approach is very time consuming so a second approach was tested. In this second approach the search for an optimal K is included into each optimization step by testing three subsequent values of K. If nothing else is specified, the starting value is chosen by calculating the mean of the eigenvalues over the groups and choosing the number of large eigenvalues which contribute at least 3/4 of the sum of all mean eigenvalues.

4 Simulation study

Two test data sets are constructed as described in the study of Friedman (1989) to make our results comparable to the findings there. Here we restrict ourselves to two settings from this study, one which should be easy for RDA and one which should not be favourable for RDA, namely Setting 1 where the mean vectors are $\mu_1 = \mathbf{0}$, $\mu_2 = (3, 0, \ldots, 0)^T$, $\mu_3 = (0, 3, 0, \ldots, 0)^T$ and covariance $\Sigma_i = diag(1, \ldots, 1)$ and Setting 4, where the eigenvalues of the covariance matrices are equal and determined by $e_j = (9(j-1)/(d-1) + 1)^2$, $j = 1, \ldots, d$ the means are $\mu_1 = \mathbf{0}$, $\mu_2 = (2.5\sqrt{e_j/d}\frac{d-j}{d/2-1})_{j=1}^d$, $\mu_3 = ((-1)^j \mu_{2j})_{j=1}^d$. So in the latter situation the mean differences are concentrated in the high-variance subspace, which makes it difficult for RDA.

For all situations described above 100 replications were sampled and evaluated. Like Friedman we trained the procedures on samples of size 40, which were randomly distributed into the three groups, but used equal priors of 1/3 in all procedures. We applied LDA and QDA as implemented in the MASS library (Venables and Ripley (1999)) for **R** and our new routines named URC and ARC are implemented in **R** (Ihaka and Gentleman (1996)) as well. We applied ARC with and without simulated annealing. The results for RDA we took from the orginal paper by Friedman.

5   Results of the simulation

Tables 1 and 2 give an overview of the results for the two settings from Friedman. The "# no results" lines give the number of test sets where the corresponding procedure yielded no result at all or in the cases of ARC or URC parameter settings which caused a singular covariance matrix when applied to the covariance estimate of the complete training set. It is obvious, that the Næs procedures can not compete with RDA. But they are better than QDA in all situations and the unified approach is equally good or even better than LDA.

The results give rise to the question, why the results of URC and ARC are so similar to LDA. A possible explanation are high values of the shrinkage parameter towards the pooled covariance. Figure 1 shows indeed, that δ is nearer to 1 in dimensions $d = 20$ and $d = 40$ and with $d = 6$ and $d = 10$ the median still lies above 0.5. Therefore, it is not surprising, that the unified approach can not be more effective than LDA, since with a high δ the effect of most of the other parameters is diminished.

Setting 1: "Equal spherical covariance matrices"

Misclassification risk	Number of variables			
$\hat{\mu}$ $(\hat{\sigma})$	6	10	20	40
RDA	0.11 (0.03)	0.12 (0.04)	0.16 (0.05)	0.19 (0.05)
δ	.77 (.037)	.79 (.035)	.75 (.037)	.78 (.034)
γ	.74 (.034)	.72 (.032)	.74 (.028)	.80 (.022)
LDA	0.13 (0.04)	0.16 (0.05)	0.26 (0.06)	0.48 (0.08)
QDA	0.25 (0.07)	0.46 (0.08)	- (-)	- (-)
# no result	2	53	100	100
URC	0.13 (0.04)	0.17 (0.07)	0.30 (0.16)	0.39 (0.13)
# no result	0	0	0	0
ARC	0.12 (0.03)	0.16 (0.04)	0.26 (0.07)	- (-)
# no result	0	0	0	100
ARC + SimAnn.	0.14 (0.06)	0.16 (0.04)	0.26 (0.08)	- (-)
# no result	0	0	3	100

Table 1. Results from setting 1 by Friedman; the numbers in paranentheses are the standard deviations

A second possible question is if ARC or URC favour parameter settings similar to RDA in these settings. This would mean that parameters c_j and α_j, $j \in \{1, \ldots, G\}$ would behave like the outer convex combination in RDA done by γ. This is not the case as can be seen from Figure 2, where approximate values of the parameters c_1 and α_1 for the case that URC does the same as RDA are added to the boxplots of the observed values as stars. Obviously α_1 is estimated too low for an equal effect as in RDA and c_1 is estimated too high.

The parameters $\alpha_j, j \in \{1, \ldots, G\}$ show an interesting behaviour: They are similar to the constant weight of the identity matrix in RDA, $\frac{1}{d} tr(S_j(\delta))$. We approximate the trace by the sum of the true eigenvalues of the covariance matrices, and plot these points – marked by X – into the boxplots of the results from URC for α_1, which is taken as an example because the other α_j, $j = 2, 3$, do not differ much. This shows, that URC does select values for α_j as optimal, which are near to a value considered sensible from a theoretical point of view.

Setting 4: "Equal, highly ellipsoidal covariance matrices with mean differences in high-variance subspace"

Misclassification risk	Number of variables			
$\hat{\mu}$ $(\hat{\sigma})$	6	10	20	40
RDA	0.06 (0.03)	0.05 (0.02)	0.14 (0.04)	0.18 (0.05)
δ	.92 (.024)	.86 (.030)	.72 (.038)	.76 (.036)
γ	.71 (.036)	.66 (.036)	.70 (.029)	.79 (.023)
LDA	0.07 (0.03)	0.13 (0.04)	0.23 (0.06)	0.48 (0.08)
QDA	0.18 (0.08)	0.41 (0.10)	- (-)	- (-)
# no result	0	56	100	100
URC	0.07 (0.04)	0.13 (0.07)	0.24 (0.15)	0.33 (0.12)
# no result	1	0	0	0
ARC	0.07 (0.04)	0.14 (0.06)	0.25 (0.07)	- (-)
# no result	0	0	4	100
ARC + SimAnn.	0.07 (0.03)	0.14 (0.05)	0.27 (0.06)	- (-)
# no result	0	0	4	100

Table 2. Results from setting 4 by Friedman; the numbers in parantheses are the standard deviations

ARC did not optimize very much in most cases, it stops in most cases after the first iteration. This means, that all error rates in the start simplex were identical and could not be improved by changing the parameters. This was the reason to test whether simulated annealing could help to overcome this minimum. This was not the case, the simulated annealing procedure was carried out once and then the algorithm stopped directly. So we will not discuss ARC in further detail here.

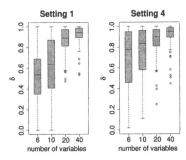

Fig. 1. Shrinkage parameter δ in the Friedman settings for URC

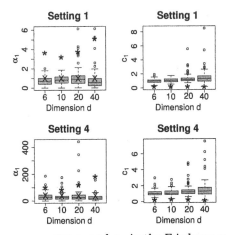

Fig. 2. Shrinkage parameter c_1 and α_1 in the Friedman settings for URC

6   Conclusion

We implemented the unified estimator and the proposed alternative estimator from Næs and Indahl with a modified Nelder Mead Simplex algorithm. The problems of restrictions on the parameter space and an integer valued parameter were solved.

In the test situation which we took from Friedman (1989) it turned out, that the procedures tend to regularize in direction of the pooled covariance matrix and therefore behave similar to LDA. Even though the number of unknown parameters is quite high, URC is quite stable in the test setting and chooses parameters which can be compared to theoretical selections of these parameter values. ARC seems to be questionable in this implementation, because it does return some arbitrary values for its parameters in most cases. Astonishingly ARC is able to improve the error rate compared to QDA in most cases. This should be investigated more thouroughly.

For future work on this implementation it is of interest whether a different optimization procedure could improve the selection of the parameters. Another idea would be to introduce a linkage between especially the α's and δ to ensure that an effect of α is not canceled out directly by a high δ.

Computations

All computations were carried out on Athlon 1800+ personal computers under Linux using **R**. A package for **R** including ARC and URC is available from www.statistik.uni-dortmund.de/leute.html?name=wtheis_en. The median of the run-times of URC was 11 minutes, for ARC 10 seconds.

References

BOHACHEVSKY, I. O., JOHNSON,M. E. and STEIN, M. L. (1986): Generalized Simulated Annealing for Function Optimization. *Technometrics, 28, 3, 209-217.*

FRIEDMAN, J.H. (1989): Regularized Discriminant Analysis. *Journal of the American Statistical Association, 84, 165–175*

IHAKA, R. and GENTLEMAN, R. (1996): **R**: A Language for Data Analysis and Graphics. *Journal of Computational and Graphical Statistics, 5, number 3, 299–314*

NÆS, T. and INDAHL, U. (1998): A Unified Description of Classical Classification Methods for Multicollinear Data. *Journal of Chemometrics, 12, 205–220.*

RÖHL, M.C., WEIHS, C., and THEIS, W. (2002): Direct Minimization of Error Rates in Multivariate Classification. *Computational Statistics, 17, 29–46*

VENABLES, W.N. and RIPLEY, B.D. (1999): Modern Applied Statistics with S-PLUS. Third Edition. *Springer*

Acknowledgments: This work has been supported by the Collaborative Research Centre "Reduction of Complexity in Multivariate Data Structures" (SFB 475) of the German Research Foundation (DFG). We like to thank Claus Weihs for helpful comments and corrections.

Two Approaches for
Discriminant Partial Least Squares

Robert Sabatier[1], Myrtille Vivien[1], and Pietro Amenta[2]

[1] Laboratoire de Physique Moléculaire et Structurale, UMR 5094,
  Faculté de Pharmacie, 15 av. Ch. Flahault, BP 14491
  34093 Montpellier Cedex 5, France.
  E-Mail: sabatier@pharma.univ-montp1.fr
[2] Department of Economics, Mathematic and Statistics,
  University of Lecce, via per Monteroni, 73100 Lecce, Italy.
  E-Mail: amenta@economia.unile.it

Abstract. In the medical sciences as well as in other contexts we often have to deal with the study of groups and with the research of their separation. The aim of this paper is to highlight how, in some situations, Partial Least Squares (PLS) Discriminant Analysis (Sjöström *et al.*, 1986) can lead to a solution that is not an answer to the given problem of discrimination. Within a PLS framework, the authors provide two extensions of it. The first is close to the Generalized PLS proposed by Cazes (1997) but used in the discrimination context. The second proposal, in the same framework, leads to consider the PLS Redundancy Analysis proposed by Tenenhaus (1995) by using suitable metrics. Some examples of data treatment are given.

1 Introduction

In the medical sciences, biology, ecology as well as in other fields, we very often have to deal with the study of groups and with the research of their separation with the aim to fix a decision role. In literature several methods have been proposed to the problem of discrimination (Tomassone *et al.*, 1988; Saporta, 1990). In some situations, a misuse of PLS Discriminant Analysis (PLS-DA) (Sjöström *et al.*, 1986) can lead to a biased solution which does not answer the given problem of discrimination. This unsuitable solution is due to several reasons.

By pointing the PLS-DA biased solution with regard to a well known real case, the authors provide two simple extensions within a PLS framework: the first is close to the Generalization of PLS proposed by Cazes (1997) but for the context of discrimination; the second proposal leads to consider the PLS Redundancy Analysis proposed by Tenenhaus (1995) by using suitable metrics. The results will be presented without reference to all the reports and graphical outputs provided by PLS method to make the paper more readable. (For all graphical outputs see: Umetri (1996), Tenenhaus (1998)).

2 Notation

Let (X, Q_X, D) be the statistical study associated with the $(n \times p)$ matrix X, collecting a set of p quantitative explanatory variables observed on n statistical units. Q_X is the $(p \times p)$ metric in $\Re^p$ and D is the (diagonal) weights metric into vectorial space of variables $\Re^n$. We assume that all the explanatory variables have zero means as regards the weights diagonal metric D. P_A is the D-orthogonal projection operator onto the vectorial subspace spanned by the column vectors of matrix A.

Let (Y, Q_Y, D) be the statistical study associated with the $(n \times q)$ matrix Y, collecting a set of q (quantitative/qualitative) criterion variables observed on the same n statistical units. Q_Y is the $(q \times q)$ metric of the statistical units in $\Re^q$. If Y is a qualitative variable with q categories then U is the D-uncentered binary indicator matrix related to the complete disjunctive coding of this variable. In this case, $D_Y = U^T D U$ is the $(q \times q)$ diagonal matrix of the each category relative frequencies, $G = D_Y^{-1} U^T D X$ is the $(q \times p)$ matrix collecting the explanatory variables averages for each categories and $B = G^T D_Y G$ is the between groups variance matrix.

Let further $V_{XY} = V_{YX}^T = X^T D Y$ be the covariance matrix among the variables of matrices X and Y with $V_{XX} = X^T D X$ and $V_{YY} = Y^T D Y$.

Finally, we denote with $s = 1, \ldots, S$ the step index; S is both the number of the retained axis and the rank of the selected PLS model. Let c_s (u_s) and w_s (t_s) be, the PLS weight (score) vectors, of order s, respectively associated with the matrices Y and X.

3   The PLS Methods

3.1   Generalized Partial Least Squares

We recall the PLS definitions according to Tenenhaus (1995, 1998), which have been generalized by Cazes (1997). The PLS regression of (Y, Q_Y, D) with respect to (X, Q_X, D) uses two statistical studies (triplets) observed on the same statistical units and weighted by means of the metric $D = diag(p_i)$ with $\sum_{i=1}^{n} p_i = 1$ and $0 \le p_i \le 1$.

The PLS regression is an iterative method maximizing the objective function $cov(Y Q_Y c, X Q_X w)$ with constraints on the axes $\|c\|_{Q_Y}^2 = \|w\|_{Q_X}^2 = 1$. At each step s this objective function is maximized by replacing Y and X, respectively, with the residual matrices $Y^{(s-1)}$ and $X^{(s-1)}$ obtained by the D-orthogonal projections of Y and X onto the subspace spanned by the $s-1$ PLS components of X of inferior order $(t_k = X^{(k-1)} Q_X w_k; k = 1, \ldots, (s-1))$. At step $s = 1$, we have $X^{(0)} = X$ and $Y^{(0)} = Y$. The axis w_s, associated with X, is given by the eigenvector corresponding to the highest eigenvalue λ^2 of $X^{(s-1)'} D Y^{(s-1)} Q_Y Y^{(s-1)'} D X^{(s-1)} Q_X$ and the objective function maximum equals to λ. By permuting X and Y (Q_X and Q_Y) into previous equation, it is possible to compute the axis c_s. Alternatively, axis c_s can be obtained by the transition formula $c_s = (1/\lambda) Y^{(s-1)'} D X^{(s-1)} Q_X w_s$ with an analogous formula to pass from c_s to w_s. Note that the $u_k = Y^{(k-1)} Q_Y c_k$ PLS components of Y ($k = 1, \ldots, s$) are only computed in order to make graphical representation. They are not used in the models building. Let's recall, among the others, the main properties of PLS:

- The system of S components $(X^{(s-1)}Q_x w_s)$ is D-orthogonal into $\Re^n$.
- c_s is given by the diagonalization of $Y^{(s-1)'}DX^{(s-1)}Q_X X^{(s-1)'}DY^{(s-1)}Q_Y$. We have $Y^{(s-1)} = P_{T_s}^\perp Y$ and $X^{(s-1)} = P_{T_s}^\perp X$ where T_s is the $\Re^n$ subspace spanned by $(t_1, \ldots, t_s)$ and $P_{T_s} = \sum_{s=1}^{S} P_{t_s}$. Therefore we can diagonalize the matrix $Y'DX^{(s-1)}Q_X X^{(s-1)'}DYQ_Y$ where it is evident that components t_s are unchanged without deflation of matrix Y.
- The linear model for each y_j is given by $\hat{y}_j^S = \sum_{s=1}^{S} P_{t_s} y_j = X\hat{\beta}_j^S$ and its variance is decomposed as $\|\hat{y}_j^S\|_D^2 = \sum_{s=1}^{S} \|P_{t_s} y_j\|_D^2$ $(j = 1, \ldots, q)$.
- The usual PLS (Wold, 1966) uses the metrics: $D = Id_n/n$, $Q_X = Id_p$ and $Q_Y = Id_q$.
- S can be chosen in different ways: the percentages of explained variance of y_j modelled at each step s, or, in a better way, the PRESS and/or Q_s criterion obtained by cross validation (Tenenhaus, 1998).

3.2   PLS Discriminant Analysis: light and shade

Following Sjöström *et al.* (1986) and Tenenhaus (1998), PLS Discriminant is the PLS analysis of the triplets $(U, Id_q, Id_n/n)$ and $(X, Id_p, Id_n/n)$ where U is the D-uncentered matrix related to the complete disjunctive coding of the class membership of the units. Additional PLS-DA properties are:

- The maximum number of PLS-DA components that can be obtained is higher than $q - 1$ (with $p > q$). On the contrary, the maximum number of Discriminant Factorial Analysis (DFA) discriminant axes is less than or equal to $min(p, q-1)$. This leads to a weak and not intuitive geometrical interpretation of higher than $q - 1$ order components. We can reach a suitable S value by cross validation but it can be higher than $q - 1$ too.
- The PLS-DA axis w_1, at the first step, is given by the diagonalization of the matrix $X'DUU'DX$. This matrix is not equivalent to the DFA between groups variance matrix. In fact, we have $B = G'D_y G$. By replacing G in the previous expression, we obtain $B = X'DUD_y^{-1}U'DX$. It is absolutely impossible to interpret PLS-DA with respect to the between groups variance except if we have the same number of units for each group (then $D_y = Id_q$). In this sense we do not have an optimality condition for PLS-DA.
- DFA discriminant components maximize the between groups variance with respect to the global variance. This property warrants a good separation for the groups as well as for units from their centre of gravity. The lack of properties for PLS-DA leads to a difficulty to appreciate the discrimination quality through the percentage of well classified units. In fact, this procedure tries to group each unit to the nearest centres of gravity even if they have no properties. In this sense, neither does the well classified percentage have optimal property.
- As we model the binary matrix U, the modelling formula $\hat{U}^S$ of U allows to interpret the adjusted model in term of class membership frequency.

This is a good property for PLS-DA even if we have always the problem to get a suitable value for S (see previous remark).

- The $\hat{U}^S$ modelling is conditioned by the preliminary treatment of X and this property is theoretical difficult to justify while no conditioning is in DFA.

4 PLS-DA alternatives

Within the PLS framework with discrimination, we propose two similar alternatives to overcome the previous remarks for the PLS-DA. First proposition is to use the Cazes's Generalized PLS with a optimal choice for the metrics whereas the second is to consider the PLS Redundancy Analysis (Tenenhaus, 1995) by using suitable metrics. The choice of using a suitable metric with respect to the usual ones can be conditioned by the dimension of the study but, in all the case, it is left in charge to the user.

4.1 The choice of suitable metrics

We define *Generalized PLS Discriminant Analysis* (GPLS-DA) as the PLS analysis of the triplets $(U, D_Y^{-1}, Id_n/n)$ and $(X, V_{XX}^{-1}, Id_n/n)$. Additional GPLS-DA properties are:

- At the first step, the axis w_1 is given by the diagonalization of the matrix BV_{XX}^{-1} and it is in this sense equivalent to DFA. In the same way, the components t_1 and u_1 associated with the first axes are the eigenvectors of $P_X P_U$ and $P_U P_X$, respectively, where P_U and P_X are the D-orthogonal projection operators onto the vectorial subspaces $Im(U)$ and $Im(X)$. The condition of unitary norm for c and w leads to unitary variances for t and u so as to maximize $cov(.,.)$ criterion is analogous to maximize $r(.,.)$.
- The other GPLS-DA steps use the residual matrix of the regression of X onto the obtained component t_s as new X whereas U is keeping the same. This allows again to find the remaining DFA components.
- The maximum number of GPLS-DA axes is less or equal to $min(p, q-1)$, like in DFA.
- The components t_s and u_s have unity norm and are independent from any X pretreatment.
- When p is higher than n, the matrix V_{XX} is not invertible. In order to overcome this problem, several approaches can be followed: a) to use the generalized inverse of V_{XX}, b) to use a lower rank spectral decomposition $V_{XX} = \sum_\ell \nu_\ell z_\ell z_\ell'$ (PCR smoothing) and c) to choose the identity matrix. The last point seems to be the more reasonable choice because the discrimination factors estimation is very unstable due to the few cases in each class, like in DFA. It suits better, then, to have more stable coefficients instead of an interpretation based on within group and between groups variances. We stress that the PLS of the triplets $(U, D_Y^{-1}, Id_n/n)$

and $(X, Id_p, Id_n/n)$, for the first axis w_1, is equivalent to diagonalize the matrix B and so to a Between PCA.

Remark: In the same context, it is possible to use the PLS Redondancy Analysis (Tenenhaus, 1995) (by adding suitable metrics) in order to have another generalization of PLS-DA. In this sense, we define as *Generalized PLS Redondancy Analysis* (GPLS-RA) of the triplets (Y, Q_Y, D) and (X, Q_X, D) the research of a set of S vectors $(t_s = XQ_Xw_s)$ $(s = 1, \ldots, S)$ such to form a D-orthogonal system in $Im(X)$. This system is chosen as solution to the maximization problem of $cov(YQ_Yc_s, X^{(s)}Q_Xw_s)$. At each step s, $X^{(s-1)} = XP^{\perp'}_{\{X'Dc_1, \ldots, X'Dc_{s-1}\}}$ where $X^{(s-1)'}$ is the residual matrix obtained by the Q_X-orthogonal projection of X' onto the vectorial subspace spanned by the set $\{X'Dc_1, \ldots, X'Dc_{s-1}\}$ while Y is unchanged. The axis w_s associated with X is the eigenvector corresponding to the highest eigenvalue μ^2 of $X^{(s-1)'}DYQ_YY'DX^{(s-1)}Q_X$ with μ equal to the maximum of $cov(.,.)$ criterion. c_s is given by the transition formula $c_s = (1/\mu)Y'DX^{(s-1)}Q_Xw_s$. We see how GPLS-RA can be easily placed in the same framework as GPLS-DA by choosing suitable metrics.

5 Example data

5.1 The Thymallus thymallus data

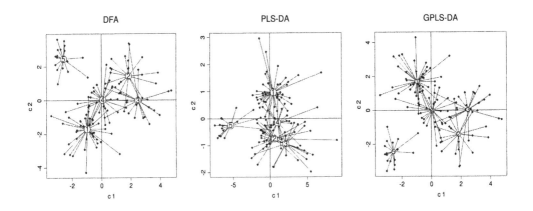

Fig. 1. DFA, PLS-DA and GPLS-DA units representations. First factorial plane.

The *Thymallus thymallus* belongs to the Salmoneide species and it is present into the higher part of the side bassin of the Rhone in France even if we can find them in other rivers of the districts (Persat, 1978). We use the

DFA as reference study in order to discriminate 5 geographically different populations with respect to 13 morphometric variables (sizes and shapes) and 120 statistical units. Data are free available with the statistical software ADE (Chessel, Doledec, 1993). The first four eigenvalues of $V_{XX}^{-1}B$ (discriminant power) are equal to: 0.7484, 0.6959, 0.4367 and 0.1503. These eigenvalues are equally associated, for each component (discriminant variable), to a between and within classes variance ratio: 2.9742, 2.283, 0.7751 and 0.1769. They are also the eigenvalues of $W^{-1}B$ with $W = V_{XX} - B$ within variance matrix. Figure 1 shows the statistical units plot for the first two DFA discriminant variables: the first axis opposes the population 5 to 2 and 3 while the second one compares the populations 5 and 1. Table 1 gives the percentage of well classified units after the cross validation for the first factorial plane. Note as the percentage of good classification for each group results unstable (from 94.44% of group 5 until 65.22% of class 4 with respect to the global value (78.33%). The total percentage of well classified for all axes results is equal to 87.50%.

We have performed a PLS-DA on the same data. According to Sjöström, the

	GPLS-DA [DFA]						PLS-DA					
	Gr 1	Gr 2	Gr 3	Gr 4	Gr 5		Gr 1	Gr 2	Gr 3	Gr 4	Gr 5	
Gr 1(*)	**36**	0	0	3	0	*39*	**36**	0	0	4	1	*41*
Gr 2(*)	1	**12**	3	3	0	*19*	1	**10**	4	4	1	*20*
Gr 3(*)	0	4	**14**	2	0	*20*	0	4	**12**	3	0	*19*
Gr 4(*)	4	2	3	**15**	1	*25*	4	4	4	**12**	1	*25*
Gr 5(*)	0	0	0	0	**17**	*17*	0	0	0	0	**15**	*15*
	41	*18*	*20*	*23*	*18*	*120*	*41*	*18*	*20*	*23*	*18*	*120*

Table 1. *Thymallus thymallus Data.* Prediction (*) of the geographical area by means of the GPLS-DA and PLS-DA Analysis. Well classified units are boldfaced

matrix U (120×5) is scaled and centered with respect to uniform weights. We see in table 1 a lower percentage of well classified (70.83%) due to the no optimal PLS-DA property of the percentage of well classified. For the first four PLS-DA components, the between/within variance ratios are (1.0544, 1.7855, 0.5623 and 0.4209) lower than DFA ones, with similar values of those of a simple scaled and centered PCA of X (1.0195, 1.5866, 0.1922 and 0.1676) for the same number of principal components. These remarks highlight the non optimality of PLS-DA. It is possible to determine 13 axes of unvoid information to model U. The correlations between the first DFA discriminant variables v_s and the PLS-DA components t_k are poor: $r(t_1, v_1) = 0.6270$ and $r(t_2, v_2) = -0.6991$. Cross validation (PRESS criterion) highlights the first four PLS-DA components as the significant ones (it is equal to $q - 1$ by change). If we consider a scaled and centered X, the cumulative percentage of reconstruction for $\hat{U}^S$ are 12.18%, 29.86%, 38.43% and 45.68%, for the first four steps, while, with a centered X, they are 11.42%, 25.14%, 30.73% and 34.58% (51.16% for both cases by using all components). We can see as PLS-DA output is influenced by the pre-treatment of matrix X unlike DFA. The Figure 1 shows a very different PLS-DA cloud. We see, by reversing the second PLS-DA axis, as the clouds for each group have an higher dispersion with respect to own's centre of gravity as well as the overlap for the clouds 2, 3 and 4. All these remarks happen as PLS-DA does not optimize any criteria (within, between or their ratio). Naturally, when we apply GPLS-DA to the data we find again the DFA results. For example, by referring to the first four couples of GPLS-DA components, the optimal squared covariances (0.7484, 0.6959, 0.4367 and 0.1503) are exactly equal to the DFA discriminant powers, the units representation is the same as well as the percentage of well classified.

5.2   The Bordeaux Wines data

We have explored the use of PLS-DA and GPLS-DA on another dataset related to a study on the quality of the Bordeaux wines (Esposito & Tenenhaus, 2001). The objective of the study is to highlight the methods differences in quality prediction of wine (good, average, poor) on the basis of four influently (centred and reduced) meteorological variables (Temperature, Sunshine, Heat, Rain) measured during 34 years (1924-1957).

The Figure 2 shows as the PLS-DA clouds for each group have an higher

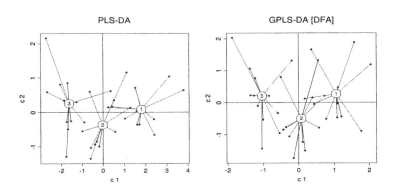

Fig. 2. *Bordeaux wines data.* DFA, PLS-DA and GPLS-DA units representations. First factorial plane

dispersion along the first axis with respect to the centres of gravity as well as a little bit more overlap for the clouds 2 and 3.

PLS-DA yields 7 misclassified objects while GPLS-DA (or DFA) only 5 (see table 2) by leading a lower percentage of well classified (79.41% vs. 85.29%) due to the no optimal properties for PLS-DA.

	GPLS-DA [DFA]				PLS-DA			
	Gr 1	Gr 2	Gr 3	Gr 1	Gr 2	Gr 3		
Gr 1(*)	11	3	0	*14*	11	3	1	*15*
Gr 2(*)	0	7	1	*8*	0	6	1	*7*
Gr 3(*)	0	1	11	*12*	0	2	10	*12*
	11	*11*	*12*	*34*	*11*	*11*	*12*	*34*

Table 2. *Bordeaux wines data.* Prediction of the Quality (*) by means of GPLS-DA and PLS-DA Analysis

Conclusions

In some situations, a misuse of PLS Discriminant Analysis can lead to a discriminant biased solution. This unsuitable solution is due to several reasons and it was pointed out with a pair of well known real cases. The authors provide two extensions within a PLS framework finding again the DFA results. We have obtained better results with GPLS-DA than with PLS-DA.

References

CAZES, P. (1997): Adaptation de la régression PLS au cas de la régression aprés analyse des correspondances multiples. *Revue de Statistique Appliquées,* XLV(2), 89-99

CHESSEL, D., DOLEDEC, S. (1993): *ADE Version 3.6: HypercardStack and Program library for the Analysis of Environment Data.* User's Manual

ESPOSITO VINCI, V., TENENHAUS, M. (2001): PLS Logistic Regression. In V. Esposito Vinci, C. Lauro, A. Morineau and M. Tenenhaus (Eds.): *Pls and related methods.* Cisia 89-99.

PERSAT, H., (1978): Ecologie de l'Ombre commun. *Bulletin de la Revue Francaise de Pisciculture,* 26,11-20.

SAPORTA, G. (1990): *Probabilité, analyse des données et statistique.* Editions Technip, Paris, 493p.

SJÖSTRÖM, M., WOLD S. and SÖDERSTRÖM, B. (1986): PLS Discrimination plots. In E.S. Gelsema and L.N. Kanals (Eds.): *Pattern Recognition in Practice II.* Elsevier, Amsterdam

TENENHAUS, M. (1995): A partial least squares approach to multiple regression, redundancy analysis and canonical analysis. *Les Cahiers de Recherche de HEC,* CR 550/1995.

TENENHAUS, M. (1998): *La Régression PLS. Théorie et pratique.* Editions Technip, Paris, 254p.

TOMASSONE, R., DANZART, M., DAUDIN, J.J. and MASSON, J.P. (1988): *Discrimination et classement.* Masson, Paris, 172p.

WOLD, H. (1966): Estimation of principal components and related models by iterative least squares. In P.R. Krishnaiah (Eds.) *Multivariate Analysis*. Academic Press, New York.

Acknowledgement: The authors whish to thank P. Cazes and M. Tenenhaus for their interest in this paper. The partecipation of Pietro Amenta to this research was supported by the PRIN 99 grant (Resp: Prof. P.Amenta)

Improving the Classification Performance of a Discriminant Rule by Dealing With Data Cases Having a Substantial Influence on Variable Selection

Sarel Steel and Nelmarie Louw

Department of Statistics and Actuarial Science,
University of Stellenbosch, Private Bag X1, Matieland, South Africa

Abstract. An important problem in discriminant analysis that has received little attention in the literature is the effect of outliers when variable selection forms part of the analysis. In this paper we argue that variable selection and outlier identification should not be done sequentially, but should rather be integrated. We investigate an integrated approach, and compare its classification performance to that of a sequential approach in a limited simulation study.

1 Introduction

Consider a classification problem in which a potentially large set of feature variables is available. Frequently, an important part of the analysis is to select a subset of the feature variables to use in the classification of future cases. In discriminant analysis the selected variables are used to construct a discriminant rule. Apart from having the advantage of being simpler than the rule based on all the feature variables, it is also frequently found that this rule yields a smaller error rate. Many techniques for variable selection in discriminant analysis appear in the literature (cf. for example Le Roux, Steel and Louw, 1997, and the references therein).

It is well known that a dataset may contain cases that markedly influence the results of a statistical analysis of the dataset. The effect of such outliers has been well examined in multiple linear regression, and methods have been proposed for dealing with such cases (see for example Andrews and Pregibon, 1978, and Rousseeuw and Leroy, 1987). The same is true in discriminant analysis (see e.g. Fung, 1995, for diagnostic measures in the linear case). Hawkins and McLachlan (1997) discuss the sensitivity to one or more outlying data cases of the maximum likelihood estimates used in constructing a discriminant rule, and they propose a robust discriminant analysis technique to reduce this sensitivity.

Variable selection is known to be an unstable process in the sense that slight perturbations of the data may lead to changes in the set of variables that is selected. It therefore seems to be especially important to investigate the effect of individual cases in a variable selection context. In a multiple linear regression setting, Rousseeuw and Leroy (1987, p.106) remark that variable selection is considerably complicated by the presence of influential points. Their recommendation is to apply a standard selection technique to the "cleaned" data, i.e. the dataset from which identified outliers have been removed. Since such an approach identifies influential cases from the data on all the feature variables, such cases are influential conditional on the model containing all the feature variables. However, this approach is unsatisfactory. A case may seem influential as a result of extreme values in variables that "do not really matter", i.e. variables that do not discriminate well between the groups and will typically not be selected. In Section 3 we present an example that illustrates this well. It is therefore insufficient when investigating influential cases in a selection context to look at the data only in terms of all the available variables. This may suggest an approach of first doing variable selection, using all the data, and subsequently identifying influential cases based on the set of selected variables. The disadvantage of such an approach is that it ignores the effect that certain cases may have on the selection process. This effect may result in an entirely different set of variables being selected than without these cases being present, placing the value of a subsequent post selection influence analysis in doubt. The best strategy therefore seems to be an integrated approach, combining variable selection and the identification of influential cases, rather than considering these issues sequentially. In this paper we investigate such a procedure and compare its performance to that of a procedure dealing sequentially with variable selection and identification of outliers.

2 Methods for dealing with influential cases

Many papers have appeared in the literature proposing methods for dealing with influential cases. In a regression context, Andrews and Pregibon (1978) proposed a strategy for finding the "outliers that matter". They consider the linear model $\mathbf{y} = X\beta + noise$ with X an $(n \times p)$ matrix of observations of independent variables, and $\mathbf{y}$ the n-vector of observations of the dependent variable. To assess the influence of deleting the m observations $(i, j, ...)$ from the dataset, Andrews and Pregibon (1978) propose the measure

$$R_{ij...}^{(m)}(X^*) = D_{ij...}^{(m)}(|X^{*\prime}X^*|) / |X^{*\prime}X^*|, \qquad (2.1)$$

where $X^* = (X : \mathbf{y})$, and the operator $D_{ij...}^{(m)}$ deletes the m observations $(i, j, ...)$ from the dataset. Small values of $R_{ij...}^{(m)}(X^*)$ are associated with influential observations. This measure can readily be applied in two-group discriminant analysis. Consider training data $\mathcal{T} = \{(\mathbf{x}_{ij}, y_{ij}), i = 1, 2; j = 1, ..., n_i\}$ from populations Π_1 and Π_2 respectively. Here, $\mathbf{x}_{ij}$ is a $p \times 1$ vector of observations of the feature variables, and y_{ij} is a group membership indicator variable. Let S denote the usual pooled covariance matrix. Then it can easily be shown that the Andrews-Pregibon criterion becomes

$$\left\{ \tilde{n}_1 \tilde{n}_2 (n_1 + n_2 - m - 2)^p D_{ij...}^{(m)}(|S|) \right\} / \{ n_1 n_2 (n_1 + n_2 - 2)^p |S| \}, \qquad (2.2)$$

where $\tilde{n}_1$ and $\tilde{n}_2$ are n_1 and n_2 respectively, appropriately adjusted to reflect the m points being omitted from the dataset. Clearly, if we wish to minimise (2.2) for a fixed value of m, we should omit the m points whose omission minimises $|S|$. We see that application of the Andrews-Pregibon criterion to identify influential points is equivalent to applying the so-called minimum covariance determinant (MCD) criterion (cf. Rousseeuw and Leroy, 1987). This idea was applied in a discrimant analysis context by Hawkins and McLachlan (1997). They describe and investigate high-breakdown linear discriminant analysis, obtained by replacing the usual maximum likelihood estimates by outlier resistant alternatives. The minimum with-in group covariance determinant criterion (MWCD) is used to identify outliers. A certain coverage percentage is specified and the remaining cases are omitted from the training data. The cases to be omitted are those cases whose omission minimises the MWCD. Finally in this section, we refer to an interesting contribution by Riani and Atkinson (2001). They explore a forward search method, originally proposed by these authors in a regression context, to study the influence of data cases and to identify outliers in discriminant analysis. Their methodology enables one to identify at the same time the variable transformations that lead to approximately normal feature variables with approximately the same covariance matrix in each group. Extending this obviously powerful method to cases where variable selection is of primary interest is an important problem for further research.

3 Influential cases in a variable selection context: an illustrative example

In this section we consider a simulated example illustrating some of the problems encountered when attempting to identify influential cases in discriminant analysis when variable selection forms part of the analysis. Data were simulated from two multivariate (using 4 feature variables) normal populations with $\Sigma = \mathbf{I}$. The mean vectors $\mu_1 = \mathbf{0}$ and $\mu_2 = [a/4, 0, a, a]$ were used. Using $a = 2.45$ resulted in the squared Mahalanobis distance between the two populations being $\Delta^2 = 12.4$. According to this parameterisation, the two groups differ substantially with respect to X_3 and X_4, and only slightly with respect to X_1. The fairly large separation between the two groups w.r.t. X_3 and X_4 should lead to these variables being selected by any reasonable selection procedure. Twenty-five values were generated from the first normal population, and 24 from the second. An additional value, simulated from a normal population with $\mu_2 = [a, 0, a, a]$ and $\Sigma = \mathbf{I}$ was added to the data from group 2. This case (labelled case 50 in the discussion below) represents an outlier in the group 2 data with respect to X_1 only. Its effect is to increase the difference between the two samples w.r.t. X_1, which may well lead to this variable being selected. For each of the 15 possible models the influence measure (2.2) with $m = 1$ was calculated, to identify the 5 most influential single cases. The results are summarised in Table 1. In this table, the cases appear in each row in order of decreasing influence.

MODEL	CASES				
X_1	50	9	3	8	13
X_2	11	21	42	38	14
X_3	4	30	10	2	20
X_4	46	24	1	48	43
X_1, X_2	50	11	3	6	21
X_1, X_3	50	30	20	4	9
X_1, X_4	50	18	46	9	3
X_2, X_3	11	21	4	10	30
X_2, X_4	11	46	21	27	25
X_3, X_4	20	4	46	30	1
X_1, X_2, X_3	50	11	6	21	3
X_1, X_2, X_4	50	11	6	46	3
X_1, X_3, X_4	50	20	18	46	4
X_2, X_3, X_4	11	20	4	21	25
X_1, X_2, X_3, X_4	50	11	6	20	21

Table 1. Simulated dataset: The five most influential cases for every possible model

Case 50 is the most prominent outlier in the full model. An analyst attempting to identify one outlier by investigating the data on all the feature variables, will therefore identify case 50 as the most likely candidate. If such an analyst decides to omit this case, subsequent variable selection and the discriminant function formed from the selected variables, will be based on the remaining 49 cases only. In addition, it should be noted that in all lower dimensional models containing X_1, case 50 is also identified as the most prominent outlier. However, in none of the models that do not include X_1, does case 50 appear amongst the 5 identified most influential cases. Clearly, case 50 is influential conditional on the underlying model containing variable X_1.

As a next step, variable selection was applied to the full dataset, as well as to the dataset without case 50. Forward, backward and fully stepwise selection were employed. On the full dataset, variables X_1, X_3 and X_4 were selected by all three methods. A sequential approach, with variable selection preceding outlier detection, would therefore identify the model containing X_1, X_3 and X_4. However, on the dataset without case 50, only variables X_3 and X_4 were selected. Hence, if outlier detection precedes variable selection, the identified model changes, with variable X_1 no longer being selected. Clearly, the order in which variable selection and outlier identification takes place in a sequential approach applied to our example dataset, influences the final selected model. Therefore, a better option seems to be an approach integrating variable selection and outlier identification.

4 An integrated approach

The following method for identifying influential cases in discriminant analysis, taking the effect of variable selection into account, was recently proposed by Steel and Louw (2001). Consider a random vector $\mathbf{X} : p \times 1$, consisting of measurements on p feature variables. The entity corresponding to $\mathbf{X}$ belongs to one of two populations, Π_1 and Π_2. We assume that $E(\mathbf{X}) = \mu_i$ and $Cov(\mathbf{X}) = \Sigma$ in $\Pi_i, i = 1, 2$. In practice, the parameters are unknown, and are estimated from the training data. Fisher's sample linear discriminant rule (SLDR) can be used to classify new cases. Denote the estimated posterior probability of belonging to Π_i by $t_i(\mathbf{X}) \equiv t_i(\mathbf{X}, \mathcal{T})$. We write $t = [t_1(\mathbf{X}), t_2(\mathbf{X})]$.

Our proposal for quantifying the selection influence of a data case is based on the following rationale. Suppose a variable selection technique is applied to $\mathcal{T}$, thereby identifying a data-dependent subset $\mathcal{V}(\mathcal{T})$ of the indices in $\{1, 2, ..., p\}$. The SLDR and the posterior probabilities are now based only on the variables corresponding to the indices in $\mathcal{V}(\mathcal{T})$. The posterior probability estimates are accordingly denoted by $t_i(\mathbf{X}^{\mathcal{V}(\mathcal{T})}, \mathcal{T}), i = 1, 2$.

Different measures can be used to evaluate the quality of the identified model. Following Breiman et al. (1993, p.122) we use

$$R^{\mathcal{V}(\mathcal{T})}(t) = \frac{1}{n_1 + n_2} \sum_{i=1}^{2} \sum_{j=1}^{n_i} \left\{ \left[t_1\left(\mathbf{x}_{ij}^{\mathcal{V}(\mathcal{T})}\right) - z_{ij}^{(1)} \right]^2 + \left[t_2\left(\mathbf{x}_{ij}^{\mathcal{V}(\mathcal{T})}\right) - z_{ij}^{(2)} \right]^2 \right\}$$
(4.1)

for this purpose. In (4.1), $z_{ij}^{(k)} = \delta_{ik}$, $j = 1, ..., n_i$; $i, k = 1, 2$, where the Kronecker delta, $\delta_{ik} = 1$, if $i = k$ and $\delta_{ik} = 0$, if $i \neq k$. Note that $R^{\mathcal{V}(\mathcal{T})}(t)$ is a measure of the error with which the group membership values of the training data cases are estimated by the post-selection posterior probability estimates.

Now consider the training data without case k, denoted by $\mathcal{T}_k \equiv D_{k...}^{(1)}(\mathcal{T})$, $k = 1, ..., n_1 + n_2$. Application of the same variable selection technique used on the full dataset, yields a set of selected variables, $\mathcal{V}(\mathcal{T}_k)$. It is important to note that the sets $\mathcal{V}(\mathcal{T})$ and $\mathcal{V}(\mathcal{T}_k)$ need not be identical, and that the sets $\mathcal{V}(\mathcal{T}_k)$ may vary with k. The measure (4.1) becomes

$$R^{\mathcal{V}(\mathcal{T}_k)}(t) = \frac{1}{n_1 + n_2} \sum_{i=1}^{2} \sum_{j=1}^{n_i} \left\{ \left[t_1\left(\mathbf{x}_{ij}^{\mathcal{V}(\mathcal{T}_k)}\right) - z_{ij}^{(1)} \right]^2 + \left[t_2\left(\mathbf{x}_{ij}^{\mathcal{V}(\mathcal{T}_k)}\right) - z_{ij}^{(2)} \right]^2 \right\}$$
(4.2)

We propose

$$Q_k(t) = \frac{R^{\mathcal{V}(\mathcal{T}_k)}(t) - R^{\mathcal{V}(\mathcal{T})}(t)}{R^{\mathcal{V}(\mathcal{T})}(t)}$$
(4.3)

as a measure of the influence of case k in the selection process. Note that $Q_k(t)$ quantifies the relative change in the error with which group membership is estimated by post-selection posterior probability estimates if case k is omitted from the training data. Therefore a negative value of $Q_k(\mathbf{t})$ suggests that $\mathbf{t}$ based on $\mathcal{V}(\mathcal{T}_k)$ is a more accurate group membership indicator than $\mathbf{t}$ based on $\mathcal{V}(\mathcal{T})$. One would expect this to translate into more accurate classification of future cases if the classification rule is based on $\mathbf{X}^{\mathcal{V}(\mathcal{T}_k)}$ instead of $\mathbf{X}^{\mathcal{V}(\mathcal{T})}$ (cf. Steel and Louw, 2001, for confirmation of this supposition in two examples). Suppose $Q_{(1)}(\mathbf{t}) \leq Q_{(2)}(\mathbf{t}) \leq ... \leq Q_{(n)}(\mathbf{t})$, and that $Q_{(1)}(\mathbf{t}) < 0$. The so-called Q-method for dealing with influential cases in a selection context now omits the case corresponding to $Q_{(1)}(\mathbf{t})$ from the data and applies variable selection to the reduced dataset. It is important to note that this procedure identifies an influential case taking the effect of variable selection into account. In Section 5 the merit of this method is investigated by means of a Monte Carlo simulation study, in which two approaches to dealing with outliers in a variable selection context in discriminant analysis are compared with respect to their error rate performance. The first approach "cleans" the data using the high-breakdown estimates proposed by Hawkins and McLachlan (1997), followed by variable selection on the "cleaned" data. This method is called the HB-method (high-breakdown) in the remainder of the paper. The second approach uses the Q-method described above.

5 Simulation study

To compare the two methods mentioned in Section 4 with respect to their classification performance, a Monte Carlo simulation study was performed. The methods were evaluated for training data from the normal, double exponential and lognormal distributions. Training samples of size $n_1 = n_2 = 25$ were used. Two covariance structures were investigated: $\Sigma = \mathbf{I}$, and the matrix $\Sigma^{0.5}$ with elements $\sigma_{ij} = 0.5(1 + \delta_{ij})$. Six feature variables and mean vectors $\mu_1 = \mathbf{0}$ and $\mu_2 = [0, 0, 0, a, a, a]$ were used. Using $a = \Delta/\sqrt{\sum_{i=4}^{6}\sum_{j=4}^{6}\sigma^{ij}}$, where σ^{ij} are the elements of Σ^{-1}, ensures that the squared Mahalanobis distance between the two populations is equal to Δ^2, for which the values 1,2,3,4,6 and 9 were used. Note that the two groups do not differ with respect to the first three variables. Cases where the training data contain 1, 5 and 9 outliers, were considered. These outliers were inserted as follows into the training data for group 2. In configuration A referred to below, the fourth component of μ_2 was set equal to zero (instead of a), in configuration B, the fourth and fifth components of μ_2 were set equal to zero (instead of a), and in configuration C, the last three components of μ_2 were all set equal to zero. This implies that such a case, belonging to group 2, resembles a group 1 case with respect to 4 (in configuration A), 5 (in configuration B) and 6 (in configuration C) variables, respectively.

For each of the cases above, the two methods described in Section 4 were applied to the training data to construct a classification rule based only on the selected variables. To obtain approximate error rates for each of these rules, 1000 (500 per group) new test cases were generated from the same distribution as the training data (excluding outliers). The test cases were classified

$\sum = I$		1 Outlier		5 Outliers		9 Outliers	
	Δ^2	HB	Q	HB	Q	HB	Q
A	1	.3688	.3565	.3738	.3604	.3740	.3603
	3	.2396	.2274	.2453	.2315	.2535	.2396
	9	.0943	.0853	.1053	.0942	.1183	.1045
B	1	.3691	.3569	.3790	.3646	.3900	.3743
	3	.2404	.2286	.2580	.2420	.2796	.2609
	9	.0957	.0873	.1284	.1129	.1562	.1382
C	1	.3718	.3576	.3909	.3736	.4118	.3955
	3	.2461	.2313	.2767	.2498	.3176	.2886
	9	.0974	.0850	.1434	.1081	.2050	.1673
$\sum^{(0.5)}$		1 Outlier		5 Outliers		9 Outliers	
	Δ^2	HB	Q	HB	Q	HB	Q
A	1	.3792	.3664	.3831	.3753	.3928	.3811
	3	.2566	.2424	.2646	.2545	.2796	.2661
	9	.1080	.0979	.1145	.1116	.1325	.1253
B	1	.3791	.3671	.3862	.3785	.4020	.3929
	3	.2585	.2434	.2700	.2617	.2947	.2834
	9	.1100	.0991	.1245	.1233	.1559	.1554
C	1	.3790	.3687	.3913	.3842	.4174	.4033
	3	.2590	.2452	.2802	.2689	.3187	.3031
	9	.1099	.0973	.1388	.1314	.1941	.1800

Table 2. Error rates for high breakdown and Q-Method: Normal distribution, different outlier configurations

using each of the two rules, and a misclassification rate was calculated for each rule. The estimated error rates were obtained by averaging the respective misclassification rates over 1000 Monte Carlo repetitions. The estimated error rates for the normal and lognormal distributions are shown in Tables 2 and 3 respectively. For the double exponential distribution, the results were largely similar to the normal case.

6   Conclusions and open problems

First consider the results for symmetrically distributed training data, for example the normal case summarised in Table 2. In all cases, the Q-method performs better than the HB-method, sometimes significantly so. Similar conclusions are valid for the double exponential training data. For asymmetrical training data, in our study the lognormal case, the HB-method outperforms the Q-method in the uncorrelated case, except at large Δ^2-values, where the Q-method performs better (cf. Table 3). At small separations the error rate yielded by the HB-method is considerably smaller than that of the other method. When correlation is present, the same behaviour is observed in the configuration A- and B-cases, but at medium to large spacings in the configuration C-cases, the Q-method is often best (cf. Table 3).

$\sum = I$	Δ^2	1 Outlier		5 Outliers		9 Outliers	
		HB	Q	HB	Q	HB	Q
A	1	.2536	.2750	.2521	.2701	.2542	.2722
	3	.1133	.1223	.1180	.1226	.1275	.1312
	9	.0508	.0471	.0577	.0531	.0615	.0591
B	1	.2512	.2728	.2594	.2729	.2743	.2847
	3	.1127	.1214	.1271	.1285	.1446	.1461
	9	.0511	.0474	.0649	.0608	.0751	.0702
C	1	.2574	.2763	.2674	.2749	.2948	.3000
	3	.1156	.1222	.1425	.1364	.1876	.1854
	9	.0506	.0455	.0837	.0713	.1304	.1209
$\sum^{(0.5)}$	Δ^2	1 Outlier		5 Outliers		9 Outliers	
		HB	Q	HB	Q	HB	Q
A	1	.2295	.2456	.2347	.2493	.2447	.2595
	3	.1233	.1281	.1306	.1407	.1399	.1518
	9	.0600	.0611	.0660	.0700	.0709	.0778
B	1	.2321	.2462	.2389	.2531	.2545	.2678
	3	.1225	.1281	.1350	.1437	.1507	.1597
	9	.0620	.0613	.0714	.0748	.0813	.0869
C	1	.2345	.2471	.2450	.2546	.2705	.2767
	3	.1262	.1239	.1475	.1468	.1712	.1729
	9	.0624	.0607	.0852	.0757	.1103	.0998

Table 3. Error rates for high breakdown and Q-Method: Lognormal distribution, different outlier configurations

Although this was a limited simulation study, several general trends are evident. No method is best in all the cases that were studied. This makes it difficult to formulate a general recommendation. It is however clear that the HB-method is recommendable for training data from a skew distribution, but not for training data from a symmetric distribution. This is especially so when the two populations are not well separated. It seems that in these cases the HB-method is particularly adept at identifying outlying cases. For training data from symmetric distributions, however, the Q-method is always better than the HB-method. This suggests that training data that do not show a symmetric distribution could perhaps first undergo a suitable transformation aimed at making the data more symmetric. The forward search method of Riani and Atkinson (2001) could be used to find such a transformation. Investigating the properties of the Q-method after transformation of the data is an interesting problem for further research. There are a number of other open problems. Firstly, our simulation study was limited. What can be said about the relative merit of the two methods in other configurations? Secondly, identifying the number of significant outliers is important for method HB, since then the coverage can be specified accordingly. Finally, it is desirable to extend the Q-method to enable it to omit more than one influential case. This would most likely make the method more competitive in cases where there are more than one outlier in the training data.

References

ANDREWS, D.F. and PREGIBON, D. (1978): Finding the outliers that matter. *Journal of the Royal Statistical Society B, 40, 85–93.*

BREIMAN, L., FRIEDMAN, J.H., OLSHEN, R.A. and STONE, C.J. (1993): *Classification and Regression Trees.* Chapman and Hall, New York.

FUNG, W.K. (1995): Diagnostics in linear discriminant analysis. *Journal of the American Statistical Association, 90, 952–956.*

HAWKINS, D.M. and MCLACHLAN, G.J. (1997): High-breakdown linear discriminant analysis. *Journal of the American Statistical Association, 92, 136–143.*

LE ROUX, N.J., STEEL, S.J. and LOUW, N. (1997): Variable selection and error rate estimation in discriminant analysis. *Journal of Statistical Computation and Simulation, 59, 195–219.*

RIANI, M. and ATKINSON, A.C. (2001): A unified approach to outliers, influence and transformations in discriminant analysis. *Journal of Computational and Graphical Statistics, 10, 513–544.*

ROUSSEEUW, P.J. and LEROY, A. (1987): *Robust regression and outlier detection.* Wiley, New York.

STEEL, S.J. and LOUW, N. (2001): Variable selection in discriminant analysis: measuring the influence of individual cases. *Computational Statistics and Data Analysis, 37, 249–260.*

Classification and Clustering of Vocal Performances

Claus Weihs[1,3],

Uwe Ligges[1], Jörg Güttner[1], Petra Hasse-Becker[2,4], and Sonja Berghoff[1]

[1] Fachbereich Statistik, Universität Dortmund, 44221 Dortmund
[2] Institut für Musik und ihre Didaktik, Universität Dortmund, 44221 Dortmund
[3] weihs@statistik.uni-dortmund.de
[4] PetraHasse@aol.com

Abstract. In order to find objective criteria for the assessment of the quality of vocal performance, time series of voice generated vibrations (so called waves) were measured in a standardised experiment where 17 singers sang the same two songs. *Classification*: Based on a segmentation of the waves into notes (Ligges et al., 2002), the intonation purity of individual tones was judged on the basis of the halftone distance of the estimated frequencies of the sung notes from their ideal frequencies. *Clustering*: In order to analyse the quality of the performances, various measures were derived from the spectrum of the sung notes, the so-called voice print. These voice characteristics build the basis for clustering the voices (Güttner, 2001).

1 Introduction

This paper deals with the finding of objective quality criteria for the assessment of the quality of singing presentations. For this purpose *time series of voice generated vibrations* (so called *waves*) are measured.

We are interested in properties of such time series related to the quality of singing. In order to find such properties we carried out an experiment with singers with voices of apparently very different quality (including laymen and professionals). This way we intended to identify rough differences, at least. This study should only be seen, however, as a first step on the way to *characterize the different interpretations of professional singers*.

Related literature is scarce. The most relevant reference (Rossignol et al., 1999) deals with the characterization of vibrato. Other related literature discuss the relationship between the anatomy of the human voice and the corresponding audio event. These references are quite important to understand the generation of vocal sound. E.g., in Titze et al. (1994) the acoustic of the high pitched tenor voice is described, Bergan und Titze (2001) have worked on the perception of pitch and roughness, and Titze et al. (2002) did some modelling of the generation of vibrato.

The paper is structured as follows. In section 2 the experiment is described by which we generated our data. Sections 3 and 4 introduce the basics of frequency analysis for singing presentations. Notice that we use the term *"note"* for the graphical sign and the corresponding ideal musical sound planned by the composer, and *"sung note"* or *"tone"* for the realized audio event corresponding to a note. In section 5 linear discriminant analysis is introduced, and its result for our experimental data, i.e. a so-called classification rule intending to reproduce the judgements of an expert corresponding to purity of intonation by means of properties of the observed time series. The term *"voice print"*, which characterizes a voice by a collection of different measures, e.g., for clustering, is introduced in section 6. In section 7 the clustering of singers from the experiment by their voice prints is described. Finally, a conclusion is given in section 8.

2   The experiment

The classical song "Tochter Zion" (Händel) was sung by 17 singers to a standardized piano accompaniment played back by headphones at the recording studio of the University of Dortmund. The interpreters could choose between two accompaniment versions transposed by a third in order to take into account the different *voice types*.

Voice and piano were recorded at different channels in CD quality, i.e. the amplitude of the corresponding vibrations was recorded with constant sampling rate 44100 hertz in 16-bit format, i.e. wave data consists of 44100 integers per second between -32767 and 32766 ($= 2^{16}$ possibilities). The *audio data sets* were transformed by means of a computer program into *wave data sets*[1]. For time series analysis the waves were reduced to 11 kHz (in order to restrict the number of data), and standardized to the interval $[-1, 1]$. Since the volume of recording was already controlled individually, a comparison of loudness of the different recordings was not sensible anyway. Therefore, by our standardization no additional information was lost.

If we could now listen to presentations of "Tochter Zion" in the different versions of an amateur and a professional (of the same voice type), we might immediately be able to identify the different quality. Our target is, however, to filter such quality differences out of the corresponding wave representations. Figures 1 exemplify the wave representations of the syllable "Zi" in "Tochter Zion" (corresponding to a c'' with 523.25 Hz) by means of the performance of an amateur and a professional soprano. The waves obviously look quite different, but how should these differences be related to the different aspects of sound quality?

3   Frequency analysis of singing presentations

In order to be able to relate differences in time series to tone characteristics of sung notes, we, naturally, have to identify what makes a melodious sound, first. Proposals for desirable sound properties could be

- purity of intonation,
- vowel purity,
- natural vibrato,
- solidity of tone,

---

[1] We would like to thank Niklas Büdenbender for his tireless support of the recording of the singing presentations and for the transformation from audio to wave data sets.

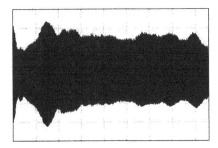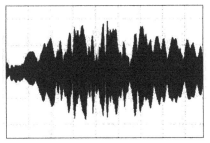

Fig. 1. Wave representation of an amateur and a professional soprano

- softness / brilliance of tone.

These characteristics are then to be "measured" on the basis of vocal time series, i.e. the *"sound information"* in the time series has to be identified. In this paper we restrict ourselves to

a) *purity of intonation*, i.e. we intend to determine a classification rule for purity of intonation from vocal time series, and to
b) a global *voice print* in order the cluster the global differences between the voices.

The analysis of intonation is essentially based on the analysis of regular oscillations of time series in order to use the identified frequencies of such oscillations for the estimation of the pitch of the analyzed tone. Such a *frequency analysis* is a standard method in time series analysis (cp. e.g. Brockwell and Davis, 1991).

For vocal time series analysis, however, there are some peculiarities. *Sung notes* consist of a simple superposition of frequencies, namely the *fundamental frequency*, twice the fundamental frequency (1st *overtone*), three times the fundamental frequency (2nd overtone), etc. e.g., for a' at 440 Hz the overtones are a'' at 880 Hz, e''' at 1320 Hz, a''' at 1760 Hz, etc. Apart from the fundamental frequency and the frequencies of the overtones noise might be included in the observed time series as well. Nevertheless, the structure of the periodogram is mainly determined by the fundamental frequency of the produced tone.

In particular, apart from the location of the fundamental frequency different singers of one note mainly differ by the *shares and the "purity" of their fundamental frequency and overtones*, i.e. by the height and width additional to the location of the peaks in the periodogram. Figure 2 shows the form of the periodogram of the amateur and the professional soprano corresponding to the "time domain" representations in Figure 1. The main difference is the larger width of the peak for the professional in contrast to the amateur caused by a natural *vibrato*. Indeed, this peak of the professional appears to be a superposition of two peaks which might be caused by different parts of

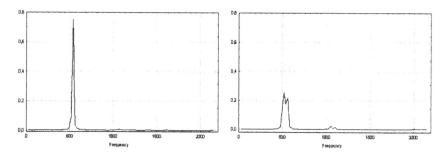

Fig. 2. Periodogram of the amateur and the professional soprano

the tone caused by the vibrato. For the amateur the absence of the vibrato causes a pure narrow peak.

4   Distance between tones

Let us now tackle the automatic assessment of the purity of the sung notes' intonation based on corresponding vocal time series. In order to get an idea about a wave property corresponding to purity of intonation, we now consider the *audio distance between different tones*. This is characterized by *DHT* (distance in halftones), the number of halftones between these tones. Unfortunately, this audio distance is not linearly proportional to the distance of the corresponding fundamental frequencies. Instead, the relationship between DHT and the fundamental frequencies of a target note and a reference note (like C) is given by:

$$frequency(target\ note) = 2^{DHT/12} \cdot frequency(reference\ note). \qquad (1)$$

Example
The audio distance of c' from a' is DHT $= -9$. Therefore, if a' corresponds to 440 Hz, frequency$(c') = 2^{-9/12} \cdot 440$ Hz $= 261.63$ Hz.

Naturally, the audio distance in halftones, DHT, can be computed by inversion of (1) from the transformed difference of the fundamental frequencies:

$$DHT = 12 \cdot \log_2 \left(\frac{frequency(target\ tone)}{frequency(reference\ tone)} \right). \qquad (2)$$

5   Discriminant analysis

After having characterized the audio distance between two sung notes, we are able to solve our original problem, namely the assessment of purity of intonation. For this purpose, a *singing expert* (the 4th author) classified 132 (self selected) tones of the 17 versions of "Tochter Zion" into the so-called *correctness classes* "flat", "correct", and "sharp". For these tones periodograms were determined, and from these the corresponding fundamental frequencies,

Class	"flat"	"correct"	"sharp"
Mean	−0.62	0.05	0.52

Table 1. Class means of predictor P.

based on a segmentation of the waves into notes and an estimator in Ligges et al. (2002).

As a so-called *natural predictor* of purity of intonation we used, based on the results of section 4, the difference between actual and target frequencies of the sung notes in halftones (*hts*):

$$P = \quad \text{actual number of } hts \text{ from } a' \quad - \text{ target number of } hts \text{ from } a'$$
$$= 12 \cdot (\log_2(\text{actual frequency(tone)}) - \log_2(\text{target frequency(note)})).$$

Please notice that the correct frequency of the tone has to be known in order to be able to compute P, and that P will not be integer, in general. Moreover notice that the target frequency will generally not be equal to the "ideal frequency" (i.e. 440 Hz for a', e.g.), since the accompaniment will not be ideally pitched, in general. In our experiment it turned out, e.g., that the piano frequency for a' was 443.5 Hz. Therefore, the target frequencies of the sung notes had to be adjusted accordingly using the formulas in section 4:

$$\text{target frequency(note)} = 2^{\text{DHT}/12} \cdot \text{piano frequency}(a') = 2^{\text{DHT}/12} \cdot 443.5 \text{ Hz}$$
$$\text{with} \quad \text{DHT} = \text{audio distance of the note to } a' \text{ in halftones.}$$

These frequencies were used to determine the predictor P. This predictor was then used to build a *classification rule* (prediction rule) for the correctness class of newly realized tones analogously as in *linear discriminant analysis* (cp. Figure 3). Notice that in standard linear discriminant analysis the predictor would be automatically generated as a linear combination of the two characteristics "actual frequency" and "target frequency" of the sung notes. Such predictors always have to be expected to be suboptimal since domain (here musical) knowledge is (at least partly) ignored. After having identified the predictor, linear discriminant analysis works as follows:

- Draw the expert class at the x-axis of a scatter plot.
- Draw the predictor values of the corresponding tones at the y-axis.
- Average the predictor values corresponding to the same correctness class (see Table 1).
- Separate the values of the predictor at the averages of the class averages (*classification rule*).
- Compare the expert classification with the classification obtained by this separation.
- "Color" the points in the plot corresponding to the correctness of the result of the classification rule (e.g. "+" = misclassified, "o" = correct).

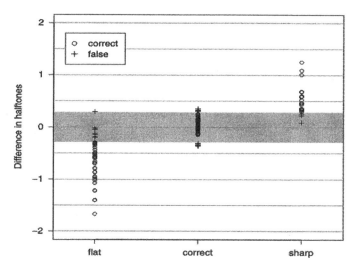

Fig. 3. Classification by means of predictor P.

- Determine the so-called (apparent) *error rate*, i.e. the share of incorrectly classified tones = number of incorrect classifications / 132. Notice that this error rate tends to be too optimistic because the same observations are used for the determination of the classification rule and of the error rate. This is particularly true for small samples. Because the size of the sample (= 132) appeared to be sufficiently large, we decided to avoid more costly, but possibly more correct methods of error rate determination like cross validation (cp. Weiss and Kulikowski, 1991).

Analyzing the result of the analysis of our data as illustrated in Figure 3, a very positive outcome has to be mentioned first, namely that all tones that were classified by the expert as "flat" or "sharp" correctly have negative and positive values, respectively, with the predictor P derived from the identified fundamental frequencies, with the exception of one tone only. Moreover, the predictor mean of those tones which were classified by the expert as "correct" is 0.05 halftones, and thus very near to its ideal value zero. Thus, one can say that the expert and the derived classification rule are in agreement.

The derived *classification rule* looks as follows: The permissible error in halftones which is just accepted to classify a tone as "correct" is 0.29 halftones below and above the target tone (indicated as the grey zone in Figure 3). Rounded the tolerance is thus approximately 0.3 halftones in both directions. Unfortunately, the estimated (apparent) error rate is 16.7%, and thus not very low. (Note that with linear discriminant analysis the optimal error rate is 24.2% and the corresponding predictor is equal to "actual frequency - target frequency" explaining 99% of the variation between the class means.)

If one is willing to consider the automatic classification as the truth, reversing, in a way, the assumption in linear discriminant analysis that the expert's classification is true, then the result of this project can be stated as follows:

The expert is willing to accept a note sung in a melody, i.e. neither separated from the neighboring tones, nor directly compared to the ideal tone, as *"correct", if its frequency deviation from the ideal tone is not larger than 0.3 halftones.* This may be considered as a result of its own worth.

6   Voice prints

Let us now consider the second task indicated in the beginning of the paper, i.e. the clustering of the singers concerning global differences in their voices. This task is tackled in Güttner (2001) in what follows the main results are discussed. The periodogram itself is not appropriate to serve as a basis for clustering, since the differences in the height of the sung tones of the different voice types hinder comparability. What is needed are heuristic descriptions of the periodogram, or a better estimator of the spectrum, corresponding to location deviation, weight and form of the peaks which are independent of the voice type.

In order to determine the location of peaks it is sufficient to estimate the fundamental frequency since then the overtones are determined also. Therefore, as a first measure the half tone distance of the estimated and the ideal frequency is determined (see section 4).

In order to measure the size of the peaks in the spectrum, the mass (weight) of the peaks of the fundamental frequency and the first 12 overtones are determined as the sum of the percentage shares of those parts of the corresponding peak in the spectrum, which are higher than a pre-specified threshold.

The shape of a peak can often not easily be described. Therefore, we only use one simple characteristic of the shape, namely the width of the peak, of the fundamental frequency and the first 12 overtones. The width of a peak is measured by the half tone distance between the smallest and the biggest frequency of the peak with a height above a pre-specified threshold.

Overall, every tone is characterized by the above 27 measures, the so-called *voice print*. Table 2 shows some characteristics of a part of the voice print, namely the weights of fundamental frequency and overtones. It is obvious that the professionals (No. 1, and 11) have the least weight on the fundamental frequencies within the corresponding voice group and the most weight on high overtones. This is especially true for singer 1 who is a singer at the opera.

The 27 measure of the voice print are used as a basis for clustering. For details on the computation of the measure see Güttner (2001).

7   Clustering the singers

The Euclidean distances of the singers corresponding to the above 27 characteristics build the basis for the "average-linkage-method" for clustering the

No.	voice	Weight on fundamental frequency and overtones			
		fund.	2nd	3rd	6th
1	*basso*	*0.03*	*0.79*	*0.68*	*0.57*
2	basso	0.20	0.52	0.35	0.21
3	basso	0.22	0.53	0.37	0.21
12	basso	0.15	0.58	0.42	0.25
6	tenor	0.20	0.56	0.45	0.29
9	**tenor**	**0.11**	**0.56**	**0.44**	**0.28**
17	tenor	0.28	0.42	0.30	0.17
4	alto	0.39	0.32	0.20	0.11
8	alto	0.52	0.25	0.16	0.09
13	alto	0.48	0.29	0.17	0.12
14	alto	0.41	0.34	0.21	0.11
15	**alto**	**0.38**	**0.41**	**0.32**	**0.20**
16	alto	0.52	0.33	0.26	0.17
5	soprano	0.61	0.14	0.07	0.05
7	soprano	0.57	0.26	0.18	0.10
10	soprano	0.56	0.13	0.06	0.06
11	*soprano*	*0.43*	*0.26*	*0.18*	*0.11*

Table 2. Voice prints characteristics

(**bold face**: minimum share of fundamental frequency in voice type,
  italics: real professionals)

singers. In order to give all characteristics the same weight, they are mean centred and normalized by their standard deviations before hand. The results are illustrated by means of a dendrogram in Figure 4.

Obviously, the voice types are clustering nearly ideally together, and the two professionals build "singular branches" in the dendrogram. Thus, the voice print appears to build a reasonable first step for the discrimination of voices.

8 Conclusion

We presented first steps of an automatic analysis of vocal time series in order to identify global differences corresponding to various kinds of sound properties of different singers. Next steps should be the identification of time series properties corresponding to individual sound properties.

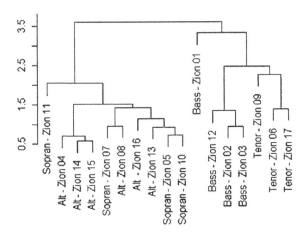

Fig. 4. Dendrogram of clustered singers

References

BERGAN, C.C., TITZE, I.R. (2001): Perception of Pitch and Roughness in Vocal Signals with Subharmonics. *Journal of Voice, 15, 165–175.*

BROCKWELL, P.J., DAVIS, R.A. (1991): *Time Series: Theory and Methods.* Springer, New York.

GÜTTNER, J. (2001): *Klassifikation von Gesangsdarbietungen.* Diploma Thesis, Fachbereich Statistik, Universität Dortmund.

LIGGES, U., WEIHS, C., HASSE-BECKER, P. (2002): Detection of Locally Stationary Segments in Time Series – Algorithms and Applications. *Technical Report 11/2002.* SFB 475, Department of Statistics, University of Dortmund, Germany. See also: http://www.sfb475.uni-dortmund.de/de/tr-d.html.

ROSSIGNOL, S., DEPALLE, P., SOUMAGNE, J., RODET, X., COLLETTE, J.-L. (1999): Vibrato: Detection, Estimation, Extractiom, Modification. *Proceedings 99 Digital Audio Effects Workshop.*

TITZE, I.R., MAPES, S., STORY, B. (1994): Acoustics of the Tenor High Voice. *Journal of the Acoustic Society of America, 95, 1133–1142.*

TITZE, I.R., STORY, B., SMITH, M., LONG, R. (2002): A Reflex Resonance Model for Vocal Vibrato. *Journal of the Acoustic Society of America, 111, 2272–2282.*

WEIHS, C., BERGHOFF, S., HASSE-BECKER, P., LIGGES, U. (2001): Assessment of Purity of Intonation in Singing Presentations by Discriminant Analysis. In: J. KUNERT and G. TRENKLER (Eds.): *Mathematical Statistics and Biometrical Applications.* Josef Eul, Bergisch-Gladbach, Köln, 395–410.

WEISS, S.M., KULIKOWSKI, C.A. (1991): *Computer Systems That Learn.* Morgan Kaufmann, San Francisco.

Cluster- and Discriminant Analysis With Both Metric and Categorial Data

Michael Wodny, Bernd Jäger, and Karl-Ernst Biebler

Institute of Biometry and Medical Informatics,
Ernst-Moritz-Arndt-University, D-17487 Greifswald, Germany

Abstract. Questions in medicine and biological sciences which require a cluster or discriminant analysis frequently appear. If there isn't clarity concerning a probability theoretical data model, topologically based methods should be preferred. In this paper, a topological data model is defined for both metric and categorial variables. Every categorial character can be transformed into dichotomous characters. Therefore, we restrict the description to continuous and binary variables. A cluster analysis regarding this data space topology is illustrated on hand of a data set from forensic medicine.
For the discriminant analysis, a n-nearest-neighbours method is a standard technology and of topological character. The method will be modified due to the topological properties of the subset of binary data of the introduced topological data model. The given example from internal medicine also contains variable selection.
The computations are carried out in a SAS environment. The programs can be requested by the authors.

1 Data space topology

At first we define what should be understood by a distance and a metric.
Definition

Let be X an arbitrary set and D (*, *) a function, which uniquely assigns every two elements of X a real number. The function D is called distance if it has the following properties:

i) D(x, y)$\geq$0 for all x, y in X and $D(x,x) = 0$ for all x in X
ii) D(x, y)=D(y, x) for all x, y in X
iii) D(x, y)$\leq$D(x, z)+D(z, y) for all x, y, z in X.

D is called a metric, if $x = y$ follows from $D(x,y) = 0$. Every object $Y_i := (x_{i1}, x_{i2}, \ldots, x_{is}, b_{i1}, b_{i2}, \ldots, b_{ir})$, i=1,2,...m, of a dataset of size m may consist of s real numbers x_{ij} and r binary values b_{ij} either 0 or 1, respectively. The finite data set is a subset of the data space composed as the orthogonal sum of the s-dimensional real space and the r-dimensional binary space. One can define several distances for $X_i := (x_{i1}, x_{i2}, \ldots, x_{is})$ and $X_k := (x_{k1}, x_{k2}, \ldots, x_{ks})$ on the subspace spanned by the continuous variables, for example the Euclidian distance or the Mahalanobis distance

$$D_M(X_i, X_k) := \sqrt{(X_i - X_k) \circ COV^{-1} \circ (X_i - X_k)^T}$$

COV^{-1} denotes the inverse of the empirical covariance matrix, which is estimated from x_{ij}, i=1,2,...,m, j=1,2,...,s. Concerning the subspace spanned by the binary variables, some examples of distances will be given. Let $B_i = (b_{i1}, b_{i2}, \ldots, b_{ir})$ and $B_k = (b_{k1}, b_{k2}, \ldots, b_{kr})$ be the binary coordinates of two observations. By comparing the corresponding coordinates, a, b, c, d in the following contingency table are the number of coordinates with the concerned property, respectively:

		B_k	
		1 present	0 present
B_i	1 present	a	b
	0 present	c	d

The simple matching metric is
$D_{sm}(B_i, B_k) := 1 - \frac{(a+d)}{(a+b+c+d)} = 1 - \frac{(a+d)}{r}$,
the Jaccard metric (also called Tanimoto metric) is
$D_T(B_i, B_k) := 1 - \frac{a}{(a+b+c)}$.
The so called Czekanowsky-"distance" $D_C(B_i, B_k) := 1 - \frac{2a}{(2a+b+c)}$
does not fulfil the triangle inequality and therefore it is not a distance in the sense of the definition above. Other examples are found in SPÄTH (1975).
From the point of view of topological classification procedures, metrics on binary spaces have a certain disadvantage: The number of their different possible values is relatively small. For instance, for the simple matching metric it is $r + 1$. This number is insignificantly larger for the Tanimoto metric. If the number m of observations is large in the comparison with the dimension r, then there are many different pairs of objects of the same distance.
This disadvantage is of principle nature and has its cause in the relatively small amount of information, which can be encoded in binary variables. If we consider the binary vectors in the r dimensional space Rr, their position is always in a corner of an r dimensional cube. The values 0, 1 as well as the lengths of all diagonals are the possible distances. D_T ranges from 0 to 1, D_M ranges from 0 to infinity. To make both metrics comparable, the Mahalanobis metric is transformed by
$D_{co}(X_i, X_k) := \frac{D_M(X_i, X_k)}{(1+D_M(X_i, X_k))}$.
This is a strictly increasing function which therefore makes it easy to check that Dco is a metric again. The suggested metric, which unites the continuous and binary characters, is for example the sum
$D_{sum}(Y_i, Y_k) := D_{co}(X_i, X_k) + D_T(B_i, B_k)$,
ranging from 0 to 2. A proof isn't necessary here. The data space is therefore a topological space with a topology induced by D_{sum}.

2   The cluster analysis

Basis of the topological classification methods is the supposition, that objects being alike have small distances in the data space. Realizations of cluster methods basing on the above defined topological data space were carried out in the SAS statistical software package. An arbitrary distance matrix can be imported to PROC CLUSTER. Several cluster methods are available (FALK (1995)).

However, it has to be checked which of the possible methods are meaningful. So the centroid method uses the Euclidean distance between the clusters centres. This is not in agreement with the data space topology resulting from D_{sum}.

We choose the single linkage method. In this case the distances are used directly for the calculation of a distance between the clusters.

- PROC CORR calculates the empirical correlation matrix for the continuous variables.
- The calculations of the Mahalonobis distances $D_M(X_i, X_k)$, its transformed values $D_{co}(X_i, X_k)$, the binary character distances $D_T(B_i, B_k)$ and the sum of the distances $D_{sum}(Y_i, Y_k)$ are carried out by the SAS module IML.
- The distances $D_{sum}(Y_i, Y_k)$ are handed over to the PROC CLUSTER.
- PROC TREE makes the evaluation of the cluster history possible.
- The output file of PROC TREE delivers the clusters and makes possible the assignments of the individuals to the clusters.

Example: The introduced method was applied to the analysis of forensic data. We investigated parameters of 1015 conspicuous road users. There was strong drunkenness suspicion of these persons. The aim of the explanatory data analysis was the search for characteristic subgroups in the data.

Investigated metric characters were gamma glutamyl transferase concentration, carbohydrate deficient transferrin concentration, ethanol concentration and methanol concentration.

Binary characters concern, especially, young or old, male or female, week or weekend and day or night of the forensic examination.

Finally, 968 complete data records were analyzed. The cluster analysis was stopped when 106 clusters were reached. At this level, 810 records were concentrated into two clusters containing 712 and 98 records, respectively. The remaining 158 observations are split into 104 clusters. The cluster of the 98 drunken drivers allows for a unique characterization: They were all suspicious during the week at night, less than 30 years old and male.

If one leaves the ethanol parameter out of the cluster analysis, the same 98 records yield a cluster. 508 records are summarized into the second cluster.

3   The discriminant analysis

The discriminant analysis is well known for continuous variables. In the following we consider only binary variables.

The n-nearest-neighbours method is one of the most used discriminant analysis procedures. It will be applied to the situation of the data space topology introduced in this paper. We confine ourselves to the case of two groups.

In the binary subspace, several different objects can exist with the same distance to the object looked at. The n-nearest-neighbours rule is therefore varied:

Let be $n = 2k + 1$. If the classification of the object is possible regarding the 2k nearest neighbours, the classical rule remains unchanged. Otherwise, all neighbours with the same distance to the object like the subsequent (2k+1)th nearest neighbour are taken into account for the classification.

Interest lies in identifying an informative subset of variables. First, an order of the variables is established according to the classification result which is produced by each of the variables alone. This may reduce bias of the following variable selection.

The variable selection consists in one-step reductions of the set of variables. This process is assessed by reclassification. For estimation the true error rate, e.g. the leave-one-out method, should be used. A stopping rule was not established.

Example: In a case-control study, data of 27 Morbus Wegner patients and 28 controls were investigated. The number of the cases is small because the illness is very rare. The questionnaire for the patients covers 56 binary variables. The aim of the explorative data analysis was a variable selection. At the optimal point of the procedure, 9 variables were chosen. At this stage, 2 of the cases and 4 of the controls were misclassified. A medical assessment of the result isn't carried out here.

References

ASPAROUKHOV, O.K. and KRZANOWSKI, W.J. (2001): A comparison of discriminant procedures for binary variables. *Comput. Stat: Data Anal. 38, 139-160.*

BOCK, H.-H. and DIDAY, E. (Eds.) (2000): Analysis of Symbolic Data. *Springer Berlin, Heidelberg.*

FALK, M. et al (1995): Angewandte Statistik mit SAS. *Springer Verlag Berlin, Heidelberg, New York.*

JÄGER, B. at al (2001): Clusteranalyse mit Binärdaten. *In: Schumacher, E.; Streichfuss, K. (Eds.): Proceedings der 5. Konferenz für SAS-Anwender in Forschung und Entwicklung (KSFE). Hohenheim, 181-190.*

LIPKUS, A.H.(1999): A proof of the triangle inequality for the Tanimoto distance *J.Math.Chem, 26, 263-265.*

SPÄTH, H. (1975): Cluster-Analyse-Verfahren. *Oldenbourg, München.*

Part II

Data Analysis and Statistics

Multivariate Mixture Models Estimation: A Genetic Algorithm Approach

Roberto Baragona[1] and Francesco Battaglia[2]

[1] Dip. Sociologia e Comunicazione,
Università di Roma La Sapienza, I-00198 Roma, Italy
[2] Dip. Statistica, Probabilità e Statistiche Applicate,
Università di Roma La Sapienza, I-00185 Roma, Italy

Abstract. We propose genetic algorithms in order to estimate the parameters of a multivariate mixture model. Their design is analogue to the evolutionary techniques for the maximization of the likelihood function. The links with both the EM algorithm and the cluster analysis are examined. The case where the number of mixture components is unknown is investigated and some estimation procedures are suggested. Real data examples and simulated data sets are used to illustrate the merits of the proposed procedure and for comparison purpose.

1 Introduction

Let us consider the array $\mathbf{Y} = (\mathbf{Y}_1', \ldots, \mathbf{Y}_n')'$, where the $\mathbf{Y}_j$, $j = 1, \ldots, n$, are i.i.d. p-dimensional random variables, with density $f(\mathbf{y}_j)$, $\mathbf{y}_j \in \mathbb{R}^p$. Let $\mathbf{y} = (\mathbf{y}_1', \ldots, \mathbf{y}_n')'$ denote a realization of $\mathbf{Y}$. We assume that the density $f(\mathbf{y}_j)$ may be written as a g components multivariate mixture density

$$f(\mathbf{y}_j) = \sum_{i=1}^{g} \pi_i f_i(\mathbf{y}_j),$$

where $0 \leq \pi_i \leq 1$, $i = 1, \ldots, g$, and $\sum_{i=1}^{g} \pi_i = 1$. The weights $\pi_1, \ldots, \pi_g$ are the mixing proportions, while the $f_i(\mathbf{y}_j)$ are the multivariate mixture component densities.

If the component densities are multivariate normal, the likelihood function for given $\mathbf{y}$ is

$$L(\theta|\mathbf{y}) = \prod_{j=1}^{n} \sum_{i=1}^{g} \pi_i (2\pi)^{-\frac{p}{2}} |\mathbf{\Sigma}_i|^{-\frac{1}{2}} \exp\{-\frac{1}{2}(\mathbf{y}_j - \mu_i)' \mathbf{\Sigma}_i^{-1}(\mathbf{y}_j - \mu_i)\}. \quad (1)$$

The array θ includes the mixing proportions π_i, the mean vectors μ_i and the variance-covariance matrices $\mathbf{\Sigma}_i$. As the weights are constrained to be non-negative and sum to unity, and by the symmetry property of the variance-covariance matrices, the array θ has $g - 1 + gp + gp(p+1)/2$ essential elements.

According to the likelihood approach, estimating the multivariate mixture parameter vector is done by maximizing (1) with respect to θ. The introduction of the well-known EM-algorithm, and its variants, makes the maximization of (1) easier to be performed than using the usual estimation devices, such as the Marquardt algorithm or the quasi-Newton methods, for instance (see McLachlan and Peel (2000) for a comprehensive review). Bayesian approaches have also been experienced, especially when the Markov chain Monte Carlo methods have been introduced to perform the generally heavy computational task (see, for instance, Bensmail et al. (1997)). Estimating the parameter vector θ, however, still remains a difficult task, and it is worth the while to explore either alternative or complementary approaches. In this paper, we propose using the genetic algorithm approach (see Mitchell (1996) or Michalewicz (1996) for an introduction) either to directly estimate the parameter vector θ or to provide the EM algorithm with appropriate starting points to efficiently initialize the iterative procedure. Also, when the number of component densities g is unknown, we propose using the cluster analysis based on genetic algorithm as an efficient device to find the appropriate value for g. Then, estimates may be further refined by using the EM algorithm with starting points provided by the genetic algorithm. Using cluster analysis methods for initialization is a common feature in the practice of the EM algorithm.

The paper is organized as follows. The next Section is devoted to the illustration of the genetic algorithm procedure for estimating the parameter vector θ in (1). In Section 3 we present some procedures based on genetic algorithm to simultaneously estimate the number of components g and the parameter vector θ. Examples are given in Section 4 concerned with both simulated and real data sets. In the last Section conclusions are drawn.

2   Estimating multivariate normal mixture parameters with genetic algorithms

Let n p-dimensional observations be available as the array $\mathbf{y}$. In order to fit a multivariate normal mixture model to the data, we first define the component indicator array X with g rows and n columns. We may give X either of the two following definitions.

$$X(i,j) = \begin{cases} 1 \text{ if the component of origin of } \mathbf{y}_j \text{ in the mixture is (possibly) } i \\ 0 \qquad\qquad\qquad\qquad\qquad\qquad\qquad\qquad \text{otherwise} \end{cases}$$

(2)

where no constraints are imposed but any observation has to originate from one component at least. Some uncertainty is allowed, however, whether which the component of origin of $\mathbf{y}_j$ may be.

$$X(i,j) = \begin{cases} v_{ij} \text{ if the component of origin of } \mathbf{y}_j \text{ in the mixture is (possibly) } i \\ 0 \qquad\qquad\qquad\qquad\qquad\qquad\qquad\qquad \text{otherwise} \end{cases}$$

(3)

where v_{ij} is a nonnegative integer in a pre-specified interval $[0, q]$. The integer v_{ij} may be regarded as a score assigned to the confidence that the observation $\mathbf{y}_j$ originates from the component i.

Given the values of $X(i,j)$, the probability that the component of origin of $\mathbf{y}_j$ in the mixture is i may be estimated

$$z(i,j) = \frac{X(i,j)}{\sum_{i=1}^{g} X(i,j)}, \qquad i = 1,\ldots,g, \qquad j = 1,\ldots,n. \qquad (4)$$

Then, for the given observations matrix $\mathbf{y}$, the parameter vector estimate $\hat{\theta} = (\hat{\pi}_i, \hat{\mu}_i, \hat{\Sigma}_i; i = 1,\ldots,g)$ is computed as usual by taking the weights $z(i,j)$ into account (see, for instance, McLachlan and Peel (2000)).

We will now model the procedure expounded above as a genetic algorithm. The genetic algorithms have been introduced by Holland (1975) for modeling the evolution of a given population towards its best adaptation to the environment. To put this complicated process into a systematic arrangement, three main operators have been devised, selection, crossover and mutation, to evolve s, say, individuals that form the population through a sequence of generations. Each individual is given a sequence of characters (chromosome) that encodes its characteristic features. To measure the adaptation level of each individual to the environment, a non-negative real function has to be defined on chromosomes which is called "fitness function." The "schema theorem" constitutes the basic result concerned with the convergence of the genetic algorithms. The genetic algorithms have been recognized to be able to find near-optimal solutions for multi-variable functions maximization. Their main advantage, compared to the traditional maximization methods, resides in that no assumptions about the objective function (strict continuity, differentiability, convexity, for instance) have to hold, except that the fitness (objective) function has to be non-negative. Furthermore, the genetic algorithm stochastic nature and its inherent parallel-like processing of many proposal solutions have some useful implications. Generally, in the current population some candidate solutions are possibly present near the global maximum, while even candidate solutions near some local maximum are given a chance to move from such region of the solution space to the region which includes the global maximum. Convergence of the genetic algorithm has been further studied by Rudolph (1994) by means of the homogeneous finite Markov chain model (for connection with Holland's schema theorem, see also Jennison and Sheehan (1995)). It has been shown that, for convergence to the global maximum, the latest found best solution has to be maintained in the current population until a better one is discovered. This is implemented by the elitist strategy, or elitist selection. If the largest fitness function at iteration $t+1$ happens to be less than the one computed at iteration t, then the best solution from the past generation replaces the poorest one within the population at iteration $t+1$.

Conditional to X, the weights (4) allow a tentative solution to the optimization problem be determined. So, it is natural to encode X as a binary, in case (2), or integer, if (3) is assumed, string (chromosome), and seeking for the string that leads to the optimal solution. To change the matrix X to the vector string x, we may stack either its columns or its rows. Let $\ell = g \times n$ denote the length of x. The fitness function is defined that maps x to the logarithm of the likelihood (1). The simple genetic algorithm, as described by Goldberg (1989), may fit to the present context as follows. It is assumed that s candidate solutions are available (chosen at random). Then, the matrix X is translated to the chromosome x column by column. Let, for instance, $g = 2$ and $n = 6$. The chromosome

$$0\,1 \mid 0\,1 \mid 1\,0 \mid 1\,1 \mid 1\,0 \mid 0\,1$$

has to be read so that the observations (3,4,5) originates from component 1, and (1,2,4,6) from 2.

Selection. Current population chromosomes are copied into chromosomes in the next generation with probability proportional to their fitness function.

Crossover. A new chromosome is built from two chromosomes chosen at random. Probability is p_c for pair. Let such pair be, for instance

$$0\,1\,0\,1\,1\,0\,1\,1\,1\,0\,0\,1$$
$$0\,1\,1\,0\,0\,1\,1\,0\,1\,1\,0\,1$$

An integer c (the cutting point) is chosen uniformly randomly between 1 and $\ell - 1$, 11 here. If $c = 8$, say, then the new chromosomes are

$$0\,1\,0\,1\,1\,0\,1\,1 \mid 1\,1\,0\,1$$
$$0\,1\,1\,0\,0\,1\,1\,0 \mid 1\,0\,0\,1$$

The first chromosome now encodes the components 1 (3,4,5) and 2 (1,2,4,5,6), instead of (3,4,5) and (1,2,4,6) respectively.

Mutation. Each bit in the string of each individual chromosome is flipped independently with usually small probability p_m.

These three steps are repeated for a pre-specified number m of iterations (generations). In the sequel we will call this algorithm GA11 if the encoding (2) is used, and GA21 in case of encoding (3).

Evolutionary techniques, however, often need some additional heuristics for a successful implementation (Michalewicz, 1996, p. 311). To form the initial population, the following procedure may be used: (i) generate a binary string of length n with g 1's placed at random, while the remaining characters equal 0, (ii) aggregate each point (observation) to the nearest one that corresponds to 1 in the binary string, (iii) define the matrix X accordingly, and (iv) repeat this procedure s times. Let us call these modified versions of the simple genetic algorithm GA12 (binary encoding) and GA22 (integer encoding). Further, if the chromosome x is built by stacking the rows of the matrix X, let us call GA13 and GA23 the corresponding procedures.

A different genetic algorithm approach may be developed along the guidelines provided in Chatterjee et al. (1996) and Chatterjee and Laudato (1997). Their procedure addresses the maximization of the likelihood function for a statistical model parameter estimation by direct encoding of the parameter vector into a chromosome. A one-to-one correspondence between any real parameter θ and a binary string ξ is established according to the formula

$$\theta = a + \xi(b - a)/(2^\ell - 1),$$

where θ is assumed to belong to the interval (a, b) and ℓ is the pre-specified length of the binary string ξ. The multivariate mixture model (1) contains $h = g - 1 + gp + gp(p + 1)/2$ entries, that is h distinct scalar parameters. These parameters are represented by a sequence of h binary strings of length ℓ each. Lower and upper bounds have to be pre-specified for each parameter to estimate, and some obvious constraints need to be imposed, for instance on the entries in each variance-covariance matrix. As for the rest, the steps of the genetic algorithm are much alike that of the simple genetic algorithm.

The genetic algorithms may well be used to provide other local search algorithm, the EM algorithm, for instance, with suitable starting points. A similar device has been proposed by Brooks and Morgan (1995) for simulated annealing. If we want to obtain exactly the global maximum, or at least a figure not far from it, the genetic algorithm is used to search the space of the candidate solutions to locate the subsets that are likely to include the global maximum. Then, confining to these subsets only, some specific maximization algorithm is started for refining the search (Mitchell, 1996, p. 124).

3 Finding the number of mixture components

If the number g of the components of the multivariate mixture model is unknown, then we may assume g as a further parameter and try to simultaneously estimate both g and the parameter vector θ. Often this is accomplished by using either the AIC or the BIC criterion. Let

$$\text{AIC} = -2logL + 2h, \qquad \text{BIC} = -2logL + log(n)h, \qquad (5)$$

where L is the likelihood function (1), h is the total number of parameters and n the number of observations. Genetic algorithms for cluster analysis are available that simultaneously estimate the number of groups and the group membership. Usually, such algorithms seek for a partition of the observations into g groups. If the number of observations n is large, however, this is not a severe limitation, and we are allowed to apply genetic algorithms to estimate the parameter vector of the multivariate mixture model when the number of components g is unknown. Either AIC or BIC in (5) may replace (1) to provide the genetic algorithm with the fitness function. We investigate this procedure by using two versions of the genetic algorithm. The first one (GCUK-clustering) has been proposed by Bandyopadhyay and Maulik (2002), and uses a floating point encoding instead of the binary (or integer) one. The second version has been developed by Baragona et al. (2001) along the guidelines provided by Falkenauer (1998). This latter uses an integer encoding. The problem, however, is rather difficult to handle, and we expect to obtain only an approximate solution, unless the number of generations is taken very large. Then, we may exploit the population yielded by the genetic algorithm, not only the individual with the largest fitness function. From the first 10, say, best individuals in the final population, we may take 10 estimated parameter vectors to use as initial values to start some steps of the

EM algorithm. Note that such "hybrid" solution not necessarily has to come from the best chromosome found by the genetic algorithm. This procedure is likely to yield more accurate solutions than using either the genetic algorithm or the EM algorithm alone.

4 Simulation results and application to real data

Checking the proposed procedures is done by using two simulated data set, already considered in the literature (see McLachlan and Peel, 2000, p. 218). Set 1 is generated by a multivariate normal mixture model with 625 observations, 4 variables and 5 components, and diagonal variance-covariance matrices. Set 2 is generated by a multivariate normal mixture model with 300 observations, 3 variables and 3 components, while not all the off-diagonal entries of the variance-covariance matrices equal zero.

In Table 1 we compare the performance of the versions GA11, GA12 and GA13, and GA21, GA22 and GA23 of our implementation of the simple genetic algorithm. For each of the six algorithms, and each of the two sets, 100000 iterations are performed. The genetic algorithm parameters are $s = 50$, $p_c = 0.8$ and $p_m = 0.005$. The figures given in Table 1 are the logarithm of the likelihood function that is computed from the best chromosome in the final population, and the generation t where we last recorded an increase of the fitness function.

The algorithm GA12 performs better than the others with respect both the final figure of the logarithm of the mixture likelihood function and the number of generations needed to obtain its largest value. It is important to point out, however, that the typical behavior of the fitness function computed for the fittest individual in each generation exhibits a sudden increase (often within no more than 10% of the total number of iterations) followed by considerably smaller increments. As a matter of fact, it is widely recognized that (i) the genetic algorithm identifies in a relatively short time the "promising regions" in the solution space, then slowly evolves the chromosomes towards further improvements, and (ii) the screening performed at the beginning is even more efficient if heuristics for creating an initial population are employed.

For illustrating hybrid techniques that combine the genetic algorithm and the EM algorithm, let us consider the Chatterjee et al. (1996) procedure and the algorithm GA11. In either cases, only 10000 generations are allowed. The fitness function seems sufficiently "smooth" so that diversity is maintained in the population and a set of alternative starting points is available. The EM algorithm performs 10 iterations. As far as the former procedure is concerned, the maximum value of the mixture likelihood is attained from 44 chromosomes out of 50. The mean vectors and mixing proportions given by the genetic algorithm require only some minor adjustments. On the contrary, the variance-covariance matrices are further improved significantly by the

EM algorithm. Similar results are obtained by using the GA11 algorithm, where the best likelihood is attained from 46 chromosomes out of 50.

genetic algorithm version	Set 1		Set 2	
	largest log-likelihood	obtained at generation	largest log-likelihood	obtained at generation
GA11	-5689	99967	-1820	92762
GA12	-5572	95077	-1820	41043
GA13	-5577	99468	-1820	67890
GA21	-5840	99843	-2040	99328
GA22	-5684	99983	-1820	84234
GA23	-5595	99223	-1820	54058

Table 1. Comparison between some versions of the genetic algorithm for parameter vector multivariate normal mixture models estimation. The number of components is assumed known.

In Table 2 the case when the number of components g is unknown is considered. The results are concerned with the Set 2 simulated data, and the genetic clustering algorithms GCUK and GGA. Either algorithm provides its best solution that includes both the number of components g and the multivariate mixture density parameter vector estimates $(\hat{\pi}_i, \hat{\mu}_i, \hat{\Sigma}_i), i = 1, \ldots, g$. The search for the number of components is confined to the interval $(2, 30)$, which seems rather large if compared with the number of observations $n = 300$. Hybridization may take place advantageously in this case as well. In fact, the more important task for the genetic algorithm is finding an appropriate proposal value for the number of components g. Our experience shows that only part of the final population needs to be exploited, the best 10 chromosomes, for instance, but, as noted already, the best hybrid solution not necessarily has to come from the best chromosome found by the genetic algorithm. For each procedure, the best solution found by the genetic algorithm is reported in the first line of Table 2, then the solution yielded by the EM algorithm, starting from such tentative solution, is reported in the next line. A another solution from the genetic algorithm is reported in the third line which allows the EM algorithm to yield the best, or the next best, overall solution. For instance, according to the BIC criterion, the algorithm GCUK indicates $g = 4$ components as best solution. Nevertheless, the best overall solution that minimizes the BIC criterion is found by the EM algorithm starting from a another solution given by the genetic algorithm. In fact, the least BIC given by the GCUK equals 3930, and this figure is reduced to 3855 by the EM algorithm. A another solution in the same population, however, gives the BIC criterion equal to 4055, but the EM algorithm, using the corresponding parameter vector estimates as starting points, gives the overall minimum BIC equal to 3805. Of course, it may happen that the best solution given by the genetic algorithm leads to the best solution given by the EM algorithm as well, as is the case of the GGA algorithm with the BIC criterion. The AIC criterion overestimates the number of components. In addition, the GGA algorithm, using the AIC criterion, is able to find only a single solution that may be handled successfully by the EM algorithm.

	g	AIC	g	BIC
GCUK	7	3860	4	3930
+EM		3729		3855
GCUK	7	3879	3	4055
+EM		3724		3805
GGA	5	3950	3	4098
+EM		3726		3805
GGA			4	4102
+EM				3858

Table 2. Multivariate normal mixture models estimation from simulated data (Set 2) when the number of components g is unknown. The genetic algorithm, either GCUK or GGA, finds proposal g values in the interval $(2, 30)$ and provides the EM algorithm with starting points.

Two well-known real data sets are considered to test the proposed procedures, the Iris data and the Diabetes data. Data are available, for instance, in the package MCLUST (Fraley and Raftery, 1999) which may be downloaded at http://cran.r-project.org/. The Iris data consist of 4 measurements on 50 plants from each of 3 species of Iris: Iris setosa, Iris versicolor, and Iris virginica. Measurements are sepal length, sepal width, petal length and petal width (cm). The two classes Versicolor and Virginica have a large amount of overlap while the class Setosa are well separated from the others. The Diabetes data consists of 3 measurements: the area under a plasma glucose curve (degree of glucose intolerance), the area under a plasma insulin curve (insulin response to oral glucose), and steady-state plasma glucose response (SSPG, insulin resistance) for 145 subjects. The subjects are clinically classified into 3 groups, chemical diabetes, overt diabetes and normal. The shape of the data set in three dimensions is that of a "boomerang with two wings and a fat middle." The parts differ in that one of the "wings" is almost planar, the other is linear with some curvature, the "fat middle" is nearly spherical.

In Table 3 the performances of the algorithms GA11, GA12, GA13, and GA21, GA22, GA23 for the Iris data and the Diabetes data are reported. The number of components is assumed known $g = 3$, the genetic algorithm parameters are $s = 50$, $p_c = 0.8$, $p_m = 0.005$, and 100000 generations are allowed. We may see that the simple genetic algorithm performs rather poorly while fairly good results are yielded by our modified versions. In fact, the best solution is found by all algorithms, but GA11 (Diabetes data) and GA11,

GA21 (Iris data). Using algorithms GA12, GA22, GA13 and GA23 may allow the best solution be reached in much less than 100000 iterations. Note that, computed by assuming the known partition, the logarithm of the likelihood is equal to -182.92 for the Iris data, and -2329 for the Diabetes data.

genetic algorithm version	Iris data		Diabetes data	
	largest log-likelihood	obtained at generation	largest log-likelihood	obtained at generation
GA11	-189.38	74406	-2304	52576
GA12	-180.25	95744	-2304	56437
GA13	-180.23	19721	-2304	43184
GA21	-297.85	93230	-2371	94824
GA22	-180.21	24566	-2304	97625
GA23	-180.20	99319	-2304	61407

Table 3. Genetic algorithm for parameter vector multivariate normal mixture models estimation. Application to the Iris data and Diabetes data. The number of components is assumed known.

In Table 4 the performances of GCUK and GGA when the number of components g is unknown are displayed. For the Diabetes data, the two genetic algorithms performs nearly the same. For the Iris data, the GGA performs better than the GCUK, which tends to explore solutions with smallest number of components. The AIC criterion seems not suitable for the two data sets as it markedly overestimate the number of components.

	Iris data		Diabetes data	
GCUK	2	600	3	4790
+EM		574		4774
GCUK	3	643	3	4815
+EM		585		4751
GGA	4	564	3	4782
+EM		521		4774
GGA	3	513	3	4809
+EM		506		4751

Table 4. Multivariate normal mixture models estimation (BIC criterion) for the Iris data and the Diabetes data. The number of components g is unknown, $2 \leq g \leq 30$. The genetic algorithm, either GCUK or GGA, finds proposal g values and provides the EM algorithm with starting points.

5 Conclusions

Genetic algorithms may turn useful in multivariate mixture models estimation. They either are able to provide good estimates on their own or may provide other algorithms, the EM-algorithm for instance, with good starting points. Finally, genetic clustering is effective for automatically estimating the number of the components of a multivariate mixture model.

References

BANDYOPADHYAY, S. and MAULIK, U. (2002): Genetic clustering for automatic evolution of clusters and application to image classification. *Pattern Recognition, 35, 1197–1208.*

BARAGONA, R., CALZINI, C. and BATTAGLIA, F. (2001): Genetic algorithms and clustering: an application to Fisher's iris data. In: S. Borra, R. Rocci, M. Vichi and M. Schader (Eds.): *Advances in Classification and Data Analysis.* Springer, Heidelberg, 109–118.

BENSMAIL, H., CELEUX, G., RAFTERY, A.E. and ROBERT, C.P. (1997): Inference in model-based cluster analysis. *Statistics and Computing, 7, 1–10.*

BROOKS, S. P. and MORGAN, B. J. T. (1995): Optimization using simulated annealing. *The Statistician, 44, 241-257.*

CHATTERJEE, S. and LAUDATO, M. (1997): Genetic Algorithms in Statistics: Procedures and Applications. *Communications in Statistics - Simulation and Computation, 26(4), 1617–1630.*

CHATTERJEE, S., LAUDATO, M. and LYNCH, L.A. (1996): Genetic Algorithms and their Statistical Applications: An Introduction. *Computational Statistics & Data Analysis, 22, 633–651.*

FALKENAUER, E. (1998): *Genetic Algorithms and Grouping Problems.* Wiley.

FRALEY, C. and RAFTERY, A.E. (1999): MCLUST: software for model-based cluster analysis. *Journal of Classification, 16, 297–306.*

GOLDBERG, D.E. (1989): *Genetic Algorithms in Search, Optimization and Machine Learning.* Addison-Wesley.

HOLLAND, J. H. (1975): *Adaptation in Natural and Artificial Systems.* University of Michigan Press, Ann Arbor (Second edition: The MIT Press, 1992).

JENNISON, C. and SHEEHAN, N. (1995): Theoretical and empirical properties of the genetic algorithm as a numerical optimizer, *Journal of Computational and Graphical Statistics, 4, 296-318.*

McLACHLAN, G. and PEEL, D. (2000): *Finite Mixture Models.* Wiley.

MICHALEWICZ, Z. (1996): *Genetic Algorithms + Data Structures = Evolution Programs* (Third ed.) Springer-Verlag.

MITCHELL, M. (1996): *An Introduction to Genetic Algorithms.* The MIT Press.

RUDOLPH, G. (1994): Convergence analysis of canonical genetic algorithms, *IEEE Transactions on Neural Networks, 5, 96-101.*

Two-Way Clustering for Contingency Tables: Maximizing a Dependence Measure

Hans-Hermann Bock

Institute of Statistics, Aachen University, D-52056 Aachen, Germany

Abstract. We consider the simultaneous clustering of the rows and columns of a contingency table such that the dependence between row clusters and column clusters is maximized in the sense of maximizing a general dependence measure. We use Csiszár's ϕ-divergence between the given two-way distribution and the independence case with the same margins. This includes the classical χ^2 measure, Kullback-Leibler's discriminating information, and variation distance. By using the general theory of 'convexity-based clustering criteria' (Bock 1992, 2002a, 2002b) we derive a k-means-like clustering algorithm that uses 'maximum support-plane partitions' (in terms of likelihood ratio vectors) in the same way as classical SSQ clustering uses 'minimum-distance partitions'.

1 Two-way clustering for a contingency table

There exists a large variety of methods for clustering simultaneously the rows and columns of a rectangular data matrix into classes $A_1, ..., A_m$ and $B_1, ..., B_l$, respectively. For example, in the case of a *real-valued* data matrix $X = (x_{kt})_{n \times p}$ with n objects and p variables a typical approach proceeds by approximating the data in each 'block' $A_i \times B_j$ by a common value ξ_{ij} and minimizing the approximation error $g(\mathcal{A}, \mathcal{B}) := \sum_{i=1}^{m} \sum_{j=1}^{l} \sum_{k \in A_i} \sum_{t \in B_j} (x_{kt} - \xi_{ij})^2$ with respect to both partitions $\mathcal{A} = (A_1, ..., A_m)$ and $\mathcal{B} = (B_1, ..., B_l)$ and all parameters ξ_{ij} (see, e.g., Bock 1968, 1972, Govaert 1983, Gaul and Schader 1996, Castillo and Trejos 2002).

In contrast, in this paper we will consider a contingency table $\mathcal{N} = (f_{uv})_{a \times b}$ for two *categorical* variables U and V with domains $\mathcal{U} = \{1, ..., a\}$ (rows) and $\mathcal{V} = \{1, ..., b\}$ (columns) and look for two partitions $\mathcal{A} = (A_1, ..., A_m)$ of $\mathcal{U}$ and $\mathcal{B} = (B_1, ..., B_m)$ of $\mathcal{V}$ which are, simultaneously, optimal for detecting possible dependencies between U and V in a sense to be specified below. The table $\mathcal{N}$ will usually result from n observed samples of the pair (U, V) such that f_{uv} is the relative frequency of samples for which the configuration (u, v) has been recorded (with $\sum_u \sum_v f_{uv} = 1$).

An example is provided by a marketing study where the dependence between the life style (variable U) and the purchased article (variable V) should be determined from data for $n = 500$ customers. If we have only $a = 7$ life styles and $b = 15$ articles, say, this problem can be easily resolved by classical tools from statistics, e.g., with χ^2 coefficients, graphical models etc. However, when a warehouse wants to analyze data observed for $n = 100\,000$ customers where each customer belongs to one of $a = 200$ listed occupations (variable U) and buys one of $b = 1000$ articles (variable V) from an electronic catalogue such a direct way is neither possible nor desirable.

In this case, a *simultaneous clustering approach* might be appropriate which compresses the huge amount of data to a reasonable size. In this approach, we aggregate the rows and columns of $\mathcal{N}$ into a given (small) number of clusters $A_1, ..., A_m \subset \{1, ..., a\}$ and $B_1, ..., B_l \subset \{1, ..., b\}$, respectively, and consider the aggregated contingency table $\mathcal{N}(\mathcal{A}, \mathcal{B}) := (\ f(A_i \times B_j)\ )$ with entries $f(A_i \times B_j) := \sum_{u \in A_i} \sum_{v \in B_j} f_{uv}$ and a size $m \times l$ which is now small enough for a direct statistical analysis. If this clustering strategy should be useful for detecting possible dependencies between U and V, it will be reasonable to choose the partitions $\mathcal{A}$ and $\mathcal{B}$ in a such way that the dependence between the classes A_i and B_j is maximum and insofar highlights as much as possible an underlying dependence between U and V in the original table $\mathcal{N}$.

We will formalize this idea in section 2 in a quite general way and introduce suitable dependence measures as a clustering criterion $g(\mathcal{A}, \mathcal{B})$. An alternating maximization algorithm is proposed in section 3. The main result of this paper resides in the fact that the *partial* maximization steps of this algorithm lead directly to the theory of 'convexity-based clustering criteria' as proposed by Bock (1983, 1992, 1994, 2002a, 2002b) and Pötzelberger and Strasser (2001). This theory is briefly sketched in section 4, and section 5 applies it to the present case. This yields a k-means-like algorithm termed *k-tangent* or *MSP algorithm* which involves *maximum-support-plane (MSP) partitions* (*maximum-tangent-plane partitions*) in analogy to minimum-distance partitions in SSQ clustering. As two particular cases we consider the classical χ^2 criterion and the Kullback-Leibler discriminating information. Section 6 points to some generalizations.

2 Dependence measures as a clustering criterion

We formalize the simultaneous clustering problem in terms of a categorical random vector (U, V) with $U \in \mathcal{U} = \{1, ..., a\}$ and $V \in \mathcal{V} = \{1, ..., b\}$ whose two-dimensional distribution P is given by the probabilities $f(u, v) := P(U = u, V = v)$[1]. We look for a m-partition $\mathcal{A} = (A_1, ..., A_m)$ of the set $\mathcal{U}$ and a l-partition $\mathcal{B} = (B_1, ..., B_l)$ of the set $\mathcal{V}$ such that the dependence between U and V in P is optimally reproduced by the aggregated two-dimensional distribution $P^{\mathcal{A}, \mathcal{B}}$ with probabilities

$$P(A_i \times B_j) := P(U \in A_i, V \in B_j) = \sum_{u \in A_i} \sum_{v \in B_j} f(u, v) \qquad (1)$$

for $i = 1, ..., m$ and $j = 1, ..., l$ which are collected in the two-dimensional $m \times l$ contingency table $\mathcal{N}(\mathcal{A}, \mathcal{B}) := (\ P(A_i \times B_j)\ )_{m \times l}$. For later use we introduce

---

[1] In section 1 we have considered an empirical distribution with $f(u, v) = f_{uv}$. We tacitly assume that $P(U = u) > 0$ and $P(V = v) > 0$ for all u and v.

the margins P_1 and P_2 of P with $P_1(A_i) := P(U \in A_i) = \sum_{u \in A_i} \sum_{v \in V} f(u,v)$ and $P_2(B_j) := P(V \in B_j) = \sum_{u \in U} \sum_{v \in B_j} f(u,v)$ as well as conditional probabilities such as $P(B_j|A_i) := P(V \in B_j|U \in A_i) = P(A_i \times B_j)/P_1(A_i)$ (which will play an important role below).

A general measure for the dependence between the classes of A and B under $P^{A,B}$ is provided by the ψ-divergence of Csiszár (1967) between $P^{A,B}$ and the product distribution $P_1 \otimes P_2$ (independence case):

$$g(A,B) := \sum_{i=1}^{m} \sum_{j=1}^{l} P_1(A_i)P_2(B_j) \cdot \psi\left(\frac{P(A_i \times B_j)}{P_1(A_i)P_2(B_j)}\right) \rightarrow \max_{A,B} \qquad (2)$$

where $\psi(\lambda)$ is a given convex function of $\lambda > 0$. In the previous context it makes sense to consider g as a clustering criterion to be maximized with respect to the pair (A, B).

By a suitable specification of the function ψ we obtain various well-known dependence measures, e.g.:

(1) The *classical* χ^2 *index* for the aggregated contingency table $N(A, B)$ by putting $\psi(\lambda) = (\lambda - 1)^2$:

$$g(A,B) := \sum_{i=1}^{m} \sum_{j=1}^{l} \frac{(P(A_i \times B_j) - P_1(A_i) \cdot P_2(B_j))^2}{P_1(A_i) \cdot P_2(B_j)} \rightarrow \max_{A,B} . \qquad (3)$$

(2) *Kullback-Leibler's discriminating information* for $\psi(\lambda) = -\log \lambda$:

$$g(A,B) := -\sum_{i=1}^{m} \sum_{j=1}^{l} P_1(A_i)P_2(B_j) \cdot \log \frac{P(A_i \times B_j)}{P_1(A_i)P_2(B_j)} \rightarrow \max_{A,B} . \qquad (4)$$

(3) The convex function $\psi(\lambda) := |\lambda - 1|$ yields the *variation distance criterion*:

$$g(A,B) := \sum_{j=1}^{l} \sum_{i=1}^{m} |P(A_i \times B_j) - P_1(A_i) \cdot P_2(B_j)| \rightarrow \max_{A,B} . \qquad (5)$$

(4) The function $\psi(\lambda) := \lambda - \lambda^s$ (with a specified parameter $0 < s < 1$) generates the *Hellinger coefficient* $1 - g(A, B)$ and (for $s = 1/2$) the *Bhattacharyya distance*.

For other choices of ψ see Bock (1992). Note that the χ^2 criterion (3) has been used in the clustering context by Celeux et al. (1989).

3   An alternating maximization algorithm

Since an *exact* (enumerative or combinatorial) maximization of the clustering criterion (2) is obviously impossible for a large number of rows and/or columns, we consider here an *alternating* maximization strategy: Starting with an arbitrary pair $(\mathcal{A}^{(0)}, \mathcal{B}^{(0)})$ of partitions it proceeds by *partially* maximizing the criterion $g(\mathcal{A}, \mathcal{B})$ with respect to $\mathcal{B}$ and $\mathcal{A}$ in turn, thereby obtaining a sequence of steadily improving partitions $\mathcal{B}^{(t)}, \mathcal{A}^{(t)}$ (with $t = 0, 1, 2, ...$). This algorithm is specified in section 5.

So it remains to develop a procedure for the *partial* (exact or at least approximate) maximization of the criterion (2) with respect to $\mathcal{B}$ or $\mathcal{A}$ which seems to be a non-trivial problem. Due to the symmetry of the criterion (2) with respect to rows and columns, $\mathcal{A}$ and $\mathcal{B}$ etc., it is sufficient to consider the partial maximization with respect to $\mathcal{B}$ for a fixed partition $\mathcal{A}$. It is the main idea of this paper to write this partial maximization problem in a form which fits the framework of the theory of *convexity-based clustering criteria* (Bock 1992, 2002a) and then to derive a recursive maximization algorithm in analogy to the classical k-means algorithm in cluster analysis.

Our method resides in the fact that the maximization problem (2) for the criterion $g(\mathcal{A}, \mathcal{B})$ with respect to $\mathcal{B}$ can be written in the form

$$g(\mathcal{A}, \mathcal{B}) = \sum_{j=1}^{l} P_2(B_j) \cdot \sum_{i=1}^{m} P_1(A_i) \cdot \psi\left(\frac{P(B_j|A_i)}{P_2(B_j)}\right) = \sum_{j=1}^{l} P_2(B_j)\phi_{\mathcal{A}}(y_j)$$

$$= \sum_{j=1}^{l} P_2(B_j) \cdot \phi_{\mathcal{A}}(E_{P_2}[\lambda(V|\mathcal{A}) \mid V \in B_j]) \to \max_{\mathcal{B}} \qquad (6)$$

where we have introduced the convex function

$$\phi_{\mathcal{A}}(y) := \sum_{i=1}^{m} P_1(A_i) \cdot \psi(\eta_i) \qquad (7)$$

of $y = (\eta_1, ..., \eta_m)' \in R^m$ and substituted for y the vectors $y_j \in R_+^m$ with components $y_{ji} := P(B_j|A_i)/P_2(B_j)$ $(i = 1, ..., m)$ for $j = 1, ..., l$. The y_{ji}'s can be written as a conditional expectation $E_{P_2}[\lambda(V|A_i)|V \in B_j]$ with the 'local' likelihood ratios

$$\lambda(v|A_i) := \frac{P(V = v|U \in A_i)}{P_2(V = v)} = \frac{\sum_{u \in A_i} f(u, v)}{P_1(A_i)P_2(V = v)}, \qquad i = 1, ..., m. \quad (8)$$

In fact:

$$E_{P_2}[\lambda(V|A_i)|V \in B_j] = \left[\sum_{v \in B_j} P_2(V = v) \cdot \lambda(v|A_i)\right] / P_2(B_j)$$

$$\overset{(8)}{=} \left[\sum_{v \in B_j} \sum_{u \in A_i} f(u, v)/P_1(A_i)\right] / P_2(B_j)$$

$$= \frac{P(A_i \times B_j)}{P_1(A_i)P_2(B_j)} = \frac{P(B_j|A_i)}{P_2(B_j)} = y_{ji}. \qquad (9)$$

Now we collect the $\lambda(v|A_i)$ in the local likelihood ratio vector

$$\lambda(v|\mathcal{A}) := \begin{pmatrix} \lambda(v|A_1) \\ \vdots \\ \lambda(v|A_m) \end{pmatrix} \in R_+^m \qquad (10)$$

and see that for a fixed j the equations (9), $i = 1, ..., m$, can be written in the form $y_j = E_{P_2}[\lambda(V|\mathcal{A})|V \in B_j]$ which proves the last equality in (6).

We conclude here that the criterion (6) is a special case of the 'convexity-based clustering criterion' described below and can therefore be maximized by applying the MSP algorithm described in the next section.

4   Maximizing a convexity-based clustering criterion

Convexity-based clustering criteria have been introduced by Bock (1983, 1992) for the situation where X is a random vector with values in an arbitrary domain $\mathcal{X}$ (e.g., $\mathcal{X} = R^p$ or $\{0,1\}^p$) which may have one of two distributions Q_0 (hypothesis) and Q_1 (alternative) with densities $q_0(x)$ and $q_1(x)$, respectively. If $y = \lambda(x) := q_1(x)/q_0(x)$ denotes the corresponding likelihood ratio and $Y := \lambda(X) \in R_+^1$ the corresponding random variable, we have, in analogy to (9), for any subset $B_j \subset \mathcal{X}$:

$$E_{Q_0}[Y|X \in B_j] = E_{Q_0}[\lambda(X) \mid X \in B_j] = Q_1(B_j)/Q_0(B_j). \qquad (11)$$

In order to characterize an optimum l-partition $\mathcal{B} = (B_1, ..., B_l)$ of $\mathcal{X}$, a *convexity-based clustering criterion* is defined here by

$$G(\mathcal{B}) := \sum_{j=1}^{l} Q_0(X \in B_j) \cdot \phi(E_{Q_0}[\lambda(X) \mid X \in B_j])$$

$$= \sum_{j=1}^{l} Q_0(X \in B_j) \cdot \phi(\frac{Q_1(B_j)}{Q_0(B_j)}) \rightarrow \max_{\mathcal{B}} \qquad (12)$$

where ϕ is a given convex function on R_+^1. This is, in fact, *the ϕ-divergence* of Csiszár (1967) for measuring the distinction of the two discretized distributions $(Q_0(B_1), ..., Q_0(B_l))$ and $(Q_1(B_1), ..., Q_1(B_l))$ and (12) can be interpreted as looking for a partition $\mathcal{B}$ which distinguishes best between Q_0 and Q_1 after discretization of $\mathcal{X}$. In another interpretation, (12) means maximizing the power of a discretized test when testing Q_0 versus Q_1. For details see Bock (1992) where a k-means-like alternating maximization technique for solving (12) is proposed which works with *maximum-tangent-plane partitions* in the λ-space R_+^1.

Pötzelberger and Strasser (2001) and Strasser (2000) have considered an analogous clustering criterion for the situation where Y is a random vector with values in R^m and probability distribution P. They look for an optimum clustering (*quantization, segmentation*) $\mathcal{B} = (B_1, ..., B_l)$ of R^m in the sense:

$$H(\mathcal{B}) := \sum_{j=1}^{l} P(Y \in B_j) \cdot \phi(E_P[Y|Y \in B_j]) \rightarrow \max_{\mathcal{B}} \qquad (13)$$

with a given convex function $\phi(y)$ on R^m. This is a generalization of the classical problem of minimizing the continuous *sum-of-squares clustering criterion* (*variance criterion*) given by

$$SSQ(\mathcal{B}) := \sum_{j=1}^{l} P(Y \in B_j) \cdot E_P \left[|| \, Y - E[Y|Y \in B_j] \, ||^2 \right]$$

$$= E[||Y||^2] - \sum_{j=1}^{l} P(Y \in B_j) \cdot ||E_P[Y|Y \in B_j]||^2 \rightarrow \min_{\mathcal{B}} \qquad (14)$$

(Bock 1974). In fact, the latter problem is obviously equivalent to (13) for the special choice $\phi(y) := ||y||^2$.

Finally, Bock (2002b) generalized the segmentation problem (12) with a view to our partial maximization problem (6): He considers $m + 1$ probability distributions $Q_0, Q_1, ..., Q_m$ for X on $\mathcal{X}$ with densities $q_0(x), q_1(x), ..., q_m(x)$. The m likelihood ratios $\lambda_i(x) := q_i(x)/q_0(x)$ $(i = 1, ..., m)$ are compiled in the vector $\lambda(x) := (\lambda_1(x), ..., \lambda_m(x))' \in R_+^m$. Now, given a convex function $\phi(x)$ on R_+^m, we may formulate the maximization problem

$$G(\mathcal{B}) = \sum_{j=1}^{l} Q_0(B_j) \cdot \phi(E_{Q_0}[\lambda(X)|X \in B_j]) \rightarrow \max_{\mathcal{B}}. \qquad (15)$$

It has exactly the form of the partial maximization problem (6) in our two-way classification approach of section 3 if we introduce in (15) the random vector $X = V$, the space $\mathcal{X} = \mathcal{V}$, the distributions $Q_0 = P_2$, $Q_i = P(\cdot|U \in A_i)$ with corresponding counting densities $q_0(v) := P_2(V = v)$ and $q_i(v) := P(V = v|U \in A_i)$ for $i = 1, ..., m$, and the convex function $\phi = \phi_A$ on R_+^m.

Thus, when solving (6), we may use the theorems derived in Bock (2002b) for the general problem (15). For ease of presentation we assume here that $\phi(y)$ is differentiable with gradient vector $a(z) := grad_y\phi(z)$ in each point $z \in R_+^m$. Then the function

$$\eta = t(y; z) := \phi(z) + a(z)'(y - z) \qquad\qquad y \in R_+^m \qquad (16)$$

describes the tangent (or support) hyperplane of the manifold $\eta = \phi(y)$ in $R_+^m \times R^1$ at the support point $z \in R_+^m$. Since ϕ is convex this hyperplane lies always below the manifold: $t(y; z) \leq \phi(y)$ for all $y \in R_+^m$ with equality for $y = z$. Below we will assign to each class B_j of $\mathcal{B}$ a support point $z_j \in R_+^m$.

Theorem 4.1
The one-parameter maximization problem (15) is equivalent to the two-para-meter minimization problem (minimum-volume problem):

$$F(\mathcal{B}, \mathcal{Z}) := \sum_{j=1}^{l} \int_{B_j} [\phi(\lambda(x)) - t(\lambda(x); z_j)] \, dQ_0(x) \; \to \; \min_{\mathcal{B}, \mathcal{Z}} \qquad (17)$$

where minimization is over all l-partitions $\mathcal{B} = (B_1, ..., B_l)$ of $\mathcal{X}$ and all choices of a system $\mathcal{Z} = (z_1, ..., z_l)$ of support points $z_1, ..., z_l$ from R_+^m.

Theorem 4.2
Given a fixed l-partition $\mathcal{B}$ of $\mathcal{X}$, the criterion $F(\mathcal{B}, \mathcal{Z})$ is minimized with respect to $\mathcal{Z}$ for the special choice $\mathcal{Z}(\mathcal{B}) := \mathcal{Z}^* := (z_1^*, ..., z_m^*)'$ given by the likelihood ratio vectors $z_j^* := E_{Q_0}[\lambda(X)|X \in B_j] = (Q_i(B_j)/Q_0(B_j))_{i=1,...,m}$, i.e., for all support systems $\mathcal{Z}$ we have:

$$F(\mathcal{B}, \mathcal{Z}) \leq F(\mathcal{B}, \mathcal{Z}(\mathcal{B})) = \int_{\mathcal{X}} \phi(\lambda(x)) dQ_0(x) - \sum_{j=1}^{l} \int_{B_j} t(\lambda(x); z_j^*) dQ_0(x)$$

$$= E_{Q_0}[\phi(\lambda(X))] - \sum_{j=1}^{l} Q_0(B_j)\phi(z_j^*) = E_{Q_0}[\phi(\lambda(X))] - G(\mathcal{B}). \; (18)$$

Here the last line establishes the equivalence of the problems (15) and (17).

Theorem 4.3
*Given a fixed system $\mathcal{Z}$ of support points $z_1, ..., z_l \in R_+^m$, the criterion $F(\mathcal{B}, \mathcal{Z})$ is minimized with respect to the partition $\mathcal{B}$ for the so-called **maximum-tangent-plane partition** $\mathcal{B}(\mathcal{Z}) := \mathcal{B}^* := (B_1^*, ..., B_l^*)$ of $\mathcal{X}$ where the class B_j^* comprizes all elements $x \in \mathcal{X}$ such that the tangent $t(\lambda(x); z_j)$ in the support point z_j and evaluated at $y = \lambda(x)$ is maximum with respect to all other tangents $t(\lambda(x); z_r)$, $r = 1, ..., l$, i.e., for all l-partitions $\mathcal{B}$ we have:*

$$F(\mathcal{B}, \mathcal{Z}) \leq F(\mathcal{B}(\mathcal{Z}), \mathcal{Z}) = E_{Q_0}[\phi(\lambda(X)) - \max_{r=1,...,l} \{t(\lambda(x); z_r)\}] \qquad (19)$$

with classes

$$B_j^* := \{x \in \mathcal{X} \mid t(\lambda(x); z_j) = \max_{r=1,...,l} t(\lambda(x); z_r)\} \qquad j = 1, ..., m. \qquad (20)$$

The theorems 4.1, 4.2, and 4.3 show that we may maximize the general clustering criterion $G(\mathcal{B})$, (15), by minimizing the criterion $F(\mathcal{B}, \mathcal{Z})$, (17), with respect to *both* parameters $\mathcal{B}$ and $\mathcal{Z}$, and that the latter problem can be (approximately) solved by starting with an initial partition $\mathcal{B} = \mathcal{B}_0$ and then minimizing F with respect to $\mathcal{Z}$ and $\mathcal{B}$ in turn. This creates a sequence $\mathcal{B}_0, \mathcal{Z}_0, \mathcal{B}_1, \mathcal{Z}_1, \mathcal{B}_1, \mathcal{Z}_2, ...$ of steadily improving support systems $\mathcal{Z}_s$ (generated by $\mathcal{B}_s$ by theorem 4.2) and l-partitions $\mathcal{B}_{s+1}$ (maximum-tangent-plane partitions for $\mathcal{Z}_s$ from theorem 4.3), for $s = 0, 1, ...$ In the next section we will formulate the resulting *k-tangent algorithm* explicitly for the case of the partial maximization problem (6) and insofar solve definitely our two-way clustering problem (2).

Remark 4.1:
If the convex function $\phi(y)$ is not differentiable at some $y = z \in R_+^m$ (see, e.g., our example (5)), we have to replace the *tangent* hyperplane $t(y; z)$ in z (see (16)) by an arbitrary *support* hyperplane $t(y; a, z) = \phi(z) + a'(y - z)$ for $\phi(y)$ in z (there might be several choices for the slope vector $a \in R^m$). With this modification the theorems 4.1, 4.2, 4.3 remain true, and the partition $\mathcal{B}$ with classes (20) is therefore called a *maximum-support-plane (MSP) partition*. Then the described maximization algorithm is called the *MSP algorithm*. For details see Pötzelberger and Strasser (2001) and Bock (2002a, 2002b).

5   The two-loop alternating simultaneous clustering algorithm using MSP partitions

We now come back to our original two-way clustering problem (2) where the criterion $g(\mathcal{A}, \mathcal{B})$ is to be maximized for a given distribution P of the random vector $(U, V) \in \mathcal{U} \times \mathcal{V}$. We have sketched, in section 3, an approach which improves iteratively an initial pair $\mathcal{A}^{(0)}, \mathcal{B}^{(0)}$ of partitions by an alternating partial maximization strategy with two iterated steps (a) and (b) where g is maximized with respect to $\mathcal{B}$ and $\mathcal{A}$, respectively. After having seen that both partial maximization problems involve a special convexity-based criterion, we can include, in both steps and as an 'inner iteration loop', the k-tangent or MSP algorithm for partial maximization as sketched at the end of section 4. In the following we formulate explicitly the resulting *simultaneous MSP clustering algorithm*.

$t = 0$:
Choose a pair of initial partitions $\mathcal{A}^{(0)} = (A_1^{(0)}, ..., A_m^{(0)})$ of $\mathcal{U} = \{1, ..., a\}$ (rows) and $\mathcal{B}^{(0)} = (B_1^{(0)}, ..., B_l^{(0)})$ of $\mathcal{V} = \{1, ..., b\}$ (columns).

$t \to t + 1$:
In this step the partitions $\mathcal{A}^{(t)} = (A_1^{(t)}, ..., A_m^{(t)})$ of $\mathcal{U}$ and $\mathcal{B}^{(t)} = (B_1^{(t)}, ..., B_l^{(t)})$ of $\mathcal{V}$ are updated as follows:

Step (a): Maximize the convexity-based criterion

$$g(\mathcal{A}^{(t)}, \mathcal{B}) = \sum_{j=1}^{l} P_2(B_j) \cdot \phi_{\mathcal{A}^{(t)}}(E_{P_2}[\lambda(V|\mathcal{A}^{(t)}) \mid V \in B_j]) \qquad (21)$$

with respect to the l-partition $\mathcal{B}$ of $\mathcal{V}$ (the columns) by using, as an 'inner loop', the MSP algorithm with the convex function

$$\phi_{\mathcal{A}^{(t)}}(y) := \sum_{i=1}^{m} P_1(A_i^{(t)}) \cdot \psi(\eta_i) \qquad (22)$$

of $y = (\eta_1, ..., \eta_m)' \in R_+^m$ (cf. (7)) and starting with the l-partition $\mathcal{B}_0 := \mathcal{B}^{(t)}$ of $\mathcal{V}$. This yields a sequence $\mathcal{B}_0, \mathcal{B}_1, \mathcal{B}_2, ...$ of steadily improving l-partitions of $\mathcal{V}$ ending with a stationary MSP partition which is denoted by $\mathcal{B}^{(t+1)}$.

Step (b): Maximize the convexity-based criterion

$$g(\mathcal{A}, \mathcal{B}^{(t+1)}) = \sum_{i=1}^{m} P_1(A_i) \cdot \phi_{\mathcal{B}^{(t+1)}}(E_{P_1}[\tilde{\lambda}(U|\mathcal{B}^{(t+1)}) \mid U \in A_i]) \quad (23)$$

with respect to the m-partition $\mathcal{A}$ of $\mathcal{U}$ (the rows) by using, as an 'inner loop', the MSP algorithm with the convex function

$$\phi_{\mathcal{B}^{(t+1)}}(x) := \sum_{j=1}^{l} P_2(B_j^{(t+1)}) \cdot \psi(\xi_j) \quad (24)$$

of $x = (\xi_1, ..., \xi_l)' \in R_+^l$ and starting with the m-partition $\mathcal{A}_0 := \mathcal{A}^{(t)}$ of $\mathcal{U}$. Here $\tilde{\lambda}(u|\mathcal{B}) \in R_+^l$ denotes the likelihood ratio vector with components $\tilde{\lambda}(u|B_j) := P(U = u|V \in B_j)/P_1(U = u)$ in analogy to (8) and (10). This iteration yields a sequence $\mathcal{A}_0, \mathcal{A}_1, \mathcal{A}_2, ...$ of steadily improving m-partitions of $\mathcal{U}$ ending with a stationary m-partition which is denoted by $\mathcal{A}^{(t+1)}$.

Stopping criterion:
The previous steps (a) and (b) are iterated in turn for $t = 0, 1, 2, ...$ until a stationary pair $(\mathcal{A}^{(t)}, \mathcal{B}^{(t)})$ of partitions is attained (or another stopping criterion is fulfilled).

Now we have to describe the 'inner loops' for both steps (a) and (b). Since (b) follows from (a) by simply inverting the roles of U and V, $\mathcal{B}$ and $\mathcal{A}$ etc., we describe only the 'inner loop' for step (a), i.e., for maximizing $g(\mathcal{A}^{(t)}, \mathcal{B})$ with respect to $\mathcal{B}$. This loop proceeds as follows:

$s = 0:$
Begin with the l-partition $\mathcal{B}_0 := \mathcal{B}^{(t)}$ of $\mathcal{V}$ (the columns). Then a sequence $\mathcal{B}_0, \mathcal{B}_1, \mathcal{B}_2, ...$ of partitions of $\mathcal{V}$ with increasing values of $g(\mathcal{A}^{(t)}, \mathcal{B}_s)$ is determined as follows:

$s \to s + 1:$
Update the current l-partition $\mathcal{B}_s = (B_{s1}, ..., B_{sl})$ of the columns:

(i) First we calculate the support points $z_{s1}, ..., z_{sl} \in R_+^m$ generated by $\mathcal{B}_s$ where z_{sj} has components

$$z_{sj|i} := E[\lambda(V|A_i^{(t)})|V \in B_{sj}] = \frac{P(B_{sj}|A_i^{(t)})}{P_2(B_{sj})} \quad i = 1, ..., m \quad (25)$$

(see theorem 4.2) such that

$$z_{sj} := \begin{pmatrix} z_{sj|1} \\ \vdots \\ z_{sj|m} \end{pmatrix} = E[\lambda(V|\mathcal{A}^{(t)})|V \in B_{sj}] \in R_+^m \quad j = 1, ..., l. \quad (26)$$

(ii) Then we determine the MSP partition $\mathcal{B}_{s+1}$ of $\mathcal{V}$ generated by these support points $z_{s1}, ..., z_{sl}$, i.e. with classes

$$\mathcal{B}_{s+1,j} := \{ v \in \mathcal{V} | t_{\mathcal{A}^{(t)}}(\lambda(v|\mathcal{A}^{(t)}); z_{sj}) = \max_{r=1,...,l} t_{\mathcal{A}^{(t)}}(\lambda(v|\mathcal{A}^{(t)}); z_{sr}) \} \quad (27)$$

$(j = 1, ..., l)$ where $t_{\mathcal{A}^{(t)}}(y; z_{sr})$ denotes the tangent (support) hyperplane for $\phi_{\mathcal{A}^{(t)}}(y)$ in the support point $z_{sr} \in R^m$.

(iii) We iterate (i) and (ii) in turn until a stationary partition $\mathcal{B}_s$ is obtained which is denoted by $\mathcal{B}^{(t+1)}$.

Remark 5.1:
In (27) we need an explicit formula for the tangent hyperplane $t_{\mathcal{A}^{(t)}}(y; z_{sj})$. From the definition of $\phi_{\mathcal{A}^{(t)}}$ we obtain with $y = (\eta_1, ..., \eta_m)'$ and $z = (\zeta_1, ..., \zeta_m)'$:

$$t_{\mathcal{A}^{(t)}}(y; z) = \sum_{i=1}^{m} P_1(A_i^{(t)}) \cdot [\psi(\zeta_i) + \dot{\psi}(z_i)(\eta_i - \zeta_i)] \quad (28)$$

where $\dot{\psi}$ is the derivative of the convex function ψ on R_+^1. Substituting here $y = \lambda(v|\mathcal{A}^{(t)})$ and $z = z_{sj}$ we obtain the explicit tangent formula in (27):

$$t_{\mathcal{A}^{(t)}}(\lambda(v|\mathcal{A}^{(t)}); z_{sj})$$
$$= \sum_{i=1}^{m} P_1(A_i^{(t)}) \cdot \left[\psi(z_{sj|i}) + \dot{\psi}(z_{sj|i}) \left\{ \frac{P(V=v|A_i^{(t)})}{P_2(V=v)} - \frac{P(B_{sj}|A_i^{(t)})}{P_2(B_{sj})} \right\} \right] \quad (29)$$

The new class $\mathcal{B}_{s+1,j}$ comprizes just those columns v for which this expression is maximum in the sense of (27).

Two special cases:

In section 2 we have listed various dependence measures which can be used as a clustering criterion. They result from (2) by different choices of the convex function ψ. We specify the previous maximality condition for two special cases:

The χ^2 criterion (3):
With $\psi(\lambda) = (\lambda - 1)^2$ maximizing (29) is equivalent to

$$\sum_{i=1}^{m} P_1(A_i^{(t)}) \frac{P(B_{sj}|A_i^{(t)})}{P_2(B_{sj})} \cdot \left[\frac{P(V=v|A_i^{(t)})}{P_2(V=v)} - \frac{1}{2} \frac{P(B_{sj}|A_i^{(t)})}{P_2(B_{sj})} \right] \to \max_j .$$

The Kullback-Leibler criterion (4):
With $\psi(\lambda) = -\log \lambda$ maximizing (29) is equivalent to

$$\sum_{i=1}^{m} P_1(A_i^{(t)}) \left[\frac{P(V=v|A_i^{(t)})/P_2(V=v)}{P(B_{sj}|A_i^{(t)})/P_2(B_{sj})} + \log \frac{P(B_{sj}|A_i^{(t)})}{P_2(B_{sj})} \right] \to \min_j .$$

6   Final remarks

In this paper we have shown that the maximum-tangent-plane (maximum-support-plane, MSP) algorithm of Bock (1983, 1992, 1994, 2002a) and Pötzelberger and Strasser (2001) can be used for clustering simultaneously the rows and columns of a contingency table. Thereby, the clustering criterion is chosen as a dependence measure for the classes of rows and columns and the clustering algorithm improves a given initial pair of partitions in several outer and inner iteration loops (a) and (b), and (i) and (ii) and converges typically to a 'local' optimum of the underlying criterion.

It appears that our simultaneous clustering method applies also to more general sample spaces than just the finite sets $\mathcal{U} = \{1, ..., a\}$ and $\mathcal{V} = \{1, ..., b\}$ considered here. For example, to the case where U and V are multidimensional random vectors with values in $\mathcal{U} = R^p$ and $\mathcal{V} = R^q$ and we look for an optimum pair of partitions $\mathcal{A}$ and $\mathcal{B}$ of R^p and R^q, respectively. Then we have to modify the previous criteria and definitions insofar as, e.g., the counting density $f(u,v) = P(U = u, V = v)$ is replaced by a joint probability (Lebesgue) density $f(u,v)$ of (U,V), sums like $P_1(A_i) = \sum_{u \in A_i} \sum_{v \in V} f(u,v)$ are replaced by integrals $P_1(A_i) = \int_{A_i} \int_{R^q} f(u,v) du dv$ and discrete likelihood ratios such as $\lambda(v|A_i) = P(V = v, U \in A_i)/(P_1(A_i)P_2(V = v))$ by density ratios such as $\lambda(v|A_i) = f(u,v)/(P_1(A_i)f_2(v))$ etc. For details see Bock (2002b).

Finally, we remark that our approach works also for clustering n data points $(u_\nu, v_\nu) \in R^{p+q}$ ($\nu = 1, ..., n$) into m classes $A_i \subset U := \{u_1, ..., u_n\}$ and l classes $B_j \subset \{v_1, ..., v_n\}$ such that the dependence between these classes is maximized: In this case we have just to use, for (U,V) in section 2, the empirical distribution $P = P^{(n)}$ of the n data points.

References

BOCK, H.-H. (1968): Statistische Modelle für die einfache und doppelte Klassifikation von normalverteilten Beobachtungen. Dissertation, Univ. of Freiburg, 1968

BOCK, H.-H. (1972): Statistische Modelle und Bayes'sche Verfahren zur Bestimmung einer unbekannten Klassifikation normalverteilter zufälliger Vektoren. *Metrika* 18, 120-132

BOCK, H.-H. (1974): Automatische Klassifikation. Mathematische und statistische Methoden zur Strukturierung von Daten (Clusteranalyse). Vandenhoeck & Ruprecht, Göttingen.

BOCK, H.-H. (1983): A clustering algorithm for choosing optimal classes for the chi-squared test. Bull. Intern. Statist. Inst., 44th Session, Madrid 1983, Vol. II: Contributed papers, 758-762

BOCK, H.-H. (1992): A clustering algorithm for maximizing ϕ-divergence, non-centrality and discriminating power. In: M. Schader (ed.): *Analyzing and modeling data and knowledge.* Springer-Verlag, Heidelberg, 1991, 19-36

BOCK, H.-H. (1994): Information and entropy in cluster analysis. In: H. Bozdo-gan et al. (eds.): *The Frontiers of statistical modeling: an informational approach.* Proc. First US/Japan Conference on Statistical Modeling, Knoxville, Tennessee, May 1992. Kluwer Academic Press, Dordrecht, 1994, Vol. II, 115-147

BOCK, H.-H. (2002a): Clustering methods with convexity-based clustering criteria with applications. *Statistical Methods and Applications* (submitted)

BOCK, H.-H. (2002b): Two-way clustering for probability distributions: maximally dependent clusters. (Preprint)

CASTILLO, W. and TREJOS, J. (2002): Two-mode partitioning: review of methods and applicatons in tabu search. In: K. Jajuga, A. Sokolowski, H.-H. Bock (eds.): Classification, clustering, and related topics. Recent advances and applications. Studies in Classification, Data Analysis, and Knowledge Organization. Springer-Verlag, Heidelberg, 43-51

CELEUX, G., DIDAY, E., GOVAERT, G., LECHEVALLIER, Y. and RALAM-BONDRAINY, H. (1989): *Classification automatique des données.* Dunod, Paris. Chapitre 2.6

CSISZÁR, I. (1967): Information-type measures of difference of probability distributions and indirect observations. *Studia Scientiarum Mathematicarum Hungarica* **2**, 299-318

GAUL, W. and SCHADER, M. (1996): A new algorithm for two-mode clustering. In: H.-H. Bock, W. Polasek (eds.): Data analysis and information systems. Studies in Classification, Data Analysis, and Knowledge Organization. Springer-Verlag, Heidelberg, 15-23

GOVAERT, G. (1983): *Classification croisée.* Thèse d'Etat, Université de Paris VI.

PÖTZELBERGER, K. and STRASSER, H. (2001): Clustering and quantization by MSP-partitions. *Statistics and Decisions* 19, 331-371

STRASSER, H. (2000): Towards a statistical theory of optimal quantization. In: W. Gaul, O. Opitz, and M. Schader (eds.): *Data analysis. Scientific modeling and practical application.* Springer-Verlag, Heidelberg, 2000, 369-383

Localised Mixtures of Experts
for Mixture of Regressions

Guillaume Bouchard

Institut National de Recherche en Informatique et en Automatique,
Projet IS2 – ZIRST – 655 avenue de l'Europe
38330 Montbonnot Saint-Martin, France

Abstract. In this paper, an alternative to Mixture of Experts (ME) called localised mixture of experts is studied. It corresponds to ME where the experts are linear regressions and the gating network is a Gaussian classifier. The underlying regressors distribution can be considered to be Gaussian, so that the joint distribution is a Gaussian mixture. This provides a powerful speed-up of the EM algorithm for localised ME. Conversely, when studying Gaussian mixtures with specific constraints, one can use the standard EM algorithm for mixture of experts to carry out maximum likelihood estimation. Some constrained models are useful, and the corresponding modifications to apply to the EM algorithm are described.

1 Introduction

Let consider a regression model, where the dependent variable Y can be fully explained with a given set of variables $X_1, \cdots, X_{d+1}$. Assume that X_{d+1} is a not observed discrete variable. This regressor is called a latent variable. A natural way of carrying out regression is to explain Y with the d remaining regressors. But the latent variable can carry much information and it could be important to try to recover it. For example, for each value of the latent variable X_{d+1}, the conditional model is completely different. The missing information can be estimated in a mixture of regressions model (Quandt and Ramsey (1978)). Categories of clusterwise regression models were studied by Hennig (1999).

Switching regression is well known in econometrics literature; it is a special case of mixture of linear regressions, assuming that the mixture proportions do not depend on the regressors. This model was first examined in Quandt (1972) and Kiefer (1978) gave consistency proof of maximum likelihood (ML) estimators. See Hurn et al. (2000) for Bayesian analysis of this model.

In a general framework, mixtures of regressions are often referred as *Mixtures of Experts* (ME), due to their first introduction in the machine learning community (Jacobs et al. (1991)). ME considers a gating network which is the conditional distribution of the hidden variable given the regressors. These models are therefore called *conditional mixture models*. Some useful results have been established, regarding the convergence rate of EM algorithm (Jordan and Xu (1995)) or identifiability (Jiang and Tanner (1999)). Direct extension is Hierarchical ME where the gating network, that is to say the conditionnal distribution of the classes given the regressors, has a tree structure (Jordan and Jacobs, 1994).

The motivation of this paper is to study mixtures of regressions where we assume a Gaussian distribution for the regressors. It leads to the so-called *localized mixture of experts* (Moerland (1999)) first introduced by Xu et al. (1995). It is also referred as normalized Gaussian networks by Sato and Ishii (2000). Our approch was to work on the joint distribution of the observations. It enables us to link localized mixture of experts with mixture models in their standard form, and thus to take profit of well established theoretical results (McLachlan and Peel (2000)). In this way, we provide a version of the EM algorithm that dramatically decreases the computing time. Conversely, mixtures of experts can be used in the mixture model context to estimate models with specific constraints on parameters. Detailed formula of the EM algorithm for such models are given in this paper.

2   The model

We consider relationships between three variables X, Y and H:

- X in $\mathbb{R}^d$ is a vector of d real regressors,
- Y in $\mathbb{R}$ is the dependent variable,
- H in $\{1, \cdots, K\}$ is the latent or hidden discrete variable.

Let $(x, y) = \{(x_i, y_i)_{i=1,\cdots,n}\}$ be iid observations of the couple (X, Y). Since H is not observed, the density of (X, Y) is obtained by marginalization:

$$p(X, Y) = \sum_{k=1}^{K} p(X, Y, H = k). \tag{1}$$

Applying the Bayes rule on $p(X, Y, H)$, we derive two useful expressions of the joint probability:

$$p(X, Y) = \sum_{k=1}^{K} p(X) p(H = k|X) p(Y|X, H = k) \tag{2}$$

$$p(X, Y) = \sum_{k=1}^{K} p(H = k) p(X|H = k) p(Y|X, H = k). \tag{3}$$

For these two parametrizations, the distribution of Y conditionally on $H = k$ and $X = x$ is, as usual in linear regression, an univariate Gaussian with mean $\beta'_k x + \alpha_k$ and variance τ_k^2:

$$Y|X = x, H = k \sim \mathcal{N}(\beta'_k x + \alpha_k, \tau_k^2). \tag{4}$$

We now present models that find estimators of β_k, α_k and τ_k.

2.1   Standard mixture of experts

The expression (2) corresponds to the conditional mixture model, since maximizing its log-likelihood does not require knowledge of the distribution of X. It is equivalent to work with the conditional probability of Y given X:

$$p(Y|X) = \sum_{k=1}^{K} \underbrace{p(H = k|X)}_{gating\ network}\ \underbrace{p(Y|X, H = k)}_{expert} \tag{5}$$

In this case, the gating network classifier $p(H|X)$ has to be specified. The multinomial logit model is usually chosen. It is a generalised linear model with conditional density

$$p(H = k|X) = \frac{p_k e^{v_k x}}{\sum_{l=1}^{K} p_l e^{v_l x}}, \quad k = 1, \cdots, K, \tag{6}$$

where vectors v_k and proportions p_k are parameters such that $v_K = 0$ and $\sum_{k=1}^{K} p_k = 1$.

2.2   Localized mixture of experts

In the sequel, we opt for parametrization (3), which corresponds to a standard *mixture model* where each component has density $p(X|H = k)p(Y|X, H = k)$. A multinomial distribution is assumed for H:

$$H \sim \mathcal{M}(1, p), \tag{7}$$

where $p = (p_1, \cdots, p_K)'$ is a vector of component proportions such that $\sum_{k=1}^{K} p_k = 1$. Knowing mixture component H, the regressors X are assumed to arise from a multivariate Gaussian distribution:

$$X|H = k \sim \mathcal{N}(\mu_k, \Sigma_k). \tag{8}$$

With the Gaussian parametrization, components can be interpreted in a more natural way than the standard ME (Xu and Jordan, 1995), since the means μ_k summarize the regressors. The corresponding gating network classifier can be obtained by direct application of the Bayes rule:

$$p(H = k|X = x) = \frac{p(H = k)p(X = x|H = k)}{p(X = x)} \tag{9}$$

$$= \frac{p_k|\Sigma_k|^{-\frac{1}{2}}e^{-\frac{1}{2}(x-m_k)'\Sigma_k^{-1}(x-m_k)}}{\sum_{l=1}^{K} p_l|\Sigma_l|^{-\frac{1}{2}}e^{-\frac{1}{2}(x-m_l)'\Sigma_l^{-1}(x-m_l)}}. \tag{10}$$

This is exactly the gating network with Gaussian kernel proposed by Xu et al. (1995). This parametrization differs from the usual *softmax* fonction

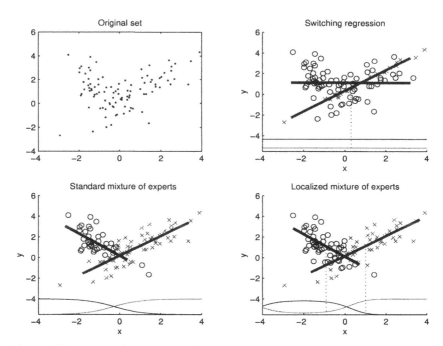

Fig. 1. Illustration of a mixture of two regression: from a dataset where a simple linear regression is not suitable (top left), switching regression (top right) finds two optimal regression lines equally distributed on the regressors. Standard mixture of experts (bottom left) expresses the proportions from a linear logistic model on the regressors. Localized ME (bottom right) assume that the distribution of the regressors is normal with parameters depending on the latent variable. We see that the last two models give similar results. Proportions are represented at the bottom of the graphs.

$1/(1 + \exp(\beta x)$ primarily by the quadratic form of the canonical link. We refer this model as *localized mixture of experts*, following Moerland (1999), who compared Gaussian and standard gating network for classification and noted a slight superiority of standard ME. Localized ME was successfully exploited in Fritsch (1996) and Fritsch, Finke and Waibel (1997) for speech recognition. They show that such kernels can reduce significantly the time of convergence of the EM algorithm for large databases. They obtain near optimal initial parameter values μ_k and Σ_k by an unsupervised learning applied on regressors only. We should stress that originally, introduction of localized ME was for convenience, but we give a natural justification of their use in terms of probability assumption.

It can easily be proved that the joint distribution of the observations (X', Y), $X \in \mathbb{R}^p$, $Y \in \mathbb{R}$ is a mixture of $(d + 1)$-dimensional Gaussian distributions. The proportions are the p_k, $k = 1, \cdots, K$ defined above, the mean and covariance matrix of the kth component are

$$m_k = \begin{pmatrix} \mu_k \\ \mu_k' \beta_k + \alpha_k \end{pmatrix}, \quad \Gamma_k = \begin{bmatrix} \Sigma_k & \Sigma_k \beta_k \\ \beta_k' \Sigma_k & \tau_k^2 + \beta_k' \Sigma_k \beta_k \end{bmatrix}. \tag{11}$$

Then, localised ME is just a Gaussian mixture with a specific parametrization.

2.3 Adding constraints

The previous model has $(\frac{d^2}{2} + \frac{5}{2}d + 3)K - 1$ parameters. It can be excessive since the number of parameters grows as a quadratic function of the dimension d of the data. To avoid overfitting, we can derive more parsimonious models by adding constraints on parameter values. The first assumption would be to constrain the component covariance matrix Σ_k to be diagonal. This assumption corresponds to the conditional independence of regressors given the component, and we claim that it may not be very severe since regression focuses essentially on coefficients β_k. We then obtain a particular covariance matrices Γ_k of the joint distribution for each component k:

$$\Gamma_k = \begin{bmatrix} \sigma_{k1}^2 & 0 & \cdots & & \sigma_{k1}^2 \beta_{k1} \\ \vdots & \ddots & 0 & & \vdots \\ 0 & \cdots & \sigma_{kd}^2 & & \sigma_{kd}^2 \beta_{kd} \\ \sigma_{k1}^2 \beta_{k1} & \cdots & \sigma_{kd}^2 \beta_{kd} & & \tau_k^2 + \prod_{i=1}^d \beta_{ki}^2 \sigma_{ki}^2 \end{bmatrix}. \tag{12}$$

To our knowledge, this type of covariance matrix was never mentioned in the literature on Gaussian mixtures. It can yet be useful for specific problems. This model has now $K(2d+3) - 1$ parameters which is linear in d, so that it can be more suitable in high dimension problems.

Another class of models can be obtained by constraining some parameters to be equal between groups:

i) $p_k = p$: components proportions are equal. This assumption can be regarded as unrealistic. However, maximum likelihood estimator can be expected to be more stable since the number of local maxima of likelihood dramatically decreases when proportions are equal.

ii) $\beta_k = \beta$: common slope between components. The model is then a linear regression for which the error term can be dependent on regressors values (top left in figure 2).

iii) $\tau_k = \tau$: common error term beetween regressions. This constraint forces the model to have a constant error term in each component (top right in figure 2).

iv) $\Sigma_k = \Sigma$: common covariance matrix for the regressors. This assumption is useful when we want a linear separations between groups instead of a quadratic one. This is illustrated in the bottom right of figure 2 with $\sigma_k = \sigma$. The probabilities of each component are split between left and right, contrary to other models.

Some other constraints would be to set $\alpha_k = \alpha$ or $\mu_k = \mu$ (left of figure 2), i.e. assuming that components have a common intercept or a common mean. They correspond to very specific models, as it can be viewed on Figure 2. Combinations of these constraints leads to a large variety of different models. Note that some of these constraints may be very severe and only applicable to specific situations.

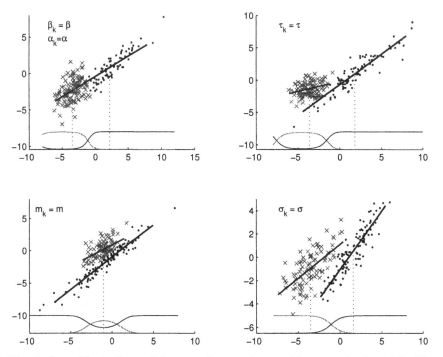

Fig. 2. Some illustrations of data sets in accordance with constrained models. The above line is the conditionnal probability of class 2 given x.

3   Maximum likelihood estimation

Before carrying out ML estimation, we must ensure that the model is identifiable. Hennig (2000) gives necessary conditions for the existence of consistent estimators in mixture of regressions with random regressors: the regressor distribution must not give positive probability to any $(d-1)$-dimensional hyperplanes. Of course, this does not occur as soon as the Σ_k are not singular, which is not a mild condition. Following Dempster et al. (1977), we now describe the EM algorithm for the Gaussian mixture of experts. We write $\tilde{\beta}_k = (\alpha_k, \beta'_k)'$ for $k = 1, \cdots, K$. Let θ be the vector of parameters containing $p_k, \tilde{\beta}, \tau_k, \mu_k$ or Σ_k for $k = 1, \cdots, K$.

E step. The expectation step requires the computation of the conditional expectation of the complete log likelihood

$$Q(\theta|\theta^{(t)}) = E\{L_c(\theta; x, y)|x, y, \theta^{(t)}\} \tag{13}$$

where $\theta^{(t)}$ is the value of the parameter vector at iteration t and $L_c(\theta; x, y)$ is the complete log likelihood of the model. Denoting with h the density of $X|H$ and g the density of $Y|X, H$, we have

$$L_c(\theta; x, y) = \sum_{i=1}^{n} \sum_{k=1}^{K} c_{ik} \log\left(p_k h(x_i; \mu_k, \Sigma_k) g(y_i; x_i, \tilde{\beta}_k, \tau_k)\right). \tag{14}$$

Here, c_{ik} equals to 1 if data i comes from component k, and 0 otherwise. Its expectation conditionally on the parameters $\theta^{(t)}$ is

$$w_{ik}^{(t)} = \frac{p_k^{(t)} h(x_i; \mu_k^{(t)}, \Sigma_k^{(t)}) g(y_i; x_i, \tilde{\beta}_k^{(t)}, \tau_k^{(t)})}{\sum_{l=1}^{K} p_l^{(t)} h(x_i; \mu_l^{(t)}, \Sigma_l^{(t)}) g(y_i; x_i, \tilde{\beta}_l^{(t)}, \tau_l^{(t)})}. \tag{15}$$

M step. The maximization step is

$$\theta^{(t+1)} = \underset{\theta}{argmax}\, Q(\theta|\theta^{(t)}). \tag{16}$$

From equations (13) and (14) we get

$$Q(\theta|\theta^{(t)}) = \sum_{i=1}^{n} \sum_{k=1}^{K} w_{ik}^{(t)} \log\left[p_k^{(t)} h(x_i; \mu_k^{(t)}, \Sigma_k^{(t)}) g(y_i; x_i, \tilde{\beta}_k^{(t)}, \tau_k^{(t)})\right] \tag{17}$$

Let $X = [x_1, \cdots, x_n]'$ be the matrix of regressors and $\tilde{X} = [\mathbb{1}_n\ X]$ where $\mathbb{1}_n$ is a $n \times 1$ vector of ones. Y is the vector of y_i and $W_k^{(t)}$ are $n \times n$ diagonal matrices with $w_{ik}^{(t)}$ on their diagonal. Expression (17) is maximised by setting its partial derivatives on $p_k, \tilde{\beta}, \tau_k, \mu_k$ and Σ_k to zero. We obtain closed form solutions:

$$p_k^{(t+1)} = \frac{1}{n} tr W_k^{(t)}, \tag{18}$$

$$\tilde{\beta}_k^{(t+1)} = (\tilde{X}' W_k^{(t)} \tilde{X})^{-1} \tilde{X} W_k^{(t)} Y, \tag{19}$$

$$\tau_k^{2\,(t+1)} = \frac{1}{tr W_k^{(t)}} (Y - \tilde{X}\tilde{\beta}_k^{(t+1)})' W_k^{(t)} (Y - \tilde{X}\tilde{\beta}_k^{(t+1)}), \tag{20}$$

$$\mu_k^{(t+1)} = \frac{1}{tr W_k^{(t)}} X' W_k^{(t)} \mathbb{1}', \tag{21}$$

$$\Sigma_k^{(t+1)} = \frac{1}{tr W_k^{(t)}} (X - \mathbb{1}\mu_k^{'(t)})' W_k^{(t)} (X - \mathbb{1}\mu_k^{'(t)}). \tag{22}$$

We can notice that equations (19) and (20) correspond to a weighted least square fit and equations (21) and (22) give weighted mean and variance.

3.1   ML estimation of constrained models

To adapt the previous algorithm to the constraint models defined above, the procedure is the same. Derivatives of expression (17) are slightly different, but except for $\tilde{\beta}_k^{(t+1)}$, the modifications are straightforward and not included here, except for the constraint $\tilde{\beta}_k = \tilde{\beta}$: we have to solve the nonlinear system

$$
\begin{cases}
\tau_k^{2\,(t+1)} = \frac{1}{tr\,W_k^{(t)}} (Y - \tilde{X}\tilde{\beta}_k^{(t+1)})' W_k^{(t)} (Y - \tilde{X}\tilde{\beta}_k^{(t+1)}), \\
\tilde{\beta}^{(t+1)} = \left(\tilde{X}'(\sum_{k=1}^K \frac{1}{\tau_k^{2\,(t+1)}} W_k^{(t)}) \tilde{X} \right)^{-1} \tilde{X}(\sum_{k=1}^K \frac{1}{\tau_k^{2\,(t+1)}} W_k^{(t)}) Y.
\end{cases}
\tag{23}
$$

Since closed form solution of this system is not available, we simply replace the term $\tau_k^{2\,(t+1)}$ by its previous value $\tau_k^{2\,(t)}$ in the expression of $\tilde{\beta}_k^{(t+1)}$. It can be proved that acting in such a way, the modified M step still increases the likelihood. The proof requires to prove that the vector $\tilde{\beta}_k^{(t+1)} - \tilde{\beta}_k^{(t)}$ has a positive dot product with $grad\,L(\tilde{\beta}_k^{(t)})$, L beeing the log-likelihood. Thus, we have defined a Generalised EM algorithm which have the same convergence properties than EM in its classical form (see Dempster et a. (1977)).

3.2   Reducing the computing time

If no constraint on component parameters is applied, ML estimation is straight-forward since the model is a mixture of normal distributions. This approach differs from Fritsch's one (1996) in the sense that we directly obtain ML estimators by an unsupervised learning on the joint distribution $p(X, Y)$ instead of $p(X)$. There exists various effective ways of finding ML estimators of μ_k and Γ_k, but the most used is the EM algorithm (McLachlan and Peel (2000)). Once we get the ML estimators $\hat{\mu}_k$ and $\hat{\Gamma}_k$, we write $\hat{\mu}_k = \begin{bmatrix} e_k \\ f_k \end{bmatrix}$ and $\hat{\Gamma}_k = \begin{bmatrix} A_k & b_k \\ b_k' & c_k \end{bmatrix}$, A_k being a $d \times d$ matrix, b_k and e_k vectors of $\mathbb{R}^d$ and f_k and e_k real values. We solve equations (11), getting $\hat{\mu}_k = e_k$, $\hat{\Sigma}_k = A_k$, $\hat{\beta}_k = \hat{\Sigma}_k^{-1} b_k$, $\hat{\tau}_k = c_k - \hat{\beta}_k' \hat{\Sigma}_k \hat{\beta}_k$, and finally $\alpha_k = f_k - \hat{\mu}_k' \hat{\beta}_k$. This estimation is simpler and faster than the previous EM algorithm. Namely, in the first algorithm, two inversions of matrices are needed for each EM step and each component (one in the evaluation of the density $h((x_i; \mu_k^{(t)}, \Sigma_k^{(t)})$ in the E step and one for the weighted least square fit (19) in the M step). By constrast, in this new version, each step requires one matrix inversion (evaluation of the Gaussian density in the E step), thus dividing the computing time by 2 when the dimension d is large. It shows that this specific parametrization can appreciably simplify estimation.

4   Discussion

We studied a mixture of Gaussian distributions used in a regression purpose, and showed that it can be viewed as a mixture of experts with Gaussian gating network. The specific parametrization provide a natural interpretation of clusters and enable us to add constraints that were never mentioned in Gaussian mixture literature. A wide variety of clusterwise regression models is therefore available, that can be used for multiple purposes. Robust linear regression is possible, so that non-Gaussian error terms can be handled easily. Some further work is needed to provide results on this topic. Independence constraints also permit to reduce significantly the number of parameters, and this can be particulary desirable in high dimensions. Finally, on the model without constraints on component parameters, we gave a powerful way of estimating ML parameters.

References

DEMPSTER, A. P., LAIRD, N. M. and RUBIN, D. B. (1977): Maximum likelihood from incomplete data via the EM algorithm. *Journal of the Royal Statistical Society*, Series B, 39, 1–38.

J. FRITSCH. (1996): Modular neural networks for speech recognition. Master's thesis, Carnegie Mellon University & University of Karlsruhe.
ftp://reports.adm.cs.cmu.edu/usr/anon/1996/CMU-CS-96-203.ps.gz.

FRITSCH, J., FINKE, M. and WAIBEL, A. (1997): Adaptively growing hierarchical mixtures of experts. In M. C. Mozer, M. I. Jordan and T. Petsche (Eds.), *Advances in Neural Informations Processing Systems*, 9. MIT Press.

HENNIG, C. (1999): Models and Methods for Clusterwise Linear Regression. Gaul, W. and Locarek-Junge, H. (Eds): *Classification in the Information Age.* Springer, Berlin, 179–187.

HENNIG, C. (2000): Identifiability of Models for Clusterwise Linear Regression. *Journal of Classification*, 17, 273–296.

HURN, M. A., JUSTEL, A. and C. P., ROBERT. (2000): Estimating mixtures of regressions. Technical report, CREST, France.

JACOBS, R. A., JORDAN, M. I., NOWLAN, S. J. and HINTON, G. E. (1991): Adaptive mixture of local experts. *Neural Computation*, 3(1), 79–87.

JIANG, W. and TANNER, M.A. (1999): Hierarchical mixtures-of-experts for exponential family regression models: approximation and maximum likelihood estimation. *Ann. Statistics*, 27, 987–1011.

JORDAN, M. I. and JACOBS, R. A. (1994): Hierarchical mixtures of experts and the EM algorithm. *Neural Computation*, 6, 181–214.

QUANDT, R. E.(1972): A new Approach to Estimating Switching Regressions *Journal of the American Statistical Association*, 67, 306–310.

KIEFER, N. M.(1978): Discrete Parameter Variation: Efficient Estimation of a Switching Regression Model, *Econometrica*, 46, 427–434.

QUANDT, R. E. and RAMSEY, J. B. (1978): Estimating mixtures of normal distributions and switching regressions, *JASA*, 73, 730–752.

McLACHLAN, G. J. and PEEL., D. (2000): *Finite Mixture Models*, Wiley.

MOODY, J. and DARKEN, C.J. (1989): Fast learning in networks of locally-tuned processing units *Neural Computation*, 1, 281–294.

MOERLAND, P. (1999) Classification using localized mixtures of experts. In proc. of the *International Conference on Artificial Neural Networks*.

SATO, M. and ISHII, S. (2000): On-line EM algorithm for the normalized gaussian network. *Neural Computation*, 12(2), 407–432.

XU, L. and JORDAN, M.I. (1995): On convergence properties of the EM algorithm for Gaussian mixtures. *Neural Computation*, 8(1), Jan.

XU, L., HINTON, G. and JORDAN, M. I. (1995): An alternative model for mixtures of experts. In G. Tesauro et al., *Advances in Neural Information Processing Systems*, 7, 633–640, Cambridge MA, MIT Press.

A Bayesian Approach for the Estimation of the Covariance Structure of Separable Spatio-Temporal Stochastic Processes

Silvia Bozza[1] and Anthony O'Hagan[2]

[1] Dipartimento di Statistica,
Università di Venezia, I-30125 Venezia, Italy
[2] Department of Probability and Statistics
University of Sheffield, S3 7RH Sheffield, England

Abstract. In this paper, we address the problem of estimating the dependence structure of spatio-temporal stochastic processes. Starting from the assumption of separability, we propose a Bayesian semiparametric model that allows non-stationary spatial-temporal dependence structures. The model provides an estimation of the spatial and temporal covariance structures, with a hierarchical model internally to model the temporal dependence. A simulated case study is reported.

1 Introduction

Space-time models have gained an increasing popularity in the last decade, due partly to the growth in the environmental and health sciences, and partly to the increasing computational powers nowadays available. Data sets can be very large and difficult to handle, and substantial computational power is often required to fit even a very simple model. Many environmental processes involve variability over space and time. Such processes typically have complicated spatial structure, temporal structure and spatio-temporal interactions. Most of the literature on space-time modelling is motivated by specific applications and each model appears to be unique and to have little in common with others, but in general we can recognize two distinct ways of approaching a space-time problem: the prioritizing and the conjoint method. The prioritizing method models the spatial and temporal components separately: it begins by modelling one dimension and then making the parameters of that model depend on the coordinates of the other dimension (Waller *et. al.* (1997)). Prioritizing models are typically hierarchical. The conjoint method models the spatial and temporal components jointly, but modelling a massive joint covariance matrix can become very complicated. A rather common assumption is that of stationarity in time and isotropy in space. Many applications in fact are based on classes of stationary spatio-temporal covariance functions. The problem of inference is then greatly simplified, parametric models for the spatial and temporal domain (see for example Cressie (1993), Hamilton (1994)) allow forecasting at any location in space and time. Cressie and Huang (1999) starting from the statement of Bochner's theorem have proposed an analytic method to derive classes of stationary non-separable valid spatio-temporal covariance functions. Nevertheless, while there are heuristic arguments underlying assumptions of stationarity in time series, there is little reason to expect spatial covariance to be stationary over the spatial scales of interest. There are several proposals in the literature to solve this problem, but they generally involve only the spatial dimension, while we need to estimate the spatio-temporal covariance structure.

Separability or additivity of the spatial and temporal dimensions, when admissible, simplifies the model and greatly reduces the number of unknown parameters (Gneiting and Schlather (2001)). The hypothesis of separability in particular allows the spatial and temporal dimensions to be written as product of a purely spatial component and a purely temporal component, for which there are standard and flexible classes of models. Separability can be a strong assumption since it asserts that all the locations in space have the same temporal covariance structure, but we believe that separability can provide the possibility to define and estimate non-stationary spatio-temporal dependence structure. Our aim is to provide a new approach for the conjoint estimation of the spatio-temporal covariance. A Bayesian hierarchical model is proposed in section 2, while a specific application is presented on section 3. Experimental results are reported in section 4.

2   A Bayesian semi-parametric hierarchical model

Space-time data are often modelled as a realization of a spatio-temporal stochastic process $Y(\mathbf{s};t)$, indexed in space by $\mathbf{s} \in \mathbb{R}^d$ and in time by $t \in \mathbb{R}$. Now suppose we collect a sample from a Gaussian random process with separable dependence structure at S sites and T time instants, and unknown mean. Let Y be the $S \times T$ matrix of observations whose generic element is $y(\mathbf{s},t)$, i.e. the observation at site $\mathbf{s}$ and at time t, and let the matrix mean be MX, where M is a $S \times K$ matrix of unknown regression coefficients, while X is a $K \times T$ matrix of covariates. If we stack the columns of Y into a vector, then we can write $\mathbf{y} = \mathbf{vec}(\mathbf{Y}) = (\mathbf{y}_1', \dots \mathbf{y}_t')'$, in the same way we can stack the columns of M into a vector, $\mathbf{m} = \mathbf{vec}(\mathbf{M}) = (\mathbf{m}_1', \dots \mathbf{m}_k')'$. We have $E(\mathbf{y}) = (X' \otimes I_{s,s})\mathbf{m}$ and the assumption of separability corresponds to a covariance structure of the form $cov(\mathbf{y}, \mathbf{y}') = \Omega \otimes \Delta$, where Ω $(t \times t)$ is a purely temporal covariance component and Δ $(s \times s)$ is a purely spatial covariance component. Then Y has a matrix-normal distribution and the likelihood can be written as

$$\mathcal{L}(M, \Omega, \Delta \mid Y)$$

$$\propto \frac{1}{\mid \Omega \mid^{\frac{s}{2}} \mid \Delta \mid^{\frac{t}{2}}} \exp\left\{-\frac{1}{2}tr\left[\Omega^{-1}(Y - MX)'\Delta^{-1}(Y - MX)\right]\right\}. \quad (1)$$

We assume inverse Wishart prior densities for the unknown spatial and temporal covariance matrices, allowing them to take values in the space of all positive definite symmetric matrices. For the regression coefficients we assume a multivariate normal distribution. The Bayesian choice adopted guarantees the existence of proper posteriors, but with the drawback that they depend strongly on the prior assumptions, because of the large number of parameters to be estimated compared to the available observations.

The number of parameters can be reduced dramatically by imposing a specific temporal structure, for instance by assuming that the temporal covariance matrix Ω has a simple autoregressive form. Then we replace the $t(t-1)/2$ parameters of Ω by a small number of autoregressive parameters. However, in practice there will generally be uncertainty about whether such a model holds exactly. We therefore propose a hierarchical model in which Ω may take any positive-definite form but we have a prior expectation that it will be close to the form given by a specific time series model.

Let θ denote the parameters of the time series model. The expectation of the inverse Wishart prior for Ω is then defined conditionally on θ, the vector of second level hyper-parameters.

The joint posterior distribution can be then decomposed as:

$$p(M,\Delta,\Omega \mid Y) = \int_{\Theta} p(M,\Delta,\Omega \mid Y,\theta)p(\theta \mid Y)\mathrm{d}(\theta) \qquad (2)$$

where

$$p(M,\Delta,\Omega \mid Y,\theta) = \frac{f\,(Y \mid M,\Delta,\Omega)\,p\,(M,\Delta,\Omega \mid \theta)}{\int f\,(Y \mid M,\Delta,\Omega)\,p\,(M,\Delta,\Omega \mid \theta)\,\mathrm{d}(M,\Delta,\Omega)}$$

$$p(\theta \mid Y) = \frac{p(M,\Delta,\Omega \mid Y,\theta)p(\theta)}{\int p(M,\Delta,\Omega \mid Y,\theta)p(\theta)\mathrm{d}(\theta)}.$$

The hierarchical model allows an easy decomposition of the posterior distribution, with the drawback that it prevents an explicit derivation of the corresponding Bayes estimators, although the successive levels are conjugate, and therefore calls for numerical approximations.

3   An application with an autoregressive process of order 1

Let us consider a zero mean gaussian process and suppose that the temporal dependence structure is thought to be related to the autocovariance structure of a stationary autoregressive process of order 1 (Hamilton (1994)), denoted by AR(1). Consequently the scale matrix will be fully specified by two parameters: the autoregressive parameter ϕ and the innovation variance σ^2 of the AR(1) process. Thus $\theta = (\phi, \sigma^2)$. The spatial dependence is allowed to be anything, so we impose no further structure on Δ.

At the first level of the hierarchy we have:

$$\Delta \sim IW_s\,(R, n_\delta) \qquad (3)$$
$$\Omega \mid \phi, \sigma^2 \sim IW_t\,(T(\phi,\sigma^2), n_\omega) \qquad (4)$$

where R and $T(\phi, \sigma^2)$ are the scale matrices, with

$$T(\phi, \sigma^2) = (n_\omega - 2t - 2)\frac{\sigma^2}{1 - \phi^2}\begin{bmatrix} 1 & \phi & \dots & \phi^{t-1} \\ \phi & 1 & \dots & \dots \\ \dots & \dots & \dots & \dots \\ \phi^{t-1} & \dots & \dots & 1 \end{bmatrix},$$

so that $E(\Omega \mid \phi, \sigma^2)$ is the covariance matrix of the AR(1) process with parameters ϕ and σ^2. The degrees of freedom n_δ and n_ω specify the strength of prior information, and in particular we will set n_ω to a high value in order to reflect a prior belief that the temporal covariance structure will be close to that of an AR(1) process for some ϕ and σ^2.

The second level parameters are assumed to be independent. For the autoregressive parameter ϕ we specify $\phi = 2\eta - 1$, $\eta \sim Be(a, b)$, so that ϕ lies in the stationary region $|\phi| < 1$, with parameters a and b fixed in order to have a weak prior. The prior for the innovation variance σ^2 must naturally have positive domain, and we choose a Gamma distribution with fixed parameters α and β.

The joint posterior looks quite intractable:

$$p(\Delta, \Omega, \phi, \sigma^2 \mid Y) = f(Y \mid \Delta, \Omega)p(\Delta, \Omega \mid \phi, \sigma^2)\, p(\phi)p(\sigma^2) \qquad (5)$$

$$\propto \frac{1}{\mid \Delta \mid^{\frac{n_\delta + t}{2}}} \frac{\mid T(\phi, \sigma^2) \mid}{\mid \Omega \mid^{\frac{n_\omega + s}{2}}} \exp\left[-\frac{1}{2}tr\Omega^{-1}Y'\Delta^{-1}Y\right] \sigma^{2(\alpha - 1)}e^{-\beta\sigma^2}$$

$$\exp\left[-\frac{1}{2}tr\Delta^{-1}R - \frac{1}{2}tr\Omega^{-1}T(\phi, \sigma^2)\right]\left(\frac{\phi + 1}{2}\right)^{a-1}\left(\frac{1 - \phi}{2}\right)^{b-1}$$

so that we cannot obtain marginal posteriors analytically.

We need to employ Markov chain Monte Carlo techniques to determine the relevant posterior distributions. Since we have chosen Gaussian distributions with conjugate priors, the derivation and implementation of the full conditional distributions needed for the Gibbs sampling are, with one exception, quite straightforward. The full conditional distributions for Ω and Δ are inverse Wishart so we do not have any difficulties in sampling from them (Ripley (1997)):

$$\pi(\Delta \mid \Omega) = IW_s\left(R + Y\Omega^{-1}Y', n_\delta + t\right)$$
$$\pi(\Omega \mid \Delta, \phi, \sigma^2) = IW_t\left(T(\phi, \sigma^2) + Y'\Delta^{-1}Y, n_\omega + s\right).$$

The full conditional distribution of σ^2 is Gamma, and we can easily sample from it (Devroye (1986)). A general problem of MCMC is that proper prior densities can hide problems of model identifiability since the resulting posterior densities are proper. The hierarchical Bayesian model introduced is non-identifiable. In fact, given the Kronecker product structure of the joint covariance, if we multiply and then divide by a same positive constant, the product does not change: $\Omega \otimes \Delta = c\Omega \otimes c^{-1}\Delta$, $\forall c > 0$. A possible way to handle the problem of non-identifiability consists in introducing constraints on the covariance structure. Constraints on the diagonal of the spatial or temporal covariance matrix have been found to be effective (as for example fixing the first element of the diagonal equal to one). Nevertheless instead of constraining some elements of the covariance matrix we have decided to constrain the innovation variance σ^2 to be equal to one. The innovation variance is a second level parameter, so in this way we are not constraining an element of the covariance structure, but we are linking the temporal and the spatial component. Since we are interested in joint estimation, this constraint does not represent an excessive arbitrary choice.

The full conditional of the autoregressive parameter is more complicated, with the consequence that we are not able to sample directly from it. For this purpose we implement a random-walk Metropolis step. The candidate value for ϕ cannot be sampled from a normal distribution directly, since we need to respect the stationarity condition. We can, however, sample a value for the transformed variable

$$\psi = log\left(\frac{1+\phi}{1-\phi}\right) \qquad \phi \in (-1,1)$$

which is clearly defined over the interval $(-\infty, +\infty)$.
The candidate is then

$$\psi^{prop} \sim N(\psi^{curr}, \tau^2) \qquad \text{with } \psi^{curr} = log\left(\frac{1+\phi^{curr}}{1-\phi^{curr}}\right).$$

If the candidate is accepted then put

$$\phi^{curr} = \phi^{prop} = g^{-1}(\psi^{prop}) = \frac{\left(e^{\psi^{prop}} - 1\right)}{\left(1 + e^{\psi^{prop}}\right)}.$$

The proposal variance τ^2 must be chosen carefully as it determines the acceptance rate, on which depends the success of the method. If the variance is too large, an extremely large proportion of iterations will be rejected and the algorithm will therefore be inefficient. Conversely if the variance is too small, the random walk will accept nearly all proposed moves but will move around the space slowly and it will therefore take many iterations to converge (Gilks et. al. (1996)).

The Gibbs sampling can be applied in a straightforward way, with the only complication being the Metropolis-Hastings step. Until convergence is achieved it proceeds as follows:

i) sample $\Omega_{(i)}$ from $IW\left(Y'\Delta_{(i-1)}Y + T(\phi_{(i-1)}, \sigma^2)\right)$ with $(n_\omega + s)$ d.f.;
ii) sample $\Delta_{(i)}$ from $IW\left(Y\Omega_{(i)}Y' + R\right)$ with $(n_\delta + t)$ d.f.;

iii) implement a Metropolis-Hastings step in order to generate a candidate for $\phi_{(i)}$, denoted ϕ^{prop}, which will be accepted with a probability given by the Metropolis ratio

$$\alpha\left(\psi^{curr}, \psi^{prop}\right) = min\left\{1, \frac{\pi(\psi^{prop} \mid \psi^{curr})}{\pi(\psi^{curr} \mid \psi^{prop})}\right\}$$

where $\pi(\psi) = \left|\frac{d}{d\psi}g^{-1}(\psi)\right|\pi\left(g^{-1}(\psi)\right)$.

4 Results

We have simulated a data set with separable spatio-temporal structure, with $i = 12$ locations located over a regular grid on the space, at each of which data are collected at $j = 100$ equally-spaced time points. The temporal dependence structure is thought to be related to that of an AR(1) process with $\phi = 0.7$, $\sigma^2 = 1$, while the scale matrix R is chosen assuming that the spatial covariance is dependent on distance. The degrees of freedom of the Wishart distributions are respectively $n_\delta = 36$, $n_\omega = 300$. The parameters of the Beta are fixed to be $a = 1.5$, $b = 1.5$, while for the Gamma we have fixed $\alpha = 3.5$, $\beta = 3.5$. The variance of the proposal τ^2 has been fixed equal to 0.05.

We ran different simulations with different starting points. Visual assessment of the simulations suggested that all parameters have converged. We then ran a single long chain (20000 iterations), with a burn-in of 10000 iterations. Results of the Gibbs-sampler algorithm are given in Table 1. For the temporal and spatial covariance matrix we have decided to represent the norm between the theoretical value, Δ_{th} and Ω_{th}, and the prior and the posterior mean respectively. The M-H showed a rate of acceptance around 30-35%. The estimated posterior mean of ϕ is 0.6912, and the trace-plot and autocorrelation plot generated suggest convergence. The trace-plot for the spatial covariance matrix, Fig. 3, and the temporal covariance matrix, Fig. 4, and the relative autocorrelations that drop out after a few iterations, Figg. 5 and 6, also suggest we have achieved convergence.

Model parameter	True value	Prior mean	MCMC post mean	Standard error
ϕ	0.7	0	0.6912	1.5332e-006
$\|\Delta_{th} - \Delta\|/\|\Delta_{th}\|$	-	0.1010	0.0503	2.0011e-005
$\|\Omega_{th} - \Omega\|/\|\Omega_{th}\|$	-	0.9094	0.2591	1.0839e-005

Table 1. Gibbs-sampler results.

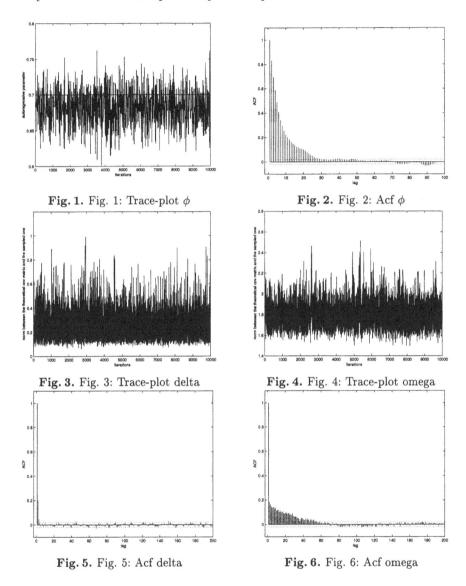

Fig. 1. Fig. 1: Trace-plot ϕ

Fig. 2. Fig. 2: Acf ϕ

Fig. 3. Fig. 3: Trace-plot delta

Fig. 4. Fig. 4: Trace-plot omega

Fig. 5. Fig. 5: Acf delta

Fig. 6. Fig. 6: Acf omega

5   Conclusions

The approach proposed has been found effective in estimating the spatial and the temporal dependence structure jointly, without assuming either isotropy in space or stationarity in time. The model proposed can obviously be applied for processes of higher order: the full conditional distributions of the second level parameters will be more complicated, but we can still define a Metropolis-Hastings step which allows us to draw a sample from them. It is clear that as the observations in time grow, the number of parameters to estimate increases, but the hierarchical structure concentrates the distribution of Ω near a space of small dimension. In practice, sampling from a very high-dimensional inverted Wishart distribution will be computationally onerous. However, by utilizing efficient algorithms for the inversion of matrices, significant speed improvements can be realized. We believe that this approach might represent an important investigative tool. In particular, the non-parametric estimation of the spatial covariance might suggest anisotropy in the space, and so indicate a spatial deformation approach. Furthermore, a spatio-temporal analysis can provide benefits not possible from a spatial only-approach.

References

CRESSIE, NOEL A.C. (1993): *Statistics for spatial data*, Wiley, N.Y., revised edition.

CRESSIE, NOEL A.C. (1999): Classes of nonseparable spatio-temporal stationary covariance functions. *J. Amer. Statist. Soc.* 94, 448, 1330-1340

DEVROYE, L. (1986): *Non-Uniform random variate generation*, Springer Verlag.

GILKS, W.R. and RICHARDSON, S. and SPIEGELHALTER, D.J. (1996): *Markov chain Monte Carlo in practice*, Chapman & Hall.

GNEITING, T. and SCHLATER, M. (2001): Space-time covariance models. In: *Encyclopedia of Environmetrics*. New York, Wiley.

HAMILTON, J.D. (1994): *Time series analysis*, Princeton University Press, New Jersey.

RIPLEY, B. (1987): *Stochastic simulation*, Wiley, N.Y.

WALLER, L.A. and CARLIN, B.P. and HONG, Xia and GELFAND, A.E. (1997): Hierarchical spatio-temporal mapping of disease rates. *J. Amer. Statist. Soc.*, 92, 438, 607-617.

An Algorithm for the HICLAS-R Model

Eva Ceulemans and Iven Van Mechelen

Department of Psychology
Katholieke Universiteit Leuven, B-3000 Leuven, Belgium

Abstract. The HICLAS-R model is a model for two-way two-mode rating data, that includes a hierarchical classification of the elements of each mode and a linking structure among the two hierarchies. In this paper, we present an algorithm for fitting HICLAS-R models, based on a recoding of the two-way two-mode rating data into three-way three-mode binary data. The performance of the algorithm is evaluated in an extensive simulation study.

1 Introduction

Hierarchical classes models are models for N-way N-mode data, that include N linked hierarchical classifications of the elements of the N modes. Although originally developed for the modelling of binary data [i.e., two-way two-mode HICLAS (De Boeck and Rosenberg, 1988); three-way three-mode INDCLAS (Leenen, Van Mechelen, De Boeck and Rosenberg, 1999), Tucker3-HICLAS (Ceulemans, Van Mechelen and Leenen, in press) and Tucker2-HICLAS (Ceulemans and Van Mechelen, 2002)], Van Mechelen, Lombardi and Ceulemans (2002) recently extended the hierarchical classes approach to rating data (HICLAS-R). In this paper we present an algorithm for fitting a HICLAS-R model based on a recoding of the two-way two-mode rating data into three-way three-mode binary data. Furthermore, the HICLAS-R algorithm is evaluated in an extensive simulation study.

The remainder of this manuscript is organized as follows: Section 2 briefly recapitulates the HICLAS-R model. In Section 3, the HICLAS-R algorithm is described. Section 4 discusses the results of an extensive simulation study. Section 5 contains some concluding remarks.

2 The HICLAS-R model

A HICLAS-R model approximates an $I \times J$ object by attribute rating data matrix $\mathbf{D}$, with entries taking values from a data value set $\{0, 1, \ldots, V\}$, by an $I \times J$ rating model matrix $\mathbf{M}$, with entries taking values from a model value set that contains 0 and R different values from the set $\{1, 2, \ldots, V\}$. As a guiding example in this section we will make use of the matrices $\mathbf{D}$ and $\mathbf{M}$ presented in Table 1; the data value set consists of the integers 0 through 4, the model value set of the integers 0, 2 and 4.

A HICLAS-R model represents two types of relations in $\mathbf{M}$: (1) quasi orders $\preceq$ among the elements of each mode, and (2) an association relation between the two modes.

	D						M				
	a_1	a_2	a_3	a_4	a_5		a_1	a_2	a_3	a_4	a_5
o_1	0	0	4	4	0	o_1	0	0	4	4	0
o_2	0	0	4	4	0	o_2	0	0	4	4	0
o_3	1	2	2	2	0	o_3	2	2	2	2	0
o_4	2	2	4	4	0	o_4	2	2	4	4	0
o_5	2	2	4	3	0	o_5	2	2	4	4	0
o_6	4	4	4	4	0	o_6	4	4	4	4	0

Table 1. Hypothetical matrices **D** and **M**.

(1) A quasi order $\preceq$ is defined on each mode of **M**. In particular, object $i \preceq$ object i' iff $\mathbf{M}_{i.} \leq \mathbf{M}_{i'.}$. Similarly, attribute $j \preceq$ attribute j' iff $\mathbf{M}_{.j} \leq \mathbf{M}_{.j'}$. Note that the quasi order implies a hierarchical classification of the objects (attributes) in that objects (attributes) with identical rows $\mathbf{M}_{i.}$ (columns $\mathbf{M}_{.j}$) constitute object (attribute) classes; furthermore, the classes can be hierarchically organized in terms of the strict order relations $<$ among the corresponding rows (columns) of **M**. For example, from Table 1 appears $\mathbf{M}_{4.} = \mathbf{M}_{5.}$; therefore, o_4 and o_5 constitute an object class. Furthermore, the latter class is hierarchically higher than $\{o_3\}$, since $\mathbf{M}_{3.} < \mathbf{M}_{4.}$.

(2) The association relation is the mapping defined by the entries in **M**, which maps each (object, attribute) pair onto the corresponding value in the model value set. For example, as appears from Table 1, in **M** o_3 is associated with a_1 with association strength 2.

A rank (P,Q,R) HICLAS-R model decomposes **M** into an $I \times P$ binary matrix **A**, a $J \times Q$ binary matrix **B** and a $P \times Q$ rating matrix **G**, with entries that take values from the model value set. For example, Table 2 shows a rank $(3,2,2)$ HICLAS-R model for the model matrix **M** of Table 1.

	A				B			G	
	$\mathbf{A}_{.1}$	$\mathbf{A}_{.2}$	$\mathbf{A}_{.3}$		$\mathbf{B}_{.1}$	$\mathbf{B}_{.2}$		$\mathbf{B}_{.1}$	$\mathbf{B}_{.2}$
o_1	1	0	0	a_1	0	1	$\mathbf{A}_{.1}$	4	0
o_2	1	0	0	a_2	0	1	$\mathbf{A}_{.2}$	0	2
o_3	0	1	0	a_3	1	1	$\mathbf{A}_{.3}$	0	4
o_4	1	1	0	a_4	1	1			
o_5	1	1	0	a_5	0	0			
o_6	0	0	1						

Table 2. Rank $(3,2,2)$ HICLAS-R model for **M** in Table 1.

A, **B** and **G** represent the quasi orders and the association relation as follows:

(1) The quasi order among the objects is represented in **A** in that $i \preceq i'$ iff $\mathbf{A}_{i.} \leq \mathbf{A}_{i'.}$. Similarly, the quasi order among the attributes is represented in

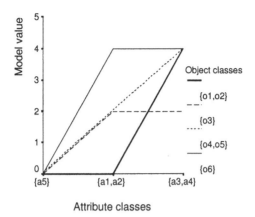

Fig. 1. Graphical representation of the HICLAS-R model matrix **M** of Table 1.

B in that $j \preceq j'$ iff $\mathbf{B}_{j.} \leq \mathbf{B}_{j'.}$. With respect to the hierarchical classification of the objects (attributes), the latter implies that elements of the same object (attribute) class have identical rows in **A** (**B**), and that the hierarchical organization of the classes is represented in terms of $<$ relations among the rows of **A** (**B**). For example, in Table 1, o_4 and o_5, which constitute an object class, have identical rows in **A**, $\mathbf{A}_{4.} = \mathbf{A}_{5.}$. Furthermore, the latter class is hierarchically higher than the class $\{o_3\}$, since $\mathbf{A}_{3.} < \mathbf{A}_{4.}$.

(2) The association relation in **M** is represented by **A**, **B** and **G** as follows:

$$m_{ij} = \max_{p=1...P} \max_{q=1...Q} a_{ip} b_{jq} g_{pq}. \tag{1}$$

For example, from Table 2 one may derive that o_3 is associated with a_1 with association strength 2. Note that by the representation of the association relation, the model matrix **M** may be fully reconstructed from the HICLAS-R model.

A HICLAS-R model can be given a graphical representation from which one may derive the association relation between the object and attribute classes. As an example, one may read from Figure 1, which graphically represents the HICLAS-R model of Table 2, that the object class $\{o_4, o_5\}$ and the attribute class $\{a_1, a_2\}$ are associated with association strength 2.

3   Algorithm

Given a rating data matrix **D** and a rank (P,Q,R), the HICLAS-R algorithm aims at finding a rating model matrix **M**, that can be represented by a (P,Q,R) HICLAS-R model and that minimizes the loss function

$$L = \sum_{i=1}^{I} \sum_{j=1}^{J} |d_{ij} - m_{ij}|. \tag{2}$$

The latter goal is achieved by successively executing three main routines: In the *first main routine* (R_1), the $I \times J$ rating data matrix $\mathbf{D}$ is recoded into an $I \times J \times V$ binary data array $t(\mathbf{D})$ as follows:

$$t(\mathbf{D})_{ijv} = \begin{cases} 1 & \text{if} \quad d_{ij} \geq v \\ 0 & \text{otherwise} \end{cases}. \tag{3}$$

Note that the latter recoding implies that the value planes of $t(\mathbf{D})$ inversely reflect the natural order on the values:

$$v \leq v' \Leftrightarrow t(\mathbf{D})_{..v} \geq t(\mathbf{D})_{..v'}. \tag{4}$$

In the *second main routine* (R_2), the algorithm looks for an $I \times J \times V$ binary model array $\underline{\mathbf{M}}'$ that minimizes

$$L = \sum_{i=1}^{I} \sum_{j=1}^{J} \sum_{v=1}^{V} |t(\mathbf{D})_{ijv} - m'_{ijv}| \tag{5}$$

and that can be decomposed into an $I \times P$ binary matrix $\mathbf{A}$, a $J \times Q$ binary matrix $\mathbf{B}$, a $V \times R$ binary matrix $\mathbf{C}$ and a $P \times Q \times R$ binary array $\underline{\mathbf{G}}'$, making use of the following decomposition rule:

$$m'_{ijv} = \bigoplus_{p=1}^{P} \bigoplus_{q=1}^{Q} \bigoplus_{r=1}^{R} a_{ip} b_{jq} c_{vr} g'_{pqr}, \tag{6}$$

where $\bigoplus$ denotes the Boolean sum. Furthermore, $\mathbf{A}$ and $\mathbf{B}$ are restricted to represent the quasi orders among the objects and attributes and $\mathbf{C}$ is constrained to inversely represent the natural order on the values:

$$v \leq v' \Leftrightarrow \mathbf{C}_{v.} \geq \mathbf{C}_{v'.}. \tag{7}$$

Finally, in the *third main routine* (R_3), $\mathbf{C}$ and $\underline{\mathbf{G}}'$ are combined into the rating matrix $\mathbf{G}$ as follows:

$$g_{pq} = \max_{r=1...R} g'_{pqr} \sum_{v=1}^{V} c_{vr}. \tag{8}$$

Van Mechelen et al. (2002) proved that the matrices $\mathbf{A}$, $\mathbf{B}$ yielded by the second routine, and $\mathbf{G}$ as obtained from the third routine, constitute a (P,Q,R) HICLAS-R model with model matrix $\mathbf{M}$ that minimizes (2).

In the following paragraphs, we will discuss the second main routine, R_2, in more detail. R_2 consists of two subroutines: $R_{2.1}$ and $R_{2.2}$.

$R_{2.1}$ starts from an initial configuration for $\mathbf{A}$, $\mathbf{B}$ and $\mathbf{C}$. Such an initial configuration may be obtained by performing (a) INDCLAS analyses (Leenen et al., 1999) on $t(\mathbf{D})$ in ranks P, Q and R; and (b) HICLAS analyses (De Boeck et al., 1988) on the matricized $I \times JV$, $J \times IV$ and $V \times IJ$ binary data array $t(\mathbf{D})$ in ranks P, Q and R, respectively. The INDCLAS as well as the HICLAS analyses yield an $I \times P$ binary matrix $\mathbf{A}$, a $J \times Q$ binary matrix $\mathbf{B}$, and a $V \times R$ binary matrix $\mathbf{C}$ (in general, the latter 'rational' initial configurations yield HICLAS-R models with lower values on the loss function (5) than random initial configurations). Starting from an initial configuration for $\mathbf{A}$, $\mathbf{B}$ and $\mathbf{C}$, $R_{2.1}$ alternatingly optimizes $\mathbf{A}$, $\mathbf{B}$, $\mathbf{C}$ and $\underline{\mathbf{G}}'$, conditional upon all the others. Since an update of $\mathbf{A}$, $\mathbf{B}$, $\mathbf{C}$ or $\underline{\mathbf{G}}'$ is only retained if it yields a lower value on the loss function (5) than the previous estimate of the array under consideration, $R_{2.1}$ continues until no updating of $\mathbf{A}$, $\mathbf{B}$, $\mathbf{C}$ or $\underline{\mathbf{G}}'$ further improves (5). Hence, $R_{2.1}$ always converges in a finite number of steps to at least a local minimum.

As in the other hierarchical classes algorithms, $\mathbf{A}$, $\mathbf{B}$ and $\underline{\mathbf{G}}'$ are optimized by means of Boolean regression (Leenen and Van Mechelen, 1998); note that in (5) the contribution of each row of $\mathbf{A}$ (resp. $\mathbf{B}$) can be separated from the contribution of the other rows, which implies that $\mathbf{A}$ (resp. $\mathbf{B}$) can be optimized through a separate Boolean regression for each row. To optimize $\mathbf{C}$ subject to the constraint (7), the following novel estimation procedure is used: First, row $\mathbf{C}_{1.}$ is optimized; subsequently, rows $\mathbf{C}_{2.}$ to $\mathbf{C}_{V.}$ are consecutively optimized under the restriction that $\mathbf{C}_{v.} \leq \mathbf{C}_{(v-1).}$. The optimal rows $\mathbf{C}_{v.}$ are found by enumerating and evaluating all alternatives.

Regarding $R_{2.2}$, the $\mathbf{A}$ and $\mathbf{B}$ that are obtained at the end of $R_{2.1}$ are not restricted to represent the quasi orders among the objects and attributes. Therefore, in $R_{2.2}$, $\mathbf{A}$ and $\mathbf{B}$ are transformed (without altering the value on the loss function) so as to make them represent the quasi orders correctly. As in all hierarchical classes algorithms, $R_{2.2}$ boils down to applying a closure operation to $\mathbf{A}$ and $\mathbf{B}$ (see, De Boeck and Rosenberg, 1988).

4   Simulation study

In this section we present a simulation study in which the HICLAS-R algorithm is evaluated with respect to goodness of fit (i.e., how well succeeds the algorithm in minimizing the loss function) and goodness of recovery (i.e., how well succeeds the algorithm in recovering the underlying truth, that is, the true HICLAS-R relations as manipulated and known by the simulation researcher).

4.1   Design and procedure

Three different types of $I \times J$ rating matrices are involved in the evaluation of the algorithm: a true matrix $\mathbf{T}$, which can be perfectly represented by a (P,Q,R) HICLAS-R model; a data matrix $\mathbf{D}$, which is $\mathbf{T}$ perturbed with error; and the model matrix $\mathbf{M}$ that results from a (P,Q,R) HICLAS-R analysis of $\mathbf{D}$.

Three parameters were systematically varied in a complete trifactorial design:

(a) the *Size*, $I \times J \times V$, of the recoded binary data array $t(\mathbf{D})$, at 3 levels: $15 \times 15 \times 15$, $30 \times 20 \times 10$, $60 \times 30 \times 20$;
(b) the *True rank*, (P,Q,R), of the HICLAS-R model for $\mathbf{T}$, at 23 levels: (2,2,2), (2,2,3), (2,2,4), (2,3,2), (2,3,3), (2,3,4), (2,3,5), (2,4,2), (2,4,3), (2,4,4), (2,4,5), (3,3,2), (3,3,3), (3,3,4), (3,3,5), (4,3,2), (4,3,3), (4,3,4), (4,3,5), (4,4,2), (4,4,3), (4,4,4), (4,4,5);
(c) the *Error level*, ε, which is defined as

$$\varepsilon = \frac{\sum_{i=1}^{I} \sum_{j=1}^{J} |t_{ij} - d_{ij}|}{IJV}, \tag{9}$$

at 7 levels: .00, .05, .10, .15, .20, .25, .30.

For each combination of Size, True rank, and Error level, 20 true matrices $\mathbf{T}$ were constructed by (1) randomly generating the binary entries of $\mathbf{A}$ and $\mathbf{B}$, with in this and all following random procedures making use of discrete uniform distributions; (2) randomly selecting each entry of $\mathbf{G}$ from a randomly chosen model value set; (3) combining $\mathbf{A}$, $\mathbf{B}$ and $\mathbf{G}$ by (1) into $\mathbf{T}$. Next, a data matrix $\mathbf{D}$ was constructed from each true matrix $\mathbf{T}$ in the following way: (1) randomly select an entry of $\mathbf{D}$ which value v was not yet changed; (2) randomly determine whether the entry will be increased or decreased; (3) randomly choose the new value of the selected entry out of the set $(v+1,\ldots,V)$ in case of an increase and out of the set $(0,\ldots,v-1)$ in case of a decrease. This procedure was repeated until ε equalled the Error level. On each of the resulting data matrices a HICLAS-R analysis in the True rank was performed.

4.2   Goodness of fit

To study how well the HICLAS-R algorithm succeeds in minimizing the loss function (2), the following badness-of-fit (BOF) statistic was used:

$$BOF = \frac{\sum_{i=1}^{I} \sum_{j=1}^{J} |d_{ij} - m_{ij}|}{IJV}. \tag{10}$$

The mean value of $BOF - \varepsilon$ across the 9660 observations amounts to -.012. As the Error level ε reflects the distance between the data and the truth, the latter implies that, on the average, the algorithm succeeds in finding a model that is at least as close to the data as the truth is. An analysis of variance with $BOF - \varepsilon$ as the dependent variable yielded intraclass correlations $\hat{\rho}_I$ (Haggard, 1958) of .63 and .08 for the main effects of Error level and Size: The higher ε and the smaller the Size, the easier it is for the algorithm to find a model that is closer to the data than the truth is. Furthermore, the Size $\times$ Error level interaction $(\hat{\rho}_I = .08)$ has to be taken in account, indicating that

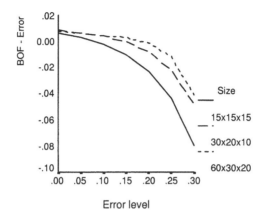

Fig. 2. Mean $(BOF - \varepsilon)$-values at levels of Error and Size.

the effect of Error level increases with smaller Size (See Figure 2). In this and the following analyses of variance only effects accounting for at least 5% of the variance of the dependent variable will be considered (i.e., $\hat{\rho}_I \geq .5$).

4.3   Goodness of recovery

Goodness of recovery will be evaluated with respect to (1) the quasi orders $\preceq$ among the objects and attributes and (2) the association relation.

(1) To measure the recovery of the quasi orders $\preceq$, we define the object quasi order matrix associated with $\mathbf{M}$ (resp. $\mathbf{T}$) as the $I \times I$ binary matrix $\mathbf{U}^M$ (resp. $\mathbf{U}^T$), with $u_{ii'}^M = 1$ (resp. $u_{ii'}^T = 1$) iff $i \preceq i'$ in $\mathbf{M}$ (resp. $\mathbf{T}$). Subsequently, the proportion of discrepancies between $\mathbf{U}^T$ and $\mathbf{U}^M$ was calculated yielding a badness-of-quasi-order-recovery $(BOQOR)$ statistic for the objects:

$$BOQOR = \frac{\sum\limits_{i=1}^{I} \sum\limits_{i'=1}^{I} \left(u_{ii'}^T - u_{ii'}^M\right)^2}{I^2}.$$

Similarly, a $BOQOR$ statistic for the attributes was defined. A weighted average of the two statistics (weighted by the number of elements in each mode), denoted $c\text{-}BOQOR$, was calculated and used in the following analyses.

The mean value on $c\text{-}BOQOR$ across the 9660 observations amounts to .172, implying that, on average, 82.8% of the true quasi orders are recovered. An analysis of variance with $c\text{-}BOQOR$ as the dependent variable shows main effects of True rank $(\hat{\rho}_I = .10)$ and Error level $(\hat{\rho}_I = .63)$: the higher the Error level and the higher (P,Q), the lower the $c\text{-}BOQOR$ (See Figures 3 and 4, respectively).

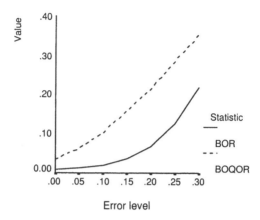

Fig. 3. Mean BOR and $c - BOQOR$-values at levels of Error.

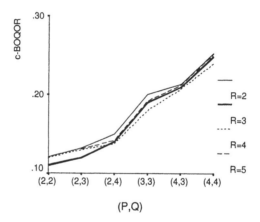

Fig. 4. Mean $c - BOQOR$-values at levels of True rank (P,Q,R).

(2) To assess the badness of recovery of the association relation (BOR) the following statistic was used:

$$BOR = \frac{\sum\limits_{i=1}^{I} \sum\limits_{j=1}^{J} |t_{ij} - m_{ij}|}{IJV}. \tag{11}$$

The mean BOR across the 9660 observations equals .069, implying that the model yielded by the algorithm differs on average 6.9% from the underlying truth. An analysis of variance with BOR as the dependent variable yields a huge main effect of Error level ($\hat{\rho}_I = .85$): Figure 3 clearly shows that the recovery of the association relation deteriorates with higher Error levels. However, except for errorfree data, these mean BOR levels are smaller than the corresponding value of ε, indicating that the model yielded by the algorithm is closer to the truth than the data are.

5 Conclusions

In this paper, we proposed an algorithm for fitting a HICLAS-R model based on a recoding of the two-way two-mode rating data into three-way three-mode binary data. A simulation study was conducted to evaluate the performance of this algorithm. The simulation results suggest that the algorithm succeeds reasonably well in minimizing the loss function, as it seldom yields a model that fits the data worse than the underlying truth. With respect to the recovery of the underlying truth, it was found that the models yielded by the algorithm are considerably closer to the underlying truth than the data are. Both goodness of fit and goodness of recovery were mainly influenced by the amount of error in the data: In particular, the greater the amount of error, the easier it is for the algorithm to find a solution that is closer to the data than the underlying truth is, but the harder it is to recover the underlying true HICLAS-R relations.

References

CEULEMANS, E. and VAN MECHELEN, I. (2002): *Tucker2 hierarchical classes analysis.* Manuscript submitted for publication.

CEULEMANS, E., VAN MECHELEN, I., and LEENEN, I. (in press): Tucker3 hierarchical classes analysis. *Psychometrika.*

DE BOECK, P., and ROSENBERG, S. (1988): Hierarchical classes: Model and data analysis. *Psychometrika, 53, 361–381.*

HAGGARD, E.A. (1958): *Intraclass correlation and the analysis of variance.* Dryden, New York.

LEENEN, I. and VAN MECHELEN, I. (1998): A branch-and-bound algorithm for Boolean regression. In: I. Balderjahn, R.Mathar and M. Schader (Eds.): *Data highways and information flooding, a challenge for classification and data analysis.* Springer, Berlin, 164–171.

LEENEN, I., VAN MECHELEN, I., DE BOECK, P., and ROSENBERG S. (1999): INDCLAS: A three-way hierarchical classes model. *Psychometrika, 64, 9–24.*

VAN MECHELEN, I., LOMBARDI, L., and CEULEMANS, E. (2002): *Hierarchical Classes Modeling of Rating Data.* Manuscript submitted for publication.

Some Applications of Time-Varying Coefficient Models to Count Data

Monica Chiogna and Carlo Gaetan

Dipartimento di Scienze Statistiche,
Università di Padova, I-35121 Padova, Italy

Abstract. In this work, we discuss usefulness of time-varying coefficients models in Environmental Epidemiology. In this context, data mostly consist of counts recording events in time or in space-time. Temporal or spatio-temporal dependence is generally treated as nuisance. By making use of two real data examples, we illustrate that time-varying coefficients models can provide a unifying framework to take appropriately account of the dependence structure of the data.

1 Introduction

The aim of this paper is to explore the potential of the time-varying coefficients modelling approach to tackle the modelling tasks typically approached in Environmental Epidemiology.

We will illustrate our points by making use of two case studies: the analysis of the relationship between daily non accidental deaths and air pollution in the city of Birmingham (Alabama) in the period 1985–1988 and the analysis of measles epidemics in London from 1960 to 1970. Each of the examples concerns problems for which a large literature has been developed; we shall only give major references here, while focusing on the unifying features of the examples.

In the next section we introduce the practical examples that we will consider in the following analyses. In Section 3 we introduce the modelling framework and discuss methods for inferences. Section 4 presents our modelling strategies and Section 5 presents the results that we obtained. Finally, we discuss some advantages of the general approach.

2 Two motivating examples

Modelling effects of air pollution on human health. We will consider the relationship between mortality and air pollution for the city of Birmingham, Alabama, in the period January 1, 1985 through December 31, 1988. This relationship was extensively analyzed in the literature (see Smith *et al.* (2000) and references therein for a survey of previous analyses), which reports some controversial results about significance of the association between particulate matter and mortality. Our analysis is based on the same dataset as Smith *et al.* (2000); we refer to the authors for a detailed description of the variables included in the dataset and of their construction.

Figure 1 shows the time series of daily counts for the study period. For exploratory purposes, the loess smoothed series of PM10 concentrations has been added to the plot. It appears that there is seasonality in the mortality series, although periodicity is not regular and that there is not a clear correlation between the behaviour of PM10 and mortality.

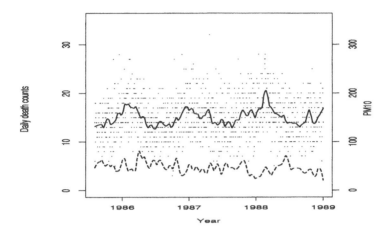

Fig. 1. Time series of the observed daily death counts along with the loess smoother of the counts (solid line) and of the PM10 (μg/m^3) values (dotted line).

Modelling infectious diseases. Measles is probably one of the most studied human diseases from the point of view of epidemiological dynamics. The development of models for behaviour of infectious diseases and epidemic has principally been focused on stochastic theoretical models (see, for example, Anderson and May (1992)), which, although stimulating, often rely on simplifying assumptions. The comprehension of the spatio-temporal dynamics might be helped by the construction of statistical models which might throw some insight into the interactions between space and time.

The dataset that we will use comprises weekly observations on the reported number of childhood measles cases in the 29 metropolitan boroughs of London over a ten years period from 1960. Figure 2 shows the spatio-temporal spread of the disease for one of the main epidemics. It appears that the disease starts in the North and then propagates to the East and next it moves to the South before fading away. In general, at the peak of all five epidemics, it is possible to see that there is a cluster of boroughs in the South of London which are all highly infected. In non-epidemic time periods, sites seem to behave independently from one another, showing low coupling.

Start of the outbreak   Main epidemic grows

Peak of epidemic   Epidemic fades away

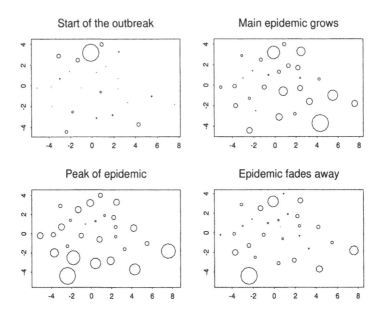

Fig. 2. Spatio-temporal plot of the epidemics at four time points. Radii of the circles are proportional to the number of infected people at the chosen time points.

3   A general framework

Model description. Consider a series of counts $\{Y(t,s), t = 1, \ldots, T, \ s \in S \subset \mathbb{R}^2\}$ where s denotes a spatial location, and a vector of covariates $x(t,s)$. At each time t we suppose that:

1. $\lambda(t,s)$ is a Gaussian random field with $\mathrm{E}[\lambda(t,s)] = \mu(t,s)$, and $\mathrm{Cov}[\lambda(t,s), \lambda(t,s')] = \sigma(t, t', s - s')$,
2. conditionally on $\lambda(t,s)$, $Y(t,s)$ is a Poisson random variable with expectation $\exp\{\lambda(t,s)\}$. We denote $Y(t,s)|\lambda(t,s) \sim \mathcal{P}(\exp\{\lambda(t,s)\})$.

Then, assume that it is reasonable to divide the vector of covariates into two components $x(t,s) = (x_1'(t,s), x_2'(t,s))'$, where the first component, $x_1(t,s)$, includes covariates which we expect to contribute to the latent mean tendency of the counts and the second component, $x_2(t,s)$, includes perturbing factors, whose influence can be thought of as being constant over space and time. If the central tendency of the counts may be thought of as resulting from the influence of both types of covariates, then it is reasonable to model the effect of $x_1(t,s)$ by a random process $\phi(t,s) = \phi(x_1(t,s))$ and to treat the effects of $x_2(t,s)$ as ordinary fixed effects. Therefore, we might employ the following specification: $\lambda(t,s) = \phi(t,s) + x_2'(t,s)\beta_2$, with β_2 representing the unknown regression coefficients for $x_2(t,s)$.

To the random process $\phi(t,s)$ is assigned the role of governing the temporal, spatial, spatio-temporal dependence shown by $Y(t,s)$. Therefore, it can take on different specifications, according to the degree of complexity of the phenomenon under study. In many applications, we only have to deal with temporal dependence. In the simplest of these cases, $\phi(t,s)$ includes only a random temporal trend. Simple random trend models are for example random walks of first–order: $\phi(t,s) = \omega(t)$, $\omega(t) = \omega(t-1) + \delta(t)$, where $\delta(t)$ is an independent Gaussian random variable, i.e. $\delta(t) \sim N(\mu_\delta, \sigma_\delta^2)$, or of second–order: $\omega(t) = 2\omega(t-1) - \omega(t-2) + \delta(t)$. According to the second formulation, $\phi(t,s)$ is the discrete version of a spline for a trend component.

In more complex situations, the random process includes also some temporal covariates. A simple model with one covariate $x_1(t)$ is: $\phi(t,s) = \omega(t) + \gamma(t)x_1(t)$, where $\omega(t)$ is a second order random walk as defined above, $\gamma(t) = \gamma(t-1) + \xi(t)$ and $\xi(t) \sim N(\mu_\xi, \sigma_\xi^2)$ is a Gaussian random variable uncorrelated with $\delta(t)$. In this formulation, the coefficient of $x_1(t)$ varies dynamically in time. This is a crucial aspect of the model. Firstly, it is possible to express long term changes in the effects of the covariates. Secondly, the dynamic on the coefficients captures the "carry-over" effect of the covariates which usually causes the effect at time t to be influenced by covariates at previous times. This seems of extreme relevance for the applications that we consider.

In the most general settings, we need to cope with spatio-temporal dependencies. In these cases, the random process $\phi(t,s)$ needs to include terms allowing interactions between space and time. This can be achieved by inserting information about the underlying spatial structure of the data and allowing temporal changes in this structure by making use of time varying coefficients. Following Mardia *et al.* (1998), we represent the spatial structure of the data by making use of surfaces $h_i(s)$, $i = 1, \ldots, q$, called spatial fields, estimated via Kriging techniques. Once the spatial fields have been estimated, they can be combined in a linear time-varying combination, which is then inserted into $\phi(s,t)$. We might for example insert spatio-temporal dependence in the model previously defined as follows: $\phi(t,s) = \omega(t) + \gamma(t)x_1(t) + \sum_{i=1}^{q} \beta_i(t)h_i(s)$, where the coefficients $\beta_i(t)$, $i = 1, \ldots, q$ are first or second order random walks.

The previous settings fall into the general framework of varying coefficients models (Hastie and Tibshirani, 1993). In our applications, we make use of time-varying coefficients (TVCs) models that relate the series $\{Y(t,s), t = 1, \ldots, T, s \in S\}$, to a sequence of unobservable states or parameters $\alpha(t) \in R^n$ on the extended time periods $t = 0, \ldots, T$. The relationship is given by an observation model

$$Y(t,s)|\alpha(t) \sim \exp\{\lambda(t,s)y(t,s) - \exp(\lambda(t,s))\}/y(t,s)!, \qquad (1)$$

with $\lambda(t,s) = z'(t,s)\alpha(t)$.

The observation model is supplemented by a Gaussian transition model

$$\alpha(t)|\alpha(t-1) \sim \mathcal{N}(F(t)\alpha(t-1), Q), \qquad (2)$$

with known transition matrix $F(t)$ and Q diagonal matrix. In a Bayesian setting, equations (1) and (2) define the two first stages of a hierarchical model. In the last stage of the hierarchy, priors for the hyperparameters have to be chosen. In our applications, we choose diffuse prior for $\alpha(0)$, i.e $\alpha(0) \sim \mathcal{N}(0, kI)$ with large k, and hyperpriors for the p unknown entries of Q, $\psi_1, \ldots, \psi_p$, are inverse gamma distributions, i.e. $\psi_i \sim \mathcal{IG}(a_i, b_i)$.

Inference. We can write the joint posterior distribution of all parameters $A = \{\alpha(t), t = 0, \ldots, T\}$ and $\Psi = \{\psi_i, i = 1, \ldots, p\}$, given the observations $Y = \{Y(s, t), s \in S, t = 1, \ldots, T\}$ as being proportional to the product of the likelihood and the priors:

$$[A, \Psi | Y] \propto \left(\prod_{s \in S} \prod_{t=1}^{T} [Y(s,t)|\alpha(t)] \right) [\alpha(0)] \prod_{t=1}^{T} [\alpha(t)|\alpha(t-1), \Psi] \prod_{i=1}^{p} [\psi_i], \quad (3)$$

where $[Z]$ denotes the distribution of the random variable Z. Obtaining the posterior distribution in (3) as well as the marginal distributions of individual parameters requires evaluation of integrals that are analytically intractable and numerically infeasible. However, Markov chain Monte Carlo inference (Robert and Casella, 1999) is feasible. The most straightforward method for sampling the parameters is the Gibbs sampler, in which each parameter is visited in turn and sampled from its full conditional distribution. However, more general sampling algorithms are required since there may be strong positive correlations between the components. In this work, we adopt a Metropolis-Hastings algorithm, where convergence and mixing is considerably improved by updating blocks $\alpha[t, t'] = (\alpha(t), \ldots, \alpha(t'))$ of state vectors instead of a single vector $\alpha(t)$ (Knorr-Held, 1999).

4   In practice

This section follows the lines described in Section 3, showing how each of our examples can be modelled by specifying the hierarchical structure described above. The first stage concerns the conditional distribution of the counts, which depends on time-varying coefficients. The second stage describes the temporal dynamic of the coefficients according to a Gaussian transition model. The final stage defines hyperpriors for the parameters of the second stage. In both examples, inference is performed by making use of Markov chain Monte Carlo methods and we choose highly dispersed inverse gamma priors for the variances ψ_i, i.e. $a_i = b_i = 0.000001$, $i = 1, \ldots, p$.

Our model building strategy starts from the 'full' models, i.e. models including all the most relevant temporal and spatial covariates, each of which equipped with a time-varying coefficient. If covariates result to be not significant, i.e. the corresponding time-varying confidence bands always include zero, they are removed from the models. Moreover, if effects of the covariates do not show evidence of changes in time, they are treated as ordinary fixed effects.

Modelling effects of air pollution on human health. As we assumed that the counts reflected an underlying tendency of the severe air pollution events, combined with adverse meteorological conditions, to cause non-accidental death, we included in the $x_1(t, s)$ component vector covariates measuring exposure to pollution and meteorological conditions, i.e. minimum temperature (Tmin), maximum temperature (Tmax), the average daily specific humidity (Hum) and particulate matter (PM10). We chose to include the pollutant's concentration at lag 1, as previous analyses (Smith *et al.*, 2000) showed the existence of a spurious association between the response and the pollutant's concentration at lag 0. Specifically, we assumed:

1 $Y(t)|\lambda(t) \sim \mathcal{P}(\exp\{\lambda(t)\})$ with $\lambda(t) = \phi(t)$,
2 $\phi(t) = \omega(t) + b_1(t)\mathrm{Tmax}(t) + b_2(t)\mathrm{Tmin}(t) + b_3(t)\mathrm{Hum}(t) + b_4(t)\mathrm{PM10}(t - 1)$, where $\omega(t)$ is a second order random walk and $b_i(t)$, $i = 1, \ldots, 4$ are first order random walks.

Intermediate analyses highlighted the non significant effect of Tmax, so this variable was removed from the model. Moreover, as confidence bounds about the trajectory of the effect of Tmin did not show variation in time, although they indicated significance of the minimum temperature, in the subsequent analyses the parameter of this covariate was treated as an ordinary fixed effect.

Modelling infectious diseases. To approach the modelling task, we needed first to recover the spatial fields. Generally speaking, the choice of the spatial fields is driven both by a priori modelling considerations and by the data. The q spatial fields $h_i(s)$, $i = 1, \ldots, q$ are divided into two sets: r trend fields and $q - r$ principal fields. Principal fields can be selected from a basis of the space of all possible spatial Kriging estimates for given s_j^*, $j = 1, \ldots, m$, normative sites and for a given covariogram $\sigma(s, s')$ (Mardia *et al.*, (1998)).

In order to identify a parametric form for $\sigma(s, s')$, we considered the empirical variogram for the data aggregated into windows centred at the peak of the epidemics, each window comprising about 40 weeks. Note that if $Y(s)|\lambda(s)$ is a Poisson random variable with mean $\exp\{\beta + \lambda(s)\}$ and $\lambda(s)$ is a stationary Gaussian random field with $E[\lambda(s)] = 0, \mathrm{Cov}[\lambda(s), \lambda(s')] = \eta^2 \rho(s - s')$, where $\rho(\cdot)$ is a correlation function, then the following expression for the semi-variogram, $\nu(\cdot)$, holds:

$$\nu(s - s') = \exp\left(\beta + \frac{\eta^2}{2}\right) + \exp\left(2\beta + \eta^2\right)\left\{\exp(\eta^2) - \exp[\eta^2\rho(s - s')]\right\}.$$

We selected the parametric form for the semi-variogram by superimposing on the semi-variogram cloud the smoothed estimate of the semi-variogram and a theoretical semi-variogram. The most satisfactory agreement was obtained by adopting an exponential powered correlogram: $\rho(s - s') = \exp\{-\sqrt{||s - s'||/\tau}\}$. where $\tau = 1.6$ and $|| \cdot ||$ is the Euclidean norm in $\mathbb{R}^2$. Therefore, the hierarchical model that we considered was as follows:

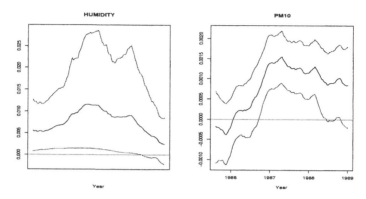

Fig. 3. Estimated trajectories for the coefficients of humidity and PM10 with pointwise 95% confidence intervals.

1 $Y(t,s)|\lambda(t,s) \sim \mathcal{P}(\exp\{\lambda(t,s)\})$ with $\lambda(t,s) = \phi(t,s) + \gamma x(s)$, where $x(s)$ represents the logarithm of the size of the young population (aged 0 to 24 years), as derived from the 1961 Census, used as a proxy to evaluate the dimension of the susceptibles pool,

2 $\phi(t,s) = \sum_{i=1}^{q} \beta_i(t)h_i(s)$, where $\beta_1(t)$ is a second order random walk, $h_1(s) = 1$, $\beta_i(t)$, $i = 2,\ldots,q$ are first order random walks and the $h_i(s), i = 2,\ldots,q$ are the first $q-1$ principal fields. (see Mardia *et al*, (1998) for details).

In the modelling phase, we chose $m = 16$ normative sites on a regular grid on the region S and $q - 1 = 4$ principal fields were used to form the evolving surface.

5 Results

The models were estimated using BayesX (Lang and Brezger, 2000) a software package that can analyse such models using MCMC simulation techniques. The MCMC specification for each model was 23000 iterations, the first 3000 discarded and every 10th subsequent sample point saved for estimation of posterior medians and quantiles. Convergence to the stationary distribution was checked adapting to R language the functions provided on the BayesX home page. These functions allow the routine plotting of autocorrelations of the samples from all parameters calculated within BayesX.

Modelling effects of air pollution on human health. Figure 3 shows the estimated coefficients for the relevant variables along with pointwise 95% confidence intervals in the TVCs setting. Inspection of the figure highlights the time-varying effect of humidity and PM10, which appear to be significant in the central period of time. The roughness of the estimates and of the relative confidence bands indicate a small carry-over effect of the variables,

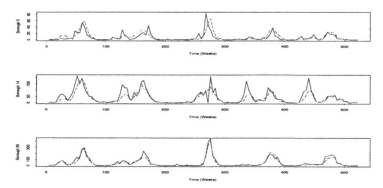

Fig. 4. Observed (solid line) and estimated (dotted line) values for the time series of measles counts for boroughs number 5, 14, 26.

showing that the effect at time t depends on previous values of the variables. We have detected, as in other studies, a positive effect of particular matter on mortality, but we have found that this effect is time-varying and that the significance of this effect might change in time. This might explain some of the controversy highlighted by re-analyses of these data based on different strategies for controlling temporal and confounding effects (Smith *et al.*, 2000).

Modelling infectious diseases. The model shows an excellent marginal fit to the data, reproducing fairly faithfully irregularities in the time trend. To incorporate the spatial dimension, let us consider the observed and estimated time series of counts for three boroughs, i.e. number 5, 14 and 26. These sites were chosen because they are quite different in terms of marginal distribution of cases and exemplify three different situations: low (number 5), medium (number 14) and high (number 26) mean number of cases and variability. It is encouraging that the model is able to grasp differences in the time behaviour of the series: for example, for borough 14, the model catches the rise in cases between the third and the fourth main epidemics, which is not visible in boroughs 5 and 14. In all boroughs, the model seems to follow quite closely the temporal structure of the five epidemics and in particular of the last one, which has a quite different behaviour

6   Conclusions

The aim of this paper has been to show that time-varying coefficients models provide a natural framework to tackle modelling tasks in environmental epidemiology, allowing realistic models to be constructed and appropriate conclusions to be drawn. In particular, we have emphasized the great flexibility of this formulation, which allow us to accommodate complex dependence structures whilst keeping transparency of the models and interpretability of the results.

The examples show that the models can be used either to make inference on time varying effects of covariates, as in the air pollution example, or for describing complex behaviour avoiding unnecessary restrictive assumptions such as stationarity, isotropy or separability between space/time correlation functions, as in the measles epidemics application. We believe that this framework provides a valuable addition to the existing methodology for gaining insight into the spatio-temporal features of the data.

However, there are some drawbacks which have to be pointed out. Firstly, inference requires approximation based on MCMC methods, which rely on convergence of a simulation which can be difficult to check, although many diagnostic tools are nowadays available to this aim. Secondly, the approach is computationally demanding, which could make its application not easily accessible.

References

ANDERSON, R.N., MAY, R. (1992). *Infectious Diseases of Humans: Dynamics and Control*, Oxford University Press, London.

HASTIE, T., TIBSHIRANI, R. (1993). Varying-coefficient models. *Journal of the Royal Statistical Society, B, 55*, 757–796.

KNORR-HELD, L. (1999). Conditional prior proposals in dynamic models. *Scandinavian Journal of Statistics, 26*, 129-144.

LANG, S., BREZGER, A. (2000). BayesX: software for Bayesian inference based on Markov chain Monte Carlo simulation technique. University of Munich, Available at http://www.stat.uni-muenchen.de/~lang/bayesx/bayesx.html.

MARDIA, K.V., GOODALL, C.R., REDFERN, E. and ALONSO, F.J. (1998). The Kriged Kalman filter (with discussion). *Test, 7*, 217-285.

ROBERT, C.P., CASELLA, G. (1999). *Monte Carlo Statistical Methods.* Springer, New York.

SMITH, R.L., DAVIS, J.M., SACKS, J., SPECKMAN, P., and STYER, P. (2000). Regression models for air pollution and daily mortality: analysis of data from Birmingham, Alabama. *Environmetrics, 11*, 719-743.

On Ziggurats and Dendrograms

Frank Critchley

Department of Statistics, The Open University
Walton Hall, Milton Keynes, MK7 6AA, UK
E-Mail: F.Critchley@open.ac.uk

Abstract. The indeterminacy in the horizontal ordering of the objects in the usual tree diagram representation of a dendrogram, and the associated dangers of misinterpretation, are well-known. A systematic choice of ordering is presented and seen to have a variety of attractive features. In particular, it induces a strengthened form of the Robinson property of the associated ultrametric matrix, permitting an *exact* one dimensional visual display of maximal subsets of objects. These systematic orderings are based upon the ziggurat decomposition of an arbitrary binary dendrogram. Worked examples motivate and illustrate the development. Connections with 'chaining' in single-link hierarchical cluster analysis are noted.

1   Introduction

The end product of most hierarchical classification procedures is a tree diagram representation of a dendrogram. There is considerable freedom of choice in the horizontal ordering of the objects in such a diagram. This indeterminacy is well described in Gower (1968) who likens it to the freedom in arranging the elements of a 'mobile'. He further notes that adjacent objects can be highly dissimilar relative to objects far apart, so that the horizontal ordering can be a misleading one dimensional representation of the dendrogram as a whole. In practice a choice of ordering has to be made and, rather than leave it to chance, it seems as well to have a systematic choice with as many desirable properties as possible.

The orderings presented here rest upon the notion of a maximal subset of objects in a dendrogram whose ultrametric dissimilarities can be exactly reproduced as distances in a *one* dimensional configuration. A famous result due to Holman (1972) – that a definite ultrametric dissimilarity on n objects is a Euclidean distance in $(n-1)$ *but no fewer* dimensions – shows that if Euclidean distances are used such a subset can never comprise more than two objects. Accordingly, we need to work with distances which are non-Euclidean in some sense – but wish to keep that sense minimal, since the eye is trained to read distances in Euclidean terms. The key idea is to represent the ultrametric dissimilarity $u(a, b)$ between two distinct objects as a Euclidean distance, not between a and b, but rather between one of them (the rightmost in the associated tree diagram) and a 'base' object, which serves as a local origin. In sharp contrast to Holman's result, there is *no* a priori limit to the maximal size of a subset that can be exactly represented in one dimension in this new way. The term *ziggurat* is used for this type of subset, since the subtree which it defines has the appearance of an end-on view of an, in general, irregular pyramid.

We emphasise that the aim of the present paper is the identification of special orderings implicit in a dendrogram *itself,* and that this is quite different from the aim, pursued elsewhere, of finding a good ordering in terms of other information *external* to it.

The paper is organised as follows. Necessary preliminaries are given in Section 2. Sections 3 and 4 present two worked examples which motivate and illustrate the development of the ziggurat decomposition of an arbitrary binary dendrogram, presented in Section 5, whose general properties are noted. The paper finishes with a short discussion.

This paper is based on the unpublished research report Critchley (1983). The ziggurat ordering of objects is implemented in the Genstat macro `zigord` (Digby (1984)). See also Van Cutsem (1983) for a cognate, alternative decomposition based on a maximal simplex of minimal diameter.

2   Preliminaries

2.1   Dendrograms and ultrametric functions

Throughout, S denotes an unordered set of $n \geq 2$ labels for the n objects under study. Formally, a dendrogram $\mathcal{D}$ on S is a nested collection of partitions of S satisfying certain well-known axioms (Jardine and Sibson, (1971)). The subsets comprising each partition are the *clusters* at the corresponding dissimilarity level.

There is a fundamental $1-1$ correspondence between the dendrograms on S and the ultrametric functions u on S. These are the functions $u : S \times S \to [0, \infty)$ satisfying

$$u(a, a) = 0 \leq u(b, a) = u(a, b) \leq \max(u(a, c), u(b, c))$$

in which $a, b, c, ...$ denote general members of S. This classical $1 - 1$ correspondence is entirely natural, $u(a, b)$ being the smallest dissimilarity level at which objects a and b belong to the same cluster. For a unified review and extension of this and related bijections in mathematical classification, see Critchley and Van Cutsem (1994).

2.2   Tree diagrams

Throughout, $\mathcal{T}$ denotes a tree diagram representation of a dendrogram $\mathcal{D}$, the nodes of $\mathcal{T}$ being identified with the clusters in $\mathcal{D}$ in the obvious way.

We restrict attention to dendrograms $\mathcal{D}$ which are (i) definite and (ii) binary. That is, to those for which (i) the terminal nodes of $\mathcal{T}$ are the singleton clusters $\{a\}$ (equivalently, $a \neq b \Rightarrow 0 < u(a,b)$) and (ii) exactly two clusters fuse at each of the $(n-1)$ non-terminal nodes of $\mathcal{T}$.

The first of these restrictions is made without essential loss, replacing 'a singleton cluster' by 'a cluster at the zero dissimilarity level' throughout.

2.3   Orderings and ultrametric matrices

From now on, we suppose that a definite binary dendrogram $\mathcal{D}$ on $\mathcal{S}$ – equivalently, its corresponding ultrametric function u – is given.

Let $\mathcal{N}$ denote $\{1, ..., n\}$ endowed with the natural order on the integers. Then, an *ordering* of $\mathcal{S}$ is a $1-1$ correspondence $\phi : \mathcal{S} \to \mathcal{N}$ or, equivalently, a vector with n components each of which is a different element of $\mathcal{S}$, the equivalence being given by

$$(\mathcal{S}, \phi) \overset{1\text{-}1}{\leftrightarrow} \mathcal{S}^\phi := (\phi^{-1}(1), ..., \phi^{-1}(n)).$$

This second, vectorial form is more convenient here. We take such an ordering to correspond to the left-to-right ordering of terminal nodes used in a tree diagram representation $\mathcal{T}$ of $\mathcal{D}$. For example, in Figure 1(a), $\mathcal{S}^\phi = (E, C, A, B, D)$.

A tree diagram representation $\mathcal{T}$ of $\mathcal{D}$ – equivalently, of u – is not unique in general, varying with the choice of ordering ϕ used for its terminal nodes. However, $\mathcal{T}$ *does* correspond to a unique $n \times n$ ultrametric *matrix* $U^\phi = (u_{ij}^\phi)$ induced by the given ultrametric function u via

$$u_{ij}^\phi := u(\phi^{-1}(i), \phi^{-1}(j)).$$

In particular, changing the ordering ϕ of $\mathcal{S}$ corresponds to permuting the rows and columns of U^ϕ, in the obvious way. When the ordering is clear from the context, we may drop the superscript and simply write $U = (u_{ij})$. Note that, since any such matrix is symmetric and vanishes on the diagonal, it is completely determined by its above diagonal elements $\{u_{ij}^\phi : 1 \le i < j \le n\}$.

Among the $n!$ possible orderings ϕ of $\mathcal{S}$, it is natural to restrict attention to those that are *compatible* with $\mathcal{D}$. That is, to those for which horizontal and vertical lines do not cross in $\mathcal{T}$, as in Figure 1(a). These are precisely the orderings ϕ for which U^ϕ has the *Robinson* property that:

the $\{u_{ij}^\phi : 1 \le i < j \le n\}$ do not decrease as you move away from the diagonal along any row or column.

For a general, formal discussion of compatibility, see Critchley and Fichet (1994).

However, there are a large number of compatible orderings of $\mathcal{D}$: $2^{(n-1)}$, a number which exceeds a million for $n = 21$. Whereas we may halve this number by adopting a rule to choose between a tree diagram and its 'dual' obtained by reflection in the vertical axis (that is, to choose between an ordering and its converse), we are still left with a choice between an exponentially large number of orderings. Fortunately, within these $2^{(n-2)}$ possibilities, there is a much smaller number of 'special' orderings implicit in the ultrametric function u itself, as we now develop.

3   A first example

Consider the tree diagram shown in Figure 1(a). Objects A and B are the first to join and, in terms of $\mathcal{D}$ alone, there is no sense in which either precedes the other. However, the other objects then join this cluster *one at a time*. This special property suggests the ordering $(\{A, B\}, C, D, E)$, in which the braces denote the arbitrariness of placing A before B. Figure 1(b) shows the same dendrogram with the objects arranged in this natural *ziggurat* ordering, which we denote by ϕ_*.

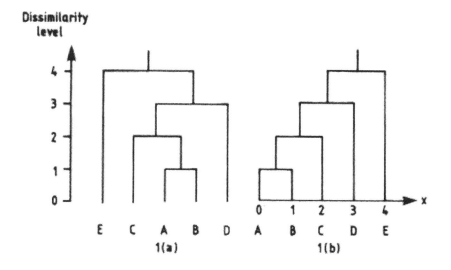

Fig. 1. A first example

This reordering of Figure 1(a) into Figure 1(b) has the effect of permuting the corresponding ultrametric matrix as follows:

$$
\begin{pmatrix}
0 & 4 & 4 & 4 & 4 \\
  & 0 & 2 & 2 & 3 \\
  &   & 0 & 1 & 3 \\
  &   &   & 0 & 3 \\
  &   &   &   & 0
\end{pmatrix}
\begin{matrix} E \\ C \\ A \\ B \\ D \end{matrix}
\;\rightarrow\;
\begin{pmatrix}
0 & 1 & 2 & 3 & 4 \\
  & 0 & 2 & 3 & 4 \\
  &   & 0 & 3 & 4 \\
  &   &   & 0 & 4 \\
  &   &   &   & 0
\end{pmatrix}
\begin{matrix} A \\ B \\ C \\ D \\ E \end{matrix}
$$

The Robinson property, noted above, of the first matrix is strengthened to the following *ziggurat* property of the second:

the $\{u_{ij}^{\phi_*} : 1 \le i < j \le n\}$ are *constant* in columns and *strictly* increasing along rows as you move away from the diagonal.

(Our choice between an ordering and its converse is made here in taking these above diagonal elements to be constant in columns rather than rows.) This stronger property permits an x-coordinate axis to be added, as shown, to the tree diagram as an exact one dimensional visual representation of the entire dendrogram. Object A, which was arbitrarily placed before B, is given coordinate zero. Object B, and all succeeding objects, are given coordinate equal to the dissimilarity level at which they join the 'base' A. Thus, these x-coordinates appear as the first row of U^{ϕ_*}, the ultrametric dissimilarity $u_{ij}^{\phi_*}$ between any two distinct objects with coordinates x_i and x_j being given by

$$
u_{ij}^{\phi_*} = \max\{x_i, x_j\}.
$$

But x_i is the Euclidean distance between $\phi_*^{-1}(i)$ and $\phi_*^{-1}(1)$ along this axis. Thus, the ultrametric dissimilarity between two objects is exactly represented visually by the one dimensional Euclidean distance between the rightmost of them and the base object. For example,

$$
u(C, D) = \max\{2, 3\} = 3 = e(A, D)
$$

where $e(\cdot, \cdot)$ denotes Euclidean distance along the x-axis.

In this sense, the x-axis of Figure 1(b) is an exact, highly visual, one dimensional representation of the given definite ultrametric dissimilarity on S – whose Euclidean dimensionality, we recall, is four.

Finally, we note that this one dimensional representation treats the ultrametric dissimilarities as being on a ratio scale. We may take advantage of situations where they have only ordinal significance by performing a strict monotone rescaling of them so that all positive jumps between successive transformed values are equal (to one), as in Figure 1. When permitted, such standardisation has the advantage of avoiding 'stragglers' such as object 23 in Figure 2 below.

4   A second example

4.1   Ziggurats of degree 0 and 1

Of course, it is not possible in general to visually represent all of a given definite binary dendrogram $\mathcal{D}$ in the way just described. However, we *can* always so represent maximal sub-dendrograms of $\mathcal{D}$, as follows.

A *ziggurat of degree zero* is defined to be a singleton cluster. The correspondence $a \leftrightarrow \{a\}$ is used now to identify S with its partition into ziggurats of degree zero, denoted S_0. In particular, $u : S \times S \to [0, \infty)$ is identified with $u_0 : S_0 \times S_0 \to [0, \infty)$ defined by $u_0(\{a\}, \{b\}) := u(a, b)$.

A *ziggurat of degree one* is defined to be a maximal cluster in $\mathcal{D}$ formed by fusing ziggurats of degree zero (singleton clusters) *one at a time*. This fusing process therefore stops when either there are no singleton clusters left to join, or when the cluster which joins next is not itself a singleton. Thus, a ziggurat of degree one can comprise anything from a singleton to (as in Figure 1) all of S.

The ziggurats of degree zero comprising a ziggurat of degree one are called its *members*. A degree one ziggurat comprising a single member is called *unitary* and coincides with the corresponding degree zero ziggurat. In a *non-unitary* degree one ziggurat, one of the two degree zero ziggurats which fuse first is arbitrarily chosen as the base, and the remaining members are then placed after it in the order of the dissimilarity levels at which they join the base.

A non-unitary degree one ziggurat always exists, as $n > 1$. There are, therefore, strictly fewer degree one than degree zero ziggurats.

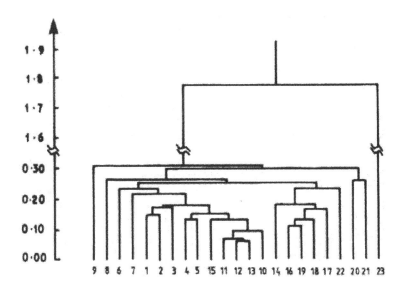

Fig. 2. A second example

The degree one ziggurats also form a partition of $\mathcal{S}$, $\mathcal{S}_1$ say, albeit at different dissimilarity levels. Consider, for example, Figure 2 which shows the tree diagram of the single-link dendrogram reported as Figure 4 in Appendix 7 of Jardine and Sibson (1971). This refers to a famous set of data on $n = 23$ local caste groups in Upper Bengal analysed by Mahalanobis et al. (1949).

Inspection shows that there are ten ziggurats of degree one here, five of which are unitary. From left to right, these ziggurats forming the partition $\mathcal{S}_1$ are:

$\{9\}; \{8\}; \{6\}; \{7\}; (\{1,2\},3); \{4,5\}; (\{12,13\},11,10,15);$
$(\{16,19\},18,17,14,22); \{20,21\}$ and $\{23\}$.

For convenience, we label these now as A to J. Each of these gives rise, as above, to a ziggurat ultrametric matrix. For example, in an obvious notation:

$$U(H) = \begin{pmatrix} 0 & 0.11 & 0.13 & 0.16 & 0.18 & 0.23 \\ & 0 & 0.13 & 0.16 & 0.18 & 0.23 \\ & & 0 & 0.16 & 0.18 & 0.23 \\ & & & 0 & 0.18 & 0.23 \\ & & & & 0 & 0.23 \\ & & & & & 0 \end{pmatrix} \begin{matrix} 16 \\ 19 \\ 18 \\ 17 \\ 14 \\ 22 \end{matrix}$$

4.2   Ziggurat induction

The induction on ziggurat degree, performed above from 0 to 1, can be repeated. Before proceeding to the general case, we continue this second worked example.

Further inspection of Figure 2 shows that $\mathcal{D}$ itself is a single *degree two ziggurat*, in the sense that it is formed by fusing its degree one ziggurats *one at a time* in the ziggurat ordering $(\{G,F\},E,D,C,H,B,I,A,J)$. This is made clear in the re-ordered tree diagram shown in Figure 3 in which, horizontally, there is a series of 10 'local' coordinate axes (one for each degree one ziggurat), interpreted exactly as in Figure 1(b). These local axes are punctuated by the '$\|$' symbol as a visual warning against trying to interpret horizontal distances across them, even in non-Euclidean terms.

Formally regarding the degree one ziggurats A to J as new 'objects', we may define $u_1 : \mathcal{S}_1 \times \mathcal{S}_1 \to [0,\infty)$ by

$$u_1(Z_1, \widetilde{Z}_1) := u_0(\{a\}, \{\widetilde{a}\}), (\{a\} \subseteq Z_1, \{\widetilde{a}\} \subseteq \widetilde{Z}_1)$$

where $Z_1, \widetilde{Z}_1$ are any two degree one ziggurats in $\mathcal{D}$. By construction, the function u_1 is well-defined and ultrametric.

In view of the overall degree two ziggurat structure of $\mathcal{D}$ here, the ziggurat-ordered ultrametric matrix $U_1^{\phi*}$ corresponding to these new 'objects' has the stronger-than-Robinson ziggurat property defined above, being given by

$$
U_1^{\phi_*} = \begin{pmatrix}
0 & 0.15 & 0.18 & 0.22 & 0.23 & 0.25 & 0.27 & 0.30 & 0.31 & 1.78 \\
& 0 & 0.18 & 0.22 & 0.23 & 0.25 & 0.27 & 0.30 & 0.31 & 1.78 \\
& & 0 & 0.22 & 0.23 & 0.25 & 0.27 & 0.30 & 0.31 & 1.78 \\
& & & 0 & 0.23 & 0.25 & 0.27 & 0.30 & 0.31 & 1.78 \\
& & & & 0 & 0.25 & 0.27 & 0.30 & 0.31 & 1.78 \\
& & & & & 0 & 0.27 & 0.30 & 0.31 & 1.78 \\
& & & & & & 0 & 0.30 & 0.31 & 1.78 \\
& & & & & & & 0 & 0.31 & 1.78 \\
& & & & & & & & 0 & 1.78 \\
& & & & & & & & & 0
\end{pmatrix}
\begin{matrix}
G \\ F \\ E \\ D \\ C \\ H \\ B \\ I \\ A \\ J
\end{matrix}
$$

There is a natural way to 'unpack' this matrix to recover the $n \times n$ ultrametric matrix U^{ϕ_*} in an overall ziggurat order ϕ_*, as follows: U^{ϕ_*} is the partitioned matrix with entries indexed by a pair of degree one ziggurats $(Z_1, \widetilde{Z}_1)$, each off-diagonal sub-matrix having constant elements equal to $u_1(Z_1, \widetilde{Z}_1)$ as given in $U_1^{\phi_*}$ above, and each diagonal sub-matrix being the corresponding square matrix $U(Z_1)$.

5   The ziggurat decomposition of a binary dendrogram

As above, let $\mathcal{D}$ be a definite binary dendrogram on $\mathcal{S}$, with corresponding ultrametric function u, and recall that the definiteness condition is without essential loss. The ziggurat decomposition of $\mathcal{D}$ is defined inductively as follows.

The ziggurats of degree zero are defined as the singleton clusters in $\mathcal{D}$ and comprise the partition of $\mathcal{S}$ denoted $\mathcal{S}_0$. In particular, $|\mathcal{S}_0| = n > 1$.

For any strictly positive integer k, the ziggurats of degree k – comprising the partition $\mathcal{S}_k$ of $\mathcal{S}$ – are defined as the maximal clusters in $\mathcal{D}$ formed by

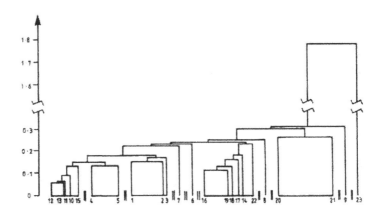

Fig. 3. A ziggurat re-ordering of Figure 2.

fusing ziggurats of degree $(k-1)$ *one at a time*. These latter are called the *members* of the degree k ziggurat. A degree k ziggurat comprising a single member is called *unitary* and coincides with the corresponding degree $(k-1)$ ziggurat. In a *non*-unitary degree k ziggurat, one of the two degree $(k-1)$ ziggurats which fuse first is arbitrarily chosen as the base, and the remaining members are then placed after it in the order of the dissimilarity levels at which they join the base. Clearly,

a non-unitary degree k ziggurat exists $\Leftrightarrow |\mathcal{S}_{k-1}| > 1 \Leftrightarrow |\mathcal{S}_k| < |\mathcal{S}_{k-1}|$.

The minimal value of k for which $\mathcal{S}$ itself is a degree k ziggurat is called *the ziggurat degree of the dendrogram* $\mathcal{D}$, denoted $k(\mathcal{D})$, and the ordering of objects within it is called *a ziggurat ordering of* $\mathcal{S}$, denoted ϕ_*. Typically, the ziggurat degree of $\mathcal{D}$ is very much less than its Euclidean dimensionality $(n-1)$.

In the first example (Section 3), the dendrogram has ziggurat degree one and its objects have ziggurat ordering $(\{A, B\}, C, D, E)$. In the second example (Section 4), $k(\mathcal{D}) = 2$ while, in an obvious and convenient shorthand, $(\{G, F\}, E, D, C, H, B, I, A, J)$ is a ziggurat ordering in which, for example, $H = (\{16, 19\}, 18, 17, 14, 22)$.

Again, let $u_0 : \mathcal{S}_0 \times \mathcal{S}_0 \to [0, \infty)$ be defined by $u_0(\{a\}, \{b\}) := u(a, b)$, as above. Then, for each integer $k > 0$, the function $u_k : \mathcal{S}_k \times \mathcal{S}_k \to [0, \infty)$ given inductively by

$$u_k(Z_k, \widetilde{Z}_k) := u_{k-1}(Z_{k-1}, \widetilde{Z}_{k-1}), (Z_{k-1} \subseteq Z_k, \widetilde{Z}_{k-1} \subseteq \widetilde{Z}_k),$$

where $Z_k, \widetilde{Z}_k$ are any two degree k ziggurats in $\mathcal{D}$, is well-defined and ultra-metric. Using a ziggurat ordering ϕ_*, the ultrametric matrix $U_{k(\mathcal{D})-1}^{\phi_*}$ has the ziggurat property that its above diagonal elements are constant in columns and strictly increasing along rows, while unpacking this matrix $(k(\mathcal{D}) - 1)$ times – as described at the end of Section 4 – we arrive at the $(k(\mathcal{D}) - 1)$-fold nestedly-partitioned $n \times n$ ultrametric matrix U^{ϕ_*}.

Finally, we note that a given ziggurat ordering ϕ_* of $\mathcal{S}$ induces a unique corresponding ziggurat ordering of the nodes in an associated tree diagram, as follows. Within each degree one ziggurat, list the nodes in order of increasing dissimilarity level and then concatenate these lists in the order of the degree one ziggurats in ϕ_*. These nodes are then followed by the similarly ordered nodes of degree two ziggurats and the process repeated until completion, increasing the ziggurat degree by one at each stage.

6   Discussion

The ziggurat decomposition of a definite binary dendrogram $\mathcal{D}$ on $\mathcal{S}$ defines a ziggurat ordering ϕ_* of $\mathcal{S}$ unique up to the choice, from among two candidates, of a base for each non-unitary ziggurat which it contains. For ziggurats of degree greater than one, this lack of uniqueness can usually be removed by adopting the natural convention that the member which forms at the lower dissimilarity level be used as the base.

In terms of $\mathcal{D}$ itself, a ziggurat ordering ϕ_* is, then, maximally determinate and, in view of its strengthened Robinson property, produces a modified visual display (such as Figure 3) that is minimally misleading.

The use of such systematic orderings can be particularly helpful when comparing several dendrograms on the same set of objects. They also serve to highlight the 'chaining' effect so prevalent in single-link cluster analysis: see, for example, the re-ordered displays of ziggurats G and H in Figure 3 and the display in Digby (1984). It is tempting to conjecture that the ziggurat degree of a single-link analysis of a given dissimilarity matrix will never exceed that of, say, a complete-link analysis.

Again, a ziggurat ordering ϕ_* and its unique induced node ordering together clarify the Euclidean structure of a dendrogram: see Critchley (1988).

Finally we note that, at least in principle, the ziggurat decomposition of a binary dendrogram $\mathcal{D}$ could be used to define an exact non-Euclidean representation of it in $k(\mathcal{D})$ dimensions (Critchley, (1983)).

References

CRITCHLEY, F. (1983): Ziggurats and dendrograms. *University of Warwick Statistics Research Report*, 43.

CRITCHLEY, F. (1988): The Euclidean structure of a dendrogram, the variance of a node and the question: 'How many clusters really are there?'. In: H. H. Bock (Ed.): *Classification and Related Methods of Data Analysis*. Elsevier, North-Holland, 75-84.

CRITCHLEY, F. and FICHET, B. (1994): The partial order by inclusion of the principal classes of dissimilarity on a finite set, and some of their basic properties. In: B. Van Cutsem (Ed.): *Classification and Dissimilarity Analysis*, Lecture Notes in Statistics, 93. Springer, New York, 5-65.

CRITCHLEY, F. and VAN CUTSEM, B. (1994): An order-theoretic unification and generalisation of certain fundamental bijections in mathematical classification – I. In: B. Van Cutsem (Ed.): *Classification and Dissimilarity Analysis*, Lecture Notes in Statistics, 93. Springer, New York, 87-119.

DIGBY, P. G. N. (1984): Dendrograms and ziggurats. *Genstat Newsletter*, 14, 14-18. Numerical Algorithms Group, Oxford.

GOWER, J. C. (1968): Multivariate analysis and multivariate geometry. *The Statistician*, 17, 13-28.

HOLMAN, E. W. (1972): The relation between hierarchical and Euclidean models for psychological distance. *Psychometrika*, 37, 417-423.

JARDINE, N. and SIBSON, R. (1971): *Mathematical Taxonomy*. John Wiley, London.

MAHALANOBIS, P. C., MAJUMDAR D. M. and RAO, C. R. (1949): Anthropometric survey of the United Provinces. *Sankhyā*, 9, 89-324.

VAN CUTSEM, B. (1983): Décomposition d'une ultramétrique: ultramétriques simples et semi-simples. *Laboratoire IMAG (Grenoble) Rapport de Recherche*, 388.

A Dimensionality Reduction Method Based on Simple Linear Regressions

Luigi D'Ambra[1], Pietro Amenta[2], and Rosaria Lombardo[3]

[1] Department of Mathematic and Statistics,
University of Naples, via Cinzia-Monte S. Angelo, 80126 Napoli, Italy.
E-Mail: dambra@unina.it
[2] Department of Economics, Mathematic and Statistics,
University of Lecce, via per Monteroni, 73100 Lecce, Italy.
E-Mail: amenta@economia.unile.it
[3] Department of Accounting and Quantitative Methods,
Second University of Naples, Napoli, Italy.
E-Mail: rosaria.lombardo@unina2.it

Abstract. After a review of the mainly dimensionality reduction methods as well as of the Shrinkage Regression Methods, authors provide a different multivariate extension of the univariate PLS Garthwaite's approach (1994) highlighting a different use and interpretation.

1 Introduction

The traditional approach to the study of modelling relationships between a dependent variable and other explanatory variables is to estimate the coefficients by ordinary least squares (OLS). In this case, when the number of explanatory variable is very large, as well as, in presence of more dependent variables, it may be advantageous to find linear combinations of the explanatory variables, called latent variables having some properties in term of correlation or in term of variance. In other word, the study of modelling relationships is led by referring to a subspace of the space spanned by the explanatory variables. The use of dimensionality reduction methods (DRM) consists, than, of substituting the set of observed explanatory variables with a fewer sequence of orthogonal latent variables.

The commonly used DRM methods are Reduced Rank Regression (RRR), Principal Component regression (PCR), Canonical Correlation Regression (CCR) and the Partial Least Squares (PLS). The study of multivariate predictions could be, also, dealt with other several approaches, for example, as 1) Constrained Principal Component Analysis (CPCA) (D'Ambra, Lauro, 1982) or 2) Canonical Analysis. From a geometrical point of view, CPCA consists in carrying out a PCA of the image of the criterion variables onto the subspace spanned by the explanatory subset through a suitable orthogonal projection operator and an orthogonal decomposition of total inertia. As highlighted before in the univariate approach, also the multivariate approaches consist of determining orthogonal latent variables. Anyway, most of them are based on an inversion matrix and in case of low observation/variable ratio and collinearity among predictors is not possible to invert the matrix.

This problem lead to an instability of the results as well as the OLS estimates fail to give good predictions. A possible approach to overcome the singularity is to put in the context of Ridge Regression (RR), of PCR or PLS.

The main purpose of this paper, after a review of the dimensionality reduction methods, is to provide a multivariate extension of the univariate PLS approach of Gartwhite (1994) (different from his multivariate proposal) highlighting a different use and interpretation.

2   Notation

Let $\Re^n$ be vectorial space of dimension n and consider the matrix $Y_{(n\times q)}$ where y_{ik} $(i = 1, \ldots, n)$ $(k = 1, \ldots, q)$ denotes the value of the k-th criterion variable observed on the $i - th$ statistical unit. Let $X_{(n\times p)}$ be the matrix where x_{ij} $(i = 1, \ldots, n)$ $(j = 1, \ldots, p)$ is the value of the j-th explanatory variable observed on the same i-th statistical unit. In this paper we assume that all variables have zero means as regards the weights diagonal metric D_n whose general term is $1/n$. Let $t_j = X a_j$ (latent variable) $(j = 1, \ldots, p)$ be an ordered sequence of orthogonal linear combinations and let $T_{(g)} = X A_{(g)}$ be an orthogonal matrix of order $(n \times g)$ containing g latent variables $(g = 1, \ldots, p)$ such that to obtain the fitted response matrix by $\hat{Y}_{(g)} = T_{(g)}(T_{(g)}^T T_{(g)})^{-1} T_{(g)}^T Y = X B_{(g)}$. Let, also, be $H_{(g)} = X^T T_{(g-1)}(T_{(g-1)}^T X X^T T_{(g-1)})^{-1} T_{(g-1)}^T X$.

3   DRMs for multivariate prediction

Several DMRs have been proposed for different purposes for multivariate prediction even if some of them can be applied also for the univariate case. They obtain the latent variables by optimizing a different objective function with good solutions, for some of them, for the situations where the explanatory variables are near collinear. In this case, in multiple regression, we know that the ordinary least square regression (OLS) predictor $b = b^{OLS} = (X^T X)^{-1} X^T y_k$ $(k = 1, \ldots, q)$, even though unbiased, has large variance leading to unrealistic and shaky predictor coefficients with possible incoherent signs.

Well-know shrinkage regression methods are PCR, PLS, RR and Continuum Regression (CR) (Stone, Brooks, 1990; Frank, Friedman, 1993; Brown, 1993; Brooks, Stone, 1994). When is almost singular, its inverse will contain several extremely large elements. A useful strategy, to avoid this problem, is to replace the factor $(X^T X)^{-1}$ in expression of b^{OLS} by a better-conditioned matrix G such to write $b = G X^T y$. PCR smoothes $(X^T X)^{-1}$ by making a spectral decomposition $X^T X = \sum_j \lambda_j v_j v_j^T$ and it truncates the sum $(X^T X)^{-1} = \sum_j \lambda_j^{-1} v_j v_j^T$ after some number of terms smaller than the rank of X. PLS finds a vector c with $\|c\| = 1$ such that the scalar product $y^T X c$ is maximal and takes $b \propto c$. This leads to consider the predictor $b^{PLS} \propto X^T y_k$ replacing $(X^T X)^{-1}$ with a better-conditioned matrix $G \propto I_p$.

In order to avoid the instability problem associated with the ill conditioned OLS estimate of β, Hoerl (1962) and Hoerl and Kennard (1970) suggest, with RR, to consider the predictor $b^{RR} = (X^T X + \delta I_p)^{-1} X^T y_k$ with $\delta \geq 0$ leading to a matrix G proportional to $(X^T X + \delta I_p)^{-1}$ (Table 3).

Stone and Brooke (1990), with the CR, (a DRM method for predicting univariate responses), pointed out a formal resemblance between OLS, PLS and PCR. They highlight as, with all three methods, the predictor b is determined by simple regression of y on a one dimensional regressor Xc, where the coefficient vector c is chosen by maximising different criteria: the squared correlation $r^2(y, Xc)$, the covariance $cov(y, Xc)$ and the sample variance of Xc ($\| Xc \|^2$), respectively. They suggest a general principle and choose the coefficient vector c, for fixed $\gamma \geq 0$, by maximising $T(\gamma, c) = (y^T Xc)^2 \| Xc \|^{2(\gamma-1)} \propto r^2(y, Xc) \| Xc \|^2$ subject to $\| c \| = 1$. In this sense, we have for $\gamma = 0$, $\gamma = 1$ and $\gamma \to \infty$ the OLS, PLS and PCR solution, respectively, with a continuum solution between them even if it does not always constitute a connected trajectory. Sundberg (1993) showed that first-factor CR is equivalent to a modified form of RR consisting of a scale adjustment of the scale predictor in order to minimize the sum of squares of residuals over the training data. The CR predictor is proportional to the RR predictor $c_\gamma \propto b^{RR}(\delta)$ where $b^{RR}(\delta)$ is a continuous function of δ and δ is a monotone function of γ: $\delta = [\gamma/(1 - \gamma)]/(\| Xc_\gamma \|^2 / \| c_\gamma \|^2)$. Discontinuities in CR so can occur because the optimal value of δ may change discontinuously with γ. It is possible to change the parametrization so that one can avoid the risk of jumps (Björkström, Sundberg , 1996, 1999).

Many of these shrinkage regression methods can be seen in a more general multivariate framework based on a common objective function for the DRMs (Abraham, Merola, 2001). All the DMRs objective functions are measures of associations between couples of latent variables of unit norm, linear combinations of the responses ($r_j = Yd_j$) and of the explanatory variables ($t_j = Xa_j$). These measures are expressed (see Table 1, with SIMPLS instead of PLS) in term of squared covariance between the latent variables t_j and r_j as well as their variance, respectively.

Method	Object function	Solution matrix
PCA	$max(a_j^T X^T X a_j)$	$X^T X$
CCR	$max[(a_j^T X^T Y d_j)^2/(\| t_j \|^2 \| r_j \|^2)]$	$(X^T X)^{-1} X^T Y (Y^T Y)^{-1} Y^T X$
RRR	$max[(a_j^T X^T Y d_j)^2/ \| t_j \|^2]$	$(X^T X)^{-1} X^T Y Y^T X$
CPCA	$max(d_j^T Y^T P_X Y d_j)$	$Y^T X (X^T X)^{-1} X^T Y$
SIMPLS	$max(a_j^T X^T Y d_j)^2$	$(I - H_j)^{-1} X^t Y Y^T X$
with the constraints $a_j^T a_j = d_j^T d_j = 1$, $a_j^T X^T X a_i = 0$, $j > i$.		

Table 1. Objective functions of the DRMs.

We can see as there is a trade-off between the objectives of RRR and the PCR: the former tries to maximize the variance of the criterion variables retained by the predictors latent subspace while the latter only that of the predictors with PLS considered as a compromise. We remark that, within these methods, if $X^T X$ is almost singular, it is possible to utilise the "PCR smooth" criteria of this matrix obtaining mixed DRM approaches (i.e. for CPCA we obtain as solution matrix $Y^T X(\sum_j \lambda_j^{-1} v_j v_j^T) X^T Y$ which is equivalent to PCR).

Abraham and Merola (2001) generalize CR to the multivariate case (MCR) maximizing the following objective function:

$$f(a_j, d_j, \alpha, \beta) = \begin{cases} (a_j^T X^T Y d_j)^2 \, \|Y d_j\|^{2\beta} \, \|X a_j\|^{2\alpha} & \alpha, \beta \geq -1 \\ a_j^T a_j = d_j^T d_j = 1, a_j^T X^T X a_i = 0, j > i \end{cases}$$

They show (Table 2) as it is possible to obtain, for fixed values of both parameters, the objective functions of the various DRMs. We remark as we can obtain also, in this framework, the CPCA approach by setting both parameters to zero with $a_j^T X^T X a_j = 1$. Brooks and Stone (1994) propose a similar multivariate generalization of CR (Joint Continuum Regression) which can be obtained, by the former, by setting β to zero and letting α vary from -1 to infinite. Both approaches find the several solutions by iterative algorithms (Books, Stone, 1994; Abraham, Merola, 2001).

Finally, we highlight as all the DRM criteria can be read within the framework of the H-Principle (Höskuldsson, 1992) which defines how we should proceed when finding solution to the mathematical model of data.

	CCA	RRR	SIMPLS	PCR	CPCA(*)
α	-1	-1	0	∞	0
β	-1	0	0	Finite	0
(*) with $a_j^T X^T X a_j = 1$.					

Table 2. Special cases of MCR.

A similar continuum can be obtained with an extension of the Principal Co-variates Regression (PCovR) (or "Weighted maximum overall redundancy") (de Jong, Kiers, 1992; Merola, Abraham, 2001). In order to find a low-dimensional subspace of the predictor space spanned by the columns of X accounting the maximum of the variations of X and Y, we propose to consider the model

$$\begin{cases} T = XW \\ X = TZ_X + E_X \\ Y = TZ_Y + E_Y \end{cases}$$

where T contains scores on g components, W is the $p \times g$ matrix of component weights with Z_X and Z_Y loading matrices, of order $g \times p$ and $g \times q$, containing the regression parameters that relate the predictors and the response variables to the components in T, respectively. Following De Jong and Kiers, we propose to maximise the following criterion

$$\alpha \|X - TZ_X\|^2 + \mu \|X^TY - Z_X^TZ_Y\|^2 + (1 - \alpha - \mu) \|Y - TZ_Y\|^2$$

such that $T^TT = I$ and $T^TE_X = T^TE_Y = 0$. The least-squares solutions are given by the first g eigenvectors of matrix $Q = \alpha XX^T + (1 - \alpha - \mu)\hat{Y}\hat{Y}^T + \mu XX^TYY^T$ if X $(p > n)$ spans the complete space and T contains scores on all components with $\hat{Y} = X(X^TX)^-X^TY$. W may be computed by regression of T on X, if X^TX is not of full rank or, otherwise, with $W = X^-T$ where X^- is any generalized inverse of X.

We introduce two parameters (α and μ), both varying between 0 and 1, so that μ tells how much the model is PLS like and $(1 - \alpha - \mu)$ determines its Multiple Linear Regression (MLR) nature. We highlight some special cases:

- for $\alpha = 0$ and $\mu = 0$ the solution leads to MLR if $g = min[rank(X), rank(Y)]$, with an emphasis on fitting Y, otherwise to RRR if $g < min[rank(X), rank(Y)]$;
- for $\alpha = 1$ and $\mu = 0$ the solution puts an emphasis on reconstructing X with a PCA of X or with PCR if we use the principal components as predictors for Y;
- for $\alpha = 0$ and $\mu = 1$ the solution leads to Partial Least Squares of X and Y (Remark: de Jong and Kiers find, with $\alpha = 0.5$, a compromise situation that perhaps compares to PLS regression).
- finally, for $\mu = 0$ and for any admissible value for α, we have the original PCovR solution.

4   A multivariate extension of Gartwaite's approach

Garthwaite (1994) shows that the latent variables of PLS are obtained as the weighted averages of simple linear regressions. In the univariate PLS, this author obtains an estimation of y_k $(k = 1, \ldots, q)$ by using the simple linear coefficients $\hat{y}_k = \sum_{j=1}^{p} f_j x_j b_j^k$ with $b_j^k = \left(x_j^T x_j\right)^{-1} x_j^T y_k$ and weight f_j $(j = 1, \ldots, p)$.

We can generalize this approach, in a different way respect to the multivariate original one, with two set of variables X and Y by regressing each column vectors of Y against each column vectors of X. The pq univariate OLS regressions are:

$$x_1 \left(x_1^T x_1\right)^{-1} x_1^T y_1 \ldots x_p \left(x_p^T x_p\right)^{-1} x_p^T y_1$$
$$\vdots \qquad \ddots \qquad \vdots \qquad\qquad (1)$$
$$x_1 \left(x_1^T x_1\right)^{-1} x_1^T y_q \ldots x_p \left(x_p^T x_p\right)^{-1} x_p^T y_q$$

In order to display the structure of dependence between Y and X in a best approximation subspace, in a PCA framework, we look for the principal axes

t_g such that

$$\min_{t_g} \sum_{j=1}^{p} \sum_{k=1}^{q} \left\| P_{x_j} y_k - t_g t_g^T P_{x_j} y_k \right\|^2$$

subject to the constraints $t_g^T t_g = 1$ and $t_{g'}^T t_g = 0$ for $g' \neq g$. This leads us to the extraction of the eigenvalues λ_g and eigenvectors t_g associated to the eigen-system $\hat{Y}^T \hat{Y} t_g = \lambda_g t_g$ with $\hat{Y} = [\hat{y}_1 | \dots | \hat{y}_q]$ column linked matrix of order $(n \times q)$ where each column is the sum of orthogonal projections onto single rank subspaces $\hat{y}_k = \sum_{j=1}^{p} x_j b_j^k = \sum_{j=1}^{p} x_j \left(x_j^T x_j \right)^{-1} x_j^T y_k = \sum_{j=1}^{p} P_{x_j} y_k$ ($k = 1, \dots, q$).

This matrix can be also express in several ways: $\hat{Y} = P_{\dot{X}} Y$, $\hat{Y} = X M^{-1} X^T Y$ and $\hat{Y} = XB$ where $P_{\dot{X}} = \sum_{j=1}^{p} P_{x_j}$, $M = diag(x_1^T x_1, \dots, x_p^T x_p)$ and

$$B = M^{-1} X^T Y = \begin{bmatrix} b_1^1 & \cdots & b_1^q \\ \vdots & \ddots & \vdots \\ b_p^1 & \cdots & b_p^q \end{bmatrix}$$

We remark as the matrix $\hat{Y} = [\hat{y}_1 | \dots | \hat{y}_q]$ can be considered as a multivariate extension of the Garthwaite's univariate approach with unitary weights even if, in this sense, other types of weight can be taken into account (i.e. $f_j = x_j^T x_j$). This matrix leads to interesting properties:

- **[Var($\hat{Y}$) criterion]** PCA of $\hat{Y}$ is equivalent to develop a PCA of the coefficient matrix B with metric $X^T X$ as well as to a PCR of matrix X with solution matrix $Y^T X M^{-1} V \Lambda V^T M^{-1} X^T Y = Y^T X_g X_g^T Y$ where $X_g = X M^{-1} V \Lambda^{1/2}$ is a matrix containing the first g λ-normed principal components of X;
- **[Cov($Y, \hat{Y}$) criterion]** It is possible to highlight the role of the matrix $\hat{Y}$ within the PLS framework by developing the PLS of X and Y subject to the constraints $a_j^T M a_j = 1$ and $d_j^T d_j = 1$. This is equivalent to consider the covariance between the matrices Y and $\hat{Y}$. The PLS solution is, also, equivalent to consider the criterion $\max_{a_j} \sum_j \left\| Y^T X a_j \right\|^2$ subject to the constraint $a_j^T M a_j = 1$.
- **[Proj($Y, \hat{Y}$) criterion]** Matrix $Y^T \hat{Y} (\hat{Y}^T \hat{Y})^{-1} \hat{Y}^T Y$ can be used for an alternative approach to CPCA based on simple regressions
- **[Cov($X, \hat{Y}$) criterion]** The approach based on the $\hat{y}_k$ as sum of orthogonal projections onto single rank subspaces spanned by the x_j's, $\hat{y}_k = \sum_{j=1}^{p} x_j b_j^k = \sum_{j=1}^{p} P_{x_j} y_k$, leads to consider a conditioned matrix G for the predictor $b = GX^T y$ (sec. 3). If we consider the covariance between the x_j's and the $\hat{y}_k$'s, we have $cov(X, \hat{Y}) = HX^T Y$ where

$$H = \begin{bmatrix} 1 & \cdots & h_{j,j'} \\ \vdots & 1 & \vdots \\ h_{j',j} & \cdots & 1 \end{bmatrix}$$

of order $(p \times p)$ which general element is the paired regression coefficients among the x_j's: $(j, j' = 1, \ldots, p)$

$$h_{j,j'} = \frac{\text{cov}(x_j, x_{j'})}{\text{var}(x_{j'})}$$

If we refer to the k-th column of Y, we obtained the predictor $b^{\hat{Y}} = HX^T y_k$ by assuming the matrix H as conditioned matrix G which takes into account all the paired relationships between the x_j's. We remark as this approach try to get back the relationships among the predictor variables that are loosed with the simple linear regressions $\hat{y}_k = \sum_{j=1}^{p} x_j b_j^k$.

General solution $b = GX^T y_k$				
OLS	PCR	PLS	RR	$\hat{Y}$
Conditioned matrix G				
$G = (X'X)^{-1}$	$G = \sum_j \lambda_j^{-1} v_j v_j^T$	$G \propto I_p$	$G \propto (X'X + \delta I_p)^{-1}$	$G = H$
Predictor b				
$(X'X)^{-1} X^T y_k$	$(\sum_j \lambda_j^{-1} v_j v_j^T) X^T y_k$	$\propto X^T y_1$	$(X'X + \delta I_p)^{-1} X^T y_k$	$HX^T y_k$

Table 3. Several conditioned matrices.

A different approach can be performed by using the $p \times q$ univariate OLS regressions (1). We can write q matrices $XB^1, \ldots, XB^k, \ldots, XB^q$ where XB^k is diagonal matrix containing the regression coefficients of k-th row of (1).

To analyze the structure of these q matrices, in the context of PLS, we can consider a generalization of covariance criterion $\max_{a_k} \sum_{k=1}^{q} (XB^k a_k, v)^2$ (D'Ambra, Sabatier, Amenta, 1988) with $a_k^T a_k = 1$ $(k = 1, \ldots, q)$ where v is eigenvector of $\sum_{k=1}^{q} (XB^K B^{kT} X^T)$ and a_k are the axes of $\Re^q$. The sum of the explained variances by each x_j's, $\sum_k (y_k^T P_{x_j} y_k)$, is the generic element of the diagonal matrix $B^k B^{kT}$ which can be used as weight within the Garthwaite's univariate approach.

At generic step s we compute the Q_k orthogonal projector $I - P_{t_k}$, onto the vectorial subspace spanned by t_k (to the step $s - 1$) and the residual matrix $X_k B_k - X_k B_k P_{t_k} = X_k B_k (I - P_{t_k})$

Finally, we remark that, for the first component, this approach can be considered as "weighted" version of the Multiple Coinerzia Analysis (Chessel, Hanafi,1996).

References

ABRAHAM, B. and MEROLA, G. (2001): Dimensionality reduction approach to multivariate prediction. In: Esposito Vinzi V. et al (Eds.): *PLS and related methods*, CISIA ceresta.

BJÖRKSTRÖM, A. and SUNDBERG, R. (1996): Continuum regression is not always continuous. *Journal of the Royal Statistical Society, Series B, 58:4, 703-710.*

BJÖRKSTRÖM, A. and SUNDBERG, R. (1999): A generalized view on continuum regression. *Scandinavian Journal of Statistics, 26:1, 17-30.*

BROOKS, R. and STONE, M. (1994): Joint continuum regression for multiple predictands. *JASA, 89,1374-1377.*

BROWN P.J. (1993): *Measurement, Regression and Calibration.* Oxford Univ. Press, Oxford.

CHESSEL, D. and HANAFI, M. (1996): Analyse de la co-inertie de K nuages de points. *RSA, XLIV, 35-60.*

D'AMBRA, L. and LAURO, N.C. (1982): Analisi in componenti principali in rapporto ad un sottospazio di riferimento. *Rivista di Statistica Applicata, n.1, vol.15.*

D'AMBRA, L., SABATIER, R. and AMENTA, P. (1998): Analisi fattoriale delle matrici a tre vie: sintesi e nuovi approcci. *Italian Journal of Applied Statistics, vol.13, n.2, 2002).*

DE JONG, S. and KIERS, H.A.L. (1992): Principal covariates regression. *Part I. Theory, Chemometrics and Intelligent Laboratory Systems, 14, 155-164.*

FRANK, I.R. and FRIEDMAN, J.H. (1993): A statistical view of some chemometrics regression tools. *Technometrics, 35, 109-148.*

GARTHWAITE, P.H. (1994): An interpretation of partial least squares. *JASA, 89.*

HOERL, A.E. (1962): Application of ridge analysis to regression problems. *Chemical Engineering Progress, 58, 54-59.*

HOERL, A.E. and KENNARD, R.W. (1970): Ridge regression: biased estimation for nonorthogonal problems. *Technometrics, 12, 55-67.*

HSKULDSSON, A. (1992): The H-principle in modelling with applications to chemometrics. *Chemometrics and Intelligent Laboratory Systems, 14, 139-153.*

STONE, M. and BROOKS, R.J. (1990): Continuum regression: cross validated sequentially constructed prediction embracing ordinary least squares and principal component regression. *J. Royal Stat. Soc., B, 2.*

SUNDBERG, R. (1993): Continuum regression and ridge regression. *J. R. Statist. Soc., B 55, 653-659.*

WOLD, H. (1966): Estimation of principal components and related models by iterative least squares, In: Krishnaiah P. R. (Ed.): *Multivariate Analysis*, Ac. Press, New York.

Acknowledgement: The partecipation of L. D'Ambra and P. Amenta to this research was supported by the PRIN 2001 grant (Resp: Prof. L.D'Ambra) and PRIN 2001 grant (Resp: Prof. P.Amenta), respectively.

Evolutionary Strategies
to Avoid Local Minima
in Multidimensional Scaling

Stefan Etschberger and Andreas Hilbert

Institut für Statistik und mathematische Wirtschaftstheorie
Universität Augsburg, 86135 Augsburg, Germany

Abstract. Multidimensional scaling is very widely used in exploratory data analysis. It is mainly used to represent sets of objects with respect to their proximities in a low dimensional Euclidean space. Widely used optimization algorithms try to improve the representation via shifting its coordinates in direction of the negative gradient of a corresponding fit function. Depending on the initial configuration, the chosen algorithm and its parameter settings there is a possibility for the algorithm to terminate in a local minimum.

This article describes the combination of an evolutionary model with a non-metric gradient solution method to avoid this problem. Furthermore a simulation study compares the results of the evolutionary approach with one classic solution method.

1 Introduction

Multidimensional scaling is very common in exploratory data analysis. It is mainly used to represent sets of objects with respect to their proximities in a low dimensional Euclidean space to get a better insight into the underlying structure of the data. The low dimensional configuration X of the data is measured with respect to its goodness of fit for example by a non-metric stress function $S(X)$ (see Kruskal(1964a)). Widely used optimization algorithms try to improve $S(X)$ via shifting each configuration's coordinates in direction of the negative gradient of $S(X)$ (see e.g. Kruskal(1964b), Johnson(1973), Meulman and Verboon(1993), Busing et al.(1997)). Depending on the initial configuration, the chosen algorithm and its parameter settings there is a possibility of the algorithm to terminate in a local stress minimum. Thus, the resulting final configuration may not represent the structure of the data accordingly.

Recent publications try to address this problem by proposing algorithms which use models like e.g. neural networks (in van Wezel et al.(2001)) or simulated annealing (Klock and Buhmann(1997)) to overcome that problem. An often suggested alternative to avoid local minima of the stress function is to use more than one starting configuration (see e.g. Opitz(1980), Webb(1999), Young(1987)). The aim of this study is to explore the capabilites of an evolutionary based algorithm with regard to this problem. Therefore a combination of an evolutionary model using a classic non-metric gradient solution method has been developed and implemented to

- achieve more heterogeneity on the solution search space,
- to enable configurations to exchange informations with crossover techniques and
- to randomly change the algorithm's parameters with mutation

and therefore prevent solutions from becoming trapped in a local minimum.

2 The gradient method

We assume n multivariate data objects y_i $(i \in \{1, \ldots, n\})$ have to be represented with respect to their proximities in a low dimensional Euclidean space. Each iteration of the algorithm leads to a configuration

$$X^l = (x_{ij})^l_{n,k},$$

j denoting each object's position in $\mathbb{R}^k$, k usually $\in \{1, 2, 3\}$ and l counting the number of the actual iteration. X^0 will be chosen randomly and the gradient step factor of the 0th iteration λ_0 will be initiated to a small positive real number (e.g. $\lambda_0 \in [10^{-3}, 10^{-1}]$). The original dissimilarity data matrix has the form

$$D = (d_{ij})_{n,n} \in \mathbb{R}^{n \times n}_+$$

Additionally we assume that

- there are no missing values in D,
- $d_{ii} = 0$ $\forall i \in \{1, \ldots, n\}$
- (i', j') is more similar than $(i, j) \Leftrightarrow d_{i'j'} < d_{ij}$.

The lth iteration of the algorithm can be described as follows:

i) Calculation of $S(X^l)$ (Kruskal(1964a))
   - Calculation of dissimilarity $\hat{d}(i, j)$ with a L_p norm
   - Monotonic transformation of $\hat{d}(i, j)$ into $\delta(i, j)$ in such a way that

$$d(i, j) \leq d(i', j') \Rightarrow \delta(i, j) \leq \delta(i', j')$$

   - Calculation of raw Stress function $S^*(X^l)$ and scaling it with maximal Stress

$$S(X^l) = \frac{S^*(X^l)}{S_{\max}(X^l)} = \frac{\sum\limits_{i<j} \left(\hat{d}(i, j) - \delta(i, j) \right)^2}{\sum\limits_{i<j} \left(\hat{d}(i, j) - \frac{2}{n(n-1)} \sum\limits_{i<j} \hat{d}(i, j) \right)^2}$$

ii) Shifting points along the negative gradient of X^l (∇S):

$$X^{l+1} = X^l - \lambda_l \nabla S|_{X^l}$$

iii) $\lambda_{l+1} = q\lambda_l$, with $q \in (0, 1)$

Iterations will be repeated till a termination criterion (e.g. minimal Stress) is fulfilled.

3   The evolutionary algorithm

Evolutionary strategies are based on biologically motivated reproducing and selection strategies and proved to be useful for solving a large range of problems which occur with optimization algorithms (see e.g. Nissen(1997)). For the given problem we put s MDS configurations in a population $P = \{I(1), I(2), \ldots, I(s)\}$. This Population contains individuals $I(i) = \{X(i), S(i)\}$ with $X(i)$ a randomly generated start configuration and $S(i) = \{\sigma(i)_1, \ldots, \sigma(i)_n\}$ as a set of uniform distributed standard deviations $(\sigma(i)_j \sim U(0, r), r \in \mathbb{R}_+)$. We speak of a generation of this population as one iteration step of the algorithm. Each generation passes the following steps:

i) Calculation of the fitness $F(X(i)) = f(S(X(i)))$ of each individual with a monotonic decreasing function $f : \mathbb{R}_+ \to \mathbb{R}_+$ of the stress, e.g. $f(r) = r^{-1}$ or $f(r) = ln^{-1}(r)$

ii) Random selection of the mating pool and the parents:

- Save the individual with the best fitness into the mating pool
- Select randomly $s-1$ (with $\frac{s}{2} \in \mathbb{N}$) individuals out of P into a mating pool $M = \left\{\tilde{I}(1), \ldots, \tilde{I}(s)\right\}$ with selection probabilities

$$p(I(i)) = \frac{f(I(i))}{\sum\limits_{i=1}^{s} f(I(i))}$$

- Divide mating pool in randomly selected pairs of parents:

$$M = \left\{I(1)_{px}, I(1)_{py}, \ldots, I\left(\frac{s}{2}\right)_{px}, I\left(\frac{s}{2}\right)_{py}\right\}$$

iii) Generation of the **children** through

- **Direct Crossover**
  Each pair of parents I_{px} and I_{py} exchange rows in their configurations X_p and Y_p with a certain probability at randomly chosen crossover point(s) c_i ($0 < c_i < n$). Thus the configurations X_c and Y_c of the children I_{cx} and I_{cy} will be set depending on the strategy type (see figures 1 and 2) to

$$X_c(i) = \begin{cases} X_p(i), & \text{if } i \geq c \\ Y_p(i), & \text{if } i < c \end{cases}, Y_c(i) = \begin{cases} Y_p(i), & \text{if } i \geq c \\ X_p(i), & \text{if } i < c \end{cases} \text{ (Strategy 1), or}$$

$$X_c(i) = \begin{cases} X_p(i), & \text{if } i \neq c \\ Y_p(i), & \text{if } i = c \end{cases}, Y_c(i) = \begin{cases} Y_p(i), & \text{if } i \neq c \\ X_p(i), & \text{if } i = c \end{cases} \text{ (Strategy 2)}$$

- **Intermediate or Discrete Recombination and Mutation**
  A standard deviation $\sigma(i)_j$ ($j \in \{1, \ldots, n\}$) is assigned to each individual's point. Those standard deviations serve as a base for the random mutation process:

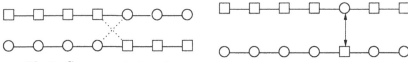

Fig. 1. Crossover strategy 1   **Fig. 2.** Crossover strategy 2

(a) The Children's standard deviations of mutation $(\sigma_c(i_1)_j, \sigma_c(i_2)_j)$ are calculated according to:
   i. An intermediate recombination of the parent's standard deviations $(\sigma_p(i_1)_j, \sigma_p(i_2)_j)$, e.g. $\sigma_c(i_1)_j = \sigma_c(i_2)_j = \frac{1}{2}(\sigma_p(i_1)_j + \sigma_p(i_2)_j)$ for all $j \in \{1, ..., n\}$ or
   ii. A Discrete recombination $\sigma_c(i_1)_j = \sigma_p(i_2)_j$ and $\sigma_c(i_2)_j = \sigma_p(i_1)_j$ for randomly selected $j \in \{1, ..., n\}$
(b) randomly select points to mutate
(c) $\widetilde{X}_c(i)_{jk} = X_c(i)_{jk} + Z(i)_{jk}$ with $Z(i)_{jk} \sim N(0, \sigma(i)_j)$

- **Mutation of Gradient Factor**
   (a) $\widetilde{\lambda}$ is the gradient factor of the parental individual with the highest fitness value
   (b) Set the gradient factor of each child to $\lambda(i) = \widetilde{\lambda} \cdot b^Z$ with $Z \sim U(-1, 1)$ and b a positive real constant
   (c) Set $\widetilde{\widetilde{X}}_c(i) = \widetilde{X}_c(i) - \lambda(i) \cdot \nabla S|_{\widetilde{X}_c(i)}$

Generations will be calculated by starting over at (1) till a termination criterion has been reached. The fittest individual, i.e. the one containing the configuration with the smallest stress, is taken as the stress value assigned to the generation.

4   The simulation study

To compare both the evolutionary and the classic approach, sets of randomly generated data objects served as a source for three simulation experiments. The representation space was chosen to be $\mathbb{R}^2$. Each experiment consisted of 500 MDS solution runs and was terminated either by reaching a given minimal stress value or by exceeding a given time limit. Some of the algorithm's parameters have been set to fixed values throughout the simulation runs (see table 1). The parameters controlled by the Monte Carlo Analysis are set by uniformly distributed random variables (see table 2).

The input data sets for each experiment type have been generated randomly as well:

Type A: 30 normally distributed objects y with attributes $y(i) \sim N(0, 1)$,
Type B: 6 sharp clusters of 5 objects each with

$$y(i) = c_j(i) + Z, \quad c_j(i) \in \{0, 1\}, \quad Z \sim N(0, 0.1)$$

	Data Type		
Parameter	A	B	C
Random Mutation Jump width	0.1	0.1	0.1
Crossover Strategy	2	2	2
Recombination Type	discrete	discrete	discrete
Mutation Probability	1	1	1
Maximal Time [sec.]	200	50	200
Initial Gradient Factor λ	0.5	0.5	0.5
Max. Factor for Gradient Change	10	10	10
Minimal Stress	$6 \cdot 10^{-3}$	$6 \cdot 10^{-3}$	$1 \cdot 10^{-4}$

Table 1. Setting of fixed parameters

Parameter	min	max	step
Population Size	2	40	2
Classic or Evolutionary	c	e	-
$\Delta\lambda$ (Classic)	0.2	1	1e-5
Crossover Probability	1e-3	1	1e-4

Table 2. Monte carlo analysis: Uniformly distributed parameters

Type C: 5 sharp clusters of 5 objects each and 5 wide spread objects as outliers

$$y(i) = c_j(i) + Z_j \quad \text{with } Z_j \sim \begin{cases} N(0, 0.1), \text{ if } j \in \{1, ..., 5\} \\ N(0, 10) \text{ , if } j = 6 \end{cases}$$

($i \in \{1, 2, 3\}$ denoting dimension, $j \in \{1, ..., 6\}$ number of cluster and c_j center of cluster)

The dissimilarity matrix D of the generated input data is calculated by aggregating the normed values of each attribute with a L_2 norm:

$$d_{ij} = \sqrt{\sum_{k=1}^{3} \frac{(x_{ik} - x_{jk})^2}{\frac{1}{n} \sum_{i=1}^{n} (x_{ik} - \bar{x}_k)^2}}, \text{ with } \bar{x}_k = \frac{1}{n} \sum_{i=1}^{n} x_{ik}$$

5 Results

Figure 3 shows a histogram of the stress values reached after termination of each run. The results of the classic runs have been collected in the grey bars, the black bars show the results of the evolutionary based runs. The classic results show a distribution with greater variance and larger worst case values in comparison to the evolutionary ones. The worst, best, average and median stress values are summarized in table 3. The worst case runs of the evolutionary approach resulted in final stress values with factor 0.12-0.35

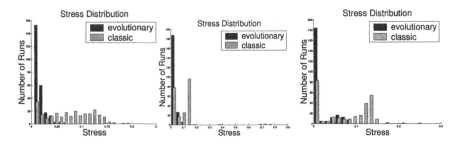

Fig. 3. Monte carlo simulation results of data types (left to right) **A, B, C**

smaller than the runs of the classic algorithm. The resulting configurations of the worst case runs for 2 dimensional representations have been plotted exemplarily for data type **B** in figures 4 and 5 (for details of the other data types see Etschberger and Hilbert(2002)). The 6 clusters are distinguishable in the evolutionary result only.

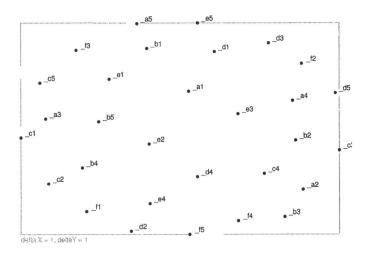

Fig. 4. Worst configuration of classic runs with data type B

6   Drawbacks and outlook

One drawback of the evolutionary approach could be the high computation costs at large number of individuals in one population in comparison to the classic algorithm. If one algorithmic termination criterion is a maximum time, a large population could result in a small number of generations with a final stress not representing the capabilities of the algorithm. So the number of individuals together with the maximal time limit should be chosen carefully.

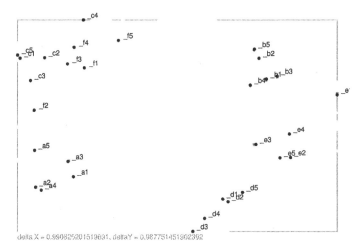

Fig. 5. Worst configuration of evolutionary runs with data type B

		Data Type		
		A	**B**	**C**
evolutionary	worst	0.069	0.10	0.089
	best	0.0056	0.0019	0.00067
	average	0.014	0.014	0.015
	median	0.0096	0.0042	0.0076
classic	worst	0.20	0.78	0.25
	best	0.0057	0.0020	0.00068
	average	0.076	0.096	0.075
	median	0.076	0.10	0.092

Table 3. Stress value results of simulation runs

Potential for improvement of the algorithm could lie in the direct crossover of points: If the similarity of each pair of configurations could be quantified except for rotation and/or translation the efficiency of the direct crossover step should increase.

Therefore the algorithm is planned to be improved and optimized with regards to the following points:

- Optimization of the algorithm:
  - Transform each individual into a rotation and translation invariant form.
  - Set up a measure for similarity of individuals to assign a penalty function to individuals similar to the ones already selected in the mating pool, i.e. change the fitness of those e.g. to $\widetilde{F}(I(i)) = \frac{F(I(i))}{p}$, with $p \in (1, \infty)$ as a penalty coefficient.

- Individualize the evolutionary changed gradient scaling factor for each point and adapt cross-over routines accordingly.
- Optimize the default values of the algorithm's parameters with a larger simulation study.
- Compare results with other actual algorithmic approaches (e.g. as in van Wezel et al.(2001), Busing et al.(1997) or in Klock and Buhmann(1997))
- Include software module in a Java and R based data mining system under work

7 Conclusion

Evolutionary algorithms seem to be promising for solving non-metric multidimensional scaling problems. With the first version of the algorithm presented with this study the quality of the resulting configurations with respect to smaller stress values could be improved significantly in comparison to one classic algorithm. A simulation study shows that the worst case runs of the evolutionary approach result in final stress values for the given sets of simulated data which are by factor 0.12-0.35 smaller than the classic algorithm's runs.

References

BUSING, F., COMMANDEUR, J., and HEISER, W. (1997): PROXSCAL: A multidimensional scaling program for individual differences scaling with contraints. *Softstat.*

ETSCHBERGER, S. and HILBERT, A. (2002): Multidimensional scaling and genetic algorithms: A solution approach to avoid local minima. *Arbeitspapiere zur Mathematischen Wirtschaftsforschung, Universität Augsburg, Heft 181.*

JOHNSON, R. M. (1973): Pairwise nonmetric multidimensional scaling. *Psychometrika, 38*, pages 11–18.

KLOCK, H. and BUHMANN, J. M. (1997): Multidimensional scaling by deterministic annealing. In Pelillo, M. and Hancock, E. R., editors, *Energy Minimization Methods in Computer Vision and Pattern Recognition*, pages 245–260.

KRUSKAL, J. B. (1964a): Multidimensional scaling by optimizing goodness of fit to a nonmetric hypothesis. *Psychometrika, 29*, pages 1–27.

KRUSKAL, J. B. (1964b): Nonmetric multidimensional scaling: A numerical method. *Psychometrika, 29*, pages 115–129.

MEULMAN, J. and VERBOON, P. (1993): Points of view analysis revisited: fitting multidimensional structures to optimal distance components with cluster restrictions on the variables. *Psychometrika, 58*, pages 7–35.

NISSEN, V. (1997): *Einführung in evolutionäre Algorithmen.* Vieweg, Braunschweig u.a.

OPITZ, O. (1980): *Numerische Taxonomie.* Gustav Fischer Verlag, Stuttgart, New York.

VAN WEZEL, M. C., KOSTERS, W. A., VAN DER PUTTEN, P., and KOK, J. N. (2001): Nonmetric multidimensional scaling with neural networks. *Lecture Notes in Computer Science*, 2189:pp. 245–260.

WEBB, A. (1999): *Statistical Pattern Recognition.* Oxford University Press, Inc, New York.

YOUNG, F. W. (1987): *Multidimensional Scaling - history, theory and applications.* Lawrence Erlbaum Associates, Inc., Publishers.

Principal Component Analysis of Boolean Symbolic Objects

Paolo Giordani

Department of Statistics, Probability and Applied Statistics,
University of Rome 'La Sapienza', I-00185 Rome, Italy

Abstract. In this paper we extend the well known principal component analysis (PCA) to deal with Boolean symbolic objects (SO's). We generalize the procedure by Ichino and Yaguchi (1994) by means of the dissimilarity functions introduced by De Carvalho and Souza (1999). In this way we extend PCA to deal with constrained SO's. In addition we propose to extend the above procedure to deal with three-way SO's applying three-way methods such as Tucker3 and Parafac. Finally, a visualization procedure that takes into account the SO's complexity is suggested.

1 Introduction

In real life, many phenomena are complex and cannot be explained by using traditional single valued variables. Instead, they might be dealt with by utilizing different kinds of variables: quantitative (discrete or continuous) or qualitative (nominal or ordinal), single or interval or set valued. We refer to this kind of data as symbolic data and to each observation unit as Boolean symbolic object (hereafter SO).

Many authors proposed extensions of PCA to deal with SO's. Ichino and Yaguchi (1994) presented a procedure in order to suitably extend PCA to mixed features variables based on their generalized Minkowski metrics. In this work we generalize their procedure considering the dissimilarity functions proposed by De Carvalho and Souza (1999) in order to take into account dependencies among variables and applying three-way methods such as Tucker3 and Parafac, in order to detect the underlying structure of three-way SO's.

2 Boolean symbolic objects

Let Ω be a set of I SO's $\omega_i, i = 1, \ldots, I$. Each SO is characterized by J variables (or descriptors) $Y = (Y_1, \ldots, Y_J)$ whose domains are $D = (D_1, \ldots, D_J)$. For each SO, the J variables take the values $d = (d_1, \ldots, d_J)$ where $d_j \subseteq D_j, j = 1, \ldots, J$. Thus we can refer to a generic SO as $a = [y_1 \in d_1] \wedge \ldots \wedge [y_J \in d_J] = \wedge_{j=1}^{J} [y_j \in d_j]$. See, for more details, Bock and Diday (2000).

When there are dependencies among variables, we talk about constrained SO's. We can define two type of dependencies:

Hierarchical: if the variable $Y_{j'}$ takes its value in a subset $[S_{j'} \subseteq D_{j'}]$, the variable $Y_{j''}$ may be inapplicable (NA). In this case we have the rule $r_{l'} : [Y_{j'} \in S_{j'}] \Rightarrow [Y_{j''} = NA]$;

Logical: if the subset $S_{j'} \subseteq D_{j'}$ of the variable $Y_{j'}$ is related to the subset

$S_{j''} \subseteq D_{j''}$ of the variable $Y_{j''}$. In this case we have the rule $r_{l''} : [Y_{j'} \in S_{j'}] \Rightarrow [Y_{j''} \in S_{j''}]$.

A SO whose description does not contradict the set of rules $\{r_1, \ldots, r_T\}$ is coherent.

The *Description Potential* is a positive measure defined on a generic SO $a = \wedge_{j=1}^{J} [y_j \in d_j]$. In fact, two different expressions are available according to the presence/absence of dependencies among variables. If there is no set of rules we have $\pi(a) = \prod_{j=1}^{J} \mu(d_j)$ and, in the latter case, we have

$$\pi(a/r_1 \wedge \ldots \wedge r_T) = \prod_{j=1}^{J} \mu(d_j) - \pi(a \wedge (\neg(r_1 \wedge \ldots \wedge r_T))) \text{ where } \mu(d_j) \text{ is}$$

the range of d_j if Y_j is continuous quantitative, or the cardinality of d_j if Y_j is discrete quantitative or qualitative. The above measures are a sort of volume of the coherent description of a SO. Therefore, if there are dependencies among variables, we subtract the volume given by the description which is not coherent.

If we have two generic SO's $a = \wedge_{j=1}^{J} [y_j \in d_j^a]$ and $b = \wedge_{j=1}^{J} [y_j \in d_j^b]$, we can define the following operations:

Join: $a \oplus b = \wedge_{j=1}^{J} [d_j^a \oplus d_j^b]$ where $d_j^a \oplus d_j^b$ is the union between the sets d_j^a and d_j^b (Y_j nominal qualitative) or the interval $[\min(d_{jL}^a, d_{jL}^b), \max(d_{jU}^a, d_{jU}^b)]$ where $[d_{jL}^a, d_{jL}^b]$ and $[d_{jU}^a, d_{jU}^b]$ are the lower and upper bound of, respectively, the sets d_j^a and d_j^b (Y_j quantitative or ordinal qualitative).

Union: $a \cup b = \wedge_{j=1}^{J} [d_j^a \cup d_j^b]$.

Conjunction: $a \wedge b = \wedge_{j=1}^{J} [y_j \in d_j^a \cap d_j^b]$.

We note that the *Join* operator differs from the *Union* operator only when the descriptor involved is quantitative or ordinal qualitative and the intersection between $[d_{jL}^a, d_{jL}^b]$ and $[d_{jU}^a, d_{jU}^b]$ is empty. In fact, in these cases, we have that $(d_j^a \oplus d_j^b) \supset (d_j^a \cup d_j^b)$.

3   The dissimilarity functions by De Carvalho and Souza (1999)

In this section, we recall the dissimilarity functions proposed by De Carvalho and Souza (1999). They suggested two dissimilarity functions based on the following different comparison functions between two SO's $a = \wedge_{j=1}^{J} [y_j \in d_j^a]$ and $b = \wedge_{j=1}^{J} [y_j \in d_j^b]$, according to the presence/absence of dependencies among variables. With respect to the j-th descriptor, if there are not dependencies, we have

$$\phi_{j\gamma}(a_j, b_j) = \left\{ \frac{1}{2} \left[\left(\frac{\theta_{1\gamma}(a_j, b_j)}{\mu(D_j)} \right)^l + \left(\frac{\theta_{2\gamma}(a_j, b_j)}{\mu(D_j)} \right)^l \right] \right\} \qquad (1)$$

where

$$\theta_{1\gamma}(a_j, b_j) = (1 - 2\gamma)\,\mu\left(d_j^a \cap \bar{d}_j^b\right) + \\ + \mu\left(\bar{d}_j^a \cap d_j^b\right) + \mu\left(\bar{d}_j^a \cap \bar{d}_j^b \cap \mu\left(d_j^a \oplus d_j^b\right)\right), \quad (2)$$

$$\theta_{2\gamma}(a_j, b_j) = (1 - 2\gamma)\,\mu\left(\bar{d}_j^a \cap d_j^b\right) + \\ + \mu\left(d_j^a \cap \bar{d}_j^b\right) + \mu\left(\bar{d}_j^a \cap \bar{d}_j^b \cap \mu\left(d_j^a \oplus d_j^b\right)\right), \quad (3)$$

in which $0 \leq \gamma \leq 0.5$. If $l = 1$, (1) is the comparison function proposed by Ichino and Yaguchi (1994). If there are dependencies among variables, (1) is replaced as follows. If the j-th variable is *NA* for both SO's, then $\phi_{j\gamma}(a_j, b_j) = 0$, if the j-th variable is NA for one SO, then $\phi_{j\gamma}(a_j, b_j) = 1$, and, otherwise,

$$\phi_{j\gamma}(a_j, b_j) = \left\{\frac{1}{2}\left[\left(\frac{\psi_{1\gamma}(a_j, b_j)}{\psi_{3\gamma}(a_j, b_j)}\right)^l + \left(\frac{\psi_{2\gamma}(a_j, b_j)}{\psi_{3\gamma}(a_j, b_j)}\right)^l\right]\right\}^{\frac{1}{l}} \quad (4)$$

where

$$\psi_{1\gamma}(a_j, b_j) = (1 - 2\gamma)\,\mu\left(d_j^a \cap \bar{d}_j^b\right)\eta(a_j, b_j) + \\ + \mu\left(\bar{d}_j^a \cap d_j^b\right)\tau(a_j, b_j) + \mu\left(\bar{d}_j^a \cap \bar{d}_j^b \cap \mu\left(d_j^a \oplus d_j^b\right)\right), \quad (5)$$

$$\psi_{2\gamma}(a_j, b_j) = (1 - 2\gamma)\,\mu\left(\bar{d}_j^a \cap d_j^b\right)\tau(a_j, b_j) + \\ + \mu\left(d_j^a \cap \bar{d}_j^b\right)\eta(a_j, b_j) + \mu\left(\bar{d}_j^a \cap \bar{d}_j^b \cap \mu\left(d_j^a \oplus d_j^b\right)\right), \quad (6)$$

$$\psi_{3\gamma}(a_j, b_j) = \mu\left(d_j^a \cap d_j^b\right)(\lambda(a_j, b_j) - 1) + \mu\left(d_j^a \cap \bar{d}_j^b\right)(\eta(a_j, b_j) - 1) + \\ + \mu\left(\bar{d}_j^a \cap d_j^b\right)(\tau(a_j, b_j) - 1) + \mu(D_j), \quad (7)$$

in which, to take into account the set of rules $\{r_1, \ldots, r_T\}$,

$$\lambda(a_j, b_j) = \left\{\frac{\pi((a \wedge a_j) \wedge b_j / r_1 \wedge \ldots \wedge r_T)\pi((b \wedge a_j) \wedge b_j / r_1 \wedge \ldots \wedge r_T)}{\pi((a \wedge a_j) \wedge b_j)\pi((b \wedge a_j) \wedge b_j)}\right\}^m \quad (8)$$

$$\eta(a_j, b_j) = \left\{\frac{\pi((a \wedge a_j) \wedge \neg b_j / r_1 \wedge \ldots \wedge r_T)}{\pi((a \wedge a_j) \wedge \neg b_j)}\right\}^m, \quad (9)$$

$$\tau(a_j, b_j) = \left\{\frac{\pi((b \wedge \neg a_j) \wedge b_j / r_1 \wedge \ldots \wedge r_T)}{\pi((b \wedge \neg a_j) \wedge b_j)}\right\}^m, \quad (10)$$

with $l \in \{1, 2, \ldots\}$ and $m \in \{\ldots 1/2, 1, 2, \ldots\}$ whose role is to increase ($m > 1$) or to decrease ($m < 1$) the emphasis of the rules.

Using (1) or (4) we can calculate the dissimilarity between two unconstrained or constrained SO's, a and b, as

$$d_n(a, b) = \frac{\left(\sum_{j=1}^{J} \phi_{j\gamma}(a_j, b_j)^n\right)^{\frac{1}{n}}}{\sum_{j=1}^{J} \delta(j)} \quad (11)$$

where $n = \{1, 2, \ldots\}$ and $\delta(j) = 0$ if a_j and b_j are *NA*, $\delta(j) = 1$ otherwise.

4   Two-way and three-way methods

The ordinary PCA is the factorization of the two-way quantitative single valued matrix $\mathbf{X}$ of order $(I \times J)$, where I is the number of units and J is the number of variables, whose generic element is x_{ij}. We have

$$x_{ij} = \sum_{s=1}^{S} a_{is}b_{js} + e_{ij} \tag{12}$$

where a_{is} and b_{js} are the generic elements of, respectively, the component scores matrix $\mathbf{A}$ and the component loadings one $\mathbf{B}$, while e_{ij} is the error term and S is the number of extracted components.

In three-way generalizations of PCA we deal with an $(I \times J \times K)$ three-way array $\mathbf{X}$, where K is the number of occasions. Tucker3 and Parafac are well-known methods which extend PCA to analyze three-way numerical data sets. The Parafac model is, probably, the most natural extension of PCA, by adding the component loadings of the occasion mode (c_{ks}). Thus, with respect to the generic element of $\mathbf{X}$, we have:

$$x_{ijk} = \sum_{s=1}^{S} a_{is}b_{js}c_{ks} + e_{ijk} \tag{13}$$

PCA can be considered as a special case of Parafac when $K = 1$ defining the component loadings as $b_{js}c_{ks}$. The Tucker3 model can be written as

$$x_{ijk} = \sum_{p=1}^{P}\sum_{q=1}^{Q}\sum_{r=1}^{R} a_{ip}b_{jq}c_{kr}g_{pqr} + e_{ijk} \tag{14}$$

where, in contrast to Parafac, different numbers of components $(P, Q$ and $R)$ can be extracted in the different modes and g_{pqr} is the generic element of the $(P \times Q \times R)$ core matrix which shows the interactions among the components of each mode. The Parafac model can be seen as a constrained version of the Tucker3 imposing $P = Q = R = S$ and $g_{pqr} = 1$ if $p = q = r, g_{pqr} = 0$ otherwise. See, for an overview, Kiers and Van Mechelen (2001).

5   New approaches of PCA on SO's

Ichino and Yaguchi (1994) presented their generalization of PCA to deal with SO's as follows:

I. Find the so-called reference event, the SO which has minimum distance according to (11) with respect to the remaining SO's. The reference event can be considered the average SO, a sort of gravity center of the data set, as noted by Ichino and Yaguchi (1994).

II. Define the coded data matrix by calculating the comparison function in

(1) with $l = 1$, for each variable, between the reference event and the other SO's and by inserting the negative sign when the SO involved is smaller than the reference event. In fact, y_{ij}, the generic element of the obtained coded matrix $\mathbf{Y}$, shows how much the score of the generic i-th SO on the j-th variable differs from that of the reference event on the j-th variable. It is useful to remark that this coding procedure does not modify the data dimension.

III. Apply PCA to the quantified data matrix $\mathbf{Y}$.

In this paper we extend the above procedure considering the comparison function in (1) or, if there are dependencies among variables, the one in (4). Therefore, our procedure represents an attempt to perform PCA on constrained SO's. In fact, we apply PCA on the coded matrix $\mathbf{Y}$ obtained in Step II, whose elements take into account the set of rules $\{r_1, \ldots, r_T\}$. As a consequence, the extracted components take into account not only the variables but also the dependencies among them. Finally, we note that the procedure involved can be extended to three-way data. In this context, we apply Tucker3 or Parafac instead of PCA in step III. Now the reference event is obtained as the SO at a specific occasion which has minimum distance with respect to the remaining SO's at each occasion. Thus, the generic element of the coded matrix has the same meaning of the two-way case except that the reference event is not an overall average SO, but the average SO at a specific occasion.

6   The visualization procedure

PCA offers the possibility to represent the observation units in the low dimensional space spanned by $\mathbf{B}$, using as coordinates the columns of $\mathbf{A}$, provided that $\mathbf{B}$ is columnwise orthonormal in order to have an adequate plot. In the three-way case, we can represent the entities of the unit mode by means of procedures which are very similar to that for plots of PCA solutions. See, for more details, Kiers (2000).

The above procedures can be applied in our PCA extensions but the visualization loses the intrinsic features of SO's. In fact, as each SO is represented as a point, it follows that the data complexity is not taken into account. Several proposals are available in literature about visualization tools that consider the SO's complexity in their low dimensional projection. See, for instance, Lauro and Palumbo (2000) in PCA for interval valued data, Palumbo and Benedetto (1999) in Multidimensional Scaling for mixed feature data and Cazes (2002) in PCA for data matrices whose elements are probability laws. In order to consider the SO's complexity, we suggest to make use of the concept of *Description Potential* already introduced that represents a measure of the variability of SO's. Going into detail, we consider, for each SO, the vector of the normalized contribution of each variable to the *Description Potential*. In fact, with respect to the generic i-th SO, we suggest to deal with the vector $\mathbf{\Pi}_i = \left[\frac{\mu(d_1^i)}{\mu(D_1^i)} \cdots \frac{\mu(d_j^i)}{\mu(D_j^i)} \right]$, $i = 1, \ldots, I$. Considering this vector as supplementary point, we can now compute its component scores according to the (two-way or three-way) model at hand. In the two-way case, we get

$$\mathbf{a}_i^{DP} = [\, a_{i1}^{DP} \ \cdots \ a_{iS}^{DP} \,] = \left[\frac{\mu(d_1^i)}{\mu(D_1^i)} \ \cdots \ \frac{\mu(d_J^i)}{\mu(D_J^i)} \right] \mathbf{B}, \qquad (15)$$

$i = 1, \ldots, I$, where we use the property that $\mathbf{B}$ is columnwise orthonormal. The vector $\mathbf{a}_i^{DP}$ provides a low dimensional representation of the complexity associated to the generic i-th SO in the low dimensional space spanned by $\mathbf{B}$. In order to have a plot of SO's taking into account their complexity in its wholeness, we construct, for each SO, an ellipsoid (an ellipse if $S = 2$). In fact, with respect to the i-th SO, the ellipsoid is constructed using $\mathbf{a}_i$, the i-th row of $\mathbf{A}$, as center and $\mathbf{A}_i + \mathbf{H}_t \frac{1}{2} \mathbf{a}_i^{DP}, t = 1, \ldots, 2^S$, as vertices. Here $\mathbf{A}_i$ is a matrix of order $(S \times S)$ whose rows are equal to the vector $\mathbf{a}_i$ and $\mathbf{H}_t$'s, $t = 1, \ldots, 2^S$, are diagonal matrices of order $(S \times S)$ whose elements are ± 1 in order to refer exactly to every vertex. They allow us to consider all the vertices of the ellipsoid associated with each SO. The case $S = 2$ can help to clarify these matrices. We have $(2^S = 4)$:

$$\mathbf{H}_1 = \begin{bmatrix} -1 & 0 \\ 0 & -1 \end{bmatrix}, \mathbf{H}_2 = \begin{bmatrix} -1 & 0 \\ 0 & 1 \end{bmatrix}, \mathbf{H}_3 = \begin{bmatrix} 1 & 0 \\ 0 & -1 \end{bmatrix}, \mathbf{H}_4 = \begin{bmatrix} 1 & 0 \\ 0 & 1 \end{bmatrix}. \qquad (16)$$

From (16) we can note that each matrix is related to a different vertex. In fact, using $\mathbf{A}_i + \mathbf{H}_t \frac{1}{2} \mathbf{a}_i^{DP}, t = 1, \ldots, 4$, leads to considering all the four vertices which identify the ellipse pertaining to the i-th SO, $i = 1, \ldots, I$.

7 Application

In this section we present an application of our procedure on real symbolic data. The data set is known as 'Biological knowledge base' (Vignes (1991)). It describes $I = 12$ Tristichaces species characterized by means of 12 nominal and 13 ordinal descriptors ($J = 25$.) It is a two-way data set in which there are eight hierarchical dependencies between pairs of variables. The number of modalities of each descriptor is from two to four. Each datum is a finite set which takes on from one to three values. Using external information, we know that the 12 species belong to five genera (Tristicha, hereinafter 'T', Indotristicha 'I', Dalzellia 'D', Malacotristicha 'M', Weddellina 'W'). Performing our procedure (using PCA) we aim at finding subgroups of SO's, according to the above genera.
We find the reference event as the SO which has minimum distance, using (11) where we take $n = 2$, with respect to the remaining SO's. The average SO is 'Tristicha Trifaria Trifaria' which belongs to genus 'T'. We code the symbolic data matrix in a numerical way. Each element is obtained using (4) or setting 0 if the variable involved is NA for both SO's and 1 if it is NA for only one SO. In (4) we take $l = 1$ and $m = 1$. The obtained numerical matrix has order (12×25) as the symbolic one.
In spite of the fact that the fit is not very high (52% is the percentage of

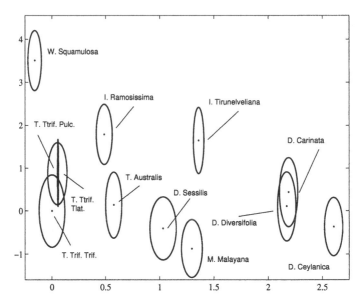

Fig. 1. Species visualization by using the proposed procedure (performing PCA).

explained sum of squares), we extract $S = 2$ components in order to have a two-dimensional plot of the observation units and we rotate the component scores matrix to simple structure. The first component is related to the presence of Bracteoles, the features of the Ovaries and some peculiarities of the Stamens. The second component takes into account others descriptors of the species. In fact, it depends on the Bracts, the Tepals and the Stipules of the leaves.

The plot in Figure 1 shows that our procedure works correctly. In fact, we are able to recover subgroups of species according to the five genera except for a few species. We can note that the misclassifications do not depend on a poor performance of our procedure but on the features of the species involved. 'Dalzellia Sessilis' (genus 'D') is characterized by features which differ considerably from those of the remaining species belonging to the same genus. In addition the two species belonging to genus 'I' are very heterogeneous and have not distinctive features with respect to the other genera. From Figure 1 we can also study the complexity of the species. We can see that 'Tristicha Trifaria Trifaria' is represented by the biggest ellipse. In fact, this species is recognized by descriptors that take the highest number of modalities. The ellipses differ according to the number of modalities of the original variables which describe the species. In fact, the size of the ellipses is consistent with the features of SO's except for 'Tristicha Trifaria Pulchella', whose *Description Potential* first component score does not reflect the complexity of the SO involved.

8   Conclusion

In this paper we proposed a procedure to perform (two-way and three-way) component models on (constrained and unconstrained) SO's. We also illustrated a visualization tool that is able to plot SO's taking into account their complexity. We provided an example in order to show how our method works.

References

BOCK, H.H. and DIDAY, E. (2000): *Analysis of symbolic data: exploratory methods for extracting statistical information from complex data.* Springer Verlag, Heidelberg.

CAZES, P. (2002): Analyse factorielle d'un tableau de lois de probabilité. *Revue de Statistique Appliquée,* 50, 5-24.

CAZES, P., CHOUAKRIA, A., DIDAY, E. and SCHEKTMAN, Y., (1997): Extension de l'analyse en composantes principales è des donnes de type intervalle. *Revue de Statistique Appliquée,* 45, 5-24.

DE CARVALHO, F.A.T. and SOUZA, R.M.C. (1999): New metrics for constrained Boolean symbolic objects. In: *Knowledge extraction and symbolic data analysis (KESDA '98),* EUROSTAT, Luxembourg, 175-187.

KIERS, H.A.L. (2000): Some procedures for displaying results from three-way methods. *Journal of Chemometrics,* 14, 151-170.

KIERS, H.A.L. and VAN MECHELEN, I. (2001): Three-way component analysis: principles and illustrative application. *Psychological methods,* 6, 84-110.

ICHINO, M. and YAGUCHI, H. (1994): Generalized Minkovski metrics for mixed feature-type data analysis. *IEEE Transaction on system, man and cybernetics,* 24, 698-708.

LAURO, C. and PALUMBO, F. (2000): Principal Component Analysis of interval data: a symbolic data analysis approach. *Computational Statistics,* 15, 73-87.

PALUMBO, F. and BENEDETTO, M. (1999): A generalisation measure for symbolic objects. In: *Knowledge extraction and symbolic data analysis (KESDA '98),* EUROSTAT, Luxembourg, 265-276.

VIGNES, R. (1991): Caractérisation automatique de groupes biologiques. *Thèse de Doctorat.* Université Paris-VI, Paris.

Multivariate Analysis for Variables of Arbitrary Information Level

Jürgen Hansohm

Lehrstuhl für Methodengestützte Planung,
Universität der Bundeswehr München, 85577 Neubiberg, Germany
http://www.UniBw-Muenchen.de/Campus/WOW/Hansohm.html
E-Mail: Juergen.Hansohm@UniBw-Muenchen.de

Abstract. Multivariate Analysis, like canonical correlation or principal component analysis with a mix of metric, nominal and ordinal data can be done by the classic method in combination with an optimal scaling technique described by Young (1981) and others. Variables with even more complex information levels, like hierachies, lattice orders, etc. are usually described by distances, but because distances have no directions and are rescaled by a different rescaling procedure, they cannot be compared equivalently with metric, nominal or ordinal variables. Here a method is proposed with fully generalizes the above mentioned methods to a set of variables of any above mentioned kind.

1 Introduction

Qualitative data plays a big role in exploratory data analysis. Often an analysis should be done with a mix of metric, nominal and ordinal variables. One approach to do this is to use a classic method, like regression for example, with a rescaling technique as described by Young et al. (1976).

In some cases one has variables with even more complex information levels. For example, a hierarchical structure with generic terms *(see below)* or a lattice order or a (total) preorder $\preceq$ on the set of the pairs of objects.

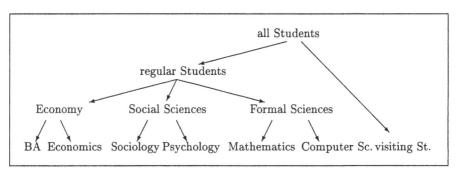

Fig. 1. Hierarchy structure of the variable "course of study" (Opitz 1980, p. 39).

In generalization of Young's approach consider now a regression or canonical correlation approach with a mix of metric, nominal, ordinal variables and variables with a more complex information level as mentioned above. On the first glance the use of distances for pairs of objects for all variables may be an adaequate method to compare the different information levels but this approach leads to unsatisfactory results.

One reason is, that by use of distances for metric and ordinal variables the information about the direction is lost. The distance between the object values "good" and "bad" for example, is the same as between "bad" and "good". The other reason lies in the transformation process by the rescaling technique. Consider an ordinal variable. For an ordinal variable the original scaling is rescaled by a monotone transformation. But distances, computed by a monotone transformation of the original ordinal scaling may differ from a monotone transformation of a distance, computed by the original ordinal scaling. For more details see the remark after theorem 1.

In the following a method is proposed which fully generalizes the quantitative analysis of qualitative data to variables with the above mentioned complex information levels by use of differences.

2   Definition of the problem

It's assumed that for any variable a set of differences according to the information level of that variable can be defined. Differences are similar to distances which were normally used for characterizing complex informations. In general, a difference set for n objects is defined as a set (cone) of $n \times n$-matrices with

$$\mathcal{D} = \{(d_{ij})_{nn} \mid d_{ij} \in I\!R, d_{ij} = -d_{ji}, (i,j = 1, \ldots, n)\} \qquad (1)$$

For any information level a subcone of $\mathcal{D}$ is defined as follows:
For a metric variable $a = (a_i)_n \in I\!R^n$ the set is defined by

$$\mathcal{D}_{metric} = \{(d_{ij})_{nn} \mid d_{ij} = y_i - y_j, y_i, \gamma \in I\!R, \gamma > 0, y_i = \gamma(a_i - \bar{a})\} \subseteq \mathcal{D} \,(2)$$

For an ordinal variable $a = (a_i)_n \in I\!R^n$ with a total preorder $\preceq$ on $\{a_i \mid i = 1, \ldots, n\}$ the set is defined by

$$\mathcal{D}_{ordinal} = \{(d_{ij})_{nn} \mid d_{ij} = y_i - y_j, y_i \in I\!R, a_i \prec a_j \Rightarrow y_i \leq y_j,$$
$$\sum_i^n y_i = 0\} \subseteq \mathcal{D} \qquad (3)$$

or with rank ties by

$$\mathcal{D}_{rank\ tied} = \{(d_{ij})_{nn} \mid d_{ij} = y_i - y_j, y_i \in I\!R, a_i \preceq a_j \Rightarrow y_i \leq y_j,$$
$$\sum_i^n y_i = 0\} \subseteq \mathcal{D} \qquad (4)$$

and for a nominal variable $a = (a_i)_n \in \mathbb{R}^n$ by

$$D_{nominal} = \{(d_{ij})_{nn} \mid d_{ij} = y_i - y_j, y_i \in \mathbb{R}, a_i = a_j \Rightarrow y_i = y_j,$$
$$\sum_i^n y_i = 0\} \subseteq \mathcal{D} \qquad (5)$$

For variables with more complex information levels like a hierarchy or a lattice order the difference set is defined by

$$D_{complex} = \{(d_{ij})_{nn} \mid d_{ij} \in \mathbb{R}, (i,j) \text{ "more similar than" } (\tilde{i}, \tilde{j})$$
$$\Rightarrow |d_{ij}| \leq |d_{\tilde{i}\tilde{j}}|, d_{ij} = -d_{ji}, (i,j = 1, \ldots, n)\} \subseteq \mathcal{D} \qquad (6)$$

This works in case of an arbitrary information level.

In order to compare the different variables we define a norm $\|\cdot\|$ on $\mathcal{D}$ by

$$\|d\| = \sqrt{<d,d>} = \sqrt{\sum_{i,j} d_{ij}^2} \qquad (7)$$

and define the correlation between two elements d and δ of $\mathcal{D}$ by

$$<d, \delta> /(\|d\| \cdot \|\delta\|) = \sum_{ij} d_{ij}\delta_{ij}/(\|d\| \cdot \|\delta\|) \qquad (8)$$

Consider the following

Problem of the canonical correlation:

Find weights $\alpha_k \in \mathbb{R}$ and differences $d^k \in D^k \subseteq \mathcal{D}(k = 1, \ldots, p)$ and $\beta_l \in \mathbb{R}, \delta^l \in \Delta^l \subseteq \mathcal{D}(l = 1, \ldots, q)$ so that the

correlation between $\sum_k \alpha_k d^k$ and $\sum_l \beta_l \delta^l$ is maximized $\qquad$ (9)

where w.l.o.g. $\|d^k\| = 1$ $(k = 1, \ldots, p)$, $\|\delta^l\| = 1$ $(l = 1, \ldots, q)$, $\|\sum_k \alpha_k d^k\| = \|\sum_l \beta_l \delta^k\| = 1$ and D^k, resp. Δ^l are the corresponding difference sets for the k-th dependent, resp. l-th independent variable[1].

The next canonical correlation is then defined by the same way under the additional condition that the solution must be uncorrelated to $\sum_k \alpha_k d^k$, resp. $\sum_l \beta_l \delta^l$. The third and following canonical correlations are defined in an analogous way.

3   Relationship to ordinary multivariate analysis

The problem of canonical correlation stated in (9) contains a lot of multivariate techniques as shown by the table below:

These well-known results can be easily verified with the help of (19).

---

[1] it should be noticed that for a variable with a nominal or complex information level the sign of the corresponding weight is meaningless

information level of the variables		method
dependent side	independent side	
metric	metric	classical canonical correlation or regression in the univariate case
one nominal	metric	linear discriminant analysis
metric	one nominal (and metric)	variance analysis (with covariates)
one ordinal	metric	method of Kruskal and Carmone (1968)
one ordinal, nominal or metric	a mix of ordinal, nominal and metric	method of Young et al.(1975, 1976, 1981)

Table 1. Relationship to other multivariate techniques

4 Computing

The problem (9) can be rewritten as

$$\text{minimize} \sqrt{\frac{\sum_{i,j}(d_{ij} - \delta_{ij})^2}{\sum_{i,j} d_{ij}^2}} \tag{10}$$

with $(d_{ij})_{nn} = d = \sum_k \alpha_k d^k$, $(\delta_{ij})_{nn} = \delta = \sum_l \beta_l \delta^l$ (Hansohm 1987).

Remark 1. (10) is the well known stress formula (one and two) introduced by Kruskal (1964a, 1964b).

Problem (10) equals

$$\text{minimize} \sum_{i,j}(d_{ij} - \delta_{ij})^2 \ (= \|d - \delta\|^2) \tag{11}$$

subject to $d = \sum_k \alpha_k d^k$, $d^k \in D^k$, $\|d^k\| = 1$, $\|d\| = 1$, $(k = 1, \ldots, p)$ and $\delta = \sum_l \beta_l \delta^l$, $\delta^l \in \Delta^l$, $\|\delta^l\| = 1$, $(l = 1, \ldots, q)$ which is obviously a least squares problem[2].

Remark 2. Because the upper diagonal elements of $(d_{ij})_{nn}$ (or $(\delta_{ij})_{nn}$) contains all the information, the computer program needs only $\frac{n(n-1)}{2}$ memory elements for storing $(d_{ij})_{nn}$.

The standard method for computing the minimum of the objective function of (11) is the ALS-algorithm. For fixed $d^k \in D^k$, $(k = 1, \ldots, p)$, $\delta^l \in \Delta^l$, $(l = 1, \ldots, q)$ the best α_k, $(k = 1, \ldots, p)$, β_l, $(l = 1, \ldots, q)$ minimizing (11) are computed *(model phase)* followed by a minimization of (11) over D^s subject to $d^s \in D^s$, $\|d^s\| = 1$ for fixed α_k and fixed d^k, $(k = 1, \ldots, p, k \neq s)$,

---

[2] notice that the condition $\|\delta\| = 1$ is omitted

$\beta_l, \delta^l, (l = 1, \ldots, q)$. This is sucessively done for all $s \in \{1, \ldots, p\}^3$ and after that for all sets Δ^l $(l = 1, \ldots, q)$ *(monotone regression phase(s), p+q times)*. Model phase and monotone regression phase(s) are then alternated iterated until the stress cannot be improved further on. For a more detailed discussion on the convergence properties of the ALS algorithm see Hansohm (1988).

Obviously, the model phase can be easily computed by a classic canonical correlation with an eigenvalue and eigenvector algorithm and for the monotone regression phase(s) one thinks at Kruskal's monotone regression algorithm. But for the last it is necessary that the minimization is done over a closed convex cone. Unfortunately, D^k is not a convex cone in all cases. Nevertheless, by the following lemmatas the computing can be done as usual.

Lemma 1. *If* $Y \subseteq \mathbb{R}^n$ *is a closed convex cone then* $D = \{(d_{ij})_{nn} \mid d_{ij} = y_i - y_j, y = (y_1, \ldots, y_n) \in Y\}$ *is a closed convex cone.*

Proof. Obviously, the difference set D is closed. Let $d^1, d^2 \in D$ and $y^1, y^2 \in Y$ with $d_{ij}^1 = y_i^1 - y_j^1, d_{ij}^2 = y_i^2 - y_j^2 \Rightarrow d_{ij}^1 + d_{ij}^2 = (y_i^1 + y_i^2) - (y_j^1 + y_j^2) \Rightarrow d^1 + d^2 \in D$ and also $\alpha d^1 \in D$ for $\alpha \geq 0$ by the same argument.$\square$

Corollary 1. *For metric, ordinal or nominal variables the difference scaling sets are closed convex cones.*

Lemma 2. *If* $\preceq$ *is a total preorder on the pairs of objects and* $D = \{(d_{ij})_{nn} \mid d_{ij} \in \mathbb{R}, (i, j) \prec (\tilde{i}, \tilde{j}) \Rightarrow |d_{ij}| \leq |d_{\tilde{i}\tilde{j}}|, d_{ij} = -d_{ji}\}$ *then* $|D| = \{|d_{ij}| \mid d_{ij} \in D\}$ *is a closed convex cone.*

Proof. Obviously, $|D|$ is a closed set and with $d \in |D| \Rightarrow \alpha d \in |D|$ for all $\alpha \geq 0$. Let $d^1, d^2 \in |D|$ with $d^1 = |\tilde{d}^1|, d^2 = |\tilde{d}^2|, \tilde{d}^1, \tilde{d}^2 \in D$ then $(i, j) \prec (\tilde{i}, \tilde{j}) \Rightarrow (d^1 + d^2)_{ij} = |\tilde{d}_{ij}^1| + |\tilde{d}_{ij}^2| \leq |\tilde{d}_{\tilde{i}\tilde{j}}^1| + |\tilde{d}_{\tilde{i}\tilde{j}}^2| = (d^1 + d^2)_{\tilde{i}\tilde{j}} \Rightarrow d^1 + d^2 \in |D|.\square$

Remark 3. $|D|$ is a dissimilarity set usually considered by methods in data analysis.

So for all variables the ALS-algorithm is well defined.

Theorem 1. *If* δ *is a difference,* D *a difference set defined by (6) and* $\hat{d}$ *a solution[4] of*

$$\min\{\sum_{ij}(|\delta_{ij}| - d_{ij})^2 \mid d \in |D|\}$$

then $d^* \in D$ *with* $d_{ij}^* = \mathrm{sgn}(\delta_{ij})\hat{d}_{ij}$ *is a solution of*

$$\min\{\sum_{ij}(\delta_{ij} - d_{ij})^2 \mid d \in D\} \quad (*)$$

---

[3] α_k $(k = 1, \ldots, n)$ are then adjusted in order to get $\|d\| = 1$
[4] in fact, $\hat{d}$ is unique

Proof. Obviously, $d^* \in D$. Let $\tilde{d} \in D$ be the minimum solution of $(*)$ then
$\sum_{ij}(|\delta_{ij}| - \hat{d}_{ij})^2 \leq \sum_{ij}(|\delta_{ij}| - |\tilde{d}_{ij}|)^2 \leq \sum_{ij}(\delta_{ij} - \tilde{d}_{ij})^2 \leq \sum_{ij}(\delta_{ij} - d^*_{ij})^2 = \sum_{ij}(|\delta_{ij}| - |d^*_{ij}|)^2 = \sum_{ij}(|\delta_{ij}| - \hat{d}_{ij})^2.\square$

The standard monotone regression algorithm formulated by Kruskal (1964a, 1964b) can be applied because the solution of the normed problem (11) with fixed δ is determined by the unnormed problem (11) with fixed δ but without the condition $\|d\| = 1$ and a norming procedure after that (Hansohm 1987, 1988).

For variables with a complex information level where a total preorder $\preceq$ on the pairs of objects describes the information level Kruskal's monotone regression algorithm can be used directly. For nominal and ordinal variables the case is a little bit more complicated. In case of an ordinal variable for example we are looking for a scaling $y \in \mathbb{R}^n$ on the n objects (and not on pairs of objects) with $a_i \prec a_j \Rightarrow y_i \leq y_j$ which is different to a monotone transformation of $d_{ij} = |y_i - y_j|$.[5]

Nevertheless the computation can be done by standard algorithms in two steps.

Firstly, for a given difference $\delta = (\delta_{ij})_{nn}$ we compute a metric multidimensional scaling $z \in \mathbb{R}^n$ for one dimension; i.e.

$$min\{\sum_{i,j}(\delta_{ij} - (z_i - z_j))^2 \mid z = (z_i)_n \in \mathbb{R}, \ \bar{z} = 0\} \qquad (12)$$

Secondly, for the above computed $z \in \mathbb{R}^n$ a monotone regression algorithm is used to determine the scalings $y \in \mathbb{R}^n$; i.e.

$$min\{\sum_{i}(z_i - y_i)^2 \mid y = (y_i)_n \in \mathbb{R}^n, \ \bar{y} = 0, \ a_i \prec a_j \Rightarrow y_i \leq y_j\} \qquad (13)$$

or with rank ties

$$min\{\sum_{i}(z_i - y_i)^2 \mid y = (y_i)_n \in \mathbb{R}^n, \ \bar{y} = 0, \ a_i \preceq a_j \Rightarrow y_i \leq y_j\} \qquad (14)$$

Instead of a monotone regression the means over the categories are used for nominal variables.

This method leads to the optimal solution because of the following theorem

Theorem 2. *Let H be a finite dimensional Hilbert space with the scalar product $< \cdot, \cdot >$ ($\|\cdot\| = \sqrt{< \cdot, \cdot >}$), T a subspace of H and $K \subseteq T$ a closed convex nonempty set. For any $x \in H$ the map*

$$P_K : H \to H, \ P_K x = \{k \in K \mid \|x - k\| \leq \|x - \tilde{k}\| \text{ for all } \tilde{k} \in K\} \qquad (15)$$

---

[5] if, for example, $a_1 \prec a_2 \prec a_3$ then $|y_2 - y_1| + |y_3 - y_2| = |y_3 - y_1|$ whereas $|d_{21}| + |d_{32}| = |d_{31}|$ isn't true in general

is defined as the projection of x on the subset $K \subseteq H$. Then

$$P_K x = P_K P_T x \text{ for all } x \in H \tag{16}$$

Proof. Because K and T are closed , convex and non empty P_K and P_T are well defined and we have $|P_K z| = |P_T z| = 1$ for all $z \in H$. Let $t_0 = P_T x$, then

$$< t_0 - x, t >= 0 \text{ for all } t \in T \tag{17}$$

Further, let $k_0 = P_K P_T x = P_K t_0$, then

$$< k_0 - t_0, k - k_0 >\geq 0 \text{ for all } k \in K \tag{18}$$

and because of (17) one gets $< t_0 - x, k - k_0 >= 0 \Rightarrow < k_0 - t_0 + t_0 - x, k - k_0 >\geq 0 \Rightarrow < k_0 - x, k - k_0 >\geq 0$ for all $k \in K \Rightarrow k_0 = P_K x.\square$

Because of the fact that

$$\sum_{i,j}((z_i - z_j) - (y_i - y_j))^2 = 2n \sum_i (z_i - y_i)^2 \tag{19}$$

the theorem can be applied to the above stated method.

Although the standard procedure for multidimensional scaling can be applied for (12) the solution here is much easier. It is simply

$$z_i = \frac{1}{n} \sum_j \delta_{ij} \ (i = 1, \ldots, n) \tag{20}$$

Proof. Obviously, $\bar{z} = \frac{1}{n^2} \sum_{i,j} \delta_{ij} = 0$ because $\delta_{ij} = -\delta_{ji}$. We show that with $\tilde{d}_{ij} = z_i - z_j$ and an arbitrary $d_{ij} = x_i - x_j$ one gets $< \tilde{d}, d >=< \delta, d >$. The right hand side equals

$$< \delta, d > = \sum_k x_k \sum_l \delta_{kl} - \sum_l x_l \sum_k \delta_{kl} = \sum_k x_k \sum_l \delta_{kl} - \sum_k x_k \sum_l \delta_{lk}$$

$$= \sum_k x_k \sum_l \delta_{kl} - \sum_k x_k \sum_l (-\delta_{kl})$$

$$= \sum_k x_k \sum_l \delta_{kl} + \sum_k x_k \sum_l \delta_{kl} \tag{21}$$

and the left hand side

$$< \tilde{d}, d > = \frac{1}{n}(\sum_{k,l} x_k \sum_j \delta_{kj} - \sum_{k,l} x_k \sum_j \delta_{lj} - \sum_{k,l} x_l \sum_j \delta_{kj} + \sum_{k,l} x_l \sum_j \delta_{lj})$$

$$= \sum_k x_k \sum_j \delta_{kj} + \sum_l x_l \sum_j \delta_{lj} = \sum_k x_k \sum_l \delta_{kl} + \sum_k x_k \sum_l \delta_{kl} \tag{22}$$

which completes the proof. $\square$

Theorem 2 is also helpful in order to compute the second canonical correlation to a given solution of (9). If $d^* = \sum_k \alpha_k^* d^{*k}$, resp. $\delta^* = \sum_k \beta_k^* \delta^{*k}$ is an optimal solution of (9) then the second canonical correlation is defined as a solution $\tilde{d} = \sum_k \tilde{\alpha}_k \tilde{d}^k$, resp. $\tilde{\delta} = \sum_k \tilde{\beta}_k \tilde{\delta}^k$ of (9) subject to the extra condition that $\tilde{d}$ is uncorrelated to d^*, resp. $\tilde{\delta}$ is uncorrelated to δ^*. In order to compute the second (and the third and so on ...) canonical correlation with the help of Theorem 2 the monotone regression phase is done after the least-squares solution (projection) on the subspace of all differences orthogonal to d^*, resp. after the projection on the subspace of all differences orthogonal to δ^*. These least-square problems (projections) can be solved very easily.

5   Conclusions and remarks

The above method of a canonical correlation differs from the approach given by Burg and de Leeuw (1983). Burg and de Leeuw compute two or more canonical correlations with **one** scaling for each variable for **all** canonical correlations whereas here the scaling for each variable for the first canonical correlation can be different from the scaling of the variables for the following ones. The disadvantage of the approach by Burg and de Leeuw is that the solution of the first canonical correlation changes if a second canonical correlation is computed or if not and that this approach is not a generalization of the classical methods. which can be seen in the case of one dependent nominal variable with more than two groups and some metric independent variables.

The methods of multivariate analysis for quantitative data can be generalized to qualtative data - even with a complex information level - by using the optimal scaling approach. The computation can be done by the standard ALS and monotone regression algorithms used for the optimal scaling of nominal and ordinal data. Although this was shown only for the model of canonical correlation it can easily be transfered to other models, like principal component analysis for example.

References

BURG, E. van der and DE LEEUW, J. (1983): Non-linear canonical correlation. *British Journal of Mathematical and Statistical Psychology, 36, 1983, p. 54-80.*

HANSOHM, J. (1987): *Die Behandlung qualitativer Datenstrukturen in quantitativen Analysemethoden durch das Prinzip der optimalen Skalierung.* Lang, Frankfurt, New York.

HANSOHM, J. (1988): Some Properties of the Normed Alternating Least Squares (ALS) Algorithm. *Optimization, 19, 1988, Vol. 5, p. 683-691.*

KRUSKAL, J.B. (1964a): Multidimensional Scaling by Optimizating Goodness of Fit to a Nonmetric Hypothesis. *Psychometrika, 29, 1964, p. 1-27.*

KRUSKAL, J.B. (1964b): Nonmetric Multidimensional Scaling: A Numerical Method. *Psychometrika, 29, 1964, p. 115-129.*

KRUSKAL, J.B. and CARMONE (1968): Use and Theory of MONANOVA - a Program to Analyze Factorial Experiments by Estimating Monotone Transformations of the Data. *unpublished paper, Bell Laboratories, 1968.*

OPITZ, O. (1980): *Numerische Taxonomie.* UTB Betriebswirtschaftslehre, Gustav Fischer, 1980, Stuttgart, New York.

YOUNG, F.W. (1975): Methods for Describing Ordinal Data with Cardinal Models. *Journal of Mathematical Psychology, 12, 1975, 416-536.*

YOUNG, F. W., DE LEEUW, J., TAKANE, Y. (1976): Regression with Qualitative and Quantitative Variables: An Alternating Least Squares Method with Optimal Scaling Features. *Psychometrika, 41, 4, 1976, 505-529.*

YOUNG, F.W. (1981): Quantitative Analysis of Qualitative Data. *Psychometrika, 46, 4, 1981, p. 357-388.*

How Wrong Models Become Useful - and Correct Models Become Dangerous

Christian Hennig

Seminar für Statistik,
ETH-Zentrum, CH-8092 Zürich, Switzerland

Abstract. The conceptual background of statistics and data analysis is considered from the viewpoint of constructivist philosophy. The relation of formal models to observable reality is discussed as well as the role of model assumptions and especially probability models in data analysis. I argue that approximate correctness of models is an ill-posed problem. The relation of model assumptions to observer-independent reality can never be assessed objectively. Instead, formal models are useful to learn about the derived statistical methods and to enable clear understanding between different observers. Some illustrations are given.

1 Introduction

All models are wrong - but some are useful. This famous statement of George Box is often cited to justify the work with models that clearly do not fit the circumstances exactly. But of course he did not say that wrong models are always useful and we are still left with the decision which wrong models are useful for a problem at hand, and in which sense they are useful. In classification and clustering, this problem arises, e.g., if we have to decide about the normal assumption or if we want to estimate the number of clusters and we wonder if a unique true number of clusters exists in reality.

In the present paper I will discuss the issue from a constructivist viewpoint. Constructivism is an epistemology which considers reality only dependent of its observers. Objective reality can never be observed, and perception is considered as a means of self-organization, not as a representation of objective reality. I give a brief introduction to constructivist philosophy in Section 2. This paper is a companion paper to Hennig (2002) and there is some intersection. But while Hennig (2002) discusses many aspects of the relation of constructivism to data analysis briefly, here I focus on the relation between formal (especially probability) models and reality.

The content of the paper may be somewhat provoking, and it should be said that it is not meant as the last word on the subject. It should simply serve to stimulate discussion about a too often neglected aspect of statistics and data analysis.

2 A short introduction into constructivism

A naive interpretation of perception can be characterized as follows: The reality outside is full of information, and to observe reality means to build a particular kind of representation of it in our brain. In the same manner science would be interpreted as building as objective representations as possible of reality in (more or less) formal language. From this point of view, the role of the observers is mainly passive. One problem of this interpretation is that the question of objectivity cannot be assessed in an objective manner. That is, to recognize the inadequacy of a particular observers' representation of reality, another observer is needed, whose objectivity again can be doubted.

The constructivist interpretation of perception is much different. Constructivists consider the role of the observer as active. Perception is interpreted as a means of self-organization of an individual, a social system, respectively. The reality outside acts as a perturbation of the observer, i.e., it forces the observer to perceive her reality in such a way that unfavorable situations such as touching a heated hot-plate are avoided. But it is by no means necessary that the observer-independent reality matches the personal reality, and the relation between these two realities cannot be observed.

There are two main principles of constructivism:

- There is no observation without observers. This means in particular that we have to take a look at the observer if we want to analyze observations.
- Observations are constructed in social dependence. Most of us probably feel that there is so much agreement between different observers that the first principle alone would not suffice to explain it. But the strong dependency of an individual on the society and in particular on the closest persons such as the parents in the first years of her life enforces an important role of communication and agreement for the construction of the personal perception. As a consequence, we also have to analyze communication if we want to analyze observations.

I refer to Watzlawick (1984) for a more comprehensive introduction into constructivism. There are various schools of constructivism, but they agree about the above mentioned principles. Some more literature can be found in Hennig (2002).

3 Reality, language and formal models

I use the term personal reality for the whole world of perception of a person. This includes sense impressions, thoughts and feelings, all of which are to be thought as interdependent. Personal reality changes in every moment, at least to some extent. It is useful to think about the relation between personal reality and language, because language is the most important carrier of communication (at least in science) and the relation of formal models to social reality is somewhat analogous to the relation of language to personal reality.

Imagine that you are asked to explain as precisely as possible your present perceptions (which cannot clearly be separated from thoughts and feelings). Probably, the first aspects which come to your mind are the aspects you can clearly describe in words: You are reading a book, the paper is white,

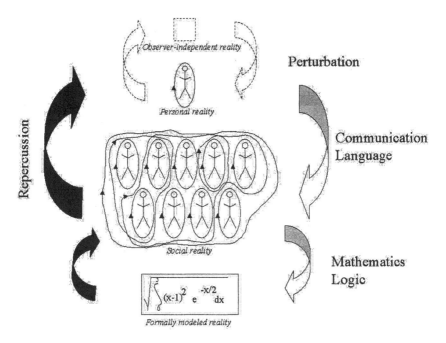

Fig. 1. "Semi-formal" model of the relation between reality and formal models.

here are letters etc. If you concentrate more deeply, then you will recognize that language is not able to describe precisely your detailed perceptions, e.g., how this particular letter "r" and the surface of the paper surrounding it are characterized, how they differ from other "r"s and other areas of this page, and what exactly your hands and your nose perceive while observing precisely this letter and this page. There are at least two reasons for this inability. Firstly, language is linear and digital as opposed to perception. Secondly, time is needed to give a static description, while perception is essentially dynamic.

In conclusion, I have two basic theses:

- Language and personal observations operate on distinct domains. Thus, language is never able to explain adequately the personal reality.
- The repercussion of language to personal reality is crucial. Once we have words, these words highlight and bundle some impressions and down-weight others, so that we are no longer able to observe reality in a way we would do without language.

The same theses apply to formal models with respect to social reality, which I will discuss now. Consider the scheme given in Figure 1. Social reality can be thought as to be made up by the whole amount of communication between human beings, of which language is an important part - and most accessible to scientific analysis. It is useful to distinguish different social realities of different social systems. For example, the reality of the social system of German classification researchers present at the annual GfKl meetings will differ from the reality of the system of teachers of a particular school. Obviously, individuals belong to more than one social system and the resulting social realities are not clearly separated.

While social realities can be analyzed by observing the system's discourse, such analysis has to take into account that the words of ordinary language are not well defined, and members of the same social system do not necessarily mean the same thing when they use, e.g., the term "democracy". At this point, scientific formal language, i.e., (often) mathematics enter. The main difference between mathematics and ordinary language is that the mathematical concepts are aimed to be uniquely defined. Science, at least where it is formalized, aims to be a social system where absolute agreement is possible because the concepts are cleaned from every connotation which is dependent on the individual and its social background. The problem is that the mathematical unification moves language one step further away from the primary personal observations. That is, observations have to be further reduced and communication has to deviate more from the original perception in order to fit into the mathematical framework. On the other hand, there is again repercussion. Formal models, once introduced in the scientific community, react on the discourse of the affected social systems, and they react also on the personal realities of the individuals who use them. For example, a "probability of rain" is nowadays accepted as understandable term in common language. As long as we believe that there exists an observer-independent reality which is affected by our actions, formal models as well as language will even react on this reality.

4   Are all models wrong?

4.1   General aspects

In the light of the previous section, all formal models are wrong in the sense that they operate on domains distinct from reality (no matter if observer-independent, personal or social). Interpreted in this way, they cannot even be approximately true (this is further discussed in the two following subsections). However, it is possible that individuals or social systems are influenced so much by the formalized discourse and the repercussion of the models, that they reduce their reality to the formalized aspects and, in the most extreme case, that they are no longer able or willing to observe deviations. That is, models can match an observer's reality, but this does not say that they fit any observer-independent reality. Instead, it says something about the reduction of the perceptions of the observers. To formulate it provoking: While wrong models may be useful, "correct" models are dangerous.

In general, a researcher or a group of researchers suggesting a model will have a more complex perception of the phenomenon of interest. There will be modeled and non-modeled aspects. The act of modeling highlights the modeled aspects and weights down the others. The non-modeled aspects are always in danger of vanishing from the scientific discourse. Thus, conscious ignorance is crucial for a reasonable work with models. By this I mean that the non-modeled aspects (including deviations between model and the researchers' perceived realities) either should be kept explicitly in the discussion, or that a clear and conscious decision is made that these aspects are not important with respect to the problem at hand.

The benefits and dangers of modeling are closely connected: Models enable understanding, clarification and communication of the researchers' perceptions and concepts, but this comes to the price that these perceptions must be adapted and reduced to the formal language.

4.2   The role of measurement

I stated that formal models cannot even be approximately true. It could be objected that it is possible, however, to calculate distances between empirical distributions of datasets and probability distributions or between dissimilarities on sets of objects and approximating ultra-metrics as generated by hierarchical clustering methods. Such distances could be interpreted in terms of a better or worse approximation of the data by the models.

It is important in this respect to consider the role of measurements. Measurement can be considered as a particular kind of language in the framework given above, which mediates between personal and unified scientific reality. Again it can be observed that measurements do not fit personal reality adequately, but that at the same time they react strongly on individual and social perception (an example for the implications of this repercussion is given in Hennig (2002)). The design and choice of measurements involves importance judgments, the construction of particular and often artificial environments and social negotiation. It is almost always more or less explicitly model based. That is, measurement can be interpreted as a social construction, and the question of the approximation of measures by models is to be distinguished sharply from the question of the approximation of personal or observer-independent reality.

Furthermore, the approximation of data by models can only be measured under some implicit model assumptions, which in itself can neither be verified nor approximated. For example, approximation of empirical distributions by probability models is only reasonable if the observations are assumed to be i.i.d.. Dependency structures of sufficient complexity and non-identical distributions can by no means be excluded. The general idea of the approximation of data by probability models refers always to the impression that there is something like a (possibly very complicated) random mechanism generating the data, which can be expected to produce stable relative frequencies if repeated long enough. The following subsection discusses the question if there is evidence in favor of such a view.

4.3   Interpretation of probability models

The usual argumentation supporting the frequentist interpretation of probability says that apparently converging relative frequencies are an empirical fact (see e.g. von Mises(1936)). This is often illustrated by plots of stabilizing sequences of the relative frequency of events such as throwing a 6 with a dice with increasing number of throws. But this stabilization can be explained purely by the definition of the relative number of successes, where the increasing denominator enforces the decrease of the variation, while this does not allow any diagnosis of convergence. More formally, Fine (1973) proves that "apparent convergence" of relative frequencies follows from "apparent randomness". The validity of such a statement depends of course on the concrete formalization of these two concepts, which I do not discuss here. The meaning is that we would judge the outcomes of a sequence as too regular to be random if the relative frequencies of success would not seem to be convergent. Thus, apparent convergence is a consequence of how we assign the attribute "random" and has nothing to do with concrete data. By the way, this argument is an example of the mechanism of self-affirmation of well established scientific models, methods and results. The judgment of such a scientific concept as "experientially successful" is often based at least partly on the following technique: Whenever the application of the concept is apparently a failure, this is attributed to the violation of assumptions or other scientific working standards (in this case "too regular to be random"), while such problems are neglected in the case of success.

The laws of large numbers also do not work as a justification of the existence of converging relative frequencies of success. The most obvious reason is that the laws are given in terms of probability models. Thus, a valid interpretation of such models must be *assumed* to apply the laws to real data, and therefore they cannot provide a *foundation* for such an interpretation.

From this discussion I do not draw the conclusion that the frequentist interpretation of probability is useless and should be rejected. Not the interpretation itself is misled, but the belief that it should and could be connected to observer-independent reality in a scientific or logical manner. Such a connection can also not be established for any other interpretation of probability models, and every attempt to do so would suffer from similar defects.

De Finetti (1972) tries to give an operational justification for his subjectivist Bayesian interpretation of probability in terms of the betting behavior of individuals. But this does not mean that there is any objective relation of subjective probabilities to the states of mind of an individual, which are claimed to be modeled. If an individual does not obey de Finettis' betting rules, it is simply judged as "non-coherent", according to the above mentioned technique of self-affirmation. Hennig (2002), and, more detailed, Walley (1991) give arguments why the demand of Bayesian coherence is not necessarily rational.

Nevertheless I think that researchers, who work with probability models, should explicitly choose an interpretation of probability. Models are most useful to enable understanding and agreement among scientists, and this does not work if the interpretation is obscured.

A "constructivist frequentism" would mean that a researcher communicates clearly that she imagines the phenomenon of her interest as repeatable, and that she interprets the assigned probabilities as tendencies which would manifest themselves as limit values of converging relative frequencies in case that the imagined replications would take place. Some sources of variation are judged as non-essential (or non-observable). The researcher would call these sources "random". She would acknowledges that objective randomness is essentially non-observable and a correct representation of the (objective, personal, or social) real reasons for the variation is out of reach of formal modeling. Instead, a constructive frequentism would say something about how the researcher observes and how she judges the phenomenon, and this is accessible to scientific discussion. In the same manner, a constructivist Bayesianism and a constructivist interpretation of other concepts of probability can easily be imagined.

5   The benefits of incorrect model assumptions

It follows from the previous discussion that the (approximate) correctness of a model assumption for given data or a given setup is an ill-posed problem. Goodness-of-fit tests and graphical assessment can never check all important aspects of a model (this is also discussed in Hennig 2002). At most, data can give strong evidence against a model. This does not mean that "a method is not allowed if the model assumptions are not fulfilled", which would be a meaningless statement. Instead, the method should be rejected if the inspection of the data leads to the suspicion that the methods derived under the model assumption may lead to non-adequate conclusions. This holds, e.g., for mean and standard error under the occurrence of outliers (as long as there are no subject-matter reasons in favor of giving the outliers high influence), but not under seemingly rectangular distributed data.

This shows one of the two main uses of model assumptions: They allow us to learn about the methods. The other benefit of explicitly stated model assumptions is that they communicate clearly the researcher's perceptions and judgments about the phenomenon of interest. This leads to understanding and often to agreement and new ideas.

To illustrate this, consider the use of normal mixture models for clustering. If a researcher assumes them, this means that

- she wants to explain the data as coming from a (usually) small number of homogeneous groups,
- she interprets a cluster as a bell-shaped point cloud with moderate tails,
- she wants to characterize the clusters only by their means and covariance matrices,

- she judges dependencies between points and the reasons for within-group variation as non-essential.

All these decisions, which cannot be justified from data or other observations alone, can now be discussed critically. This is one of the most important stages of scientific work, and at this stage, model diagnostics become useful. Often, the discovery of discrepancies between the data and the structures judged important by the researcher leads to interesting new findings. That is, model assumptions are often useful *because* they lead to the detection of clear deviations. If model based methods are a priori rejected because the assumptions are suspected not to hold, this key feature of model assumptions is ignored. (Of course, it is nevertheless often reasonable to replace unstable model-based methods by more stable ones.)

6   Concluding example

Based on constructivist epistemology, I developed an attitude towards models, for which the question of the correctness of the model is an ill-posed problem. Formal models and observer-independent, personal, and social reality operate on distinct domains. All attempts to verify objectively models or even probability interpretations such as the frequentist one are doomed to fail. Instead, formal models communicate the perceptions of researchers in a unified, clear manner, and they enable us to learn about data analytic methods.

Here is an example for the implications of this attitude: Often data are transformed in order to get a more normal-shaped distribution. According to the ideas given here, this is useless, as long as the only aim is to fulfill the normal assumption. A better rationale is as follows:

Data should be transformed in order to achieve correspondence between the treatment of the differences of the values by the data analytic method and the subject-matter meaning of these differences as judged by the researchers.

Suppose that a social scientist wants to compare two groups with respect to the answers to a question, for which five ordered alternatives are given. Often this is done by use of the Wilcoxon test, which is preferred over the *t*-test because the data is ordinal and non-normal. Suppose further that the scientist argues that the linguistic difference between the first four categories is approximately equal while the fifth category is somewhat extreme. Under the assumption that the scientist's judgment is sufficiently precise, I suggest that a transformation of the categories to, say, 1, 2, 3, 4 and 8, followed by application of the *t*-test, will be clearly superior to the standard treatment, except under very extreme distributions of the answers.

While the Wilcoxon test seems to be "allowed" for ordinal data, it nevertheless treats the categories as numbers, whose effective differences are determined from the distribution. If there is additional information about these differences stemming from the personal or social reality of the scientists, it seems to be a bad choice to ignore this information only because there is no objective rationale how to translate it into numbers.

Further, we know from statistical theory that the t-test is approximately valid in i.i.d. settings with existing variances, that it is fairly good for light tailed distributions, and that it suffers mainly from extreme outliers and extreme skewness, which should not be present in this setup (but it would not be a good idea to score the highest category as 1000 and to apply the t-test, even if the subject-matter researcher would judge this to be the adequate value). Thus, we should rather trust the outcome of the t-test in this case than in some other experiments, where distributional shapes occur, which are very similar to the normal with moderately heavier tails. This is where the use of (well understood) model assumptions enters.

References

DE FINETTI, B. (1972): *Probability, Induction and Statistics*. Wiley, London.

FINE, T. L. (1973): *Theories of Probability*. Academic Press, New York.

HENNIG, C. (2002): Confronting Data Analysis with Constructivist Philosophy. In: K. Jajuga, A. Sokolowskij and H.-H. Bock (Eds.): *Classification, Clustering, and Data Analysis*. Springer, Berlin, 235–244.

VON MISES, R. (1936): *Wahrscheinlichkeit, Statistik und Wahrheit*. Springer, Vienna.

WALLEY, P. (1991): *Statistical Reasoning with Imprecise Probabilities*. Chapman and Hall, London.

WATZLAWICK, P. (1984) (Ed.): *The Invented Reality*. Norton, New York.

Visualizing Symbolic Data by Closed Shapes

Antonio Irpino[2], Carlo Lauro[1] and Rosanna Verde[2]

[1] Dip. di Matematica e Statistica, Università di Napoli Federico II,
Monte S. Angelo, I-80126 Naples, Italy
[2] Dip. di Strategie Az. e Metod. Quantitative, Seconda Universitá di Napoli,
Piazza Umberto I, 81043 Capua, Italy

Abstract. In the framework of Factorial Data Analysis on Symbolic Objects (SO's), we propose new kinds of SO's visualizations on factorial planes alternative to rectangular shapes (*Minimum Covering Area Rectangle* MCAR). MCAR were mainly proposed in PCA on SO's to represent in reduced bi-dimensional subspace symbolic data described by interval variables and represented by hypercubes. The new representations of SO's are based on the convex hulls (CH) of the projected hypercube vertices. In particular, we propose a compromise between the MCAR and CH visualizations by means of particular closed shapes, that contains the CH and it is contained by MCAR. The main advantage of this kind of SO representation is its interpretation and lower over-fitting than MCAR. Furthermore, some indexes of quality of representation and over-fitting are developed.

1 Introduction

In the framework of Symbolic Data Analysis, the factorial techniques (SO-Principal Component Analysis without (Cazes et al (1998)) or with Cohesion Constraints (Lauro & Palumbo (2000)), So-Generalized Canonical Analysis, So-Factorial Discriminant Analysis (Lauro et al. (2000)) are based on the representation of the vertices of hypercubes associated to the description of the SO's to analyze. In fact, in the geometrical space generated by the SO's descriptors, each hypercube represents the internal variability of the SO description due to the presence of intervals of real values, multiple discrete values, multiple categories, distributions, as showed in Boch & Diday (2000). Among all the factorial techniques developed to treat SO's, in this paper we refer to SO-Principal Component Analysis under Cohesion Constraint (Lauro & Palumbo (2000), SO-Factorial Discriminant Analysis) which decomposes the inertia of the hypercubes vertices projected in the SO's space by means of the vertices belonging (to hypercube) constraint, when SO's are described by interval variables. The following considerations are always valid when SO's are represented in the original space as convex shapes.

Let $y_1, \ldots, y_p$ be p interval variables which describe n SO's; $\mathbf{Y}$ is the matrix of the coordinates. in the original descriptors space, of the vertices of the hypercubes (with $n \times 2^p$ rows and p columns); A $(n\dot{2}^p \times n)$ is the cohesion matrix: it is a Boolean matrix which specifies the belonging of the vertices to the corresponding SO.

Principal Component Analysis on SO's consists in maximizing the variance between the hypercube vertices solving the following eigenequation:

$$\frac{1}{n2^p}\mathbf{Y}'\mathbf{A}(\mathbf{A}'\mathbf{A})^{-1}\mathbf{A}'\mathbf{Y}\mathbf{v}_m = \lambda_m\mathbf{v}_m \tag{1}$$

under the orthonormality constraints $\mathbf{v}'_m\mathbf{v}_{m'} = 0$ for $m \neq m'$ and $\mathbf{v}_m\mathbf{v}_m = 1$ for $m = m'$ and $(1 < m < p)$.

The coordinates of the vertices which represent the generic SO_i on the axis m, are given by the vector $\phi_{i,m} = \mathbf{Y}_i\mathbf{v}_m$, i.e., the original coordinates are transformed by means of a linear combination of the original variables. Then, being an hypercube a convex representation of a SO in the original space, its projection onto the subspace spanned by the factorial axes will also be a convex shape. In figure 1 we show an example of a SO described by means of the symbolic assertion a where the three descriptors are interval variables.

$$a = \left[Y_1 \subseteq \left[\underline{y_{1a}}; \overline{y_{1a}}\right]\right] \wedge \left[Y_2 \subseteq \left[\underline{y_{2a}}; \overline{y_{2a}}\right]\right] \wedge \left[Y_3 \subseteq \left[\underline{y_{3a}}; \overline{y_{3a}}\right]\right]$$

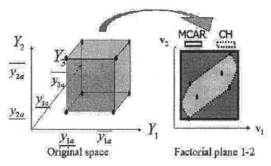

Fig. 1. A symbolic assertion in the original descriptors space and in the projection space

However, the visualization of SO's on factorial plane by minimal covering area rectangles (MCAR), proposed in Principal Component Analysis on SO's - and extended to the others Factorial techniques proposed in Symbolic Data Analysis - does not seems adequate to represent the projections of the hypercubes associated to the SO's. In fact, even if it allows to provide simple descriptions of the SO's by means of a symbolic assertions described only by the real intervals that the projection can assume for each $\mathbf{v}_i$ new variable, it also provides an overfitted description of the projected SO (Lauro et al.(2000)). An alternative visualization can be furnished by Convex Hulls (CH) (Porzio et al (1998)) of the projected hypercubes vertices. Nevertheless, even if it seems the best way to visualize SO's, from a geometrical point of view, its interpretation is complex in terms of symbolic assertions. In fact, as we can see in section 2, the description of the CH is given by the simplex generated by its edges, where each of them is a linear bounded combination of the new variables (i.e. an edge is described by a linear combination of linear combination of the original descriptors).

Then, our proposal is to find a compromise between the MCAR and CH visualizations by means of particular closed shapes, that contains the CH and is contained by MCAR. The new shape is called PECS (Parallel Edges Connected Shape) and is applicable for the visualization of SO when a factorial analysis is performed on vertices. The main advantage of PECS is that its interpretation is done in terms of intervals variables as well as logical rules. Then, it is better interpretable than CH and contains less overfitting than MCAR.

In order to identify PECS we need to generate the CH of the projected vertices on the factorial plane. In this paper we present a fast algorithm for the generation of a 2d convex-hull. Then we show the algorithm to build PECS and some indexes for evaluating the overfitting for each SO.

2   A faster 2D convex hull algorithm

Given p interval variable the vertices of the hypercube which describe a SO is equal to $n = 2^p$. From a computational point of view the number of projected points (vertices), on which we have to compute the convex hull, increase exponentially with the number of variable (for example, given 10 intervals the vertices are 1024). The computational problems is critical for the generation of convex hull. In fact, the best algorithm for the generation of a 2D convex hull have to do at least $n^2 = 2^{2p}$ comparison operations if no structure on data are defined. In this paper we present a faster algorithm that has a lower number of comparison operations due to the geometrical properties of hypercubes and to the linearity of the projection operator onto the factorial planes.

The algorithm (2DPP-CH , 2D Parallelotope Projected Convex Hull) is based on the following principles:

i)   An hypercube in the original space is a geometrical shape that is symmetric whit respect to its barycenter.

ii) It is possible to demonstrate that the edges of the CH of the vertices projected onto a factorial plane are projections of the edges of the hypercube in the original space.

iii) As the projection operator is a linear combination of the original variables, the vertices projected onto a factorial plane are symmetric to the projection of the hypercube barycenter. Then, given p interval variables the maximum number of edges of the 2D convex hull will be $2p$. Once we calculated p consecutive points or edges, the other p are given by means of the property of barycentric symmetry. It is possible to demonstrate that from a point (that is the projection of a vertex of the original hypercube) is possible to go only in p different direction, or in other words, it is an extreme point of only p different edges.

The algorithm is based on the following two steps:

First step Identification of a starting extremal point
We have to calculate an extremal point that we call **Point$_1$**. For the barycentric, **Point$_{p+1}$** is determinated as in Figure 2.

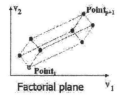

Factorial plane

Fig. 2. 2DPP-CH step 1

Second step Searching the other extremal points (Figure 3)
$i = 1$
While $(i < p)$ {
- Search the $p - i + 1$ candidate extreme points linked to **Point$_i$**
- Calculate angles between v_1 and the $p - i + 1$ edges where **Point$_i$** and the candidate points are vertices
- The minimum angle allow to identify an extreme edge; **Point$_{i+1}$** is determinated and its symmetrical **Point$_{p+i+1}$** too
$i = i + 1$ }

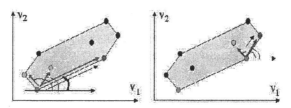

Fig. 3. 2DPP-CH step 2

Given p interval variables the number of comparisons in step 1 and 2 is equal to $\sum_{i=1}^{p} (p - i)$ that is lesser than 2^{2p}.

The convex hull, as shown in Figure 4, allows to have the better visualization of the projection of the hypercube which describes a SO, but, at same time, its interpretation in terms of symbolic assertion is not so easy. In

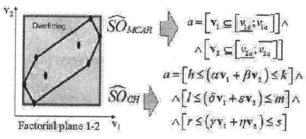

Fig. 4. $\widehat{SO}_{MCAR}$ vs. $\widehat{SO}_{CH}$

fact, the CH is interpreted by means of its edges that are linear combinations of the factors. Choosing the CH as visualization shape, it is important to understand how good the SO is represented on the factorial plane, taking into account a measure that represent the projected internal variability of the SO onto the factorial plane and onto the subspace generated by all the eigenvectors. The measure that we introduce is based on the same concept of the Linear Description Potential (LDP)of De-Carvalho(1994) developed in order to describe the internal variability of a SO in its original space. The LDP measure is the proportional to the perimeter of hypercube described by p variables, as we can deduct by its formula:

$$LPD(SO) = \sum_{i=1}^{p} \left| \overline{y_{i,a}} - \underline{y_{i,a}} \right|$$

As the SO-PCA looks at the best space spanned by orthonormal components which minimizes the sum of square of the distances between SO's vertices, we propose a new index based on the square of the edge for each variable that we call SSDP (Sum of square Descriptor Potential), that is coherent with the analysis, more than LPD.

$$SSPD(SO) = \sum_{i=1}^{p} \left(\overline{y_{i,a}} - \underline{y_{i,a}} \right)^2 \tag{2}$$

The projection of the edges, being its measure the distance between two vertices, is always less than than its length in the original space. Then, we can compute the $SSPD(\widehat{SO}_{CH})$ as the sum of square of p consecutive edges of the CH.

$$SSPD(\widehat{SO}_{CH}) = \sum_{i=1}^{p} (edge_i)^2 \tag{3}$$

In this way we can define an index for the quality of representation of the projected SO visualized by means of a CH as follows:

$$\frac{SSPD(\widehat{SO}_{CH})}{SSPD(SO)} \tag{4}$$

3   Parallel edge connected shapes (PECS)

Once calculated the CH of the projected vertices of the hypercube we are able to introduce a new geometric shape that allows a better visualization of the SO onto a factorial plane than MCAR (i.e. has a lower overfitted area representation) and, at the same time, that is better interpretable in terms of symbolic assertion than CH. The chosen shape contains the CH and is contained by MCAR. It is not a convex shape but connected whit edges parallel to the factorial axes. The interpretation of PECS is done in terms of logical rules (*if* $\mathbf{v}_m > a$ *then* $\mathbf{v}_m > b$). In fact each point that generates a 270 angle can be described by a rule (Figure 5). The principle for the identification of the points that generates a concave angle is based on the maximization of the overfitting rectangular area that can be cut out from the MCAR but not from CH.

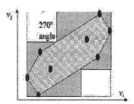

Fig. 5. PECS, convex and concave vertices

In order to identify the concave angle which maximize the cut area, by means of symmetric properties of CH, we have to solve, for p consecutive edges of the CH, the following optimization problem.

$$(\overline{x} - x)\left(y - \underline{y}\right) \text{MAX!}$$
$$s.a.$$
$$\begin{cases} \frac{x-x_1}{x_2-x_1} = \frac{y-y_1}{y_2-y_1} \\ x_1 \leq x \leq x_2 \\ y_1 \leq y \leq y_2 \end{cases} \tag{5}$$

The objective function to be maximized is the area A cut out from the MCAR, while the constraints represent the working edge (which goes from $(x_1, y_1$ to (x_2, y_2) as in Figure 6. Being a quadratic optimization problem with linear constraints it admits only a maximum for each edge. Once calculated the points (x, y) which generates the concave angles for each edge, we chose that points which generates the maximum cut of the overfitted area. By means of the symmetry of the CH exist a symmetric point to the barycenter that generates a cut area of the same dimension. The generic step i of the algorithm generates a shape as in Figure 5. The further steps of the algorithm search for other concave angles solving the same optimization problem (6) taking into account that the cut area to be maximized is between the CH and PECS

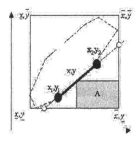

Fig. 6. Optimization problem for an edge

generated at the step $i - 1$. The search is done on convex sub-zones of the PECS generated in step $i - 1$. In figure 7 we show an example of a PECS with two concave angles and its description in terms of symbolic assertion. As the

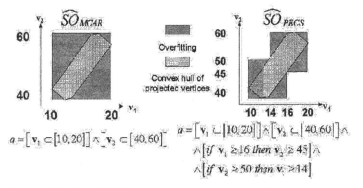

Fig. 7. MCAR vs PECS, visualization and symbolic interpretation

algorithm does not converge in a finite number of rules, it is important to set a stop criterion. We propose two criteria, the former one is based on the percentage of overfitting area of the PECS, while the latter is based on an interpretability criterion in terms of parsimony.

Overfitting criterion Given the following measure of over-fitting for a PECS, defined in $[0; 1]$ (0="No over-fitting"; 1="Max over-fitting") :

$$OF(PECS) = \frac{area(PECS) - area(CH)}{area(CH)} \qquad (6)$$

we may set a soil $\alpha \in [0; 1]$ and then generate those rules which allow to have PECS with a proportion of overfitting less than α.

Parsimony criterion We may fix a suitable number of rules (in practice less then five), in order to better interpret the PECS in terms of symbolic assertion, and then we can observe the associated $OF(PECS)$ measure of overfitting.

4 Conclusions end future issues

The interpretation of the shape of visualization of SO's in the context of dimensionality reduction, such as in Symbolic Factorial Analysis techniques, may be considered from different points of view. In fact, an easy visual interpretation is not always the easier interpretable visualization. This kind of problem is much more relevant in symbolic data analysis, where it is important that the output of a treatment can be described in terms of SO's in order to do further symbolic analysis. In the present paper we proposed to solve the visualization-interpretation dilemma with PECS. For the future works, it is important to take into account structures in SO's descriptors space, such as the presence of rules or taxonomies. In fact, particular structures can modify the symmetrical and convex hypothesis of the SO in the original descriptor space. It is possible to generalize the shapes of visualization proposed taking into account not global SO symmetry and convexity, but local ones by means of particular decompositions.

References

BOCK, H. H. and DIDAY, E. (eds) (2000): Analysis of Symbolic Data, Springer Verlag. Heidelberg.

CAZES, P., CHOUAKIA, A., DIDAY, E., SHECKTMAN, Y.: (1997) Extension de l'analyse en composante principales des donnes de type intervalle, *Revue de Statistique Applique* **XIV**(3),5-24.

DE CARVALHO, F.A.T.: (1992)Mthodes descriptives en Analyse de Donnes Symboliques, Thse de doctorat, Universit Paris IX Dauphine, Paris.

LAURO, N.C., PALUMBO, F. : (2000): Principal Components Analysis of Interval Data: a symbolic Data Analysis Approach In: *Computational Statistics*,Vol. 15 n.1,73-87.

LAURO, N.C., VERDE, R., PALUMBO, F. : (2000): Factorial Data Analysis on Symbolic Objects under cohesion constrains In: *Data Analysis, Classification and related methods*, Springer-Verlag, Heidelberg.

PORZIO, G., RAGOZINI, G., VERDE, R. : (1998) Generalization of Symbolic Objects by Convex Hulls. In Proc. ASU98.

LBGU-EM Algorithm for Mixture Density Estimation

Bambang Heru Iswanto[1] and Bernd Fritzke[2]

[1] Neural Information Processing Group,
Fakultät IV Elektrotechnik und Informatik,
Technische Universität Berlin,
Franklinstr. 28/29, D-10587 Berlin, Germany
[2] Neural Computation Group, Fakultät Informatik,
Technische Universität Dresden,
D-01307 Dresden, Germany

Abstract. We present a novel method for mixture density estimation. It is combination of the well known EM algorithm and a recently proposed vector quantization method called LBG-U. By using LBG-U to initialize the centers of the mixture components we were able to achieve better density estimates than with randomly initialized centers or with centers initialized by traditional LBG (a.k.a. batch k-Means). The empirical study performed two (of three) investigated data sets also indicated that the variance of the results for the new method is significantly lower than for the other two methods. Therefore our novel approach makes estimations from different initializations more consistent.

1 Introduction

Mixture models have been extensively studied and applied to clustering of multivariate data. An important special case is the Gaussian mixture model where each component is a Gaussian normal distribution and all components are combined using mixing parameters which form a partition of unity. The standard method for determining the optimal parameter values for the Gaussians and the mixing components is the EM algorithm (Dempster et al., 1977). EM starts from the given initial parameter values and modifies them iteratively such that the likelihood of the data is increased in every step. EM is a local optimization method and thus very sensitive to initialization.

To overcome this initialization dependence problem, the k-Means algorithm is often used to determine initial positions for the Gaussian mixture components: after random initialization k-Means is run until convergence and thereafter the actual EM algorithm starts from the positions determined by k-Means. However, since k-Means is itself a local method (actually it can be seen as efficiently computable special case of EM in the limit of vanishing Gaussian variance) the strong dependence on initialization persist.

In this paper we investigate a possibility to remedy the initialization problem by using the LBG-U algorithm (Fritzke, 1997) to initialize the parameters of the mixture model. The LBG-U algorithm is a generalization of the LBG method (Linde et al., 1980). In contrast to LBG, LBG-U has shown only a weak dependence on initialization and generates in many cases codebooks with considerably lower quantization error. The codebooks can never be worse than those generated by LBG, since the initial iteration of LBG-U is LBG.

Nevertheless it is not at all self-understood that LBG-U is also a good initialization method for mixture density estimation, since the error function (the negative log-likelihood of the data) is different from that used by LBG and LBG-U (the mean square quantization error). Experiments with EM using different initializations (namely LBG-U, LBG and random initialization) have been performed on several data sets with different dimensionality. The results indicate, that LBG-U can indeed be very useful as initialization method for EM.

2 EM algorithm for mixture model

In mixture model, the density function of the data is formed from a linear combination of M kernel functions

$$p(\mathbf{x}|\Psi) = \sum_{j=1}^{M} P(j)p(\mathbf{x}|\theta_j), \tag{1}$$

where $\mathbf{x}$ is d-dimensional data vectors. Here vector Ψ consist of unknown parameters: $P(j)$ and θ_j. The parameters $P(j)$ are called the mixing parameters, and can be regarded as *prior* probabilities of the data point having been generated from component j of the mixture model. These priors are chosen to satisfy the constraints $\sum_{j=1}^{M} P(j) = 1$ and $0 \leq P(j) \leq 1$. The functions $p(\mathbf{x}|\theta)$ represent the conditional density function, and are normalized so that $\int p(\mathbf{x}|\theta)d\mathbf{x} = 1$. The corresponding *posterior* probabilities can be expressed by using Bayes' theorem as

$$P(j|\mathbf{x}) = \frac{P(j)p(\mathbf{x}|\theta_j)}{\sum_{i=1}^{M} P(i)p(\mathbf{x}|\theta_i)}. \tag{2}$$

There are various choices for the possible kernel functions. However, for the purpose of this paper, we shall restrict attention to kernel functions which are Gaussian and each have a mean vector μ_j of dimension d and a covariance matrix $\Sigma_j = \sigma_j^2 \mathbf{I}$, hence the conditional densities are given by

$$p(\mathbf{x}|\theta_j) = \frac{1}{(2\pi\sigma_j^2)^{d/2}} \exp\left\{-\frac{||\mathbf{x} - \mu_j||^2}{2\sigma_j^2}\right\}. \tag{3}$$

The parameters of the mixture model Ψ can be determined by using maximum likelihood approach. In practice, instead of maximizing the likelihood, often the negative log-likelihood is used as error function

$$E(\Psi) = -\ln \mathcal{L}(\Psi) = -\sum_{i=1}^{N} \ln \sum_{j=1}^{M} P(j)p(\mathbf{x}_i|\theta_j) \tag{4}$$

and is minimized accordingly (minimizing an error function is equivalent to maximizing the corresponding likelihood). In particular, the EM algorithm is well suited this purpose.

The EM algorithm is an iterative method starting from some initial parameter values. Each iteration consists of two steps, E (expectation)-step and M (maximization)-step. By using the current parameter values $\Psi^{(t)}$ we compute the posterior probabilities $P^{(t)}(j|\mathbf{x})$ calculated according to Bayes' theorem in (2). This is the E-step of the EM algorithm. In the M-step, we compute new parameter values, $\Psi^{(t+1)}$, that minimize the expected error (4) with respect to the parameters. The update equations for the parameters of the mixture model are given by

$$\mu_j^{(t+1)} = \frac{\sum_{i=1}^{N} P^{(t)}(j|\mathbf{x}_i)\mathbf{x}_i}{\sum_{i=1}^{N} P^{(t)}(j|\mathbf{x}_i)} \tag{5}$$

$$(\sigma_j^2)^{(t+1)} = \frac{1}{d} \frac{\sum_{i=1}^{N} P^{(t)}(j|\mathbf{x}_i)\|\mathbf{x}_i - \mu_j^{(t+1)}\|^2}{\sum_{i=1}^{N} P^{(t)}(j|\mathbf{x}_i)} \tag{6}$$

$$P(j)^{(t+1)} = \frac{1}{N} \sum P^{(t)}(j|\mathbf{x}_i) \tag{7}$$

The E- and M-steps are alternated repeatedly until convergence. EM algorithm guarantees convergence to local maximum of likelihood. The details of the EM algorithm can be found in (Dempster et al., 1977), (Bishop, 1995) and (McLachlan and Krishnan, 1997).

The EM algorithm

- **Initialization:** Let $\Psi^{(0)}$ be an initial values of the likelihood parameters and repeat the following EM steps for t = 1, 2, ...
- **repeat(EM)**
  E-step: calculate the posterior probabilities $P^{(t)}(j|\mathbf{x})$ using Eq.(2)
  M-step: choose $\Psi^{(t+1)}$ that minimize expected error (4) using update equations: Eq.(5), Eq.(6), and Eq.(7)
- **until** $|\mathcal{L}(\Psi^{(t+1)}) - \mathcal{L}(\Psi^{(t)})| \leq \epsilon$, where ϵ is an arbitrary small account.

3   LBG-U algorithm

The LBG-U algorithm (Fritzke, 1997) is an improvement of LBG algorithm for vector quantization (VQ). The underlying problem in VQ is to construct a *codebook* (a set of reference vectors $\{\mathbf{w}_c | c \in \mathcal{A}\}$, where $\mathcal{A} = \{c_1, ..., c_M\}$ is a set of units) which minimizes the quantization error

$$E(\mathcal{D}, \mathcal{A}) = \frac{1}{|\mathcal{D}|} \sum_{c \in \mathcal{A}} \sum_{\mathbf{x} \in \mathcal{R}_c} \|\mathbf{x} - \mathbf{w}_c\|^2, \tag{8}$$

where $\mathcal{R}_c$ is Voronoi set of unit c, namely a set of data vectors for which a particular codebook vector $\mathbf{w}_c$ is nearest.

The learning algorithm of LBG involve an iteration of the following two steps (called Llyod iteration) in its inner loop: computation of the Voronoi sets $\{\mathcal{R}_c | c \in \mathcal{A}\}$ and moving of the reference vectors $\mathbf{w}_c$ to the centroid of its Voronoi set

$$\mathbf{w}_c = \frac{1}{|\mathcal{R}_c|} \sum_{\mathbf{x} \in \mathcal{R}_c} \mathbf{x}. \tag{9}$$

The theoretical foundation for this is that a *necessary* (not sufficient) condition for a set of reference vectors to minimize the quantization error is that (9) holds for all reference vectors. The complete LBG algorithm is given by:

i) Initialize the unit set $\mathcal{A} := \{c_1, ..., c_M\}$ and the reference vector of all units: $\mathbf{w}_c :=$ (from data set $\mathcal{D}$ randomly) $\forall c \in \mathcal{A}$.
ii) Save the current error: $E_{\mathbf{LBG}} := E(\mathcal{D}, \mathcal{A})$
iii) Compute for each unit $c \in \mathcal{A}$ its Voronoi set $\mathcal{R}_c$.
iv) Move the reference vector of each unit to the mean of its Voronoi set (9)
v) If $E(\mathcal{D}, \mathcal{A}) < E_{\mathbf{LBG}}$ continue with step 2
vi) Return the current set of reference vectors $\{\mathbf{w}_c | c \in \mathcal{A}\}$.

LBG-U consists of repeated runs of LBG. Each time LBG has converged, however, a particular measure of utility

$$\mathcal{U}(c) = E(\mathcal{D}, \mathcal{A}\backslash c) - E(\mathcal{D}, \mathcal{A}) \tag{10}$$

and a local distortion error

$$E(c) = \sum_{\mathbf{x} \in \mathcal{R}_c} \|\mathbf{x} - \mathbf{w}_c\|^2 \tag{11}$$

is assigned to each codebook vector. The utility indicates how important $\mathbf{w}_c$ is for error reduction. Thereafter, the vector with minimum utility is moved to a Voronoi region of a vector with maximum local distortion error, LBG runs on the resulting modified codebook until convergence is reached, another vector is moved, and so on. It can be proved that LBG-U (as LBG) converges in a finite number of iterations. In practice usually a small number of iterations suffices. The complete of LBG-U algorithm is the following:

i) Initialize the unit set $\mathcal{A} := \{c_1, ..., c_M\}$ and the reference vector of all units: $\mathbf{w}_c :=$ (from data set $\mathcal{D}$ randomly) $\forall c \in \mathcal{A}$.
ii) Save the error: $E_{\mathbf{LBGU}} := E(\mathcal{D}, \mathcal{A})$
iii) Save the best codebooks: $\mathcal{K}_{\mathbf{LBGU}} := \{\mathbf{w}_c | c \in \mathcal{A}\}$
    stop := FALSE
iv) WHILE ($\neg$ stop) REPEAT:
    • run LBG until convergence
    • memorize the current error: $E_{\mathbf{LBG}} =: E(\mathcal{D}, \mathcal{A})$
    • IF ($E_{\mathbf{LBG}} \geq E_{\mathbf{LBGU}}$) THEN stop := TRUE
    ELSE
    • memorize the current error $E_{\mathbf{LBGU}} := E_{\mathbf{LBG}}$
    • save the best current codebook: $\mathcal{K}_{\mathbf{LBGU}} := \{\mathbf{w}_c | c \in \mathcal{A}\}$

- determine $a := \arg \min_{c \in \mathcal{A}} U(c)$ (the unit with minimum utility) using Eq.(10)
- determine $b := \arg \max_{c \in \mathcal{A}} E(c)$ (the unit with maximum error) using Eq.(11)
- move a beside b: $\mathbf{w}_a := \mathbf{w}_b + \hat{\mathbf{u}}\epsilon\sqrt{E(b)/|\mathcal{D}|}$, where ϵ is a small constant and $\hat{\mathbf{u}}$ is a random vector from d-dimensional unit sphere.

$v)$ Return the current set of codebook $\mathcal{K}_{\mathbf{LBG}U}$

4   LBGU-EM algorithm

The EM algorithm introduced above starts with some initial guess at the maximum likelihood parameters, $\mathbf{\Psi}^{(0)}$, and then proceeds to iteratively generate successive estimations, $\mathbf{\Psi}^{(1)}, \mathbf{\Psi}^{(2)}, \ldots$ by repeating the E-step and M-step. Each EM iteration increases the log-likelihood (or decreases the negative log-likelihood) as shown by Dempster *et al.* For the mixture model, the EM algorithm will converge to a local maximum of the likelihood. Only data points with large posterior probabilities for a given kernel do affect the new parameters. This is the local aspect of EM makes EM sensitive to initial parameter values and leads to high variance of the results for different initializations.

In this paper we propose LBGU-EM algorithm. It consists of an initial run of LBG-U to find a codebook $\{\mathbf{w}_j | j = 1, ..., M\}$ and Voronoi sets of the data vectors $\{\mathcal{R}_j | j = 1, ..., M\}$. Thereafter the parameters of the mixture model are initialized as follows:

$i)$ the centers of kernels μ_j are set to the reference vectors $\mathbf{w}_j$.
$ii)$ the parameters σ_j^2 for each component are initialized to the variance of each Voronoi sets, and finally
$iii)$ the mixture parameters $P(j)$ are set to $|\mathcal{R}_j|/N$.

Thereafter, standard EM is run until convergence.

5   Experiments and results

A number of experiments have been performed to compare the negative log-likelihood of the result of the LBGU-EM, LBG-EM, and random-EM algorithms using three data sets:

Data set A 2-dimensional noisy 11-modal Gaussian mixture
Data set B 3-dimensional noisy 4-modal Gaussian mixture
Data set C 34-dimensional data set (Ionosphere data from UCI Machine Learning repository)

For data set A experiments were performed using 16 different codebook sizes (2, 3, ..., 17), for data set B with sizes (2, 3, ..., 19) and for data set C with sizes (2, 3, 4 and 5). For each codebook size we considered 20 trials. For data set C on trials up to size 5 were performed because beyond this size degenerate solutions with infinite likelihood occurred for all methods.

The same initialization for the parameters σ_j^2 and $P(j)$ was used in each case. The initializations of σ_j^2 and $P(j)$ are according to the Voronoi sets of their reference vectors as defined by LBGU-EM algorithm. Initialization for LBG and LBG-U was based on randomly sampling from the data set $\mathcal{D}$.

In each experiment we monitored the log-likelihood and the number of EM iterations required until convergence. The log-likelihood was used as a performance measure to compare LBGU-EM, LBG-EM and random-EM algorithm. The experiment results are shown in Fig. 2, 3, 4, and 5.

As shown in Fig. 2, 3 and 4, it is evident that for data sets A, B and C the mean error of the proposed LBGU-EM method is in general lower than the other two methods. Even more clear is the result for the variance: LBGU-EM exhibits a much smaller variance for different initializations.

Furthermore, in Fig. 5 as we see, using the LBGU-EM, the number of EM iterations required until convergence is in general less than using the LBG- and random-EM for the same data sets. For data set B, however, there are number of cases - in particular with high number of Gaussians (16, 17, 19) - where LBGU-EM need more EM iterations than LBG-EM (while the means and variances is still lower).

6   Discussion

In our contribution we have shown how LBG-U can be used to improve the performance of the EM algorithm comparing to LBG and randomly initialized EM. Our experiment results using three data sets indicate that the use of LBG-U for EM initialization leads to dramatically lower variances of the resulting log-likelihood error function and thus to better reliability of the results. Moreover, the achieved mean error values were lower than those both for LBG and randomly initialized EM. LBGU-EM outperformed LBG-EM on these data. An additional advantage of using LBGU-EM is the required number of EM iteration, as shown in our experiment results. The number of EM iterations required using LBGU-EM is in general less than the other two methods.

A better characterization of the data sets, however, for which LBGU-EM gives an improvement is still an open problem. Since LBG-U minimize a different error function than density estimation, it may also be possible to create variants of LBG or LBG-U which take this into account.

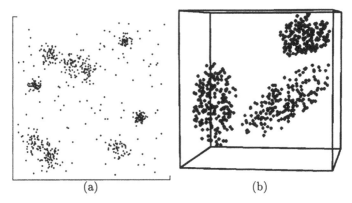

Fig. 1. (a) Two-dimensional data, data set A. (b) Three-dimensional data, data set B.

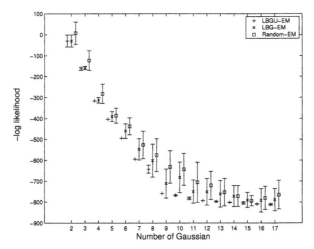

Fig. 2. Means and variances of negative log-likelihood for different number of Guassian for data set A.

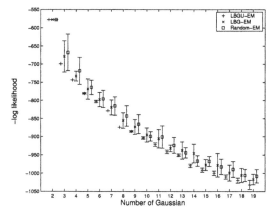

Fig. 3. Means and variances of negative log-likelihood for different number of Guassian for data set B.

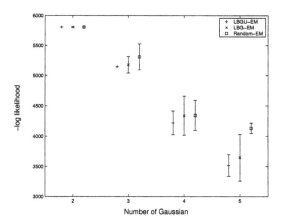

Fig. 4. Means and variances of negative log-likelihood for different number of Guassian for data set C.

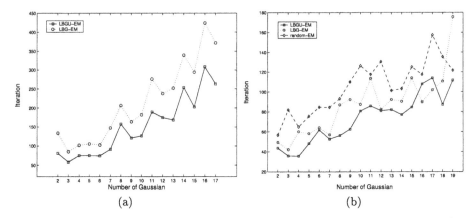

(a)   (b)

Fig. 5. Means of number of EM iterations required until convergence as function of the number of mixture components (Gaussians) (a) with data set A and (b) with data set B.

References

BISHOP, C. (1995): *Neural Networks for Pattern Recognition.* Oxford University Press, New York.

DEMPSTER, A.P., LAIRD, N.M. and RUBIN, D.B. (1977): Maximum Likelihood from Incomplete Data via the EM Algorithm. *Journal of Royal Statistical Society. Ser. B: 39, pp. 1-38.*

FRITZKE, B. (1997): The LBG-U Method for Vector Quantization - an Improvement over LBG Inspired from Neural Network. *Neural Processing Letters, vol. 5, no. 1, pp. 35-45, 1997.*

LINDE, Y., BUZO, A., and GRAY, R.M. (1980): An Algorithm for Vector Quantization Design. *IEEE Transactions on Communication, vol. COM-28, pp. 84-95.*

MCLACHLAN, G.J. and KRISHNAN, T. (1997): *The EM Algorithm and Extensions.* John Willey & Sons, New York.

Change-Points in Bernoulli Trials With Dependence

Joachim Krauth

Department of Psychology
University of Düsseldorf, D-40225 Düsseldorf, Germany

Abstract. Many authors have studied the problem of estimating the parameters in Bernoulli trials with dependence. Here, we extend this problem and derive modified maximum likelihood estimates to identify change-points and changed segments in this situation. This problem is of interest, e.g., in molecular biology when analyzing DNA sequences, where one of the four bases is coded as 1 and the other three as 0.

1 Introduction

The analysis of deoxyribonucleic acid (DNA) sequences is an important topic in molecular analysis. These sequences carry the hereditary information of essentially all living organisms (with the exception of certain RNA viruses). They consist of complementary chains of deoxyribonucleotides which are twisted around each other into a double-helical structure. The major components of DNA samples are four nitrogenous bases, the two purines adenine (A) and guanine (G) (with a double ring structure) and the two pyrimidines thymine (T) and cytosine (C) (with only a single ring). Though these four bases predominate, DNA may contain other minor components in addition. However, in most cases DNA samples are described by a sequence of the letters A, G, T, and C. The nucleotides in a DNA macromolecule are joined together by means of diester links in which one phosphoric acid molecule forms bounds between the 3' and 5' positions of consecutive molecules. The DNA chain is always read in the direction from the 5' to the 3' end.
Molecular biologists are interested in finding subsequences of bases in a DNA chain which might be functionally important. In order to detect change-points or changed segments in DNA sequences, the sequences are often recoded in such a way that one of the four bases is identified with a 1 and the other three bases with zeros. A change-point is then defined as a point after which the probability of the occurrence of a 1 is altered. Similarly, in a changed segment the probability of a 1 differs from the corresponding probability outside the segment.
If we assume that the recoded chain can be modeled by independent random variables, i.e. if we assume a Bernoulli sequence, statistical tests and estimates are available for detecting and locating change-points and changed segments (Krauth (1999, 2000), Avery and Henderson (1999b)). However, Avery and Henderson (1999a) fitted Markov chain models to four-state DNA sequences and found that fitting a first-order model works well for most sequences while for some of the longer sequences second- and higher order models were needed. That this kind of dependence can influence the tests for change-points and

changed segments for the recoded binary sequences is obvious, though Avery (2001) is optimistic if only weak dependence is present and the "significance levels are used judiciously".

2   Estimates for the change-point problem

We consider a sequence of $n(n \geq 4)$ random variables $X_1, ..., X_n \epsilon \{0, 1\}$, where

$$P(X_i = 1) = 1 - P(X_i = 0) = \begin{cases} \pi_1 \text{ for } i = 1, ..., \tau, \\ \pi_2 \text{ for } i = \tau + 1, ..., n, \end{cases}$$

with $\tau \epsilon \{2, ..., n - 2\}, 0 < \pi_1, \pi_2 < 1$. Further, we define first-order transition probabilities

$$\pi_{st,i} = P(X_i = t | X_{i-1} = s) \text{ for } i = 2, ..., n; s, t \epsilon \{0, 1\}.$$

If we assume stationarity of the transition probabilities before and after the change-point (τ) we can consider the following reparametrization:
For $i = 2, ..., \tau$:

$$\pi_{11}(1) = \pi_{11,i} = \lambda_1, \ \pi_{10}(1) = \pi_{10,i} = 1 - \lambda_1,$$
$$\pi_{01}(1) = \pi_{01,i} = \frac{(1 - \lambda_1)\pi_1}{1 - \pi_1}, \ \pi_{00}(1) = \pi_{00,i} = \frac{1 - 2\pi_1 + \lambda_1\pi_1}{1 - \pi_1},$$

for $i = \tau + 1$:

$$\pi_{11}(\tau) = \pi_{11,\tau+1} = \lambda_\tau, \ \pi_{10}(\tau) = \pi_{10,\tau+1} = 1 - \lambda_\tau,$$
$$\pi_{01}(\tau) = \pi_{01,\tau+1} = \frac{\pi_2 - \lambda_\tau\pi_1}{1 - \pi_1}, \ \pi_{00}(\tau) = \pi_{00,\tau+1} = \frac{1 - \pi_1 - \pi_2 + \lambda_\tau\pi_1}{1 - \pi_1},$$

for $i = \tau + 2, ..., n$:

$$\pi_{11}(2) = \pi_{11,i} = \lambda_2, \ \pi_{10}(2) = \pi_{10,i} = 1 - \lambda_2,$$
$$\pi_{01}(2) = \pi_{01,i} = \frac{(1 - \lambda_2)\pi_2}{1 - \pi_2}, \ \pi_{00}(2) = \pi_{00,i} = \frac{1 - 2\pi_2 + \lambda_2\pi_2}{1 - \pi_2}.$$

From this, we derive the correlations

$$\rho_1 = \rho[X_i, X_{i+1}] = \frac{\lambda_1 - \pi_1}{1 - \pi_1}, \ \rho[X_i, X_j] = \rho_1^{j-i} \text{ for } 1 \leq i < j \leq \tau,$$
$$\rho[X_\tau, X_{\tau+1}] = \frac{(\lambda_\tau - \pi_2)\pi_1}{\sqrt{\pi_1(1 - \pi_1)\pi_2(1 - \pi_2)}},$$
$$\rho_2 = \rho[X_i, X_{i+1}] = \frac{\lambda_2 - \pi_2}{1 - \pi_2}, \ \rho[X_i, X_j] = \rho_2^{j-i} \text{ for } \tau + 1 \leq i < j \leq n.$$

If $X_1, ..., X_n$ are independent, we have $\lambda_1 = \pi_1, \lambda_\tau = \lambda_2 = \pi_2$.
If we assume for the moment that τ is fixed and known, and if we define

$$n_{11}^j = \sum_{i=2}^j x_{i-1} x_i, \quad n_{10}^j = \sum_{i=2}^j x_{i-1}(1 - x_i),$$

$$n_{01}^j = \sum_{i=2}^j (1 - x_{i-1}) x_i, \quad n_{00}^j = \sum_{i=2}^j (1 - x_{i-1})(1 - x_i)$$

for $j = 2, ..., n$, the likelihood function is given by

$$L(\pi_1, \pi_2, \lambda_1, \lambda_2, \lambda_\tau, \tau) = \pi_1^{x_1}(1 - \pi_1)^{1-x_1}$$
$$\pi_{11}(1)^{n_{11}^\tau}(1 - \pi_{11}(1))^{n_{10}^\tau}(1 - \pi_{00}(1))^{n_{01}^\tau}\pi_{00}(1)^{n_{00}^\tau}$$
$$\pi_{11}(\tau)^{x_\tau x_{\tau+1}}(1 - \pi_{11}(\tau))^{x_\tau(1-x_{\tau+1})}$$
$$(1 - \pi_{00}(\tau))^{(1-x_\tau)x_{\tau+1}}\pi_{00}(\tau)^{(1-x_\tau)(1-x_{\tau+1})}$$
$$\pi_{11}(2)^{n_{11}^n - n_{11}^\tau - x_\tau x_{\tau+1}}(1 - \pi_{11}(2))^{n_{10}^n - n_{10}^\tau - x_\tau(1-x_{\tau+1})}$$
$$(1 - \pi_{00}(2))^{n_{01}^n - n_{01}^\tau - (1-x_\tau)x_{\tau+1}}$$
$$\pi_{00}(2)^{n_{00}^n - n_{00}^\tau - (1-x_\tau)(1-x_{\tau+1})}.$$

As has been observed by many authors (e.g. Klotz (1973), Devore (1976),
Price (1976), Lindqvist (1978), Moore (1979), Kim and Bai (1980), Budescu
(1985)) who studied the model above in the case of no change-point, i.e. for
$\pi_1 = \pi_2, \lambda_1 = \lambda_\tau = \lambda_2$, no simple explicit maximum likelihood estimates
can be derived. Therefore, we consider in a manner similar to that of Devore
(1976) the modified likelihood function

$$L^*(\pi_1, \pi_2, \lambda_1, \lambda_2, \tau) = \pi_{11}(1)^{n_{11}^\tau}(1 - \pi_{11}(1))^{n_{10}^\tau}(1 - \pi_{00}(1))^{n_{01}^\tau}\pi_{00}(1)^{n_{00}^\tau}$$
$$\pi_{11}(2)^{n_{11}^n - n_{11}^\tau - x_\tau x_{\tau+1}}(1 - \pi_{11}(2))^{n_{10}^n - n_{10}^\tau - x_\tau(1-x_{\tau+1})}$$
$$(1 - \pi_{00}(2))^{n_{01}^n - n_{01}^\tau - (1-x_\tau)x_{\tau+1}}$$
$$\pi_{00}(2)^{n_{00}^n - n_{00}^\tau - (1-x_\tau)(1-x_{\tau+1})}$$

instead of the full likelihood given above. Here, we neglect the distribution of
X_1 and the transition from X_τ to $X_{\tau+1}$. Following the argument in Billingsley (1968, pp. 4 - 5) this should be of no great importance, if n is large.
The modified MLE's derived from L* are given by

$$\hat{\lambda}_1(\tau) = \hat{\pi}_{11}(1), \quad \hat{\pi}_1(\tau) = \frac{1 - \hat{\pi}_{00}(1)}{2 - \hat{\pi}_{00}(1) - \hat{\pi}_{11}(1)},$$

$$\hat{\lambda}_2(\tau) = \hat{\pi}_{11}(2), \quad \hat{\pi}_2(\tau) = \frac{1 - \hat{\pi}_{00}(2)}{2 - \hat{\pi}_{00}(2) - \hat{\pi}_{11}(2)},$$

$$\hat{\rho}_1(\tau) = \hat{\pi}_{11}(1) + \hat{\pi}_{00}(1) - 1, \quad \hat{\rho}_2(\tau) = \hat{\pi}_{11}(2) + \hat{\pi}_{00}(2) - 1,$$

where

$$\hat{\pi}_{11}(1) = \frac{n_{11}^\tau}{n_{11}^\tau + n_{10}^\tau}, \quad \hat{\pi}_{00}(1) = \frac{n_{00}^\tau}{n_{00}^\tau + n_{01}^\tau},$$

$$\hat{\pi}_{11}(2) = \frac{n_{11}^n - n_{11}^\tau - x_\tau x_{\tau+1}}{n_{11}^n - n_{11}^\tau - x_\tau x_{\tau+1} + n_{10}^n - n_{10}^\tau - x_\tau(1 - x_{\tau+1})},$$

$$\hat{\pi}_{00}(2) = \frac{n_{00}^n - n_{00}^\tau - (1 - x_\tau)(1 - x_{\tau+1})}{n_{00}^n - n_{00}^\tau - (1 - x_\tau)(1 - x_{\tau+1}) + n_{01}^n - n_{01}^\tau - (1 - x_\tau)x_{\tau+1}}.$$

The modified MLE $\hat{\tau}$ of the change-point (τ) is that value of τ for which $L^*(\hat{\pi}_1(\tau), \hat{\pi}_2(\tau), \hat{\lambda}_1(\tau), \hat{\lambda}_2(\tau), \tau)$ is maximum for $2 \leq \tau \leq n - 2$.

By considering the size of the difference between $\hat{\pi}_1(\hat{\tau})$ and $\hat{\pi}_2(\hat{\tau})$ we can judge whether the observed change is important. By considering $\hat{\lambda}_1(\hat{\tau})$ and $\hat{\lambda}_2(\hat{\tau})$ or $\hat{\rho}_1(\hat{\tau})$ and $\hat{\rho}_2(\hat{\tau})$, respectively, it is possible to judge for the observed sequence the degree of deviation from the assumption of independence.

Some additional remarks seem to be appropriate. First, our estimate of a change-point may be biased if higher-order dependencies are present. Second, if we calculate the estimates given above for short sequences, it may be necessary to modify them in such a way that all estimates are well defined. Third, in particular for short sequences, the estimate of τ may be not unique.

3 Estimates for the changed-segment problem

We consider a sequence of $n(n \geq 6)$ random variables $X_1, ..., X_n \epsilon \{0, 1\}$, where

$$P(X_i = 1) = 1 - P(X_i = 0) = \begin{cases} \pi_1 \text{ for } i = 1, ..., \tau_1, \tau_2 + 1, ..., n \\ \pi_2 \text{ for } i = \tau_1 + 1, ..., \tau_2, \end{cases}$$

with $\tau_1 \epsilon \{2, ..., n-4\}, \tau_2 \epsilon \{\tau_1 + 2, ..., n-2\}, 0 < \pi_1 < \pi_2 < 1$. Further, we define first-order transition probabilities $\pi_{st,i}$ as above. If we assume stationarity of the transition probabilities before the first change-point (τ_1), after the first change-point and before the second change-point (τ_2), and after the second change-point, we can consider the following reparametrization:

For $i = 2, ..., \tau_1, \tau_2 + 2, ..., n$:

$$\pi_{11}(1) = \pi_{11,i} = \lambda_1, \quad \pi_{10}(1) = \pi_{10,i} = 1 - \lambda_1,$$

$$\pi_{01}(1) = \pi_{01,i} = \frac{(1 - \lambda_1)\pi_1}{1 - \pi_1}, \quad \pi_{00}(1) = \pi_{00,i} = \frac{1 - 2\pi_1 + \lambda_1\pi_1}{1 - \pi_1},$$

for $i = \tau_1 + 1$:

$$\pi_{11}(\tau_1) = \pi_{11,\tau_1+1} = \lambda_{\tau_1}, \quad \pi_{10}(\tau_1) = \pi_{10,\tau_1+1} = 1 - \lambda_{\tau_1},$$

$$\pi_{01}(\tau_1) = \pi_{01,\tau_1+1} = \frac{\pi_2 - \lambda_{\tau_1}\pi_1}{1 - \pi_1}, \quad \pi_{00}(\tau_1) = \pi_{00,\tau_1+1} = \frac{1 - \pi_1 - \pi_2 + \lambda_{\tau_1}\pi_1}{1 - \pi_1},$$

for $i = \tau_1 + 2, ..., \tau_2$:

$$\pi_{11}(2) = \pi_{11,i} = \lambda_2, \ \pi_{10}(2) = \pi_{10,i} = 1 - \lambda_2,$$

$$\pi_{01}(2) = \pi_{01,i} = \frac{(1 - \lambda_2)\pi_2}{1 - \pi_2}, \ \pi_{00}(2) = \pi_{00,i} = \frac{1 - 2\pi_2 + \lambda_2\pi_2}{1 - \pi_2},$$

for $i = \tau_2 + 1$:

$$\pi_{11}(\tau_2) = \pi_{11, \tau_2+1} = \lambda_{\tau_2}, \ \pi_{10}(\tau_2) = \pi_{10,\tau_2+1} = 1 - \lambda_{\tau_2},$$

$$\pi_{01}(\tau_2) = \pi_{01, \tau_2+1} = \frac{\pi_1 - \lambda_{\tau_2}\pi_2}{1 - \pi_2}, \ \pi_{00}(\tau_2) = \pi_{00, \tau_2+1} = \frac{1 - \pi_1 - \pi_2 + \lambda_{\tau_2}\pi_2}{1 - \pi_2}.$$

From this, we derive the correlations

$$\rho_1 = \rho[X_i, X_{i+1}] = \frac{\lambda_1 - \pi_1}{1 - \pi_1},$$

$$\rho[X_i, X_j] = \rho_1^{j-i} \text{ for } 1 \le i < j \le \tau_1, \tau_2 + 1 \le i < j \le n,$$

$$\rho[X_\tau, X_{\tau+1}] = \frac{(\lambda_{\tau_1} - \pi_2)\pi_1}{\sqrt{\pi_1(1 - \pi_1)\pi_2(1 - \pi_2)}},$$

$$\rho_2 = \rho[X_i, X_{i+1}] = \frac{\lambda_2 - \pi_2}{1 - \pi_2},$$

$$\rho[X_i, X_j] = \rho_2^{j-i} \text{ for } \tau_1 + 1 \le i < j \le \tau_2,$$

$$\rho[X_{\tau_2}, X_{\tau_2+1}] = \frac{(\lambda_{\tau_2} - \pi_1)\pi_2}{\sqrt{\pi_1(1 - \pi_1)\pi_2(1 - \pi_2)}}.$$

If $X_1, ..., X_n$ are independent, we have $\lambda_1 = \lambda_{\tau_2} = \pi_1, \lambda_2 = \lambda_{\tau_1} = \pi_2$.
If we assume for the moment that τ_1 and τ_2 are fixed and known and if we
define $n_{11}^j, n_{10}^j, n_{01}^j$, and n_{00}^j as above, the likelihood function is given by

$$L(\pi_1, \pi_2, \lambda_1, \lambda_2, \lambda_{\tau_1}, \lambda_{\tau_2}, \tau_1, \tau_2) =$$

$$\pi_1^{x_1}(1 - \pi_1)^{1-x_1}$$

$$\pi_{11}(1)^{n_{11}^{\tau_1}}(1 - \pi_{11}(1))^{n_{10}^{\tau_1}}(1 - \pi_{00}(1))^{n_{01}^{\tau_1}}\pi_{00}(1)^{n_{00}^{\tau_1}}$$

$$\pi_{11}(\tau_1)^{x_{\tau_1}x_{\tau_1+1}}(1 - \pi_{11}(\tau_1))^{x_{\tau_1}(1-x_{\tau_1+1})}(1 - \pi_{00}(\tau_1))^{(1-x_{\tau_1})x_{\tau_1+1}}$$

$$\pi_{00}(\tau_1)^{(1-x_{\tau_1})(1-x_{\tau_1+1})}\pi_{11}(2)^{n_{11}^{\tau_2}-n_{11}^{\tau_1}-x_{\tau_1}x_{\tau_1+1}}(1-\pi_{11}(2))^{n_{10}^{\tau_2}-n_{10}^{\tau_1}-x_{\tau_1}(1-x_{\tau_1+1})}$$

$$(1 - \pi_{00}(2))^{n_{01}^{\tau_2}-n_{01}^{\tau_1}-(1-x_{\tau_1})x_{\tau_1+1}}\pi_{00}(2)^{n_{00}^{\tau_2}-n_{00}^{\tau_1}-(1-x_{\tau_1})(1-x_{\tau_1+1})}$$

$$\pi_{11}(\tau_2)^{x_{\tau_2}x_{\tau_2+1}}\left(1-\pi_{11}(\tau_2)\right)^{x_{\tau_2}(1-x_{\tau_2+1})}\left(1-\pi_{00}(\tau_2)\right)^{(1-x_{\tau_2})x_{\tau_2+1}}$$

$$\pi_{00}(\tau_2)^{(1-x_{\tau_2})(1-x_{\tau_2+1})}\pi_{11}(1)^{n_{11}^n-n_{11}^{\tau_2}-x_{\tau_2}x_{\tau_2+1}}\left(1-\pi_{11}(1)\right)^{n_{10}^n-n_{10}^{\tau_2}-x_{\tau_2}(1-x_{\tau_2+1})}$$

$$\left(1-\pi_{00}(1)\right)^{n_{01}^n-n_{01}^{\tau_2}-(1-x_{\tau_2})x_{\tau_2+1}}\pi_{00}(1)^{n_{00}^n-n_{00}^{\tau_2}-(1-x_{\tau_2})(1-x_{\tau_2+1})}.$$

If we neglect the distribution of X_1 and the transitions from X_{τ_1} to X_{τ_1+1} and from X_{τ_2} to X_{τ_2+1} we derive the modified likelihood function $L^*(\pi_1,\pi_2,\lambda_1,\lambda_2,\tau_1,\tau_2)$ and from this the modified MLE's

$$\hat{\lambda}_1(\tau_1,\tau_2)=\hat{\pi}_{11}(1),\ \hat{\pi}_1(\tau_1,\tau_2)=\frac{1-\hat{\pi}_{00}(1)}{2-\hat{\pi}_{00}(1)-\hat{\pi}_{11}(1)},$$

$$\hat{\lambda}_2(\tau_1,\tau_2)=\hat{\pi}_{11}(2),\ \hat{\pi}_2(\tau_1,\tau_2)=\frac{1-\hat{\pi}_{00}(2)}{2-\hat{\pi}_{00}(2)-\hat{\pi}_{11}(2)},$$

$$\hat{\rho}_1(\tau_1,\tau_2)=\hat{\pi}_{11}(1)+\hat{\pi}_{00}(1)-1,$$

$$\hat{\rho}_2(\tau_1,\tau_2)=\hat{\pi}_{11}(2)+\hat{\pi}_{00}(2)-1,$$

where

$$\hat{\pi}_{11}(1)=\frac{n_{11}^n+n_{11}^{\tau_1}-n_{11}^{\tau_2}-x_{\tau_2}x_{\tau_2+1}}{n_{11}^n+n_{11}^{\tau_1}-n_{11}^{\tau_2}-x_{\tau_2}x_{\tau_2+1}+n_{10}^n+n_{10}^{\tau_1}-n_{10}^{\tau_2}-x_{\tau_2}(1-x_{\tau_2+1})},$$

$$\hat{\pi}_{00}(1)=\frac{n_{00}^n+n_{00}^{\tau_1}-n_{00}^{\tau_2}-(1-x_{\tau_2})(1-x_{\tau_2+1})}{n_{00}^n+n_{00}^{\tau_1}-n_{00}^{\tau_2}-(1-x_{\tau_2})(1-x_{\tau_2+1})+n_{01}^n+n_{01}^{\tau_1}-n_{01}^{\tau_2}-(1-x_{\tau_2})x_{\tau_2+1}},$$

$$\hat{\pi}_{11}(2)=\frac{n_{11}^{\tau_2}-n_{11}^{\tau_1}-x_{\tau_1}x_{\tau_1+1}}{n_{11}^{\tau_2}-n_{11}^{\tau_1}-x_{\tau_1}x_{\tau_1+1}+n_{10}^{\tau_2}-n_{10}^{\tau_1}-x_{\tau_1}(1-x_{\tau_1+1})},$$

$$\hat{\pi}_{00}(2)=\frac{n_{00}^{\tau_2}-n_{00}^{\tau_1}-(1-x_{\tau_1})(1-x_{\tau_1+1})}{n_{00}^{\tau_2}-n_{00}^{\tau_1}-(1-x_{\tau_1})(1-x_{\tau_1+1})+n_{01}^{\tau_2}-n_{01}^{\tau_1}-(1-x_{\tau_1})x_{\tau_1+1}}.$$

The modified MLE's $\hat{\tau}_1$ and $\hat{\tau}_2$ of the change-points (τ_1) and (τ_2) are those values of τ_1 and τ_2 for which $L^*(\hat{\pi}_1(\tau_1,\tau_2),\hat{\pi}_2(\tau_1,\tau_2),\hat{\lambda}_1(\tau_1,\tau_2),\hat{\lambda}_2(\tau_1,\tau_2),\tau_1,\tau_2)$ is maximum for $\tau_1\epsilon\{2,...,n-4\},\tau_2\epsilon\{\tau_1+2,...,n-2\}$.

The location of the changed segment is estimated by $\hat{\tau}_1$, while its length is estimated by $\hat{\tau}_2-\hat{\tau}_1$. The size of the difference between $\hat{\pi}_1(\hat{\tau}_1,\hat{\tau}_2)$ and $\hat{\pi}_2(\hat{\tau}_1,\hat{\tau}_2)$ indicates whether the observed change is of importance. The sizes of $\hat{\lambda}_1(\hat{\tau}_1,\hat{\tau}_2)$ and $\hat{\lambda}_2(\hat{\tau}_1,\hat{\tau}_2)$ or of $\hat{\rho}_1(\hat{\tau}_1,\hat{\tau}_2)$ and $\hat{\rho}_2(\hat{\tau}_1,\hat{\tau}_2)$, respectively, are measures of the degree of deviation from the assumption of independence for the observed sequence.

Similarly as for the change-point problem, our estimates may be biased if higher-order dependencies are present. For short sequences it may be necessary to modify the estimates in such a way that they are well defined and there may be more than one solution for $(\hat{\tau}_1,\hat{\tau}_2)$.

4   Example

In Robb et al. (1998, Fig. 1) a nucleotide sequence which is 1,200 nt in length is reported. This is a composite sequence constructed from overlapping clones. The result is based on the analysis of up to 181 mice embryos.

	A = 1	G = 1	C = 1	T = 1	A = G = 1
$\hat{\tau}$	865	798	988	918	425
$\hat{\pi}_1$	.215	.291	.309	.185	.509
$\hat{\lambda}_1$	.274	.330	.326	.200	.662
$\hat{\rho}_1$	.075	.056	.024	.018	.311
$\hat{\pi}_2$	.356	.147	.114	.352	.483
$\hat{\lambda}_2$	.353	.100	.120	.320	.520
$\hat{\rho}_2$	-.005	-.055	.007	-.050	.071

Table 1. Change-point analysis for five ways of transforming the four-letter sequence into a binary sequence

	A = 1	G = 1	C = 1	T = 1	A = G = 1
$\hat{\tau}_1$	1005	217	11	49	991
$\hat{\tau}_2$	1041	798	988	918	1026
$\hat{\pi}_1$	.247	.168	.109	.347	.491
$\hat{\lambda}_1$	.311	.198	.120	.325	.583
$\hat{\rho}_1$	.085	.036	.013	-.034	.181
$\hat{\pi}_2$	.543	.321	.311	.177	.500
$\hat{\lambda}_2$	.211	.332	.326	.181	.118
$\hat{\rho}_2$	-.727	.016	.021	.004	-.765

Table 2. Changed-segment analysis for five ways of transforming the four-letter sequence into a binary sequence

We coded the letter A by 1 and the other three letters by 0 and generated in this way a binary sequence. For this sequence we identified a change-point and a changed segment as described above. In the same way we proceeded in the case of the letters G, T, and C. Finally, we coded the two purines (A and G) by 1 and the two pyrimidines (T and C) by 0. The results are given in Tables 1 and 2.

It can be observed that for the sequences with G = 1, C = 1, and T = 1 no evidence for a dependence exists if we consider the small values of $\hat{\rho}_1$ and

$\hat{\rho}_2$. This is no longer true for the sequence with A = G = 1, where a certain degree of dependence cannot be ruled out. Similar effects were also observed by other authors (Avery (2001)) for other DNA-samples.

For the sequence with A = 1, a certain degree of dependence was observed in the changed-segment analysis for the observations within the segment ($\hat{\rho}_2 = -.727$). However, this may be an artifact because the segment contains only 36 nucleotides and a spurious correlation cannot be ruled out in this case.

A comparison of the values of $\hat{\pi}_1$ and $\hat{\pi}_2$ in Table 1 reveals that there is some evidence for the existence of a change-point in the sequences with A = 1, G = 1, C = 1, T = 1, while for the sequence with A = G = 1 this evidence is weak. Considering the first four sequences, the existence of a change-point between 798 and 918 is plausible.

A comparison of the values of $\hat{\pi}_1$ and $\hat{\pi}_2$ in Table 2 gives likewise some evidence for a changed segment in the sequences with A = 1, G = 1, C = 1, T = 1, and no evidence for the sequence with A = G = 1. In this case we find similar (large) segments in the sequences with G = 1, C = 1, and T = 1, while for A = 1 a comparatively small segment is detected.

One problem with our kind of analysis is certainly the assumption that only one change-point or only one changed segment, respectively, exists. If this assumption does not hold it cannot be ruled out that the identification of change-points or changed segments may be misleading. In particular, it may occur that we select from several distinct maxima of the modified likelihood function that one which is only by chance the largest one. Therefore, as a kind of control, we considered not only the largest, but also the second and third largest values of the modified likelihood function with respect to the selection of τ or of τ_1 and τ_2, respectively. However, in most cases rather similar values of the estimates resulted. Only in the sequence with A = 1 we found for the change-point analysis the estimate $\hat{\tau} = 865$ for the maximum and the estimates $\hat{\tau} = 995$ and $\hat{\tau} = 989$ for the second and third largest values of the likelihood function. This might be an indication for the existence of two change-points in this situation.

5   Discussion

Modified MLE's were derived for change-points and changed segments in the situation of Bernoulli trials with dependence. This extends previous results for the stationary situation. Avery and Henderson (1999b) and Krauth (1999, 2000) derived tests for change-points and changed segments in independent Bernoulli trials. It is to be hoped that these results may be extended some day to the situation with dependent trials. Then it might also be possible to derive approximate confidence intervals for change-points. For the parameters of a stationary binary Markov chain approximate confidence intervals were derived by Bedrick and Aragon (1989). However, these results cannot be extended in a straightforward way to derive confidence intervals for change-points.

From a biological point of view it may be criticized, that DNA sequences have to be reduced to binary sequences in order to be analyzed, though this transformation has also been advocated by other authors (e.g. Avery and Henderson (1999b), Avery (2001)). However, in contrast to binary sequences the definition of change-points and changed segments becomes difficult for sequences with four bases and such definitions may lack plausibility from a biological point of view.

References

AVERY, P.J. (2001): The effect of dependence in a binary sequence on tests for a changepoint or a changed segment. *Applied Statistics, 50, 243–246.*

AVERY, P.J., HENDERSON, D.A. (1999a): Fitting Markov chain models to discrete state series such as DNA sequences. *Applied Statistics, 48, 53–61.*

AVERY, P.J., HENDERSON, D.A. (1999b): Detecting a changed segment in DNA sequences. *Applied Statistics, 48, 489–503.*

BEDRICK, E.J., ARAGON, J. (1989): Approximate confidence intervals for the parameters of a stationary binary Markov chain. *Technometrics, 31, 437–448.*

BILLINGSLEY, P. (1961): *Statistical inference for Markov processes.* The University of Chicago Press, Chicago, London.

BUDESCU, D.V. (1985): Analysis of dichotomous variables in the presence of serial dependence. *Psychological Bulletin, 97, 547–561.*

DEVORE, J.L. (1976): A note on the estimation of parameters in a Bernoulli model with dependence. *Annals of Statistics, 4, 990–992.*

KIM, S., BAI, D.S. (1980): On parameter estimation in Bernoulli trials with dependence. *Communications in Statistics - Theory and Methods, A9, 1401–1410.*

KLOTZ, J. (1973): Statistical inference in Bernoulli trials with dependence. *Annals of Statistics, 1, 373–379.*

KRAUTH, J. (1999): Discrete scan statistics for detecting change-points in binomial sequences. In: W. Gaul and H. Locarek-Junge (Eds.): *Classification in the Information Age.* Springer, Heidelberg, 196–204.

KRAUTH, J. (2000): Detecting change-points in aircraft noise effects. In: R. Decker and W. Gaul (Eds.): *Classification and Information Processing at the Turn of the Millenium.* Springer, Heidelberg, 386–395.

LINDQVIST, B. (1978): A note on Bernoulli trials with dependence. *Scandinavian Journal of Statistics, 5, 205–208.*

MOORE, M. (1979): Alternatives aux estimateurs à vraisemblance maximale dans un modèle de Bernoulli avec dépendance. *Annales des Sciences Mathématiques du Québec, 3, 119–133.*

PRICE, B.(1976): A note on estimation in Bernoulli trials with dependence. *Communications in Statistics - Theory and Methods, A5, 661–671.*

ROBB, L., MIFSUD, L., HARTLEY, L., BIBEN, C., COPELAND, N.G., GILBERT, D.J., JENKINS, N.A., HARVEY, R.P. (1998): epicardin: A novel basic helix-loop-helix transcription factor gene expressed in epicardium, branchial arch myoblasts, and mesenchyme of developing lung, gut, kidney, and gonads. *Developmental Dynamics, 213, 105–113.*

Two-Mode Clustering Methods: Compare and Contrast

Sabine Krolak-Schwerdt

Department of Psychology,
Saarland University, D-66041 Saarbrücken, Germany

Abstract. In this paper methods to cluster analyze two-mode data are discussed which assume that both objects and attributes contribute to the uncovering of meaningful patterns of clusters. Two-mode methods are reviewed and criteria are proposed which aim at a comparison and evaluation of the reviewed methods. The selected criteria show that most two-mode approaches suffer from drawbacks concerning interpretation of the data, convergence of algorithms, uniqueness of solutions or applicability to larger data sets. They imply some suggestions for future directions in the development of two- and three–mode cluster analysis.

1 Introduction

This paper is concerned with the cluster analysis of two-mode data which consist of two sets of entities (e.g., objects and attributes) and which indicate the relationship between the sets of entities such as profile data (e.g., scores of objects on attributes). The perspective that is taken here concerns one specific problem from applying classical one-mode approaches which may be stated in the following way: Classical methods of cluster analysis assume that objects to be classified belong to heterogenous populations and an adequate partition of the objects consists of clusters which are homogeneous with respect to the underlying attributes. Due to this assumption, it is difficult to deal with any problem of object classification involving clusters which are homogenous with respect to a subset of attributes only. Thus, not all attributes but rather specific combinations of attributes constitute homogeneity of a cluster and these combinations may change from one cluster to another.

In these cases, both objects and attributes will contribute to the uncovering of meaningful patterns of clusters. Psychology offers several substantive domains, where representations are requested that simultaneously display the structure of the objects, the structure of the attributes, and their associative relations. These include cognition, person perception and clinical classifications. To mention an example from social cognition, it is well known that people organize person attributes cognitively in terms of discrete categories or stereotypes which consist of beliefs about how certain subsets of attributes tend to go together or cluster in specific types of persons. In order to adequately analyze these cognitive representations, objects and attributes must be treated as entities with the same theoretical status.

The following exposition will focus on those approaches to two-mode classification which have been designed to jointly clustering objects and attributes. In the next section, a review of methods in two-mode clustering is given. Subsequently, some criteria are proposed which may be helpful in comparing and evaluating the reviewed methods. It turns out that most two-mode approaches suffer from drawbacks concerning interpretation of the data, uniqueness of solutions or applicability to larger data sets. What might be even more critical, these methods have been introduced in different subdisciplines, and as a consequence, there is no common frame of reference to integrate or relate them to each other. This contrast and comparison yields some suggestions for future developments in the last section.

2   Two-mode clustering methods

Research on two-mode clustering frequently subdivides corresponding methods into three categories (De Soete et al. (1984), Schwaiger (1997)). The first category consists of methods which are generalizations of the ADCLUS model proposed by Shepard and Arabie (1979; see DeSarbo (1982)). The second category contains methods which are fitting additive or ultrametric tree structures to two-mode data. Methods belonging to the third category may be termed 'reordering approaches'. They perform a reorganization of the data matrix by permuting rows and columns.

Methods within the first category are mainly designed to analyze nonsymmetric similarity data such as confusion data or brand-switching data (c.f. Both and Gaul (1987)) and they allow for overlapping as well as nonoverlapping clusters. The basic assumption is the following: The similarity of two entities is an additive function of weights which are associated to those clusters the two entities jointly belong to.

DeSarbo (1982) developed the first method within this category called the GENNCLUS approach. It requires the number k of clusters to be specified in advance. Given a rectangular nonsymmetric similarity matrix $S = (s_{ij})$ of order $n \times m$, GENNCLUS aims at finding a best fitting matrix $\hat{S} = (\hat{s}_{ij})$

$$\hat{S} = PVQ' + C,$$

where

$P : (n \times k)$ matrix designating membership of n objects in k clusters,
$V : (k \times k)$ matrix of weights,
$Q : (m \times k)$ matrix designating membership of m attributes in k clusters,
$C : (n \times m)$ matrix where each element is an additive constant c.

GENNCLUS allows the matrix of weights V to be constrained to a diagonal form or to be unconstrained. Thus, the GENNCLUS approach qualifies as a flexible tool which can estimate very different data models in specifying type of clustering (overlapping vs. nonoverlapping) and type of model (that is, V unconstrained vs. V constrained). Major drawbacks of GENNCLUS concern interpretation of input data and properties of the algorithm. First, GENNCLUS assumes the input data to be fully metric. Second, the input data must be interpretable as nonsymmetric similarities. Thus, the applicability of the approach is restricted to very special cases of two-mode data. Finally, there is a considerable tendency of the algorithm to converge into local optima.

The PENCLUS approach proposed by Both and Gaul (1987) postulates the same model function as GENNCLUS to predict the similarity data $\hat{S}$, but differs from the GENNCLUS method in the estimation procedure. Within the PENCLUS approach the matrices V and C are estimated via regression while a penalty function is implemented for the estimation of the parameters of P and Q subject to the condition of establishing either overlapping or nonoverlapping clustering solutions. As Both and Gaul (1987) have shown in applications to data from marketing research, PENCLUS yields classifications with valuable recovery characteristics of the basic data structures.

The model proposed by Baier, Gaul und Schader (1997) introduces several new features within the category of ADCLUS generalizations. First of all, in the model function to predict the data an error term is introduced

$$S = PVQ' + C + error$$

which renders the approach into a probabilistic model subject to the assumption that the error terms are normally distributed with $N(0, \sigma^2)$. Furthermore, the model offers the possibility to constrain cluster membership in P (or Q) due to a-priori information and then to test which bundles of attributes have contributed to the a-priori classification of objects. However, a-priori knowledge about the data structure must be presupposed in any case, since the user must specify the number of relevant clusters in advance.

Models within the second category estimating ultrametric tree structures have been proposed by De Soete et al. (1984), by Espejo and Gaul (1986) and by Schwaiger (1997). Starting with a two-mode data matrix, the algorithms construct a sort of 'grand matrix' in the first step which contains three types of similarities: between objects and attributes, between object pairs and between attribute pairs. Using the grand matrix, classical one-mode algorithms are applied in the second step. The clustering solution is always nonoverlapping.

The models proposed within this category differ in the way the grand matrix is constructed. Espejo and Gaul's missing value approach starts with a given two-mode dissimilarity matrix $D = (d_{ij})$ and treats the unknown object/object-distances $d_{ii'}$ and attribute/attribute-distances $d_{jj'}$ as missing values. De Soete et al. (1984) calculate from the input data first a dissimilarity matrix which satisfies the two-mode analogue of the ultrametric inequality and transform this matrix subsequently into a grand matrix satisfying the one-mode ultrametric inequality. However, though this approach is computationally more complex than the missing value approach, the algorithm performed much poorer (cf. Espejo & Gaul, 1986). Therefore, the details of the method will not be presented.

Schwaiger (1997) extended the ultrametric tree approach in the following way. Starting with a two-mode matrix $X = (x_{ij})$ of profile data, the grand matrix is constructed by calculating distances between any pair of entities

$$d_{ii'} = \frac{1}{m} \sum_{j=1}^{m} | x_{ij} - x_{i'j} |, \qquad i, i' = 1, \ldots, n,$$
$$d_{jj'} = \frac{1}{n} \sum_{i=1}^{n} | x_{ij} - x_{ij'} |, \qquad j, j' = 1, \ldots, m,$$
$$d_{ij} = max_{i,j} \, x_{ij} - x_{ij}, \qquad i = 1, \ldots, n, j = 1, \ldots, m,$$

which are subsequently normalized by the respective block maxima. The resulting symmetric distance matrix is analyzed by one-mode clustering methods in the second step.

The basic idea developed by Espejo and Gaul (1986) in conjunction with Schwaiger's (1997) procedure to construct the grand matrix appear promising for solving the two-mode classification problem. First of all, the input data are not restricted to dissimilarities which comes much closer to a genuine two-mode classification. Second, using clustering algorithms with well-known properties such as the average–linkage procedure omits the use of cumbersome estimation procedures and there is no a-priori knowledge on the number of clusters required to perform the analysis.

The origins of 'reordering methods' go back to the 'bond-energy-algorithm' developed by McCormick et al. (1972). Approaches of this category assume two-mode profile data as input and provide overlapping as well as nonoverlapping solutions. Depending on the specific method, the data values x_{ij} are interpreted as categorical or even restricted to a binary format.

The bond energy algorithm (BEA) provides a permutation of rows and columns of the data matrix such that numerically larger cells are pushed together. In this way, an ensemble of dense submatrices or blocks within the data matrix will result which consist of numerical large values. Objects and attributes corresponding to the rows and columns of a block constitute a cluster. The most serious objection against this method is that its algorithm is not fully explicated in formal terms. Instead, a heuristics is utilized which provides an at least locally optimum solution (cf. De Soete et al. (1984), p. 379). This renders the approach into the most suboptimal method.

The 'modal block method' introduced by Hartigan ((1972)) also extracts a set of submatrices or blocks from the input data. Each block is defined by a subset of objects and a subset of attributes such that each attribute within the block is constant over the objects in the same block. This constant value c is called the 'modal value' for that block. The goal of the analysis is to represent the data by a few large blocks with corresponding block modal value c.

With larger data sets, many blocks fulfil the definition of a modal block. Hence, selection of a few blocks to represent the data is performed by iteratively finding those patterns of attributes which occur most frequently. The objection against this method is that the procedure may not guarantee to yield unique solutions or to find an exhaustive solution in which each entity is in at least one cluster.

The idea of finding blocks of maximum size in the data matrix is also inherent in the GRIDPAT method (Krolak-Schwerdt, Orlik and Ganter (1994), Krolak-Schwerdt and Orlik (1998)). The method was originally formulated to analyze self concept data from Kelly grids which is also valid for the HICLAS method (Rosenberg, Van Mechelen and De Boeck (1996)). Thus, both approaches are designed for binary data matrices. The rationale of GRIDPAT to construct a cluster is described in the following by using the terminology of Formal Concept Analysis (FCA; Ganter and Wille, 1999).

In the FCA framework, the data structure is presented by (A, B, V), where $V \subseteq A \times B$ is a binary relation, and the presence of attribute b_j for object a_i is denoted by $(a_i, b_j) \in V$. Given a subset A_r of objects, the set $A_r^V := \{b_j \in B \mid (a_i, b_j) \in V \text{ for all } a_i \in A_r\}$ contains all attributes of B the objects in A_r possess. In an analogous way, $B_r^V := \{a_i \in A \mid (a_i, b_j) \in V \text{ for all } b_j \in B_r\}$ is the set of all objects of A which have the attributes of B_r in common. A block (in V) is a subset $W_r \subseteq V$

$$W_r = A_r \times B_r,$$

where $A_r^V = B_r$ and $B_r^V = A_r$. That is, all attributes of a block apply to all objects of the same block and vice versa.

The GRIDPAT procedure successively determines blocks from the data array each of which fulfils the requirement of being of maximum size and having a minimum set of attribute–object–pairs in common with other blocks:

$$\mid W_r - \cup_{s=1}^{r-1} W_s \mid = max \ .$$

The basic idea of GRIDPAT is to select from the many blocks of a data set those which give an exhaustive, but simultaneously parsimonious representation of the data. The major drawback of this approach is that it may yield nonunique solutions, especially with larger data sets.

The final method to be discussed is HICLAS (Rosenberg, Van Mechelen and De Boeck (1996)). For reasons of simplicity, the terminology of FCA is used to introduce its basic concepts. In HICLAS, subsets of objects A_r are defined by the attributes they share (i.e. A_r^V) and vice versa, corresponding subsets of attributes need to apply to the same subset of objects (i.e. B_r^V, where $A_r^V = B_r$ and $B_r^V = A_r$). A_r and B_r are termed a 'class' in HICLAS.

Moreover, HICLAS defines an order relation '$\leq$' between different classes in a similar way as does FCA in terms of subconcept- superconcept-ordering: A class involving the object set A_r is hierarchically below another class involving A_s (i.e. a subconcept of), that is $(A_r, B_r) \leq (A_s, B_s)$, if $A_r \subseteq A_s$ which is equivalent to $B_r \supseteq B_s$.

3   Criteria for comparison and evaluation

In the discussion of two-mode approaches, four major criteria evolved which may serve as an aid in comparing and critically evaluating the reviewed methods. These are: 1) interpretation of input data and their scale values, 2) the question, if the methods involve major computational problems, 3) their applicability to larger data sets and 4) finally the derivation of a three-mode version of the method. Table 1 gives a summary of the proposed criteria.

	Interpretation of data i_1 i_2	Scale value s_1 s_2	Computational problems c_1 c_2 c_3	Applicable to large data sets app	three-mode version mod_3
ADCLUS extensions:					
GENNCLUS	x	x	x		
PENCLUS	x	x		x	
Baier et al.	x	x		x	
Ultrametric tree fitting:					
De Soete et al.	x	x			x
Missing value method	x	x		x	
Schwaiger's method	x			x	
Reordering methods:					
Bond energy (BEA)	x	x	x x x	x	
Modal block method	x	x	x x	x	
GRIDPAT	x	x	x	x	x
HICLAS	x	x	x		x

Table 1. Comparison of two-mode clustering methods

Abbrevations. Interpretation of data: i_1: two-mode similarity, i_2: 'genuine' two-mode; Scale value: s_1 metric, s_2: non-metric; Computational problems: c_1: local optima, c_2: nonunique solutions, c_3: heuristics; Applicable to large data sets: app; Three-mode version: mod_3.

The first aspect involving interpretation of input data yields a separation of one group of approaches consisting of mainly ADCLUS generalizations and some ultrametric tree fitting approaches which may be applied to the special case of two-mode similarity data. The goal of a genuine two-mode classification is achieved only by reordering approaches, Schwaiger's approach and the method introduced by Baier et al. (1997).

The scale values criterion characterizes the ADCLUS generalizations as having the drawback of requiring metric data while every other approach besides this group is applicable to the broad range of non-metric input data.

Computational problems concern the major objection against the group of reordering approaches. The most serious drawback is that nearly all approaches yield nonunique solutions. On the other hand, these methods are quite popular because they offer the advantage of being easy to handle: They operate directly on the input data and thus avoid additional transformations of the data into appropriate similarity values. Furthermore, the clustering solution may be interpreted directly on the input data in that clusters are visualized as object–attribute–blocks.

If the analysis of large data sets is requested, the only methods which do not fulfil this objective are GENNCLUS, the De Soete et al. (1984) approach and HICLAS while the other methods are designed to treat data sets of considerable magnitude.

A very different view on two-mode approaches concerns the question, if their theoretical underpinnings allow for an extension to analyze three-mode data which consist of objects, variables and conditions. There are three approaches which offer a three-mode version: the De Soete et al. (1984) approach, GRIDPAT and HICLAS. The other methods have not been extended in this direction as yet.

How do the reviewed methods relate to each other, and is there a frame of reference that might help to integrate them? In current research there is no such frame of reference available. In order to demonstrate how peculiar the methods are with respect to their basic rationale and to the resulting clustering solution, experimental data on the cognitive representation of social stereotypes and their attributes were analyzed. The data consist of subjects' assignments of attributes from the domains of physical appearance, intelligence, dominance and attitudes to gender stereotypes. The main organizing principles in the data involve a grouping of career oriented stereotypes (e.g., career woman, career man) on the basis of appearance, dominance and intelligence, a grouping of politically committed stereotypes (e.g., feminist, intellectual) by their attitudes and a subset of traditional types (e.g., housewife, senior citizen). Thus, an adequate two-mode representation should replicate these stereotype-by-attribute patterns. Table 2 shows the clustering solutions.

Both GRIDPAT and HICLAS using dichotomized data yield the same solution of four clusters, where clusters 1, 2 and 4 consist of the expected grouping into career oriented, politically committed and traditional stereotypes with their corresponding features.

The main structure provided by the modal block method is composed of career oriented stereotypes in three clusters, while there is no representation of the politically committed and the traditional stereotype groups.

Ultrametric tree fitting gives a solution which amalgamates the stereotypes on the basis of intelligence and dominance into a cluster comprising career man and - woman, intellectual and senior citizen. However, the partition contains two clusters referring to stereotype labels without having any characterizing attribute (e.g., confident type and housewife).

In summary, three different solutions are obtained each of which pronounces a different classification criterion, while there is no obvious relation between them such as a kernel of shared structures.

GRIDPAT and HICLAS:
1) career woman, career man, *fashionable, orderly, strong, dominant, intelligent, ambitious*
2) feminist, intellectual, *idealistic, progressive, intelligent, selfless*
3) feminist, confident type, *outgoing, dominant, progressive*
4) housewife, senior citizen, *orderly, selfless, conservative*

Modal block method:
1) career woman, *fashionable, strong, dominant, intelligent*
2) career woman, career man, senior citizen, *ambitious, orderly*
3) career woman, career man, senior citizen, confident type, *egoistic, hides feelings, materialistic*
4) housewife, *weak, submissive, not ambitious, idealistic, reserved*
5) confident type, *egoistic, materialistic, progressive*

Ultrametric tree fitting:
1) career woman, career man, intellectual, senior citizen, *intelligent, strong, dominant, outgoing, ambitious*
2) feminist, *progressive, idealistic, shows feelings, selfless*
3) confident type, –
4) housewife, –

Table 2. Classification of social stereotypes

4   Suggestions for future developments

One of the major issues concerns the resolution of computational problems. In some cases such as GENNCLUS, this may be accomplished by improving the corresponding algorithms. In other cases, a more thorough revision of clustering criteria is requested. Especially, the modal block method and GRIDPAT might gain from further specifications of their criteria. This might render their nowadays vaguely defined amalgamation rules into well defined schedules. The second issue concerns possible extensions of the approaches to analyze three–mode data. As the review has shown, there is only a small group of methods offering such a generalization. However, three–mode data are frequently collected in the behavioral and cognitive domain and thus, three–mode approaches are paramount to offer a more realistic and theoretically meaningful representation of data.

Another prevalent future development is the deduction of a common frame of reference to integrate or relate the methods to each other. Within the category of reordering methods, this might be accomplished by FCA. At least GRIDPAT and HICLAS obviously refer to basic notions which are the defining features of FCA, and may thus be integrated within this framework. What might be the connecting link to ultrametric tree fitting methods and the ADCLUS extensions, remains to be specified. In addition, such a common frame of reference needs to extend to three-mode data and data of different scale values.

References

BAIER, D., GAUL, W. and SCHADER, M. (1997): Two–Mode Overlapping Clustering with Applications to Simultaneous Benefit Segmentation and Market Structuring. In: R. Klar and O. Opitz (Eds.): *Classification and Knowledge Organization*. Springer, Berlin, 557–566.

BOTH, M. and GAUL, W. (1987): Ein Vergleich zweimodaler Clusteranalyseverfahren. *Methods of Operations Research, 57, 593–605.*

DESARBO, W.S. (1982): Gennclus: New Models for General Nonhierarchical Clustering Analysis. *Psychometrika, 47, 449–475.*

DE SOETE, G., DeSARBO, W.S., FURNAS, G.W. and CARROLL, J.D. (1984): The Representation of Rectangular Proximity Matrices. In: E. Degreef and J. Van Buggenhaut (Eds.): *Trends in Mathematical Psychology.* North–Holland, Amsterdam, 377–392.

ESPEJO, E. and GAUL, W. (1986): Two-Mode Hierarchical Clustering as an Instrument for Marketing Research. In: W. Gaul and M. Schader (Eds.): *Classification as a Tool of Research.* North–Holland, Amsterdam, 121–128.

GANTER, B. and WILLE, R. (1999): *Concept Analysis – Mathematical Foundations.* Springer, Berlin.

HARTIGAN, J. (1972): Direct Clustering of a Data Matrix. *Journal of the American Statistical Association, 67, 123–129.*

KROLAK-SCHWERDT, S. and ORLIK, P. (1998): *Direct Clustering of a Two-Mode Binary Data Matrix* (Report No. 186). Arbeiten der Fachrichtung Psychologie, Universität des Saarlandes, Saarbrücken.

KROLAK-SCHWERDT, S., ORLIK, P. and GANTER, B. (1994): Tripat: A Model for Analyzing Three–mode Binary Data. In: H.H. Bock, W. Lenski and M.M. Richter (Eds.): *Information Systems and Data Analysis.* Springer, Berlin, 298–307.

McCORMICK, W.T., SCHWEITZER, P.J. and WHITE, T.W. (1972): Problem Decomposition and Data Reorganization by a Clustering Technique. *Operations Research, 20, 993–1009.*

ROSENBERG, S., VAN MECHELEN, I. and DE BOECK, P. (1996):A Hierarchical Classes Model: Theory and Method with Applications in Psychology and Psychopathology. In: P. Arabie, L.J. Hubert and G. De Soete (Eds.): *Clustering and Classification.* World Scientific Publications, River Edge, 123–155.

SCHWAIGER, M. (1997): Two–Mode Classification in Advertising Research. In: R. Klar and O. Opitz (Eds.): *Classification and Knowledge Organization.* Springer, Berlin, 596–603.

Sensitivity of Graphical Modeling
Against Contamination

Sonja Kuhnt and Claudia Becker

Fachbereich Statistik, Universität Dortmund, D-44221 Dortmund, Germany

Abstract. Graphical modeling as a form of multivariate analysis has turned out to be a capable tool for the detection and modeling of complex dependency structures. Statistical models are related to graphs, in which variables are represented by points and associations between each two of them as lines. The usefulness of graphical modeling depends of course on finding a graphical model, which fits the data appropriately. We will investigate how existing model building strategies and estimation methods can be affected by model disturbances or outlying observations. The focus of our sensitivity analysis lies on mixed graphical models, where both discrete and continuous variables are considered.

1 Introduction

Graphical models turned out to be a helpful tool for detecting and modeling dependency structures (e.g. Cox and Wermuth, 1996, Edwards, 2000, Lauritzen, 1996, Whittaker, 1990). Up to now not much work has been done with respect to considering model disturbances or the effect of outlying observations on the estimation in such models. Since usually estimation is performed by the maximum likelihood method, it can be expected that – similar to other model situations – also in graphical models outliers or contaminated data will disturb the estimation. Hence, with the growing acceptance of using graphical models for analyzing dependency structures there will also be a growing need for sensitivity analyses of the existing estimation methods and for the construction of robust estimates for these models.

We consider here first approaches to sensitivity analyses and robustness in graphical models, where we focus on the case of mixed random vectors containing both discrete and continuous elements. There exists already work on robustness and the effect of outliers for either purely discrete or purely continuous cases – more with respect to the continuous case, less with respect to the discrete case (see e.g. Barnett and Lewis, 1994, for an overview). We try to put together ideas from both branches for the usage in mixed graphical models, concentrating on graphical interaction models, where an undirected graph shows the association structure between the variables.

The paper is organized as follows. In Section 2 we briefly recollect the main ideas of graphical modeling and introduce in more detail the distributional assumptions. Section 3 provides an example data set illustrating the effect of a certain disturbance in the data on the model building process. To expand the findings of the example, we show the results of a simulation study in Section 4, where the effect of contamination on the model building process is

investigated in more detail. We conclude with some remarks on the definition
of outliers and possible robustifications of the modeling in graphical mixed
models.

2 Graphical models: Distributional assumptions

The notion of graphical independence models visualizes conditional indepen-
dences inherent in a statistical model by a graph. A graph in the mathematical
sense is a pair $G = (V, E)$, where $V = \{1, ..., n\}$ is a finite set of vertices and
the set of edges E is a subset of the set of ordered pairs of distinct vertices.
In an undirected graph it follows from $(a, b) \in E$ that also $(b, a) \in E$.

Given a random vector $X = (X_1, ..., X_n)'$ and an undirected graph $G =
(V, E)$ with $V = \{1, ..., n\}$ the notion of a graphical independence model is
defined by the class of all distributions of X, for which $X_a \perp X_b \mid \mathbf{X}_{V \setminus \{a,b\}}$
holds iff (a, b) is not element of the set E. Here, $X_a \perp X_b \mid \mathbf{X}_{V \setminus \{a,b\}}$ denotes
the conditional independence of X_a and X_b given all other variables.

We consider a set $X = (X_1, ..., X_n)'$ of random variables, where the first
p variables are discrete and the following q continuous, $n = p+q$. Denote the
vector of discrete variables by X_Δ and the vector of of continuous variables
by X_Γ. If a purely discrete vector X_Δ is considered, graphical models provide a new way to demonstrate well-established log linear models (Edwards
and Kreiner, 1983, Whittaker, 1990). In the purely continuous case graphical
models based on the assumption of a normal distribution are characterized
by restrictions on the covariance matrix (Edwards, 2000, Chap.3). An extension of the distributional assumptions of the pure cases to the mixed case
has been provided by Lauritzen and Wermuth (1989) with the notion of a
conditional gaussian (CG-) distribution, where the continuous variables given
the discrete variables are normally distributed. Let a typical observation of
$X = (X'_\Delta, X'_\Gamma)'$ be written as $(i', y')'$, where i is a p-tuple containing the
values of the discrete variables and y is a real-valued vector of length q. Let
further $\mathcal{I}$ denote the set of all possible outcomes of X_Δ. The density of a
CG-distribution is then defined by $f_{X_\Delta, X_\Gamma} = f_{X_\Delta}(i) \, f_{X_\Gamma \mid X_\Delta}(i|y)$, yielding

$$f_{X_\Delta, X_\Gamma}(i, y) = p_i \, (2\pi)^{-\frac{q}{2}} \, \det(\Sigma_i)^{-\frac{1}{2}} \, \exp\{-\frac{1}{2}(y - \mu_i)' \Sigma_i^{-1}(y - \mu_i)\}, \quad (1)$$

where p_i denotes the probability of the occurrence of i, and μ_i, Σ_i are the
conditional mean and covariance of Y given i. The distribution is called homo-
geneous, if for some Σ it holds that $\Sigma_i = \Sigma \ \ \forall i \in \mathcal{I}$. The set $\{p_i, \mu_i, \Sigma_i\}_{i \in \mathcal{I}}$
is called the set of moment parameters, their structure determines the inde-
pendence properties between the random variables. Applications of graphical
independence models usually aim at finding a simple model in the sense of
a sparse dependency structure, which is still consistent with the data. Various strategies have been proposed for the selection of an appropriate model.
These are of course to be seen with the appropriate caution and should always

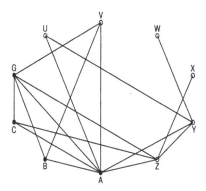

Fig. 1. Independence graph resulting from stepwise model selection

be accompanied by background knowledge. Reviews can be found in Edwards (2000, Chap. 6) and Blauth (2002, Chap. 2). They encompass backward and forward selection strategies as well as alternative search algorithms. As a typical example we look at a backward-selection procedure. The procedure starts with a saturated model, where no conditional independence holds, hence every pair of vertices is joined by an edge in the corresponding independence graph. Then, step by step, individual edges are removed. At each step a criterion is calculated for every model resulting from the removal of a further edge from the present graph. Such a criterion can e.g. be Akaike's Information Criterion (AIC), $-2\ln\widehat{\ell}_M + 2r$, where $\widehat{\ell}_M$ is the maximum likelihood unter the model M and r is the dimension (number of free parameters) of the model. Also the χ^2 test based on the deviance difference $-2(\ln\widehat{\ell}_{M_0} - \ln\widehat{\ell}_{M_1})$ between two models M_0 and M_1, $M_0 \subseteq M_1$, is frequently used. The edge corresponding to the largest value of the AIC-criterion or the largest p-value is deleted and the procedure continues until there is no further improvement in the AIC-criterion or the p-value stays below a given level α. Often, the model search is restricted to models with a decomposable graph, such that maximum likelihood estimates can be explicitly calculated. The aim of this paper is to explore the sensitivity of such a procedure to contaminated data.

3   Data example: Breast cancer

As an example we consider a data set dealing with ablative surgery for breast cancer. The main variable (G) classifies each of 186 patients by the treatment success as either successful / intermediate (G=1) or failure (G=2). The data set further contains six continuous variables (U-Z) and three binary variables (A-C) describing various characteristics of the patients. This data set has originally been described by Krzanowski (1975) in the context of discriminant analysis. The data set provides an illustrative example of the mixed case and has already been analyzed using the graphical model approach (see e.g. Edwards, 2000, p. 119 ff.). We start with the homogeneous saturated model and apply the backwards model selection strategy described in Section 2 based on the χ^2 test. This procedure gives the independence model described by the graph in Figure 1. Note, that the principle of coherence has been followed, meaning that an edge with a p-value below the chosen level $\alpha = 0.05$ at any step will not be removed in a later step. Also, only models with decomposable graphs have been considered. The model search has been conducted using the computer program MIM (Edwards, 2000).

We repeat the same procedure after changing the value of variable U for the first observation in the data set. The values of variable U vary between 23 and 69 with a median of 47.14 and a variance of 78.5. The value 35 of the first observation is replaced by the maximum value 69 for U in the data set, hence by an observation not obviously presenting a contaminated value. Still, it suffices to change the result of the model search selection procedure, compare Figure 2. Concentrating on the main variable (G) we see in Figure 1, that the corresponding vertex is connected with the vertices for the variables A,B,C and Z. In Figure 2, however, variable V is also connected with G. Changing a single value in only one observation hence already changed the identified model, yielding an additional edge in the resulting graph.

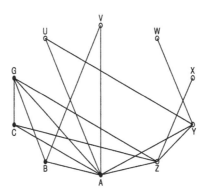

Fig. 2. Independence graph resulting from stepwise model selection on the data with a single changed observation

4   Simulation study for a mixed homogeneous model

The example of the foregoing section gives rise to the question whether this is a singular effect or may happen rather often. In general, we have to investigate what happens to the model building process if some observations do not fit into the pattern built by the majority of the data. To expand the findings of the example, we perform a simulation study. We generate 100 data sets with 1000 observations each according to a graphical mixed model with dependency structure according to Figure 3. The four-dimensional random vector X with observation $x = (i', y')' = (i_1, i_2, y_1, y_2)'$ follows a CG-distribution with density according to (1). The moment parameters for the simulation are given in Table 1. The data generated in this way will also be called the

p_{i_1,i_2}	$i_2 = 1$	2	3
$i_1 = 1$	0.3712	0.0087	0.0219
2	0.3799	0.1101	0.0032
3	0.0912	0.0007	0.0131

μ_{i_1,i_2}	$i_2 = 1$	2	3
$i_1 = 1$	$\begin{pmatrix} -15.38 \\ 27.77 \end{pmatrix}$	$\begin{pmatrix} 11.41 \\ 19.48 \end{pmatrix}$	$\begin{pmatrix} -18.45 \\ 34.19 \end{pmatrix}$
2	$\begin{pmatrix} -11.07 \\ 18.76 \end{pmatrix}$	$\begin{pmatrix} -7.11 \\ 10.47 \end{pmatrix}$	$\begin{pmatrix} -14.14 \\ 25.18 \end{pmatrix}$
3	$\begin{pmatrix} -17.35 \\ 31.91 \end{pmatrix}$	$\begin{pmatrix} -13.39 \\ 23.62 \end{pmatrix}$	$\begin{pmatrix} -20.42 \\ 38.33 \end{pmatrix}$

$$\Sigma = \begin{pmatrix} 10.78 & -14.22 \\ -14.22 & 29.74 \end{pmatrix}$$

Table 1. Moment parameters of the simulated model

"true" data. Next, we disturb the true data in several ways, creating five data situations:

(A) true data
(B) y_1 replaced by -30 in 10 randomly chosen observations
(C) y_1 replaced by 1000 in 10 randomly chosen observations
(D) y_1 replaced by -30 if $i = (1,1)$
(E) i replaced by $(3,2)$ in 10 randomly chosen observations.

To each of the simulated data sets we apply the same backwards selection strategy as for the breast cancer data, but without the restriction to decomposable models. Since the focus of this investigation lies on the effect of contamination in the data we stay with this selection procedure. Generally, it would also interesting to compare results from backward selection with other procedures.

Fig. 3. Independence graph of the simulated model

The results of the model selection procedure are reported in Table 2. Several conclusions can be drawn from these results. First, we see that certainly

	(graph 1)	(graph 2)	(graph 3)	(graph 4)	Others
(A)	95	1	0	0	4
(B)	96	1	1	0	2
(C)	6	0	1	82	1
(D)	0	0	100	0	0
(E)	0	98	1	0	1

Table 2. Simulation results: number of samples out of 100 resulting in respective graphs in situations (A) to (E)

contamination of the data has an influence on the results of the model selection. The observed effects of the data example in Section 3 seem to be no singular event. Second, obviously the degree of contamination is important. Comparing the results for situations (B) and (C), we find that the moderate contamination scheme (B), where we change some observed values to a value which lies at the border of what we may expect under the model, does seldom change the outcome of the model selection. On the other hand, the very extreme contamination of situation (C) drastically changes the results. We expect that there will be some degree of extremeness in the contamination where the behaviour of the model selection procedure changes. It will be one aspect of further research to determine this "change point" more exactly. Third, the type of contamination matters. Different disturbances have different effects in the sense that different graphs are found to represent the dependency structure. There is no general direction of change, we find graphs with additional edges as well as graphs with less edges than for our true model. Again, further research is needed to investigate these effects in more detail. This includes the question, in which cases it might actually be desirable to find a different model than the true model. Although only few observations are contaminated compared to the total number of observations, the resulting data might actually be much better explained by a different model due to the structural nature of the models. For example situation (D) definitely induces a dependence between Y_1 and the two discrete variables, which is reflected in the selected models.

5   Further directions: Outliers and robust model selection

The results of the simulation study show how severely "outliers" in the data can affect the model selection process in graphical modeling. These findings yield two interesting directions of further research: first, the concept of outlyingness has to be investigated conceptionally in the context of graphical modeling, especially with respect to mixed models. Second, a robust alternative for model selection should be found which is less sensitive to contamination in the data.

Concerning the first point, we give a few comments. It is not immediately obvious how to characterize an observation as outlying with respect to a mixed graphical model. If we restrict to the marginal (resp. conditional) distributions, it is of course possible to define outliers with respect to the normal distribution (continuous variables) as well as with respect to the contingency table model (discrete variables), cf. Barnett and Lewis (1994), Becker and Gather (1997, 1999), Gather, Kuhnt and Pawlitschko (2002), Kuhnt (2002). A special aspect of the combination of both is that it is possible to have a single outlier in the continuous variables, whereas in the contingency table we find a whole cell and hence a set of observations to be outlying. From this follows a certain asymmetry. When looking at both types of variables together, it is necessary to define an outlier with respect to the CG-distribution. Several questions arise. Could it happen that we have observations contributing with their discrete part to the same cell of the contingency table, where some of these observations are outliers with respect to the distribution of the continuous variables, but some are not? On the other hand, does it make sense to declare all observations contributing with their discrete part to an outlying cell as outliers, if their continuous parts fit in the structure of the continuous variables quite well? Although we have some sort of intuitive knowledge of what is an outlying observation, a formalization for CG-distributions is a challenge to be followed.

For the general problem of stability of model selection we know that applying different selection procedures to the same data will often lead to inconsistent results. In this sense the variation in the selected models due to the chosen model selection method would be worth an investigation on its own. Although this would exceed the scope of this paper it should be kept in mind.

In the area of "robust" ways of model selection, first approaches for general parametric models are given by Ronchetti (1997), especially on robust versions of the Akaike Information Criterion. When fitting graphical models as described above, maximum likelihood estimation is used. It is well known that maximum likelihood estimators are sensitive against contamination in the data under many distributional assumptions. Hence, a natural way to robustify the model selection process would be to replace the maximum likelihood estimators by more robust alternatives. This approach may also be applicable in graphical modeling. Look at the case of investigating continuous variables only. The analysis of the dependency structure is based mainly on the concentration matrix, i.e. the inverse of the covariance matrix. This has to be estimated appropriately. In the saturated model, this does not pose any problem, but when deleting edges, the concentration matrix estimation has to be performed under restrictions (certain entries in the matrix have to be equal to zero). When calculating maximum likelihood estimators, the so-called modified iterative proportional scaling is used (Frydenberg and Edwards, 1989), where, starting from an initial estimate, the concentration matrix is adjusted iteratively to reflect the dependency structure of the data on the one hand and to fulfill the restrictions on the other hand. To our knowledge there does not exist a robustified version of the iterative proportional scaling algorithm up to now. Since in this algorithm empirical covariance matrices for certain choices of subsets of the variables are calculated, a robustification seems possible by using robust covariance estimators like e.g. the MCD covariance estimator (Rousseeuw, 1985). Of course, this would be a solution for the continuous variables only. There exists a respective version of iterative proportional scaling for mixed models which has to be modified also with respect to estimating the discrete probabilities and the dependency between discrete and continuous variables robustly. Here, the proposal of a modification is less obvious and still under investigation.

References

BARNETT, V. and LEWIS, T. (1994): *Outliers in Statistical Data.* 3rd ed. Wiley, Chichester.

BECKER, C. and GATHER, U. (1997): Outlier Identification and Robust Methods. In: G.S. Maddala and C.R. Rao (Eds.): *Handbook of Statistics 15: Robust Inference.* Elsevier, Amsterdam, 123–143.

BECKER, C. and GATHER, U. (1999): The Masking Breakdown Point of Multivariate Outlier Identification Rules. *Journal of the American Statistical Association, 94, 947–955.*

BLAUTH, A. (2002): *Model Selection in Graphical Models With Special Focus on Genetic Algorithms.* Logos Verlag, Berlin.

COX, D.R. and WERMUTH, N. (1996): *Multivariate Dependencies.* Chapman & Hall, London.

EDWARDS, D. (2000): *Introduction to Graphical Modelling.* 2nd ed. Springer, New York.

EDWARDS, D. and KREINER, S. (1983): The Analysis of Contingency Tables by Graphical Models. *Biometrika, 70, 553-565.*

FRYDENBERG, M. and EDWARDS, D. (1989): A Modified Iterative Proportional Scaling Algorithm for Estimation in Regular Exponential Families. *Comp. Statist. Data Analysis, 8, 143-153.*

GATHER, U., KUHNT, S. and PAWLITSCHKO. J. (2002): Outlier Regions for Various Data Structures. To appear as invited Chapter to the Volume *"Emerging Areas in Probability, Statistics and Operations Research", Mathematical Sciences Series.*

KRZANOWSKI, W.J. (1975): Discrimination and Classification Using Both Binary and Continuous Variables. *Journal of the American Statistical Association, 70(352), 782-790.*

KUHNT, S. (2002): Outlier Identification Procedures for Contingency Tables using Maximum Likelihood and L_1 Estimates. Submitted.

LAURITZEN, S.L. (1996): *Graphical Models.* Clarendon Press, Oxford.

LAURITZEN, S.L. and WERMUTH, N. (1989): Graphical Models for Associations Between Variables, Some of Which are Qualitative and Some Quantitative. *Annals of Statistics, 17, 31-54.*

RONCHETTI, E.M. (1997): Robustness Aspects of Model Choice. *Statistica Sinica* *1, 327-338*.

ROUSSEEUW, P.J. (1985): Multivariate Estimation With High Breakdown Point. In: W. Grossmann, G. Pflug, I. Vincze and W. Wertz (Eds.): *Mathematical Statistics and Applications*. Reidel, Dordrecht, 283–297.

WHITTAKER, J. (1990): *Graphical Models in Applied Mathematical Multivariate Statistics*. Wiley, Chichester.

Acknowledgments: The financial support of the Deutsche Forschungsgemeinschaft (SFB 475) is gratefully acknowledged.

New Graphical Symbolic Objects Representations in Parallel Coordinates

Carlo N. Lauro[1], Francesco Palumbo[2], and Alfonso Iodice D'Enza[1]

[1] Dipartimento di Matematica e Statistica
Università "Federico II" – Napoli, Italy
clauro@unina.it
[2] Dipartimento di Istituzioni Economiche e Finanziarie
Università di Macerata – Macerata, Italy
palumbo@unimc.it

Abstract. Data visualization plays an outstanding role in descriptive statistics. Human eye has a strong ability in detecting regularities in the data and, in many cases, the analysis of graphed data can drive the analyst towards the choice of the most suitable analytical tools. Symbolic Data Analysis (SDA) aims at defining statistical methods to analyze complex data structures no longer based on the classical tabular model. In the SDA context, this paper proposes a thinking on the Symbolic Data visualization and, at the same time, new methods capable of representing complex data and preserving the statistical interpretation.

1 Introduction

Modern *Object Oriented Databases* store complex information, which are no longer represented by a set of records, but by Symbolic Objects (SO). These data bases represent a collection of objects, corresponding to entities of the real world described by attributes. Values, assumed by the attributes, represent the object state. Under this paradigm, each state does not necessary corresponds to a quantitative or categorical single-valued variable, but to any generic function that satisfies a set of given constraints. This situation implies that we deal with interval-valued variables, set-valued variables, multiattribute variables, etc. This model of database allows to store real or abstract concepts (Bock and Diday; 1999). From a theoretical point of view, this new concept of data base could store any kind of information if any numerical representation exists. In addition, being the data base capable of storing data and functions, it also allows to postulate taxonomies and logical rules defined on the data.

This framework opened new and unforeseeable possibilities in statistical data analysis, which lately gave a great upsurge of scientific publications in the treatment and analysis of such kind of data. On the other hand, statistical analysis of these data has to take into account more aspects: positioning, size and shape, orientation (in case of multivariate data).

In the present paper we focus our attention on the graphical representation of complex data that aims at preserving the statistical interpretation. In particular we identify the following main aspects to be investigated: *synthesis of SO's, identification of main features, comparisons tools among SO's* and *identification of relations among/between descriptors.*

There is no getting away from that graphic representations give us an easy and quick insight into the real world phenomena. The SO's were represented by "*Zoom Stars*" diagrams (Noirhomme and Rouard; 1998), these *iconic* representations make difficult any (statistical) interpretation in case of a large number of SO's.

Taking into account the complexity of the information we are going to deal, we identify some suitable tools to represent these data: the parallel coordinates as geometric support (Inselberg; 1981); standardization methods for symbolic descriptors, in order to make them homogeneous; basic definition of *average* SO; ordering criteria.

2 Symbolic objects descriptors

In SDA the data matrix is replaced by the *Symbolic Data Table* (Diday; 1996) whose columns correspond to *symbolic descriptors* (or variables) and rows are called *symbolic descriptions*. In symbolic data base language, they correspond to the world state and to the object state, respectively.

Among all the possible descriptors definitions, most authors restrict their attention to two kinds of symbolic descriptors: Multi–valued and Interval; Modal.

Hereinafter, we introduce an example of symbolic data set, constituted by Italian wines (in the meaning of typologies). The description associated to the Amarone wine, given by an experts pool, is represented by the set of the following assertions in symbolic object language:

$$Amarone = \{[\ alcohol(grades) = (12.5, 17.5)]\ \wedge \qquad (1)$$
$$[\ aging(months) = (24, 48)]\wedge$$
$$[\ price(ItL) = (28, 135)]\wedge$$
$$[\ smell = \{flowery = 0.3; spiced = 0.7\}]\wedge$$
$$[\ color = \{ruby - red\}]\}$$

In the Italian wines example we have five descriptors: *alcohol, aging* and *price* are interval valued variables, smell and color are multimodal and multivalued variables, respectively.

2.1 Interval valued descriptors

We start to describe the interval valued variables properties. An interval-valued variable $I[Y] \subset \mathbb{R}$ is represented by a series of sets of values delimited by ordered couples of bounds referred as *minimum* and *maximum*: $I[y] = \{I[y]_1, I[y]_2, \ldots, I[y]_n\}$, where $I[y]_i \equiv [\underline{y_i}, \overline{y_i}]\ \forall i \in [1, \ldots, n]$ and $\underline{y_i} \leq \overline{y_i}$. The generic interval $I[y]_i$ can also be expressed by the couple $\{y_i^c, y_i^r\}$ and that this is a biunivocal relationship, where: $y_i^c = \frac{1}{2}(\overline{y_i} + \underline{y_i})$ and $y_i^r = \frac{1}{2}(\overline{y_i} - \underline{y_i})$.

Interval valued variables are standardized according to the following procedure proposed by (Lauro and Palumbo; 2001). These results were obtained by referring to some basic interval arithmetic concepts that are not reported. We refer everybody interested to the Neumaier's book for an exhaustive treatment (Neumaier; 1990).

Let us introduce two basic concepts: mean interval and distance among intervals. Mean interval $I[\bar{y}]$ is defined as:

$$I[\bar{y}] = \frac{1}{n} \sum_i I[y]_i, \tag{2}$$

where $I[y]_i \subset \mathbb{R} \ \forall i \in \{1, \dots, n\}$.

We refer to the following distance measure for interval data:

$$d\left(I[y]_i, I[y]_{i'}\right) = |x_i^c - x_{i'}^c| + |x_i^r - x_{i'}^r|, \tag{3}$$

where $d\left(I[y]_i, I[y]_{i'}\right)$ satisfies the Euclidean distance properties.

Taking into account the definition 3, the following properties can be verified. Let $\{I[y]_1, \dots I[y]_n\}$ be a set of finite interval, so that $I[y]_i \subset \mathbb{R} \ \forall i \in \{1, \dots, n\}$ and $I[\bar{y}]$ is their corresponding mean interval, then: $\sum_{i=1}^{n} [(x_i^c - \bar{x}^c) + (x_i^r - \bar{x}^r)] = 0$. and $\sum_{i=1}^{n} d^2 \left(I[y]_i, I[c]\right)$ is minimized *iff* the constant interval $I[c]$ corresponds to $I[\bar{y}]$.

Definition 3 allows to introduce the notation of *scalar variance* for interval-valued data. We define the deviance as the sum of squared distances with respect to the mean interval, as a consequence the variance σ_j^2 for interval-valued data is defined as follows: $\sigma^2 = \frac{1}{n} \sum_{i=1}^{n} d^2 (I[y]_i, I[\bar{y}])$.

Variance definition can also be written according to the following formula:

$$\sigma^2 = \frac{1}{n} \sum_{i=1}^{n} \left(|y_i^c - \bar{y}^c| + |y_i^r - \bar{y}^r|\right)^2. \tag{4}$$

With a little algebra we obtain:

$$\sigma^2 = \frac{1}{n} \left[\sum_{i=1}^{n} (y_i^c - \bar{y}^c)^2 + \sum_{i=1}^{n} (y_i^r - \bar{y}^r)^2 + 2 \sum_{i=1}^{n} |y_i^c - \bar{y}^c||y_i^r - \bar{y}^r| \right] \tag{5}$$

The expression in 5 affirms that the variance for interval-valued data can be decomposed into three components: variance among midpoints, variance among ranges and twice the connection between midpoints and ranges, given by $\gamma = \sum_{i=1}^{n} |y_i^c - \bar{y}^c||y_i^r - \bar{y}^r| \geq 0$.

The remarked properties in the definition 3 indicate that the distance between intervals can be generalized to the Euclidean distance in the space $\mathbb{R}^p$.

A standardized interval $I[z]_i$ is given by:

$$I[z]_i = \left[\frac{1}{\sigma} \left(y_i^c - \bar{y}^c - |y_i^r - \bar{y}^r|\right), \frac{1}{\sigma} \left(y_i^c - \bar{y}^c + |y_i^r - \bar{y}^r|\right) \right]. \tag{6}$$

2.2   Multivalued and modal descriptors treatment

According to the SO definition, qualitative descriptors are of two kinds, depending on the presence of a probability or a frequency measure associated to each modality. Let us define the generic multivalued Y variable. Its numerical representation is a matrix $n \times K$, where n is the number of SO's and K the number of modalities. The generic term $y_{i,k} = 1$ in case of presence of the kth modality and 0 otherwise. Analogously, a modal variable Y is represented by a $n \times K$ matrix, $y_{i,k} \in [0,1]$ and $\sum_k y_{i,k} = 1$.

We propose an unique treatment of these two different kinds of variables that is based on the standardization of the contingency table, computed assuming the χ^2 distance between each modality and the column marginal. In order to trace these measures of deviation on the same system of axes for the standardized interval-valued variables, we standardize them with respect to each modality.

Let us assume Y^j a generic categorical variable, the generic distance measure $\tilde{y}^j_{i,k}$ is computed as:

$$\tilde{y}^j_{i,k} = \frac{y^j_{i,k}}{y^j_{\cdot,k}} - \frac{y^j_{i,\cdot}}{n}. \tag{7}$$

This data coding, which represents one among all possible treatments, allows to exploit an useful interpretation. As a consequence of the proposed coding, modalities assume values that represent a *"deviance"* from the marginal condition. This is the most interesting aspect of the treatment. If an object has an over represented modality, with respect to the marginal profile, this will assume a highly positive coordinate. On the contrary, under-represented modalities will have negative coordinate. The higher is the module of the coordinate the more significative is its over/under representation in the SO.

3   SO's graphical representation

One of the most common SO's graphic representation is due to Noirhomme-Fraiture and Rouard (1997,1998) and it is named *Zoom Star* representation and is derived from the Kiviat diagrams. This representation is based on radial diagrams, and can combine different types of descriptors. Its most remarkable properties, with respect to other different diagrams, is the possibility of representing more than three descriptors at the same time and of preserving a good visualization of axes and categories in 3D representations (3D Stars). The latter is outstanding if we take into account the possibility of representing histograms over each axis in 3D visualization. Of course, the 3D representation is specially effective if the user has interaction capabilities with the graph, but has low performance in printed documents. On the other hand, it is worthy to notice, the Zoom Star representation admits difficult interpretation of the statistical relationships among variables because of no standardization of variables and because the radial schema loses any kind of relation among variables. This because of two aspects: angles between variables are only determined by the number of variables itself; the variables order is subject to no statistical criteria.

3.1   A new visualisation approach on n parallel axes

Parallel axes can be defined as a visualization support derived from the *parallel coordinates* schema, firstly proposed by Inselberg (1981,1999) and then improved and popularized in the statistical community by Wegman (1990). The parallel coordinates representation exploits the projective geometry properties which consist in the definition of duality between the $\mathbb{R}^n$ Euclidean space and a system of n parallel axes in $\mathbb{R}^2$. It can be proved that these relationships correspond to a duality *point* $\leftrightarrow$ *line*; each point in $\mathbb{R}^n$ corresponds to (n-1)-segments polygonal line in the projective $\mathbb{R}^2$ parallel coordinates system.

The most appealing aspect in our proposal, with respect to other graphic visualization methods for symbolic data, is the relevance given to the possibility of comparing syntheses of SO's, as well as single variables on different parallel axes systems.

Homogeneity of the standardized descriptors allows to define any generic SO's synthesis. The following section shows examples based on the comparisons of "*means*" and "*histograms*" of SO's. Other different measures of synthesis can also be defined in order to give relevance to other specific aspects.

SO's ordering criterion plays a prime role for the identification of regularities in the data. With respect to single valued data, in the case of symbolic data analysis there are several new aspects to take into account.

Ordering criteria can be classified into two types: based on the definition of a distance measure, that implies the definition of the most representative SO (mean object) and of a ranking measure based on the distance from this SO. Among the distances defined for complex data structure we identified the ones proposed by Ichino and Yaguchi (1994) or by Gower and Krzanowski (1999) as suitable measures. On the other hand, SO's can be ordered from left to right according to either the midpoint value or the range value.

An ordered representation of syntheses of SO's can help to easily catch different aspects. The distance criterion takes into account SO's as a whole, whereas midpoint or range ordering tends to evaluate only one aspect of the SO's at once.

In Figure 1, in the two graphics in the top, we observe a set of syntheses of SO's ordered according to the midpoint values, whereas, two graphics on the bottom show SO's ordered with respect to the ranges. Figure 1 is a clear example of how evident is the absence (on the top) or presence (in the bottom) of association between ranges and midpoints. At, the same time, we easily notice the presence of anomalous SO's in the two examples on the right side of Figure 1.

The histogram representation is the most complete synthesis of SO's. Histogram representation in Figure 2 summarizes the SO's as a whole and allows to compare them on the basis of statistical criteria. Symbolic descriptors, differently from classical single valued variables, assume a set of values for each

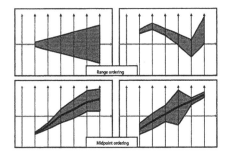

Fig. 1. Syntheses of SO's: midpoints and ranges graphics

observation. So, as shown in Figure **2**, each observation (SO) can be described by a histogram.

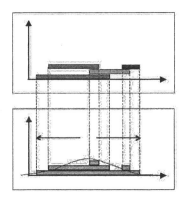

Fig. 2. SO's histogram representation

4 Italian wines representation

In order to illustrate our proposal we use the Italian wines data set. It consists of the following wines (that are described by the five descriptors mentioned in 1): Amarone, Barolo, Brunello, Barbaresco, Aglianico, Cabernet, Chianti (red wines), Verdicchio, Fiano, Chardonnay and Falanghina (white wines).

Color is a Boolean multivalued variable, and its six modalities are associated to three shadings of red wines: purple, garnet and ruby; and to three white shadings of white wines: straw, gold and pale green yellow. Smell is a modal variable, its modalities represent the different adjectives that characterize smell analysis. In particular: flowery, fruity, herbaceous, spiced, ethereal, aromatic, wide.

Figure **3** represents a system of parallel axes, where to each axis is associated a histogram obtained by the synthesis of the five descriptors considered in the Italian wines data set (as shown in Figure **2**). As general rule, in SDA is

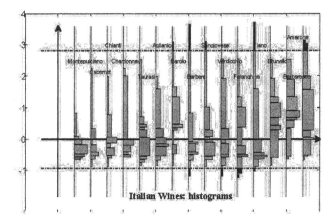

Fig. 3. Variable SO's histogram representation

quite rare the case of a large number of SO's. The histogram-representation capability to synthesize information is really amazing. Italian wines in Figure **3** are ordered with respect to the midpoint values. Looking at the figure from right to left we observe that there is association between ranges and midpoints. SO's on the left side are characterized by small midpoints values as well as by small ranges values. Whereas, on the right side we observe SO's characterized by large midpoint values, as well as by wide intervals.

·Midpoints order and range order can consider all the coded descriptors simultaneously (as a synthesis) or each descriptor individually represented in separate graphics; in these cases axes are ordered in increasing way, according to the distance from the midpoints of each SO's from a 'mean' midpoint, or to the *magnitude* of the objects, respectively.

The Barbera red wine (in the middle of the graphic) represents an anomalous SO. In fact, its histogram width appears with extreme values out of the 5th and 95th percentiles (dashed horizontal lines). The reasons of this can be easily understood looking at the single variables graphics (for sake of shortness plots of single variables are not reported). Barbera red wine is characterized by two descriptors that assume wide ranges: color and aging.

5 Final remarks

Differently from classical variables, symbolic descriptors may assume set of values and characterize the SO's with respect to different aspects: position, size, shape. This paper proposes several visualization approaches that were designed to ensure the comparison among SO's. As showed in the paper it turns out difficult to take into account all the SO's aspects at the same time. In the classical data analysis (with single-valued data) it can be difficult to choose the best representation, the choice becomes even more difficult when we have to compromise our visualization needs. An useful tool to get more aspects at the same time should be based on interactive and dynamic graphic representations.

References

BOCK, H.H. and DIDAY, E. (1999); eds. *Analysis of Symbolic Data*. Springr Verlag, Hiedelberg.

DIDAY, E. (1996): Une introduction á l'analyse des données symboliques. In *SFC*, Vannes, France.

GOWER, J.C. and KRZANOWSKI, W.J. (1999): Analysis of distance for structured multivariate data and extensions to multivariate analysis of variance. *Applied Statistics*, 48:505–519.

ICHINO M., and YAGUCHI, H. (1994): General Minkowski metrics for mixed features type data analysis. *IEEE Transaction on System, Man and Cybernetics*, 24:698–708.

INSELBERG, A. (1981): N-dimensional graphics, part I lines and hyperplanes. G320-2711, IBM LASC.

INSELBERG, A. (1999): Don't panic ... just do it in parallel! *Computational Statistics*, 14:53–77.

LAURO, N.C. and PALUMBO, F. (2001): Principal component analysis on subpopulations: an interval data approach. In *Abstracts of the IMPS2001 Conference*, Osaka (Japan), July 2001.

NEUMAIER, A.(1990): *Interval methods for systems of Equations*. Cambridge University Press, Cambridge.

NOIRHOMME-FRAITURE, M. and RUARD, M. (1997): Computer graphics for symbolic objects. In *App. Stoch. Models and Data Analysis*, volume 2, Anacapri, Rocco Curto Editore.

NOIRHOMME-FRAITURE, M. and RUARD, M. (1998): Representation of subpopulations and correlation with zoom star. In *Int.Seminar on New Techniques & Technologies for Statistics, NTTS'98*, pages 357 – 362, Sorrento.

WEGMAN, E.(1990): Hyperdimensional data analysis using parallel coordinates. *J. Amer. Stat.Ass.*, 85:664–675.

Acknowledgments: This paper was realized in the framework of the Esprit project Vitamin-s and of PRIN2000 "*Analisi Simbolica e Data Mining*" at the Dipartimento di Matematica e Statistica - University Federico II of Naples

A Hierarchical Classes Approach to Discriminant Analysis

Luigi Lombardi[1,2], Eva Ceulemans[1], and Iven Van Mechelen[1]

[1] Department of Psychology,
   Katholieke Universiteit Leuven, Tiensestraat 102, B-3000 Leuven, Belgium
[2] Department of Developmental Psychology,
   Università di Padova, via Venezia 8, 35100, Padova, Italy

Abstract. Given an $I \times J$ object by attribute binary data matrix, and a predefined partition of the I objects into K partition classes, one may wish to characterize each of the K partition classes in terms of a set of singly necessary and jointly sufficient attributes; from the latter sets one may further derive attributes or attribute patterns that discriminate among the partition classes. In this paper, we propose how this goal may be achieved by fitting a new type of constrained hierarchical classes model, called D-HICLAS, to the data matrix. An algorithm for fitting D-HICLAS models is presented and an application to real data is discussed.

1 Introduction

Consider the following situations

- A marketing manager is interested in determining product qualities that best describe a given bunch of product categories.
- A medical researcher is interested in determining symptoms that significantly differentiate among known groups of psychiatric patients.
- A psychologist wants to investigate which cognitive profiles best characterize different given groups of students in primary school.

Each of these examples involves a characterization of given categories in terms of a predefined set of descriptors.

A particular case is the situation in which one wants to characterize each of K possible categories by means of a set of *singly necessary* and *jointly sufficient* binary attributes. From these sets one may further derive attributes or attribute patterns that possibly discriminate among the categories.

More formally, consider an $I \times J$ binary data matrix $\mathbf{D}$ defining a binary relation between a set of I objects and a set of J attributes, and an $I \times K$ binary partition matrix $\mathbf{P}$ defining a K–partition of the object set where, in particular, $p_{ik} = 1$ denotes that object i belongs to class k. Assume further that all classes of the K–partition are homogeneous with respect to each of the J attributes. The *characterization problem* then boils down to finding a $K \times J$ binary matrix $\mathbf{C}$, called the *characterization matrix*, such that the quantity

$$E = \sum_{i=1}^{I} \sum_{j=1}^{J} |d_{ij} - \sum_{k=1}^{K} p_{ik} c_{kj}| \qquad (1)$$

is minimal. It is straightforward to show that (1) is minimal if, given the proportion π_{kj} $(\forall k = 1, \ldots, K; \forall j = 1, \ldots, J)$ of objects in class k which possess attribute j, the entries c_{kj} of $\mathbf{C}$ are replaced with

$$z_{kj} = \begin{cases} 1 & \text{if} \quad \pi_{kj} \geq .50 \\ 0 & \text{if} \quad \pi_{kj} < .50 \end{cases} \qquad (\forall k = 1, \ldots, K; \ \forall j = 1, \ldots, J) \qquad (2)$$

The matrix $\mathbf{Z}$ yields an exact solution to the minimization of (1). However, an exact representation of $\mathbf{C}$ itself may be troublesome in empirical data matrices. In particular, in case of data sets that are not very small and with a large number of attributes, the high complexity of the characterization sets can be very difficult to interpret. A possible way out consists of approximating $\mathbf{C}$ by means of a matrix that has a much simpler structural representation.

The method to be presented here, which is called D-HICLAS (HICLAS model for descriptive Discriminant analysis), is a novel extension of the conjunctive HICLAS model (Van Mechelen et al., 1995) to deal with the problem of approximating the characterization matrix $\mathbf{C}$. A D-HICLAS model yields a simplified approximation of $\mathbf{C}$ by reducing the original set of attributes to a few binary variables, called bundles. Moreover a D-HICLAS analysis guarantees also that the K–partition is well represented in the model.

Section 2 of this paper outlines the general theory of D-HICLAS model and the associated data analysis. Section 3 illustrates the new model with an application to real psychological data. Finally in Section 4 some possible model extensions are discussed.

2   Descriptive discriminant HICLAS approach

2.1   The model

We assume an $I \times J$ object by attribute data matrix $\mathbf{D}$ and an $I \times K$ binary partition matrix $\mathbf{P}$ defining a K–partition on the objects (K–categories). A descriptive discriminant hierarchical classes analysis will approximate $\mathbf{D}$ by an $I \times J$ reconstructed binary matrix $\mathbf{M}$ that can be decomposed into $\mathbf{P}$ and a $K \times J$ binary matrix $\mathbf{M}^*$ that approximates the characterization matrix $\mathbf{C}$. $\mathbf{M}^*$ can be further decomposed into a $K \times R$ binary matrix $\mathbf{A}$ and a $J \times R$ binary matrix $\mathbf{B}$, where R denotes the rank of the model. In particular, $\mathbf{A}$ defines R, possibly overlapping, clusters of the K–categories, whereas $\mathbf{B}$ defines R, possibly overlapping, clusters of attributes. As a guiding example we use the hypothetical matrices shown in Tables 1–3.

2.2   Relations represented in D-HICLAS model

The D-HICLAS model represents three types of relations defined in $\mathbf{M}^*$: association, equivalence and hierarchy.

The *association relation* is the binary relation between the categories and the attributes of $\mathbf{M}^*$ as defined by the 1–entries of $\mathbf{M}^*$. *Equivalence relations* are defined on the categories and on the attributes of $\mathbf{M}^*$. Categories are equivalent iff they are associated with the same set of attributes. Likewise attributes are equivalent iff they are associated with the same set of categories. A *hierarchical relation* is defined among the categories and among the attributes of $\mathbf{M}^*$. A category is hierarchically below another, iff the respective sets of associated attributes are in a subset/superset relation. Similarly, an attribute is hierarchically below another, iff the respective set of associated categories are in a subset/superset relation.

The matrices $\mathbf{A}$ and $\mathbf{B}$ of a D-HICLAS model represent the three relations as follows

i) *Association relation*:

$$\mathbf{M} = \mathbf{P}\mathbf{M}^* \tag{3}$$

with $\mathbf{M}^* = [\mathbf{A}^c \otimes \mathbf{B}']^c$ (where $\otimes$ denotes the Boolean matrix product (Kim, 1982)). This association rule means that for an arbitrary entry m_{ij} of $\mathbf{M}$,

$$m_{ij} = \sum_{k=1}^{K} p_{ik} m_{kj}^*$$
$$= \sum_{k=1}^{K} p_{ik} \left(\bigoplus_{r=1}^{R} a_{kr}^c b_{jr} \right)^c \tag{4}$$

where m_{kj}^* indicates the (k, j)–entry of $\mathbf{M}^*$ and $\bigoplus$ denotes the Boolean sum (Kim, 1982). Moreover (3) implies that for an arbitrary entry m_{ij} of $\mathbf{M}$,

$$m_{ij} = 1 \quad \Leftrightarrow \quad \exists k : 1, \dots, K \quad : \quad p_{ik} = 1 \quad \wedge \quad m_{kj}^* = 1 \tag{5}$$

where

$$m_{kj}^* = 1 \quad \Leftrightarrow \quad \forall r : 1, \dots, R \quad : \quad b_{jr} = 1 \quad \Rightarrow \quad a_{kr} = 1 \tag{6}$$

In (6) the $\mathbf{B}$ row vector of an attribute can be considered to denote a set of formal requisites stemming from that attribute; these requisites are to be jointly met by a category to be associated with the attribute in question. For example, from the model in Table 3, it can be derived that category C_1 is associated with attribute c. This further implies that all objects in category $C_1 = \{1, 2, 3\}$ are also associated with attribute c.

ii) *Equivalence relations*: A category k (resp. an attribute j) is equivalent to another category k' (resp. another attribute j') if and only if $\mathbf{A}_{k:} = \mathbf{A}_{k':}$ (resp. $\mathbf{B}_{j:} = \mathbf{B}_{j':}$). For example, categories C_1, C_2 and C_3 are associated with different set of attributes, and, hence, those categories are not equivalent and have different row vectors in the $\mathbf{A}$ matrix of the D-HICLAS model of Table 3. On the other hand, notice that by (3) all objects belonging to the same category share the same attribute pattern.

iii) *Hierarchical relations*: A category k (resp. an attribute j) is hierarchically below to another category k' (resp. another attribute j') if and only if $\mathbf{A}_{k:} \leq \mathbf{A}_{k':}$ (resp. $\mathbf{B}_{j:} \geq \mathbf{B}_{j':}$). Note that for $\mathbf{B}$ this reversal ($\geq$) reflects the fact that the more requisites stem from an attribute, the fewer categories that attribute is associated with. For example, attribute c is hierarchically above attribute d; consequently, the bundle patterns of attributes c and d are in a subset/superset relation in the D-HICLAS model of Table 3.

Graphic representation. Figure 1 presents a graphic representation for the D-HICLAS model of Table 3. In Figure 1 category and attribute classes are displayed as paired boxes, the upper box of each pair being a category class and the lower box an attribute class. The top of the category hierarchy is at the top of the representation, whereas the attribute hierarchy is represented upside down. The association relation can be read from the representation as a dominance relation: A category is associated with all attributes below it, and an attribute is associated with all categories above it.

	D Attributes				**M** Attributes			
Objects	a	b	c	d	Objects	a	b	c	d
Obj 1	1	0	1	0	Obj 1	1	0	1	0
Obj 2	1	1	1	0	Obj 2	1	0	1	0
Obj 3	1	0	1	0	Obj 3	1	0	1	0
Obj 4	0	0	1	1	Obj 4	0	0	1	0
Obj 5	0	0	1	0	Obj 5	0	0	1	0
Obj 6	0	1	1	0	Obj 6	0	1	1	0
Obj 7	0	0	1	0	Obj 7	0	1	1	0

Table 1. Hypothetical data matrix $\mathbf{D}$ and related D-HICLAS model matrix $\mathbf{M}$

	P Categories				**M*** Attributes			
Objects	C_1	C_2	C_3		Categories	a	b	c	d
Obj 1	1	0	0		C_1	1	0	1	0
Obj 2	1	0	0		C_2	0	0	1	0
Obj 3	1	0	0		C_3	0	1	1	0
Obj 4	0	1	0						
Obj 5	0	1	0						
Obj 6	0	0	1						
Obj 7	0	0	1						

Table 2. D-HICLAS Model decomposition for matrix $\mathbf{M}$ in Table 1

	A			**B**	
	Bundles			Bundles	
Categories	*I*	*II*	Attributes	*I*	*II*
C_1	0	1	a	0	1
C_2	0	0	b	1	0
C_3	1	0	c	0	0
			d	1	1

Table 3. D-HICLAS Model decomposition for matrix $\mathbf{M}^*$ in Table 2

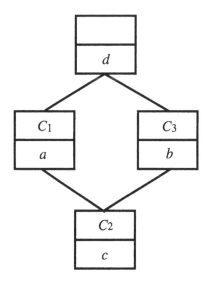

Fig. 1. Graphic representation of the conjunctive D-HICLAS model of Table 3. Empty boxes denote empty classes.

2.3   Data analysis and algorithm

The aim of a D-HICLAS analysis in rank R of a binary data matrix $\mathbf{D}$ and a given partition matrix $\mathbf{P}$ is to approximate $\mathbf{D}$ as closely as possible by a reconstructed binary model matrix $\mathbf{M}$, in terms of the loss function

$$L = \sum_{i=1}^{I}\sum_{j=1}^{J}|d_{ij} - m_{ij}| \tag{7}$$

and such that $\mathbf{M}$ can be represented by a rank R D-HICLAS model.

The routine which looks for matrices $\{\mathbf{A}, \mathbf{B}\}$, such that (7) is minimal is a modified version of the alternating greedy procedure for ordinary HICLAS analysis (Leenen and Van Mechelen, 2001). In particular, the D-HICLAS algorithm successively executes two main routines.

i) Given an initial random configuration, $\mathbf{A}^0$ for $\mathbf{A}$, the procedure looks, conditionally upon $\mathbf{A}^0$, for the optimal matrix $\mathbf{B}^0$, which is such that

(7) is minimal. In the next steps, $\mathbf{A}^w$ is reestimated conditionally upon $\mathbf{B}^{w-1}$, and $\mathbf{B}^w$ is reestimated conditionally upon $\mathbf{A}^w$ ($w = 1, 2 \ldots$). This procedure continues until no further improvement in the loss function (7) is observed.

A conditional estimate for $\mathbf{A}$ (resp. $\mathbf{B}$) is obtained by a greedy heuristic which successively estimates each row of $\mathbf{A}$ (resp. $\mathbf{B}$). In particular, given $\mathbf{A}$, the j-th row $\mathbf{B}_{j:}$ of $\mathbf{B}$ ($\forall j = 1, \ldots, J$) is optimized by means of a Boolean regression that minimizes

$$L_{(j)} = \sum_{i=1}^{I} |d_{ij} - m_{ij}| \tag{8}$$

Whereas, given $\mathbf{B}$, the k-th row $\mathbf{A}_{k:}$ of $\mathbf{A}$ ($\forall k = 1, \ldots, K$) is optimized by means of a generalized form of Boolean regression that minimizes

$$L_{(k)} = \sum_{i:p_{ik}=1} \sum_{j=1}^{J} |d_{ij} - m_{kj}| \tag{9}$$

More precisely, in this regression the values of each predictor variable are $N_k = \sum_i^I p_{ik}$ concatenated copies of each column of $\mathbf{B}$, whereas the values of the criterion vector are the data–entries d_{ij} ($\forall i : p_{ik} = 1; \forall j = 1, \ldots, J$).

ii) In the second main routine the matrices $\mathbf{A}$ and $\mathbf{B}$ obtained at the end of the first routine are modified such as to make them consistent with the equivalence and hierachical relations in the model matrix $\mathbf{M}$, that $\mathbf{A}$ and $\mathbf{B}$ yield by (3). For this, a closure operation (Barbut and Monjardet, 1970) is successively applied to each of the two matrices $\mathbf{A}$ and $\mathbf{B}$. This operation implies that zero–entries in the two matrices are turned into one if this change does not alter $\mathbf{M}$ (and, hence, neither the value of the loss function).

3   An empirical application

In this section we present a D-HICLAS analysis of data from a study on archetypal psychiatric patients (Mezzich and Solomon, 1980). In this study each of 11 psychiatrists was invited to think of a typical patient for each one of four diagnostic categories: manic–depressive depressed (MDD), manic–depressive manic (MDM), simple schizophrenic (SS) and paranoid schizophrenic (PS). These four diagnostic categories are part of the nomenclature of mental disorders (DSM-II) issued in 1968 by the American Psychiatric Association. The 11 psychiatrists characterized each archetypical patient by $0 - 6$ severity ratings on 17 symptoms from the Brief Psychiatric Rating Scale (BPRS).

In order to yield a D-HICLAS analysis each symptom of the original data base was trichotomized into two dummy variables indicating at least a medium severity rating $(1-6)$ and an high severity rating $(3-6)$, respectively.

This resulted in a 44 × 34 patient by symptom data matrix **D**. Next, **D** was analyzed by means of the D-HICLAS algorithm in ranks 1 to 5.

On the basis of a scree test, the rank 3 solution with a proportion of discrepancies of .167 was retained. Figure 2 shows the graphic representation of the conjunctive D-HICLAS rank-3 solution.

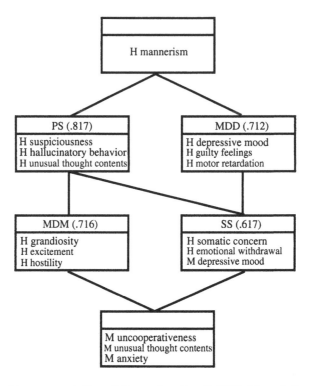

Fig. 2. Graphic representation of the conjunctive D-HICLAS rank-3 solution. Diagnostic categories are displayed in the upper boxes, symptoms in the lower boxes. M and H denote medium rating and high rating, respectively.

The graphic representation reads as follows:

Diagnostic categories and symptom classes are displayed as paired boxes, the upper box of each pair containing diagnostic categories and the lower box containing symptoms. The top of the diagnostic category hierarchy is at the top of the representation, whereas the symptom hierarchy is represented upside down. In order to simplify the graphic representation we inserted in each symptom class the three best fitting symptoms only. Moreover, for each diagnostic category we displayed both the label and the goodness of fit in the upper boxes.

Notice that the association relation can be read from the representation as a dominance relation: A psychiatric category is associated with all symptoms below it, and a symptom is associated with all psychiatric categories above it.

In substantive terms Figure 2 reads as follows: The grouping of symptoms in the graphic representation is in line with the classical distinction between negative and positive psychotic symptoms (Andreasen and Olsen, 1982; Stuart, Malone, Currie, Klimidis and Minas, 1995). In particular, the left side of the symptoms hierarchy contains extreme positive psychotic symptoms and extreme positive affective disorder symptoms that are typical of the paranoid schizophrenic type (PS). Whereas the right side of the symptoms hierarchy contains negative psychotic symptoms and extreme negative affective disorder symptoms that are typical of the manic–depressive depressed type (MDD). Finally, notice that the paranoid schizophrenic type (PS) can be represented as the conjunctive combination of the manic–depressive manic type (MDM) and the simple schizophrenic type (SS), with the latter diagnostic category being characterized by negative psychotic symptoms.

4   Possible extensions

Several possible extensions of the descriptive discriminant hierarchical classes model may be considered.

In the present paper, D-HICLAS has been proposed as a model for two-way Boolean data. However, the current approach can be straightforwardly extended to rating–valued data. In particular, a D-HICLAS model for rating data would be considered as a particular constrained instance of the HICLAS-R model family (Van Mechelen, Lombardi and Ceulemans, 2002). In the rating–valued context the *characterization problem* then would boil down to finding a simplified rating–valued matrix that approximates the characterization matrix C.

Another further extension of the D-HICLAS model could be derived modifying the nature of the association relation (5). In fact, likewise the standard two-way HICLAS model for binary data (De Boeck and Rosenberg, 1988) a disjunctive variant of the conjunctive D-HICLAS model can be formulated by means of the following disjunctive association rule

$$m_{ij} = \sum_{k=1}^{K} p_{ik} \left(\bigoplus_{r=1}^{R} a_{kr} b_{jr} \right) \tag{10}$$

Finally, a possible D-HICLAS model relaxation would imply hierarchical representations in which objects in the same category do not necessarily share the same attribute pattern.

References

ANDREASEN, N.C. and OLSEN, S. (1982): Negative v positive shizophrenia: definition and validation. *Archives of General Psychiatry, 39, 789–794.*

BARBUT, M. and MONJARDET, B. (1970): *Ordre et classification: Algèbre et combinatoire* (2 Vols.) Hachette, Paris.

DE BOECK, P. and ROSENBERG, S. (1988): Hierarchical classes: Model and data analysis. *Psychometrika, 53, 361–381.*

KIM, K.H. (1982): *Boolean matrix theory.* Marcel Dekker, New York.

LEENEN, I. and VAN MECHELEN, I. (2001): An evaluation of two algorithms for hierarchical classes analysis. *Journal of Classification, 18, 57–80.*

MEZZICH, J.E. and SOLOMON, H. (1980): *Taxonomy and behavioral science: comparative performance of grouping methods.* Academic Press, London.

STUART, G.W., MALONE, V., CURRIE, J., KLIMIDIS, S. and MINAS, I.H. (1995): Positive and negative symptoms in neuroleptic–free psychotic inpatients. *Schizophrenia Research, 16, 175–188.*

VAN MECHELEN, I., DE BOECK, P. and ROSENBERG, S. (1995): The conjunctive model of hierarchical classes. *Psychometrika, 60, 505–521.*

VAN MECHELEN, I., LOMBARDI, L. and CEULEMANS, E. (2002): Hierarchical classes modeling of rating data. Submitted for publication.

Prediction Optimal Data Analysis by Means of Stochastic Search

Karsten Luebke and Claus Weihs

Lehrstuhl Computergestützte Statistik
Fachbreich Statistik
Universität Dortmund, Germany

Abstract. In this work a new procedure for the determination of multiple multivariate linear models with latent factors is proposed with the aim of prediction optimal projections on latent factors. In order to compare the new method with 'classical' methods like Ordinary Least Squares, Principal Components Regression, Partial Least Squares and Reduced-Rank Regression, a factorial experimental design is used in which important characteristics of the model are varied.

1 Introduction

In multivariate linear regression q response variables are related to k explanatory variables within a linear model. Sometimes, when the two groups of variables are correlated, there are numerical problems in estimating the regression coefficient matrix. Then the model is combined with a dimension reduction technique as for example Canonical Correlation Analysis. With assumptions about the structure of the error terms the estimator found by this method is optimal – for the given data (see Schmidli (1995) or Reinsel and Velu (1998)). The estimator that fits the data best need not to be the best estimator to predict from new explanatory variables the response variables, though.

The new algorithm for optimal prediction in a multiple multivariate linear model with latent factors is based on the computer intensive direct minimization of the mean squared error of prediction (MSEP) (see Hothorn and Weihs (2002)). The optimization is carried out by simulated annealing (see Bochachevsky et al. (1996) and Röhl et al. (2002)) within the space of possible projection matrices on latent factors. It is distribution free as it does not use any assumptions on the error structure.

Within an extensive simulation study the new method is compared to 'classical' methods. By doing an experimental design more general results can be found than by comparing just one or two specific examples. In the latter case it might happen that the new method performs very well in one example and rather poor in another one. With a proper experimental design it is possible to find potential factors that influence the performance of the method.

This paper is organized as follows: In section 2 we introduce the latent factor model. The prediction criterion is investigated in section 3. In section 4 the new latent factor prediction pursuit method is explained. The simulation study and the results thereof are shown in the sections 5 and 6. The paper is concluded in section 7.

2   Latent Factor model

The basic multiple linear model looks as follows:

$$Y = 1_n\mu + XM + E \tag{1}$$

with

- $Y \in \mathbb{R}^{n \times q}$ the data of the response variables
- $\mu \in \mathbb{R}^q$ the mean column vector of the responses
- $X \in \mathbb{R}^{n \times k}$ the data of the explanatory variables. For simplicity it is assumed that X is of full column rank and mean centered
- $M \in \mathbb{R}^{k \times q}$ the unknown regression coefficient matrix
- $E \in \mathbb{R}^{n \times q}$ the matrix of the errors.

In a latent factor model instead of the variables X in model (1) so-called latent variables Z under the side-condition $Z'Z = I_r$ $(r \leq k)$ with $Z = XG$ are used. The model with latent factors is:

$$Y = 1_n\mu + XM + E = 1_n\mu + (XG)B + E \tag{2}$$

$$\text{with the side condition } (XG)'(XG) = I$$

The space of possible projection matrices G that fulfill the side condition is needed both for the new method (see section 4) and for the design of experiment to test the new method (see section 5).

Lemma 3 (J. Groß). *Let* $X \in \mathbb{R}^{n \times k}$ *with full column rank. The general solution of* $(XG)'(XG) = I_r$ *is*

$$G = X^+A,$$

with $A \in \mathbb{R}^{n \times r}$ *where* $span(A) \subset span(X)$ *and* $A'A = I_r$.

The proof is omitted here but can be seen in Groß et al. (2002) where the Lemma is also extended to the case where X is not of full column rank.

Given an estimate of G and μ it is assumed that the estimate of B is the usual least square estimate.

$$\hat{B} = [(X\hat{G})'(X\hat{G})]^{-1}(X\hat{G})'(Y - 1_n\hat{\mu}) = (X\hat{G})'(Y - 1_n\hat{\mu})$$

Note that we made use of the side-condition $(X\hat{G})'(X\hat{G}) = I_r$. The ordinary least squares estimator for B is used by all reduced rank regression techniques investigated in the simulation study (compare section 6). Thus the methods differ only in the way they estimate G.

3 Prediction criteria

Suppose that the mean and the regression matrix are estimated on a training set but that it is interesting how this estimator will perform on future values X_0, Y_0. The point prediction of the future response value is:

$$\hat{Y}_0 = 1_{n_0}\hat{\mu}_Y + X_0\hat{M}_{X,Y}.$$

M is estimated on the training set x, Y. With a known test set X_0, Y_0 the loss in n_0 observations can be measured by

$$L = \frac{1}{n_0}\|(Y_0 - \hat{Y}_0)\Gamma^{-\frac{1}{2}}\|^2 \tag{3}$$

where Γ is a fixed $q \times q$ weight matrix. One possible choice is the diagonal matrix of the variances of the response variables (compare Schmidli (1995), page 22). This was used here.

Usually one is not only interested in the performance of the estimator for some observation but also in the 'general' or average performance. The corresponding mean loss (mean squared error of prediction) is defined as (see Schmidli (1995), page 24):

$$MSEP = \frac{1}{n_0}E_{Y|X}E_{Y_0|X_0}\|(Y_0 - \hat{Y}_0)\Gamma^{-\frac{1}{2}}\|^2$$

$$= \frac{1}{n_0}E_{Y|X}E_{Y_0|X_0}\|(Y_0 - (1_{n_0}\hat{\mu} + X_0\hat{M}_{Y,X}))\Gamma^{-\frac{1}{2}}\|^2$$

$$= \frac{1}{n_0}E_{Y|X}E_{Y_0|X_0}\|(Y_0 - (1_{n_0}\hat{\mu} + X_0(\hat{G}_{X,Y}\hat{G}'_{X,Y}X'(Y - 1_n\hat{\mu}))))\Gamma^{-\frac{1}{2}}\|^2 \tag{4}$$

Equation 4 shows that the $MSEP$ can be seen as a function of the projection matrix G.

As the $MSEP$ is a conditional expectation where the distribution is at least partially unknown it is necessary to do a kind of bootstrap estimation. When $\hat{G}$ is not a linear function of X, Y one needs to generate different Y, Y_0 for the same X, X_0 (see Lübke (2002), page 10).

4 Latent factor prediction pursuit

The new latent factor prediction pursuit method (LaFaPP) tries to minimize the $MSEP$ given in equation (4) within the possible solution space of the side-condition (see Lemma 3). The conditional expectations $E_{.|.}$ within (4) are estimated by a 50% bootstrap. This means that the given data is randomly split in X, Y and X_0, Y_0 respectively.

The computer intensive minimization is done by means of simulated annealing on the basis of a Nelder-Mead algorithm (see Press et al. (1992), page 451). The Nelder-Mead algorithm is an optimization method that does not need any gradients. In contrast to the pure downhill simplex method of the Nelder-Mead algorithm the simulated annealing method accepts with a probability proportional to a parameter T (called temperature) a trial point even if it is worse than the points in the simplex (a better point is always accepted). By this it is hoped that local minima can be overcome. By reducing the temperature slowly the algorithm will converge to the next minima.

In LaFaPP the simulated annealing is applied to the vectorized projection matrices G. The stochastic search by means of simulated annealing is done within the solution space of the side condition. In order to guarantee the side condition we optimized on orthonormal matrices F so that $A = U_X F$ where U_X are the left eigenvectors of X (compare Groß et.al. (2002)). This way, obviously $span(A) \subset span(X)$ and $A'A = F'U_X'U_X F = F'F = I$. Orthonormal F are generated by Gram-Schmidt post-orthonormalization.

So the LaFaPP method can be described as follows:

$i)$ Split the data in a Train- and Test set
$ii)$ Minimize the estimated $MSEP$ within the possible solution space of G by means of simulated annealing
$iii)$ Repeat step 2 for ranks $r = 1, \cdots, k$
$iv)$ Repeat step 1-3 sufficiently often (i.e. 200 times)
$v)$ Calculate for every rank the matrix $\hat{M}_r = \hat{G}_r \hat{B}_r$ as a weighted mean. The weight is determined by the prediction error of the run.
$vi)$ Find the rank with minimum $\widehat{MSEP}$

Note that we calculated the overall $\hat{M}_r$ and not the overall $\hat{G}_r$ as there are equivalent projection matrices G. This means that different projection matrices can lead to the same M (compare Weihs and Hothorn (2002)). As the optimization-routine is repeated 200 times it is computational time demanding. We implemented the algorithm in the statistical program R where on a Unix computer one optimization based on 200 replications took about 7 hours.

5   Design of experiment of the simulation study

In order to obtain most general results, important characteristics of the model are varied by using a $2^4 \times 3^1$ experimental design.

The numerical stability was tested by means of the degree of multicollinearity of the matrix X (see Belsley et al. (1980), page 86). As a measure of the degree of multicollinearity the condition number was used (compare Belsley et al. (1980), page 104p.). In order to generate various kinds of projection matrices G the eigenvectors of the matrix X were transformed. As a measure of the correlation between the latent factors Z and the original eigenvectors of X we used the angle between the vectorized latent factors and the eigenvectors. By the proper choice of B, different correlations between the target variables Y were tested. The influence of error variances was assessed by different variances of E varying the signal-to-noise ratio (compare Frank and Friedman (1993)). Also we used two different numbers of underlying latent factors.

The chosen values of characteristics of the model (2) are shown in Table 1. We used train- and test data sets consisting of 50 observations, and 10

Matrix	Characteristic	measurement	Realization
B	Correlation between Y_1, Y_2	angle	5,85
E	Error variance	Signal-to-noise	1,3
X	Multicollinearity	Condition number	10,100
G	Number of latent factors		2,4
G	Relation X and Z	(vec) angle	5,45,85

Table 1. Design of experiment of simulation study

explanatory variables X as well as two responses Y. Before they were transformed (to fulfill the needs of the experimental design) the matrix X and B consisted of the realizations of an i.i.d. standard normal distribution. The validation data set had 500 observations.

6   Results of the simulation study and an biometric example

The new LaFaPP method is compared to Ordinary Least Squares Regression (OLS) and to reduced rank regression methods like Canonical Correlation Analysis (CCA) and Redundancy Analysis (RDA). Also the more heuristically motivated procedures Principal Component Regression (PCR) and Partial Least Squares (PLS) are used. All these methods are described in Schmidli (1995).

The results of the simulation study are very promising. In Table 6 the estimated $MSEP$ is shown relative to the optimal (true regression coefficient) $MSEP$. The classical methods are clearly outperformed by the new LaFaPP

Method	OLS	PCR	PLS	CCA	RDA	LaFaPP
Relative $MSEP$	1.91	1.64	1.51	1.73	1.70	1.02

Table 2. Results of the simulation study on 200 Train- and Test data splits

method which is almost optimal.

In order to analyze the results of the experiment we made a regression of the relative $MSEP$ on the coded influencing factors. In Table 3 the at 10% level significant factors with the estimated coefficients are shown. As the regression is made on the coded factors the variances are equal for all factors so the values of the estimators can be compared directly.

Factor	OLS	PLS	PCR	CCA	RDA	LaFaPP
Intercept	1.91	1.52	1.64	1.73	1.70	1.02
Condition	$-4\ 10^{-4}$	-	-	-	-	-
Rank	-	-	-	$-4\ 10^{-3}$	$-4\ 10^{-3}$	-
Corr. eigenv.	$9\ 10^{-4}$	0.118	0.139	-	-	0.002
Corr. Y	$-3\ 10^{-4}$	-	-	0.174	0.202	0.009
S - N	-	0.092	0.101	-0.004	-	-0.002
R^2	0.37	0.71	0.73	0.99	0.99	0.86

Table 3. Significant influence on the relative $MSEP$

Looking at Table 3 it is surprising that the relative $MSEP$ of OLS is getting better with a higher condition number, though the coefficient is very small. Note, however, that the high condition (100) is not that high. In Frank and Friedman (1993) the prediction of OLS is not getting worse with a higher condition number. Also note that the R^2 is low, so it may be a random result.

PLS and PCR are getting worse when the correlation between the latent factors and the eigenvectors is reduced. This could have been expected, as especially PCR directly depends on the eigenvectors of X. The fact, that the relative $MSEP$ of these two methods is getting worse with a higher signal-to-noise ratio, is similar to a result found by Frank and Friedman (1993).

RDA and CCA perform better when there is a higher correlation in Y. Probably this can be explained by the fact that both calculate latent factors in Y as well and when the correlation is low the information in the latent factors is lower than in the case of high correlation.

The coefficients in the new LaFaPP-method are all rather small so that it seems that LaFaPP is stable under the situations tested in this simulation study.

In order to make a fair competition we also tested the relative loss (3) on the 500 observations of the validation set. The data of the validation set was unknown to all methods. Remember that LaFaPP used knowledge of the test set for making an optimal prediction. The results are shown in Table 6. Also with the validation set LaFaPP is significantly better than the classical

Method	OLS	PCR	PLS	CCA	RDA	LaFaPP
Relative Loss	1.21	1.19	1.14	1.16	1.17	1.01

Table 4. Results of the simulation study on Validation set

methods.

The superiority of LaFaPP was also found in a real life biometric example. In this example chemotaxonomical markers were investigated whether they could be used as biomarkers of bacteria (see Auling (1992) and Hirashi et al. (1998)). Since markers for the same group of bacteria should behave coherent a linear relationship was assumed. If the prediction would be good, the chemical effort may be reduced. Also, this would give evidence that the chemotaxonomical components could be used as biomarkers so that the groups of bacteria could be classified by these markers.

Altogether the chemotaxonomical markers consists of 11 different quinones and 6 different polyamines (369 obs). The data was collected at the 'Institut für Umweltmedizin und Krankenhaushygiene' of the Universtät Freiburg. The data comes from tests where the influence of hospital sewage was investigated on a laboratory scale sewage treatment plant. The experiments were supported by the Bundesministerium für Bildung und Forschung and the Umweltbundesamt.

Table 5 shows the estimated $MSEP$ for the prediction of the polyamines from the quinones. It can be seen that the prediction is poor (the best average

Method	$\widehat{MSEP}_{Test,Train}$	$\widehat{MSEP}_{Validation}$
OLS	4.508	4.72
PLS	4.479	4.746
PCR	4.504	4.71
CCA	4.501	4.743
RDA	4.508	4.72
LaFaPP	4.035	4.664

Table 5. Estimated error in prediction of the polyamines

R^2 achieved is 0.34) in all the methods, but the new $LaFaPP$ method is best. The relatively high error may be caused by the fact that the variances are very high. A conclusion can be that according to this data at least one of the chemotaxonomical groups is not a good biomarker for the bacteria.

7 Conclusion

Concerning predictive power, the new LaFaPP method turns out to outperform the classical reduced rank methods clearly – in all situations tested in the simulation study. It has several advantages like small $MSEP$ and the fact that it doesn't make any assumptions of the data. By now it has the disadvantage that it is very computation time demanding. It can be made much faster, though, by using a computer language like C. In a future work the not yet implemented case of not full column rank will be covered. Also possible influencing factors like the number of observations and variables in the explanatory and response data should be investigated.

References

AULING, G. (1992): Polyamines, biomarker for taxonomy and phytopathogénic and other bacteria belonging to the protobacteria. *Belgian Journal of Botany, 125, 203–209.*

BELSLEY, D.A., KUH, E. and WELSCH, R.E. (1980): *Regression diagnostics.* Wiley, New York.

BOCHACHEVSKY, I.O., JOHNSON, M.E. and STEIN, M.L. (1986): Generalized simulated annealing for function optimization. *Technometrics, 35, 109–135.*

GROSS, J., LUEBKE, K. and WEIHS, C. (2002): A note on the general solution for a projection matrix in latent factor models. *Technical Report 28, SFB 475, Universität Dortmund.*

HIRASHI, A., UEDA, Y. and ISHIHARA, J. (1998): Quinone profiling of bacterial communities in natural and synthetic sewage sludge for enhanced phosphate removal. *Applied and Environmental Microbiology, 64, 992–998.*

LÜBKE, K. (2002): Optimale Prognose am Beispiel der Differenzierungsgüte verschiedener chemotaxonomischer Marker in komplexen biologischen Matritzen. *Diplomarbeit, Universität Dortmund, Fachbereich Statistik.*

PRESS, W.H., FLANNERY, B.P., TEUKOLSKY, S.A. and VETTERLING, W.T. (1992): *Numerical Recepies in C.* Cambridge University Press, Cambridge.

REINSEL, G.C. and VELU, R.P. (1998): *Multivariate Reduced-Rank Regression, Theory and Applications.* Springer, New York.

RÖHL, M.C., WEIHS, C. and THEIS, W. (2002): Direct minimization of error rates in multivariate classification. *Computational Statistics, 17, 29–46.*

SCHMIDLI, H. (1995): *Reduced Rank Regression* Physica, Heidelberg.

WEIHS, C. and HOTHORN, T. (2002): Determination of optimal prediction oriented multivariate latent factor models using loss functions. *Technical Report 15, SFB 475, Universität Dortmund.*

Acknowledgment: This work has been supported by the Collaborative Research Center 'Reduction of Complexity in Multivariate Data Structures' (SFB 475) of the German Research Foundation (DFG).

System Error Variance Tuning in State-Space Models

Pietro Mantovan and Andrea Pastore

Dipartimento di Statistica
Università Ca' Foscari Venezia, I-30125 Venezia, Italy

Abstract. The multivariate dynamic regression model is a particular specification of the dynamic linear model. For this model, we propose a recursive equation for the estimation of the system error variance matrix. The solution can be used when more observation are available at each state of the system. In these cases, the algorithm allows to define a recursive procedure for the estimate of both the state vector (the regression coefficients) and the other *hyperparameters* of the model. The performances of the proposed method are evaluated by means of Monte Carlo experiments.

1 Introduction

The state-space representation of a dynamic regression model may be seen as a particular specification of dynamic models as well as of varying coefficient models (Hastie and Tibshirani (1993)). For these models, the definition of the system equation can be considered as a subjective element in model specification. In some operational contexts (for instance environmental monitoring applications) the state-space model has to provide *many-step-ahead* real-time predictions where the time series of interest are sampled with high-frequency. In these cases, the accuracy of the predictions may be influenced by the transition timing and by the specification of the system equation.

Even if in the applications the distribution of the system error is often assumed as known (for instance Marrs, 2001), some problems arise when a real-time (recursive) estimation method is required for both the state vector and the other unknown parameters, even if both the measurement and the system equations of the model are linear:

- In the Kalman filter the state vector has a transition each time that a new value of y_t is observed. In other words, the frequency of sampling is also the frequency of the transition of the state vector. But in many automatic monitoring systems, the frequency of measurement (or sampling) is defined by the characteristics of the measuring instruments or as a function of the measures cost and it can be considered *independent* from the frequency of transition of the state vector. In this case the *transition timing* becomes one of the main points (see Mantovan 2001)
- In many cases, with high frequency data, the researcher is interested in *many-step-ahead* prediction. For instance, for hourly data, 24-hours-ahead (one-day-ahead) predictions could be interesting. If possible, the learning rule on the state vector should also include the *many-step-ahead* prediction error. In the Kalman filter the posterior distribution of the state vector depends on the one-step-ahead prediction error.

In order to avoid these problems, it is possible to consider a more flexible definition of the system equation. Some instances are discussed by Mantovan (2001).

A simple but effective solution is to define the transition at a fixed lag, that is every n times, $n \geq 1$ (for instance, for hourly data, with $n = 12$ or $n = 24$) or after some fixed intervals choosen considering some of the characteristics of the variables (transition timing). This is equivalent to assume that, in the state-space model, more observations are available at each state of the system. For instance, in a model for prediction of the nitrogen dioxide hourly concentration the transition could be fixed in specific hours with respect to the vehicle traffic. The idea is quite simple, but it could improve the *many-step-ahead* prediction.

In the paper, we consider a multivariate dynamic linear regression model and propose a method for real-time system error variance matrix estimation. We follow the approach proposed by Mantovan et al. (1999). Given the linear state-space model, two auxiliary parallel state-space models are defined. With two mutually interactive filters, the first auxiliary model is used for the estimation of both the state vector and the measurement error variance matrix, while the second auxiliary model is used for the estimation of both the system matrix and the system error variance matrix. The proposed method is recursive and allows to obtain real-time estimation and prediction.

In section 2 we give short a description of the multivariate dynamic regression model and show how it can be written in state-space form. In section 3 we introduce a model with more observation at each state of the system and recall the *AMA* algorithm (Mantovan and Pastore (1999)). In section 4, the updating equations for the system matrix and for the system error variance matrix are described. Section 5 contains an overview of the estimation method for the state vector and all the other parameters. The results of some Monte Carlo experiments are then shown in section 6.

2   The multivariate dynamic regression model

Dynamic linear models give a relationship between a sequence of $c-$variate observable random vectors y_t $(t = 1, 2, \ldots)$ and a sequence of $k-$variate unobservable random vectors θ_t, usually referred as *state vector*, as defined by the following stochastic system:

$$y_t = H_t \theta_t + v_t \tag{1}$$
$$\theta_t = M_t \theta_{t-1} + u_t \tag{2}$$

where H_t is a known matrix, M_t is the system or transition matrix, $v_t \sim N(0, S_t)$ is the measurement error, $u_t \sim N(0, \Omega_t)$ is the system error. Here t is counter for the *states* of system. It is usually assumed that: v_t and u_t are mutually and serially uncorrelated; u_t is uncorrelated with θ_j, $j < t$; v_t is uncorrelated with θ_j, for all j and t, $t = 1, 2, \ldots$. Here, we will assume $S_t = S$ and $\Omega_t = \Omega$, for all t.

The dynamic regression model is defined by the following stochastic system:

$$y_t = B_t' x_t + v_t \tag{3}$$
$$\text{vec}(B_t) = M_t \, \text{vec}(B_{t-1}) + u_t \tag{4}$$

where B_t is a (h, c) matrix of regression coefficients and x_t is a h−dimensional vector of regressors. This model can be written in the form of equations (1) and (2) setting $H_t = I_c \otimes x_t'$ and $\theta_t = \text{vec}(B_t)$.

If S_t, Ω_t and M_t are known for all t, at the state t of the system, given $Y_t = (y_1, y_2, ..., y_t)$, the Kalman filter provides updating equations for the estimate $\hat{\theta}_t(t)$ of the state vector θ_t and the estimate $\hat{P}_t(t)$ of the associated variance matrix. If the random errors v_t and u_t are mutually and serially uncorrelated, the updating equations of the Kalman filter are deducible from the condition of research of the linear and unbiased minimum total variance estimator (Kalman, 1960; Kalman and Bucy, 1961). When the errors and the state vector at the time $t = 0$ are Gaussian, then the Kalman filter is deducible from Bayes's theorem (Jazwinski, 1970; Harrison and Stevens, 1976; Gelb, 1974). In this case, it is easy to define the predictive distributions of the state vector θ_{t+s} and of the observable vector y_{t+s} given Y_t, $s = 1, 2, \dots$.

3   A dynamic regression model with replications at each state of the system

We introduce an extension of the dynamic regression model defined above. Let us assume that, at each state t of the system, n_t independent (conditionally on the state vector) observations are available for both the vectors y_t and x_t. We denote with $y_{t,i}$ and $x_{t,i}$ these observations, $i = 1, \dots, n_t$. Moreover, let $H_{t,i} = I_c \otimes x_{t,i}'$. A dynamic regression model with replications at each state of the system can be defined as follows:

$$y_{t,i} = H_{t,i}\theta_t + v_{t,i}, \quad i = 1, \dots, n_t \tag{5}$$
$$\theta_t = M_t\theta_{t-1} + u_t \tag{6}$$

where $v_{t,i} \sim N(0, \Sigma_t)$ are uncorrelated observation errors and $u_t \sim N(0, \Omega_t)$ is the system error. We will assume $\Sigma_t = \Sigma$ and $\Omega_t = \Omega$, for all t.

This model can be written in the form of equations (1) and (2) as follows. Let $_j h_{t,i}$ be the c−dimensional column vector defined by the j−th row of the matrix $H_{t,i}$. Then, define the (c, n_t) matrix:

$$_j\Phi_t = (_j h_{t,1}, \; _j h_{t,2}, \dots, \; _j h_{t,n_t}) \tag{7}$$

whose columns are the j−th rows of the matrices $H_{t,i}, i = 1, \dots, n_t$. Setting: $Y_t = (y_{t,1}, y_{t,2}, \dots, y_{t,n_t})$, $H_t = (_1\Phi_t, \; _2\Phi_t, \dots, \; _c\Phi_t)'$, $V_t = (v_{t,1}, v_{t,2}, \dots, v_{t,n_t})$, $y_t = \text{vec}(Y_t')$, $v_t = \text{vec}(V_t')$, equation (1) follows from equation (5), with $S_t = \Sigma \otimes I_{n_t}$. Note that S_t depends on t only via n_t.

For the model defined by equation (5) and (6), conditionally on M_t, Σ and Ω, the Kalman filter estimate $\hat{\theta}_t(t)$ can be obtained. But for the same model, an Approsimated MArginal recursive updating equation system, *(AMA)*, (Mantovan and Pastore, 1999) was propopsed in order to estimate the state vector θ_t and the measurement error variance matrix Σ_t, conditionally only on M_t and Ω. The AMA algorith has been obtained by considering a generalization of a result proposed by Press (1992). We will denote with $\hat{\theta}_t^A(t)$ and $\hat{\Sigma}^A(t)$ the AMA-estimates respectively of θ_t and Σ at the t-th state of the system.

4   Updating equations for the system matrix and for the system error variance matrix

To set up the algorithm for the estimation of the system matrix and the system error variance matrix, we consider an *auxiliary* model obtained from the multivatiate dynamic regression model defined accordingly to equations (5)-(6). The idea ia s generalization of the algorithm proposed by Mantovan et al. (1999). Substituing θ_t as defined in equation (6) in equation (5) we can define the following stochastic system:

$$y_t = G_{t,i}\phi_t + e_{t,i}, \quad i = 1,\ldots,n_t \tag{8}$$

$$\phi_t = \phi_{t-1} + \epsilon_t \tag{9}$$

where: $G_{t,i} = G_{t,i}(\theta_{t-1}) = H_{t,i}\left(I_k \otimes \theta_{t-1}'\right)$, $\phi_t = \text{vec}\left(M_t'\right)$,

$$e_{t,i} = H_{t,i} \cdot u_t + v_{t,i} \tag{10}$$

and ϵ_t is a k^2-variate random vector such that $Pr(\epsilon_t = 0) = 1$, for all t.

Equations (8) and (9) define a new dynamic linear model where ϕ_t can be treated as the state vector, conditionally on the state vector θ_{t-1} and the measurement error variance matrix Σ.

¿From this model, two updating equation systems can be defined, conditionally on the estimates $\hat{\theta}_{t-1}^A(t-1)$ and $\hat{\Sigma}^A(t-1)$ obtained with the AMA algoritm from the model (5)-(6):

- for Ω, conditionally on M_{t-1} (or on $\phi_{t-1} = vec(M_{t-1}')$)
- for both Ω and M_t.

4.1   Estimation of the system error variance, conditionally on the system matrix

The estimate $\hat{\Omega}(t)$ of Ω at the t-th state of the system is obtained via a recursive equation and it require the estimate $\hat{\Omega}(t-1)$ at the previous state.

The substitution of θ_{t-1} with its estimate $\hat{\theta}_{t-1}^A(t-1)$ in the expression which defines $G_{t,i}$ gives an *estimate* $\hat{G}_{t,i}$ of $G_{t,i}$:

$$\hat{G}_{t,i} = \hat{G}_{t,i}(\hat{\theta}_{t-1}) = H_{t,i}\left(I_k \otimes \hat{\theta}_{t-1}'^A(t-1)\right).$$

for $i = 1, \ldots, n_t$. Then, an *estimate* $\hat{e}_{t,i}$ of the error $e_{t,i}$ can be obtained by substituing in equation (8) $G_{t,i}$ with its *estimate* $\hat{G}_{t,i}$, and ϕ_{t-1} with its estimate $\hat{\phi}_{t-1}(t-1)$.

$$\hat{e}_{t,i} = y_{t,i} - \hat{G}_{t,i}\hat{\phi}_{t-1}(t-1) \tag{11}$$

Let us consider again equation (10) and substitute herein $e_{t,i}$ with its *estimate* $\hat{e}_{t,i}$. Then, the quantity:

$$\hat{u}_t = \left(\sum_{i=1}^{r} H'_{t,i} \, H_{t,i} \right)^{-1} \left(\sum_{i=1}^{r} H'_{t,i} \, \hat{e}_{t,i} \right) \tag{12}$$

can be interpreted as a ordinary least squares estimate of the error u_t.
 The estimate $\hat{\Omega}(t)$ is obtained by the following recursive equation:

$$\hat{\Omega}(t) = \frac{t-1}{t} \cdot \hat{\Omega}(t-1) + \frac{1}{t} \cdot \hat{u}_t \hat{u}'_t. \tag{13}$$

It is worth noting that, if the system matrix is known, then equation (11) will be defined with the true known value of ϕ_{t-1}.

4.2   Estimation of the system matrix

From equation (10), the following relation holds:

$$\Xi_{t,i} = \mathrm{VAR}\,(e_{t,i}) = H_{t,i}\Omega H'_{t,i} + \Sigma \tag{14}$$

for $i = 1, \ldots, n_t$. An estimate $\hat{\Xi}_{t,i}(t)$ of $\Xi_{t,i}$ can be obtained by substituing Ω with its estimate $\hat{\Omega}(t)$ and Σ with its estimate $\hat{\Sigma}^A(t-1)$, for $i = 1, \ldots, n_t$.
 Then, conditionally on $\hat{\Xi}_{t,i}(t)$ for $i = 1, \ldots, n_t$, $\hat{\theta}_{t-1}^A(t-1)$ and $\hat{\Omega}(t)$, an estimate $\hat{\phi}_t(t)$ of ϕ_t can be obtained with the Kalman filter applied to the model (8)-(9).

5   An overview of the estimation method for the state vector and all the hyperparameters

The proposed estimation method for the system error variance matrix, allows to define an algorithm for the recursive estimation, from the model (5)-(6), of both the state vector θ_t and all the other *iperparametri* Σ, Ω, and M_t. The algorithm requires the estimate at the $(t-1)$−th state of the system:

- $\hat{\Sigma}^A(t-1)$,
- $\hat{\Omega}(t-1)$,
- $\hat{\phi}(t-1) = \mathrm{vec}\left(\hat{M}'(t-1) \right)$
- $\hat{\theta}_{t-1}^A(t-1)$,

and is made up of the following steps:

step 1 the estimate $\hat{\Omega}(t)$ is obtained using equations (12) and (13), conditionally on: $\hat{\Omega}(t-1)$, $\hat{\Sigma}^A(t-1)$, $\hat{\phi}(t-1)$, $\hat{\theta}^A_{t-1}(t-1)$,

step 2 the estimate $\hat{\phi}(t)$ is obtained with the Kalman filter considering the model (8)-(9), conditionally on $\hat{\Sigma}^A(t-1)$, $\hat{\phi}(t-1)$, $\hat{\theta}^A_{t-1}(t-1)$, $\hat{\Omega}(t)$,

step 3 the estimates $\hat{\theta}^A_t(t)$ and $\hat{\Sigma}^A(t)$ are obtaines with the AMA algorithm considering the model (5)-(6), conditionally on $\hat{\Sigma}^A(t-1)$, $\hat{\theta}^A_{t-1}(t-1)$, $\hat{\Omega}(t)$ and $\hat{\phi}(t)$.

6 Monte Carlo experiments

The method summarized in section 5 has been applied to simulated data from a multivariate regression model as described by equations (3) and (4), with $c = 2$ and $h = 3$. Each regressor was simulated following a first order autoregressive process AR(1) process $x_{j,t} = \alpha \cdot x_{j,t-1} + \eta_t$, with $\alpha = 0.7$ and $\eta_t \sim WN(0, 0.1^2)$. The regression coefficient matrix B_t at time $t = 1$ was set as follows:

$$B_1 = \begin{bmatrix} 1 & 1 & 0 \\ 0 & 1 & 1 \end{bmatrix}.$$

The measurement error matrix was fixed at: $\Sigma = 0.01 \cdot I$. Different values were considered for the system error matrix: $\Omega = \omega \cdot I$, $\omega = 0.1, 0.5, 1, 2$. The system matrix was fixed at $M_t = I$, for all t, and considered both as known and as unknown. The number T of states of the system was set to 100, with a number of replication $n_t = 6, 12, 24$ for each state.

For each experiment, 1000 replication were simulated. The performances of the algorithm have been measured by means of the euclidean norm of $\text{vec}(\hat{\Omega}(T)) - \text{vec}(\Omega)$, denoted with δ_Ω, and, when the system matrix has been assumed as unknown, of the euclidean norm of $\text{vec}(\hat{M}_T(T)) - \text{vec}(M_T)$, denoted with δ_M. Since Ω and M_t are both matrix of the same order $c \cdot h = 6$, δ_Ω and δ_M are comparable measures.

Moreover, the predictive performances have been also evaluated as follows. The mean (among each component of y_t) of the squared correlation coefficients between the one–step–ahead prediction $\hat{y}_{t+1}(t)$ and the observed values y_{t+1} has been compared, by a ratio denoted with ρ, with the mean (among each component of y_t) of the R-squared coefficients obtained via ordinary least squares regression.

The results are presented as follows. Table 1 contains the values of δ_Ω, for different values of n_t and ω, obtained in experiments where the system matrix was assumed as known. Similarly, values of δ_Ω and δ_M obtained in experiments where the system matrix was assumed as unknown are shown in Table 2. Table 3 contains the values of ρ for the two set of experiments (system matrix known and unknown).

ω	$n_t = 6$	$n_t = 12$	$n_t = 24$
0.1	0.1851	0.1194	0.0598
0.5	0.2052	0.1442	0.0748
1	0.2382	0.1790	0.0890
2	0.3232	0.2827	0.1056

Table 1. Results of the Monte Carlo experiments: values of δ_Ω, system matrix assumed as unknown.

ω	$n_t = 6$		$n_t = 12$		$n_t = 24$	
	δ_Ω	δ_M	δ_Ω	δ_M	δ_Ω	δ_M
0.1	0.2225	0.1189	0.1606	0.1842	0.1019	0.2076
0.5	0.2498	0.1477	0.1916	0.2101	0.1316	0.2388
1	0.2877	0.1893	0.2211	0.2485	0.1522	0.2775
2	0.4294	0.2454	0.3689	0.2933	0.1918	0.3346

Table 2. Results of the Monte Carlo experiments: values of δ_Ω and δ_M.

ω	$n_t = 6$		$n_t = 12$		$n_t = 24$	
	M known	M unknown	M known	M unknown	M known	M unknown
0.1	1.1812	1.1403	1.1786	1.1246	1.1798	1.0615
0.5	1.2307	1.1892	1.2212	1.1587	1.2366	1.0856
1	1.2446	1.1915	1.2553	1.1723	1.2427	1.1244
2	1.2732	1.2111	1.2685	1.1823	1.2698	1.1678

Table 3. Results of the Monte Carlo experiments: values of ρ.

It is worth to note from table 3 that the proposed algorithm has a predictive performance always better than the linear regression model, used as a benchmark. As expected, the algorithm behaves better when the system matrix is assumed as known and the effect of n_t is not considerable. Instead, high values of n_t has effect on the estimate of the system matrix.

References

ANDERSON B.D., MOORE J.B. (1979): *Optimal Filtering*, Prentice-Hall, Englewood Cliffs.

HASTIE T., TIBSHIRANI R. (1993): Varying coefficient model. *Journal of the Royal Statistical Society, B, 55(4), 757–796.*

GELB A. (1974): *Applied Optimal Estimation.* The M.I.T. Press, Cambridge.

JAZWINSKI A.H. (1970): *Stochastic processes and filtering theory.* Academic Press, New York.

KALMAN R.E., (1960): A new approach to linear filtering and prediction problems. *Journal of Basic Engineering, 82D, 33–45.*

MANTOVAN, P. (2001): State Space Modelling for Bayesian Learning and Forecasting of on Line Environmental Data. In: C. Provasi (Ed.): *Modelli Complessi e Metodi Computazionali Intensivi per la Stima e la Previsione*, Cleup, Padova, 17–26.

MANTOVAN P., PASTORE A. (1999): Marginal Updating Equations for Measurement Error Variance Matrix and State Vector Estimates in the Dynamic Linear Model. In: H. Bacelar-Nicolau et al. (Eds.), *VIII International Symposium on Applied Stochastic Models and Data Analysis*, Instituto Nacional del Estatistica, Portugal Lisboa, 212–217.

MANTOVAN, P., PASTORE, A. and TONELLATO, S. (1999): Recursive estimation of system parameter in environmental time series models. In: M. Vichi and O. Opitz (Eds.): *Classification and Data Analysis*. Springer, Heidelberg, 311–318.

MANTOVAN, P., PASTORE, A. and TONELLATO, S. (2000): A comparison between parallel algorithms for system parameter identification in dynamic linear models. *Applied Stochastic Models in Business and Industry, 15, 369 – 378*.

MARSS, A.D. (2001): In-Situ Ellipsometry Solutions using Sequential Monte Carlo. In: A Doucet et al. (Eds.): *Sequential Monte Carlo Methods in Practice*, Springer - New York, 465–477.

PRESS S.J. (1982): *Applied Multivariate Analysis*. Krieger, Malabar, Florida.

Corrado Gini and Multivariate Statistical Analysis: The (so far) Missing Link

Paola Monari and Angela Montanari

Dipartimento di Scienze statistiche
Università di Bologna, I-40126 Bologna, Italy

Abstract. In this paper we present a review of Corrado Gini's contributions to statistical methodology which have been or may be profitably employed in multivariate analysis, with a special attention to classification and regression trees, multiple regression, discriminant analysis and robust location estimators.

1 Introduction

Corrado Gini (1884-1964) is the founder of the Italian statistical school. During his long scientific career he wrote 87 books and more than 800 papers and brought a lot of new ideas into many aspects of statistical theory and practice, but he almost never explicitly addressed multivariate issues. It was a precise choice of interest.

Recently, however, larger and larger data sets, also as far as the number of observed variables is concerned, have become available thus requiring the development of new techniques also capable to face the so called curse of dimensionality. The result has been the flourishing of methods whose common feature is the reinterpretation of the solution of multivariate problems as the solution of a sequence of suitably posed univariate ones. In this new setting Gini's contribution emerges as original and fundamental.

2 Classification and regression trees

Perhaps the Gini's idea which is best known to statisticians working in multivariate statistical analysis is what is generally called Gini index, largely employed in the context of classification tree methodology (Brieman *et al.*, 1984).

A binary tree structured classifier requires a partition of the covariate space X which is reached by repeated splits of subsets of it into two descendant subsets (nodes) beginning with X itself. A first interesting feature of the method is that the splits are formed by conditions on the coordinates of x, thus translating a multivariate problem into a sequence of suitably posed univariate ones. A second aspect worth underlining here, as it directly leads to Gini index, is that each split is to be selected so that the data in each of the descendant subsets are "purer" than the data in the parent subset.

This requires to define an impurity function which, according to Brieman *et al.*, is a function ϕ defined on the set of all J-tuples of numbers $(p_1, ..., p_J)$

(in a J class problem) satisfying $p_j \geq 0$, $j = 1, .., J$, $\sum_j p_j = 1$ with the properties:

i. ϕ is maximum only at the point $\left(\frac{1}{J}, \frac{1}{J}, ..., \frac{1}{J}\right)$;
ii. ϕ achieves its minimum only at $(1, 0, ..., 0); (0, 1, ..., 0); ...(0, 0, ..., 1)$;
iii. ϕ is a symmetric function of $(p_1, ..., p_J)$.

Given an impurity function ϕ, the impurity measure of any node t, may be defined as $i(t) = \phi\left(p(1|t), ..., p(j|t), ..., p(J|t)\right)$ where $p(j|t)$, $j = 1, ..., J$, denotes the proportion of cases in node t belonging to class j.

One possible choice for $i(t)$ is indeed represented by the Gini index, which is defined as:

$$i(t) = \sum_{j \neq i} p(j|t) p(i|t) = \left(\sum_j p(j|t)\right)^2 - \sum_j p^2(j|t) = 1 - \sum_j p^2(j|t) \quad (1)$$

It can be easily proved to satisfy properties (i)-(iii) and to be a concave function of class probabilities, thus guaranteeing that, for any split s, impurity is never increasing. This index has many interesting interpretations. If one assigns an object selected at random from a node t to class i with probability $p(i|t)$, given that the estimated probability the item is actually in class j is $p(j|t)$, the estimated probability of misclassification associated to this assignment rule is the Gini index (1).

A further interpretation in terms of variances is possible: in a node t, assign all class j objects the value 1, and all other objects the value 0. Than the sample variance of these values is $p(j|t)\left[1 - p(j|t)\right]$. If this is repeated for all the J classes and the variances summed, the result is again Gini index.

Besides these two interpretations a third one is possible, which is indeed the one Gini gave in his almost never quoted paper "Variabilità e Mutabilità" (1912), where he first introduced his index. It is deeply rooted in Gini's theory of variability and so a short digression is here necessary in order to view it in the proper light.

In Gini's view, the goal of a variability measure differs according to the nature of the characters which are being studied. If the character keeps its intensity, but appears with different values only because of random or systematic measurement errors, the goal of a variability measure is that of determining how much the observed quantities differ from the true one. While if the character really takes different values for different statistical units the goal of a variability measure is that of determining how much the observed quantities differ from each other.

To solve the latter problem Gini proposed a measure, known as Gini's mean difference, which, given n observed values of a variable X, is defined as the average of all the possible differences between those values (also including the comparison of a unit with itself):

$$\Delta = \sum_{i=1}^{n} \sum_{j=1}^{n} |x_i - x_j| / n^2 \qquad (2)$$

It can be easily computed by the following equivalent expression:

$$\Delta = 2 \sum_{i=1}^{n} (2i - n - 1) x_{(i)} / n^2 \qquad (3)$$

where $x_{(i)}$ denotes the i-th observation in the ascending ranking of the observations. In the same paper Gini also proposed an extension of this measure to qualitative variables. Such are also the identifiers of the J classes in a J class classification problem. Denoted by $n_1, n_2, ..., n_J$ the frequencies of each of the J distinct attributes of a given nominal character, such that $\sum_{j=1}^{J} n_j = n$, and setting equal to 1 the diversity between any two different attributes, the sum of the differences of a case which shows the j-th attribute from all the other cases will be $n_j \cdot 0 + (n - n_j) \cdot 1$, and the sum of all the possible n^2 differences $\sum_{j=1}^{J} n_j(n - n_j)$. Gini's mean difference will then be

$$\Delta = \sum_{j=1}^{J} n_j(n - n_j) / n^2$$

or equivalently, after putting $p_j = n_j / n$: $\Delta = \sum_{j=1}^{J} p_j(1 - p_j)$ where one can easily recognise a different form of equation (1).

Gini's mean difference can also be used as a splitting criterion in the regression tree context, as an alternative to ordinary least squares or least absolute deviation fitting methods.

Ordinary least squares (OLS) regression trees produce a partition of the covariate space such that, within each element of the partition, the regression function may be approximated by the mean value of the response variable Y corresponding to those units whose covariate values belong to that partition member. This is obtained by choosing the total within node sum of squares as the split function:

$$\frac{1}{n} \sum_{t \in \tilde{T}} \sum_{x_j \int} (y_j - \bar{y}(t))^2$$

(where $\tilde{T}$ is the set of terminal nodes, y_j is the response value measured on the j-th statistical unit belonging to node t and $\bar{y}(t)$ is the node average response value) and by iteratively splitting nodes so as to maximise its decrease.

An alternative solution is to choose

$$\frac{1}{n} \sum_{t \in \tilde{T}} \sum_{x_j \int} |y_j - M(t)|$$

(where $M(t)$ is the sample median of the y values in the node). This leads to least absolute deviations (LAD) trees and amounts to approximate the regression surface, within each element of the partition, by the median of the response values in the node and to choose those splits which iteratively allow to minimise the sum of the absolute deviations from the node medians.

A further possibility is to choose a split function derived from Gini's mean difference:

$$\frac{1}{n^2} \sum_{t \in \tilde{T}} \sum_{x_j \in t;\; x_i \int} |y_j - y_i|$$

As Gini's mean difference for a variable Y may be rewritten as

$$\Delta = \frac{\sum_{i=1}^{n} d_{i,M} |y_i - M|}{\sum_{i=1}^{n} d_{i,M}}$$

(where M is the median of the n units and $d_{i,M}$ is the rank of the difference $|y_i - M|$ in the ascending sequence of absolute differences) that is as a weighted average of the absolute distances from the median, with weights equal to $d_{i,M}$, using it as a split function amounts to approximate once again the regression surface by the median of the response values in a given node and to chose those splits which iteratively allow to minimise the sum of the weighted absolute deviations from the node medians. In other words, the median is still the function approximator, as in LAD trees, but is computed on possibly different sets of units. The use of the split function based on Gini's mean difference may then lead to regression trees whose properties are intermediate between those of OLS and LAD trees, but much work has still to be done.

3   Linear regression and linear discriminant analysis

Gini's mean difference can be defined in a variety of ways, each of which provides some insight into it. Stuart (1954) has derived the expression:

$$\Delta = 4\text{cov}(X, F(X)) = \Delta_{xx} = E_{X_1} E_{X_2} |X_1 - X_2|$$

where $F(X)$ denotes the cumulative distribution function of the random variable X, that is Δ is interpreted as a function of the covariance between a variate and its rank and its empirical estimate $\tilde{\Delta}_{xx}$ is obtained by (2) or (3).

This expression suggests a possible way of defining the analogous of the classical covariance, based on the concept of mean difference. What may be called Gini co-difference (Schechtman and Yitzhaki, 1987) is then defined as

$$4\text{cov}(Y, F(X)) = \Delta_{xy} = E_{X_1,Y_1} E_{X_2,Y_2} \{[\text{sgn}(X_1 - X_2)] (Y_1 - Y_2)\}$$

or as

$$4\text{cov}(X, F(Y)) = \Delta_{yx} = E_{X_1,Y_1} E_{X_2,Y_2} \{[\text{sgn}(Y_1 - Y_2)] (X_1 - X_2)\}$$

according to which variable is ranked. (X_1, Y_1) and (X_2, Y_2) are mutually independent pairs of random variables with the same joint density function and

$$\text{sgn}(y) = \begin{cases} -1 \text{ for } x < 0 \\ 0 \text{ for } x = 0 \\ 1 \text{ for } x > 0 \end{cases}$$

Δ_{XY} can be empirically estimated as

$$\tilde{\Delta}_{XY} = \sum_i \sum_j \left\{ [\text{sgn}(x_i - x_j)] (y_i - y_j) \right\} / n^2$$

whose computational version is $\tilde{\Delta}_{XY} = 2 \sum_{i=1}^{n} (2i - n - 1) y_{r(x_i)} / n^2$ where $y_{r(x_i)}$ is the observation on Y that corresponds to the i-th lowest value of X. These concepts have been widely employed in order to develop what has been called Gini multiple linear regression, which has been approached from various perspectives.

Olkin and Yitzhaki (1992) for instance suggest to estimate the parameters of the linear multiple model $Y = \alpha + \beta_1 X_1 + \beta_2 X_2 + ... + \beta_p X_p + \epsilon$, where $E(\epsilon) = 0$, by minimizing $\tilde{\Delta}_{ee} = \text{cov}(e, R(e)) = \sum_i e_i R(e_i)$ where e represents the sample residual and $R(e)$ is the rank of the estimated error term which is an estimate of its distribution function.

The method doesn't allow to estimate α, which is therefore estimated as $a = \bar{y} - \tilde{\beta}' \bar{x}$ where $\tilde{\beta}$ is the vector estimator of β, thus causing the regression line to pass through the origin.

Minimization of Gini's mean difference of the sample error term yields the first order conditions

$$\text{cov}(X_k, R(e)) = 0 \quad k = 1, ..., p \tag{4}$$

Since the error e is a function of all the regression weights the solution of (4) yields the partial effect of X_k on Y, which is similar to that obtained from OLS.

Podder (2002) suggests a more general framework within which a different version of Gini regression can be derived. His proposal is to obtain an estimator for the vector parameter β by optimising a weighted sum of the residuals, which is a translation invariant measure of dispersion:

$$\sum_{i=1}^{n} w_i e_i \quad \text{under the constraint that } \sum_{i=1}^{n} w_i = 0. \tag{5}$$

The weights which appear in the computational expression of Gini's mean difference $w_i = 2(2i - n - 1)/n^2$ satisfy this constraint. With such weights one can easily verify that α cannot be directly estimated and Potter too suggests to estimate it as $a = \bar{y} - \tilde{\beta}' \bar{x}$. The open problem is then to identify the best variable to be ranked, that is the suitable variable to which the rank i in

Gini's weight refers. Podder proposes to weight each residual by a function of the rank of the corresponding X_k value. As minimising (5) amounts to make it vanish, by equating $\sum_{i=1}^{n} w_i e_i = \sum_{i=1}^{n} w_i(y_i - \beta_1 x_{i1} - \beta_2 x_{i2} - ... - \beta_p x_{ip})$ to 0 with respect to each of the regressors (i.e. by choosing the weights according to the rank of each of the regressors) one obtains a set of p normal equations which suggest that the residuals of the linear regression model satisfy the condition $\mathrm{cov}(R(X_k), e) = 0$ $\forall k$.

Denoting the estimated covariance between the rank of the k-th regressor and the j-th regressor as $\tilde{\Delta}_{kj}$ and the stimated covariance betwen the rank of the k-th regressor and the dependent variable as $\tilde{\Delta}_{ky}$, the k-th normal equation is

$$\tilde{\beta}_1 \tilde{\Delta}_{k1} + \tilde{\beta}_2 \tilde{\Delta}_{k2} + ... + \tilde{\beta}_p \tilde{\Delta}_{kp} = \tilde{\Delta}_{ky} \quad (k = 1, ..., p)$$

The matrix form of the set of normal equations is then $\mathbf{D}_{xx}\tilde{\beta} = \mathbf{D}_{xy}$ (where $\mathbf{D}_{xx}$ is Gini's difference-codifference matrix of the regressors and $\mathbf{D}_{xy}$ is the codifference vector between each regressor and the response variable) and its solution is $\tilde{\beta} = \mathbf{D}_{xx}^{-1}\mathbf{D}_{xy}$ whose structure closely resembles the one obtained by OLS. A more thorough study of the performances of this estimator is however still necessary.

Liner combinations of the observed variables have found a wide use also in the context of discriminant analysis. The first idea goes back to Fisher who suggested to search directly the linear combination of the p measured characteristics which maximizes group separation, defined as the ratio of "between" to "within" group variance under the condition of homoscedasticity. Apparently, it does not require any distributional assumption, but normality or at least symmetry is actually implicitly assumed. Furthermore it is well known that Fisher's function is not robust against outlying observations.

In order to maintain the ease of interpretation of Fisher's function, while avoiding the normality and heteroscedasticity assumption, Posse (1992) proposed a projection pursuit version of linear discriminant analysis based on the search of the linear combination showing the minimum total probability of misclassification.

A promising solution may also be obtained by looking for the linear combination which optimizes group separation in terms of Gini's transvariaton (Montanari, Calò 1998). According to Gini (1916), two groups are said to transvariate on a variable X, with respect to their corresponding mean values m_{x1} and m_{x2} if the sign of some of $n_1 n_2$ differences $x_{i1} - x_{j2}$ ($i = 1, 2, ..., n_1$; $j = 1, 2, ..., n_2$) which can be defined between the x values belonging to the two groups is opposite to that of $m_{x1} - m_{x2}$. Any difference satisfying this condition is called "a transvariation" and $|x_{i1} - x_{i2}|$ is its intensity. In order to measure the transvariation between two groups Gini proposed transvariation probability and transvariation area. The former is defined as the ratio of the number of transvariations (assuming the median as mean value) to its maximum. It takes value in the interval 0,1 and the more the two groups overlap, the greater values it takes.

Denoted by $f_k(x)$ $k = 1, 2$ the group probability density functions, the transvariation area is $\int_{-\infty}^{+\infty} \Psi(x)dx$ where $\Psi(x) = \min(f_1(x), f_2(x))$. When the transvariation probability is zero, the two groups do not overlap and therefore the transvariation area is also zero, but the inverse is not always true. This means that the two measures usually highlight different aspects of group transvariation.

The above description may have shown that transvariation measures can be profitably used to discriminate between two groups. A linear discriminant function can then be derived as the linear combination which minimizes transvariation probability or area. For normal data the solutions coincide and also coincide with Fisher linear discriminant function.

A closer look at the formal expression of transvariation area shows that it is but twice the total probability of misclassification, therefore minimizing transvariation area leads to the solution obtained by Posse. Based on the study of the statistical properties of transvariation measures and on simulations Montanari and Calò (1998) show that the linear disciminant function obtained by optimising transvariation probability generally gives the best results as it is robust against violations of normality and homoscedasticity assumptions and against the presence of outliers.

4 Multivariate transvariation and multivariate median

The only true Gini's contribution to multivariate analysis is confined to multivariate transvariation (Gini and Livada, 1959) and to the concept of spatial median (Gini and Galvani, 1929).

The extension of his notion of transvariation between two groups to the multivariate context requires that at least one pair of units simultaneously transvariates on each variable. Transvariation may still be measured by transvariation probability, again defined as the ratio of the number of transvariating pairs (with respect to the marginal medians) to its maximum. As opposite to the univariate case, however, transvariation probability can no longer be interpreted as a measure of group separability as it may be greater than 0 even if the groups are completely separate in the multidimensional space. On the contrary transvariation area, which for the multivariable case Gini named "transvariation space", $\int_{-\infty}^{+\infty} \Psi(x_1, x_2, ..., x_p)dx_1, dx_2, ..., dx_p$ where

$$\Psi(x_1, x_2, ..., x_p) = \min(f_1(x_1, x_2, ..., x_p), f_2(x_1, x_2, ..., x_p)),$$

with f_1 and f_2 the multivariate group densities, still maintains its meaning and its equivalence to the total probability of misclassification in the equal prior case.

Calò and Montanari (2000) have introduced a modified version of Gini's multidimensional transvariation probability which can be interpreted as a true measure of group separation in the multivariate space and have proposed a stepwise variable selection method in discriminant analysis.

Gini's spatial median is quite well known in the statistical literature on robust location measures even if he dedicated to it very little space. Given n points lying in $\mathbb{R}^p$, $x_1, x_2, ..., x_n$ the spatial median is the p-vector M which minimizes the Euclidean distance of the points from it $\sum_{i=1}^{n} \|x_i - M\|$. When $p = 1$ the definition yields the standard univariate median. Small (1990) presents a thorough survey of multidimensional medians, also highlighting the properties of Gini's spatial one and relating it to other possible definitions of medians in the multivariate space.

References

BRIEMAN, L. FRIEDMAN, J.H., OLSHEN, R.A., STONE, C.J. (1984): *Classification and regression trees*. Wadsworth International Group, Belmont, California.

CALÒ, D.G. and MONTANARI, A. (2000): On a Transvariation Based Measure of Group Separability. *Book of Short Papers COMPSTAT 2000, Utrecht University and Statistics Netherdanlds, 71-72*.

GINI, C. (1912): Variabilità e mutabilità. *Studi economico-giuridici pubblicati per cura della Facoltà di Giurisprudenza della Regia Università di Cagliari, Anno III, parte 2, also reproduced in C.Gini (1939) op. cit..*

GINI, C. (1916): Il concetto di transvariazione e le sue prime applicazioni. *Giornale degli economisti and Rivista di statistica.*

GINI, C. (1959): *Transvariazione*. Libreria Goliardica, Roma.

GINI, C. and GALVANI, L. (1929): Di talune estensioni, dei concetti di media ai caratteri qualitativi. *Metron, 8.*

GINI, C. and LIVADA, G. (1959): Transvariazione a più dimensioni. *in C.Gini, 1959.*

GINI, C. and LIVADA, G. (1959): Nuovi contributi alla teoria della transvariazione. *in C.Gini, 1959.*

MONTANARI, A. and CALÒ, D.G. (1988): Two group linear discrimination based on transvariation measures. *in A.Rizzi, M.Vichi, H.H.Bock (eds), Advances in data science and classification, Springer-Verlag Berlin, Heidelberg, 251-256.*

OLKIN, I. and YITZHAKI, S. (1992): Gini regression analysis. *International statistical review, 60, 185-196.*

PODDER, N. (2002): The theory of multivariate Gini regression and its applications. *working paper.*

POSSE, C. (1992): Projection pursuit discriminant analysis for two groups. *Communications in Statistics, Theory and Methods, 21, 1-19.*

SCHECHTMAN, E. and YITZAKI, S. (1987): A measure of association based on Gini's mean difference. *Communications in Statistics, Theory and Methods, 16, 207-231.*

SMALL, C.G. (1990): A survey of multidimensional medians. *International statistical review, 58, 263-277.*

STUART, A. (1954): The correlation between variate values and ranks in sample from continuous distribution. *British Journal of Statistical Psychology, 7, 37-44.*

On Correspondence Analysis of
Incomplete Orderings

Kalev Pärna

Institute of Mathematical Statistics,
University of Tartu, EE-50409 Tartu, Estonia

Abstract. Correspondence analysis (CA) is a method for graphical presentation of two-way data tables. We consider the following problem: how can CA be applied in a particular case when the data consists of incomplete orderings. As an example of this kind of data we refer to a contest where each member of the jury allocates ranks $1, 2, ..., k$ only to k "best" candidates (out of n). In order to apply CA for such data a restricted iterative proportional fitting procedure is proposed to modify the initial table of ranks by imputing nonzero numbers to cells that were not among the k best cells. We demonstrate the work of the method via a practical example.

1 Introduction

Correspondence analysis (CA) is an exploratory method for analysing 2-way data tables that results in displaying the rows and columns as points in a low-dimensional vector space (see, e.g., Greenacre (1984), Greenacre and Hastie (1987)). The coordinates of the row-points and column-points are chosen in such a way as to account for as much of the association between the rows and columns as possible.

For an I x J data table N, CA decomposes the departure of the initial data from the independence model which prescribes that each cell entry is proportional to the product of corresponding row and column totals. While revealing main 'dimensions' in departures of cell entries from the independence model, CA has similarities with the principal component analysis.

Algebraically, CA is a singular value decomposition (SVD) of the departure matrix from independence. As SVD assumes no missing values in the matrix, we need, before applying CA, special methods for handling cells with missing or incomplete information.

Our study is motivated by the problems of treating missing data phenomena when trying to analyze the results of a well-known Song Contest. We have 24 by 24 data matrix where each country (column of the table) gives points $12, 10, 8, 7, ...1$ only to its ten best songs (rows of the table). No country can give points to itself. This is a particular case of missing values problem where the data consists of *incomplete orderings* and the diagonal does not carry any information (a variety of sociomatrices). Our aim here is to get a graphical presentation of the data that show associations between songs and countries and possible groups of countries with similar rankings.

To be more general, let us consider a table N of incomplete rankings where each of I subjects allocates ranks only to its best K out of $I - 1$ subjects

other than itself. Then for each column of N we have:
1) K nonzero ranks (or ratings),
2) no information in the diagonal cell,
3) partial information in the remaining $I - K - 1$ cells (they are "worse" than the K best cells of that column).

So, we have two problems here: how to treat cell types 2) and 3). We have not met any paper devoted to CA for this specific case of incomplete tables. Beh (1999) describes a method for correspondence analysis of ranked data similar to our data, which is based on counts how many times the i'th row was given the rank j. However, their method concentrates on relationships between rows rather than between rows and columns (= judges) simultaneously. Still, there is a natural method worked out by de Leeuw and van der Heijden (1988) for handling diagonal cells (or other cells) that do not carry any information. In fact, we want to eliminate such elements from the analysis and concentrate on interactions caused by other cells. In their paper CA on tables with missing cells is described in the following way: if the usual CA is interpreted as a decomposition of departures from the independence model, in the case of missing cells CA is interpreted as a decomposition of departures from quasi-independence. The latter term means independence only for the cells included (see, e.g. Bishop et.al (1975)). In practice, they suggest to fill missing cells (diagonal elements, in our case) iteratively using the the independence model or, in other words, by *zero-order reconstitution* formula. After doing so these cells do not depart from independence and, therefore, they do not contribute to the decomposition of dependencies, when performing CA. Roberts (1996) discusses alternative ways of treating missing diagonal for sociomatrices with zero-one elements.

While the ideas above help us to manage with type 2) cells, the problem with the type 3) cells is that they can not be considered as 'completely ' missing. Namely, these cells carry the information that they are worse than K best cells in corresponding columns. This leads to an order restricted imputation procedure for these cells. In Section 3 we propose an unified restricted iterative proportional fitting procedure to impute values to cells of type 2) and type 3). The general idea is to introduce as less new dependencies into the data table as possible. As a part of the procedure, diagonal cells are eliminated from the analysis by treating them in term of quasi-independence. For type 3) cells our procedure tries to take into account the natural order restriction between initial ranks and imputed values – the latter should be less than initial ranks. This is achieved by a certain normalization step in the procedure. At the same time the imputed values should also fit independence model (as well as possible), since we try not to introduce new associations into the data. This is again achieved by zero-order reconstitution formula. We demonstrate the work of the method via a practical example where we analyse the results of the Eurovision Song Contest 2002.

2   Correspondence analysis and reconstitution of cells

We only give a short overview of CA here, in order to facilitate the reader to follow the description of our procedure in Section 4, and to interprete the results of an example in Section 5. Let $N = (n_{ij})$ be $I x J$ observed data matrix with grand total $n_{..}$ and let $P = N/n_{..}$ – the data in proportion form. Let $r = (p_{i.})$ and $c = (p_{.j})$ be column vectors of row and column marginals of P, respectively, and let $D_r = diag(r)$, $D_c = diag(c)$. Dividing the rows of P by respective row totals, $D_r^{-1}P$, we obtain I row profiles as points in an $J - 1$ dimensional space (since the elements of each row profile sum up to 1). The i-th row profile has mass equal to $p_{i.}$ of that row in grand total. The mass center of the 'cloud' of all row profiles is the centroid of the cloud, and it is a profile that corresponds to the marginal row of P. The distance between each profile and the centroid is measured by the chi-squared distance:

$$d^2(i) = \sum_j (\frac{p_{ij}}{p_{i.}} - p_{.j})^2 /p_{.j}$$

Inertia of the cloud is defined as weighted average of the distances of all row profiles from the centroid: $In = \sum_i d^2(i)\ p_{i.} = \chi^2/n_{..}$, where the right-hand side is classical Pearson's mean-square contingency coefficient. By analogy, we can repeat all previous with columns to obtain column profiles, centroid of column profiles, and the inertia of the cloud which is numerically equal to that of the cloud of row profiles.

Our gain in CA is to find low-dimensional sub-space which comes closest to the points of the cloud (of row profiles, for example). This is achieved by finding principal axes of inertia. Principal axes are vectors applied to the centroid of the cloud and showing the direction of largest inertia, every next being orthogonal to all previous. The complete mathematical solution is embodied in SVD of the following matrix that describes deviations from the independence model. Let Let $E = rc'$ contain cell estimates under the independence hypothesis. Usual CA is now based on the SVD of the form

$$D_r^{-1/2}(P - E)D_c^{-1/2} = U\Lambda V' \tag{1}$$

where Λ is diagonal matrix of singular values and the matrices U, V consist of (left and right) singular vectors. The latter are used to calculate unweighted row and column scores (called standard coordinates):

$$R = D_r^{-1/2}U, \qquad C = D_c^{-1/2}V$$

that are needed to plot rows and colums in two (usually) dimensions.

According to de Leeuw and van der Heijden (1988), correspondence analysis of incomplete data is based on the SVD of slightly different matrix

$$S_r^{-1/2}(P - Q)S_c^{-1/2} \tag{2}$$

where Q is the matrix of cell estimates under the quasi-independence model keeping missing values free from the independence requirement. For those cells the difference between P and Q is zero. However, they show that in practice the deviation matrix $P - Q$ can be calculated iteratively by means of reconstitution formula. Greenacre (1984) discusses general method of imputing to missing values via reconstitution of order $K \geq 0$ in full detail. For our purposes it is sufficient to apply only zero-order reconstitution. To explain that, let M be the set of all (i,j) which correspond to missing values. The algorithm starts with arbitrary values $x_{ij}^{(0)}$ for cells in M and $x_{ij}^{(0)} = p_{ij}$ for cells not in M. After finding marginals $x_{i.}^{(0)}, x_{.j}^{(0)}, x_{..}^{(0)}$ a new set of imputed values is calculated by the recursive formula

$$x_{ij}^{(s+1)} = \frac{x_{i.}^{(s)} x_{.j}^{(s)}}{x_{..}^{(s)}} \tag{3}$$

applied only for the cells in M. The other cells remain unchanged. (Note that this iterative formula is also valid if x-s are not proportions but frequencies etc.) These steps are iterated until there is no significant difference between two subsequent sets of imputed values. As a result, the imputted values is a part of the best rank 1 approximation of the initial data matrix and, therefore, the imputed values do not contribute to the departure of the initial data matrix from independence model (measured by inertia or chi-squared statistic).

This procedure is shown to converge to a matrix that we denote X. Let now Y be the matrix of estimated values under the independence model applied to X. Then $X - Y = P - Q$ and we can substitute $X - Y$ for $P - Q$ in (2). As $X - Y$ is a *complete* data matrix we can perform CA of incomplete data by standard CA programs (de Leeuw and van der Heijden (1988)).

3 Restricted zero-order reconstitution procedure

We now describe an iterative procedure which imputes values to incomplete data cells of type 2) and 3) simultaneously. Without loss of generality we only consider our ESC 2002 data. As before, let M be the set of indices of type 2) and type 3). Recall that each country (column) gives points 12, 10, 8, 7,...,2, 1 to its ten best songs (rows). As it is clear that the only information is the ordering of songs in each column (the scale 12, 10, etc. is purely prescribed by the rules of the contest) we have the right for monotone transformations of initial ranks. Ideally, if the countries would rank *all* songs, the ranks would have been the numbers from 23 to 1. Therefore, as
Step 1. we lift initial points up to the scale 23 (best song), 22 (second best), ..., 14 leaving the lower part of the scale, the values between 14 and 0, for imputed values. Let us fix some arbitrary values of $n_{ij}^{(0)}$ for the cells in M and take $n_{ij}^{(0)}$ as 'lifted ' scores for the cells not in M. Set $s = 0$.

Step 2. Calculate the marginals $n_{i.}^{(s)}$, $n_{.j}^{(s)}$, and $n_{..}^{(s)}$.

Step 3. Use the formula

$$n_{ij}^{(s+1)} = \frac{n_{i.}^{(s)} n_{.j}^{(s)}}{n_{..}^{(s)}}$$

to modify imputed values for the cells in M. Keep the cells not in M unchanged. This step creates imputed values to fit independence model as well as possible.

Step 4. To follow our order restrictions (imputed values should be between 14 and 0) we have to control the growth of imputed values in type 3) cells by normalizing them in such a way that they sum up to 91 ($=1+2+...+13$) - the ideal total for type 3) cells. That is, we re-define

$$n_{ij}^{(s+1)} := n_{ij}^{(s+1)} \frac{91}{n_{.j}^{(s+1)} - n_{jj}^{(s+1)} - 185}$$

where the denominator is the total for type 3) cells before the normalization.

Step 5. Repeat Steps 2-4 until there is no significant change in imputed values.

In practice, starting with arbitrary values for missing cells it took 15-20 iterations to reach the stationary set of imputed values. The result does not depend on the choice of initial values.

4 Results

Iterative procedure for imputing ranks was applied to ESC 2002 data (currently available at http://www.eurovision.tv/en/results/index.php). The original data and the resulting 24x24 table of 'continued' rankings are too large to bring them here and we only make some remarks on the latter. Both row and column totals were calculated for the new table. Due to the normalization, the column totals are roughly equal (276 + diagonal element, which varied from 20,6 for the winner to 5,3 for the last place). One important feature of the new table is that its row totals (i.e. new total scores for songs) create somewhat different final ranking of songs as compared to the original (official) one. However, departure from the initial ranking is only seen for the songs whose total score is relatively low, and this can be easily explained. Namely, there are two typical possibilities for low totals to come: many low points from different countries, or one-two higher points. But Step 1 of the iterative procedure gives more bonuses in the first case, since more cells are lifted up to the scale 14,...,23. Therefore, the iterative procedure works in favor of songs that received points from a larger number of countries, whereas the songs that only gained some exclusive points are 'punished' by the algorithm. This can be interpreted as a smoothing feature of the algorithm. We then applied CA on that new table.

Pearson's chi-square statistics for fitting independence model to the table is $\chi^2 = 1168.1$ (d.f.=529), which is high. The first four singular values with their

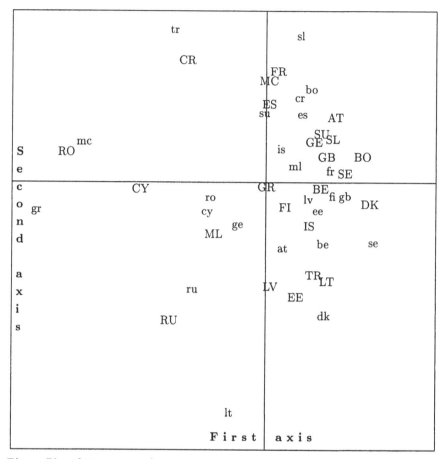

Fig. 1. Plot of 24 countries (upper case symbols) and 24 songs (lower case symbols) by first two principal axes obtained from CA applied to 'continued' rankings of ESC2002 data. The first axis describes 17.5% and the second axis 15.9% of the total inertia.

percentage of the chi–square are .171 (17.5%), .164 (15.9%), .142 (11.9%), .128 (9.7%). We see that four axes account for as much as 55.0% of the total departure from the independence, whereas the first two axes describe 33.4% of all dependencies. A plot of these two dimensions is shown in Figure 1.

As it happens often in applications of CA, the first axes are largely determined by some most 'outstanding' associations between rows and columns. On the left of Figure 1 one can see two pairs, RO–mc (12 points out of total 25 to 'mc' from RO), and CY–gr (again, 12 points). At the bottom, 'lt' received points only from RU, LV and EE, whereas at the top, 'sl' mainly gained from CR an ES. Best songs ('lv', 'ml', 'ee', 'gb') are close to the centroid of the cloud (origin) since due to their uniformly high points their profiles are similar to the marginal column profile which is flat. In a similar manner, the countries who reported rankings that correlate well with the final ranking lie in the middle of the plot, whereas countries with specific features in their orderings lie outside the centre. A horseshoe-like curve can be seen which starts with southern countries (CR, FR, MC, ES), proceeds mainly with middle-european countries (AT, SU, GE), northern countries (DK, LV, EE, LT, and, surprisingly, TR), and through RU reaches again southern countries (CY, RO). With certain reservations we can interprete the first axis as south-north axis. More precise interpretations are somewhat dangerous, since the plot describes only one third of the chi-square. It is therefore necessary to check the findings on the plot by examination initial data.

5 Discussion

There are several other possible ways to handle incomplete rankings before one applies ordinary CA. Probably the most naive method (say, method 1) is simply to impute zero values to all incomplete cells (i.e. diagonal cells and the cells that initially remained unordered). But this has a clear disadvantage that one then introduces negative associations into the diagonal (0 points to its self!). One could improve that method by filling diagonals with final ranks of respective rows, scaled to the interval 0–12 (method 2). This would be approximately the same as zero-order reconstitution of diagonal cells, and subsequent CA would treat the diagonal in a proper way (the diagonal would be excluded from the decomposition of chi-square). But the problem that remains is with type 3) cells. As they are all taken zeros, the rows with rare points (for example: 0,1,0,...,0) would have extreme profiles and they would be dominating in the analysis and plots. Therefore the next step is imputing some reasonable positive values to these cells. Due to the order restrictions we have, it is necessary to make more space for imputed values, and this leads to the lifting step (Step 1 above). After the lifting initial ranks one can take integers 1,...,13 for 13 imputed values in each column, chosen in accordance with the final ranking, since we try to avoid introducing new dependencies into the data (method 3). This idea is already very close to our iterative procedure which, in addition, takes into account the fact that each imputing step also produces new marginals. We have applied CA to the tables obtained by all the methods 1, 2, 3, and by the iterative procedure. The overall conclusion is that the iterative procedure described in this paper is the best.

References

BEH, E.J. (1999): Correspondence analysis of ranked data. *Commun. Statist.- Theory Meth., 28*, 1511–1533.

de LEEUW, J. and van der HEIJDEN, P.G.M. (1988): Correspondence Analysis of Incomplete Contingency Tables. *Psychometrika, 53*, 223–233.

GREENACRE, M.J. (1984): *Theory and Applications of Correspondence Analysis.* Academic Press.

GREENACRE, M. and HASTIE, T. (1987): The geometric interpretation of correspondence analysis. *Journal of American Statistical Association, 82,* 437–447.

ROBERTS, J. M., Jr. (1996): Alternative approaches to correspondence analysis of sociomatrices. *Journal of Mathematical Sociology, 21,* 359–368.

van der HEIJDEN, P.G.M. and de LEEUW, J. (1985): Correspondence analysis used complimentary to loglinear analysis. *Psychometrika, 50,* 429–447.

Acknowledgments: Practical part of this work was done jointly with Jelena Sõrmus.

This work was supported by the Estonian Science Foundation Grant No. 5277.

Some Statistical Issues in Microarray Data Analysis

Stéphane Robin

INA-PG / INRA, Biométrie & Intelligence Artificielle,
16 rue Claude Bernard, F-75005, Paris, France

Abstract. DNA chips give a direct access to the expression levels of thousands of genes at the same time. This promising technology is a key point of functional genomics. However, the abundance and variability of the data it provides require proper statistical analysis.
We first introduce the DNA chip technology and present what biologists hope to learn thanks to it. Some statistical problems raised by these data are then discussed with references to recent bibliography.

1 Introduction

Among the recent advances in molecular biology, the microarray technology seems to be one of the most promising. This 'high throughput' technology allows to measure the expression level of several thousands of genes in one single experiment. This information is crucial in view of understanding the function of the genes and is, therefore, a key point of functional genomics.

Large scaled sequencing programs An major biological work has been made in the last fifteen years by sequencing the genomes of numerous organisms. Sequencing means reading a very long text written with the alphabet of famous four letters (bases) $\{a, c, g, t\}$. Genome lengths vary between millions of bases for bacteria to billions for superior organisms.
The problem of finding genes in these sequences raised immediately after their publication. Both biological and bioinformatic tools to detect genes now exist; it is therefore possible to evaluate the number of genes of a given species. Table 1 shows how this number can vary.

Organism	Number of genes
Escherichia coli (Bacteria)	4 000
Saccharomyces cerevisiae (Yeast)	6 000
Caenorhabditis elegans (Nematode)	19 000
Drosophila melanogaster (Fly)	13 000
Arabidopsis thaliana (Plant)	25–30 000
Human	30–50 000

Table 1. Approximate number of genes in several species

Functional genomics One of the main issue for molecular biologists is now to understand the functions of all these genes. Although a gene is mainly characterized by its sequence (i.e. the portion of the genome sequence that corresponds to it), its function can not be directly deduced from this sequence. At the present time, in 'superior' organisms, only 5 % of the genes have a 'known' function that has been biologically confirmed by some experimental or phenotypic evidence; 65 % of the genes have a predicted function (most of the time, the prediction is based on an homology between the sequence of the gene and the sequence of few genes the functions of which are known); the functions of the remaining 30 % are still unknown. Biologists hope to be able to understand gene functions thanks to an intensive use of the DNA chip technology.

Section 2 recalls some basic biological principles and presents DNA chips. Typical biological questions are addressed in Section 3. Section 4 proposes a overview of some statistical problems raised by microarray data, emphasizing differential analysis.

2   DNA chips

We briefly describe here the aim and principle of the DNA chip technology. A large presentation is proposed by Brown and Botstein (1999).

Central dogma of molecular biology Figure 1 presents the two steps that leads from the gene to the protein, i.e. to the molecule that has an effective biological function. The gene DNA sequence is first copied (*transcripted*) and then translated (according to the genetic code) into a protein. Depending on the condition or tissue, zero, one or several copies of a given gene can be made. The expression level of a gene is related to this number, i.e. to the concentration of corresponding messenger RNA (mRNA) in the cell. The transcriptome of a cell is define as the set of all the mRNA (transcripts) present in the cell.

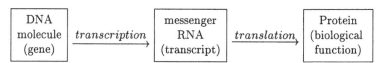

Fig. 1. Two steps from gene to protein

Transcriptome analysis measures the abundance of the transcripts corresponding to each genes and provides therefore an estimation of their expression levels. DNA chips are designed to capture separately transcripts corresponding to each of the genes.

DNA chips The separation of the transcripts is based on the hybridization reaction that leads two complementary RNA (or DNA) fragments to match spontaneously. The fragments match according to the Watson-Crick rule that associates a with t and c with g (see Figure 2). Complementary fragments

```
target (solution)   a   t   g   g   t   a   g   c   a
                    |   |   |   |   |   |   |   |   |
                    t   a   c   c   a   t   c   g   t   probe (chip)
```

Fig. 2. Hybridization of a single strain of DNA to its complementary

corresponding to each gene are spotted on a chip; all this spots constitute an array. The solution (target) containing transcripts is spread on the chip (probe). The quantity of transcripts hybridized on each spot of the array measures the expression level of the corresponding gene.

Quantification Before being spread on the chip, transcripts are labeled in order to be quantified. The two most popular labeling techniques are fluorescence and radioactivity. Most of the time, chips used with fluorescence are glass slides ('microarray') while chips used with radioactivity are nylon membranes ('macroarray', see Figure 3). A microarray can contain about 10 000 spots; a macroarray contains a bit less.

The fluorescence technique can use two different dyes at the same time (green

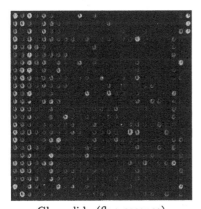
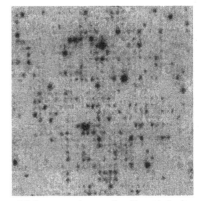

Glass slide (fluorescence)   Nylon membrane (radioactivity)

Fig. 3. Partial pictures of a microarray (left) and a macroarray (right). The left picture results from the superimposition of two pictures : one green and one red. Equal green and red signals result in yellow spots; absence of both green and red signals give black spots.

and red). In a typical experiment, transcripts extracted from tumors are labeled with the red dye while normal transcripts are labeled with the green dye; the two solutions are then spread on a same chip. The abundance of the transcripts of each type of cell is quantified by exciting the chip with two different lasers, one green and one red. Unfortunately, there are many bias in the labeling technique and normalization of the data is strongly required. Most of the time, the log-transform is applied to the signal in order to stabilized its variance. In the following, all numeric values will refer to log-signals.

3   Biological questions

A basic idea of functional genomics is that, to understand the function of a gene, one need to know in which conditions or in which tissues it is highly (or lowly) expressed. The 'high throughput' technology of DNA chips allows to explore in a reasonable time (and with a reasonable cost) many conditions or tissues.

Expression profiles Historically, one of the first question raised by microarray data has been to define groups (clusters) of genes having similar expression profiles in a given set of conditions. Gene belonging to a same cluster probably participate to the same physiologic mechanism or are involved in the same regulation network (see below). The pioneer paper of Eisen *et al.* (1998), that presents several studies of this kind, has revealed clustering techniques to the molecular biology community.

The dual clustering question is also interesting when 'conditions' are patients. In their very famous paper, Alizadeh *et al.* (2000) compare different types of lymphoma. Within patients of one type, they detect two subtypes of patients on the base of their expression profiles. Those two subtypes of patients turn out to have very different responses to the standard therapy.

Genes affected by a condition change A natural way to discover gene involved in a given mechanism is to detect 'differentially expressed' genes. For example, Tusher *et al.* (2001) study human genes affected by ionizing radiations: this study is lead by comparing the transcriptomes of exposed and non-exposed human cells. This kind of study is sometimes called 'differential analysis'.

Tissues or patients classification The DNA chip technology can also be used for diagnosis since patients can be characterized by their expression profiles. Golub *et al.* (1999) have made the most famous study of that type: their aim was to classify patients into one of two types of acute leukemia. Many supervised classification techniques have been tested on their data.

The problem of selecting a small subset of genes sufficient to make a good classification is also important in view of designing reduced chips for routine analysis.

Regulation networks The most exciting but also ambitious question for biologist is to determine regulation activities (activation or inhibition) between genes. On the base of many expression profiles, biologist hope to be able to draw huge graphs (networks) showing, for example, that gene A induces gene B that itself inhibits gene C, etc. Such a network would be a key to understand metabolic pathways. However, this project will probably require tremendous datasets and, at the present time, only reduced networks can be analyzed.

4 Statistical issues

Each biological question presented in Section 3 can be reformulated in terms of statistical analysis that has to be lead very carefully because of the high variability of microarray data. Although many of these analysis can be made with standard statistical methods, the dimension of microarray data imply a new way to look at standard statistical notions. For example, the distinction between 'individuals' and 'variables' is not clear about genes: genes will be considered as individuals in many clustering analysis and as variables in supervised classification.

Furthermore, classical statistical problems as multiple comparison or variable selection are restated by microarray data because we have to deal here with several thousands of levels (for multiple comparison) or variables (for variable selection) at the same time. This section presents a non exhaustive list of problems. Crucial steps such as probe sampling, design of experiments and image analysis are not discussed here.

Clustering The definition of genes (or tissues) having similar profiles has been one of the first problem to be treated with statistical methods. The need of automatic clustering techniques appeared very early because of the size of the datasets. The great popularity of the paper of Eisen *et al.* (1998) is partly due the free '*Cluster*' software that was associated to it (see web-sites given at the end of this paper). This software performs many analysis such as hierarchical clustering (based on correlation coefficients), K-means, self-organized maps (Kohonen's networks), etc. Many biological paper present analysis looking like Figure 4 (reproduced from Eisen *et al.* (1998)) that are sometimes called 'Eisenifications'!

The limitations of theses approaches is that they do not take into account the great experimental variability of these data, and because the result is very method-dependent and need biological assessment. Other approaches such as bootstrap on trees or mixture models are proposed by statistical papers but they still have few applications in the biological literature.

Data normalization All practitioners are now convinced that the variability of the data can not be neglected. Many papers have shown that experimental artifacts induce huge variations of the signal. For example, Sekowska *et al.*

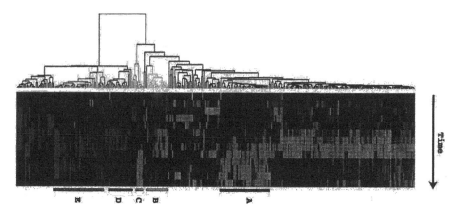

Fig. 4. Example of clustering of microarray data (reproduction of Fig. 1 of Eisen *et al.* (1998)). The red and green matrix represents the dataset: each column corresponds to a gene and each row to a condition (a time in this case); negative values are colored in green, positive are colored in red. A biological interpretation of clusters A to E is given in the original paper.

(2001) aim to detect genes affected be a change in the sulfur source in *B. subtilis*. The analysis of variance table of this experiment (not shown here) shows that the mean square of the interaction of interest (Sulfur source×Gene) is 10 000 times smaller than the variability due to the date of the experiment. This analysis (and many others) proves that the data have to be normalized in some way. The analysis of variance model is now commonly used to analyze such designs (see Kerr and Churchill (2001)). However, the status of the different effects can be discussed between fixed and random. More recently, mixed models have been introduced to deal with repeated data (Wolfinger *et al.* (2001)).

Bias in DNA labeling The analysis of variance model is often used to eliminate artifacts. A typical experimental bias is observed in experiments using two dyes (red and green) because the two dyes have not the same efficiency, and because the difference depends on the gene. The correction of the mean red/green difference can be made simply and with a good precision thanks to the size of the dataset. However, the correction of this bias for each gene can not be made so simply because of the small number of (or even sometimes 'absence of') replicates.

Figure 5 shows that this bias seems to be related to the mean signal of the gene. Let us denote R_g the signal obtained for gene g in the condition labeled in red and G_g the signal obtained for the same gene in the conditioned labeled in green. The mean signal is $M_g = (R_g + G_g)/2$ and the (half) difference is $D_g = (R_g - G_g)/2$. Dudoit *et al.* (2002) suggest to use the 'loess' (Cleveland (1979)) robust regression $D_g = f(M_g)$ to correct the Gene×Dye interaction. Such a correction reduces significantly the Gene×Dye interaction and is proposed by many commercial softwares.

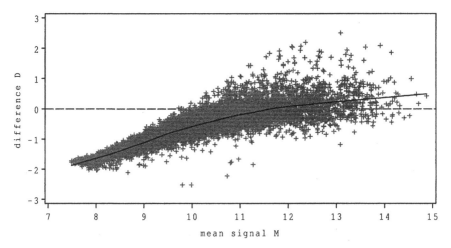

Fig. 5. Plot of the half difference D between the red and green signals versus their mean M for a microarray of A. *thaliana* (10 000 spots). Solid line = loess regression curve.

Differential analysis As said in Section 3, the discovery of genes having different expression levels under two conditions is one of the typical question in microarray data analysis. Examples of typical analysis including description of the experimental design, data normalization and differential analysis can be found in Dudoit *et al.* (2002) or Rudemo *et al.* (2002).The question can be formulated in following way: let A and B denote the two conditions and A_{gi} denote the expression level of gene g in the i-th replicate in condition A (resp. B_{gi}). The statistical problem is then to test the hypothesis $\mathbf{H_0} =$ "A_{gi}'s and B_{gi}'s have the same distribution". Let Δ_g denote the test statistic for gene g: typically $\Delta_g = \bar{A}_g - \bar{B}_g$ where $\bar{A}_g$ is the mean expression level of g in condition A (resp. $\bar{B}_g$).

Distribution of Δ_g under $\mathbf{H_0}$ A non parametric approach requires a set of non differentially expressed genes to estimate distribution of Δ_g under $\mathbf{H_0}$. Generally, one assumes that only few genes are differentially expressed, so that the distribution of Δ_g under $\mathbf{H_0}$ is estimated using all the genes. Dudoit *et al.* (2002), Tusher *et al.* (2001) or, more recently, Storey and Tibshirani (2001) propose several approaches to limit the influence of differentially expressed genes in this estimation.

Variance estimate In a parametric framework, the parameters characterizing this distribution have to be estimated. The normal distribution of the data is frequently assumed; in this framework, the question is then to estimate the variance σ_g^2 of Δ_g that appears in the statistic $T_g = \Delta_g / \sqrt{\hat{\sigma}_g}$. We present here several possible approaches.

Homoscedasticity: The simplest approach is based on the homoscedasticity hypothesis "$\sigma_g \equiv \sigma$". In this case, the common estimate $\hat{\sigma}$ has a high precision thanks to the large number of genes and the associated t-test is highly powerful. In the data of Sekowska *et al.* (2001), a careful analysis leads to set apart about 50 genes with high variance σ_g^2 among 4 600. For the to the remaining 4 550 the homoscedasticity hypothesis is quite reasonable. However, a strong heteroscedasticity is observed in many experiments and standard transforms (log, Box-Cox, etc) are unable to correct it.

Gene specific estimate: In case of heteroscedasticity, a specific estimate $\hat{\sigma}_g$ can be calculated for each gene. When the number of replicates is small (less than 5), this estimation is very bad and the power of the test is dramatically low. In the data of Sekowska *et al.* (2001) again, this approach detects only 1 differentially expressed gene instead of 50 under the homoscedasticity hypothesis. This great loss of power suggests to look for an intermediate way between the two preceeding approaches (see Rudemo *et al.* (2002) for a discussion).

Combined estimate: In order to stabilize the gene specific variance estimate $\hat{\sigma}_g$, Tusher *et al.* (2001) propose to add some constant to it and to use $s_g^2 = \sigma_0^2 + \hat{\sigma}_g^2$. σ_0^2 is chosen sufficiently high to avoid false positive due to too small estimate $\hat{\sigma}_g$.

Variance modeling: Figure 5 suggests that the variance σ_g^2 is related to the mean expression level M_g. This relation is frequently observed and Rudemo *et al.* (2002) propose a exponential modeling of the relation $\sigma_g^2 = f(M_g)$ while Huber *et al.* (2002) suggest a quadratic form.

Mixture model: The modeling of σ_g^2 can be made independently from the expression level by using a mixture model (see Delmar *et al.* (2002)). In this framework, genes are supposed to belong to one of K classes, each characterized by a variance s_k^2 ($k = 1..K$).

In the last three approaches, the distribution of the statistic T_g is still difficult to obtain and is generally approximated by a Gaussian or a Student distribution. The comparison of all these methods is also difficult to make, mainly because of the lack of test datasets in which differentially expressed genes are clearly identified. Simulation comparisons are not really satisfying since the simulation model has a major influence on the performance of the different methods. Pan (2002) compares the results obtained by several methods on Golub *et al.* (1999) data.

Mixture model / Bayesian classification The hypothesis testing framework is not the only way to detect differentially expressed genes. A mixture model approach is proposed by Efron *et al.* (2000) or Parmigiani *et al.* (2002).

The components of the mixture correspond, for example, to up-regulated ($\mathbb{E}(\Delta_g) > 0$), down-regulated ($\mathbb{E}(\Delta_g) < 0$) and non differentially expressed ($\mathbb{E}(\Delta_g) = 0$) genes. Differentially expressed genes are then detected according to their posterior probability of belonging to one of the first two components.

Multiple comparison Differential analysis always imply a multiple testing problem since several thousands of tests (one for each gene) are made at the same time. Controlling the overall level or the false positive rate is one of the most crucial statistical problem raised by microarray data. The very popular approach ('SAM' for Statistical Analysis of Microarray, Tusher *et al.* (2001)) is based on permutation tests. The same permutation is applied on all the genes at the same time to preserve the correlation structure, which is obviously necessary since the genes can not be considered as independent. Yet, it seems that the estimation of the False Discovery Rate (FDR) can be improved (Storey and Tibshirani (2001), Korn *et al.* (2001)).

Classification The problem of classifying tissues or patients is addressed by many biological papers. Many supervised classification methods (Fisher discriminant analysis, nearest neighbors, support vector machines (SVM), classification trees, etc.) have been tested and all the statisticians working in this domain know the Golub *et al.* (1999) or Alizadeh *et al.* (2000) datasets. Dudoit *et al.* (2000) or Brown *et al.* (2000) propose comparisons. The statistical renewal of SVM came together with the apparition of microarrays and these two techniques seems to be made for each other since SVM generally perform very well on transcriptome data. However, one of the key principle of SVM is to augment artificially the dimension of the data space in order to make the groups linearly separable. In microarray experiments, samples or tissues (individuals) are much less numerous as genes (variables), so the groups are linearly separable in the original data space.

In several papers, the selection of a subset of discriminating genes is made on the bases of a differential analysis. This approach is not satisfying because of the correlation between genes that may lead to a very redundant subsets. Stepwise selection can be used for Fisher discriminant analysis. A selection procedure for SVM is proposed by Weston *et al.* (2000) and applied to Golub *et al.* (1999) data by Guyon *et al.* (2002). The reduction of the number of genes improved the performance of the classifier on the test data.

Web-sites

The intense activity of the statistical community about microarray data makes it unreasonable to wait for the final publication of papers. Published papers do not give a good idea of the up-to-date bibliography. This motivates the presence of technical reports and web-sites among the references. A frequent look at some web-sites is therefore necessary. Of course, the following list is not exhaustive but proposes some interesting pages in connection with the topics discussed in this paper.

STANFORD MICROARRAY DATABASE <www.dnachip.org/>: test datasets (Alizadeh *et al.* (2000), Golub *et al.* (1999), ...) can be downloaded from this database.

EISEN-LAB <rana.lbl.gov/>: the '*Cluster*' software is available there.

GENE EXPRESSION DATA ANALYSIS (Department of Biostatistics & Medical Informatics, University of Wisconsin - Madison) <www.biostat.wisc.edu/geda/>: the seminar page presents a good up-to-date bibliography.

TERRY SPEED'S MICROARRAY DATA ANALYSIS GROUP <www.stat.berkeley.edu/users/terry/zarray/Html/>: this team is one of the most active in the field and proposes an overview of statistical problems.

SIGNIFICANCE ANALYSIS OF MICROARRAYS <www-stat.stanford.edu/~tibs/SAM/>: presentation of the SAM method for differential analysis.

References

ALIZADEH, A., EISEN, M., DAVIS, R. E., MA, C. A., LOSSOS, I., ROSENWALD, A., BOLDRICK, J., SABET, H., TRAN, T. ., YU, X., POWELL, J., YANG, L., MARTI, G., MOORE, T., HUDSON, J., CHAN, W. C., GREINER, T. C., WEISSENBERGER, D. D., ARMITAGE, J. O., LEVY, R., GREVER, M. R., BYRD, J. C., BOTSTEIN, D., BROWN, P. O. and STAUDT, L. M. (2000): Distinct types of diffuse large B-cell lymphoma identified by gene expression profiling. *Nature, 403, 503–511.*

BROWN, P. and BOTSTEIN, D. (1999): Exploring the new world of the genome with DNA microarrays. *Nature Genetics, Supplement 21, 33–37.*

BROWN, M. P. S., GRUNDY, W. N., LIN, D., CRISTIANINI, N., SUGNET, C. W., FUREY, T. S., ARES, M. and HAUSSLER, D. (2000): Knowledge-based analysis of microarray gene expression data by using support vector machines. *Proc. Natl. Acad. Sci. USA, 97, 262–267.*

CLEVELAND, W. S. (1979): Robust locally weighted regression and smoothing scatterplots. *Journal of the American Statistical Association, 74, 829–836.*

DELMAR, P., ROBIN, S. and DAUDIN, J.-J. (2002): Mixture model on the variance for the differential analysis of gene expression. *submitted.*

DUDOIT, S., FRIDLYAND, J. and SPEED, T. P. (2000): Comparison of discrimination methods for the classification of tumors using gene expression data. *Technical Report 576, Statistics Department, University of California, Berkeley.*

DUDOIT, S., YANG, Y., CALLOW, M. J. and SPEED, T. P. (2002): Statistical methods for identifying differentially expressed genes in replicated cDNA microarray experiments. *Statistica Sinica, 12, 111–139.*

EFRON, B., TIBSHIRANI, R., GOSS, V. and CHU, G. (2000): Microarrays and their use in a comparative experiment. *Technical report, Department of Statistics, Stanford University. www-stat.stanford.edu/~tibs/research.html.*

EISEN, M. B., SPELLMAN, P. T., BROWN, P. O. and BOTSTEIN, D. (1998): Cluster analysis and display of genome-wide expression patterns. *Proc. Natl. Acad. Sci. USA.* 14863–14868.

GOLUB, T. R., SLONIM, D. K., TAMAYO, P., HUARD, C., GAASENBEEK, M., MESIROV, J. P., COLLER, H., LOH, M., DOWNING, J. R., CALIGIURI, M. A., BLOOMFIELD, C. D. and Lander, E. S. (1999): Molecular classification of cancer: Class discovery and class prediction by gene expression. *Science, 286, 531–537*.

GUYON, I., WESTON, J., BARNHILL, S. and VAPNIK, V. (2002): Gene selection for cancer classification using support vector machines. *Machine Learning, 46, 389–422*.

HUBER, W., VON HEYDEBRECK, A., SLTMANN, H., POUSTKA, A. and VINGRON, M. (2002): Variance stabilization applied to microarray data calibration and to the quantification of differential expression. *Bioinformatics, 18, 96–104*.

KERR, M. K. and CHURCHILL, G. (2001): Experimental design for gene expression microarrays. *Biostatistics, 2, 183–201*.

KORN, E. L., TROENDLE, J. F., MCSHANE, L. M. and SIMON, R. (2001), Controlling the number of false discoveries:application to high-dimensional genomic data. Technical Report 003, National Cancer Institute, Biometric Research Branch, Dicision of Cancer Tratment and Diagnosis. linus.nci.nih.gov/~brb/TechReport.htm.

PAN, W. (2002): A comparative review of statistical methods for discovering differentially expressed genes in replicated microarray experiments. *Bioinformatics, 18 (4), 546–554*.

PARMIGIANI, G., GARRET, E., ANBAZHAGAN, R. and GABRIELSON, E. (2002): A statistical framework for expression-based molecular classification in cancer. *J. R. Statist. Soc. B, 64 (4), 1–20*.

RUDEMO, M., LOBOVKINA, T., Mostad, P., Scheidl, S., Nilsson, S. and Lindahl, P. (2002): Variance models for microarray data. http://www.math.chalmers.se/~rudemo/.

SEKOWSKA, A., ROBIN, S., DAUDIN, J.-J., HÉNAUT, A. and DANCHIN, A. (2001): Extracting biological information from DNA arrays: an unexpected link between arginine and methionine metabolism in *bacillus subtilis*. *Genome Biology, 2 (6)*, http://genomebiology.com/2001/2/6/research/0019.1.

STOREY, J. D. and TIBSHIRANI, R. (2001), Estimating false discovery rates under dependence, with applications to DNA microarrays. Technical Report 2001-28, Department of Statistics, Stanford University. www.stat.berkeley.edu/~storey/.

TUSHER, V. G., TIBSHIRANI, R. and CHU, G. (2001): Significance analysis of microarrays applied to the ionizing radiation response. *Proc. Natl. Acad. Sci. USA, 98, 5116–5121*.

WESTON, J., MUKHERJEE, S., CHAPELLE, O., PONTIL, M., POGGIO, T. and VAPNIK, V. (2000): Feature selection for SVMs. In *Neural Information Processing Systems, 668–674*. http://www.ai.mit.edu/people/sayan/webPub/feature.pdf.

WOLFINGER, R. D., GIBSON, G., WOLFINGER, E., BENNETT, L., HAMADEH, H., BUSHEL, P. AFSHARI, C. and PAULES, R. S. (2001): Assessing gene significance from cDNA microarray expression data via mixed models. *J. Comp. Biol., 8 (6) 625–637*.

Acknowledgments: The author thanks Pr M. Eisen for authorizing the reproduction of Figure 4 and Pr J.-J. Daudin for his comments.

Background of the Variability in Past Human Populations: Selected Methodological Issues

Arkadiusz Sołtysiak

Dept of Historical Anthropology,
Institute of Archeology, Warsaw University

Abstract. The phenotypic variability in biological populations depends on genes and environmental interactions. In case of past human populations many factors of variability are related to the cultural background, e.g. modifications of the gene flow in the population due to social stratification, or non-random character of the sample resulting from the variability of burial customs. The complexity and fluctuation of the background of variability makes the research on affinities between past populations difficult, but not impossible. In author's opinion the decisive presentation of the analytical procedure solving all problems related to variability in human populations is not possible. However, some steps towards it can simply be done by increasing attention to the preparation and interpretation stages of standard methodology.

1 Introduction

Archaeological excavations, apart from the artefacts, bring also human skeletal remains. One of the questions directed by archaeologists to physical anthropologists concerns the possibility of reconstructing ancient migrations. In general way, what is searched on is the interdependence of archaeological cultures with specified ethnic units. So far, many attempts to answer questions of that kind have been done (cf. Howells (1989); Lahr (1989)). The present paper, however, is not intended to outline the history of research of this area. Instead, it contains a brief discussion of some important difficulties in translating the archaeological question into a biological and statistical language of physical anthropology.

2 The problem

For the first glance, the question seems to be easy to answer. There are the series of human skeletons; each of them can be measured according to a given standard, including continuous and discrete morphological traits. Serological and genetic characteristics are also available, although they will not be discussed here for they are still rarely used in the studies of ancient populations. The statistical treatment of the data set should enable the decision whether there is a significant difference between the series. The classification of series in order to determine similarity degree in their set and fix the clusters of series is also possible. The lack of differences can be interpreted as proof of affinity between past populations represented by the skeletal series.

Actually, the problem is much more complicated. The morphological variability of bones and teeth, just as all other organs, is the result of interaction between genes (or rather proteins as the products of their expression) and environment. In case of mankind this interaction can be specific because of the existence of culture. Moreover, when ancient skeletons are considered, the possibility of post mortem changes cannot be precluded. Theoretical components of variability can be defined in more detail as follows:

i) *ante mortem*
  (a) genetic (DNA polymorphism)
   • adaptative (genes only)
   • neutral, including genes and non-coding sequences
  (b) ontogenetic (differentiated genes expression)
   • related to growth of the organism
   • seasonal or related to other cosmic cycles
  (c) environmental
   • nonbiotic, e.g. the influence of climatic features
   • biotic, the interactions with biosphere (e.g. food, parasites)
   • cultural, the interactions with human artefacts
    − cultural modifications of phenotypes, e.g. artificial cranial deformations
    − modifications of the gene flow in the population, e.g. due to social stratification
    − the changes in natural selection
ii) *post mortem*
  (a) differences in burial customs
  (b) deformations of bones, e.g. due to soil pressure
  (c) differences in the state of preservation
iii) statistical artefacts
  (a) non-random sampling
  (b) measurement (intraobserver) error
  (c) methodical (interobserver) error

Assuming that the affinities between populations are synonymous with the similarity of their genes pools, only the genetic component of variability should be taken into account. However, it is impossible to effectively split the variability into defined components. There are many studies on heredity rates, considering twin or family materials (Vandenberg (1962), Hiernaux (1963), Nakata et al. (1974), Sjövold (1984)) and prehistoric skeletal series as well (Varela and Cocilovo (1999)). The heritability estimate h^2 can be acknowledged as high enough in case of at least some morphological characteristics of bones, but actually it also comprises a part of environmental variability resulting from ecological homogeneity of the family. Fortunately, at least in theory this part of environmental variability should be also good indicator of affinities for its expected correlation with kinship. Experiments on rats suggest that the environmental part of h^2 can have even greater impact (Pucciarelli (1980)).

The next question is, whether the interpopulational genetic variability is sufficient to distinguish between populations. Hitherto published studies on human DNA polymorphism have shown that in most cases less than 20% of variability can be assigned to interregional or interpopulational differences, but in many loci the result is statistically significant (Barbujani et al. (1997), Brown and Armelagos (2001)). So far there is no information about the genetics of bone morphology and it remains unclear how this significance refers to skeletons. The question of adaptability and possible convergention must not also be disregarded, taking into account the factor of climatic zones and ecological strategies (Gugliemino-Matessi et al. (1979), Vark et al. (1985), Bharati et al. (2001)), as well as the changes of morphology due to migration itself (Kobyliansky and Arensburg (1977)).

Human populations are often characterized by high level of heterogeneity and for that reason their historical changes cannot be represented simply in form of phylogenetic trees. The complete replacement of one population by another in a given territory is also unlikely; migrations are only partial in most cases. It implies that it can be impossible to reconstruct them even in case of long and well documented skeletal series if the migrating group was small or if the morphological characteristics of compared populations are similar. Thus the researcher should not expect that discussed question can always be answered; some migrations simply cannot be revealed on the basis of bone morphology only.

So far, the biological factors were discussed. However, there is also the cultural influence on the morphological variability in past human populations. In some cases it may be significant. The cultural modifications can take place both ante (e.g. teeth incrustations, cranial deformations) and post mortem (e.g. burning of body, incisures on bones) and only some of them affect the variability of morphological characteristics used in anthropology. They can be a good indicator of cultural diffusion, but not of migrations in biological sense.

More important from biological point of view is the possibility of social barriers in gene flow in the population, very difficult to recognize in skeletal series. Usually the human populations - by analogy to other animals and plants - are treated as panmictic, although it may be wrong in some cases. The tests of normality in longer series can be used to check out the hypothesis of panmixia.

The last cultural factor concerns the burial customs. One can expect different treatment of the deceased in various traditions as well as specific rules of distribution. For example in ancient Mesopotamia children were frequently buried in houses, while adults were laid in cemeteries. Such lack of random sampling is increased during excavations as usually only parts of burial grounds are discovered.

Some post mortem modifications are not culturerelated. It has been proven that the humidity can be a source of significant measurement error (Albrecht (1983)). Also the deformations of bones due to soil pressure can be present. In case of the skull such deformation would mostly affect the neurocranium and, since the skull usually lie on the side, cause the elongation and narrowing. Measuring error impact has been already exhaustively discussed (Jamison and Zegura (1974), Page (1976), Utermohle and Zegura (1982)).

The problem can then be defined as follows: how to reconstruct biological affinities between past populations using morphological characteristics of the bones, and being aware that the similarity is not equal to affinity and there is a legion of factors contributing to the variability, some of them impossible to precisely define. Such problem cannot be solved automatically. What is needed is a concentration on the details and careful adaptation of statistical or taxonomical method to the specific case, without overestimation of the numerical results.

3   Methodological issues

The definition of the problem is only a starting point and it should be followed by the choice of most appropriate methodological approach. Here only some selected methodological issues will be discussed, related directly to the peculiarities of the variability in past human populations.

The skeletal series are not random samples. For that reason it may be impossible to use statistical methods without some assumptions, which cannot be proven. The researcher should be aware how far those assumptions can affect the results of analysis. For example it is clear that in most cases the random character of post mortem deformations due to humidity and earth pressure will be assumed, although actually the influence of those factors cannot be precisely measured, apart from some ideal experiments. However, the assumption, that the bones covered in coffins will be less deformed than those buried directly under the ground, will be relevant.

The skeletal series in many cases are not proper samples from a population. There is a difference between biological and statistical definition of a population. In biological sense the population is a class of intercrossing organisms, at least partially isolated from other populations. In statistical sense the population is a class of individuals living in a certain area at a certain time (Vark and Schaafsma (1992)). The definition of the area and time depends on the researcher. Since the relations between the individuals belonging to one skeletal series cannot be precisely defined, only the statistical definition of a population may be applied.

There can be distinguished four principal steps of the analytical procedure aiming at the reconstruction of the history of past populations. Here are some remarks concerning all of them:

Step one: the choice of characteristics. Two types of characteristics can be used in the research of affinities of past populations: metrical (measurements of chords, arcs, capacities, and circumferences) or nonmetrical (observations of morphological variants, e.g. sutural bones, bony bridges, foramina). The heritability estimate h^2 for metrical characteristics is often greater than for nonmetrical ones (Sjövold (1984)); the characteristics of both kinds are correlated in a small degree. Because of its morphological complexity the skull is of most usefulness. No general model for the choice of characteristics can be proposed; they should be highly hereditable, with possible normal distribution, possible highest interpopulational and lowest intrapopulational variability (Vark and Schaafsma (1992):230). The correlation between chosen characteristics should be as low as possible, although the use of Mahalonobis' distance solves this problem to some extent. Of course, in many cases the choice of characteristics will be determined by their accessibility in reports on the series which cannot be reexamined.

Step two: characteristics are turned into variables. Before the analysis, the characteristics must be turned into variables: standardized, weighted or recalculated in other way. The weighting is usually not recommended (cf. Sneath and Sokal (1973):109), contrary to standardization separately for each sex or age group, if the characteristics are dependent on them. The standardization levels the natural weighting due to scale. For the sake of uniformity, the statistics of chosen reference series (e.g. Howells (1989)) can be used for standardization. More sophisticated (although so far rarely explored) way of recalculation is principal component analysis and the use of component function scores instead of characteristics. However, it may be impossible in case of many missing variables or small data set.

Step three: multivariate analyses and classification. From the multitude of multivariate statistics and classification methods, only few have been successfully adopted in physical anthropology. Previously Penrose's distances of size and shape were used for comparing populations, later substituted by Mahalanobis distance. The last one is not recommended for small series and requests complete data set (Vark and Schaafsma (1992):238). The interpopulational distances are usually classified by using of dendrograms and interpreting them intuitively, since statistical testing is not possible for majority of classification methods (Sneath and Sokal (1973):163). The use of different distances, different sets of variables and different methods can lead to different results. For that reason it is recommended to check out the results of analysis with several procedures. The possible discordances have to be explained. The paper of B. Hemphill is an illustration of multi–procedural approach to the variability of past human population, where the affinities had been analysed by Mahalanobis distance, two types of cluster analysis, multidimensional scaling, and principal coordinate analysis (Hemphill (1999)).

Step four: interpretation of results. Since it is impossible to split the variability into its components, the researcher must reckon with danger that observed differences or similarities are the result of factors not related to the affinity. There are no general rules of solving this problem, and every case must be treated individually. If the individuals were buried in different manners, post mortem deformations can be significant. If nomadic and settled populations are compared, differences due to life style should be expected. Some factors can be not important in most cases, but appear decisive in a specific study. Thus, the need of acquaintance with cultural context and archaeological treatment of the compared series must be stressed.

4 Sumerians and Akkadians vs Amorites. A case study

It is proper to illustrate the present discussion with a simple case study showing the difficulties in reconstructing affinities between ancient populations. According to historical sources (cf. Michalowski (1989)), in $21/20^{th}$ century BCE the nomadic tribes of Amorites migrated from north to Mesopotamia and dominated over Sumerians and Akkadians, previous inhabitants of this territory. However, the written sources give no information how great was the influence of Amorites on Mesopotamian population. Thus, one can ask whether the skeletal series assigned to the periods before and after Amorite influx differ or not   the difference would be a indication of possible great impact of migration.

There are 14 skeletal series from Mesopotamia, assigned to period between 4th and 2nd millennium BCE (Table 1). Unfortunately, other matherials were published only as averages (e.g. Rathbun (1975), Swindler (1956)) and cannot be used in this study. Seven series belong to north and seven to south Mesopotamia[1]. The selection of characteristics is very limited since only few standard skull measurements were taken by all researchers. The methodical error cannot be excluded especially in case of orbital breadth. The measurements and indices taken into consideration are presented in Table 2. A majority of skulls were damaged and full set of variables is available only for 21 individuals out of 70. The number of missing cases for each variable is shown in Table 2.

Considerable number of missing variables disables the use of covariance matrices and principal component analysis. Moreover, the average small number of individuals results in necessary pooling of the series, although their relationships cannot be precisely defined. The series will be pooled into four samples: north and south Mesopotamia before and after 2000 BCE. Since the Amorites migrated from the north, it can be expected that in case of their evident influx the sample "south after" should be more similar to "north" than "south before". Since normal distribution of pooled series cannot be assumed, such hypothesis will not be tested with use of standard statistical parametric methods. Instead, the classification methods are applicable.

---

[1] The full data set is available on request

Site	Chron.	Location	male	female	uncertain	Source
Hassuna	4th mill.	north	2	1	–	Coon (1950)
Halawa	3rd mill.	north	1	2	-	Kunter (1981)
Tawi	3rd mill.	north	-	1	-	Kunter (1984)
Tell Chuera	3rd mill.	north	-	-	1	Wahl (1986)
Tell Arbid	2nd mill.	north	2	3	1	Sołtysiak unp.
Terqa	2nd mill.	north	2	1	-	Sołtysiak unp.
Bassit	2nd mill.	north	-	1	1	Le Goff (1996)
Ubaid	4th mill.	south	7	3	-	Keith (1926)
Kish	3rd mill.	south	16	2	-	Buxton-Rice (1931)
Eridu	3rd mill.	south	4	2	-	Coon (1981)
Tell ed-Der	3rd mill.	south	1		-	Burger-Heinrich (1989)
Tell ed-Der	2nd mill.	south	6	2	-	Burger-Heinrich (1989)
Isin	2nd mill.	south	1	1	-	Ziegelmayer (1987)
Ur	2nd mill.	south	3	3	-	Keith (1926)
			45	22	3	

Table 1. The skeletal series from ancient Mesopotamia

	measurements									
Martin 1928	g-op	eu-eu	b-ba	ft-ft	d-ek	or.h.	n-ns	apt-apt	n-pr	zy-zy
Martin 1928	1	8	17	9	53a	52	54	55	48	45
Howells 1989	GOL	GB	BBH	MFD	OW	OH	NH	NB	UFH	BZD
missing cases	3	5	26	7	24	21	28	22	29	30

	indices					
Martin 1928	8/1	9/8	17/1	48/45	52/53a	55/54
missing cases	5	12	26	38	25	29

Table 2. The characteristics

For cluster analysis it may be assumed that the frequency of objects belonging to random samples taken from one population tends to equality in particular clusters. From other point of view, the objects belonging to the populations which differ in many ways, probably will be more frequently included in different clusters. Thus, the similarity or dissimilarity of populations can be measured as the differences in frequency in the set of clusters, and treated with nonparametric statistical tests, such as χ^2.

In the present case study modified KlettOverall's method has been used (Sołtysiak and Jaskulski (1999)), separately for measurements and for indices. All variables have been standardized separately for each sex. Because of data incompletness the mean square Manhattan distance was applied. Eleven clusters were obtained for measurements analysis and four for indices analysis; Table 3 shows their distribution.

The number of clusters has been decreased for χ^2 testing, with use of dendrogram for their centroids. The clusters 1+3, 2+5+7 and 6+10 of measurement

	measurements analysis											indices analysis			
	C1	C2	C3	C4	C5	C6	C7	C8	C9	C10	C11	C1	C2	C3	C4
N before	1		2		1				1	1		2	1	2	
N after	3	1	2			4						5	2		
S before	8	3	8	1	5		1	1			1	14	6	6	2
S after	2	2	6	1	1							7	2	1	1
sum	14	6	18	2	7	4	1	1	1	1	1	28	11	9	3

Table 3. The results of cluster analyses

analysis and the clusters 2+4 of indices analysis were joined. For small number, all series from north have been pooled. In result two 3x3 tables could have been tested. For indices analysis $\chi^2 = 1.13$ with no significance, while for measurement analysis $\chi^2 = 14.15$ with $p < 0.01$. The last result indicates the difference in cluster 6+10 between "north" and "south". However, the number of individuals taken into consideration is so small that this result cannot be treated as a proof of regional difference. Since the difference between south samples "before" and "after" is insignificant in both analyses, there is no indication of populational change related to the migration of Amorites. Also the inversed hypothesis - that the population of south Mesopotamia did not change at all - could not be proven in that case.

The case study presented above with its negative result is a good illustration of difficulties in research of the history of human populations. Of course not all difficulties were discussed here, for example some Mesopotamian skulls had been noted as deformed post mortem, the difference in sex frequency was also ignored.

The general suggestion of this paper is that the numerical competences are important, but only together with the intimate knowledge of the problem background they can be really useful.

References

ALBRECHT, G.H. (1983): Humidity as a Source of Measurement Error in Osteometrics. *American Journal of Physical Anthropology, 60, 517-521.*

BARBUJANI, G. et al. (1997): An Apportionment of Human DNA Diversity, *Proceedings of National Academy of Sciences, 94, 4516-4519.*

BHARATI, S. et al. (2001): Climate and Head Form in India. *American Journal of Human Biology, 13, 626-634.*

BROWN, R.A. and G.J. ARMELAGOS (2001): Apportionment of Racial Diversity, *Evolutionary Anthropology, 10, 34-40.*

BURGER-HEINRICH, E. (1989a): Tell ed-Der: Sondage A und B. Anthropologische Befunde der paläobabylonischen und neosumerischen Gräber. *Northern Akkad Project Reports, 3, 47-68.*

BURGER-HEINRICH, E. (1989b): Anthropologische Befunde. In: H. Gasche: La Babylonie en 17e siècle avant notre ere. *Mesopotamian History and Environment, series II, Ghent, 67-74.*

BUXTON, L.H.D. and D.T. RICE (1931): Report on the Human Remains found at Kish. *Journal of the Royal Anthropological Institute of Great Britain and Ireland, 61, 57-119.*

COON, C.S. (1950): Three Skulls from Hassuna. *Sumer, 6, 93-96.*

COON, C.S. (1981): The Eridu Crania. A Preliminary Report. In: F. Safar et al.: *Eridu.* Baghdad, 307-309.

HEMPHILL, B.E. (1999): Biological Affinities and Adaptations of Bronze Age Bactrians: IV. A Craniometric Investigation of Bactrian Origins. *American Journal of Physical Anthropology, 108, 173-192.*

HIERNAUX, J. (1963): Heredity and Environment: Their Influence on Human Morphology. A Comparison of Two Independent Lines of Study. *American Journal of Physical Anthropology, 21, 575-589.*

LE GOFF, I. (1996): Étude des restes humains. In: P. Darcque: Trois inhumations simultanées du bronze recent I à Bassit (Syrie). *Syria, 73, 141-152.*

GUGLIEMINO-MATESSI, C.R. et al. (1979): Climate and the Evolution of Skull Metrics in Man. *American Journal of Physical Anthropology, 50, 549-564.*

HOWELLS, W.W. (1989): *Skull Shapes and Map: Craniometric Analyses in the Dispersion of Modern Homo.* Papers of the Peabody Museum of Archaeology and Ethnology, 79, Cambridge MA.

JAMISON, P.L. and S.L. ZEGURA (1974): A Univariate and Multivariate Examination of Measurement Error in Anthropometry. *American Journal of Physical Anthropology, 40, 197-204.*

KEITH, A. (1926): Report on the Human Remains. In: L. Woolley: *Ur Excavations vol. 1.* London, 214-240.

KOBYLIANSKY, E. and B. ARENSBURG (1977): Changes in Morphology of Human Populations Due to Migration and Selection. *Annals of Human Biology, 4, 57-71.*

KUNTER, M. (1981): Anthropologische Befunde: Kampagnen 1977 und 1978. In: W. Orthman: *Halawa 1977-1979.* Bonn, 67-87.

KUNTER, M. (1984): Anthropologische Untersuchung der Skelettreste. In: I. Kampschulte and W. Orthmann: *Gräber des 3. Jahrtausends v. Chr. im syrischen Euphrattal. Ausgrabungen bei Tawi 1975 und 1978.* Bonn, 115-119.

LAHR, M.M. (1989): *The Evolution of Modern Human Diversity. A Study of Cranial Variation.* Cambridge.

MARTIN, R. (1928): *Lehrbuch der Antropologie.* Jena.

MICHALOWSKI, P. (1989): *The Lamentation over the Destruction of Sumer and Ur.* Winona Lake.

NAKATA, M. et al. (1974): Multivariate Analysis of Craniofacial Measurements in Twin and Family Data. *American Journal of Physical Anthropology, 41, 423-430.*

PAGE, J.W. (1976): A Note on Interobserver Error in Multivariate Analyses of Populations. *American Journal of Physical Anthropology, 44, 521-526.*

PUCCIARELLI, H.M. (1980): The Effects of Race, Sex, and Nutrition on Craniofacial Differentiation in Rats. A Multivariate Analysis. *American Journal of Physical Anthropology, 53, 359-368.*

RATHBUN, T.A. (1975): *A Study of the Physical Characteristics of the Ancient Inhabitants of Kish, Iraq.* Miami.

SJÖVOLD, T. (1984): A Report on the Heritability of Some Cranial Measurements and Nonmetrical Traits. In: G.N. van Vark and W.W. Howells (Eds.): *Multivariate Statistical Methods in Physical Anthropology.* Dordrecht, 223-246.

SNEATH, P.H.A. and R.R. SOKAL (1973): *Numerical Taxonomy*. San Francisco.

SOŁTYSIAK, A. and P. JASKULSKI (1999): Analysis of Morphological Differences Between Prehistoric Populations with Use of a Non-Hierarchic Method of Data Clustering. *Przegląd Antropologiczny - Anthropological Review, 62, 75-83*.

SWINDLER, D.R. (1956): *A Study on the Cranial and Skeletal Material from Nippur*. Philadelphia.

UTERMOHLE, CH.J. and S.L. ZEGURA (1982): Intra and Interobserver Error in Craniometry: A Cautionary Tale. *American Journal of Physical Anthropology, 57, 303-310*.

VANDENBERG, S.G. (1962): How "Stable" are Heritability Estimates? A Comparison of Heritability Estimates from Six Anthropometric Studies. *American Journal of Physical Anthropology, 20, 331-338*.

VARELA, H.H. and J.A. COCILOVO (1999): Evaluation of the Environmental Component of the Phenotypic Variance in Prehistoric Populations. *Homo, 50, 46-53*.

van VARK, G.N. et al. (1985): The Statistical Significance of an Association between Skull Morphology and Climatic Conditions. *Homo, 36, 232-241*.

van VARK, G.N. and SCHAAFSMA, W. (1992): Advances in the Quantitative Analysis of Skeletal Morphology. In: R.S. Saunders and M.A. Katzenberg (Eds.): *Skeletal Biology of Past Peoples: Research Methods*. New York, 225-257.

WAHL, J. (1986): Anthropologische Untersuchung der Skelettfunde. In: W. Orthmann et al.: *Tell Chuera in Nordost-Syrien. 1982-1983*. Berlin, 65-80.

ZIEGELMAYER, G. (1987): Die Menschlichen Skelettreste 1983-1984 (7-8 Kampagne). In: B. Hrouda: *Isin-Išan Bahriyat III. Die Ergebnisse der Ausgrabungen 1983-1984*. München, 121-136.

Acknowledgments: The author thanks Elżbieta Jaskulska and Piotr Jaskulski for their critical comments, Polish Science Foundation (Fundacja na Rzecz Nauki Polskiej) for scholarship for the year 2001. The research has been financed by Committee for Scientific Research (KBN), grant No 5 H01H 035 21 entitled "The variability of the ancient Near Eastern human populations".

Spatial Prediction With Space-Time Models

Stefano F. Tonellato

Dipartimento di Statistica
Università "Ca' Foscari" di Venezia, S. Polo 2347, 30125 Venice, Italy

Abstract. In this paper we deal with the problem of spatial prediction for a spatio-temporal process. Our method is based on the state-space representation of the observed spatial time series and requires the implementation of MCMC techniques. We can use the mean of the predictive distribution as a point predictor and we can quantify the uncertainty of our predictions, since we can sample from the predictive distribution. We will show through an application to Ireland wind speed data (Haslett and Raftery (1989)) that although point predictions can be quite precise, the predictive distribution might show a counterintuitive behaviour when the space-time process is not temporally stationary.

1 Introduction

During the latest years, increasing attention has been focussed on the analysis of spatio–temporal stochastic processes. Desease mapping, water resources forecasting, environmental monitoring are just a few examples of human activities that require the analysis of data collected over space and time.

In this work we consider how a very well known class of models, the Bayesian dynamic linear models (West and Harrison 1997), can be employed in the analysis and prediction of space–time processes. In particular, we will focus our attention on the prediction of the realisation of a stochastic process at an unobserved site.

Consider the univariate spatio-temporal stochastic process $Y(s, t)$; $s \in \mathcal{D} \subset \mathbb{R}^2$, $t = 1, 2, \ldots$, and assume that, for each t, observations are collected over the location set $\mathcal{S} = \{s_1, s_2, \ldots, s_n\} \subset \mathcal{D}$. Provided the observed series $\mathbf{Y}_t = [Y(s_1, t), \ldots, Y(s_n, t)]'$, $t = 1, 2, \ldots, T$, can be represented as a Bayesian dynamic linear model, we are interested in the prediction of $Y(s_0, t)$, $t = 1, 2, \ldots, T$, with $s_0 \notin \mathcal{S}$. We will show how $Y(s_0, t)$ can be predicted conditionally on the whole sample information, i.e. conditionally on $\mathbf{Y}_1, \ldots \mathbf{Y}_T$. Moreover, by using MCMC techniques, a full Bayesian analysis of the models is possible.

2 Bayesian dynamic linear models for space-time processes

In Tonellato (1997) a class of Bayesian dynamic linear models has been defined in order to deal with space-time processes. In their general form, such models can be represented in terms of the following equations:

$$\mathbf{Y}_t = \mathbf{W}_t \boldsymbol{\beta} + \mathbf{H}\boldsymbol{\zeta}_t + \boldsymbol{\varepsilon}_t \tag{1}$$

$$\boldsymbol{\zeta}_t = \mathbf{G}\boldsymbol{\zeta}_{t-1} + \mathbf{u}_t, \tag{2}$$

where $\mathbf{W}_t\beta$ indicates the effect of some covariates on the mean of $\mathbf{Y}_t$, $\mathbf{W}_t \in \mathbb{R}^{n \times k}$ and $\beta \in \mathbb{R}^k$, $\mathbf{H} \in \mathbb{R}^{n \times m}$ is a known matrix, ζ_t denotes the unobservable m-dimensional state vector, ε_t indicates a measurement error distributed as a Gaussian white noise, $\varepsilon_t \sim GWN(\mathbf{0}, \sigma_\varepsilon^2 \mathbf{I}_n)$, $\mathbf{G} \in \mathbb{R}^{m \times m}$ indicates the transition matrix. The m-dimensional noise $\mathbf{u}_t$ is distributed as a $GWN(\mathbf{0}, \Sigma_\mathbf{u})$ and it is uncorrelated with ε_s, for all s, and with ζ_s, for all $s < t$. Unobservable trend, seasonal an stationary autoregressive components can be introduced in the model by suitably defining the matrices $\mathbf{H}$ and $\mathbf{G}$. Spatial interaction among sites can be modelled through both the matrices $\mathbf{G}$ and $\Sigma_\mathbf{u}$, which are not necessarely known and may depend on unknown parameters, say ϕ and θ respectively. The inclusion of covariates, of course, can also play an important role in explaining the spatial behaviour of the observed process. It is worth to note that, for these models, likelihood identifiability is guaranteed under fairly mild conditions (Tonellato (1997, 2001)). This means that the likelihood is strongly informative and that repeated observations provide useful information about spatial interaction even when data are collected over sparse sites. Moreover, under the same conditions, the state space representation is minimal, i.e. the size of the state vector cannot be reduced preserving the stochastic properties of the model given by (1) and (2).

The choice of the structure of matrices $\mathbf{H}$ and $\mathbf{G}$ in equations (1) and (2) depends on the kind of unobservable components we intend to deal with (i.e. on the kind of periodicity of a seasonal component, the non-stationary temporal behaviour of the trend, or the order of a temporally stationary autoregressive signal). In a time series context, West and Harrison (1997) give general methods for the choice of such structure, leading to the definition of a wide variety of dynamic models. Their results can be easily extended to spatio-temporal modelling, as far as we model temporal interaction through the matrices $\mathbf{H}$ and $\mathbf{G}$, whereas spatial dependence is modelled through the covariance function of the noise $\mathbf{u}_t$ in equation (2).

The unknown parameters are: ζ_t, $t = 0, 1, \ldots, T$, β, σ_ε^2, θ, and the unknown coefficients appearing in $\mathbf{G}$. For ease of notation, the vector of the unknown parameters (excluding ζ_t) will be denoted by ψ.

Once prior distributions on ψ and ζ_0 have been elicited, the implementation of the Gibbs sampler is standard (Carter and Kohn (1994)). The parameterisation of Σ_u might raise some difficulties (Tonellato (1997)) which can be overcome by the implementation of a Metropolis step whithin the Gibbs sampler.

3   Spatial prediction

Consider the model defined in (1) and (2) and suppose we can modify it as follows:

$$\mathbf{Y}_t = \mathbf{W}_t\beta + \mathbf{H}^*\zeta_t^* + \varepsilon_t \qquad (3)$$

$$\zeta_t^* = \mathbf{G}^*\zeta_{t-1}^* + \mathbf{u}_t^* \qquad (4)$$

Fig. 1. Irish Meteorological Service synoptic meteorological stations

Here the state vector has been augmented, i.e.

$$\zeta_t^* = [\zeta_t' \vdots \zeta(s_0, t)']',$$

where $\zeta(s_0, t)$ denotes the value of the state at the unobserved site s_0. Moreover, we define

$$u_t^* = [u_t' \vdots u(s_0, t)']',$$

$$H^* = [H \vdots 0] \quad \text{and} \quad G^* = \begin{bmatrix} G & G_1 \\ G_2 & G_3 \end{bmatrix}.$$

The variance matrix of u_t^* is parameterised as Σ_u, so it does not raise any estimation problems, as we will show in the next section. The elements of G_1, G_2 and G_3 are assumed to be known or to be known functions of the coefficients of G.

A K–dimensional sample ψ_j, $j = 1, 2, \ldots, K$, can be drawn from the posterior distribution of ψ by applying the Gibbs sampler to the model defined in (1) and (2). Hence, plugging the sampled values ψ_j in (3) and (4), we can draw a K–dimensional sample from the posterior distribution of $\zeta(s_0, t)$, $t = 1, 2, \ldots, T$. A sample from the predictive distribution of $Y(s_0, t)$,

$t = 1, 2, \ldots, T$, can be easily generated from the conditional distribution of $Y(s_0, t)$ given $\psi_j, \zeta_j(s_0, 1), \ldots, \zeta_j(s_0, T), j = 1, \ldots, K$, since $Y(s_0, t)$ is linked to ψ and $\zeta(s_0, t)$ by a relationship analogous to the one in eq. (1), i.e.

$$Y(s_0, t) = \mathbf{W}_t(s_0)\boldsymbol{\beta} + \mathbf{h}^{*\prime}\boldsymbol{\zeta}(s_0, t) + \boldsymbol{\varepsilon}(s_0, t), \tag{5}$$

where $\mathbf{W}_t(s_0)$ represents the row vector of the covariates at site s_0 and $\mathbf{h}^*$ is known. It is worth to note that, by suitably augmenting the dimension of the state vector, we can obtain predictions on r unobserved sites, say $s_{0_1}, \ldots, s_{0_r}$.

To obtain both parameter estimation and predictions we might use directly the model defined by eqs. (3) and (4). We prefer to define two different parameterisations in order to speed up computations: sampling from the posterior of ψ by using (1) and (2) and then using the modified parameterisation to obtain predictions is more efficient, particularly if we want to predict the behaviour of the process on more than one ungauged sites.

4   An application

In this section we present an illustrative application which, although preliminary in nature, sheds some light on the predictive performance of our method. The data are daily mean wind speeds measured by 12 meteorological stations in Ireland from 1978 January 1st to 1978 December 31st. This is a subsample of a dataset covering the period from 1961 January 1st to 1978 December 31st which has been analysed in Haslett and Raftery (1989). Site locations (Fig. 1) are quite sparse: the distances between sites range from 60 up to 420 kilometres. In our analysis we removed the station of Rosslare because of its outlying behaviour (details can be found in the paper mentioned above). We removed also the observations collected at Mullingar and used them to assess the predictive performance of our method. Fig. 2 shows the data we used in the analysis (measures are in knots). In order to stabilise the variance and to achieve an approximate Gaussian distribution, we applied a square root transformation to the original data. We show the results we obtained with two alternative models. In implementing the Gibbs sampler, we generated, for both models, 200 independent chains for 1000 iterations. Convergence of the Gibbs sampler has been assessed by comparing the behaviour of different chains.

Model 1. The first model is defined as:

$$\mathbf{Y}_t = \mathbf{W}\boldsymbol{\beta} + \boldsymbol{\mu}_t + \boldsymbol{\varepsilon}_t \tag{6}$$

$$\boldsymbol{\mu}_t = \boldsymbol{\mu}_{t-1} + \boldsymbol{\eta}_t \quad \boldsymbol{\eta}_t \sim GWN(0, \boldsymbol{\Sigma}_{\boldsymbol{\eta}}) \tag{7}$$

where $\mathbf{W} = [\mathbf{1}_{10} \vdots \mathbf{abs} \vdots \mathbf{ord}]$ (**abs** and **ord** contain rispectively the abscissae and the ordinates of the 10 site locations after fixing the origin of the plane at Valentia; note that in this case the covariates are constant with respect to time). The term $\mathbf{W}\boldsymbol{\beta}$ represents a linear spatial trend.

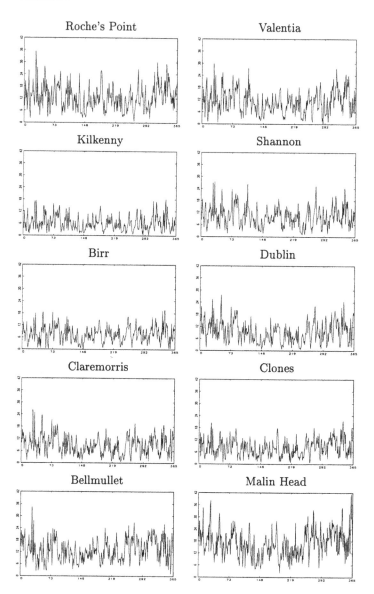

Fig. 2. Plots of observed wind speed time series (measures are in knots)

The matrix Σ_η is defined as

$$\Sigma_\eta\,[i,j] = \begin{cases} \theta_1 & \text{if } i = j, \ i,j = 1,\ldots,10 \\ \theta_1\theta_2 \exp(-\theta_3 d_{ij}) & \text{otherwise,} \end{cases} \qquad (8)$$

with $\theta_1 > 0$, $0 \le \theta_2 \le 1$ and $\theta_3 > 0$. The symbol d_{ij} indicates the Euclidean distance between s_i and s_j. This model corresponds to the one in (1) and (2) with

$$\mathbf{H} = \mathbf{G} = \mathbf{I}_{10}, \quad \zeta_t = \mu_t \quad \text{and} \quad \mathbf{u}_t = \eta_t.$$

Clearly, spatial interaction is introduced through both the spatial trend an the variance-covariance matrix Σ_η. The modified model in (3) and (4) is given by

$$\mathbf{Y}_t = \mathbf{W}\boldsymbol{\beta} + \mathbf{H}^*\boldsymbol{\mu}_t^* + \varepsilon_t$$
$$\boldsymbol{\mu}_t^* = \boldsymbol{\mu}_{t-1}^* + \boldsymbol{\eta}_t^* \quad \boldsymbol{\eta}_t^* \sim GWN(0, \Sigma_{\eta^*})$$

with $\mathbf{H}^* = [\mathbf{H} \vdots \mathbf{0}]$, $\boldsymbol{\mu}_t^* = [\boldsymbol{\mu}_t' \vdots \mu(s_0, t)]'$ (here s_0 corresponds to Mullingar station), $\mathbf{G}^* = \mathbf{I}_{11}$ and $\boldsymbol{\eta}_t^* = [\boldsymbol{\eta}_t' \vdots \eta(s_0, t)]'$ is a 11-dimensional Gaussian white noise whose variance matrix is parameterised as Σ_η. Eq. (5) becomes

$$Y(s_0, t) = \mathbf{W}(s_0)\boldsymbol{\beta} + \mu(s_0, t) + \varepsilon(s_0, t).$$

The prior distributions are the following:

$$\boldsymbol{\beta} \sim N\left(\begin{bmatrix} 2 \\ 0 \\ 0 \end{bmatrix}, 2\mathbf{I}_3\right); \mu_0 = 0 \ a.s.; \ \sigma_\varepsilon^2 \sim IG(0.5, 0.5);$$

$$\theta_1 \sim IG(25, 0.5); \qquad \theta_2 \sim U(0, 1); \theta_3 \sim U(0, 10)$$

($IG(a, b)$ indicates an Inverted Gamma distribution with parameters a and b). The prior distribution on $\boldsymbol{\beta}$ has been suggested by an exploratory analysis of the data for the period 1961-1977. The prior on θ_1 means that, a priori, we expect a smooth behaviour of the temporal trend component. The prior distribution elicited on μ_0 is degenerate. Such a prior was required in order to guarantee likelihood identifiability (summing a constant vector to the spatial trend and subtracting it from μ_t, for all t, would not change the likelihood structure) and it might seem unreasonable. Note, however, that the model defined here is equivalent to:

$$\mathbf{Y}_t = \zeta_t + \varepsilon_t$$
$$\zeta_t = \zeta_{t-1} + \eta_t$$

with $\zeta_0 = \mathbf{W}\boldsymbol{\beta}$, i.e. $\mathbf{W}\boldsymbol{\beta}$ plays the role of the initial conditions on ζ_t. It is worth to discuss also the prior distribution of θ_3. Since we assumed that $0 < \theta_3 \leq 10$ almost surely, some information in the likelihood might be lost. However, for $\theta_3 = 10$, the spatial correlation function of $\eta(s, t)$ evaluated at a distance of 1 kilometre has value no greater than $\exp(-10)$, which is quite unlikely for the data we are dealing with. We made this choice in order to simplify computations, but different priors with support in $\mathbb{R}^+$ might be used, such as a Gamma distribution for instance.

Point predictions   90% prediction interval

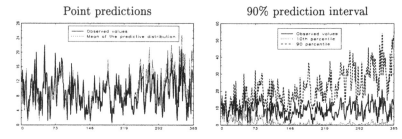

Fig. 3. Predictions at Mullingar using **Model 1**

Fig. 3 shows point predictions and the 90% forecast intervals obtained
by the model for Mullingar station. The predictive mean seems to approximate reasonably well the behaviour of the observed process, but it is worth
to note that the mean percentage error is about 18.7%. In fact, the predictive distribution, inherits the temporal nonstationarity of the model, so
that its variance increases with time. This is clearly an unpleasant feature of
this model and it suggests that very careful attention should be paid when
modelling non stationary spatial time series, since temporal non stationarity
might have very strong implications on spatial prediction.

Model 2. At the light of the predictive performance of **Model 1**, we defined
the following model:

$$\mathbf{Y}_t = \widetilde{\mathbf{W}}\boldsymbol{\beta} + \mu_t \mathbf{1}_{10} + \mathbf{x}_t + \boldsymbol{\varepsilon}_t \tag{9}$$

$$\mu_t = \mu_{t-1} + \eta_t \quad \eta_t \sim GWN(0, \sigma_\eta^2) \tag{10}$$

$$\mathbf{x}_t = \phi \mathbf{x}_{t-1} + \boldsymbol{\omega}_t \quad \boldsymbol{\omega} \sim GWN(0, \boldsymbol{\Sigma}_\omega). \tag{11}$$

where $\widetilde{\mathbf{W}}$ is defined as $\mathbf{W}$ above, but all the elements in the second row
(corresponding to Valentia station) are equal to zero. In this model the term
$\widetilde{\mathbf{W}}\boldsymbol{\beta}$ represents the differences between wind speed's mean at Valentia and
wind speed's mean at the other sites, which are not taken into account by
the common temporal trend μ_t. The variance matrix $\boldsymbol{\Sigma}_\omega$ is parameterised as
$\boldsymbol{\Sigma}_\eta$ in (8). This model corresponds to the one in (1) and (2) with

$$\mathbf{H} = [\mathbf{1}_{10} \vdots \mathbf{I}_{10}], \quad \mathbf{G} = \begin{bmatrix} 1 & 0 \\ 0 & \phi \mathbf{I}_{10} \end{bmatrix}, \quad \boldsymbol{\zeta}_t = [\mu_t \vdots \mathbf{x}_t']' \quad \text{and} \quad \mathbf{u}_t = [\eta_t \vdots \boldsymbol{\omega}_t']'.$$

The modified model in (3) and (4) is obtained by defining: $\mathbf{H}^* = [\mathbf{H} \vdots 0]$,
$\boldsymbol{\zeta}_t^* = [\mu_t \vdots \mathbf{x}_t' \vdots x(s_0, t)]'$, $\mathbf{G}^* = \begin{bmatrix} 1 & 0 \\ 0 & \phi \mathbf{I}_{11} \end{bmatrix}$, and $\mathbf{u}_t^* = [\eta_t \vdots \boldsymbol{\omega}_t' \vdots \omega(s_0, t)]'$, which is
a 12-dimensional Gaussian white noise. Eq. (5) becomes

$$Y(s_0, t) = \widetilde{\mathbf{W}}(s_0)\boldsymbol{\beta} + \mu_t + x(s_0, t) + \varepsilon(s_0, t).$$

Point predictions   90% prediction interval

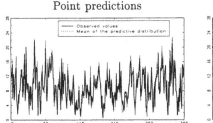
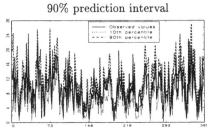

Fig. 4. Predictions at Mullingar using **Model 2**

The prior distributions are the following:

$$\beta \sim N \left(\begin{bmatrix} 1 \\ 0 \\ 0 \end{bmatrix}, 2\mathbf{I}_3 \right) ; \mu_0 \sim N(0,2) \ a.s.; \mathbf{x_0} \sim N(0,2)$$

$$\sigma_\varepsilon^2 \sim IG(0.5,0.5); \qquad \sigma_\eta^2 \sim IG(5,0.5); \quad \phi \sim N(0,1)\mathbf{1}_{]-1,1[}$$

$$\theta_1 \sim IG(0.5,0.5); \qquad \theta_2 \sim U(0,1); \qquad \theta_3 \sim U(0,10)$$

Fig. 4 shows point predictions and the 90% forecast intervals obtained by **Model 2**. The performance of **Model 2** is clearly much better than the one of **Model 1**: the mean percentage error now is 2.9%. This is due to the fact that we can estimate quite precisely the common temporal trend and that the space-time autoregressive process is temporally stationary.

It might be argued that the predictive performance of the model is good because the location of Mullingar is approximately in the middle of the region covered by the monitoring network. In Fig. 2, however we can see that in Birr and Dublin, which are the closest stations to Mullingar, wind speed means behave in quite different ways. This fact suggests that the model approximates quite well the spatial structure of the process, in spite of the sparsity of site locations.

5   Conclusions

In this paper we propose a method for the analysis and spatial prediction of space-time processes. In our illustrative application, we have shown how point predictions and forecast intervals can be easily obtained. We think that the methodology we propose presents strong advantages with respect to traditional kriging based prediction techniques. It can exploit the information provided by repeated measurements even when few spatial data are available and it allows for a precise quantification of prediction uncertainty.

References

CARTER, C. K. and KOHN, R. (1994). On Gibbs sampling for state–space models. *Biometrika, 81, 641–553*.

HASLETT, J. and RAFTERY, A. E. (1989). Space-time modelling with long memory dependence: assessing Ireland's wind power resource. *Applied Statistics, 38, 1–21*.

TONELLATO, S. F. (1997). Bayesian dynamic linear models for spatial time series. *Tech. Rep.*, Università "Ca' Foscari" di Venezia, Italy.

TONELLATO, S. F. (2001). A Multivariate Time Series Model for the Analysis and Prediction of Carbon Monoxide Atmospheric Concentrations. *Applied Statistics, 50, 187–200*.

WEST, M. and HARRISON, J. P. (1997). *Bayesian forecasting and dynamic linear models*. New York: Springer-Verlag.

Acknowledgments: We are very grateful to the Royal Statistical Society and Blackwell Publishers Ltd for their kind permission to reprint the map of Irelend in Fig. 1, which appeared in the paper by Haslett and Raftery (1989). This research has been partially supported by Consiglio Nazionale delle Ricerche, grant n. 99.01675.CT10.

Part III

Data Mining, Information Processing,
and Automation

Neural Budget Networks of Sensorial Data

Massimo Aria[1], Ab Mooijaart[2], and Roberta Siciliano[1]

[1] Dipartimento di Matematica e Statistica,
Università di Napoli Federico II, Italia, via Cintia, I-80126, Napoli
{aria; roberta}@unina.it
[2] Dept. of Psychometrics and Research Methodology,
University of Leiden, The Netherlands, Rapenburg 70 NL-2300 RA, Leiden
mooijaart@fsw.leidenuniv.nl

Abstract. This paper provides a neural network approach based on latent budget model to Sensorial Analysis of large data sets. Formally, consumer marker evaluations of products can be specified as preferences, budgets, or compositional data. For this type of data, unconditional as well as conditional latent budget analysis can be fruitfully considered. Main idea is to capture in few latent budget variables the consumer choices and the products sensorial properties. Main problem of neural network models is identification. A stabilizing algorithm within the Metropolis class is introduced. Applications of real data sets will be finally discussed.

1 The framework

Sensorial analysis is performed in order to find the best suitability between consumers taste and products sensorial properties. It is also used for the product organoleptic characteristics tracking in order to guaranty the production quality. Several other aims might be of interest such as product positioning on competitor market, interaction between sensorial aspects and consumer choices, prospective study for new product design, market evaluation and segmentation using sensorial criteria, specific sensorial characteristics determination for each product, raw material and final product conformity tracking, process or aging modifications.

A brief history about the main approach of sensory analysis, the Descriptive Analysis, is the following. Basically, it began with an *expert approach* for product evaluation in food corporations. In the 1950's this evolved to reduce panels in order to give a qualitative description of products through taste and discussion sessions, called *the Flavor Profile*, (Stone and Sidel, 1985). Two quantitative extensions, QDA (*Quantitative Descriptive Analysis*) and *Spectrum*, have been proposed in the 1970's and are today frequently applied methods. Both can be considered as a tool to measure, quantify and profile sensory properties in products in a precise and reproducible way. The modern descriptive analysis of a given set of products is performed by having a trained panel of assessors/judges: typically 8-12 persons evaluate the products one at a time with respect to a number of sensory properties under controlled and designed conditions. The QDA and Spectrum methods differ in the principles set up for panel training and sensory property vocabulary determination. Finally, another common descriptive technique is *Free Choice*

Profiling where assessors use vocabulary of their own choice.

The idea of calibrating instrumental measurements with sensory information is of major interest for food research and the food industry. In building up sensory predictive models, we face the classical problem of multicollinearity, as these components are closely related. A conventional multiple linear regression approach is not advisable owing to extreme uncertainty about the parameter estimates. Researchers have turned to the biased regression techniques, of which the most common are principal component regression, ridge regression and partial least squares regression (Hoerl and Kennard, 1970; Naes and Martens, 1989). More recently, the approach of *Continuum Regression* was proposed by Stone and Brooks (1990). The continuum regression embraces principal component regression, partial least-squares regression and ordinary least-squares multiple linear regression. This is achieved by the introduction of a parameter, varying in a continuum, in a generalized factor selection criterion.

1.1   Outline of the paper

In *section 2.* the neural budget network based on the latent budget model for sensorial data is defined. In particular, the least-squares estimation is described presenting two special cases, namely conditional and unconditional analysis. Some methods for identifying the model parameters are discussed. *Section 3.* introduces a new approach based on the so-called stabilizing algorithm. This represents an alternative identifiability method which is particularly useful within the neural network framework.

In *section 4.* a real world application of the proposed approach to sensorial data is presented in order to show the interpretation of the model parameter estimates obtained by the neural budget approach. Possible extensions of the proposed algorithm when dealing with longitudinal sensorial data are finally discussed.

2   The latent budget model

The definition. Sensorial data are organized in a matrix $\mathbf{F}$ which rows are the preference rating or ranks given to a certain number of product characteristics. This matrix can be converted into a $(I \times J)$ matrix $\mathbf{P}$ of compositional data dividing each row element by its row margin $\mathbf{P} = \mathbf{D_X}^{-1}\mathbf{F}$. In this way, we define a matrix $\mathbf{P}$ of observed budgets $\mathbf{p_i}$ which can be fitted by latent budget model. This is a reduced-rank probability model to decompose a table of compositional data through a mixture of K positive factorial terms (called *latent budgets*) satisfying restrictions likewise conditional probabilities (de Leeuw & van der Heijden, 1991). In the matrix formulation the model can be written as

$$\mathbf{\Pi} = \mathbf{A}\mathbf{B}^T \tag{1}$$

$$\mathbf{A}\mathbf{1_K} = \mathbf{1_I} \quad \mathbf{1_J}^T\mathbf{B} = \mathbf{1_K}$$

where $\mathbf{\Pi}$ is a $(I \times J)$ matrix of theoretical budgets, $\mathbf{A}$ is a $(I \times K)$ matrix of mixing parameters $\pi_{k|i}$ and $\mathbf{B}$ is a $(J \times K)$ of latent budgets $\pi_{j|k}$.

The estimation. The model parameters can be estimated by weighted least-squares method minimizing the loss function

$$f = SSQ(\mathbf{W}(\mathbf{P} - \mathbf{AB}^T)) \tag{2}$$

This estimation method has no distributional assumptions and is as well a way to generalize two different approaches to latent budget analysis:

- *Conditional Latent Budget Analysis*: $\mathbf{W} = \mathbf{I}$.
  In this case we have a classical latent budget model $\mathbf{AB}^T$ fitted by an ordinary least-squares criterion. In this approach the model parameters can be interpreted as conditional probabilities. Particulary the mixing parameter $\pi_{k|i}$ is the conditional probability of the generic element with the i-th attribute to fall into the k-th latent budget whereas the generic component $\pi_{j|k}$ is the conditional probability of the element in the k-th latent budget to assume the j-th attribute.
- *Unconditional Latent Budget Analysis*: $\mathbf{W} = \mathbf{D_X}^{-1/2}$.
  In this approach the matrix $\mathbf{W}$ is chosen in order to take into account the row frequencies giving a weight system as a measure of different importance of rows. The matrix $\mathbf{F}$ can be written as $\mathbf{F} = \mathbf{X}^T\mathbf{Y}$ where $\mathbf{X}$ and $\mathbf{Y}$ are two matrices in complete and disjunctive coding with dimensions (N x I) and (N x J) respectively. As a result, we have a special case of the weighted version of mixture model presented by Mooijaart et al. (1999) that can be understood as a supervised double-layer neural network with linear constrains. As consequence, the model parameters represent the weights of causal links connecting the nodes of a linear constrained network. In this way, the estimation of LBM becomes an alternative approach to learn the network to the classical back-propagation algorithm.

The identification. A major problem, well known in literature, is that the LBM is not identifiable. In this case, it means that the Weighted Least-Squares estimation method produces identified solution for $\mathbf{\Pi}$ but not for $\mathbf{A}$ and $\mathbf{B}$. The identifiability might seriously complicate the model interpretation because there may be another set of latent budgets that yields the same expected budgets, but with different values for the estimates of the latent components and mixing parameters yielding to a different interpretation. We use the matrix notation to explain the identifiability problem of LBM,

$$\mathbf{\Pi} = \mathbf{AB}^T = \mathbf{AT}^{-1}\mathbf{TB}^T = \mathbf{A}^\star\mathbf{B}^{\star T} \tag{3}$$

where $\mathbf{A}^\star = \mathbf{AT}^{-1}$, $\mathbf{B}^{\star T} = \mathbf{TB}^T$ and $\mathbf{T}$ is a (K x K) matrix with generic element t_{cd}. The row sum of $\mathbf{T}$ is constant equal to $\sum_d^K t_{cd} = 1$ $(c = 1, ..., K)$ to ensure the respect of linear constrains of $\mathbf{A}$ and $\mathbf{B}$.

Some methods have been proposed in order to solve the identifiability problem. We distinguish two main ways. The first one is focused on the identification of the model via *Active Constraints Method* (de Leeuw, van der Heijden, and Verboon, 1990 and Mooijaart, 1999) using a constrained estimation algorithm to find the identified model solution. Based on the geometrical properties of LBM, the second approach lies to searching the matrix **T** that maximizes (*extreme outer solution*) or minimizes (*extreme inner solution*) the distance among latent budgets through the optimization of a criterion (van der Ark, 1999). This is equivalent to choose the **B*** that contains the extreme outer (or inner) latent budgets identified in the space of possible solutions.

3   The Stabilizing Algorithm

In the following, we propose a new algorithm, called *Stabilizing Algorithm*, to identify the outer solution within the van der Ark approach. The idea is to use a method based on the structure of the class of Metropolis algorithm (Metropolis, Rosenbluth, Rosenbluth, Teller and Teller, 1953) to identify the optimal solution choosing the matrix **T**, which maximizes the sum of chi-square distances among the latent budgets, that is

$$f = \min_T (\sum_{q=1}^{Q} \delta_{\chi_q^2})^{-1} \tag{4}$$

where

$$Q = \binom{K}{2} \tag{5}$$

is the combination of K elements taken two at time, and

$$\delta_{\chi^2} = \sqrt{\sum_{j=1}^{J} (b^*_{j|k} - b^*_{j|k'})^2 / p_{+j}} \tag{6}$$

is the chi-square distance between k-th and k'-th latent budget. p_{+j} is the relative marginal frequency of the j-th column of the matrix F.

The algorithm is structured into an external and an *internal routine*. The internal routine consists of the selection of the direction to search the optima of the selected criterium. This search continues exploring the way in a certain number of iterations depending on a tolerance parameter *tol* which decreases in each iteration. The updated matrices A and B are checked to ensure the respect of the linear constrains. In this way, just the appropriate changes are considered to direct the algorithm through the right solution. The *external procedure* guarantees the ability of the algorithm to walk out of the local optima choosing in each iteration a different search direction through the recurrence of the internal procedure.

The steps of the algorithm can be described as follows:

Step 1. (Start external routine)

Set $\mathbf{T}^{(0)} = \mathbf{I_K}$ (start to unidentified solution).

Set **num** $= 1$, **delta$_{num}$** $= constant < 1$ and $\mathbf{r} = 0$;

Compute $\mathbf{A}$ and $\mathbf{B}$ with the (2) following the *unconditional approach*;

Step 2. (Start internal routine)

Set **tol** $= constant < 1$ and **delta** $= constant < 1$;

Step 3.

Compute $\mathbf{A}^{\star(r)} = \mathbf{AT}^{-1(r)}$, $\mathbf{B}^{\star(r)} = \mathbf{T}^{(r)}\mathbf{B}^\mathbf{T}$ and $\mathbf{f}^{(r)}$;

Step 4.

Choose randomly two elements of $\mathbf{T}^{(r)}$ in the same row;

Compute $\mathbf{T}^{(r+1)}$:

- add $+$**tol** to the first row;
- add $-$**tol** to the second row;

compute $\mathbf{A}^{\star(r+1)} = \mathbf{AT}^{-1(r+1)}$ and $\mathbf{B}^{\star(r+1)} = \mathbf{T}^{(r+1)}\mathbf{B}^\mathbf{T}$;

if $\mathbf{A}^{\star(r+1)}$ and $\mathbf{B}^{\star(r+1)}$ do not respect the linear constrains:

- $\mathbf{T}^{(r+1)} = \mathbf{T}^{(r)}$;
- $\mathbf{f}^{(r+1)} = \mathbf{f}^{(r)}$;
- goto step 6;

compute $\mathbf{f}^{(r+1)}$;

tol $=$ **tol** $*$ **delta** and $\mathbf{r} = \mathbf{r} + 1$;

Step 5.

if $\mathbf{f}^{(r+1)} \geq \mathbf{f}^{(r)}$:

$\mathbf{f}^{(r+1)} = \overline{\mathbf{f}^{(r)}}$;

$\mathbf{T}^{(r+1)} = \mathbf{T}^{(r)}$;

Step 6. (End internal routine)

$\mathbf{r} = \mathbf{r} + 1$;

if **tol** ≥ 0.001 goto step 3

else stop internal routine;

Step 7. (End external routine)

num $=$ **num** $*$ **delta$_{num}$**;

go to step 2;

stop when **num** < 0.01.

4   The Application

The data set concerns a sensorial test about 16 different kinds of boiled potatoes (source: http://www.dina.dk/per). The matrix is formed by the scores given by 14 subjects (assessors) on 15 different characteristics about the taste of the potatoes eaten alone or with some sauces. The aim of the analysis is the identification of the casual links existing between the preferences expressed by the experts and the sensorial characteristics of the products through a narrow number of latent budgets. To such aim, Unconditional LBM is employed, which parameters can be interpreted as the weights of a double-layer neural network with linear constrains. In order to select the complexity of the model, we use the dissimilarity index (Clogg and Shihadeh, 1994) which has two main advantages: it does not need any assumption about the distribution of data and it can be easily interpreted because the index is a percentage that expresses the proportion of miss-classified. Two types of analysis can be done, either considering *all the experts* or the subjects separately. Tables 1 and 2 describe the scores, expressed by all the experts for every sensorial characteristic relative to the different products. The mixing parameters allows to describe the characteristics which outline important rules in the expression of the judgment of every subject. For example, in table 1 we can observe that subject 1 gives more attention to the characteristics forming the fourth budget, while for subject 2 the second budget seems to be the most preferred. Table 2 shows the latent components that express the weights associated to every characteristic regarding the different budgets. In this way, returning to subject 1, it is possible to see that the fourth budget, the preferred one, is a budget in which it assumes importance the characteristics relative to the taste of the product with sauces of *mushrooms* and *celery* and the judgments about the *bitter* and the *earthy*. On the other hand, the subject 2 pays more attention on the characteristics about the taste of the product accompanied from sauce of *chestnuts* and the sensorial characteristics *herby* and *toasted*.

Tables 3 and 4 describe the scores expressed by the *subject 1* on the various characteristics respect to every product. In this way it is possible to analyze in details as the subject 1 expresses his preferences and on which characteristics it places more attention in explaining the various judgments. Analyzing the mixing parameters in table 3, it is possible to identify the budget associated to each product, while the latent components in table 4 allow to describe the single budgets. For instance, about the scores expressed for product 1, the budget associated is the second and the relevant characteristics are the taste with *butter*, the *earthy*, *herby* and the *acidity* of the product.

5   Extensions

The proposed methodology can be extended to analyze and to compare sensorial data across various day time periods as well as different product typologies or consumers groups. On this purpose, Parallel Budget Networks for Simultaneous latent budget analysis can be defined for longitudinal analysis of three-way data sets. The estimation algorithm can be extended in straightforward way by estimating in alternated way the matrices A and B so to estimate mixing parameters for the each two-way matrix being held constant the latent components. The result is a common matrix B and a different matrix A associated to each two-way matrix that composes the original data matrix. The model parameters are identified taking into account simultaneously the judgments expressed by the different subjects about the different products and the different sensorial characteristics.

Subjects	Mixing Parameters				
	k=1	k=2	k=3	k=4	indep.
Subjects 1	0.1713	0.2217	0.2922	**0.3148**	1.00
Subjects 2	0.1820	**0.5046**	0.1961	0.1173	1.00
Subjects 3	**0.3786**	0.1684	0.1726	0.2805	1.00
Subjects 4	0.0488	0.2585	0.1829	**0.5098**	1.00
Subjects 5	0.0691	0.2627	0.1955	**0.4727**	1.00
Subjects 6	0.0727	0.2756	0.1232	**0.5285**	1.00
Subjects 7	0.1362	**0.3846**	0.1860	0.2932	1.00
Subjects 8	0.1453	0.2121	0.1081	**0.5345**	1.00
Subjects 9	0.1338	0.1420	**0.4801**	0.2441	1.00
Subjects 10	0.1248	0.2945	**0.4607**	0.0.1199	1.00
Subjects 11	0.0001	0.3657	**0.5147**	0.1196	1.00
Subjects 12	0.0972	**0.4288**	0.0921	0.2883	1.00
Subjects 13	**0.6482**	0.0636	0.2281	0.0601	1.00
Subjects 14	0.0520	0.2375	**0.4222**	0.2883	1.00

Table 1. Mixing parameters estimates of conditional LBM(4) for potatoes data: *all subjects simultaneously.*

Attributes	Latent Components				
	k=1	k=2	k=3	k=4	indep.
Chestnuts	0.0287	**0.1385**	0.0432	0.0505	*0.1136*
Artichokes	**0.1278**	0.0064	0.0331	0.0278	*0.1048*
Mushrooms	0.0084	0.0121	**0.0626**	**0.1490**	*0.0327*
Peanuts	0.0002	0.0000	**0.3297**	0.0002	*0.0444*
Celery	0.0002	0.0000	0.0329	**0.2086**	*0.0460*
Butter	0.0412	0.0397	0.0205	**0.0852**	*0.0470*
Cereals	**0.1060**	**0.2555**	0.0526	0.0338	*0.0748*
Earthy	0.0526	0.0346	0.0061	**0.2512**	*0.0799*
Herby	**0.2673**	**0.2030**	0.0001	0.0000	*0.0839*
Strawy	0.0291	0.0202	0.0457	0.0611	*0.0802*
Toasted	0.0000	**0.0542**	0.0252	0.0081	*0.0240*
Metallic	0.0167	0.0240	0.0220	0.0078	*0.0421*
Sweet	**0.1946**	0.0989	0.1149	0.0049	*0.1190*
Bitter	0.0173	0.0199	**0.1995**	**0.0932**	*0.0669*
Acid	**0.1100**	0.0930	0.0119	0.0184	*0.0407*

Table 2. Latent components estimates of conditional LBM(4) for potatoes data: *all subjects simultaneously.*

Products	Mixing Parameters				
	k=1	**k=2**	**k=3**	**k=4**	*indep.*
Products 1	0.2704	**0.3756**	0.1175	0.2364	1.00
Products 2	0.0095	0.3700	0.0483	**0.5721**	1.00
Products 3	0.0391	**0.4961**	0.4595	0.0053	1.00
Products 4	**0.4124**	0.0451	0.3007	0.2419	1.00
Products 5	**0.5802**	0.0038	0.2320	0.1841	1.00
Products 6	0.0287	0.2136	**0.6053**	0.1523	1.00
Products 7	0.2526	0.2624	0.2272	0.2578	1.00
Products 8	**0.3861**	0.1223	0.2492	0.2424	1.00
Products 9	**0.5075**	0.0012	0.2135	0.2778	1.00
Products 10	0.0162	**0.5658**	0.1134	0.3046	1.00
Products 11	0.0073	**0.6063**	0.3101	0.0763	1.00
Products 12	0.0103	0.0211	0.0335	**0.9352**	1.00
Products 13	0.0272	**0.5235**	0.0442	0.4051	1.00
Products 14	**0.5310**	0.1373	0.2506	0.0811	1.00
Products 15	0.3150	0.0049	**0.6766**	0.0036	1.00
Products 16	0.0784	0.2029	**0.6966**	0.0221	1.00

Table 3. Mixing Parameters estimates of conditional LBM(4) for potatoes data: subject 1.

Attributes	Latent Components				
	k=1	**k=2**	**k=3**	**k=4**	*indep.*
Chestnuts	0.0171	0.0313	**0.2552**	0.0022	*0.0876*
Artichokes	**0.1369**	0.1006	0.0194	**0.1835**	*0.1062*
Mushrooms	0.0064	0.0019	0.0053	**0.1835**	*0.0277*
Peanuts	**0.1476**	0.0348	0.0053	0.0002	*0.0472*
Celery	0.0275	0.0016	0.0056	**0.0918**	*0.0293*
Butter	0.0000	**0.2723**	**0.1402**	0.0027	*0.1060*
Cereals	0.0119	0.0037	0.0506	0.0027	*0.0211*
Earthy	0.0332	**0.1078**	0.0122	0.0000	*0.0368*
Herby	0.0899	**0.1982**	0.0000	**0.1412**	*0.0989*
Strawy	0.0243	0.0018	**0.0270**	0.0023	*0.0173*
Toasted	0.1579	0.0014	0.0000	0.0019	*0.0355*
Metallic	**0.0774**	0.0394	0.0131	**0.0908**	*0.0545*
Sweet	0.0000	0.0000	**0.4616**	**0.2987**	*0.2024*
Bitter	**0.2671**	0.0000	0.0041	0.0001	*0.0678*
Acid	0.0028	**0.2050**	0.0001	**0.0930**	*0.0616*

Table 4. Latent components estimates of conditional LBM(4) for potatoes data: subject 1.

References

AGRESTI, A.(1990) *Categorical data analysis*, Wiley, N.Y.

BROCKHOFF, P.M. (1994) *Statistical Analysis of Sensory Data*. Ph.D. thesis, Dept. of Mathematics and Physics and Center of Food Research, Royal Veterinary and Agricultural University, Copenhagen, Denmark.

BROCKHOFF, P.M., HIRST, D. and NAES, T. (1995). Three way factor methods in sensory analysis. In: *Multivariate statistics for Sensory Data*, Ed. T. Naes and E. Risvik, Elsevier Science Publishers, Amsterdam, The Netherlands.

CLOGG, CLIFFORD C. and EDWARD S. SHIDADEH (1994). *Statistical Models for Ordinal Variables*, Thousand Oaks, CA.: Sage Publications.

DE LEEUW, J., VAN DER HEIJDEN, P.G.M., and VERBOON, P. (1990). A latent time budget model, *Statistica Neerlandica*, 44, 1, 1-21.

DE LEEUW, J., VAN DER HEIJDEN, P.G.M. (1991). Reduced-rank models for contingency tables, *Biometrika*, 78, 229-232.

HOERL, A.E. and KENNARD, R.W. (1970). Ridge regression: biased estimation for nonorthoganal problems, *Technometrics*, 12, 55-67.

METROPOLIS, N., ROSENBLUTH, A., ROSENBLTUH, M., TELLER, A., and TELLER, E. (1953). *Equations of state calculations by fast computing machines*. J Chem Phys, 21:1087-1091

MOOIJAART, A., VAN DER HEIJDEN, P.G.M., VAN DER ARK, L.A. (1999). A least-squares algorithm for a mixture model for compositional data, *Computational Statistics and Data Analysis*.

NAES, T. and MARTENS, H. (1985). Comparison of prediction methods for multicollinear data. *Communications in Statistics - Simulation and Computation*, 14, 545-576.

SICILIANO, R., MOOIJAART, A. (1999). Unconditional Latent Budget Analysis: a Neural Network Approach, in S. Borra, R. Rocci, M. Vichi, M. Schader (Eds.): *Advances in Classification and Data Analysis*, Springer-Verlag, Berlin, 127-136.

STONE, M. and BROOKS, R.J. (1990). Continuum regression: Cross validated sequentially constructed prediction embracing ordinary least squares, partial least squares and principal components regression. *J. R. Statist. Soc. B.* **52** (2),n 237-239.

STONE, H. and SIDEL, J.L. (1985). *Sensory Evaluation Practices*. Academic Press, Orlando.

Acknowledgments: This work has been partially supported by MIUR Funds

Evolutionary Model Selection in Bayesian Neural Networks

Silvia Bozza, Pietro Mantovan, and Rosa A. Schiavo

Dipartimento di Statistica, Università Ca' Foscari di Venezia
Campiello Sant'Agostin 2347–S. Polo, I-30125 Venezia, Italy

Abstract. In this paper, we address the problem of selecting the proper architecture of Bayesian neural networks. Specifically, we propose a variable architecture model where input-to-hidden connections and, therefore, hidden units are selected by using a variant of the Evolutionary Monte Carlo algorithm developed by Liang and Wong (2000). To perform the Bayesian learning of parameters we propose a hybrid Markov chain Monte Carlo algorithm which includes an Evolutionary Monte Carlo step for selecting the architecture. Simulation results show the effectiveness of the proposed approach.

1 Introduction

A crucial problem which arises when dealing with Bayesian neural networks is that of determining their most appropriate size, expressed in terms of number of computational units and/or connections. In fact, too small a network may not be able to learn the sample data, whereas one that is too large may give rise to overfitting phenomena and cause poor "generalization" performance. This implies that the model's performance on out-of-sample data is unsatisfactory (Neal, 1996). Recently, a few solutions have been proposed in the literature to solve this problem such as the use of a geometric prior on the number of hidden units (Müller and Rios Insua, 1998), and a reversible jump algorithm to move between architectures having a different number of hidden units (Rios Insua and Müller, 1998). In this paper we propose the use of an evolutionary approach for selecting input-to-hidden connections and hidden units when all the incoming connections are absent. In particular, we use a variant of the Evolutionary Monte Carlo algorithm developed by Liang and Wong (2000, 2001), which works by simulating a population of samples in parallel where a different temperature is attached to each sample. The population is updated by three genetic operators: selection, crossover and mutation. The neural model with the highest fitness is then used for Bayesian learning of parameters. The most attractive features of genetic algorithms (Mitchell, 1996) and simulated annealing (Kirkpatrick *et al.*, 1983) are thus incorporated into the framework of Markov chain Monte Carlo. Specifically, we propose a hybrid Markov chain Monte Carlo algorithm which consists in a Gibbs-sampling algorithm with Metropolis steps to update the network parameters and an Evolutionary Monte Carlo step to select the architecture. To test the effectiveness of the proposed procedure, we performed experiments on a simulated data set. The results obtained are encouraging and comparable with those of Müller and Rios Insua (1998).

The paper is organized as follows. In Section 2 we introduce our Bayesian neural network model and, in Section 3, we extend it to the variable architecture case. The proposed hybrid Markov chain Monte Carlo algorithm is described in Section 4. Section 5 presents the experimental results and, finally, Section 6 concludes the paper.

2   The Bayesian neural network model

Let us consider the following feed-forward neural network (FFNN) consisting of $L - 1$ input units with an extra "bias" unit x_0 permanently fixed at $+1$, $\mathbf{x} = (x_0, x_1, ..., x_l, ..., x_{L-1})'$, one intermediate layer of M^* hidden units, and a final layer of K output units $y_1, ..., y_k, ..., y_K$:

$$\hat{y}_k = \sum_{j=1}^{M^*} \beta_{kj} \psi \left(\gamma_j' \mathbf{x} \right) + \beta_{k0}, \qquad k = 1, .., K \qquad (1)$$

where the β_{kj}'s represent the connection weights from the hidden unit j to the output unit k, for $j = 1, ..., M^*$ and $k = 1, ..., K$, β_{k0} is the bias term of the output unit k, and the γ_j's are the vectors of connection weights from the input units to the hidden unit j. The function $\psi(\cdot)$ is usually taken to be a non linear and differentiable function such as the logistic activation function $\psi(\eta) = \exp(\eta)/(1 + \exp(\eta))$ (Bishop, 1995).

This neural network model can be analyzed from a Bayesian viewpoint. Specifically, it can be viewed as a nonlinear regression of a response $y_k^{(n)}$ on covariates $\mathbf{x}^{(n)} = (x_0^{(n)}, x_1^{(n)}, ..., x_l^{(n)}, ..., x_{L-1}^{(n)})'$:

$$y_k^{(n)} = \sum_{j=1}^{M^*} \beta_{kj} \psi \left(\gamma_j' \mathbf{x}^{(n)} \right) + \beta_{k0} + \epsilon_k^{(n)}, \qquad (2)$$

where $\epsilon_k^{(n)} \sim \mathcal{N}(0, \sigma^2)$, $n = 1, ..., N$. For the sake of simplicity β_{k0} will be set equal to 0.

Denoting $\boldsymbol{\beta}_k = (\beta_{k1}, ..., \beta_{kM^*})'$ and $\boldsymbol{\gamma} = (\gamma_1', ..., \gamma_{M^*}')'$, the Gaussian conditional distribution of the response $y_k^{(n)}$ is:

$$y_k^{(n)} \mid \boldsymbol{\beta}_k, \boldsymbol{\gamma}, \mathbf{x}^{(n)} \sim \mathcal{N} \left(\sum_{j=1}^{M^*} \beta_{kj} \psi \left(\gamma_j' \mathbf{x}^{(n)} \right), \sigma^2 \right), \qquad \forall n = 1, ..., N. \quad (3)$$

To perform the Bayesian learning of the above model (2), we shall assume the following prior distributions for network weights:

$$\beta_{kj} \sim \mathcal{N}(\mu_\beta, \sigma_\beta^2), \qquad \forall j = 1, ..., M^* \qquad \forall k = 1, ..., K$$
$$\gamma_j \sim \mathcal{N}_L(\boldsymbol{\mu}_\gamma, \mathbf{S}_\gamma), \qquad \forall j = 1, ..., M^*$$

where γ_i and γ_j are stochastically independent $\forall\ i \neq j$, β_{kj} and β_{km} are stochastically independent $\forall\ j \neq m$, and $\mathcal{N}_L(\cdot)$ denotes an L-variate normal distribution .

3   Variable architecture model

In order to extend the model (2) to the variable architecture case, we introduce an $M^* \times L$ matrix $\mathbf{D}$ which identifies the network's architecture by indicating the presence or the absence of input-to-hidden connections and, therefore, hidden units when all the incoming connections are absent. Specifically, the generic element d_{jl} of $\mathbf{D}$ can take on only two possible values 0 or 1. If $d_{jl} = 1$, the input unit l is connected to the hidden unit j, while if $d_{jl} = 0$ no connection exists. We allow the model to select the architecture by introducing the indicator d_{jl}:

$$y_k^{(n)} = \sum_{j=1}^{M^*} \beta_{kj} \psi \left(\sum_{l=0}^{L-1} d_{jl} \gamma_{jl} x_l^{(n)} \right) + \epsilon_k^{(n)}, \tag{4}$$

or, alternatively,

$$y_k^{(n)} = \sum_{j=1}^{M^*} \beta_{kj} \psi \left(\gamma_j' \mathbf{\Delta}_j \mathbf{x}^{(n)} \right) + \epsilon_k^{(n)}, \tag{5}$$

where $\mathbf{\Delta}_j$ is a diagonal matrix whose principal diagonal is given by the j-th row of matrix $\mathbf{D}$, $\mathbf{d}_j$.

Assuming that the rows of matrix $\mathbf{D}$ are stochastically independent random vectors $(\mathbf{d}_i \perp \mathbf{d}_j,\ \forall i \neq j)$ having the same probability distribution, the generic realization $\mathbf{d}_j$ will have probability:

$$p(\mathbf{d}_j) = \frac{1}{2^L} . \tag{6}$$

Let $\mathbf{y} = (y_1, ..., y_K)'$ be the response variables vector, $\boldsymbol{\beta} = \left(\boldsymbol{\beta}_1', ..., \boldsymbol{\beta}_K' \right)'$ the vector of hidden-to-output connection weights and $\mathbf{d} = (\mathbf{d}_1', ..., \mathbf{d}_{M^*}')'$ is obtained by stacking the rows of the matrix $\mathbf{D}$ into a vector, then the probability density function of $\mathbf{y}$ is given by:

$$\mathbf{y} \mid \boldsymbol{\beta}, \boldsymbol{\gamma}, \mathbf{d}, \mathbf{x} \sim \mathcal{N}_K(\boldsymbol{\mu}, \mathbf{S}_y) , \tag{7}$$

where $\boldsymbol{\mu} = (\mu_1, ..., \mu_K)'$ with $\mu_k = \sum_{j=1}^{M^*} \beta_{kj} \psi \left(\gamma_j' \mathbf{\Delta}_j \mathbf{x} \right)$, and $\mathbf{S}_y = diag(\sigma^2)$. Given N observations $\mathbf{y}^{(1)}, ..., \mathbf{y}^{(N)}$, the likelihood function is:

$$\mathcal{L}\left(\mathbf{y}^{(1)}, ..., \mathbf{y}^{(N)} \mid \mathbf{X}, \beta, \gamma, \mathbf{d}\right)$$

$$\propto \prod_{n=1}^{N} \frac{1}{|\mathbf{S}_y|^{1/2}} \exp\left[-\frac{1}{2}\left(\mathbf{y}^{(n)} - \boldsymbol{\mu}^{(n)}\right)'(\mathbf{S}_y)^{-1}\left(\mathbf{y}^{(n)} - \boldsymbol{\mu}^{(n)}\right)\right] \quad (8)$$

where $\mathbf{X} = (\mathbf{x}^{(1)}, ..., \mathbf{x}^{(N)})$.

Assuming that β, γ, $\mathbf{d}$ are stochastically independent, the joint posterior distribution for the model's parameters is

$$p(\beta, \gamma, \mathbf{d} \mid \mathbf{Y}, \mathbf{X}) \propto p(\mathbf{Y} \mid \mathbf{X}, \beta, \gamma, \mathbf{d}) p(\beta, \gamma, \mathbf{d})$$

$$\propto |\mathbf{S}_y|^{-N/2} \exp\left[-\frac{1}{2}\sum_{n=1}^{N}\left(\mathbf{y}^{(n)} - \boldsymbol{\mu}^{(n)}\right)'(\mathbf{S}_y)^{-1}\left(\mathbf{y}^{(n)} - \boldsymbol{\mu}^{(n)}\right)\right]$$

$$\cdot \frac{1}{2^{LM^*}} \left(\sigma_\beta^2\right)^{-KM^*/2} \exp\left\{-\frac{1}{2\sigma_\beta^2}\sum_{k=1}^{K}\sum_{j=1}^{M^*}(\beta_{kj} - \mu_\beta)^2\right\}$$

$$\cdot |\mathbf{S}_\gamma|^{-M^*/2} \exp\left\{-\frac{1}{2}\sum_{j=1}^{M^*}(\gamma_j - \mu_\gamma)'(\mathbf{S}_\gamma)^{-1}(\gamma_j - \mu_\gamma)\right\}, \quad (9)$$

where $\boldsymbol{\mu}^{(n)} = (\mu_1^{(n)}, ..., \mu_K^{(n)})$ with $\mu_k^{(n)} = \sum_{j=1}^{M^*} \beta_{kj}\psi\left(\gamma_j'\Delta_j\mathbf{x}^{(n)}\right)$, and $\mathbf{Y} = \left(\mathbf{y}^{(1)}, ..., \mathbf{y}^{(N)}\right)$.

The joint posterior is rather complicated, thus we can not obtain the marginal posteriors analytically. We need to implement Markov chain Monte Carlo (MCMC) techniques to determine the relevant posterior distributions (Gilks et al., 1996). The hybrid MCMC algorithm we propose in the next section consists in a Gibbs sampling algorithm with Metropolis step to update the network's parameters and an Evolutionary Monte Carlo step to select the architecture.

4   A hybrid Markov chain Monte Carlo algorithm

The MCMC algorithm we propose for inference and prediction with a variable architecture FFNN works as follows.

i) Start with β and γ equal to some initial guess, and an architecture $\mathbf{d}$ with three fully connected hidden units (as in Müller and Rios Insua, 1998).

Compute the full conditional distributions $\pi(\cdot)$ for $\beta, \gamma, \mathbf{d}$ from (9). Until convergence is achieved iterate through steps 2 through 4:

2. Update β by a random walk Metropolis step. Given the current value of β, β^{curr}, generate a proposal $\beta^{prop} \sim g(\beta^{curr})$, where $g(\cdot)$ is a multivariate normal with mean given by the current value of the parameter and variance chosen in order to have a rate of acceptance in the range $[0.15, 0.50]$ (Gilks *et al.*, 1996). Compute

$$\alpha(\beta^{prop}, \beta^{curr}) = min \left[1, \frac{\pi(\beta^{prop} \mid \mathbf{Y}, \mathbf{X}, \mathbf{d}, \gamma)}{\pi(\beta^{curr} \mid \mathbf{Y}, \mathbf{X}, \mathbf{d}, \gamma)} \right],$$

where $\alpha(\beta^{prop}, \beta^{curr})$ represents the acceptance probability. If the candidate is accepted then put β^{curr} equal to β^{prop}.

3. Update γ by a random walk Metropolis step. For each γ_j, $j = 1, ..., M^*$, generate a proposal $\gamma_j^{prop} \sim g(\gamma_j^{prop})$, where $g(\cdot)$ is a multivariate normal with mean given by the current value of the parameter and variance chosen as in step 2. Compute

$$\alpha(\gamma_j^{prop}, \gamma_j^{curr}) = min \left[1, \frac{\pi(\gamma^{prop} \mid \mathbf{Y}, \mathbf{X}, \mathbf{d}, \beta)}{\pi(\gamma^{curr} \mid \mathbf{Y}, \mathbf{X}, \mathbf{d}, \beta)} \right],$$

where $\gamma^{prop} = (\gamma_1, ..., \gamma_{j-1}, \gamma_j^{prop}, \gamma_{j+1}, ..., \gamma_{M^*})$. If the candidate is accepted then put γ_j^{curr} equal to γ_j^{prop}.

4. Update $\mathbf{d}$ by an Evolutionary Monte Carlo step. This step will be described below.

4.1 Model selection by evolutionary Monte Carlo

The selection of network architectures by using genetic algorithms, a class of well-known population-based stochastic search algorithms developed from principles of natural selection (Mitchell, 1996), requires the model's architecture to be given in matrix form. In this way a one-to-one mapping to the corresponding network architecture is established. Since in this study the neural network model is feed-forward and its architecture depends only on input-to-hidden connections as the output units are assumed to be fixed, we shall consider the $M^* \times L$ matrix $\mathbf{D}$ as defined in Section 3. Specifically, each column of the matrix will contain the binary representation of input-to-hidden connections.

In particular, we shall consider an initial population consisting of M^* fully connected layered feed-forward neural networks $\mathbf{D}^1, ..., \mathbf{D}^j, ..., \mathbf{D}^{M^*}$, where the network $\mathbf{D}^j$, $j = 1, ..., M^*$, having h_j hidden units is given by the following matrix:

$$
\mathbf{D}^j =
\begin{array}{c}
\\
h_1 \\
\\
h_j \\
h_{j+1} \\
\\
h_{M^*}
\end{array}
\begin{array}{|cccccc}
x_0 & x_1 & ... & x_l & ... & x_{L-1} \\
\hline
1 & 1 & ... & 1 & ... & 1 \\
... & ... & ... & ... & ... & ... \\
1 & 1 & ... & 1 & ... & 1 \\
0 & 0 & ... & 0 & ... & 0 \\
... & ... & ... & ... & ... & ... \\
0 & 0 & ... & 0 & ... & 0
\end{array}
$$

Each network architecture, specified in matrix form, is converted to a binary string by concatenating the successive rows, thereby yielding a chromosome. The generic chromosome $\mathbf{d}^j$ is thus obtained by stacking the rows of the matrix $\mathbf{D}^j$ into a vector, $\mathbf{d}^j = vec(\mathbf{D}^j)$, $\forall j = 1, ..., M^*$. The population of models will be denoted by $\mathbf{d}_{pop} = vec\left((\mathbf{d}^1, ..., \mathbf{d}^{M^*})'\right)$. A genetic algorithm can then be used to update a population of such models and select the one with the highest fitness function.

We use a variant of the Evolutionary Monte Carlo algorithm introduced by Liang and Wong (2000). According to it, a different temperature t_j is attached to each chromosome $\mathbf{d}^j$, where $t_1 > t_2 > ... > t_{M^*}$. A Boltzmann distribution for each individual $\mathbf{d}^j$ is defined as:

$$
f_j(\mathbf{d}^j) = \frac{1}{Z_j(t_j)} \exp\left\{-H(\mathbf{d}^j)/t_j\right\} ,
$$

where $H(\mathbf{d}^j)$ is the fitness function and $Z_j(t_j) = \sum_{\{\mathbf{d}^j\}} \exp\left\{-H(\mathbf{d}^j)/t_j\right\}$ is the normalizing constant. In particular $H(\mathbf{d}^j)$ is the negative log-full-conditional density of $\mathbf{d}^j$ which is given by:

$$
H(\mathbf{d}^j) = -\log \pi(\mathbf{d}^j \mid \mathbf{Y}, \mathbf{X}, \beta, \gamma) \tag{10}
$$
$$
\propto \left[-\frac{1}{2} \sum_{n=1}^{N} \left(\mathbf{y}^{(n)} - \boldsymbol{\mu}^{(n)}\right)' (\mathbf{S}_y)^{-1} \left(\mathbf{y}^{(n)} - \boldsymbol{\mu}^{(n)}\right) \right].
$$

Then, the Boltzmann distribution of the population of models $\mathbf{d}_{pop}$ is:

$$
f(\mathbf{d}_{pop}) = \prod_{j=1}^{M^*} f_j(\mathbf{d}^j) = \frac{1}{Z(\mathbf{t})} \exp\left\{ -\sum_{j=1}^{M^*} H(\mathbf{d}^j)/t_j \right\} , \tag{11}
$$

where $Z(\mathbf{t}) = \prod_{j=1}^{M^*} Z_j(t_j)$.

The population is updated as follows:

(a) a chromosome pair, $\mathbf{d}^j$ and $\mathbf{d}^i$, for $j \neq i$, is selected with probability p_{cr} from the current population of models according to the *roulette wheel* selection procedure. This consists in first assigning a weight to each chromosome and then selecting it with a probability proportional to that weight. Specifically, each chromosome is assigned a weight proportional to its Boltzmann probability $p(\mathbf{d}^j) = \exp(-H(\mathbf{d}^j)/t_j)/Z$ where Z represents the normalizing constant. Two offsprings $\mathbf{d}^{j,new}$ and $\mathbf{d}^{i,new}$ are generated by recombining the selected $\mathbf{d}^{j,old}$ and $\mathbf{d}^{i,old}$ chromosomes as follows. First q crossover points are drawn uniformly on $\{1,...,LM^*\}$, then $\mathbf{d}^{j,new}$ and $\mathbf{d}^{i,new}$ are constructed by swapping the genes of the two parental chromosomes in correspondence of the crossover points. A new population $\mathbf{d}^{new} = (\mathbf{d}^1,...,\mathbf{d}^{j,new},...,\mathbf{d}^{i,new},...,\mathbf{d}^{M^*})$ is thus proposed;

(b) a chromosome $\mathbf{d}^j$ is randomly selected with probability $1 - p_{cr}$ from the current population and then mutated to a new chromosome $\mathbf{d}^{j,new}$ by flipping some bits also chosen randomly. A new population $\mathbf{d}^{new} = (\mathbf{d}^1,...,\mathbf{d}^{j,new},...,\mathbf{d}^M)$ is thus proposed;

(c) the new population $\mathbf{d}^{new}$ is accepted with probability given by the Metropolis ratio:

$$\alpha(\mathbf{d}^{new}, \mathbf{d}^{old}) = min\left\{1, \frac{f(\mathbf{d}^{new})}{f(\mathbf{d}^{old})} \frac{T(\mathbf{d}^{old} \mid \mathbf{d}^{new})}{T(\mathbf{d}^{new} \mid \mathbf{d}^{old})}\right\}$$

where $\mathbf{d}^{old}$ is the old population, $f(\cdot)$ is the Boltzmann distribution given in (11), and $T(\cdot \mid \cdot)$ represents the transition probability between the old population and the new one. Specifically, the transition probability is given by the probability of selecting the chromosomes and the probability of generating the new ones according to the implemented genetic operator (crossover or mutation).

The Evolutionary Monte Carlo algorithm we propose is summarized as follows. Given an initial population of M^* chromosomes $\mathbf{d}^j$, and the temperatures $t_1 > t_2 > ... > t_{M^*}$, it consists of four steps:

i) Calculate the fitness function $H(\mathbf{d}^j)$ for each chromosome;
ii) Apply the crossover or the mutation operator to the chromosomes with probability p_{cr} and $(1 - p_{cr})$, respectively. A new population is proposed and it is accepted with probability given by the Metropolis rule;
iii) Calculate the fitness function for each new chromosome;
iv) Go to step 2.

5   Experimental results

To evaluate the effectiveness of the proposed approach we carried out experiments on the robot arm benchmark data set (Mackay, 1992). The aim is to learn the mapping from two real-valued inputs representing joint angles to two real-valued outputs representing the position for an imaginary robot arm. The relationship between the variables is:

$$y_1^{(n)} = 2.0\cos\left(x_1^{(n)}\right) + 1.3\cos\left(x_1^{(n)} + x_2^{(n)}\right) + \epsilon_1^{(n)}$$

$$y_2^{(n)} = 2.0\sin\left(x_1^{(n)}\right) + 1.3\sin\left(x_1^{(n)} + x_2^{(n)}\right) + \epsilon_2^{(n)}$$

where $n = 1, ..., 200$ and $\epsilon_k^{(n)} \sim \mathcal{N}(0, 0.05^2)$.

The data were modelled using the variable architecture neural network given in (4) with hyperbolic tangent activation function, *tanh*. We set the maximum of the number of hidden units, the values for the initialization and hyperparameters as in Müller and Rios Insua (1998). In particular we fixed $M^* = 20$, $\mu_\beta = 0$, $\mu_\gamma = 0$, $\sigma_\beta^2 = 10$, $S_\gamma = 0.05 I_L$. The variance of the proposal for the input-to-hidden and the hidden-to-output parameters was set to $\tau_\gamma = 0.09$ and $\tau_\beta = 0.1$, respectively.

The temperatures were equally spaced between 5 and 1. We employed the 1-point crossover and the 2-point mutation operators. The probabilities of applying crossover or mutation were set to 0.7 and 0.3, respectively. The Evolutionary algorithm was iterated for 50 generations.

We ran different simulations with different starting points. Visual assessment of the simulations suggested that all parameters have converged. We then ran a single long chain (10000 iterations), with a burn in of 1000 iterations. The M-H steps showed a rate of acceptance of 30% for the input-to-hidden parameters, 40% for the hidden-to-output parameters, and around 50% for the population proposed. Figures 1 and 2 show the estimated posterior distribution of **d** and the trajectory obtained using the Markov chain, respectively. As one can see, our method selects neural models having 5, 6 and 7 hidden units with probabilities equal to 0.15, 0.20 and 0.12 respectively. These results turn out to be comparable with those obtained by Müller and Rios Insua (1998).

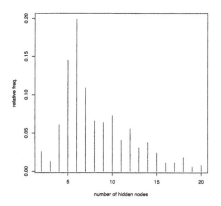

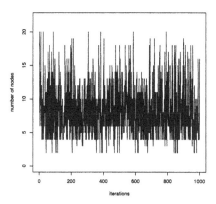

Fig. 1. *Est. post. distr.*   **Fig. 2.** *Markov chain trajectory*

6 Conclusions

In this paper, we proposed a Bayesian neural network model with variable architecture where input-to-hidden connections, and hence hidden units, were selected by using a variant of the Evolutionary Monte Carlo algorithm. The proposed model generalizes the one proposed by Müller and Rios Insua (1998) by assuming that the connections between input units and hidden nodes may vary. This generalization has been made possible by the implementation of the Evolutionary Monte Carlo algorithm. The results obtained on simulated data showed that our method is able to select models with a small number of hidden units.

References

BISHOP, C.M. (1995): *Neural Networks for Pattern Recognition*, Oxford University Press.

GILKS, W.R., RICHARDSON, S. and SPIEGELHALTER, D.J. (1996): *Markov chain Monte Carlo in practice*, Chapman & Hall.

KIRKPATRICK S., GELATT Jr., C.D. and VECCHI, M.P. (1983): Optimization by simulated annealing. *Science*, vol. 220, 671-680.

LIANG, F. and WONG, W.H. (2000): Evolutionary Monte Carlo: Applications to C_p Model Sampling and Change Point Problem. *Statistica Sinica*, vol. 10, 317–342.

LIANG, F. and WONG, W.H. (2001): Real-Parameter Evolutionary Monte Carlo with Applications to Bayesian Mixture Models. *Journal of the American Statistical Association*, vol. 96, 653–666.

MACKAY, D.J.C. (1996): A Practical Bayesian Framework for Backpropagation Networks. *Neural Computation*, vol. 4, 448–472.

MITCHELL, M. (1996): An Introduction to Genetic Algorithms. MIT Press.

MÜLLER, P. and RIOS INSUA, D. (1998): Issues in Bayesian Analysis of Neural Network Models. *Neural Computation* vol. 10, 749–770.

NEAL, R.M. (1996): *Bayesian Learning for Neural Networks.* Lecture Notes in Statistics. Springer.

RIOS INSUA, D. and MÜLLER, P. (1998): Feedforward Neural Networks for Nonparametric Regression. In Dey D.K., Müller, P. and Sinha D. (Eds.) *Practical Nonparametric and Semiparametric Bayesian Statistics.* Springer, 181–194.

Extreme Datamining

V.C. Chavez-Demoulin[1], S.A. Jarvis[2], R. Perera[3],
A.S.A. Roehrl[4], S.W. Schmiedl[4], and M.P. Sondergaard[4]

[1] Department of Mathematics, ETH, Zürich. e-mail: valerie@math.ethz.ch
[2] Department of Computer Science, University of Warwick, UK
[3] Departamento de Estadistica,
    Instituto Tecnológico Autónomo de México
[4] Approximity GmbH, Loreleystr. 5, 94315 Straubing, Germany

Abstract. In recent years there have been a number of developments in the datamining techniques used in the analysis of terrabyte-sized logfiles resulting from Internet-based applications. The information which these datamining techniques provide allow knowledge engineers to rapidly direct business decisions. Current datamining methods however, are generally efficient only in the cases when the information obtained in the logfiles is close to the average. This means that in cases where non-standard logfiles (extreme data) are being studied, these methods provide unrealistic and erroneous results. Non-standard logfiles often have a large bearing on the analysis of web applications, the information which they provide can impact on new or even well established services. In this paper a recent Extreme Value Theory methodology is applied as a unique toolkit to describe, understand and predict the non-standard fluctuations as discovered in real-life Internet-sourced log data.

1 Introduction

With the arrival of the Internet and the ability to store vast amounts of information by the millisecond, comes the need for sophisticated tools to examine and interpret this data. It is probable that extreme events form component parts of this data and, by their nature, hold potentially useful business information. Extreme events on the Internet can give rise to huge economic fallouts and for that reason they can determine the success or failure of many web-based applications. The precise estimation of such event probabilities therefore, is essential for the proper managing of web-based resources (including features such as quality of service, request routing and also security).

Analysis of application logfiles makes it is possible to estimate extreme quantiles and therefore measure the probabilities of rare events. These events have particular impact on the following:

i) Load-testing – It is important to be able to estimate target load levels for web-based applications. Estimations are often sought for the overall growth in the amount of site traffic, the peak load level which can occur within the overall traffic, the numbers of users which might ramp-up to that peak load level and how long that peak load level is expected to last.

ii) Reliability – The optimal design of new web applications require precise estimations of extreme quantiles of both the operating load and the physical properties of the system architecture.

iii) Marketing – Extreme events will effect marketing. Product trends and one off events can have a huge effect on the traffic and the patterns of users. By describing the fluctuations caused by these events and by providing precise estimation of their probabilities, marketing professionals can expose and exploit these events.

iv) Finance – Extreme data analysis is crucial in this area. Until recently volatility has been assumed constant in most models, nevertheless new models suggest that this is wrong. By analysing extreme events it should be possible to determine causes of high volatility (which will cause the extreme events) as well as predicting the time at which these events may occur.

Extreme Value Theory (EVT) offers a model in which these factors can be considered. In a number of cases it has provided useful views on aspects of extreme data and allowed the derivation of associate solutions. See Embrechts, Klüppelberg and Mikosch (1997) for detail of the mathematical theory of EVT and for a discussion of its application to financial and insurance risk management[1].

A flexible model is based on a so–called point process characterisation. The resulting Peaks Over Threshold (POT) method considers exceedances over a threshold u. Mathematical theory (see Davison 2001, Chapter 6) supports the condition of a possibly inhomogeneous Poisson process with intensity λ for the number of exceedances combined with independent excesses over the threshold. Given u, the excesses are treated as a random sample from the generalized Pareto distribution (GPD), with scale parameter σ and shape parameter κ. An advantage of the threshold method over the method of annual maxima is that since each exceedance is associated with a specific event, it is possible to let the scale and shape parameters depend on covariates. For instance, website log data can be of different types; a news website typically may belong to various subclasses (sport, news, finance etc.) and their occurrence shows a non-constant intensity, possibly depending on factors such as hit cycles, exceptional events etc. Logfile sales data from an e-shop like Amazon will typically be a function of product prices, user preferences (clusters), time and other information. Extreme log data may become more or less frequent over time and may become more or less severe. It is also the case that in general, they will show cyclic behaviour.

In this paper we focus on th eapplication of some of the more recent EVT methodology which may be useful in handling the presence of such covariates and the resulting modelling of extremal events.

The natural variability of the exceedances tends to mask any trends or other dependence on time. While variation due to the different covariates such as type of customers, type of logfiles or server locations could be summarized parametrically, changes in time need not have a specific parametric

---

[1] Other related articles can be found at www.math.ethz.ch/finance and www.risklab.ch.

form. In this paper we therefore propose to combine the point process for exceedances with smoothing methods to give a flexible exploratory approach to model changes in large values for logfiles data. In doing so, we closely apply the methodology developed by Chavez-Demoulin (1999), Chavez-Demoulin and Davison (2001) in the environmental context and Chavez-Demoulin and Embrechts (2001) in the financial and insurance context.

A possible model might consist of an inhomogeneous Poisson process for the number of exceedances, with intensity of the form $\lambda(t) = \exp\{x^T\alpha + f(t)\}$ combined with the generalized Pareto distribution for the sizes of exceedances (the excesses) with a parameterisation of the form $\kappa(t) = x^T\beta + g(t)$ and $\log\sigma(t) = x^T\gamma + s(t)$ where α, β and γ are vectors of parameters and f, g and s are smooth functions (see Section 2 for the basic POT notation). The vector of covariates x can also depend on time, in particular taking into account possible discontinuities in λ, κ and σ, due for example to events such as a worldwide Internet crisis (such as that seen in April 2000), or a stock market crash (such as that of March 2000). Other reasons for discontinuous effects include one-off events such as (in a sporting context) the Olympic games or the football world championship.

Problems can arise when statistically identifying the functions g and s. These can be avoided by working with so–called orthogonal parameters. We might use either the re-parameterisation $\{\kappa, \nu(\kappa,\sigma)\}$ such that the parameters κ and ν are orthogonal with respect to the Fisher information metric or the re-parameterisation $\{\zeta(\kappa,\sigma),\sigma\}$ such that the parameters ζ and σ are orthogonal. As κ is hard to estimate and physically more stable than σ, we prefer to use the parameterisation (κ,ν). Following the orthogonalisation technique described in Cox and Reid (1987), we find the parameter $\nu = \sigma(1+\kappa)$ to be orthogonal to κ. Below, we use $\nu(t) = \exp\{x^T\eta + s(t)\}$. Whatever statistical estimation method we use, we are faced with a mixture of a finite dimensional problem (parameters α, β, η) and an infinite dimensional one (functions f, g, s). In order to handle the latter, some smoothness assumptions must typically be made. Estimation algorithms carry a penalty component which is a function of the amount of smoothness required for the functions f, g, s. We could also restrict these functions to finitely parameterized classes of functions; we prefer however to allow the data to define this crucial time dependence and hence provide a general, versatile model. The construction of such a model requires semi-parametric techniques. Having observed $w_1, \ldots, w_n$, we might estimate α, β, η, f, g and s using maximum likelihood estimation based on penalized log-likelihood criteria. A motivation for the use of a procedure based on penalized log-likelihood is that it treats the entire dataset as a single entity. We use a Fisher scoring algorithm which has a clear justification through the penalized log-likelihood and furthermore allows for the incorporation of different smoothing methods.

The paper is organized as follows: In Section 2 the stochastic techniques underlying the threshold (POT) method are reviewed. In Section 3 we apply a new smoothing methodology, providing a new tool for practical extreme value exploration of Internet-style log data. The results are documented.

2   The Threshold Method

The approach based on the threshold method considers a characterisation of all observations which are extreme in the sense of having exceeded a high threshold u. Consider a sequence of independent and identically distributed random variables $Z_1, \ldots, Z_q$ from a distribution $F(z)$ in a wide class of continuous distribution functions. The number of exceedances over the level u has a Poisson distribution with mean λ and conditional on n exceedances, the excesses $W_j = Z_j - u$ are a random sample of size n from the generalized Pareto distribution (GPD)

$$G_{\kappa,\sigma}(w) = \begin{cases} 1 - (1 - \kappa w/\sigma)_+^{1/\kappa}, & \kappa \neq 0, \\ 1 - \exp(-w/\sigma), & \kappa = 0. \end{cases} \tag{1}$$

As $\kappa \to 0$, $G_{\kappa,\sigma}(w)$ tends to the exponential distribution with mean σ. Equation (1) can be used as the basis for a likelihood for σ and κ which is

$$l(\sigma, \kappa) \doteq -n \log \sigma - (1 - 1/\kappa) \sum_{j=1}^{n} \log (1 - \kappa w_j/\sigma)_+ \,,$$

and the Poisson Process log-likelihood in term of λ, σ, κ is then

$$l(\lambda, \sigma, \kappa) \doteq n \log \lambda - \lambda - n \log \sigma - (1 - 1/\kappa) \sum_{j=1}^{n} \log(1 - \kappa w_j/\sigma)_+ \,. \tag{2}$$

In deriving (2), the (asymptotic) independence of the frequency and sizes of the losses over a high threshold u are used. Maximum likelihood estimation of the parameters κ and σ of a generalized Pareto random variable is non–regular in the sense that the score statistic is not asymptotically normal if $\kappa > 1/2$ (Davison (1984a, 1984b), Smith (1985)). The generalized Pareto distribution s yield a practical family for statistical estimation, provided that the threshold is taken sufficiently high.

The choice of the threshold is an important aspects discussed in many papers (see for example Embrechts, Klüppelberg and Mikosch 1997, Smith 1987 and Yang 1978).

The level exceeded on average once in $1/p$ years (or any other relevant time period), called the $1/p$–year return level, is often a quantity of interest. Based on the threshold model it's value is

$$y_{1-p} = u - \frac{\sigma}{\kappa} \left\{ (\lambda/p)^{-\kappa} - 1 \right\}. \tag{3}$$

which may be estimated by replacing σ, κ and λ by their maximum likelihood estimates. Interval estimates may be obtained by the delta method or by a re-parameterisation in terms of $(y_{1-p}, \lambda, \kappa)$, treating κ and λ as nuisance parameters, and solving (3) for σ. This method is also referred to as the profile likelihood approach.

Independence of widely separated extremes seems reasonable in most applications, but they almost always display short–range dependence in which clusters of extremes occur together. Serial dependence will typically imply clustering of large values: for example, high sales of a bestseller book tend to occur together and maxima visits to the sports pages of a news website occur during the Olympic games. In these cases, it seems unrealistic to assume independence within each period (some weeks). In the threshold method, the usual solution is to fit the point process model to cluster maxima, as the use of the GPD for the peak excess in each cluster is justified. An important practical problem is the identification of clusters from data, provided that the cluster size is random and its distribution depends on the local correlation of the Z_i. The identification of clusters has been influenced by earlier work including Leadbetter *et al.* (1983), and is a topic of much current research. Following Davison and Smith (1990), Robinson and Tawn (2000) propose a run approach for both the choice of a suitable high threshold and of a method to identify independent clusters, for more details and alternative estimation procedures see Embrechts, Klüppelberg and Mikosch (1997, Section 8.1).

3   An application

The capability of the extreme value methodology is considered. We present the changing quantitative behaviour in extreme observations above some given threshold. A typical data set might include the number of hits of the k pages of a website, each recorded as an excess above some threshold value u_i, $i = 1, \ldots, k$. One could also consider the e-shop value of sales over a given time period for k different product types, or indeed losses above given retention limits (thresholds). In each case, a measure of the loading risk or risk can be given; the $1/p$ return level is then considered. Objectively, we want to model y_{1-p} as a function of time: i.e. is y_{1-p} constant or changing in time, and if the latter is the case, how does y_{1-p} change with time? We might also consider whether y_{1-p} depend on the page or type of product which the site presents?

As an example, we look at the sales across $k = 4$ types of product of a well-known website (after some preprocessing) over a period of 50 weeks. The points correspond to the values of the excess of sales, that is, the large sales figures exceeding a certain limit minus the threshold. For each product, we chose a non-parametric threshold form such that about 5% of the original data are excesses. Following the methodology developed in Chavez-Demoulin (1999), we fit different models for λ, κ and ν and compare them using tests based on the likelihood ratio statistics. After an extreme value analysis, we obtain the estimated quantile of interest as a function of time for each product type. The figure shows (in straight lines) the 8-weeks return level, that

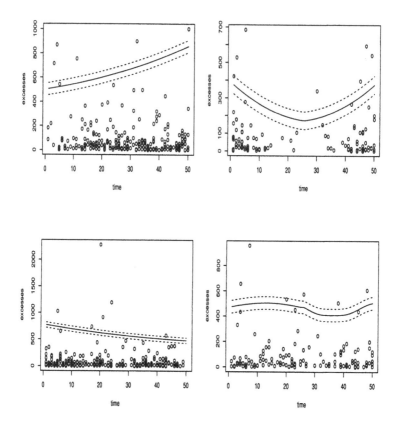

Fig. 1. e-shop data. The points are the values of the excesses of sales (big sales exceeding a certain limit minus the threshold) for four types of product of a well-known e-shop against time (50 weeks). The straight lines are the 8-weeks return levels and their 90% confidence interval (dotted lines).

is the level crossed on average once in 8 weeks. The dotted lines are the corresponding 90%-bootstrap confidence intervals based on the residuals (cf Chavez-Demoulin, 1999 for more discussion of the bootstrap methods use).

There are a number of ways in which these results can be used.

- Marketing - Understanding the extreme values which the datamining identifies allows marketing strategies to highlight and respond to future extreme periods. This might include seasons, campaigns, geography, time-zones and product segments etc.
- Managing Extreme Values - It is important to understand the impact of extreme values on the business. For example, the change in corresponding

productivity of other business areas during a period of extreme sales. This will be beneficial to choosing the right fit between strategy, customer expectations and the capabilities of the organisation.

- Security – By performing multi-scale analysis on a number of different time-frames it is possible to quickly and effectively detect *denial of service attacks* (automatic page requesting at a rate which is designed to crash the server). This analysis is possible both at the packet level and also at a level higher in the protocol stack.

- Future Planning - EVT provides the skilled strategist with a tool for making future assumptions and for deducing the strengths and opportunities of the organisation at some point in time. The identification of previous extreme values allows greater certainty in price positioning and the selection of entire value propositions.

4   Conclusion

Popular web services are now generating huge quantities of log data. The example e-shop application documented in this paper currently produces approximately 5 gigabytes of logfile-data per hour. Results on this scale are difficult to analyse with conventional tools; it is also the case that current datamining methods are generally only efficient in the cases when the information obtained in the logfiles is close to the average. Studying non-standard logfiles (extreme data) can provide important additional information to a business.

A new model for extreme datamining is presented. This is based on the recent extreme value theory methodology. Our motivation for the use of a semi-parametric procedure based on penalized log-likelihood is that it treats the entire dataset as a single entity. This provides a natural approach to the analysis of Internet-sourced log data. We provide a supporting tool-kit based on this model with which a large real-life case study is tested and documented.

The identification of extreme values can have a large bearing on web-based applications. Extreme datamining offers precision to marketing strategies, allows the management of extreme values, provides a mechanism for monitoring security and a basis on which future business plans can be honed.

References

CHAVEZ-DEMOULIN, V. (1999): *Two Problems in Environmental Statistics: Capture-Recapture Analysis and Smooth Extremal models.* Ph.D. thesis. Department of Mathematics, Swiss Federal Institute of Technology, Lausanne.

CHAVEZ-DEMOULIN V. and DAVISON A. C. (2001): Generalized Additive Models for Sample Extremes. *Submitted to Applied Statistics.*

CHAVEZ-DEMOULIN V. and EMBRECHTS P. (2001): Smooth Extremal Models in Finance *Submitted to Journal of Risk and Insurance*

COX, D. R., REID, N. (1987): Parameter orthogonality and approximate conditional inference (with Discussion). *Journal of the Royal Statistical Society, B,* **49**, 1–39.

DAVISON, A. C. (1984a): *A statistical model for contamination due to long-range atmospheric transport of radionuclides.* Ph.D. Thesis. Department of Mathematics, Imperial College of Science and Technology, London.

DAVISON, A. C. (1984b): Modelling excesses over high thresholds, with an application. *Statistical Extremes and Applications.,* Ed. J. Tiago de Oliveira, *461–482.*

DAVISON, A. C. (2001): Statistical Models. Cambridge University Press. *To appear.*

DAVISON, A. C., SMITH, R. L. (1990): Models for exceedances over high thresholds (with Discussion). *Journal of the Royal Statistical Society, B,* **52**, 393–442.

EMBRECHTS, P., KLÜPPELBERG, C. and MIKOSCH, T. (1997): *Modelling Extremal Events for Insurance and Finance.* Berlin: Springer.

GREEN, P. J., SILVERMAN, B. W. (1994): *Non-parametric Regression and Generalized Linear Models: A Roughness Penalty Approach.* Chapman and Hall, London.

GREEN, P. J., YANDELL, B. (1985): Semi-parametric generalized linear models. *Proceedings 2nd International GLIM Conference.* Lancaster, Lecture Notes in Statistics, **32**, 44–55. New York: Springer-Verlag.

LEADBETTER, M.R. (1991): On a basis for 'peaks over threshold' modelling. *Statist. Probab. Letters* **12**, 357–362.

McQUARRIE, A. D. R., TSAI, C.-L. (1998): *Regression and Time Series Model Selection.* Singapore: World Scientific.

ROBINSON, M. E., TAWN, J. A. (2000): Extremal analysis of processes sampled at different frequencies. *Journal of the Royal Statistical Society, B* **62**, 117-136.

SMITH, R. L. (1985): Maximum likelihood estimation in a class of non-regular cases. *Biometrika,* **72**, 67–90.

SMITH, R. L. (1987): Estimating tails of probability distributions. *Annals of Statistics,* **15**, 1174–1207.

YANG, G. L. (1978) Estimation of a biometric function. *Annals of Statistics,* **6**, 112–116.

Information Filtering Based on Modal Symbolic Objects

Francisco de A. T. de Carvalho and Byron L. D. Bezerra

Centro de Informatica - CIn / UFPE,
Av. Prof. Luiz Freire, s/n - Cidade Universitaria,
CEP: 50740-540 Recife - PE, Brazil, {fatc,bldb}@cin.ufpe.br

Abstract. Recommender systems aim to furnish automatically personalized suggestions based on user preferences. These systems use information filtering (IF) techniques to recommend new items by comparing them with a user profile. This paper presents an approach where each user profile is modelled by a set of modal symbolic descriptions, which summarize the information given by the set of items already evaluated by the user. The comparison between a new item and a user profile is accomplished by a new suitable dissimilarity function which takes into account differences in content and position. This new approach is evaluated in comparison with the kNN method, which is an IF technique often used in this kind of system.

1 Introduction

Computer recommender systems aim to automatize the process of recommendation of items. They are information systems that filter in relevant information for a given user based on his profile so as to provide the user with a personalized recommendation of items.

These systems use information filtering techniques. Among these techniques, those related to content based filtering recommend new items by comparing them with a user profile. This profile is usually expressed as a set of items given, directly or indirectly, by the user (e.g., the set of books bought by the user in a online bookstore). The most popular content based filtering technique used in this kind of system is the k Nearest Neighbour (kNN) method, but it presents efficiency problems as the user profile grows.

This paper presents an approach where each user profile is modelled by a set of modal symbolic descriptions, which summarize the information given by the set of items already evaluated by the user. The comparison between an item and a user profile is accomplished by a new suitable dissimilarity function which takes into account differences in content and position.

The new approach presented in this paper is related to symbolic data analysis (SDA). SDA is a new domain in the area of knowledge discovery. It is related to multivariate analysis, pattern recognition and artificial intelligence. SDA provides suitable tools for managing aggregated data described by multi-valued variables, where the entries of a data table are sets of categories, intervals, or probability distributions (more details about SDA can be found in the site http://www.jsda.unina2.it/).

To evaluate this approach our system is asked to furnish some ordered lists of recommendations from a database (MCJones (1997)) consisting of 22.867 users that entered 1.572.965 numeric ratings on a 1 to 5 interval for

638 movies. In order to perform this evaluation, the precision and speed up of the proposed approach was measured in comparison with the kNN method. These measurements are accomplished during the construction of the ordered lists of recommendations to 50 selected users, whose profiles have at least 300 evaluations of movies. Concerning the speed up, our new approach clearly outperforms the kNN method while they present roughly the same precision.

2 Symbolic data

Data analysis has as input a data table where the rows are the descriptions of the items and the columns are the variables. One cell of this data table contains a single quantitative or categorical value.

Sometimes in the real word the information recorded is too complex to be described by usual data-types. That is why different kinds of symbolic variables and symbolic data have been introduced (Bock and Diday (2000)). For example, an interval variable takes, for an item, an interval of its domain, whereas a categorical multi-valued variable takes, for an item, a subset of its domain as value.

In this paper we are mainly concerned with modal symbolic data. Let O_j be a finite set of categories. A *modal variable* y_j with domain O_j defined on a set $E = \{a, b, \ldots\}$ of objects is a multi-state variable where for each object $a \in E$ it is not only given a subset of its domain O_j, but also, for each category m of this subset, a weight $w(m)$ which indicates how relevant m is for a. Formally, $y_j(a) = (S_j(a), q_j(a))$ where $q_j(a)$ is a weight distribution defined on $S_j(a) \subseteq O_j$ such that to each category $m \in S_j(a)$ corresponds a weight $w(m)$. $S_j(a)$ is the support of the measure $q_j(a)$ in the domain O_j.

A symbolic description of an item is a vector whose descriptors are symbolic variables. In our approach, each item (and also the user profile) is described by a vector where in each component there is a weight distribution given by a modal symbolic variable.

3 Recommendation based on symbolic descriptions

Content based filtering aims to suggest items that are similar to those items that the user has liked in the past. Particularly, in the movie domain, the user profile is formed by a list of items (liked or disliked by the user in the past) with their respective grades. The description of each item is a row of a data table whose columns are usual or symbolic variables. Each cell of this data table may have a single category (single valued qualitative nominal or ordinal variable), a set of categories (multi-valued qualitative nominal or ordinal variable) or a text (textual variable).

In this paper, a textual variable, after the application of some Information Retrieval pre-treatment techniques (Baeza-Yates et al (1999)), is managed as a multi-valued qualitative nominal variable.

The item description includes also a special column (single valued ordinal variable) which furnishes the user evaluation of the item expressed by a grade between 1 (the worst evaluation) and 5 (the best evaluation).

Example 1. An example of an item (movie) description is given below:

Variable	Type	Description
Director	Single valued qualitative nominal	Steven Spielberg
Cast	Multi-valued qualitative nominal	{Tom Hanks, David Morse, Bonnie Hunt}
. . .	. . .	. . .
Grade	Single valued qualitative ordinal	5

Table 1. Item (movie) description.

In our approach, the items are recommended according to the following main steps:

1. Construction of the symbolic description of the user profile.
2. Comparison, furnished by a dissimilarity function, between the user profile and a item to be recommended.
3. Generation of a ranked list of items according to their comparison with the user profile.

Step 3 is accomplished in a straightforward way: a list of recommended items for a user is formed by sorting the items according to their dissimilarity with the user profile. Steps 1 and 2 will be described in the next sections.

4 Symbolic description of the user profile

The aim of this step is to construct a suitable representation of the user profile. In this paper, we propose to represent each user profile by a set of modal symbolic descriptions which synthesize the whole information given by the item descriptions belonging to the user profile, taking into account the user evaluation (grade) of each item of his profile.

The construction of the modal symbolic descriptions of the user profile involve two steps: pre-processing and generalization.

4.1 Pre-processing

The aim of this step is to associate with each item a modal symbolic description. This step is necessary in order to construct the set of modal symbolic descriptions used to represent the user profile and in order to compare the user profile with a new item.

Let $x_i = (X_i^1, \ldots, X_i^p)$ be the description of an item i $(i = 1, \ldots, n)$, where $X_i^j \subseteq O_j$, $j = 1, \ldots, p$, is a subset of categories of the domain O_j of the variable y_j. With each category $m \in X_i^j$, we can associate the following weight:

$$w(m) = \begin{cases} \frac{1}{|X_i^j|}, & \text{if } y_j \text{ is single or multi-valued qualitative} \\ \frac{f(m)IDF(m)}{\sum_{m \in x_i^j} f(m)IDF(m)}, & \text{if } y_j \text{ is textual} \end{cases} \tag{1}$$

where $f(m)$ and $IDF(m)$ are, respectively, the frequency and the inverse document frequency (Baeza-Yates et al (1999)) of the category (word) m and $|X_i^j|$ is the cardinality of X_i^j.

The associated modal symbolic description of item i is now $x_i = (X_i^1, \ldots, X_i^p)$ where $X_i^j = (S_j(i), q_j(i))$, $j = 1, \ldots, p$, and $S_j(i)$ is the support of the weight distribution $q_j(i)$.

Example 2. The modal symbolic description of the item (movie) of Example 1 is showed below:

Variable	Description
Director	({Steven Spielberg},{1.0})
Cast	({Tom Hanks, David Morse, Bonnie Hunt}, {0.33, 0.33, 0.33})
...	...
Grade	5

Table 2. Item (movie) modal symbolic description.

In this example, $S_{Cast}(i) = \{$Tom Hanks, David Morse, Bonnie Hunt$\}$ and $q_{Cast}(i) = \{0.33, 0.33, 0.33\}$. Notice that variable Grade is not pre-processed because this variable is used to evaluate the item and not to describe it.

4.2   Generalization

The aim of this step is to construct a suitable symbolic description of the user profile. In the movie domain, the user profile is formed by a list of items (liked or disliked by the user in the past) with their respective grades. In our approach each user profile is formed by a set of sub-profiles. Each sub-profile is modelled by a modal symbolic description which summarizes the whole information given by the set of items already evaluated by the user with the same grade.

Formally, let u_k be the sub-profile of user u which is formed by the set of items which have been evaluated with grade k. Let $y_{u_k} = (Y_{u_k}^1, \ldots, Y_{u_k}^p)$ be the modal symbolic description of the sub-profile u_k, where $Y_{u_k}^j = (S_j(u_k),$

$q_j(u_k))$, with $S_j(u_k)$ being the support of the weight distribution $q_j(u_k)$, $j = 1, \ldots, p$.

If $x_i = (X_i^1, \ldots, X_i^p)$, where $X_i^j = (S_j(i), q_j(i))$ $(j = 1, \ldots, p)$, is the modal symbolic description of the item i belonging to u_k, the support $S_j(u_k)$ of $q_j(u_k)$ is defined as

$$S_j(u_k) = \bigcup_{i \in u_k} S_j(i) \tag{2}$$

Let $m \in S_j(u_k)$ be a category belonging to O_j. Then, the weight $W(m) \in q_j(u_k)$ of the category m is defined as

$$W(m) = \frac{1}{|u_k|} \sum_{i \in u_k} \delta(i, m) \tag{3}$$

where

$$\delta(i, m) = \begin{cases} w(m) \in q_j(i), & \text{if } m \in S_j(i) \\ 0, & \text{otherwise} \end{cases} \quad \text{and } |u_k| \text{ is the cardinality of } u_k.$$

Example 3. Suppose there are only two movies in the user sub-profile u_5. Table 3 shows, for the variable Cast, their corresponding modal symbolic description. Table 4 shows the corresponding modal symbolic description of user sub-profile u_5.

Variable	Movie 1	Movie 2
Cast	({T. Hanks, D. Morse} {0.5, 0.5})	({D. Morse, B. Hunt}, {0.5, 0.5})
. . .	. . .	. . .
Grade	5	5

Table 3. Items (movies) modal symbolic descriptions.

Variable	User sub-profile 5
Cast	({Tom Hanks, David Morse, Bonnie Hunt}, {0.25, 0.50, 0.25})
. . .	. . .
Grade	5

Table 4. User sub-profile u_5 modal symbolic description.

5   Comparison between an item and an user profile

The comparison between an item and an user profile is achieved by a dissimilarity function and takes into account the user sub-profiles. Roughly, an item should be recommended by the system if it is similar to the user sub-profiles u_5 and u_4 and if it is dissimilar to the user sub-profiles u_1 and u_2. It is not clear if an item must be similar or dissimilar to the user sub-profile u_3 and it is why we do not take it into account to achieve the comparison between an item and an user profile. The dissimilarity function accomplishes this comparison first variable wise by taking into account differences in position and content, and then aggregates the partial comparison results.

Let $x = (X^1, \ldots, X^p)$, where $X^j = (S_j(z), q_j(z))$, $j = 1, \ldots, p$, be the modal symbolic description of a new item z and $y_{u_k} = (Y^1_{u_k}, \ldots, Y^p_{u_k})$, where $Y^j_{u_k} = (S_j(u_k), q_j(u_k))$, $j = 1, \ldots, p$, the modal symbolic description of the sub-profile u_k, $k \in \{1, 2, 4, 5\}$. The comparison between the new item z and the user profile u is achieved by the following dissimilarity function:

$$\Phi(z, u) = \frac{1}{4} \left[\frac{\sum_{k \in \{1,2\}} p_k (1 - \phi(x, y_{u_k}))}{\sum_{k \in \{1,2,4,5\}} p_k} + \frac{\sum_{k \in \{4,5\}} p_k \phi(x, y_{u_k})}{\sum_{k \in \{1,2,4,5\}} p_k} \right] \quad (4)$$

For the recommendation of an item, the similarity (dissimilarity) between this item and the user sub-profile u_5 (u_1) should be more relevant than the similarity (dissimilarity) between this item and the user sub-profile u_4 (u_2). To consider this last remark in the formula 4 we introduced a weight p_k, $k \in \{1, 2, 4, 5\}$. In this work we set $p_k = 3$ if $k \in \{1, 5\}$, $p_k = 2$, if $k \in \{2, 4\}$ and $p_k = 0$ if the sub-profile u_k has not been constructed because there is no item in the user profile which has been evaluated with grade k.

The function $\phi(x, y_{u_k})$, $k \in \{1, 2, 4, 5\}$, has two components: a context free component, associated to the sets $S_j(z)$ and $S_j(u_k)$, and a context dependent component, associated to the weight distributions $q_j(z)$ and $q_j(u_k)$.

5.1   Two component dissimilarity function

The two component dissimilarity function ϕ is defined as

$$\phi(x, y_{u_k}) = \frac{1}{p} \sum_{j=1}^{p} [w_{cf} \phi_{cf}(S_j(z), S_j(u_k)) + w_{cd} \phi_{cd}(q_j(z), q_j(u_k))] \quad (5)$$

where ϕ_{cf} measures the differences in position, in the case where the sets $S_j(z)$ and $S_j(u_k)$ are ordered, and ϕ_{cd} measures the differences in content between x and y_{u_k}. The weights w_{cf} and w_{cd} express the relative importance of each component ϕ_{cf} and ϕ_{cd} in the formula 5 and they are such that

$w_{cf} + w_{cd} = 1$, $w_{cf} > 0$ and $w_{cd} > 0$. In this work we considered that a priori ϕ_{cf} and ϕ_{cd} have the same importance and we set $w_{cf} = w_{cd} = 0.5$.

Table 5 expresses the agreement (α and β) and disagreement (γ and δ) between the weight distributions $q_j(z)$ and $q_j(u_k)$:

Item z

		+ (Agreement)	- (Disagreement)
User	+	$\alpha = \sum_{m \in S_j(z) \cap S_j(u_k)} w(m)$	$\gamma = \sum_{m \in \overline{S_j(z)} \cap S_j(u_k)} W(m)$
u		$\beta = \sum_{m \in S_j(z) \cap S_j(u_k)} W(m)$	
	-	$\delta = \sum_{m \in S_j(z) \cap \overline{S_j(u_k)}} w(m)$	

Table 5. Comparison between the weight distributions $q_j(z)$ and $q_j(u_k)$.

The context dependent component ϕ_{cd} is defined as

$$\phi_{cd}(q_j(z), q_j(u_k)) = \frac{1}{2} \left(\frac{\gamma + \delta}{\alpha + \gamma + \delta} + \frac{\gamma + \delta}{\beta + \gamma + \delta} \right) \quad (6)$$

The context free component ϕ_{cf} of ϕ is defined as

$$\phi_{cf}(S_j(z), S_j(u_k)) = \begin{cases} 0, & \text{if } S_j(z) \cap S_j(u_k) = \emptyset. \\ \frac{|(S_j(z) \oplus S_j(u_k)| - |S_j(z)| - |S_j(u_k)|}{|(S_j(z) \oplus S_j(u_k)|}, & \text{otherwise} \end{cases} \quad (7)$$

If the domain O_j of the categorical variable y_j is ordered, let $m_L = min\ S_j(z)$, $m_U = max\ S_j(z)$, $c_L = min\ S_j(u_k)$ and $c_u = max\ S_j(u_k)$. The join (Ichino and Yaguchi (1994)) $S_j(z) \oplus S_j(u_k)$ is defined as

$$S_j(z) \oplus S_j(u_k) = \begin{cases} S_j(z) \cup S_j(u_k), & \text{if the domain } O_j \text{ is non ordered} \\ \{min(m_L, c_L), max(m_U, c_U)\}, & \text{otherwise} \end{cases} \quad (8)$$

The agreement furnished by the system between the item z and the user u is the value of $\Phi(z, u)$.

6   Experimental evaluation

To evaluate this approach our system is asked to furnish some ordered lists of recommendations from a subset of the EachMovie database (McJones (1997)) consisting of 22.867 users that entered 1.572.965 numeric ratings on a 1 to 5 interval for 638 movies. A list of recommended items for a user is formed by sorting the items according to their dissimilarity with the user profile.

In order to perform this evaluation the precision and speed up of the proposed approach in comparison with the kNN method were measured . The prediction accuracy was measured according to Breese criterion (Breese et al (1998)). This criterion measures the utility of a sorted list produced by a recommender system for a particular user. The main advantage of this criterion for real systems is that the estimated utility takes into account the user generally consumes only the first items in the sorted list. The speed was measured by the time spent for producing the list of suggestions in milliseconds.

These measurements are accomplished during the construction of the ordered lists of recommendations to 50 selected users, whose profiles have at least 300 evaluations of movies. From the set of evaluated movies, subsets of cardinal $C \in \{20, 40, 60, 80, 100, 140, 180\}$ were selected randomly for training purposes and the other evaluated movies were used for testing purposes. For a fixed cardinality of the training and test sets, this process was repeated 30 times for each selected user and the average of the accuracy and speed was calculated based on the test set. Finally, for a fixed cardinality of the training and test sets, the average and standard deviation of the accuracy and speed on the 50 selected users was calculated.

For all experiments we considered the kNN method with 11 nearest neighbours. In the case of kNN, a list of recommended items for a user is formed by sorting the items according to their grade furnished by the system. In that case, the grade is furnished in the following way. Let L_u be the training set and T_u the test set associated to the user u. Let $V_z^k \subseteq L_u$ be the set of the k nearest neighbours of $z \in T_u$ according to dissimilarity function Φ (equation 4). Let ω_i be the grade of item $i \in V_z^k$ given by the user u. The grade ω_z of z furnished by the system is calculated as (Breese et al (1998)):

$$\omega_z = \frac{\sum_{i \in V_z^k} \omega_i \Phi(i, z)}{\sum_{i \in V_z^k} \Phi(i, z)} \tag{9}$$

Our aim is to compare the average accuracy and speed furnished by our method with that of the kNN method. To carry out this goal, we will consider the following random variables:

- X_1: the average prediction accuracy (Breese) furnished by our approach.
- X_2: the average prediction accuracy (Breese) furnished by the kNN method.
- X_3: the average speed in milliseconds furnished by our approach.
- X_4: the average speed in milliseconds furnished by the kNN method.

Let μ_i, σ_i, $\overline{X}_i$ and s_i be, respectively, the mean, standard deviation, sample mean and sample standard deviation of the random variables $X_i, i = 1, \ldots, 4$. Our aim is to test the null hypothesis $H_0 : \mu_1 = \mu_2$ and $H_0' : \mu_3 = \mu_4$ against, respectively, the alternative hypothesis $H_1 : \mu_1 < \mu_2$ and $H_1' : \mu_3 < \mu_4$. A suitable hypothesis test is the one side test concerning the difference between two means for the case of two independent samples and homogeneity of variance. The statistical variable of the test has a t-Student distribution with 98 df. Table 6 shows the results of this experiment.

TS	$\overline{X}_1$	s_1	$\overline{X}_2$	s_2	Z_1	Decision	$\overline{X}_3$	s_3	$\overline{X}_4$	s_4	Z_2	Decision
20	0,276	0,160	0,277	0,162	-0,030	Accept	1517	167	1258	195	7,124	Accept
40	0,287	0,154	0,293	0,157	-0,218	Accept	2324	313	2210	358	1,681	Accept
60	0,298	0,165	0,314	0,163	-0,490	Accept	2896	412	2985	472	-0,999	Accept
80	0,311	0,163	0,323	0,168	-0,346	Accept	3264	463	3502	573	-2,279	Reject
100	0,323	0,168	0,341	0,168	-0,540	Accept	3525	510	3951	641	-3,672	Reject
140	0,352	0,180	0,366	0,173	-0,405	Accept	3975	597	4640	809	-4,670	Reject
180	0.386	0.184	0.402	0.179	-0.447	Accept	3569	582	4724	882	-7.728	Reject

Table 6. Comparison between our approach and the kNN method.

In this table, TS means training set size, Z_1 (Z_2) is the observed value of the statistical variable of the test under the null hypothesis H_0 (H_0'). Notice that when TS grows the test set size diminishes. It is the reason why in Table 6, for TS > 140, we observe in both methods a lower average speed.

Table 6 shows that for all training sizes, the average accuracy of kNN method is slightly greater than the one supplied by our approach. Despite that, at the significance level of 5%, we can not reject the hypothesis that there is no difference in accuracy between the two methods.

On the other hand, Table 6 shows that when the training set size grows, at the significance level of 5%, we can reject the hypothesis that there is no difference in average speed between the two methods in favour of the hypothesis that the average speed of our method is smaller than the one of kNN method.

We can conclude saying that concerning the speed up, our new approach clearly outperforms the kNN method when the learning set grows, while they present roughly the same precision.

7 Final comments and conclusions

We have presented a new approach for filtering information in the framework of recommender systems which is related to symbolic data analysis. In our approach, the whole information given by the item descriptions belonging to the user profile is synthesized in a set of modal symbolic descriptions and takes into account the user evaluation (grade) of each item of his profile. To compare a user profile with an item a new dissimilarity measure which takes into consideration differences in content and position was introduced .

The experiments carried out on a subset of the EachMovie database showed the usefulness of this approach. Indeed, concerning the speed up, our new approach clearly outperforms the kNN method when the learning set grows, while they present roughly the same precision.

Among the futures issues of this work, we can detach the application of this approach to other domains beyond movies and the use, as a previous step, of some example selection methods to improve the quality of the symbolic description of the user profile. Finally, another interesting study to be carried out is the analysis of storage gain using our approach.

References

BAEZA-YATES,R. and BERTHIER,R-N. (1999): *Modern Information Retrieval.* Addison-Wesley Pub Co, Boston.

BOCK, H.H and DIDAY,E. (2000): *Analysis of Symbolic Data.* Springer, Heidelberg.

BREESE,J.S.; HECKERMAN, D.; KADIE,C. (1998): Empirical analysis of predictive algorighms for collaborative filtering. In: G. F. Cooper and S. Moral (Eds.): *Proceedings of the 14th Conference on Uncertainty in Artificial Intelligence (UAI-98).* Morgan Kaufmann Publishers, San Francisco, 43–52.

ICHINO, M and YAGUCHI, H. (1994): Generalized Minkowsky Metrics for Mixed Feature Type Data Analysis. *IEEE Transactions on System, Man and Cybernetics, 24, 698–708.*

MCJONES, P. (1997): EachMovie collaborative filtering data set. DEC Systems Research Center. http://www.research.digital.com/SRC/eachmovie/

VERDE, R.; DE CARVALHO, F.A.T; LECHEVALLIER, Y. (2001): A Dynamical Clustering Algorithm for Symbolic Data. In: E. Diday and Y. Lechevallier (Eds.): *Tutorial on Symbolic Data Analysis.* 25th Annual Conference of the Germany Classification Society, Munich (Germany), 59–72.

Acknowledgments: This paper is supported by grants from the joint project Smart-Es (COFECUB-France and CAPES-Brazil) as well as by grants from CNPq-Brazil.

Analyzing Learner Behavior and Performance

Karsten Friesen[1,2] and Hans Schmitz[2]

[1] Lehrstuhl für Wirtschaftsinformatik III,
Universität Mannheim, D-68131 Mannheim, Germany
[2] Lehrstuhl für Allgemeine Betriebswirtschaftslehre und Industrie,
insbesondere Produktionswirtschaft und Controlling
Universität Mannheim, D-68131 Mannheim, Germany

Abstract. This paper presents a method for analyzing learner behavior and performance in a simulation-based educational application. The method was developed for an experiment that has been conducted at the University of Mannheim in the summer term of 2002. The experiment was designed to study the impact of different types of instruction on the improvement of students' knowledge. To collect the appropriate data, an extension of the program was developed that logs the user interactions combined with the current state of the simulation. This enables the instructors to classify different learning strategies by their quality and user type. The experiment was conducted in cooperation with a team of psychologists and was funded by SAP AG.

1 Gathering insight into the learners' behavior

The actual behavior and performance of students using a learning application is of major importance for both instructors and developers. The information about the students' usage of the software indicates whether or not the didactical concepts improve the learning result. Knowing the users' learning strategies helps the developers concentrate their resources on key features of the software application.

There are two questions we are trying to answer. Firstly we want to explore whether or not certain features in a learning program work the way they are expected to work. In a learning program features are implemented to facilitate didactical concepts. Thus the first question is about the features' impact on the learners' behavior.

The second question is what the most effective features of a learning program are. If you can identify them, you can concentrate your development resources on them.

Thus it is sensible to take a close look at the way the learners interact with the software (Bryant, Hunton (2000), p. 134). Also, the relationship between learning behavior and the learning performance has to be examined because effectiveness is the overall goal.

There are two basic alternatives if you want to study the effectiveness of a learning program. A first approach is to simply compare a learning program with conventional training (see McInnes et al. (1995) as an example). The software is treated as a *black box*. To measure the effect of the software one has to compare the knowledge gained using the software with the results of the conventional training. We are using a second approach, that records and analyzes the learners' behavior and performance using the software during the learning process. Therefore the black box is opened up and the learners' interactions with the software become visible. In the following we refer to this scenario as the *white box view*.

2   Characteristics of the learning program

The method for analyzing learner behavior and performance was tested for the first time in an experiment with a learning program, that is designed to help learners to improve their cost accounting knowledge. The authors are members of the development team of this program. The software has been used for two years in undergraduate and graduate courses. Thus, the software itself is not an experimental prototype.

At the moment the learning program contains six learning modules dealing with different aspects of the topic. It takes about one hour on average to work through one of the learning modules. Each learning module consists of different tasks, that are presented as HTML documents, enriched by different multimedia elements. Between three and six tasks form a learning module. Each task is based on its predecessor, so there is a only one main path through a module.

The tasks have to be completed using or manipulating case study data from a model enterprise, that are stored in a database. To view or manipulate case study data, program windows have to be used, triggered by hyperlinks in the HTML documents. Some tasks require the use of cost accounting methods, also provided by the learning program. Therefore the learners have to apply their knowledge in a complex system (Mandl et al. (1994)).

The learners can consult a help function during their self-paced learning with the program. The help function contains explanations for all program functions and a glossary of cost accounting terms.

The software gives an instant feedback to the learners' solution of a task. If a wrong solution is entered by the learner, the learning program offers some clues in order to support the learning process.

What would a white box view look like in this setting? For example, it could be interesting to measure the time needed to complete the different tasks in a learning module. If you combine this information with the number of wrong inputs in every task, you can identify the major difficulties from the learners' point of view. You might also want to count the number of times a certain document was used by the learner, for example a certain help topic. A similar task is to count the number of times the learner uses different program functions.

These short examples about a white box view also show for what kind of learning program the method can be used. One scenario is that there is some kind of navigational task in the software. A second scenario includes the application to a software that provides several functions that have to be

TEST PHASE	DATA COLLECTED
Pre-Test	Preknowledge Socio-demographic data Computer literacy Mathematical skills General learning strategies
Self-paced learning	Activity logs
Post-Test	Increased knowledge
Written examinations	Marks (voluntary)

Table 1. Test structure

combined by the user to solve certain problems. The more options or choices a learning program offers, the more appropriate is the application of the white box view.

3   Collecting the data

A range of data may affect the students' learning strategy. Table 1 shows a rough outline of a sequence of tests which cover both the black box and white box view already mentioned.

In a pre-test phase, which may take place several weeks before the students actually use the program, basic data can be collected by questionnaires. The learners' preknowledge concerning the subjects covered by the program has to be measured by some kind of test. It can be used to determine an indicator for the learning success if one compares the preknowledge with the increased knowledge which is measured by the post-test. The knowledge may be measured by multiple-choice questions with different degrees of difficulty.

Furthermore, besides some relevant socio-demographic data, the information on computer literacy, mathematical skills, and general learning strategies (such as organization, elaboration, repetition, time management, etc.) is determined by standardized tests as described by Richter et al. (2001) and Wild et al. (1992).

The students' first contact with the program occurs in the self-paced learning phase. In this phase they have to complete the tasks of one selected learning module. All of their relevant activities are recorded. These data are explained more closely below and analyzed in section 4. These data provide the white box view already mentioned.

To get this extended view, the learning program needs to be extended by the ability to log the learners' activities. In the majority of cases the students work in simultaneous sessions under the controlled conditions of an experiment—but to ease the collection and administration of the records, we recommend the following client-server setup: the learning program is the logging client, records all the activities and sends them to a central logging server, which can then collect the data of all sessions in realtime. Our solution does not require a permanent connection between the server and the clients. A log entry contains

- a unique student identification key, e. g. the matriculation number
- date and time of the log entry
- client host information, e. g. IP address and host name
- a unique session id generated by the learning program
- working time from the start of the program
- activity information

It is remarkable that, in contrast to common HTTP server logs, we can clearly identify user sessions here, and once we know (through the student id) who actually worked on a certain computer, we may easily assign the log entries to the corresponding data gathered in the pre and post tests. Besides this, the *activity information* is a relatively generic term and not limited to HTML page requests. In our scenarios it may also be a database transaction, an answer to a quiz, data input, the use of the help system, or other activities in the program.

4   The analysis

As a result, there are two tables of information: the first one with the per-student data collected in the pre and post tests, and the other one with per-date/time activity information. The goal is now to condense the latter one to a per-student basis by performing various types of analysis. This allows us to find relations between the performance and strategy data.

In the following, we will introduce some useful methods to discover and check learning strategies. They may be performed by an appropriate spreadsheet application. In our case, Microsoft Excel was used for the tables and its VBA macro language to perform the analyses. However, it shall be noted that some of the analyses below are highly specific to the respective application and may have to be parameterized.

Paths through learning modules: To obtain a first rough overview on how the program is used it seems to make sense to analyze the overall paths between selected activities. As mentioned in section 2, a learning module is made up of a sequence of tasks. A learner may only proceed from one task to the next if he finds the correct answer at the end of the task. If not, he gets a help page and has to try again. By this means, typical *task cycles* are formed, whereas exceptions attract attention more easily, e. g. it should not be possible to skip a task. Table 2 shows an example of a path analysis for our learning program where task cycles can easily be identified. It shows the absolute frequency of activities (denoted by the column headings) depending on a preceding activity (the row headings). If a cell has equal column and row headings (e. g. "start"), this means that the learner reloaded the page,

from/to	start	1	1b	1f	1r	2	2b	2f	2r	3	3b	3f	3r	4	4b	4f	4r
start	67	116	15	8	3	8	5	21	1	8	7	24		9	6	12	7
1	35		55	92	38	2	1			1	3						
1b	27	15	17	91	43												
1f	2	92	97	1													
1r	3	2	8		8	82	1										
2	13				12		47	236	36								
2b	20		1			9		319	38								
2f	6					240	330		3								
2r	2					2	3			76							
3	17					1			8	6	50	452	37				
3b	15	1								17	4	393	36				
3f	8	1								460	400	10					
3r										3	3			76			
4	12												10	4	41	90	35
4b	14												7	1		71	28
4f	1												96	76			
4r	7												2				1

Table 2. Example of a path analysis

whereas an arbitrary number of other activities, which are not relevant for the analysis, may lie in between.

In general, this analysis can be used not only for HTML page requests but also to find characteristic structures in all kinds of user activities.

Number of activity cycles: In almost every computer program users have to perform some sequences of recurring, related activities. Such *activity cycles* may be as aggregate as "edit, save, edit, ..." or HTML page oriented as "1.htm, entering wrong answer, 1wrong.htm, 1.htm, ...". It is clear that activity cycles are very specific to the program being analyzed. The question that we try to answer here is how often an activity or a sequence of activities is to be performed for a given learner during a learning session.

It is up to the analyst to know where to find appropriate sequences, which can be examined. As a simple example, if the learner enters a wrong solution, he usually gets to a page that offers help, like in the introducing example above. It could be useful to count the number of failed attempts for a given task or even for the whole learning module.

A more comprehensive example that is typical for our learning program program mentioned in section 2 is the usage of cost accounting methods. In our case, it made sense to examine the typical sequence of planning functions as it is required by one task in the learning module. The correct sequence consisted of:

- editing the standard price of a raw material
- performing cost planning in order to simulate the cost changes

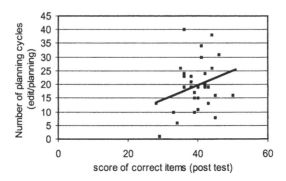

Fig. 1. Number of planning cycles and score in the post-test

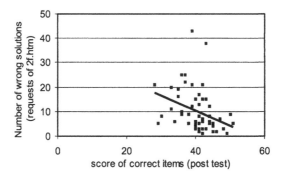

Fig. 2. Number of wrong solutions and score in the post-test

The goal of the task was to approximate the standard price of the raw material by trying to meet a given cost target. One could assume that better students need less cycles. But, comparing the number of the cycles with the number of correct items in the post-test as in fig. 1, it turned out that they needed more. At first glance, this appears to be rather surprising. However, this result only reflects that better students purposefully try to find a correct solution the expected way. The weaker students performed the cost planning procedure more rarely and tried randomly to enter various values at the end of the task, as shown in fig. 2.

Therefore an analysis of the activity cycles can indeed help to check certain behavior patterns if the relevant activities are known. As demonstrated above, it is even possible to check for common mistakes, or the number of breaks or other influences, e. g. usage of the help or general menu functions, the omission of important activities etc.

Reflection time between activities: The difference of the date/time information of two given activities is usually the reflection time. If the start and end activities of a task are defined, one can easily measure the reflection time for this task. In general, better students should accomplish a task in less time.

Approximation strategies: In tasks that require a numerical solution, it may be worthwhile to examine the method used by learners to acquire it. For tasks similar to the example above it makes sense to analyze the duration of the approximation process, the average deviation from the correct solution, how fast or if it was found after a given period of time. Our experiment suggests that this effect can easily be superposed by other influences if the learner does not use the program the expected way.

5 Summary

To use the method described in this article, one needs to have some knowledge of the learning program, ideally the ability to add the appropriate logging instructions to acquire a white box view. The logs are more comprehensive than common HTTP server log entries. The method helps to identify the role of selected features of a learning program program for a given target group. Performing the extensive surveys as mentioned in section 3 leads to a large effort. Our next step is to do a comprehensive analysis of the collected data.

References

BRYANT, S. M. and HUNTON, J. E. (2000): The Use of Technology in the Delivery of Instruction: Implications for Accounting Educators and Education Researchers. *Issues in Accounting Education, 15(1), 129–162*

MANDL, H., GRUBER, H., and RENKL, A. (1994): Knowledge Application in Complex Systems. In: S. Vosniadou, E. De Corte, and H. Mandl (Eds.): *Technology-Based Learning Environments: Psychological and Educational Foundations.* Springer, Heidelberg, 40–47

McINNES, W. M., PYPER, D., VAN DER MEER, R., and WILSON, R. A. (1995): Computer-aided learning in accounting: educational and managerial perspectives. *Accounting Education, 4(4), 319–334*

RICHTER, T., NAUMANN, J., and GROEBEN, N. (2001): Das Inventar zur Computerbildung (INCOBI): Ein Instrument zur Erfassung von Computer Literacy und computerbezogenen Einstellungen bei Studierenden der Geistes- und Sozialwissenschaften. *Psychologie in Erziehung und Unterricht, 2001(48), 1–13*

WILD, K.-P., SCHIEFELE, U., and WINTELER, A. (1992): *LIST. Ein Verfahren zur Erfassung von Lernstrategien im Studium.* Gelbe Reihe: Arbeiten zur Empirischen Pädagogik und Pädagogischen Psychologie, Nr. 20. Neubiberg: Universität der Bundeswehr München, Institut für Erziehungswissenschaft und Pädagogische Psychologie.

An Integration Strategy for Distributed Recommender Services in Legacy Library Systems

Andreas Geyer-Schulz[1], Michael Hahsler[2], Andreas Neumann[1], and Anke Thede[1]

[1] Schroff-Stiftungslehrstuhl Informationsdienste und elektronische Märkte, Universität Karlsruhe (TH), D-76128 Karlsruhe, Germany
[2] Institut für Informationsverarbeitung und Informationswirtschaft, WU-Wien, Augasse 2-6, A-1090 Wien, Austria

Abstract. Scientific library systems are a very promising application area for recommender services. Scientific libraries could easily develop customer-oriented service portals in the style of amazon.com. Students, university teachers and researchers can reduce their transaction cost (i.e. search and evaluation cost of information products). For librarians, the advantage is an improvement of the customer support by recommendations and the additional support in marketing research, product evaluation, and book selection. In this contribution we present a strategy for integrating a behavior-based distributed recommender service in legacy library systems with minimal changes in the legacy systems.

1 Introduction

In this article we present an integration strategy for distributed recommender services in legacy library systems and report about our experiences in actually introducing such a system at the library of the Universität Karlsruhe (TH). This research is motivated by the problem that scientists and students are more and more incapable of efficiently finding relevant literature in conventional database oriented catalog systems. The recent survey of Klatt et al. (2001) about the usage of electronic scientific information in academic education reports that although three quarters of students regard electronic literature research as very important, almost 60 % of them rely on asking classmates for recommendations. Furthermore, the study reveals that approximately a third complains about supply complexity and information overload, and a third reports to have troubles with the evaluation of the quality of electronic literature. Symptomatic of the situation is that for 90 % of the scientists literature research is email consultation with students and colleagues, and two thirds conduct literature research via general internet search engines like google. This reliance on personal networking is even more critical considering the current trend towards mass universities, where many universities are forced to teach a growing number of students with a more or less fixed staff size. For other applications of recommender services in a scientific and educational environment see Geyer-Schulz et al. (2001).

A recommender system like the one of the library of the Universität Karlsruhe (TH) shown in Figures 1 and 2 provides a scalable solution to these prob-

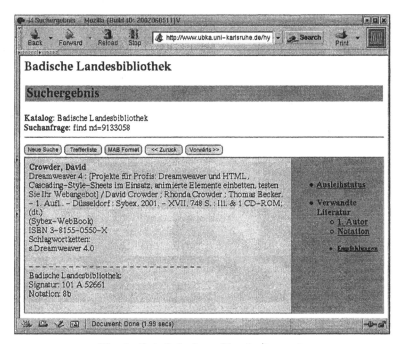

Fig. 1. Detailed view of books/journals

lems, namely more sophisticated access paths to prevent information overload of users, and the opportunity to free some of the time needed for personal networking and recommending literature. Figure 1 shows the detailed inspection page of books and journals including author (Crowder, David), title (Dreamweaver 4), publisher, keywords etc. In the darker bar on the right side the link to recommendations (Empfehlungen) appears only if recommendations can be given (as is here the case). Figure 2, for example, displays the recommendation page for Dreamweaver 4.

In this contribution we concentrate on two topics: In section 2 we describe an integration strategy for recommender services into legacy library systems and the resulting architecture of the system of the library of the Universität Karlsruhe (TH). In section 3 we give a short survey of the stochastic purchase incidence model used to generate recommendations, and discuss its validity in the context of a library. Our sample data stems from the website of the 23 libraries in the south-west of Germany hosted by the library of the Universität Karlsruhe (TH) for the observation period of 2001-01-01 to 2002-07-08. In addition we present implementation details and performance considerations.

2   Integrating recommender services into legacy library systems

The recommender services implemented at the library of the Universität Karlsruhe (TH) are based on a generic architecture whose main idea is de-

414   Geyer-Schulz et al.

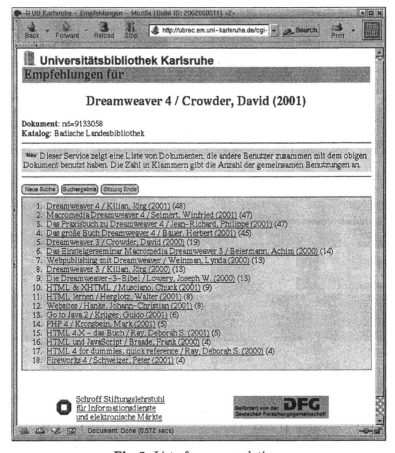

Fig. 2. List of recommendations

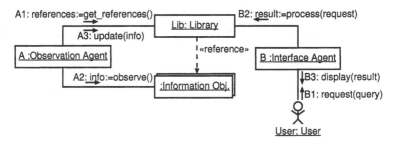

Fig. 3. Collaboration in an agency for libraries with active agents

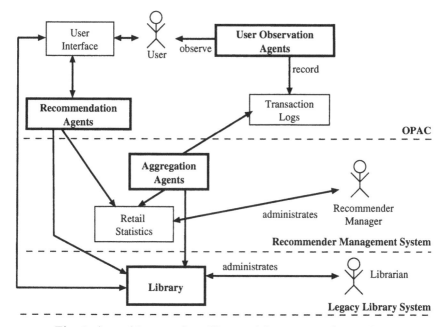

Fig. 4. An architecture for a library with recommender services

scribed by the pattern of a library with active agents (Geyer-Schulz and Hah-sler (2001)). Figure 3 shows this pattern which uses Russell's and Norvig's (1995) agent analysis pattern. In this pattern a library object, an observation agent and an interface agent interact in order to provide automated infor-mation services – in our case recommender services. The environment, which consists of the library, the referenced information objects and the users, is perceived by the agents via their sensors. The independently acting agents gather information and influence their environment by updating information of the virtual library (observation agent) or passing results to users (interface agent). This independence results in a weakening of consistency constraints which improves performance, reduces resource requirements, and simplifies the implementation of the system. The pattern strikes a balance between consistency and performance requirements.

In Figure 4 we show an architecture for recommender services which embeds the pattern of Figure 3 as an agency of software agents which consists of three layers, namely the legacy library system, the recommender management system, and the online public access catalog (OPAC). The legacy library system corresponds to the meta-data management system, the recommender management system to the broker management system, and the OPAC to the business-to-customer interface in the generic version of this architecture, see Geyer-Schulz et al. (2002). The task of the observation agent shown in Figure 3 is split in two parts and handled by the user observation agent and the aggregation agent of Figure 4. The interactions between persons, software agents and information stores is represented by arrows, where the direction indicates who starts an activity. A name near an arrow states the nature of the activity, if the arrow is unnamed, it means a simple request for information.

On the level of the legacy library system information objects are described by the library's traditional MAB format for books and journals which is the meta-data representation. However, because the interface to the other layers of this architecture is quite minimal (it requires only a method for retrieving the meta-data by a unique object key), the recommender management system and the OPAC are almost completely independent from the database technology used in this layer. Because we use a legacy library system for meta-data management, standard interfaces for external applications are not available. The software agents we need are therefore integrated in the web interface of the OPAC. This implies that because of the legacy system the meta-data of an information object is stored in a distributed fashion. Information observation agents update only meta-data stored outside the legacy library system. The distributed storage of information objects allows the integration of agent-based information services which reduce the transaction cost of meta-data management and improve the service quality of the library system. The recommender management system level and the OPAC are more tightly coupled. The recommender service we are describing in this article is based on observed user behavior. In an information market selecting an information object (e.g. following a link) is considered as a purchase of this information object. In the library environment inspection of detailed library entries reveals interest in a certain book or journal. While lending data would have been available, for privacy reasons we have chosen to regard inspection of detailed library entries as purchase equivalent. In addition lending data is currently biased by a high degree of non-availability of books (above 50 %).

The user observation agent is implemented via the session manager of the OPAC. It records market baskets in the form of http-logs with link embedded session IDs. Link embedded session IDs considerably improve the accuracy of session identification. Preprocessing by the user observation agent on the library server includes extraction of http GET requests with session IDs. Preprocessing on the recommendation server implements basic robot detection and filtering as well as session splitting after a break of 15 minutes to take care of public access terminals in the library building and session restarts from bookmarks. The aggregation agent on the recommender management system level computes market-baskets, estimates a consumer behavior model for each book described briefly in section 3, and generates statistics for assessing the quality of the recommender system. The recommendation agent resides on the recommendation server and is implemented as a CGI-script. It generates recommendation pages with the corporate identity of the university library and its associated libraries. The service is accessed via embedded links

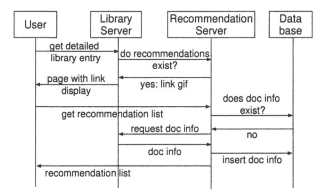

Fig. 5. Message trace

in the references of the OPAC on the library server which are only visible if recommendations are available. Fault tolerance with respect to crashes of the recommendation server is achieved by exploiting the alternate tag mechanism of the html page description language.

Figure 5 describes the message trace triggered by the first user requesting the detailed view of Dreamweaver 4 shown in Figure 1 and then consulting the webpage of the list of recommendations shown in Figure 2. In subsequent requests the generation of the recommendation list does not require access to the library server, because author, title, and year of publication are cached in a database system residing on the recommendation server in order to reduce the load of the library server.

3   The recommender system for the library of the Universität Karlsruhe (TH)

Ehrenberg's (1988) repeat-buying theory describes the frequency distribution of information product co-purchases as following a logarithmic series distribution (LSD) under the assumptions that the share of non-buyers is unspecified, that the purchases of a consumer follows a Poisson distribution, that the distribution of the means of the Poisson distributions of consumers follows a truncated Γ-distribution, and that the market is stationary. This framework with its strong indepence assumptions has been applied to describe the regularities in information product usage in the context of a virtual university for anonymous user groups by Böhm et al. (2002). Recommendations are essentially the outliers with respect to the LSD distribution of a product and its co-purchases. Generating recommendations implies identifying products bought together more often than expected by the stochastic model thus violating the indepence assumptions.

As Figure 6 for the Dreamweaver 4 example shows, this framework holds in a library context, too. The observed frequency distribution $f(x\text{ obs})$ corresponds to the ranking by the number of co-purchases seen in brackets in

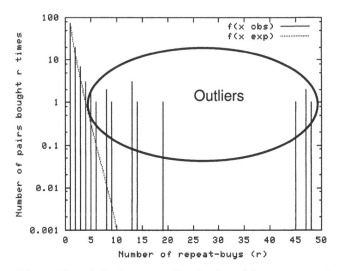

Fig. 6. Plot of the frequency distribution of Dreamweaver 4

	q undef.	no χ^2 (< 3 classes)	Sign. $\alpha = 0.05$	Sign. $\alpha = 0.01$	Not sign.	Σ
	1,533,326	231,310	11,731	20,325	31,862	1,828,554
Σ	(0)	(89,845)	(11,634)	(18,424)	(29,202)	(149,105)

(n) indicates n lists with recommendations

Table 1. Results for observation period 2001-01-01 to 2002-07-08

the recommendation list in Figure 2. More specifically, a LSD model with a robust mean of 1.29 and a parameter $q = 0.386$ passes a χ^2-goodness-of-fit test at $\alpha = 0.01$ ($\chi^2 = 3.915$ which is below 10.828, the critical value at $\alpha = 0.01$).

Table 1 summarizes the statistical results for the sample data of the 23 libraries hosted by the library of the Universität Karlsruhe (TH). From the 15 million books and journals contained in the combined library catalog 1,828,554 documents have been inspected by users together in a session with at least one other document. For 149,105 of these products lists of recommendations with a total of 1,601,656 entries have been generated. As the Dreamweaver 4 example from the Badische Landesbibliothek shows, these recommendations cross catalog boundaries and increase the awareness of users for books in other libraries hosted by the library of the Universität Karlsruhe (TH).

The current implementation allows incremental updates of market baskets with a complexity of $O(n^2)$ in time and space with n the number of items updated. LSD models are estimated only for updated market baskets. This

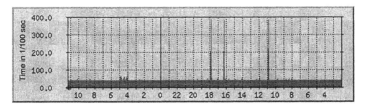

Fig. 7. Duration of HTTP requests over network

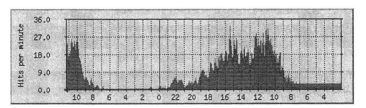

Fig. 8. HTTP requests for CGI exist_recommendations.pl

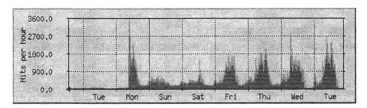

Fig. 9. HTTP requests for CGI get_recommendations.pl

improves the scalability of the algorithm because the upper bound is reduced by a reduction of the update period. Compared with simple association rule algorithms which compute market baskets essentially in the same way, the advantage of this algorithm is that the only parameter for the LSD estimation, the mean, can be computed for updated market baskets only and does not depend on global values like support and confidence. The recommendation server is currently located on a PC with a 1,2 GHz AMD Athlon processor and 1,5 GB main memory, running Mandrake Linux (Kernel Version 2.4.17), the recommender software is implemented in Perl, as database MySQL is used. For operating the system real time monitoring is a requirement. Therefore network traffic and several processor parameters are monitored with the mrtg package (http://people.ee.ethz.ch/~oetiker/webtools/mrtg/).

During the introduction the following installation problems had to be solved: First, the special configuration of firewalls and private LANs at the Universität Karlsruhe (TH) led to the problem that the recommendation server was not accessible to the general public although for the test group inside the firewalls the system worked perfectly. Second, due to sometimes unreliable and partially slow DNS the overall response time for end users varied strongly, see the peaks in Figure 7. Fixes for this problem could be a hardcoded IP number of the recommendation server in the library OPAC and a shift of the router table update routines to off-peak periods. Third, for the implementation of conditional links we encountered the problem that JavaScript exhibited a different behaviour on each tested webbrowser. The current solution, namely to hide an existence test for recommendation lists behind the loading of an image has the drawback that the appearance of the link may not conform to the rest of the webpage and that the existence test must be executed for each detailed view of a document which generates high network traffic and a high load on the external recommendation server (see Figure 8). Although no systematic evaluation of the acceptance of recommendations by end users and experts has been carried out yet due to the recency of the introduction of the system, traffic analysis of recommender usage shows that even without advertising 13,930 recommendation lists have been visited in the period from 07/09–07/31/2002 with an average of 26 visits per hour. A typical load profile is shown in Figure 9.

References

BÖHM, W., GEYER-SCHULZ, A., HAHSLER, M. and JAHN, M. (2002): Repeat-Buying Theory and Its Application for Recommender Services. In: O. Opitz and M. Schwaiger (Eds.): *Exploratory Data Analysis in Empirical Research.* Springer, Heidelberg, 229–239.

EHRENBERG, A.S.C. (1988): *Repeat-Buying: Facts, Theory and Applications.* Charles Griffin & Company Ltd, London.

GEYER-SCHULZ, A. and HAHSLER, M. (2001): Pinboards and Virtual Libraries - Analysis Patterns for Collaboration. Technical Report 1, Institut für Informationsverarbeitung und -wirtschaft, Wirtschaftsuniverität Wien, Augasse 2-6, A-1090 Wien.

GEYER-SCHULZ, A., HAHSLER, M. and JAHN, M. (2001): Educational and Scientific Recommender Systems: Designing the Information Channels of the Virtual University. *Int. Journal of Engineering Education, 17 (2), 153-163.*

GEYER-SCHULZ, A., HAHSLER, M. and JAHN, M. (2002): Recommendations for Virtual Universities from Observed User Behavior. In: W. Gaul and G. Ritter (Eds.): *Classification, Automation, and New Media.* Springer, Heidelberg, 273-280.

KLATT, R., GAVRIILIDIS, K., KLEINSIMLINGHAUS, K. and FELDMANN, M. (2001): Nutzung und Potenziale der innovativen Mediennutzung im Lernalltag der Hochschulen. Sozialforschungsstelle Dortmund, BMBF-Studie, http://www.stefi.de/.

RUSSELL, S. and NORVIG, P. (1995): *Artificial Intelligence: A Modern Approach - The Intelligent Agent Book.* Prentice-Hall, Upper Saddle River.

Acknowledgment: We gratefully acknowledge the funding of the project "Scientific Libraries in Information Markets" by the Deutsche Forschungsgemeinschaft within the scope of the research initiative "V^3D^2" (DFG-SPP 1041).

Comparing Simple Association-Rules and Repeat-Buying Based Recommender Systems in a B2B Environment

Andreas Geyer-Schulz[1], Michael Hahsler[2], and Anke Thede[1]

[1] Schroff-Stiftungslehrstuhl Informationsdienste und elektronische Märkte,
Universität Karlsruhe (TH), D-76128 Karlsruhe, Germany
[2] Institut für Informationsverarbeitung und Informationswirtschaft,
WU-Wien, Augasse 2-6, A-1090 Wien, Austria

Abstract. In this contribution we present a systematic evaluation and comparison of recommender systems based on simple association rules and on repeat-buying theory. Both recommender services are based on the customer purchase histories of a medium-sized B2B-merchant for computer accessories. With the help of product managers an evaluation set for recommendations was generated. With regard to this evaluation set, recommendations produced by both methods are evaluated and several error measures are computed. This provides an empirical test whether frequent item sets or outliers of a stochastic purchase incidence model are suitable concepts for automatically generating recommendations. Furthermore, the loss functions (performance measures) of the two methods are compared and the sensitivity with regard to a misspecification of the model parameters is discussed.

1 Introduction

In the recent past many methods and algorithms have been developed for realising recommender systems and many variants are applied in well known enterprises as book and CD stores (e. g. amazon.com), e-mail and news filtering (e. g. Siemens), and recommendation of related web sites (e. g. alexa.com). But until now the deployment of such systems has been restricted to B2C environments offering recommendations to single persons or customers. In this contribution we examine the performance of two known methods for creating recommendations in a real world B2B environment. One system works with association rules and the other is based on Ehrenberg's repeat-buying theory. We evaluate the results of the methods, compare their performance, and argue based on the evidence of our case study that B2C technologies can be transferred to B2B environments.

Our paper is structured as follows: We first repeat the basics of the two methods, followed by an introduction to the context of the B2B case study, then we present the results of the evaluation, and finally we summarize our findings.

2 Association rules and repeat-buying theory

Association rules were first introduced by Agrawal et al. (1993) and are since then well known in the data mining community. The aim of association rules is to find correlated items from a set of transactions in a database. A typical application is to find associated products from market basket data.

The problem is formalized as follows: Let $I = \{i_1, i_2, \ldots, i_m\}$ be a set of items and D be a set of transactions T with $T \subseteq I$, that is each transaction consists of a set of items. Let k-*itemset* denote an itemset with k elements.

Let $X \subseteq I$ and $Y \subseteq I$ be sets of items. A transaction T is said to contain or satisfy X if $X \subseteq T$. The support of the itemset X is defined as the fraction of transactions containing X: $supp(X) = \frac{|\{T:X \subseteq T\}|}{|D|}$. An itemset is called frequent if its support is above a specified minimum support threshold *minsupp*.

An association rule is an implication of the form $X \Rightarrow Y$ where $X \cap Y = \emptyset$. The support of a rule is defined as the support of the union of the antecedent and the consequent of the rule: $supp(X \Rightarrow Y) = supp(X \cup Y)$ and is a measure for its statistical significance. The confidence of an association rule is defined as $conf(X \Rightarrow Y) = \frac{supp(X \cup Y)}{supp(X)}$ and tells how often in transactions satisfying X also all the items from Y appear. It thus describes the strength of a rule and a minimum confidence threshold *minconf* makes sure that only rules with a minimum strength are considered.

For the comparison with the repeat-buying based recommender system we only need to calculate all frequent 2-itemsets. Normally, though, all frequent k-itemsets have to be calculated. To solve this problem, fast algorithms have been presented in several publications (Agrawal and Srikant (1994), Houtsma and Swami (1995), Brin et al. (1997)). For dense datasets proposals for improved measures, like lift or interest (Bayardo et al. (2000), Aggarwal and Yu (1998)) and conviction (Brin et al. (1997)), have been compared to the support-confidence framework. These are not applicable to our sparse product data, therefore we continue to work within the classical support-confidence framework.

For generating a recommendation list for a given item we need to compute all association rules meeting the given support and confidence thresholds with the corresponding item in the rule's antecedent. The union of all consequents yields the recommendation list. No other assumptions on the nature of the data are made. Association rules can be applied to any kind of data being available in the form of items and transactions.

The theory on the repeat-buying behavior of consumers was introduced by Ehrenberg and his co-workers (Chatfield et al. (1966), Ehrenberg (1988)). The model describes the probability that a consumer buys a product a specified number of times during an observation period by showing that these probabilities follow a negative binomial distribution (NBD). Ehrenberg and other authors empirically showed that this model holds for diverse consumer markets. This model depends on the following basic assumptions:

i) The market is stationary, i.e. the preconditions for buying a product do not change from one evaluation period to another.

ii) The purchases of two items are independent of one another.

Böhm et al. (2001) and Geyer-Schulz and Hahsler (2001) describe how to apply the Logarithmic Series Distribution (LSD), a limiting case of the NBD distribution, to web session data in order to generate recommendations for web sites. In order to translate the model to web applications web sessions are equated with market baskets and viewing a document is interpreted as consuming a product. The LSD distribution $P(r) = \frac{-q^r}{r \ln(1-q)}$, $r \geq 1$ is used to compute the probability that two independent products are used together at the same purchase occasion, in this case a web session. The mean of the LSD distribution is $w = \frac{-q}{(1-q)\ln(1-q)}$ with corresponding variance $\sigma^2 = \frac{w}{1-q} - w^2$. We estimate the LSD distribution for co-purchases of products in a robust manner and compare the resulting distribution with the actually observed values. For outliers with an observed purchase frequency beyond the expected values we can then conclude that the pair of products cannot be independent from one another and must be interrelated. Outliers so identified constitute our recommendations. To make sure that the observed values do indeed follow an LSD-distribution a χ^2-goodness-of-fit test is applied to the observed and the expected values.

3   Case study context and evaluation

The case study was conducted at Secomp[1], a B2B computer accessories wholesale merchant in Germany. It is among the leading catalog marketers of computer accessories in Europe, with approximately 50.000 customers in Germany, 12.500 products and about 200.000 orders per year. At the point of the evaluation of the recommender systems Secomp provided us with anonymous purchase histories from January 1997 until March 2002 with market basket identifications.

For measuring the performance and calculating the loss functions of the recommender systems we need information about which products are actually interrelated and good candidates for recommendations and which are not. For the evaluation scenario we thus calculated all lists of products with possible recommendation candidates from the purchase data (for each product a list of all other products being purchased together during the evaluation period). As evaluation period we chose January 2001 until March 2002 as a compromise because of the high innovation rate in the computer and technical industry and the repeat-buying model's stationary market requirement and in order to minimize the number of outdated products in the evaluated lists.

We randomly selected 200 out of the generated lists and presented them to product managers from Secomp. The product managers had to state for each pair of products whether they are interrelated and suitable for recommendations or not. Examples for interrelated products would be a printer and a parallel printer cable or a set of writable CDs together with labels for CD boxes. The result of the evaluation were a total of 4931 votes, of which

---

[1] http://www.secomp.de

945 where "fit" votes and 3986 were "don't fit" votes. This constitutes our evaluation set against which we tested the recommender systems with various parameter settings.

4 Performance measures

A survey of possible performance measures for recommender systems is presented and discussed in Geyer-Schulz and Hahsler (2002). In the following we denote by a good / bad recommendation a pair classified as interrelated / not interrelated by the product managers. A recommendation is shown / suppressed if the recommender system would / would not propose the product pair for recommendations. The basic performance values are the outcomes of a statistical experiment as shown in the following table:

	good	bad
shown	correct recommendations (a)	type II error (b)
suppressed	type I error (c)	correct rejections (d)

In information retrieval, machine learning, and related fields several combinations of these values have been used as performance measures (Geyer-Schulz and Hahsler (2002)). In statistical terms these combinations constitute application dependent loss functions. We will concentrate on the measures accuracy, precision and f-measure for the following reasons:

- Precision ($prec = \frac{a}{a+b}$, the fraction of the good among the shown recommendations): A retailer offering a recommendation service to his customers will want to be sure that the shown recommendations are helpful to the customer rather than annoying or confusing him. A high precision is thus an important aim for our systems to be applicable also in practice.
- F-measure ($fmea = \frac{2*prec*rec}{prec+rec}$, measure for the quality of the combination of precision and recall ($rec = \frac{a}{a+c}$, fraction of shown recommendations among the good)): The f-measure has to make sure that we find a reasonable combination of precision and recall.
- Accuracy ($acc = \frac{a+d}{a+b+c+d}$, the fraction of correct recommendations and rejections): As the accuracy takes into account both error rates at the same time it constitutes a suitable compromise for our application. The accuracy will be low at extreme values of precision or recall and indicates an acceptable parameter choice at its maximum value.

5 Results

The performance results of the two algorithms where obtained by executing the algorithms on a grid over promising parameter regions and comparing the results with the evaluation set. This yields the number of correct decisions by the algorithms and the number of erroneous results as compared to the assessment of the product managers from which we calculate the three performance measures introduced above.

Repeat-buying based recommender system The algorithm of the repeat-buying based recommender system takes as only parameter the threshold that influences the expected type II error rate. We varied this threshold to find the one with the maximum accuracy and got the results depicted in the following table where we can see that the algorithm reaches a maximum accuracy at a threshold of 0.01:

Threshold	0.005	0.01	0.02	0.03	0.04	0.05	0.06	0.07	0.08	0.09	0.1
Precision	0.690	0.675	0.646	0.636	0.602	0.594	0.587	0.583	0.571	0.562	0.557
F-measure	0.284	0.301	0.309	0.317	0.318	0.324	0.333	0.338	0.339	0.340	0.345
Accuracy	0.827	0.828	0.826	0.826	0.822	0.822	0.822	0.821	0.820	0.819	0.818

Association rule based recommender system For running the association rule algorithm the specification of the two parameters minimum support and minimum confidence is necessary. As these values influence the generation of rules and therefore the output of the algorithm we had to perform a grid search to find the optimal support/confidence threshold combination yielding the highest accuracy. The result of the grid search can be found in table 1 , for each combination of support and confidence threshold the results for precision, f-measure and accuracy are given.

To get a better overview over the development of the three measures three-dimensional graphs are shown in figure 1 for the accuracy and in figure 2 for the precision and f-measure. The left graph in figure 1 shows the accuracy values for all combinations from the grid whereas the graph on the right is the detailed view of the top two layers in the left graph. The detailed view shows how the accuracy changes around the maximum and how the accuracy drops when changing one of the thresholds.

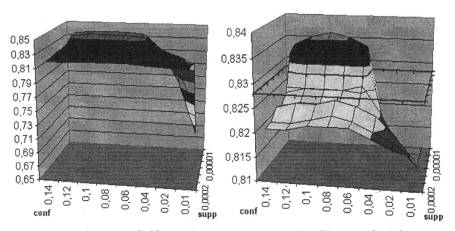

Fig. 1. Accuracy (left) and detailed accuracy with LSD plane (right)

sup\ conf		0.01	0.02	0.04	0.06	0.08	0.10	0.12	0.14
0.00001	prec	0.314	0.397	0.507	0.632	0.670	0.707	0.736	0.754
	f-me	0.407	0.445	0.426	0.411	0.384	0.365	0.326	0.301
	accu	0.676	0.758	0.810	0.833	0.835	0.836	0.835	0.833
0.00002	prec	0.344	0.439	0.538	0.660	0.698	0.727	0.755	0.761
	f-me	0.392	0.425	0.398	0.386	0.357	0.338	0.319	0.290
	accu	0.729	0.786	0.817	0.834	0.835	0.835	0.835	0.832
0.00008	prec	0.460	0.532	0.608	0.687	0.714	0.733	0.741	0.744
	f-me	0.297	0.286	0.268	0.266	0.245	0.235	0.226	0.211
	accu	0.801	0.813	0.820	0.826	0.825	0.825	0.825	0.824
0.00010	prec	0.489	0.559	0.623	0.673	0.705	0.727	0.732	0.736
	f-me	0.264	0.260	0.242	0.237	0.221	0.212	0.205	0.194
	accu	0.807	0.815	0.820	0.823	0.823	0.823	0.823	0.822
0.00012	prec	0.529	0.599	0.674	0.724	0.763	0.784	0.782	0.792
	f-me	0.239	0.240	0.222	0.220	0.212	0.201	0.193	0.185
	accu	0.812	0.818	0.822	0.824	0.825	0.824	0.824	0.823
0.00018	prec	0.598	0.650	0.720	0.780	0.830	0.832	0.833	0.843
	f-me	0.185	0.185	0.177	0.173	0.167	0.161	0.154	0.144
	accu	0.815	0.818	0.820	0.822	0.823	0.822	0.821	0.821
0.00020	prec	0.636	0.671	0.730	0.795	0.842	0.844	0.839	0.849
	f-me	0.179	0.180	0.171	0.168	0.163	0.156	0.151	0.141
	accu	0.817	0.818	0.820	0.822	0.822	0.822	0.821	0.821

marked: better results than repeat-buying

Table 1. Grid search for finding optimal threshold combination

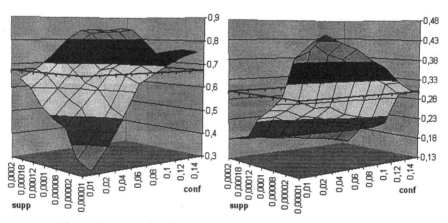

Fig. 2. Precision (left) and f-measure (right) with LSD planes

Comparison of the performance measures For the comparison of the performances we inserted into figure 1 and 2 the corresponding value of the best LSD model with a threshold of 0.01 as a plane represented by a polygone with strokes. Comparing the outcomes of the evaluations of the two algorithms we find that:

i) When fitting the parameters of the algorithms to the validation sample the association rule algorithm reaches higher performance results than the repeat-buying based algorithm.

ii) For only 6 of the 56 combinations of support/confidence thresholds the association rule algorithm yields an overall better result than the repeat-buying algorithm (see marked cells in association rule result table). Due to the irregular spacing of the grid we hesitate to draw any inferences from that.

iii) A misspecification of one or both thresholds of the association rule algorithm makes the quality of the results decrease rapidly. The thresholds depend on the composition of the data and there exists no method to automatically infer an optimal threshold combination for a given system other than such an evaluation. Moreover, as the composition of the market baskets changes over time the optimal combination can vary which means that evaluations have to be repeated on a regular basis to keep the quality level of the recommender system.

iv) The threshold for the repeat-buying algorithm seems to depend less on the specific data and seems to be more robust, and the risk of a parameter misspecification is lower. However, this needs additional validation.

5.1 Comparison with B2C evaluation results

In Geyer-Schulz and Hahsler (2002) a comparison between simple association rules and repeat-buying based recommendations is presented for an internet information broker, a B2C application. This study is based on a set of 3774 different items and 25.522 transactions. Varying thresholds were used for the two algorithms. The results compared to the ones reported in this paper can be seen in the following table:

	accuracy	precision	recall	supp/conf thres.	LSD thres.
B2C	> 0.7	0.6 − 0.9	0.4 − 0.1	0.00005/0.1	0.5
B2B	> 0.8	0.5 − 0.7	0.4 − 0.1	0.00001/0.1	0.1

The results for accuracy, precision and recall are given as well as the respective thresholds yielding the highest accuracy. Comparing these values to the results of the present evaluation we can conclude:

i) Yielding an accuracy of > 0.8 for both systems there is strong evidence that these systems can be applied to B2B environments, as well.

ii) The precision in the B2B system with 0.5 – 0.8 is lower compared to the B2C results. This is probably due to the fact that in B2B we work with cumulative market baskets because wholesalers aggregate the orders of retailers which in turn aggregate the orders of their customers.

iii) The optimal support thresholds differ in the two applications which is due to the different compositions of the transactions and sparsities of the data.

iv) The optimal repeat-buying threshold for the B2B application is lower which is probably again due to the cumulative market baskets.

v) Both algorithms yield very similar peak results in both cases. Both of them are suitable for either B2C or B2B environments.

6   Conclusions

In this paper we presented an application of two known recommender systems, based on association rules and on the repeat-buying theory, to data in a B2B environment together with a performance evaluation and a comparison of the respective results. From the results we can conclude that the application of recommender methodologies known from the B2C environment can be transferred without problems to the B2B environment with similar performance. We also found out that in this ex-post evaluation study association rules yield better peak results than the repeat-buying based recommender system. This means that association rules can be better parameterized to evaluation sets ex-post. However, no method exists for determining this parameters a priori. The repeat-buying based recommender system seems more robust to data changes and it is probably easier to specify a well performing parameter a priori. The overall performance of the two methods except for grave parameter misspecifications of the association rule method is still very similar.

For future work we would like to examine how exactly the two methods perform over time and we plan to repeat the evaluation and the performance comparison for several observation periods.

References

CHATFIELD, C. and EHRENBERG, A. S. C. and GOODHARDT, G. J. (1966): Progress on simplified model of stationary purchasing behaviour. *Journal of the Royal Statistical Society, Series A, 129(3)* 317–367.

EHRENBERG, A. S. C. (1988): *Repeat-Buying: Facts, Theory and Application.* Charles Griffin & Company Ltd., London.

AGRAWAL, R. and IMIELINSKI, T. and SWAMI, A. (1993): Mining Association Rules between Sets of Items in Large Databases. In: P. Buneman and S. Jajodia (Eds.): *Proceedings of the ACM SIGMOD International Conference on Management of Data.* ACM Press.

AGRAWAL, R. and SRIKANT, R. (1994): Fast algorithms for mining association rules. In: J. B. Bocca and M. Jarke and C. Zaniolo (Eds.): *Proceedings of the 20th international Conference on very large databases.* 487–499.

HOUTSMA, M. and SWAMI, A. (1995): Set-oriented mining for association rules in relational databases. In: P. S. Yu and A. L. P. Chen (Eds.): *Proceedings of the 11th International Conference on Data Engineering.* IEEE Computer Society, 25–33.

BRIN, S. and MOTWANI, R. and ULLMAN, J. and TSUR, S. (1997): Dynamic itemset counting and implication rules for market basket data. In: J. M. Peckman (Ed.): *Proceedings of the ACM SIGMOD International Conference on Management of Data.* ACM Press, 255–264.

AGGARWAL, C. C. and YU, P. S. (1998): A new framework for itemset generation. In: A. Mendelson and J. Paredaens (Eds.): *PODS 98, Symposium on Principles of Database Systems.* ACM press, 18–24.

BAYARDO, R. and AGRAWAL, R. and GUNOPULOS, D. (2000): Constraint-based rule mining in large, dense databases. *Data Mining and Knowledge Discovery, 4 (2/3), 217–240.*

BOEHM, W. and GEYER-SCHULZ, A. and HAHSLER, M. and JAHN, M. (2001): Repeat-buying theory and its applications for recommender services. In: *Proceedings of the 25th Annual Conference of the GfKl.* Springer-Verlag, Heidelberg.

GEYER-SCHULZ, A. and HAHSLER, M. (2001): A customer purchase incidence model applied to recommender systems. In: *ACM WebKDD 2001 Workshop on Mining Web Log Data Across All Consumer Touchpoints.* Springer-Verlag.

GEYER-SCHULZ, A. and HAHSLER, M. (2002): Evaluation of Recommender Algorithms for an Internet Information Broker based on Simple Association Rules and on Repeat-Buying Theory. In: *Proceedings of the WebKDD 2002: Web Mining for Usage Patterns and User Profiles.* Springer-Verlag.

Acknowledgments: We gratefully acknowledge the support of the Schroff Stiftung and of the Secomp GmbH, Ettlingen, Germany, especially the extensive help of Mr. Taraba and Mr. Vey.

Students' Preferences Related to Web Based E-Learning: Results of a Survey

Marc Göcks and Daniel Baier

Institute of Business Administration and Economics,
Brandenburg University of Technology Cottbus, Postbox 101344,
D-03013 Cottbus, Germany

Abstract. The importance of e-learning is more and more emphasized in the professional, school and college based education. So, e.g., at many universities, e-learning modules are currently developed for controlled as well as self-study processes. In order to investigate the students' acceptance of such modules, a survey on their preferences was conducted. Selected results of this survey – with a focus on gender-specific differences – are presented.

1 Introduction

This survey is based on a research project named eL-IT (e-learning modules for information, communication, and media technology courses) which is funded by the German BMBF (Federal Ministry of Education and Research) and focusses on information technology content and environment generation which can be used by students in a controlled as well as a self-study process. To accomplish this, it is important to design a learning environment which meets best the students' and the teachers' requirements. This paper discusses the efforts of eL-IT to analyze the students' preferences by conducting a survey. Contrary to former surveys a prototype was used for demonstrating the advantages of e-learning scenarios over traditional learning scenarios. Additionally, course of study and gender specific differences in the students' preference structures were analyzed. In section 2 requirements and results from former surveys are discussed. Section 3 presents a short outline of the eL-IT research project, section 4 selected results of our survey.

2 E-learning: terms and requests

E-learning is a fast growing market for professional, school and college based education programs which has yet a strong potential to grow (Berlecon Research (2001), Lehner (2001)). Unfortunately, a unifying technological definition of e-learning is missing. The different attempts go from computer based training (CBT) programs over web based training (WBT) programs to traditional distance learning supported by new media (for an overview on available programs see, e.g., Neibecker and Breiter (1999)). E-Learning is often used as a generic term for internet-based teaching and learning programs (Kerres (2001)). In this paper we shall attempt to use the following minimum list of requirements for an e-learning environment which has been compiled from the available literature (see, e.g., Bruns and Gajewski (1999), Schulmeister (1999), Steinmetz (1999), Bauer and Philippi (2001)):

- The educational content taught is enhanced by multimedia elements like audio, video, graphics, and animations.
- Communication channels between the students are implemented by, e.g., creating chat rooms, discussion rooms, or boards.
- Consulting of a teletutor via e-mail or video conferencing is possible.
- The e-learning modules are parts of a network which integrates a huge variety of information resources.
- The student himself and his ability to receive individually tailored information is the center of interest.

Additionally, various surveys have been conducted in a more market-oriented fashion in order to analyze the learners' preferences, certainly one of the most important success factors for the acceptance (e.g. Neibecker (2000), Frank (2001), Gaul and Schmidt-Thieme (2001), Ahuja and Rödder (2002)). So, e.g., Gaul and Schmidt-Thieme (2001) interviewed students and discovered that their preferences were – independently from demographic variables or from personal experiences – quite heterogenous. A majority of the interviewed students preferred more traditional learning environments, but most of them were open for new experiences. Frank (2001) – on the other hand – found out that most of the students wished to work independently and flexibly and that they wanted to have the opportunity to consult a teletutor for learning feedbacks. Neibecker (2000) concluded from his survey that design characteristics, e.g., navigation and service, were very important for the acceptance of the e-learning environments.

Moreover, there is an intensive discussion about gender specific differences. This survey was to investigate not the reasons for gender related differences, e.g., social or cultural influences (Winkler (1999)) but to show rather the specific differences in online-behavior. Women are still less using the internet, because they have less access possibilities than men and behave more hesitating in view of the internet, developed mainly by men. Men use the internet more playful, whereas women prefer a target orientated usage of the internet (e.g. Dorer (2001)). Women prefer entertaining medium offers and refer these more strongly than men to their own life situation (Yom (1997)). Furthermore, there are differences related to online-communication so, e.g., women tend to prefer chat rooms on a higher level and men tend to favor discussion rooms (Hochholzer (2000)). Here, the BMBF is heavily engaged in the development of gender specific study programs in education, research and new media. Following this important research focus, this survey also wants to prove potential gender related differences concerning online-behavior and online-communication.

3   Research project

The research project eL-IT is supported by the initiative "New Media in Education" of the Federal Ministry of Education and Research (BMBF). In addition to eL-IT, a total of 99 projects is supported until the end of 2003. One of the main goals of the initiative – among others – is to consider gender related differences in the development of new learning environments.

Partners of eL-IT are BTU Cottbus, TU Berlin, TU Dresden, and University of Kassel with seven participating chairs, where BTU Cottbus, with its four chairs, provides the major parts. Each chair is responsible for the development of two e-learning modules. The total of fourteen modules not only supports the present lectures but also creates a virtual study program for industrial engineering as well as information and media technology. Our chair is responsible for the development of an e-commerce and a multimedia law module. The two main target groups for these modules are students of industrial engineering courses and students of information and media technology (IMT) courses at the BTU Cottbus.

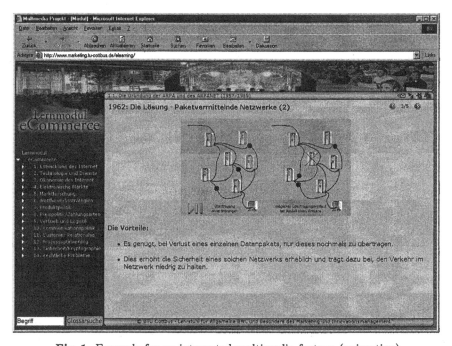

Fig. 1. Example for an integrated multimedia feature (animation)

Similar to live lectures at the university, the module contents are organized using chapters which contain lectures, exercises, tasks, and tests. So, e.g., the e-learning module e-commerce is organized in fourteen chapters which deal with the various technological and economical aspects of the e-revolution. The requirements from section 2 were considered in the development of this module. So, e.g., various multimedia elements were integrated into the module as can be seen from Fig. 1 and students can choose between different

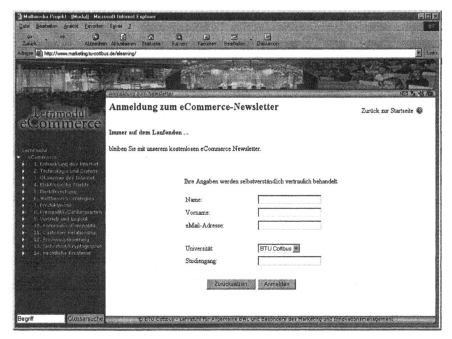

Fig. 2. Example for a communication channel registration (newsletter)

communication channels like chat rooms, discussion rooms, and a newsletter. A corresponding print screen for registration is shown in Fig. 2. The students can also contact a teletutor to whom they can send exercises and from whom they can get a feedback. Furthermore, a glossary with some hundred terms and definitions is provided.

4 Results of the survey

In order to analyze the students' preferences a sample of 105 students were interviewed, 74 students of industrial engineering and 31 IMT students at the BTU Cottbus. The female portion was 42%. The questionnaire included 20 closed questions each with a possibility to add own comments and suggestions. In order to demonstrate the advantages of e-learning scenarios over traditional learning scenarios a prototype of the e-learning module e-commerce was presented prior to handing out the questionnaire. Furthermore we used our e-commerce module not to evaluate it but to show the students how an e-learning module can look like. The intention was to get qualitative statements about their expectations and preferences concerning e-learning programs in general. To examine possible course of study and gender specific differences t-tests were used, but only for gender specific differences results are shown.

So, as can be seen from Fig. 3, graphics, animations, and simulations are the most preferred multimedia features. Text and hyperlinks (hyperlinks diff.

means: no focused search for special contents) are rated at a lower level. Men tend to prefer the multimedia features. Concerning the differences related to the course of study, the ranking of the multimedia features is very similar. Like the male students in the whole sample, IMT students tend to rate the features higher than students of industrial engineering.

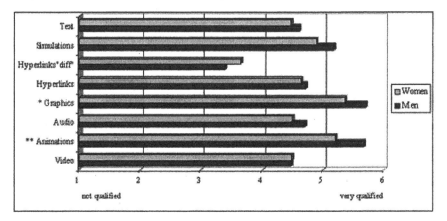

Fig. 3. Evaluation of different multimedia features (gender related differences; $\star$: α = 0.05, $\star\star$: α = 0.01)

Fig. 4 shows that e-mail, discussion rooms, and newsletter are the most preferred communication channels. There are relatively high gender related differences concerning chat rooms and discussion rooms. Men rated both channels higher. This contradicts Hochholzer (2000) who found out that women tended to prefer chat rooms on a higher level. In comparison of the gender and course of study results both rankings were nearly the same. IMT students tended to evaluate communication channels on a higher level, but the gap between both groups is very small.

As can be seen from Fig. 5, content and service (e.g., intuitive navigation, simple side structuring) are the most important characteristics of module design. In comparison with Neibecker (2000) the results are nearly the same. Concerning the rating of "multimedia items" and "interactive items", dependencies related to gender and also to the course of study are discovered. The ranking of the IMT students is comparable to the ranking of the men, and the rankings of students of industrial engineering and women are nearly the same.

Relating to the kind of knowledge transfer, over 50% of the students prefer a hybrid model, which combines specific aspects of the teacher centered and learner centered knowledge transfer. With regards to the differences related to the course of study, 61% of the IMT students prefer a hybrid model but only 47% of the students of industrial engineering. 25% of the students of

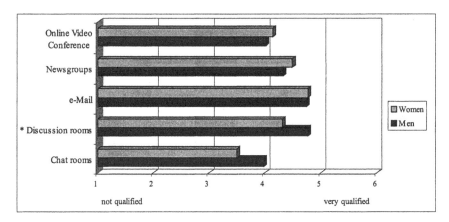

Fig. 4. Evaluation of different communication channels (gender related differences; $\star$: $\alpha = 0.05$, $\star\star$: $\alpha = 0.01$)

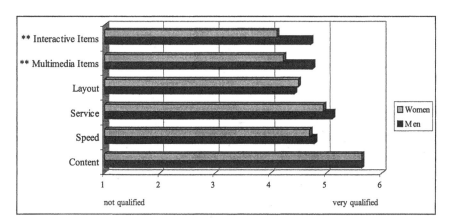

Fig. 5. Analysis of importance of module design characteristics (gender related differences; $\star$: $\alpha = 0.05$, $\star\star$: $\alpha = 0.01$)

industrial engineering want a teacher centered knowledge transfer but only 16% of the IMT students want the same. In spite of this differences, no dependency between the course of study and the evaluating of the kind of knowledge transfer could be establish.

76% of the students want a teletutor to send in exercises, to get a feedback and to ask questions. No real differences related to gender or course of study could be proven. The results are nearly identical concerning the results (69% want to have a teletutor) of Frank (2001). Students prefer a teletutor for content problems on the highest level. Women and students of industrial engineering rated a teletutor for technical problems as a little bit more important than a teletutor for organizational problems. The evaluation of IMT students and men was exactly the opposite.

Independent of the group of students, most want the module development for current (42%) or past (38%) computer technology applications. Over 80% of all interviewed students think that a combination of virtual and present lectures are the future in education.

5   Conclusion and outlook

To develop gender and course of study orientated e-learning modules, it is necessary to know more about students' needs. The results of our survey gave us important information about the students' preferences, which can be used to improve the quality of our modules. What kind of conclusions can we draw?

- In general, all groups of students support the integration of new media programs in their education.
- Men tend to rate the indicated possibilities higher. The women were more or less indifferent.
- The IMT students faced the topic more openly and prefer a higher level of new media integration.

The differences related to gender and course of study were mostly small. This supports the findings of Gaul and Schmidt-Thieme (2001) who couldn't discover clear gender specific differences. It seems to be not necessary to develop totally different module versions. But it seems important to consider the determined differences in the development of modules. We have to implement the most preferred items, i.e. graphics, animations, simulations, e-mail, discussion rooms, newsletter, and a teletutor. Concerning the module design, we have to consider first the content and service characteristics. Furthermore, we should not develop our modules for future computer applications. Blended learning programs can optimize the combination of virtual and present lectures.

In order to be able to recognize future modifications of preferences it is also necessary to evaluate the modules periodically. Only if target groups are involved in the design and development process it can be ensured that they are going to be satisfied with the developed contents and design.

References

AHUJA, A. and RÖDDER, W. (2002): Kritische Erfolgsfaktoren universitärer Multimediakurse. In: P. Chamoni, R. Leisten, A. Martin, J. Minnemann and H. Stadtler (Eds.):*Operations Research Proceedings 2001*. Springer, Berlin, 441–448.
BAUER, R. and PHILIPPI, T. (2001): *Einstieg ins E-Learning*. BW Bildung und Wissen, Nürnberg.

BERLECON RESEARCH GmbH (2001): *Wachstumsmarkt E-Learning: Anforderungen, Akteure und Perspektiven im deutschen Markt.* Berlecon Research, Berlin.

BRUNS, B. and GAJEWSKI, P. (1999): *Multimediales Lernen im Netz. Leitfaden für Entscheider und Planer.* Springer, Berlin.

DORER, J. (2001): Internet und Geschlecht. Berufliche und private Anwendungspraxen der neuen Technologie. In: E. Klaus, J. Röser, U. Wischermann (Hrsg.): *Kommunikationswissenschaft und Gender Studies.* Westdeutscher Verlag, Wiesbaden, 241–266.

FRANK, C. (2001): Learning operations research with hypermedia: students' expectations and experiences.*International Conference on Operations Research (OR 2001),* Duisburg, September 2001.

GAUL, W. and SCHMIDT-THIEME, L. (2001): Online Conjoint Analysis of Designs for Multimedia Enhanced Teaching. *Arbeitspapier, Institut für Entscheidungstheorie und Unternehmensforschung,* Universität Karlsruhe (TH).

HOCHHOLZER, B. (2000): Frauen surfen anders!?. *Medientage-München 2000.*

KERRES, M. (2001): *Multimediale und telemediale Lernumgebungen: Konzeption und Entwicklung.* 2. Aufl., Oldenbourg, München.

LEHNER, F. (2001): E-Learning - Virtueller Unterricht über das Internet am Beispiel von Hochschulen und Universitäten.*Forschungsbericht Nr. 52, Lehrstuhl für Wirtschaftsinformatik III.* Universität Regensburg.

NEIBECKER, B. (2000): Online-Befragung multimedialer Lehr-/Lernangebote bei Lehrenden und Lernenden. *Arbeitspapier, Institut für Entscheidungstheorie und Unternehmensforschung,* Universität Karlsruhe (TH).

NEIBECKER, B. and BREITER, F. (1999): Angebote und Akzeptanzmessung multimedialer Lehr-/Lernangebote. *Arbeitspapier, Institut für Entscheidungstheorie und Unternehmensforschung,* Universität Karlsruhe (TH).

SCHULMEISTER, R. (1999): *Virtuelle Universität - Virtuelles Lernen.* Oldenbourg, München.

STEINMETZ, R. (1999): *Multimedia-Technologie.* 2. Auflage, Springer, Berlin.

WINKLER, G. (1999): Geschlechtsverhältnisse und vernetzte Systeme. In: H. Götschel:*Frauen und Frauenforschung in den Naturwissenschaften.* Frauenrat der Univät Konstanz, Konstanz, 14–15.

YOM, M. (1997): *Frauen und Online-Medien.* Löw und Vorderwülbecke, Baden Baden.

MURBANDY: The (so far) Missing Link: User-Friendly Retrieval and Visualization of Geographic Information

Bernd Hermes[1], Maximilian Stempfhuber[1], Luca Demicheli[2], and Carlo Lavalle[2]

[1] Social Science Information Centre (IZ),
   Lennéstr. 30, D-53113 Bonn, Germany
[2] European Commission, Joint Research Centre, Space Applications Institute
   TP 261, Ispra (VA), I-21020, Italy

Abstract. In many situations, the search for non-textual information is driven by a specific topic rather than the values of a data record's attributes. Therefore, data is often indexed with census nomenclatures, classifications or thesauri to allow a user to search with keywords. MURBANDY is a user-friendly graphical interface which supports query formulation using this indexing languages and at the same time visualizes the semantic dependencies between them and other search attributes. The generic version of the user interface is able to display dependencies between keywords and an arbitrary number of databases during query formulation, and lets the user interactively explore and manipulate his query at a very detailed level.

1 Introduction

Retrieval in information systems is often done by comparing user-specified values with actual data. But the values the user wants to specify for searching cannot always be compared with the data he is looking for. In some domains, like market research (Stempfhuber et al. 2002) or image retrieval, he wants to specify "which" data is needed, and not how it should look like. He is interested in certain aspects of the content and wants to see dependencies in the data. To fulfill the user's information need in these cases, the data has to be described with metadata, which characterizes a record's semantic content or global features in comparison to other records (e.g. sample size in statistical data). The content is normally described by assigning terms from an indexing language (e.g. classification system or thesaurus) to each record. The description of the data with an indexing language lets the user focus on the topic of his information need when searching for data rather than on the data formats, values or types.

2 Visualizing the query process

It is the task of the user interface to visualize the dependencies in the data and to lead and support the user in the information seeking process. Normally, an application has to deal with different kinds of users (e.g. novice and expert). While the casual user prefers to enter keywords by selecting them from a list (he is not familiar with valid keywords or typing them is too error-prone) it is faster for experts to enter them by typing or to use shortcuts, like ? from official census nomenclatures. The design of the interface should support unexperienced users and experts without using different user interfaces.

In many domains the lists of keywords tend to become rather long. Since screen real estate is limited, scrollable list boxes are used to display the list of keywords. But scrolling hides parts of the list box's content and the user has to remember already selected items. There is a race condition between the space needed for presenting options (e.g. list boxes) and summarizing previous selections to lower short term memory's load, for which a user-friendly solution is needed.

Another problem arises as soon as an indefinite number of values per search attribute can be entered, which can be multiple numerical ranges or keywords. Here the number of entry fields is hard to define a priory. Providing only a few fields limits the complexity of the user's query, having too many wastes screen real estate.

Syntax and layout of graphical user interfaces often imply a combination of the individual controls (e.g. sliders or entry fields) which represent the search attributes with Boolean operators. Since the user expects the result set to shrink the more specific his query is (the more attributes he specifies), the attributes will be combined with the AND operator. As soon as there is no simple interpretation of how the attributes and their values are transformed into a (Boolean) query, e.g. values are combined with OR within attributes and with AND between them, the result of the query is hard to guess in advance. Neither a query preview nor the final result set may be able to explain relations in the data, so that the user can not easily understand how search attributes and their values interact with each other and influence the result in detail.

2.1 Dynamic screen layout and tight coupling

The dynamic spatial layout of controls on the screen solves the problems related with multivalued search attributes by adjusting the size of controls (e.g. entry fields) and rearranging them in a way so that they can hold an arbitrary number of values without wasting space that otherwise could be used for selection lists or a status display (Stempfhuber 1999). We developed a control for entering text which initially consists of one single entry field and grows or shrinks vertically with every entry that is added or deleted. Space on the screen is dynamically occupied or freed depending on the amount of data the user enters. Figure 1 shows parts of the user interface of ELVIRA, an information system for market researchers, to illustrate the idea.

To allow selection rather than manual input (recognition vs. recall), the entry field is tightly coupled with a selection list. The content of the selection list serves two functions:

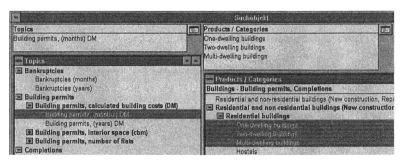

Fig. 1. Tight coupling of dynamic entry fields with selection lists

- Validation of (manual) input from the user: the entry field only accepts input which can also be found in the list, but assists the user with a thesaurus.
- Display of choices: to avoid typing errors, search terms can be selected from the list instead of being typed into the entry field.

The user can freely choose it's mode of interaction. Entering text in the entry field selects the corresponding item in the list and selecting in the list inserts the text in the entry field (same for deleting items). This tight coupling of controls together with the synchronized flow of information between them are two of the core principles of the WOB model for user interface design (Krause 1997). Both principles can directly be mapped to software design patterns and thus are clearly specified at the conceptual and the implementation level (Stempfhuber 2002). Tight coupling is also used to synchronize permissible values of multiple search attributes and therefore to eliminate combinations of values that will lead to zero-hit queries. In figure 1, the attributes "topics" and "products / categories" are synchronized in a way that when a topic is selected, all entries from "products / categories" are removed that can not be combined with the selected topic. The dependencies between attributes are bi-directional (but not recursive) so that initially selecting a "product" will reduce available "topics".

2.2   Status display to reduce memory load

The entry field at the same time serves as a status display. This is necessary, because the lists of attribute values tend to become rather long in real-life applications (up to 1.800 entries in some of the many census nomenclatures used in ELVIRA). Scrolling those hierarchically organized lists always hides parts of them, so that the user has to remember a potentially large number of already selected items. The status display summarizes the selected items, gives a comprehensible overview of the query and at the same time reduces short term memory load. When displaying query results, the selections lists are replaced by a result list, while the status display still remains visible.

Attribute	B1	B2	B3	
A1	☒		☐	Σ
A2	☐	☒		
A3	☒	☐	☒	
	Σ			

Fig. 2. Visual formalism for displaying dependencies between attributes

Again, there is no need to remember the query when reviewing results and comparing them with the search conditions.

2.3   Query refinement in a one-screen-system

Another problem in information systems is support for iterative query refinement. Many systems divide query formulation and presentation of results into separate screens which makes it not only difficult to compare query and results. It also forces the user to first develop a strategy for re-formulating the query while looking at the results (query form not visible) and then switching back to the proper screen and modifying the query (results not visible). The solution is again to use an enhanced status display that is visible together with the query result and allows modification of the query without switching screens.

2.4   Visual formalisms

The proposed solution and the systems mentioned so far fail to visualize dependencies between query attributes - or their values - and the elements of the result set. Because multiple values of an attribute are often combined with the Boolean OR operator and the attributes themselves are combined with AND, query previews give only the total of records in the result set, but may fail to visualize which combinations of search values appear in the result set. Visual Formalisms (Nardi & Zarmer 1993) are generic visualizations like maps, tables or charts which have to be adapted to a certain domain when used. They use humans' information processing capabilities - like detecting patterns from spatial arrangements - and visualize dependencies between data. They are also well known through frequent use and do - in contrast to metaphors - not require explicit transfer of knowledge between domains. What makes them useful in computer interfaces is that they are interactive, being output and input at the same time.

Our visualization uses a table - a Visual Formalism - where each axis shows one search attribute (see figure 2). The table dynamically grows or shrinks depending on the number of values specified for each attribute. The cells of the table contain one of three possible values:

- Empty cell: no dependency between the corresponding attribute values.

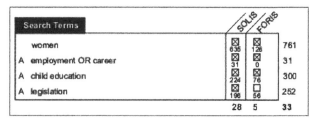

Fig. 3. Visualizing dependencies between search terms and databases

- Unmarked checkbox: dependency in the data which the user can activate to include it in the query (mark the checkbox by clicking the mouse).
- Marked checkbox: activated dependency which adds records to the result set.

The number of records resulting from an activated cell can be displayed within the cell or as sum for rows and columns. This gives the user an idea how the result set will grow or shrink when activating / de-activating a cell. Figure 3 shows this for a document retrieval system, where the two attributes to combine are the search terms and the databases to search (adapted from Stempfhuber 2002). In this example the user has excluded the term "legislation" from the database FORIS.

3   Information needs in MURBANDY

The Social Science Information Centre built a user interface prototype for the retrieval of land use data in MURBANDY (Monitoring Urban Dynamics, Lavalle et al. 2000). For urban planning models are needed that integrate historical and current data and allow to prognosticate future development. An important criteria is the change of land use and the consumption of land in urban areas. Therefore, land use data for 25 European cities has been collected and classified for four different years between 1955 and 1990. Besides the satellite images, from which part of the data has been extracted, there are colored maps for each city and year that show land use and traffic network according to the international land use classification.

Common use cases for this data are the analysis of the change of land use for a single city within a specific period, or the comparison of two cities with regard to certain classes of land use, e.g. industrial areas. In rare cases more than two cities will be compared at once. To compare or evaluate the cities, the user needs to be able to interactively explore the visualization of the land use data by selectively hiding or showing specific land use categories for every single city.

4   The MURBANDY user interface

In MURBANDY, queries can be formulated with two entry fields - serving at the same time as status displays - together with tightly coupled selection lists (figure 4). One pair of entry field and selection list can be used to specify the types of land use and the other one for the cities that should be analyzed or compared. The selection list for the types of land use is displayed as a hierarchy, the cities are listed alphabetically and as a map. The names of cities can either be typed into the entry field, selected in the selection list or marked in the map. Again, there is tight coupling between entry field, selection list, and map so that the user can freely change his mode of interaction.

When specifying search values, the height of the entry fields and their corresponding selection lists are dynamically adjusted (figure 4). This reduces the space needed for presentation of alternatives (which the user has already seen), and provides additional space for the status display to reduce short term memory load. At the same time, the status display allows deselecting search values without locating them again in the selection list. To omit zero-hit queries, the attributes "land use" and "cities" are tightly coupled, so that the selection of a type of land use reduces the list of cities and vice versa. The direction for adaptation is determined by the attribute which is selected first. If a type of land use is selected, only the list of cities will adapt and will not in turn lead to an adaptation of the list with the types of land use. This avoids recursion and therefore confusion of the user. Though a query preview is calculated behind the scenes while the query is formulated, we chose to use a "Search" button to let the user state that he believes his information needs will be met. When the query is submitted, the two selection lists are hidden and the entry field for the cities is rotated by 45 degrees, giving room for a tabular display of the query preview. The system can be configured to automatically retrieve and display the data, as seen in figure 5.

Both entry fields now serve as a status display, which can be modified by typing in or deleting search values or by clicking one of the labels "land use" or "cities" to show the selection lists again. For experienced users, this could be the only screen they work with, because it contains space saving ways of entering search values, displays preview data and visualizes the query result as map at the same time. A cell in the preview table is empty, if no data exists for the combination of land use and city. As a default, all existing combinations (marked by a checkbox) are activated (checked) so that they are displayed in the map. Removing a check hides the land use in the corresponding map of the city. Deleting the land use from the status display changes the query eliminating the line from the preview table and therefore hides the land use in all of the maps. Working with MURBANDY is a two-step process of search (selecting types of land use and cities) and refinement (filtering the result set), which can have an arbitrary number of iterations without switching screens. Even the analysis of the results (maps) is tightly integrated and allows query re-formulation if additional data is needed.

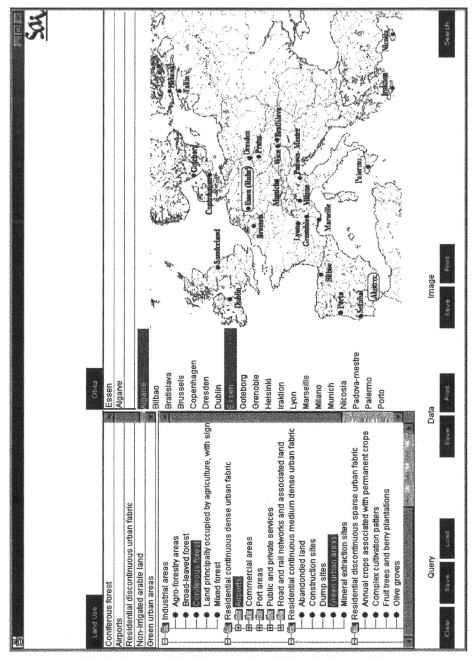

Fig. 4. Dynamically adjusted entry fields and selection lists

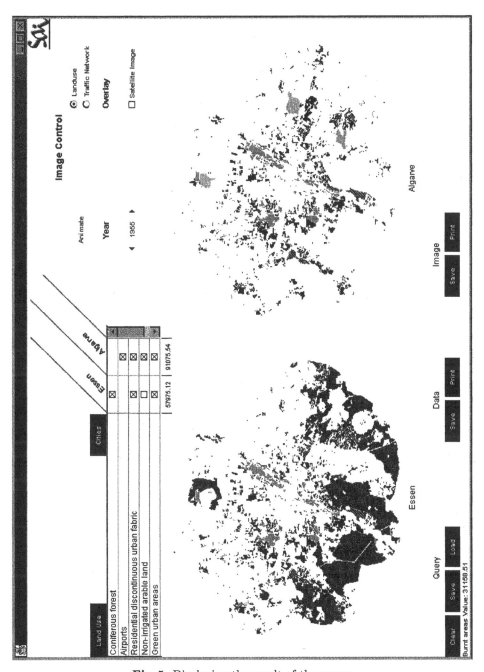

Fig. 5. Displaying the result of the query

5 Conclusion

The user interface design of MURBANDY represents a generic idea of visualizing dependencies between multiple indexing languages (e.g. nomenclatures,
classifications or thesauri) and even between indexing languages and multiple databases. It has been evaluated in controlled user tests and found to be
very comprehensive when used for searching textual and non-textual data.
Currently we are preparing a test scenario for document retrieval in multiple
databases. The goal will be to find out how our user interface can support
the user in situations where databases are indexed with different thesauri
and cross-concordances exist to map thesaurus entries between these thesauri.
Here, the relationships between multiple thesauri and multiple databases have
to be presented simultaneously to the user.

References

KRAUSE, J. (1997): Das WOB-Modell. In: Krause, J. and Womser-
    Hacker, C. (1997): *Vages Information Retrieval und graphische Be-
    nutzungsoberflächen: Beispiel Werkstoffinformation.* Konstanz. Schriften zur
    Informationswissenschaft Bd. 28, pp. 59-88.
LAVALLE, C. and DEMICHELI, L. and CARRASCO, P. C. and TURCHINI, M.
    and NIEDERHUBER, M. and McCORMICK N. (2000): Murbandy /Moland.
    Technical Report European Commission Euroreport.
NARDI, B.; ZARMER, C. (1993): Beyond Models and Metaphors: Visual For-
    malisms in User Interface Design. *Journal of Visual Languages and Computing,
    1993, 4, pp. 5-33.*
STEMPFHUBER, M. (1999): Dynamic spatial layout in graphical user interfaces.
    In: Bullinger, H. J. and Ziegler, J. (1999): *Human-Computer Interaction: Com-
    munication, Cooperation, and Application Design. Proceedings of HCI Inter-
    national '99.* Munich, Germany, August 22-26, 1999. Vol. 2, pp. 137-141.
STEMPFHUBER, M. (2002): *ODIN - Objektorientierte grafische Benutzung-
    soberflächen. Dissertation im Fachbereich für Informatik an der Universität
    Koblenz-Landau.*
STEMPFHUBER, M. and HELLWEG, H. and SCHAEFER, A. (2002): ELVIRA:
    User friendly Retrieval of Heterogeneous Data in Market Research In: Callaos,
    N. and Encinas, L.H. and Yetim, F. (Eds.): *Proc. of 6th World Multiconference
    on Systemics, Cybernetics and Informatics (SCI 2002).* Orlando, Florida, 299–
    304.

ASCAID: Using an Asymmetric Correlation Measure for Automatic Interaction Detection

Andreas Hilbert

Lehrstuhl für Mathematische Methoden der Wirtschaftswissenschaften,
Universität Augsburg, D-86135 Augsburg, Germany

Abstract. Based upon the predictive association measure λ by Goodman and Kruskal, a new algorithm for the induction of a decision tree is proposed. This algorithm cares about the asymmetric character of the classification task and enables the use of statistical inference.

1 Introduction

Decision trees are very successfully used for the classification task of objects in many fields like marketing or medicine. Like other classification procedures, for instance logistic regression or linear discriminant analysis, decision trees develop classification rules describing the correlation between independent exogenous attributes and an endogenous class membership attribute.

In case exogenous attributes are exclusively metric scaled, the procedures usually try to aggregate these attributes in a way that the so built new quantity best describes the class membership attribute. The accuracy of this classification procedure is often quantified by variance-based measurements. Regression-based procedures use the least-squares approach and enable the classification of binary scaled membership attributes. In case of mainly nominal scaled exogenous attributes the procedures divide the objects in a way that the generated partitions are as homogeneous as possible. The homogeneity itself can be quantified by deviation measurements like Entropy measure or by Gini index. Finally, CHAID algorithm by Kaas (1980) uses a special correlation measure to develop classification rules.

Even though the purpose of these procedures is to explain the correlation between one membership attribute and several exogenous attributes, only one algorithm actually uses a correlation measurement to achieve that. Furthermore, it should be emphasized that the used correlation measurement is symmetric in its nature although the classification task is asymmetric.

Therefore a new decision tree algorithm based on an asymmetric correlation measurement is introduced. It can be shown that several well-known decision tree algorithms as ID3, C4.5 or CART can be understood as special versions of a generalized decision tree based on asymmetric correlation measurements. But in contrast to these well-known procedures the new algorithm ASCAID enables the use of statistical inference.

2   Decision trees

Since the first contribution about classification of membership attributes by Sonquist et al. (1971) several standard techniques for the construction of decision trees have been developed, for instance the basic algorithm ID3 by Quinlan (1986), C4.5 by Quinlan (1993) or the above mentioned χ^2-based algorithm CHAID by Kaas (1980). The algorithm CART is described as well as the construction of decision trees in general by Breiman et al. (1984) in their important and well-known monograph to this topic.

Generally, a decision tree is built from a set of data having attributes $X_1, \ldots, X_n$ and membership attribute Y. The result of the process is represented as a flow-chart-like tree. Each internal node specifies a decision on an attribute and each branch denotes an outcome of these decisions. Furthermore, each end node or leaf of the tree corresponds with an subset of objects with identical class membership or with objects whose homogeneity is as good as requested.

The basic algorithm for the induction of a decision tree itself is a "greedy algorithm that generates decision trees in a top-down recursive divide-and-conquer manner" (Han, Kamber (2001)) and consists of the following steps:

- The tree starts with the *root* node. It represents the whole data set.

- In case all objects belong to the same class, the node becomes a leaf and is labeled with that class.

- Otherwise, the algorithm uses a *split criterion* for selecting the attribute that best separate the set of objects into subsets. This attribute becomes the *decision attribute* for the given node.

- A branch is created for each known value of the decision attribute and its data set is accordingly partitioned.

- The algorithm recursively repeats the same procedure to induce a tree for all subsets of each partition. Once an attribute has occurred at a node, it doesn't need to be considered in any of the node's descendents.

- The recursive partitioning finishes when a *stop criterion* is fulfilled. This stop criterion itself depends on the used split criterion and/or the underlying type of induction procedure.

This basic strategy can be found in most of the well-known algorithms for induction of decision trees. But only the split and the stop criteria separate the different algorithms. The most important **split criteria** are *information gain, information gain ratio* (both are based on the well-known *entropy*), *Gini index, twoing value* and χ^2 *measure of correlation*. They all attempt to partition the data set in a way that the resulting subsets are as homogeneous as possible with respect to the class membership of the objects.

When decision trees are developed, many of the branches may reflect anomalies in the data set due to noise or outliers. Tree **pruning** methods address this problem of *overfitting* data. Such methods typically use statistical measures to remove the least reliable branches and improve the ability of the tree to correctly classify unknown objects.

3   Attribute selection and correlation measures

All classification procedures try to explain the correlation between one endogenous membership attribute Y and exogenous attributes $X_1, \ldots, X_n$. The algorithms for the induction of decision tree attempt to solve this problem by an iterative bivariate analysis of pairs (X_i, Y) for all objects belonging to a given node. To consider such pairs (X_i, Y) in the manner of bivariate analysis the techniques of correlation analysis are available. Following Hilbert (1998, p. 60–78) there exist two relevant important types of correlations:

- Type 1 measures the deviation from the stochastical independence. It is symmetric in the way it uses the attributes and is based on the χ^2 measure.

- Type 2 considers the *reduction of the prediction error* for one attribute, given the value of another attribute. It is asymmetric and known as *predictive association.*

The correlation measures based on type 1, for instance χ^2 itself and its derived measures ϕ, Tschuprow's contingency measure T or Cramer's V, are very popular while the use of correlation measures of type 2 is very uncommon. The major reason why these type 1 measures are used so often is the knowledge of the (asymptotical) distribution of these measures. This knowledge enables the use of statistical inference in order to test the correlation between the attributes. But "the fact that an excellent test of independence may be based on χ^2 does not at all mean that χ^2 ... is an appropriate measure of degree of association" (Goodman, Kruskal (1954), p. 740). In fact, it is difficult to meaningfully compare that correlation measures of two pairs (X_i, Y) and (X_j, Y) and to interpret their values in an operational way.

Therefore, Goodman and Kruskal (1954) proposed another concept to measure the correlation between two attributes. It is based upon an idea of Guttman (1941) and well-known as **predictive association**. Their concept is able to reflect the extent of the ability of an attribute to predict the values of another attribute. In order to construct a correlation measurement that follows this concept the following has to be realized: Defining $\mathbf{PE}(Y)$ as the prediction error of an attribute Y with values $y_1, \ldots, y_m$ and $\mathbf{PE}(Y|X_i)$ as the equivalent prediction error of the same attribute Y given an attribute X_i with values $x_{i1}, \ldots x_{im_i}$. Then, it is obvious that the following is valid:

$$PE(Y|X_i) = \sum_{j=1}^{m_i} P_{X_i}(x_j) \cdot PE(Y|X_i = x_j) \qquad (1)$$

$P_{X_i}(x_j)$ denotes the probability or (in case of a sample) the relative frequency of an attribute X_i having the value x_j. Using this denotation the measure of **predictive association** is defined by

$$CM_{(X_i \to Y)}^{PRE} := \frac{PE(Y) - PE(Y|X_i)}{PE(Y)}. \qquad (2)$$

This quantity is a general *asymmetric measurement of correlation* between the two involved attributes with X_i as cause and Y as effect. Because of its nature to reflect the extent of the ability of an attribute to predict the values of another attribute it is also called **Proportional-Reduction-of-Error** or **PRE** coefficient. Based upon this very general definition of a PRE coefficient, only the operational form of $PE(\cdot)$ has to be specified to obtain a concrete measurement of correlation. If considering, however, the definition and meaning of the coefficient, it is easy to understand why every deviation coefficient is a good choice for the prediction error $PE(\cdot)$: the smaller the deviation of an attribute the better its prediction.

The well-known deviation coefficients for nominal scaled attributes are *Shannon's entropy* **H** (Shannon (1948)), the *deviation coefficient* S_H by Herfindahl and a measure that is based on the probability or frequency of the mode of the distribution of the considered attribute, the *modality measurement* **M** (Hilbert (1998), p. 115–122). In case Shannon's entropy **H** or the deviation coefficient S_H by Herfindahl, defined by

$$H(Y) := -\sum_{k=1}^{m} P_Y(y_k) \cdot \operatorname{ld} P_Y(y_k) \qquad S_H(Y) := 1 - \sum_{k=1}^{m} P_Y(y_k)^2 \qquad (3)$$

are used to declare the prediction error, it can easily be shown (Hilbert (2002), p. 6–7) that the measure of **information gain** by Quinlan (1986) and **Gini index** by Breiman et al. (1984) can be treated as an unstandardized asymmetric correlation measure. The proposed split criteria are nothing but predictive association coefficients.

The modality measurement

Considering information gain and Gini index as special correlation measures it is obvious that the interpretation of these quantities is very difficult. Furthermore, their values usually have no concrete meaning. Only the relative comparison of the different measures is possible and leads to a best splitting attribute. An absolute appraisal of the values, however, is not possible.

Otherwise, this characteristic is one of the most important advantages of the third deviation measurement, modality measure $\mathbf{M}$. The use of $\mathbf{M}$ to describe the prediction error for an attribute leads to a definition according to

$$\mathbf{M}(Y) := 1 - \max_{k=1,\ldots,m} \mathbf{P}_Y(y_k) \tag{4}$$

and consequently to the following PRE coefficient:

$$\mathbf{CM}_{(X_i \to Y)}^{\text{PRE, M}} := \frac{\sum_{j=1}^{m_i} \max_{k=1,\ldots,m} \mathbf{P}_{(X_i,Y)}(x_j, y_k) - \max_{k=1,\ldots,m} \mathbf{P}_Y(y_k)}{1 - \max_{k=1,\ldots,m} \mathbf{P}_Y(y_k)} \tag{5}$$

This coefficient is known as the predictive association coefficient λ by Goodman and Kruskal (1954) and has some similarities to the split criterion *theta* by Messenger and Mandell (1972) who proposed the less-known tree algorithm THAID based upon that theta coefficient. Also Breiman et al. (1984) analyzed a similar coefficient in the framework of missclassification costs.

In contrast to the other predictive association measurements Goodman and Kruskal's λ can easily be interpreted. If nothing is known about the distribution of the values of an attribute Y, the best prediction of Y is the mode y_{mod} of the attribute with a prediction error $1 - \mathbf{P}_Y(y_{\text{mod}})$. Given an exogenous attribute X_i this prediction error can be calculated according to (1) to describe the support of X_i to predict Y. Thus, λ corresponds to the proportional reduction of the prediction error of Y as long as the mode is the best prediction for an attribute. For further descriptive details also see Hilbert (1998, p. 114–126). With respect to the sample form $\hat{\lambda}$ of the coefficient, Goodman and Kruskal (1963) prove that $\hat{\lambda}$ is asymptotically unbiased and asymptotically normal distributed. Furthermore, they give the following expression for the asymptotical variance of $\hat{\lambda}$:

$$\mathbf{Var}(\hat{\lambda}) = \frac{1 - \sum_{j=1}^{m_i} \mathbf{P}_{(X_i,Y)}(x_j, y_{k_j^*})}{N \cdot \left(1 - \mathbf{P}_Y(y_{k^*})\right)^3} \tag{6}$$

$$\cdot \left(\sum_{j=1}^{m_i} \mathbf{P}_{(X_i,Y)}(x_j, y_{k_j^*}) + \mathbf{P}_Y(y_{k^*}) - 2 \cdot \sum_{\substack{j=1 \\ k_j^* = k^*}}^{m_i} \mathbf{P}_{(X_i,Y)}(x_j, y_{k_j^*}) \right)$$

N is the sample size (of a node), $\mathbf{P}(\cdot)$ the known probability or the sample estimator of the unknown probability of the (common) distribution of Y

and/or X_i, k^* the index of the mode of Y and k_j^* the index of the mode of Y given $X_i = x_j$. Using these sampling properties it is possible to calculate a *confidence interval* for $\lambda(X_i \to Y)$, to realize one- or two-sided *inferential tests* for $\lambda(X_i \to Y)$ or to test $\lambda(X_i \to Y)$ against $\lambda(X_j \to Y)$ for some i, j.

Comparison of the different split criteria

This property to realize statistical inference for this correlation measure and split criterion is very interesting and important. But it has to be analyzed which further advantages or disadvantages – compared to Gini index or information gain – Goodman and Kruskal's λ has. Therefore, it is useful to have a look at the functional form of the measurements, described for a binary membership attribute Y (Fig. 1).

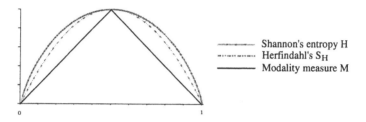

Fig. 1. Deviation measures for a binary attribute Y

First of all, it is obvious that Shannon's entropy **H** and Herfindahl's deviation measurement $\mathbf{S}_H$ are very similar. This also explains why the results of the induction of a decision tree using Gini index and information gain measure are usually identical. Furthermore, **H** and $\mathbf{S}_H$ assess all distributions, which are more or less similar to an equal distribution, in the same way. Differences are very difficult to analyze. The modality measure **M**, however, reacts in such a situation much more sensitive. Otherwise, **M** has difficulties in the discrimination of distributions which are similar to an extremely unbalanced one. In this case the other measures have the advantage to react very sensitively to a variation of probabilities. This also means that the modality measure, taken as a split criterion, does not prefer the *end-cut splits*. It is, however, not obvious if this is an advantage or disadvantage, even though Breiman et al. (1984) do not seem to approve a decision tree algorithm which has not this end-cut-split feature. Anyway, further research and simulation studies are necessary.

Finally, it can be shown that the modality measure **M** and the measures **H** and $\mathbf{S}_H$ generate a different order with respect to the deviation of two distributions. While, for instance, entropy measurement and Herfindahl's de-

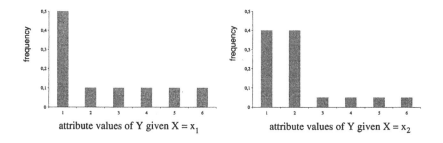

Fig. 2. Distributions of Y given two different values of an exogenous attribute X

viation measure both prefer the distribution on the right-hand side in Fig. 2 (also see Table 1), modality measure **M** prefers the left-hand distribution which is – in the author's opinion – much more desirable in the framework of decision trees. For another critical situation applying **H** and $\mathbf{S}_H$ also see Hilbert (2002, p. 10–11).

To summarize, it may be emphasized that the modality measure has the ability to induce a decision tree which differs from the ones produced by Gini index or information gain measure. In contrast to the opinion of Breiman et al. (1984) the modality measure seems to have some advantages for which it is worthwhile to analyze this measure in more detail. Considering as well the opportunity to use statistical inference the introduction of Goodman and Kruskal's λ as a split criterion is a chance to receive a new and promising algorithm for the induction of a decision tree. This might generate trees and classification rules which are, probably, much more adequate than the known ones.

	$Y|X = x_1$	$Y|X = x_2$
Modality measure **M**	0.50	0.60
Herfindahl's $\mathbf{S}_H$	0.70	0.67
Entropy **H**	1.49	1.33

Table 1. Deviation measures of Y given $X = x_1$ and $X = x_2$

4   The procedure ASCAID

Based upon these remarks a new algorithm for the induction of decision trees is proposed. This algorithm handles the asymmetric character of the classification task (in contrast to CHAID) and enables the use of statistical inference (in contrast to ID3 or CART). According to the first algorithm for the induction of classification rules, the AID procedure by Sonquist et al. (1971), this procedure is called **ASCAID**: Using an **AS**ymmetric Correlation Measure for **A**utomatic **I**nteraction **D**etection. It is also a top-down approach and consists of the following steps:

Merging Step: The aim of this optional step is to merge the categories of exogenous attributes to prevent a partition with too many subsets and/or the creation of subsets which are too similar. Both approaches lead to a decision tree which is more suitable to be used for other data sets (less overfitting). The procedure itself is similar to the one of the CHAID procedure, but has to be adopted to the measure λ (see Hilbert (2002), p. 13 – 14).

Splitting Step: Based upon the suitably merged categories of all exogenous attributes X_i, the assessment of these attributes with respect to their discrimination power for the membership attribute Y need to be analyzed. Therefore, the following steps are necessary:

- $\hat{\lambda}(X_i \to Y) := \hat{\lambda}(i)$ is to be calculated for all possible pairs (X_i, Y).
- A well-drawn and problem-adopted threshold $\lambda_{\min}$ has to be chosen which is used for the separation of high and low correlated pairs (X_i, Y).
- All exogenous attribute X_i with a value $\hat{\lambda}(i) > \lambda_{\min}$ will be chosen as a potential split criterion.
- If there is more than one potential split criterion, the different quantities can be used to construct an inferential statistic (see Hilbert (2002), p. 14). In case the adequate null hypothesis can not be rejected, there are strong hints for overfitting the data. The induction of the tree, however, can be continued, for instance by choosing attribute X_{i^*} with the largest sample value $\hat{\lambda}(i^*)$ as split criterion, but handled carefully.

Stopping Step: Based upon the best chosen split attribute, a new partition of the sample arises. The dividing will be terminated if at least one of the well-known pre-pruning rules is valid. The node becomes a leaf. In case all nodes are leaves, the algorithm stops. Finally, post-pruning techniques ensure the adaptability of the tree to other samples.

Accuracy of the Tree
To measure the accuracy of the tree, the PRE measure λ can be used again. Defining the leaves of the tree as values of a dummy attribute X_0, the predictive association $\hat{\lambda}(X_0 \to Y)$ of that X_0 and membership attribute Y can be calculated. Additionally, all tests with respect to λ are possible and useful. Thus, different induced decision trees can also be compared by using the known test statistics (see Hilbert (2002), p. 14). Furthermore, the value of $\hat{\lambda}$ can be interpreted as (estimated) missclassification rate of the decision tree for the identification of class membership attribute Y.

5   Outlook

With ASCAID, a decision tree algorithm is proposed which cares about asymmetric character of the classification task, enables the use of statistical inference and is easy to interpret. Furthermore, the accuracy of the whole tree is based on the same measure as the splits of the nodes. Besides these very promising but also theoretical features of the algorithm some intensive empirical studies are necessary to show what ASCAID is really able to perform. Furthermore, comparisons with the other well-known algorithms are needful as well as studies about the thresholds in the merging/splitting steps.

References

BREIMAN, L.; FRIEDMAN, J.H.; Olshen, R.A., and STONE, C.J. (1984): *Classification and Regression Tree*. Statistics Series. Wadsworth, Belmont.

GOODMAN, L.A. and KRUSKAL, W.H. (1954): Measures of Association for Cross Classifications. *Journal of the American Statistical Association, 49, 732 – 764*.

GOODMAN, L.A. and KRUSKAL, W.H. (1963): Measures of Association for Cross Classifications, III: Approximate Sampling Theory. *Journal of the American Statistical Association, Vol. 58, 310–364*.

GUTTMAN, L. (1941): An Outline of the Statistical Theory of Prediction. In: Horst, P. (Ed.): *The Prediction of Personal Adjustment*. Bulletin 48, Social Science Research Council, New York.

HAN, J. and KAMBER, M. (2001): Data Mining. Concepts and Techniques. Morgan Kaufmann, San Francisco.

HILBERT, A. (1998): Zur Theorie der Korrelationsmaße. Eul Verlag, Lohmar, Köln.

HILBERT, A. (2002): Some Remarks about the Usage of Asymmetric Correlation Measurements for the Induction of Decision Trees. *Arbeitspapiere zur Mathematischen Wirtschaftsforschung, Universität Augsburg, Heft 180*.

KAAS, G.V. (1980): An Exploratory Technique for Investigating Large Quantities of Categorical Data. *Applied Statistics, 29, No. 2, 119–127*.

MESSENGER, R.C. and MANDELL, L.M. (1972): A modal search technique for predictive nominal scale multivariate analysis. *Journal of the American Statistical Society, 67, 768–772*.

QUINLAN, J.R. (1986): Induction of Decision Trees. *Machine Learning, 1, 81–106*.

QUINLAN, J.R. (1993): *C4.5 Programs for Machine Learning*. Morgan Kaufmann, San Mateo, California.

SHANNON, C.E. (1948): The Mathematical Theory of Communication. *The Bell Systems Technical Journal, Vol. 27, 379–423*.

SONQUIST, J.A.; BAKER, E.L. and MORGAN, J.N. (1971): Searching for Structure. Institute for Social Research, University of Michigan, Ann Arbor, MI.

Discriminative Clustering: Vector Quantization in Learning Metrics

Samuel Kaski and Janne Sinkkonen

Neural Networks Research Centre,
Helsinki University of Technology,
FIN-02015 HUT, Finland

Abstract. Discriminative clustering uses auxiliary data to discover task-relevant characteristics of primary data. Asymptotically such clustering is equivalent to vector quantization in the primary data space, but with a new metric. It is implicitly assumed that changes in the primary data are important only to the extent they cause variation in the auxiliary data; the new metric is set up to measure the important changes. In this paper, optimization and regularization of discriminative clusters are discussed.

1 Introduction

We consider the task of clustering continuous primary data $x \in \mathbb{R}^n$ in a way that the clusters become relevant for or informative of the discrete auxiliary data c, i.e., capable of predicting $p(c|x)$. The discriminative approach is expected (and indeed found) to result in clusters more informative about c than those obtained by modeling the joint distribution (Hastie et al. (1995); Hastie and Tibshirani (1996); Miller and Uyar (1997); Hofmann (2001)). The continuity of x distinguishes the setting from that of classical distributional clustering (Pereira et al. (1993); Tishby et al. (1999); Slonim and Tishby (2000)).

The motivation for the model comes from a central problem of unsupervised learning: particularly in clustering it is not possible to distinguish between relevant and irrelevant variation after the (feature extraction and) metric has been fixed. Assumed a suitable dependent variable such as a class labeling is available, however, it might be advantageous to use it even in tasks such as clustering that are usually tacked with unsupervised learning. We have earlier suggested to learn the metric or feature extraction in a supervised fashion and carry out unsupervised learning in the new metric. The idea, called the learning metrics principle, is applicable if an appropriate paired data set is available for learning.

Charting companies based on financial indicators is one example application for discriminative clustering (Kaski et al. (2001)); in this case the bankruptcy risk (whether the company goes bankrupt or not) is natural auxiliary data. Other potential application domains are clustering of texts based on their topic areas, clustering of gene activity patterns based on their functional classes or disease types of the cells, or segmentation of customers based on what they buy.

2 Discriminative clustering

The goal of discriminative clustering is to partition the primary data space into clusters that are (i) local and (ii) homogeneous and predictive in terms of auxiliary data. (The connection between homogeneity and predictivity of the clusters is detailed below.) Locality is enforced by defining the clusters as Voronoi regions in the primary data space: $\mathbf{x}$ belongs to cluster j, $\mathbf{x} \in V_j$, if $\|\mathbf{x} - \mathbf{m}_j\| \le \|\mathbf{x} - \mathbf{m}_k\|$ for all k. The Voronoi regions are uniquely determined by the parameters $\{\mathbf{m}_j\}$.

Homogeneity is enforced by assigning a *distributional prototype* ψ_j to each Voronoi region j, and searching for partitionings capable of predicting auxiliary data with the prototypes. The resulting model is a piecewise-constant generative model of $p(c|\mathbf{x})$, with the log likelihood

$$L = \sum_j \sum_{\mathbf{x} \in V_j} \log \psi_{j,c(\mathbf{x})} \ . \tag{1}$$

The probability of class i within Voronoi region V_j is predicted to be ψ_{ji}. Asymptotically for large data

$$L = -\sum_j \int_{V_j} D_{KL}(p(c|\mathbf{x}), \psi_j) p(\mathbf{x}) d\mathbf{x} + \text{const.} \ , \tag{2}$$

where D_{KL} is the Kullback-Leibler divergence between the prototype and the observed distribution of auxiliary data. This is the cost function of K-means clustering or Vector Quantization (VQ) with the distortion measured by D_{KL}. In this sense, maximizing the likelihood of the model maximizes the distributional homogeneity of the clusters.

The cost (2) is to be minimized with respect to both sets of prototypes, $\mathbf{m}_j$ and ψ_j.

It can be shown that maximizing (2) maximizes the mutual information between the auxiliary data and the clusters considered as a random variable (Sinkkonen and Kaski (2002)).

3 Connection to learning metrics

Assuming important variation in $\mathbf{x}$ is revealed by variation in the conditional density $p(c|\mathbf{x})$, it is sensible to define a metric that measures the important aspects. The distance d between two close-by data points $\mathbf{x}$ and $\mathbf{x} + d\mathbf{x}$ is defined to be the difference between the corresponding conditional distributions of c, measured by the Kullback-Leibler divergence D_{KL}. It is well known that the divergence is locally equal to a quadratic form of the Fisher information matrix $\mathbf{J}$, i.e.

$$d_L^2(\mathbf{x}, \mathbf{x} + d\mathbf{x}) \equiv D_{KL}(p(c|\mathbf{x})\|p(c|\mathbf{x} + d\mathbf{x})) = d\mathbf{x}^T \mathbf{J}(\mathbf{x}) d\mathbf{x} \ . \tag{3}$$

The Fisher information matrix has classically been used for constructing metrics for probabilistic model families (see e.g. Amari and Nagaoka (2000)) A novelty here is that the data vector $\mathbf{x}$ is considered as the parameters of the Fisher information matrix, the aim being to construct a new metric into the *data space*.

The Kullback-Leibler divergence defines a metric locally, and the metric can in principle be extended to an information metric or Fisher metric to the whole data space. We call the idea of measuring distances in the data space by approximations of (3) the *learning metrics principle* (Kaski et al. (2001); Sinkkonen and Kaski (2002); Kaski and Sinkkonen (2002)).

The principle is presumably useful for tasks in which suitable auxiliary data are available, but instead of merely predicting the values of auxiliary data the goal is to analyze, explore, or mine the primary data.

It can be shown (Sinkkonen et al. (2002)) that under certain simplifying assumptions, discriminative clustering asymptotically performs vector quantization in the Fisher metric by Euclidean Voronoi regions: Euclidean metrics define the family of Voronoi partitionings $\{V_j\}_j$ over which the optimization is done, and the Fisher metric is used to measure distortion inside the regions. The result is theoretical in the sense that it holds only at the limit of a large number of both data and clusters, whereas in practical data analysis especially the number of clusters is usually small.

4   Estimation of clusters

The natural extension of maximum likelihood estimation of (1) is to introduce a prior and to find the maximum a posteriori (MAP) estimate. The Bayesian framework is particularly convenient for discriminative clustering: since in our case only the resulting clusters are interesting, not the distribution of the auxiliary data within them, the class distributions can be conveniently integrated out from the posterior. (Although seemingly paradoxical, the auxiliary data of course guides the clustering.)

Denote the observed auxiliary data set by $D^{(c)}$, and the primary data set by $D^{(x)}$. We then wish to find the set of clusters $\{\mathbf{m}\}$ which maximizes the marginalized posterior

$$p(\{\mathbf{m}_j\}|D^{(c)}, D^{(x)}) = \int_{\{\boldsymbol{\psi}_j\}} p(\{\mathbf{m}_j\}, \{\boldsymbol{\psi}_j\}|D^{(c)}, D^{(x)})d\{\boldsymbol{\psi}_j\} \,,$$

or equivalently $\log p(\{\mathbf{m}_j\}|D^{(c)}, D^{(x)})$. Here the integration is over all the $\boldsymbol{\psi}_j$.

Denote the number of classes by N_c, the number of clusters by K, and the total number of samples by N. Denote the part of the data assigned to cluster j by $D_j^{(c)}$, and the number of data samples of class i in cluster j by n_{ji}. Further denote $N_j = \sum_i n_{ji}$.

Assume the improper and separable prior $p(\{\mathbf{m}_j\}, \{\boldsymbol{\psi}_j\}) \propto p(\{\boldsymbol{\psi}_j\}) = \prod_j p(\boldsymbol{\psi}_j)$. Then,

$$p(\{\mathbf{m}_j\}|D^{(c)}, D^{(x)}) \propto \int_{\{\boldsymbol{\psi}_j\}} p(D^{(c)}|\{\mathbf{m}_j\}, \{\boldsymbol{\psi}_j\}, D^{(x)}) p(\{\boldsymbol{\psi}_j\}) d\{\boldsymbol{\psi}_j\}$$

$$= \prod_j \int_{\boldsymbol{\psi}_j} p(D_j^{(c)}|\boldsymbol{\psi}_j) p(\boldsymbol{\psi}_j) \, d\boldsymbol{\psi}_j \propto \prod_j \int_{\boldsymbol{\psi}_j} \prod_i \psi_{ji}^{n_{ji}} p(\boldsymbol{\psi}_j) \, d\boldsymbol{\psi}_j \equiv \prod_j Q_j \,.$$

We will use a conjugate (Dirichlet) prior, $p(\boldsymbol{\psi}_j) \propto \prod_i \psi_{ji}^{n_i^0 - 1}$, where $n^0 = \{n_i^0\}_i$ are the prior parameters common to all j, and $N^0 = \sum_i n_i^0$. Then the "partition-specific" density $p(D_j^{(c)}|\boldsymbol{\psi}_j) p(\boldsymbol{\psi}_j)$ is Dirichlet with respect to $\boldsymbol{\psi}_j$ and the factors Q_j of the total posterior become

$$Q_j = \int_{\boldsymbol{\psi}_j} p(D_j^{(c)}|\boldsymbol{\psi}_j) p(\boldsymbol{\psi}_j) \, d\boldsymbol{\psi}_j \propto \int_{\boldsymbol{\psi}_j} \prod_i \psi_{ij}^{n_i^0 + n_{ji} - 1} \, d\boldsymbol{\psi}_j = \frac{\prod_i \Gamma(n_i^0 + n_{ji})}{\Gamma(N^0 + N_j)} \,.$$

The log of the marginalized posterior probability then is

$$\log p(\{\mathbf{m}_j\}|D^{(c)}, D^{(x)}) = \sum_{ij} \log \Gamma(n_i^0 + n_{ji}) - \sum_j \log \Gamma(N^0 + N_j) + const. \quad (4)$$

In MAP estimation this function needs to be maximized.

4.1   Gradient algorithm for smoothed DC

The objective function (4) itself cannot be optimized by a gradient algorithm because the gradient would be affected only by samples at the typically zero-probability borders of the clusters. We have therefore resorted to "smoothing" the assignment of samples to the clusters during optimization by $n_{ji} = \sum_{c(\mathbf{x})=i} y_j(\mathbf{x})$. Here $c(\mathbf{x})$ is the class of $\mathbf{x}$ and $y_j(\mathbf{x})$ is a smoothed cluster "membership function," defined for example by

$$y_j(\mathbf{x}) = Z^{-1}(\mathbf{x}) e^{-\|\mathbf{x}-\mathbf{m}_j\|^2/\sigma^2}$$

with Z such that $\sum_j y_j(\mathbf{x}) = 1$, and σ governing the degree of smoothing. In the experiments, the smoothing is used only for optimization; no smoothing is used in evaluating the clustering results.

After the smoothing any standard gradient-based algorithms are applicable. We have used conjugate gradients.

4.2   Simulated annealing for DC

Alternatively, the gain function (4) can also be directly maximized by simulated annealing. In each iteration, a candidate step is generated by making small random displacements to the prototype vectors. The step is accepted if it increases the value of the gain function, and even if it decreases the gain function it is accepted with a decreasing probability.

We used normally distributed displacements, with the covariance matrix $\sqrt{T}\sigma^2 \mathbf{I}$. Here T is the "temperature" that was decreased linearly from 1 to 0.1, and the parameter σ was chosen in preliminary experiments using a cross-validation. In simulated annealing, a step that decreases the gain is accepted with the probability $\exp(-\Delta E/T)$, where ΔE is the potential decrease in the gain function.

5   Experiments

Altogether 14,994 samples were picked up from speech data in the TIMIT collection, classified into 41 groups of phones (phonetic sounds), and encoded into 12 cepstral components.

The likelihoods (4) of DC were compared with closest alternative mixture models: K-means, mixture of Gaussians, the joint distribution model MDA2 (Hastie et al. (1995)), and a mixture of Gaussians with the classes concatenated to the samples in the 1-out-of-N encoded form. The likelihood measures the clustering performance in the primary space since the parameters modeling the auxiliary information have been integrated out.

Note that the comparison is not fair since the other models besides DC do not try to optimize the same objective function. Our aim is to show that DC is better than the existing alternatives *in the task of DC*, finding a partitioning of the primary data space that is as informative as possible about the auxiliary variable.

Quality of the clustering solutions as a function of the smoothing parameter σ, or the standard deviation of the Gaussians of the mixture models, is shown in Figure 1. Either the smoothed conjugate gradient MAP algorithm or the simulated annealing algorithm is best for each cluster number, and the difference to the alternatives is mostly significant (Table 1). The older algorithm (Sinkkonen and Kaski (2002)) that maximizes empirical mutual information or, equivalently, smoothed maximum likelihood, is almost as good.

6   Regularization by K-means

We finally discuss a new approach of regularizing the DC solution. DC, as presented above, models solely the conditional probability $p(c|\mathbf{x})$ and would possibly benefit from an explicit model of $p(\mathbf{x})$, in particular for small and noisy data sets. The DC model could be complemented with a generative mixture-type model for $\mathbf{x}$, to model the joint density by $p(c, \mathbf{x}|\{\mathbf{m}_j\}\{\boldsymbol{\psi}_j\}) = p(c|\mathbf{x}, \{\mathbf{m}_j\}, \{\boldsymbol{\psi}_j\})p(\mathbf{x}|\{\mathbf{m}_j\})$.

If a special kind of model is used for $p(\mathbf{x})$ then the resulting joint density model translates into a compromise between DC and K-means cost. This

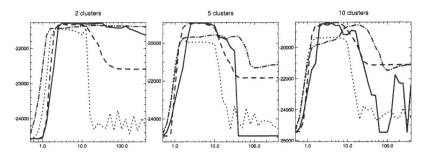

Fig. 1. The performance of the DC algorithm *(solid line)* compared to an older discriminative clustering algorithm *(dashed line)*, plain mixture of Gaussians *(dotted line)* and MDA2, a mixture model for the joint distribution of primary and auxiliary data *(dash-dotted line)*. Sets of clusters were computed with each method with several values of the smoothing parameter σ (x-axis), and the posterior log-probability (4) of the validation data is shown for a hard assignment of each sample to exactly one cluster. The smallest visible value corresponds to assigning samples of each class evenly to the clusters. Results measured by empirical mutual information (not shown) are qualitatively very similar.

	2	5	10
cjgrad MAP	-4651	**-4514**	**-4860**
SA MAP	**-4537**	-4515	-4874
max MI	-4577	<u>-4548</u>	-4885
MoG	<u>-4577</u>	<u>-4584</u>	<u>-5085</u>
MDA2	-4550	<u>-4579</u>	<u>-4953</u>
1-out-of-N	<u>-4576</u>	<u>-4684</u>	<u>-5050</u>

Table 1. Average performance (posterior log-probability; eqn 4) of the algorithms over 10-fold cross-validation trials. The best result for each cluster number is shown in bold, and significantly worse results (t-test, p<0.01) have been underlined. cjgrad MAP: MAP estimation of smoothed DC by the conjugate gradient algorithm; SA MAP: MAP estimation by simulated annealing; max MI: DC by an older algorithm that maximizes mutual information; MoG: mixture of Gaussians; MDA2: mixture model for joint probabilities; 1-out-of-N: class concatenated to the sample vectors in the 1-out-of-N-encoded form.

occurs when $p(\mathbf{x}|\{\mathbf{m}_j\})$ is defined piece-wise for the Voronoi regions as (unnormalized) Gaussians: for $\mathbf{x} \in V_j$,

$$p(\mathbf{x}|\{\mathbf{m}_j\}) = Z^{-1}(\{\mathbf{m}_j\})e^{-\lambda\|\mathbf{x}-\mathbf{m}_j\|^2} , \qquad (5)$$

where $\lambda > 0$. Despite the piecewise definition, the density is everywhere continuous with respect to $\mathbf{x}$, for the borders of Voronoi regions are always half-way between the cluster prototypes. If the normalization factor $Z(\{\mathbf{m}_j\})$ is interpreted as a prior of the model, then the posterior (4) gets the extra factor

$$\prod_j Z(\{\mathbf{m}_j\})p(D^{(x)}|\{\mathbf{m}_j\}) = \prod_j \prod_{\mathbf{x} \in V_j} \exp(-\lambda \|\mathbf{x} - \mathbf{m}_j\|^2) ,$$

and the log posterior of the joint model becomes

$$\log p(\{\mathbf{m}_j\}|D^{(c)}, D^{(x)})$$
$$\propto \sum_{ij} \log \Gamma(n_i^0 + n_{ji}) - \sum_j \log \Gamma(N^0 + N_j) - \sum_{j;\mathbf{x} \in V_j} \lambda \|\mathbf{x} - \mathbf{m}_j\|^2 . \quad (6)$$

This can be interpreted as

$$MAP \equiv \log p(\{\mathbf{m}_j\}|D^{(c)}, D^{(x)}) = MAP_{DC} - \lambda E_{VQ} , \quad (7)$$

where MAP_{DC} is given in (4) and E_{VQ} is the error of K-means clustering. A change in the value of λ makes the focus of the clustering shift between DC and K-means.

7   Discussion

In summary, we have applied the learning metrics principle to clustering, and coined the approach discriminative clustering. In the earlier work (Kaski et al. (2001)) Fisher metrics were derived from explicit conditional density estimators for clustering with self-organizing maps; discriminative clustering has the advantage that the (arbitrary) density estimator is not required.

The new marginalized MAP algorithm outperformed alternative clustering methods on extracting discriminative clusters. It was slightly better than the earlier algorithm derived from information-theoretic principles which, for finite data, is equivalent to a (smoothed) maximum likelihood algorithm.

The conjugate gradient algorithm that used heuristic smoothing to estimate gradients was slightly better than a direct simulated annealing algorithm. Hence it can be concluded that the artificial smoothing, introduced to make gradient-based optimization possible, does not cause obvious artifacts in the clusters.

References

AMARI, S.-I. and NAGAOKA, H. (2000): *Methods of Information Geometry.* American Mathematical Society and Oxford University Press.

HASTIE, T. and TIBSHIRANI, R. (1996): Discriminant analysis by Gaussian mixtures. *Journal of the Royal Statistical Society B, 58, 155–176.*

HASTIE, T., TIBSHIRANI, R., and BUJA, A. (1995): Flexible discriminant and mixture models. In: J. Kay and D. Titterington (Eds.): *Neural Networks and Statistics.* Oxford University Press.

HOFMANN, T. (2001): Unsupervised learning by probabilistic latent semantic analysis. *Machine Learning, 42, 177–196.*

KASKI, S. and SINKKONEN, J. (2002) Principle of learning metrics for data analysis. *The Journal of VLSI Signal Processing-Systems for Signal, Image, and Video Technology, special issue on Data Mining and Biomedical Applications of Neural Networks.* Accepted for publication.

KASKI, S., SINKKONEN, J., and PELTONEN, J. (2001): Bankruptcy analysis with self-organizing maps in learning metrics. *IEEE Transactions on Neural Networks, 12, 936-947.*

MILLER, D. J., and UYAR, H. S. (1997): A mixture of experts classifier with learning based on both labelled and unlabelled data. In: M. Mozer, M. Jordan, and T. Petsche (Eds.): *Advances in Neural Information Processing Systems 9,* MIT Press, Cambridge, MA, 571–577.

PEREIRA, F., TISHBY, N., and LEE, L. (1993): Distributional clustering of English words. In: *Proceedings of the 30th Annual Meeting of the Association for Computational Linguistics.* ACL, Columbus, OH, 183–190.

SINKKONEN, J., and KASKI, S. (2002): Clustering based on conditional distributions in an auxiliary space. *Neural Computation, 14, 217–239.*

SINKKONEN, J., KASKI, S., and NIKKILÄ, J. (2002) Discriminative clustering: optimal contingency tables by learning metrics. In: *Proceedings of the 13th European Conference on Machine Learning (ECML'02).* Accepted for publication.

SLONIM, N. and TISHBY, N. (2000): Agglomerative information bottleneck. In: S. A. Solla, T. K. Leen, and K.-R. Müller (Eds.): *Advances in Neural Information Processing Systems 12,* MIT Press, Cambridge, MA, 617–623.

TISHBY, N., PEREIRA, F. C., and BIALEK, W. (1999): The information bottleneck method. In: *37th Annual Allerton Conference on Communication, Control, and Computing.* Urbana, IL.

Acknowledgment: This work was supported by the Academy of Finland, in part by the grant 52123.

Neural Network Hybrid Learning:
Genetic Algorithms & Levenberg-Marquardt

Ricardo B. C. Prudêncio and Teresa B. Ludermir

Center of Informatics, Federal University of Pernambuco
P.O.Box 7851, Cidade Universitaria, Recife-PE, Brazil, 50.732-970

Abstract. The success of an Artificial Neural Network (ANN) strongly depends on its training process. Gradient-based techniques have been satisfactorily used in the ANN training. However, in many cases, these algorithms are very slow and susceptible to the local minimum problem. In our work, we implemented a hybrid learning algorithm that integrates Genetic Algorithms(GAs) and the Levenberg-Marquardt(LM) algorithm, a second order gradient-based technique. The GA-LM algorithm was used to train a Time-Delay Neural Network for river flow prediction. In our experiments, the GA-LM hybrid algorithm obtained low prediction errors within a short execution time.

1 Introduction

Artificial Neural Networks (ANNs) have been deployed in a variety of real world problems (Haykin (1994)). The success of ANNs for a particular problem depends on the adequacy of the training algorithm regarding the necessities of the problem. The existing gradient-based techniques (Battiti (1992)), in particular the Backpropagation algorithm (Rumelhart et al.(1986)), have been widely used in the training of ANNs. However, as these algorithms perform local searches, they are susceptible to the local minimum problem (Masters 1995). The use of stochastic algorithms, such as Genetic Algorithms (GAs)(Goldberg (1989)), is an interesting alternative for ANN training, since they are less sensitive to local minima. Nevertheless, they are generally slow compared to the fastest versions of gradient-based-algorithms.

In this light, we implemented a new hybrid algorithm that integrates Genetic Algorithms (GAs) and the Levenberg-Marquardt (LM) algorithm (Levenberg (1944))(Marquardt (1963)). Our algorithm aims to combine the capacity of GAs in avoiding local minima and the fast execution of the LM algorithm. In our experiments, we trained a Time Delay Neural Network (TDNN) (Lang and Hinton (1988)) for a river flow prediction problem. Our experiments revealed the following: (1) the implemented algorithm generated networks with good training performance, regarding the error obtained in the validation data, and good generalization performance, regarding the test errors; and (2) the hybrid algorithm was very efficient in terms of the execution time. Based on these results, we opted to integrate the GA-LM algorithm in a ANN design system previously proposed in (Prudêncio and Ludermir (2001a)) for river flow prediction problems.

In what follows, we present issues on training algorithms in section 2, and an overview of the hybrid GA & LM training approach in section 3. Section 4 presents the case-study of river flow prediction and section 5 presents the experiments comparing the hybrid GA-LM approach to other training procedures. Section 6 shows our final remarks.

2   Deterministic and stochastic algorithms

Neural Networks training algorithms can be classified as deterministic or stochastic (Masters (1995)), according to the optimization algorithm used to minimize the cost function. The former type, which includes the various gradient-based algorithms, such as Backpropagation(BP) (Rumelhart et al. (1986)) and Conjugate Gradient (Barnard and Cole (1989)), is characterized by the use of deterministic search operators. In general, these algorithms determine, from a starting point in the search space, a direction which minimizes the error in that given point and steps toward this direction. These algorithms are very sensitive to fall in local minima, since they perform local searches. This problem is crucial in the training of ANNs, since the error surface usually contains multiple local minima and few global minima.

A usual way to minor this effect is by random restarting the initial weights a number of times, and keeping the trained weigths with best results. However, some issues must be addressed regarding the number of restarts: (1) when this number is small, the obtained results may be unsatisfactory. This will depend on how affected is the algorithm by the weight initialization; (2) when the number of restarts is high, the training results tend to be better, however the execution time increases significantly, specially for Backpropagation. This process is probably more plausible if we consider more efficient algorithms, such as those of second-order (Battiti (1992)), including the Levenberg-Marquardt algorithm.

The stochastic algorithms, on the other hand, are characterized by performing global searches and by implementing probabilistic search operators. Among them, we highlight the use of GAs (Montana (1989)) and the Simulated Annealing algorithm (Masters (1995)) in the ANN training. These algorithms determine a new point in the search space by random operations applied to the current weights, most commonly deploying the Gaussian or the Cauchy perturbation (Yao (1995)). The following points in the search space to be examined are selected also on the basis of probabilistic criteria. Due to these characteristics, the stochastic algorithms are less vulnerable to the local minima problem. Another advantage of these algorithms is that the cost function does not need to be differentiable, since it does not use gradient information.

Despite the above-cited advantages, the stochastic algorithms are slower than the faster versions of gradient based techniques (Yao (1995)). Besides, although they are efficient to run global searches, they are less efficient to undergo more refined local searches. A very promising approach emerges in this scenario: the hybrid training, which combines the advantages of both deterministic and stochastic approaches. In the hybrid training, the ANN's weights are alternately modified by a deterministic and by a stochastic algorithm. The stochastic algorithm defines the initial weights used by a local deterministic algorithm to proceed a more fine-tuned local search. This is, in fact, an alternative approach to the random restart of the local algorithm. The ideal behavior of the hybrid algorithm should present the computational efficiency of the gradient-based techniques with the capacity of the stochastic techniques in avoiding local minima.

In (Belew et al. (1990)), the authors combined GAs to the BP algorithm obtaining better results than the use of each algorithm in isolation. In (Masters (1995)), the authors combined the Simulated Annealing and Conjugate Gradient. Other applications of hybrid training algorithms can be found in (Kinnebrock (1994)) and (Castillo et al. (2000)).

3   Hybrid GA-LM algorithm

In this work, we adopted the hybrid learning approach described above using Genetic Algorithms to define the initial weights used as input by the Levenberg-Marquardt algorithm. Hence, we use Genetic Algorithms as the global search procedure and the LM algorithm as the local search procedure. The choice for the LM algorithm is due to its better efficiency (in comparison to other gradient-based algorithms) when dealing with small ANNs, which is the case of the deployed TDNN. The choice of GA as the global procedure is due to its capability of evaluating multiple points in the search space at same time. Hence, they are less sensitive to fall in local minima (Goldberg (1989)).

In our hybrid algorithm, each GA chromosome stores a weight configuration that serves as a starting point for the LM algorithm. In each LM training, the algorithm runs until one of these criteria is verified: maximum number of 500 iterations, generalization loss of 10% or stopping in the training progress of 5%. Details of these stopping criteria can be found in (Prechelt (1994)). The GA's fitness function evaluates a chromosome through the MSE (Mean Squared Error) on the validation data after the LM training. This measure was chosen because it estimates the generalization performance of the trained network (Bishop (1995)).

Regarding the weights' representation, two main approaches must be considered: binary and real schemes. In the former, the value of each weight is stored in a string of bits with a fixed length, and the chromosome is formed by the concatenation of all strings. This scheme has problems of scalability and the precision of the results may not be satisfactory since it is limited by the number of bits in the initial string. The real scheme does not suffer from this drawback since the weights are represented by real numbers. For this reason, we opted to use the real representation in our algorithm.

Considering the genetic operators, it is possible to identify a problem when defining the crossover operator. Two ANNs can be functionally equivalent but bear considerably different genotypes, which makes it difficult the generation of children with the same fitness. This is the case, for instance, of two ANNs with the same weights however in different order. This problem is known as the permutation problem (Hancock (1992)). Although some authors suggest that this is not a difficult problem, there is still a lot to be investigated (Yao (1995)). As we are not convinced that the permutation problem effects are not severe, we opted to discard the crossover operator. Therefore, the only operator adopted in our work was the Gaussian (or Normal) mutation, where a small number obtained from a $N(0, \sigma^2)$ distribution is added to the current value of the weight. The standard deviation σ is a parameter of the operator.

We observe here that, in each execution of the hybrid algorithm, if the GA is set up to perform g generations with i chromosomes per generation, the number of weight configurations generated by the GA, and consequently the number of LM executions, is equal to i multiplied by g. The hybrid algorithm returns the trained weights with the lowest validation error, among the $i \times g$ configurations of trained weights.

4   Case study: river flow prediction

As case study, we trained a TDNN which was used to forecast the monthly river flow of a hydrographic reservoir. The relevance of working with this problem comes from the fact that the operation planning of a hydroelectric power station can be improved based on its flow forecasting system, since the latter reveals the reservoir's energetic potential. Among other works that applied ANNs to the problem of river flow prediction, we highlight (Kadowaki et al. (1997)), (Valenca (1999)) and (Prudêncio and Ludermir (2001a)).

The input data used in our work was obtained from the Guarapiranga reservoir, which is part of the Brazilian Electrical Sector. We have available 300 flow values from January 1963 to December 1986 (Valenca (1999)). This series was equally divided into training, validation and test data sets. The TDNN used in our experiments has a time-window of length 12, receiving the last 12 months flow, and 5 units in the hidden layer. This network employs the one-step prediction of the river flow based on the last 12 months.

The work presented here was developed in the context of a main work which proposes the use of Case-Initialized Genetic Algorithms (Grefensttete and Ramsey (1993)) to implement a system to design neural networks for time series prediction (Prudêncio and Ludermir (2001b)). The case-initialization of GAs consists of generating the first GA's population from well-succeeded solutions to problems which are similar to the one being tackled. The inspiration of this technique comes from the fact that similar problems have similar search spaces and, therefore, good solutions to a particular problem can provide information about the search space for similar problems.

Figure 1 shows the architecture of an implemented prototype. The CBM module maintains a case base in which each case associates a time series to a well-succeeded network architecture used to predict it. Given a new problem (new time series), the Case-Base Manager (CBM) module retrieves a prede-

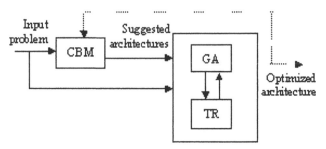

Fig. 1. NN optimization model using Case-Initialized GAs.

fined number of cases, selected on the basis of their similarity to the input problem. The Genetic Algorithm (GA) module performs an optimization of the ANN architecture, using as the initial population the architectures retrieved by the CBM module. The Training module (TR) is responsible for training the weights of each architecture. The output network will be the best architecture generated by the GA and trained by TR. Following, a new case is created and inserted in the base, in order to suggest more adequate solutions in the future. The preliminary results of this prototype for the river flow prediction problem were very promising (Prudêncio and Ludermir (2001a)).

The TR module actually implements the randomly initialized Levenberg-Marquardt algorithm. However, as the proposal of the optimization model is to develop a general system which works well in situations with different needs and constraints, we should experiment different training algorithms and choose the more robust one. The proposal of GA-LM hybrid algorithm is a tentative of developing such robust algorithm.

5   Experiments and results

In our experiments, four procedures were compared in the learning of the TDNN described above: RAND-BP(n), RAND-LM(n), GA-BP(i,g) and GA-LM(i,g). The former two procedures correspond to the usual training process where the gradient-based algorithm is executed n times with random initial weights and the configuration of trained weights with the lowest validation error is returned. RAND-BP(n) and RAND-LM(n) used the BP and the LM algorithms respectively. The procedure GA-BP(i,g) corresponds to a hybrid algorithm in which the GAs are used as the global stochastic algorithm and the BP is the local gradient-based algorithm. And finally, the procedure GA-LM(i,g) corresponds to the proposed algorithm where the LM is combined with GAs.

The random procedures were run for two different values of n (number of weight restarts): 100 and 200. To proceed with a fair comparison, we setup the parameters i and g in such a way that the procedures with GAs implement the same number of restarts as the random procedures. Hence, for $n = 100$ restarts, we used $i = 10$ and $g = 10$, and for $n = 200$, we used $i = 10$ and $g =$

20. The values for mutation rate and the standard deviation of the Gaussian perturbation were set to 0.1 and 0.3 respectively. These values were chosen in preliminary tests.

In order to compare the performance of these procedures, we ran each of them 10 times, and calculated the average values of the MSE in the validation and test sets, as well as, the average execution time.

Procedure (100 restarts)	AVG MSE Validation	Procedure (200 restarts)	AVG MSE Validation
GA-BP(10x10)	34.45	GA-BP(10x20)	32.96
GA-LM(10x10)	34.68	GA-LM(10x20)	34.04
RAND-BP(100)	35.01	RAND-BP(200)	34.82
RAND-LM(100)	35.41	RAND-LM(200)	35.51

Table 1. Ranking based on the Average MSE of the validation set.

In Table 1, we presented the ranking of algorithms for 100 and 200 restarts in terms of the MSE in the validation set, which measured the ANN training performance. As we can see, the performance of the algorithms were very similar for both numbers of restarts. We could say that the procedures are statistically equivalent with high confidence. Despite this similarity, the proposed hybrid algorithm obtained good results in this measure for both number of restarts (2nd place in the ranking of algorithms). Another observation is that, for both BP and LM algorithms, the use of GA initialization improved the results, compared to the random procedures.

Procedure (100 restarts)	AVG MSE Test	Procedure (200 restarts)	AVG MSE Test
RAND-LM(100)	34.41	RAND-LM(200)	35.63
GA-LM(10x10)	36.17	RAND-BP(100)	36.07
RAND-BP(100)	36.24	GA-LM(10x20)	36.80
GA-BP(10x10)	36.73	GA-BP(10x20)	37.53

Table 2. Ranking based on the Average MSE of the test set.

In Table 2, we presented the results in terms of the MSE in the test set. As we can see, the proposed hybrid algorithm presented an intermediate ranking in this measure (2nd place for $n = 100$ and 3rd place for $n = 200$). We observed that the ranking of the GA procedures for the test set was, in general, worse than the ranking obtained for the validation set, particularly for $n = 200$. This effect is more drastic in the GA-BP procedure, which obtained the best validation error, however, the worst test error. This observation may indicate that the use of GA initialization led to an overfitting of the validation data, however this conclusion must be better investigated. Other papers about hybrid learning did not mention this effect.

Procedure (100 restarts)	AVG Execution Time	Procedure (200 restarts)	AVG Execution Time
GA-LM(10x10)	2.4 min	GA-LM(10x20)	4.7 min
GA-BP(10x10)	6.7 min	RAND-LM(200)	12.0 min
RAND-LM(100)	6.8 min	GA-BP(10x20)	13.5 min
RAND-BP(100)	9.7 min	RAND-BP(200)	19.2 min

Table 3. Ranking based on the Average Execution Time (minutes).

The most significant result of these experiments appears when we examined the execution time obtained for each of the learning procedures (see Table 3). As we can see, our proposed algorithm was the fastest algorithm, reducing significantly the execution time compared to the other procedures. This improvement was at least 64% for 100 restarts, and 60% for 200 restarts. This characteristic is of main importance for applications with strong time constraints. The good performance of our hybrid algorithm in this point can be explained by the fact that, at each GA generation, the LM algorithm takes advantage of the optimization performed in the previous generation. Hence, it only refines the search that has already been hardly performed in the previous generations. Furthermore, the LM algorithm is a second-order algorithm, which is, in general, faster than the Backpropagation (Masters (1995)).

6   Conclusion

This paper presents the implementation of a hybrid learning algorithm for ANNs where the GAs were responsible for selecting the initial weights for the Levenberg-Marquardt algorithm. This algorithm was compared to different combinations of initialization strategies and gradient-based techniques on the training of a TDNN for a river flow prediction problem.

Based on the undergone experiments, we concluded that the GA-LM algorithm obtained good results in terms of quality of prediction and showed excellent results in terms of time execution. Despite these good results, the use of GA's initialization may sometimes led to overfitting, although the GA-LM algorithm was less sensitive to this problem. These results lead us to perform more accurate experiments with GA-LM algorithm in order to use it in our general system to design neural networks (as presented in section 4). Eventually, we will test other stochastic techniques.

Another point to investigate in the future is how to avoid the problem of overfitting in hybrid algorithms, evaluating in which situations a hybrid algorithm can be applied with a lower risk of affecting the generalization performance. It is also necessary, to undergo a more detailed study about the influence of the GA's parameters on the performance of the NN training.

References

BARNARD, E. and COLE R.A. (1989): A Neural-Net Training Program based on Conjugate-Gradient Optimization. *Technical Report CSE-89-014, Oregon Graduate Institute, Beaverton, OR*.

BATTITI, R. (1992): First and Second-Order Methods for Learning Between Steepest Descentand Newton's Method. *Neural Computation, 4, 141–166*.

BELEW, R.K., MCINERNEY, J. and SCHRAUDOLPH, N.N. (1990): Evolving Networks: Using the Genetic Algorithm with Connectionist Learning. *Technical Report CSE-CS-90-174, University of California, San Diego, CA*.

BISHOP, C. (1995): *Neural Networks for Pattern Recognition*. Oxford University Press, UK.

CASTILLO, P.A., CARPIO, J., MERELO, J. J., RIVAS, V., ROBER, G. and PRIETO, A. (2000): Evolving Multilayer Perceptrons. *Neural Processing Letters, 12, 115–127*.

GOLDBERG, D.E. (1989): *Genetic Algorithms in Search, Optimization and Machine Learning*. Addison-Wesley, Reading, MA.

GREFENSTTETE, J. and RAMSEY, C. (1993): Case-based initialization of genetic algorithms. *Proceedings of the Fifth International Conference on Genetic Algorithms, San Mateo, CA, 84–91*.

HANCOCK, P.J.B. (1992): Genetic Algorithms and Permutation Problems: a Comparison of Recombination Operators for Neural Net Structure Specification. *Proceedings of the International Workshop on Combinations of Genetic Algorithms, Baltimore, 108–122*. IEEE Computer Society Press, CA.

HAYKIN, S. (1994): *Neural Networks: A Comprehensive Foundation*. IEEE Press/Macmillan College Publishing Company, New York, NY.

KADOWAKI, M., SOARES, S. and ANDRADE, M. (1997): Montly River Flow Prediction Using Multilayer Neural Networks with Backpropagation. *Anais do IV Simpsio Brasileiro de Redes Neurais (in portuguese), 32–35, Goiana, Brazil*.

KINNEBROCK, W. (1994) Accelerating the Standard Backpropagation Method Using a Genetic Approach. *Neurocomputing, 6, 583–588*.

LANG, K and HINTON, G. (1988): Time-Delay Neural Network Architecture for Speech Recognition. *Technical Report CMU-CS-88-152, Carnegie-Mellon University, Pittsburgh, PA*.

LEVENBERG, K. (1944): A Method for the Solution of Certain Non-Linear Problems in Least Squares. *Quarterly Journal of Applied Mathematics, 2, 164–168.*

MARQUARDT, D. (1963): An Algorithm for Least-Squares Estimation of Nonlinear Parameters. *SIAM J. Applied Mathematics, 11, 431–441.*

MASTERS, T. (1995): *Advanced Algorithms for Neural Networks: a C++ Sourcebook.* John Wiley & Sons, New York, NY.

MONTANA, D. J. and DAVIS, L. (1989): Training Feedforward Neural Networks Using Genetic Algorithms. *Proceedings of the Eleventh International Joint Conference on Artificial Intelligence, Detroit, MI, 762–767.*

PRECHELT, L. (1994): Proben1 - A Set of Neural Network Benchmark Problems and Benchmarking Rules. *Technical Report 21/94, Fakultat fur Informatik, Universitat Karlsruhe, Germany, September, 1994.*

PRUDÊNCIO, R.B.C. and LUDERMIR, T.B. (2001a): Evolutionary Design of Neural Networks: Aplication to River Flow Prediction. *Proceedings of the International Conference on Artificial Inteligence and Aplications, AIA 2001, Marbella, Spain, 56–61*

PRUDÊNCIO, R.B.C. and LUDERMIR, T.B. (2001b): Design of Neural Networks for Time Series Prediction Using Case-Initialized Genetic Algorithms. *Proceedings of the 8th International Conference on Neural Information Processing, ICONIP' 01, Shanghai, China, 990–995.*

RUMELHART, D.E., HINTON, G.E. and WILLIAMS, R.J. (1986): Learning internal representations by error propagation. In: D.E. RUMELHART and J.L. MCCLELLAND (Eds.): *Parallel Distributed Processing Vol.1.* MIT Press, Cambridge, 318–362.

VALENCA, M.J.S. (1999): Analysis and Design of the Constructive Neural Networks for Complex Systems Modeling. *Ph.D Thesis (in portuguese), Federal University of Pernambuco, Recife, Brazil.*

YAO, X. (1995): Evolutionary Artificial Neural Networks. *Encyclopedia of Computer Science and Technology, 33, 137–170.* Marcel Dekker, New York, NY.

Syntagmatic and Paradigmatic Associations in Information Retrieval

Reinhard Rapp

Johannes Gutenberg-Universität Mainz, FASK
D-76711 Germersheim, Germany

Abstract. It is shown that unconscious associative processes taking place in the memory of a searcher during the formulation of a search query in information retrieval - such as the production of free word associations and the generation of synonyms - can be simulated using statistical models that analyze the distribution of words in large text corpora. The free word associations as produced by subjects on presentation of stimulus words can be predicted by applying first-order statistics to the frequencies of word co-occurrences as observed in texts. The generation of synonyms can also be conducted on co-occurrence data but requires second-order statistics. Both approaches are compared and validated on empirical data. It turns out that for both tasks the performance in the simulation is comparable to the performance of human subjects.

1 Introduction

According to Ferdinand de Saussure (1916), there are two fundamental types of relations between words that he believes correspond to basic operations of our brain: *syntagmatic* and *paradigmatic* associations[1]. There is a syntagmatic relation between two words if they co-occur in spoken or written language more frequently than expected from chance and if they have different grammatical roles in the sentences in which they occur. Typical examples are the word pairs *coffee - drink*, *sun - hot*, or *teacher - school*. The relation between two words is paradigmatic if the two words can substitute for one another in a sentence without affecting the grammaticality or acceptability of the sentence. Examples are synonyms or antonyms like *quick - fast*, or *eat - drink*. Normally, words with a paradigmatic relation are the same part of speech, whereas words with a syntagmatic relation can but need not be the same part of speech. Table 1 compares some properties of syntagmatic and paradigmatic relations.

When formulating a search query from a given natural language problem description, the searcher usually tries to use search words that optimize recall and precision. As has been examined on the basis of problem descriptions given to professional searchers and the corresponding search protocols, in their queries the searchers mostly use words that have a paradigmatic relation to the words in the problem description; however, it also frequently occurs that they use words with a syntagmatic relation.

---

[1] Since terminology was not established yet, de Saussure speaks of *syntagmatic* and *associative relations* instead of *syntagmatic* and *paradigmatic* associations.

	syntagmatic	*paradigmatic*
co-occurrence frequency	> chance	any
part of speech	any	same
substitution possible	no	yes

Table 1. Comparison of the properties of syntagmatic and paradigmatic relations.

For example, when asked to search for documents on the *theory of relativity*, in order to complement the rather unspecific words *theory* and *relativity*, a searcher may use *Einstein* as one of the search words, which has a syntagmatic relationship to the term *relativity theory*. Table 2 shows an example search protocol as provided by a German psychological information agency[2]. The searches in the agency were conducted by professional searchers in the psychological databases *PsycINFO* and *PSYNDEX* on the basis of written problem descriptions as obtained from their customers.

Problem description:
Heimarbeit in der Sozialarbeit / Sozialpdagogik
(Homework in casework / social education)

PsycINFO search protocol:
1	870	Find CT=**Paraprofessional Personel$**
2	347	Find CT=**Volunteer Personnel$**
3	142	Find CT=**Foster Parents**
5	6	Find CT=**Probation Officer$** And All [**Paraprof$**;**Volunteer**;**Lay$**]/PQ
6	272	Find [1;2] And All Social [Work;Casework;Case]/PQ
7	18	Find 6 And All [**Volunteer**;**Lay$**]/PQ
8	20	Find 1 To 3 And **Supervision**/PQ
9	97	Find [3;6] And **Training**/PQ
10	136	Find 5;7 To 9
15	36	Find CT=**Nonprofessional Personnel**
16	171	Find 10 Or 15
17	97	Find 16 And PY>1974

Table 2. Record of a database search. Search words not considered in paradigmatic relation with at least one of the words in the problem description are printed in bold. The numbers in the first column are for reference to the respective search command, those in the second column indicate the number of documents found in the database.

In previous publications, when trying to automatically generate search words from natural language problem descriptions, the emphasis has usually been on trying to generate words with similar meaning, i.e. on paradigmatic associations (Grefenstette (1994); Ruge (1995); an exception is Wettler et al.

---

[2] Zentralstelle für psychologische Information und Dokumentation in Trier.

(1995)). Although the suggested approaches work rather well, they only offer a partial solution to the problem of search word generation, as syntagmatic associations are ignored.

In this paper we want to show that the two types of relations as defined by de Saussure are reflected in the statistical distribution of words in large corpora. We present algorithms that automatically retrieve words with either the syntagmatic or the paradigmatic type of relationship from a corpus. We also perform a quantitative evaluation of our results by comparing them to human word associations and human intuitions on word similarities.

In our view, comparing the simulation results to human experimental data is a more direct way to show the effectiveness of our methods than to generate search queries, retrieve documents, and then to evaluate recall and precision. The reason is that recall and precision depend not only on the quality of the search terms, but also on the documents in the database as well as on subjective relevance judgments. These factors not directly related to our aims may blur the results. Also, as retrieval results must satisfy human information needs, the basis for quality judgments in information retrieval are human intuitions. Therefore, showing that we can simulate human intuitions gives evidence that it should be possible to successfully apply our methods in information retrieval.

2   Paradigmatic associations

Paradigmatic associations are words with high semantic similarity. According to Ruge (1995), the semantic similarity of two words can be computed by determining the agreement of their lexical neighborhoods. For example, the semantic similarity of the words *red* and *blue* can be derived from the fact that they both frequently co-occur with words like *color, flower, dress, car, dark, bright, beautiful,* and so forth. If for each word in a corpus a co-occurrence vector is determined whose entries are the co-occurrences with all other words in the corpus, then the semantic similarities between words can be computed by conducting simple vector comparisons.

Please note that this finding is in agreement with the observation from information retrieval that term similarity can be computed by comparing the term vectors in the term/document-matrix (Salton, McGill (1983)). The only difference is that in information retrieval document size is more or less arbitrary, whereas for generating a co-occurrence matrix text windows of a fixed number of words are considered instead of documents.

Our intention is to compare the results produced by our algorithm to similarity estimates obtained from human subjects. Such data was kindly provided by Thomas K. Landauer, who had taken it from the synonym portion of the *Test of English as a Foreign Language* (TOEFL). Originally, the data came, along with normative data, from the Educational Testing Service (Landauer, Dumais (1997)). The TOEFL is an obligatory test for foreign students who would like to study at universities where the teaching language is English.

The data comprises 80 test items. Each item consists of a problem word in testing parlance and four alternative words, from which the test taker is asked to choose that with the most similar meaning to the problem word. For example, given the test sentence *"Both boats and trains are used for transporting the materials"* and the four alternative words *planes, ships, canoes,* and *railroads*, the subject would be expected to choose the word *ships*, which is the one most similar to *boats*.

Our computations of word similarities are based on the *British National Corpus* (BNC), a 100 million word corpus of written and spoken English. In a pre-processing step this corpus was lemmatized and its function words were removed (for details see Rapp (1999)). Then - based on a window size of ±1 words - a co-occurrence matrix of all words in the corpus was computed.

To determine the words most similar to a given word, the co-occurrence vector of this word is compared to all other vectors in the matrix and the words are sorted according to the similarity values obtained. It is expected that the most similar words are ranked first. For vector comparison we used the city-block metric. It computes the distance between two vectors as the sum of the absolute differences of corresponding vector positions (Rapp(1999)).

To give some results, table 3 shows the top five paradigmatic associations to six stimulus words. Although these results look plausible, a quantitative evaluation would be preferable. For this reason we did a comparison with the results of the human subjects in the TOEFL test. Remember that the human subjects had to choose the word most similar to a given stimulus word from a list of four alternatives.

blue	cold	fruit	green	tobacco	whiskey
red	hot	food	red	cigarette	whisky
green	warm	flower	blue	alcohol	brandy
grey	dry	fish	white	coal	champagne
yellow	drink	meat	yellow	import	lemonade
white	cool	vegetable	grey	textile	vodka

Table 3. Paradigmatic associations to six stimulus words.

In the simulation, we assumed that the system had chosen the correct alternative if the correct word was ranked highest among the four alternatives. This was the case for 55 of the 80 test items, which gives us an accuracy of 69%. This accuracy may seem low, but it should be taken into account that the TOEFL tests the language abilities of prospective university students and therefore is rather difficult. Actually, the performance of the average human test taker was worse than the performance of the system. The human subjects were only able to solve 51.6 of the test items correctly, which gives an accuracy of 64.5%.

3 Syntagmatic associations

Syntagmatic associations are words that frequently occur together. Therefore, an obvious approach to extract them from corpora is to look for word pairs whose co-occurrence frequency is significantly higher than chance. To test for significance we used the log-likelihood test (Rapp (1999)).

As we did with the paradigmatic associations, we would like to compare the results of our simulation to human performance. Suitable data is available in the form of the Edinburgh Associative Thesaurus, a large collection of association norms compiled by Kiss et al. (1973). Kiss presented lists of stimulus words to human subjects and asked them to write after each word the first word that the stimulus word made them think of. Table 4 gives some examples of the associations the subjects came up with.

blue	cold	fruit	green	tobacco	whiskey
sky	hot	apple	grass	smoke	drink
black	ice	juice	blue	cigarette	gin
green	warm	orange	red	pipe	bottle
red	water	salad	yellow	poach	soda
white	freeze	machine	field	road	Scotch

Table 4. Some sample associations from the Edinburgh Associative Thesaurus.

As can be seen from the table, not all of the associations given by the subjects are of syntagmatic type. For example, the word pairs *blue - black* or *cold - hot* are clearly of paradigmatic type. This observation is of importance and will be discussed later.

For the computation of the syntagmatic associations we used the same corpus as before, namely the BNC. Based on a window size of ± 20 words,[3] we first compute the co-occurrence vector for a given stimulus word, thereby eliminating all words with a corpus frequency of less than 101.[4] We then apply the log-likelihood test to this vector (for details see Rapp (1999)). Finally, the vocabulary is ranked according to descending log-likelihood scores in the vector. The word with the highest value is considered to be the primary associative response.

In order to make the common properties and differences between the two algorithms for the computation of 1st and 2nd order associations more explicit, table 5 shows a comparison of the steps involved.

In table 6 a few sample association lists as predicted by our system are shown. They can be compared to the human associative responses given in

---

[3] Since the sparse data-problem is more severe for 1st than for 2nd order associations, a larger window size is required.

[4] This threshold was introduced since in the association experiment human subjects tend to respond with frequent words.

Step	1st order	2nd order
Corpus	BNC (unmodified)	BNC (lemmatized and with function words removed)
Window size	±20 words	±1 word
Association measure	log-likelihood ratio	none
Computation of strongest association to a word	highest value in association vector	vector is compared to the vectors of all other words in the vocabulary (vectors are normalized)

Table 5. Comparison of the two algorithms.

table 4. The valuation of the predictions has to take into account that association norms are conglomerates of the answers of different subjects that differ considerably from each other. A satisfactory prediction would be proven if the difference between the predicted and the observed responses were about equal to the difference between an average subject and the rest of the subjects. This is actually the case. For 27 out of the 100 stimulus words the predicted response is equal to the observed primary response. This compares to an average of 28 primary responses given by a subject in the Edinburgh Associative Thesaurus. Other evaluation measures lead to similar good results (Rapp (1996)).

blue	cold	fruit	green	tobacco	whiskey
red	hot	vegetable	red	advertising	drink
eyes	water	juice	blue	smoke	Jesse
sky	warm	fresh	yellow	ban	bottle
white	weather	tree	leaves	cigarette	Irish
green	winter	salad	colour	alcohol	pour

Table 6. Results with the 1st order approach.

We conclude from this that our method seems to be well suited to predict the free word associations as produced by humans. However, human associations are not only of syntagmatic but also of paradigmatic type. And to our surprise the co-occurrence-based method not only predicts syntagmatic but also paradigmatic associations rather well.[5] In the ranked lists produced by the system we find a mixture of both types of associations, but for a given word there is no indication as to the type of association. However, we have a simple proposal to separate the paradigmatic from the syntagmatic associations. Remember that the 2nd-order approach described in the previous section produced paradigmatic associations only. So if we simply remove the words produced by the 2nd-order approach from the word lists obtained by

---

[5] This observation, which is contrary to common belief, has also been reported in Rapp (1996).

the 1st-order approach, then this should give us solely syntagmatic associations.

4 Comparison between 1st and 2nd order approaches

Table 1 compares the top five associations to a few stimulus words as produced by the 1st-order and the 2nd-order approach. In the list, we have printed in bold those 1st-order associations that are not among the top five in the second-order lists. Further inspection of these words shows that they are all syntagmatic associations. So the method proposed seems to work in principle. However, we have not yet conducted a systematic quantitative evaluation. Conducting a systematic evaluation is not trivial, since the definitions of the terms *syntagmatic* and *paradigmatic* as given in the introduction may not be precise enough. Also, for a high recall, the word lists considered should be much longer than the top five. However, the further down we go on the ranked lists, the less typical are the associations. So it is not clear where to set a threshold. Fortunately, this problem can be avoided by sorting all associations according to the quotient

$$\frac{1st\ order\ association\ strength}{2nd\ order\ association\ strength}$$

It can be expected that this quotient is well suited to separate the syntagmatic from the paradigmatic associations, i.e. we will find the syntagmatic associations at the top and the paradigmatic association at the bottom of the list.

Stimulus	1st-order	2nd-order
blue	*red*	red
	eyes	green
	sky	grey
	white	yellow
	green	white
cold	*hot*	hot
	water	warm
	warm	dry
	weather	drink
	winter	cool
fruit	*vegetable*	food
	juice	flower
	fresh	fish
	tree	meat
	salad	vegetable

Stimulus	1st-order	2nd-order
green	*red*	red
	blue	blue
	yellow	white
	leaves	yellow
	colour	grey
tobacco	**advertising**	cigarette
	smoke	alcohol
	ban	coal
	cigarette	import
	alcohol	textile
whiskey	**drink**	whisky
	Jesse	brandy
	bottle	champagne
	Irish	lemonade
	pour	vodka

Fig. 1. Comparison between 1st-order and 2nd-order associations.

5   Discussion, conclusions, and prospects

The production of search words during the formulation of search queries is governed by unconscious processes taking place in the memory of the searcher, enabling him or her to generate syntagmatic and paradigmatic associations. In most cases, previous publications on automatic search term generation put the emphasis on paradigmatic rather than on syntagmatic relations. By giving examples where searchers used syntagmatic associations in their queries, we showed that neglecting syntagmatic associations means that some aspects of the behavior of human searchers are not accounted for. Based on observations on the statistical distribution of words in texts, we have described algorithms for the computation of both 1st-order and 2nd-order associations. The results obtained have been compared with the answers of human subjects in the free association task and in the TOEFL synonym test. It could be shown that the performance of our system is comparable to the performance of the subjects for both tasks.

We observed that there seems to be some relationship between the type of computation performed (1st-order versus 2nd-order) and the terms *syntagmatic* and *paradigmatic* as coined by de Saussure. Whereas the results of the 2nd-order computation are of paradigmatic type exclusively, those of the 1st-order computation are a mixture of both syntagmatic and paradigmatic associations. Removing the 2nd-order associations from the 1st-order associations leads to solely syntagmatic associations.

An important problem that we have not approached in this paper is the problem of ambiguity. For example, the word *palm* has senses related to *tree* and to *hand*. Some associations that we compute will be related to one sense and some to the other (or to both), but our algorithms provide no means of separating the senses.

This is the problem of sense induction for which we want to outline a possible solution. We start by assuming that the senses of an ambiguous word are best described by some of its typical associations. Our core assumption is that a set of n words then best describes the n senses of a given ambiguous word when the typical associations of the words in the set complement each other in such a way that the union of these associations is identical to the typical associations of the ambiguous word. We call this assumption the complementarity condition.

By evaluating the degree of complementarity for each possible pair of the top ten associations to *palm*, we found that the pair *tree / hand* best fulfilled the complementarity condition. Likewise, for the word *bank* we obtained the pair *account / river*. These preliminary results look encouraging.

A problem with this approach is that not only the word that we look at, but also its associations that we use as sense descriptors can be ambiguous, and that this problem goes on. We believe that independent component analysis (ICA) can solve this fundamental problem. ICA can be seen as an extension of principal component analysis (PCA) and is capable of dealing with statistical dependencies of higher than second order. In signal processing, ICA was successfully used to solve the so-called cocktail party problem, that is to recover the signals A and B if only two different mixtures of these signals are available (see Hyvärinen et al. (2001)). For ICA to work the signals A and B need to be statistically independent at any time. They are called the independent components of the two mixed signals.

In our view, ICA can be applied to the problem of sense induction if for an ambiguous word context vectors extracted from corpora of different domains are available.[6] Since it is unlikely that the different senses of a word are distributed evenly over different domains, these vectors can be seen as different mixtures of the senses. Therefore, the independent components that ICA computes should be the vectors optimally describing each sense. As the number of words in a language is limited, it will usually not be possible to find a word whose vector exactly matches a sense vector and thus makes its meaning explicit. However, since the sense vector specifies an exact position in semantic space, it is possible to approximately describe its meaning by some of its neighboring words.

To conclude, let us mention that in our view the observed relation between our statistical models and the intuitions of de Saussure is not incidental, and that the striking similarity of the simulation results with human associations also has a deeper reason. Our explanation is that human associative behavior is governed by statistical processes. It appears that first order statistics are suitable for the simulation of free word associations, that second order statistics are appropriate for computing semantic similarities between words, and that the higher order statistics dealt with by ICA may be able to solve the ambiguity problem.

However, further work is required to find out if these conjectures hold, and - as far as information retrieval practice is concerned - to what extent automatic systems simulating these processes on the basis of the above principles can assist in either generating search queries from natural language input or in optimizing suboptimal search queries.

References

de SAUSSURE, F. (1916/1996): Cours de linguistique générale. *Paris: Payot.*
GREFENSTETTE, G. (1994): Explorations in Automatic Thesaurus Discovery. *Dordrecht: Kluwer.*
HYVÄRINEN, A.; KARHUNEN, J.; OJA, E. (2001): Independent Component Analysis. *New York: Wiley.*
KISS, G.R., ARMSTRONG, C., MILROY, R., PIPER, J. (1973): An associative thesaurus of English and its computer analysis. *In: A.J. Aitken, R.W. Bailey, and N. Hamilton-Smith (eds.): The Computer and Literary Studies. Edinburgh: University Press. 153-165.*

---

[6] Since ICA is computationally expensive, it seems not realistic to simply compute the independent components for the co-occurrence vectors of all words of a language.

LANDAUER, T. K.; DUMAIS, S. T. (1997): A solution to Plato's problem: the latent semantic analysis theory of acquisition, induction, and representation of knowledge. *Psychological Review, 104(2), 211-240.*

RAPP, R. (1996): Die Berechnung von Assoziationen. *Hildesheim: Olms.*

RAPP, R. (1999): Automatic identification of word translation from unrelated English and German corpora. *In: Proceedings of the 37th Annual Meeting of the Association for Computational Linguistics, College Park. 519-526.*

RUGE, G. (1995): Wortbedeutung und Termassoziation. *Hildesheim: Olms.*

SALTON, G.; McGILL, M. (1983): Introduction to Modern Information Retrieval. *New York: McGraw-Hill.*

WETTLER, M.; FERBER, R.; RAPP, R. (1995): An associative model of word selection in the generation of search queries. *Journal of the American Society for Information Science, 46(9), 685-699.*

Acknowledgments: This research was supported by the Deutsche Forschungsgemeinschaft. I would like to thank Manfred Wettler and Gerda Ruge for their support of this work.

Finding the Most Useful Clusters: Clustering and the Usefulness Metric

Caroline St.Clair

North Central College,
30 N. Brainard St., Naperville, IL, 60540, USA,
castclair@noctrl.edu

Abstract. Algorithms that extract information from data are required to provide correct information. However, data mining algorithms have an additional requirement. The information they extract must not only be correct, but also useful. The usefulness metric was developed to meet these needs. Although it has been shown to work on classification algorithms, the usefulness metric's success lies in its ability to be applied to other data mining algorithms. This paper will show two different methods of applying the usefulness metric to a clustering algorithm in order to obtain more useful clusters.

1 Introduction

The main purpose of using data mining algorithms is to extract information from data. There are three main stages of data mining: preprocessing, data extraction, and data analysis. An excellent source of information on the stages can be found at (Fayyad, et al. (1996)). Most data extraction methods rely solely on correctness metrics to measure their effectiveness. Whether this means finding the best node in a decision tree, finding the best association rule, or finding the best attribute to cluster data on, correctness has been the driving force behind these algorithms. One cannot argue with the fact that finding the most correct solution to a problem is important. However, algorithms used in the context of data mining must extract more than just correct information; it has been argued that the information must also be useful information (Silberschatz and Tuzhilin (1996), Uthurusamy (1996)).

Useful information has also been referred to as "valuable information" (Weiss and Indurkhya (1998)). This additional constraint on data mining algorithms requires a degree of subjectiveness to be used by the algorithm. What might be useful to one person may not necessarily be useful to another. Thus, data mining algorithms cannot rely exclusively on a correctness metric when carrying out their task.

There is a fast growing market for data mining products. Generally, this group of users has a great deal of knowledge regarding their data. What does data mining have to offer any user who understands their data? If data mining is to succeed in these types of arenas, they must provide a unique service. Suppose a grocery store manager knows that stocking products at eye level sells better than stocking products at other locations on a shelf, and a software product draws the same conclusion. Since the user already had this type of knowledge, the information would not be very useful, regardless of how correct it is. Certainly there are situations in which a user would like their knowledge verified, but more often, the case is to obtain new knowledge.

In (St.Clair et al. (1998)) it was shown that a classification algorithm could be modified to seek out useful information. A usefulness metric was developed to encapsulate the objective and subjective measures needed for this process to succeed (St.Clair (2000)). The usefulness metric is composed of three measurements: actionability, newness and correctness. The combination of these provides both objective and subjective measures. Actionability and newness are both subjective measures. Actionability is determined by measuring a particular user's ability to "act on" information. Is the user able to make a decision in their best interest with the information? If so, then the actionability of the information is high. Newness is determined by measuring how novel the information is to the user. Does the user already know this information? If so, the newness of the information is low. Of course, maintaining a level of correctness is important, and the usefulness metric does allow for a correctness component. This objective component is determined by measuring the accuracy of the information.

Although it has been shown that this metric can be successfully applied to classification algorithms, the question of whether it can be extended to other data mining algorithms remains. This paper will show how the usefulness metric can be applied to clustering algorithms in order to find more useful clusters in the data. The metric will be used at the front-end of a clustering algorithm to search for more useful clusters. In addition, the metric will be used at the back-end of a clustering algorithm to find more useful descriptions for the clusters.

2   Applying the usefulness metric to clustering

Clustering algorithms are used to determine patterns in data. In order to determine patterns, a clustering algorithm groups together *like* tuples. These groups are called *clusters*. The user may predetermine the number of clusters. Generally, a distance metric is used to determine the *likeness* between tuples. There are a number of clustering methods, including partitioning methods, hierarchical methods, density-based methods, grid-based methods, and model-based methods. A discussion of these methods along with various distance metrics can be found in (Han and Kamber (2001), Berry and Linoff (1997)).

In this paper, an agglomerative based hierarchical method will be used with the usefulness metric; although, this metric can be easily applied to any clustering method, including k-means. The agglomerative method is a bottom-up approach to clustering. The following steps outline the agglomerative approach used in this paper:

i) Create an NxN matrix, where N represents the number of tuples and the matrix is lower triangular. Initially, each tuple represents its own cluster. As tuples are merged, their values are replaced with the mean values of all tuples in the merged cluster. These mean values are the centroid values.

ii) Populate each cell in the lower triangular portion of the matrix with the distance between the two clusters represented by the row and column of the matrix. For example, the cell at row 5 column 3 represents the distance between cluster 5 and cluster 3. Centroid values are used to determine the distance between clusters.

iii) Merge the two clusters that have the smallest distance. This is done by replacing each attribute of one of the clusters with the average attribute values of the two clusters. The other cluster is eliminated.

iv) Repeat steps 2-3 until *k* clusters remain.

A front-end application of the usefulness metric is to weight the distance during step 2. In order to apply the usefulness metric, actionability and newness values must be assigned to each attribute and weight factors determined for actionability and newness. For example, the user may choose an equal weight factor for actionability and newness, or the user may decide that newness is more important than actionability and assign a larger weight factor to newness. The sum of these two factors must equal 1. This paper assumes an equal weight factor.

A new weighted distance for tuples can now be calculated using Equation 1. This equation assumes interval distance is used and *n* attributes exist. T_i and T_j represent particular tuples, T_{ia} represents the *a*th attribute value for tuple *i*, Act_a represents the actionability value assigned by the user to the *a*th attribute, $ActF$ represents the actionability factor assigned by the user, New_a represents the newness value assigned by the user to the *a*th attribute, and $NewF$ represents the newness factor assigned by the user. By weighting the distance with the usefulness metric, attribute distance is biased by the actionability and newness values assigned to the attribute, while the distance itself represents the correctness component. Thus, the algorithm will cluster the data based on actionability and newness, in addition to distance, rather than solely on distance.

$$d(T_i, T_j) = \sum_{a=1}^{n} (|T_{ia} - T_{ja}| * ((Act_a * ActF) + (New_a * NewF))) \quad (1)$$

In addition to using the usefulness metric at the front-end of a clustering algorithm, it can also be used to help analyze clusters at the back-end of a clustering algorithm. Once clusters are formed, information is conveyed to the user about the similarities of the data within the clusters. Attributes most responsible for developing the clusters are found by determining the attributes with the largest difference from the total dataset population. For example, a cluster may be described as "commuter students" if the attributes representing "commuter" and "students" have a high variance from the total dataset population. Although the accuracy of this information may be high, it may not be useful. What if the user knows this information and is seeking out new information? What if the user cannot act on the information provided?

Actionability and newness values, along with the mean difference from the total dataset population can be combined to determine the attributes that would best describe the clusters.

Once clusters are created, a usefulness value is assigned to each attribute. This is shown in Equation 2 where $UValue_a$ represents the usefulness value for attribute a. *Diff* is the mean difference of this attribute value from the total dataset population. *New, NewF, Act, ActF* are the same as in Equation 1. A correctness factor, represented by *CorF* is introduced. For the back-end application, the user must determine a correctness factor in addition to the actionability and newness factors.

$$UValue_a = (Diff_a * CorF + Act_a * ActF + New_a * NewF) \qquad (2)$$

Determining actionability and newness values for each attribute is very user dependent. Newness and actionability are ranged between 0 and 1. Each user will have different experiences with the data, different knowledge bases and different job descriptions. In (St.Clair (2000)), newness values were generated using user's existing knowledge statements, and actionability values were assigned using a brute force method of painstakingly assigning each attribute an actionability value. Determining the newness values for attributes in a clustering algorithm is a simpler process. Users may have a general idea or even actual statistical data of an attribute's ability to cluster. The user may already know that the data can be clustered into "commuter students" and "non-commuter students". If this is the case, the user may assign a low newness value to these attributes. If the user has previously analyzed the data using a clustering algorithm, the values for the mean difference from the population can be easily transferred into newness values. For example, assume a clustering algorithm has found clusters and .8 is assigned as the mean difference from the population for a particular attribute. It is assumed that these values are scaled from 0 to 1. If this is the highest value assigned to any attribute, then the clusters are described using this attribute. A user may wish to then assign .2 (1 - .8) as the newness value for this attribute.

Actionability values for clustering algorithms can be handled using the brute force method; however, this may be an unrealistic task for a user given a dataset containing a large number of attributes. In this case, it may be more beneficial to assign each attribute a neutral value of .5. A user may have an opinion regarding the actionability of a few attributes and can easily raise or lower the actionability value on those attributes accordingly. New methods for determining actionability are currently being investigated by the author. The brute force method is used to assign both actionability and newness values for the simple example presented in this paper. To clarify how these equations can be used, the next section provides a specific example showing how the usefulness metric can be applied to the back-end of a clustering algorithm, while Section 4 shows how the usefulness metric can be applied to the front-end of a clustering algorithm.

3   Back-end example

Once clusters are found, they are analyzed in order to find the attributes responsible for their creation. This is determined by comparing the mean of each attribute in the cluster to the mean of the total dataset population. It may be more feasible to base this on the most useful attributes. In order to determine the most useful attributes, the usefulness metric is incorporated into the mean difference. A simple example will help demonstrate how the usefulness metric can be applied. Table 1 represents a few personal statistics for a fictitious group of people. The dataset is kept small to make it easy for the reader to analyze and is considered the total dataset population. The four attributes used are married, gender, income and age. Married and gender are binary attributes. Income and age are interval scaled. If the person is married, a 1 will appear in the married column, otherwise a 0 is used. For the gender attribute, a 1 will represents female and 0 male.

PERSON	MARRIED AV .2 NV 0	GENDER AV 0 NV 0	INCOME AV 1.0 NV 1.0	AGE AV .35 NV 1.0
1	1	0	58000	48
2	1	0	43000	30
3	0	1	60000	53
4	0	1	40000	27

Table 1. Personal statistics

Actionability and newness values for each attribute are also shown. Although these are fabricated values, they are certainly possible scenarios. If the user knows clusters exist based on "married" and "gender", a 0 may be assigned as newness values. No new information would be presented to the user if these attributes were used for cluster formation. If the user has no knowledge of clusters formed using "income" and "age", a 1 may be assigned as newness values. These attributes would supply new information to the user regarding the clusters. Of course, any value within the range is also possible. Various values are set for the actionability of these attributes. The higher the action-ability value, the more the user can act on information presented regarding this attribute. A number of attributes may be considered unactionable and should be rated lower. For example, gender may be considered unactionable in particular settings because of gender discrimination issues. If the user has no opinion regarding the actionability of an attribute .5 can be assigned. Correctness, actionability and newness are all assigned factors of .33, thus equally biasing the results.

A test was conducted using the agglomerative method of clustering to seek out 2 clusters using the steps outlined in Section 2. Data was normalized, since two different types of attributes were used. Table 2 shows the results of this test. The first column of each cluster shows the centroid values, or mean values for the cluster's attributes. The second column, "Mean Attr Variance", represents the average variance of all tuples in the cluster from the centroid for that attribute. The lower this value, the more *like* the attribute values are for this cluster. The third column, "Mean Diff from Pop", helps to describe the cluster. This value shows the average variance of all tuples in the cluster from the total dataset population for that attribute. The higher this value, the greater the attribute contributed to the development of the cluster. The final column, "Usefulness Value", shows the results of incorporating the usefulness metric into the "Mean Diff from Pop". This value is calculated using Equation 2, shown in Section 2. The usefulness value should also be used to determine the attribute that best describes the clusters to the users. We will see how the combination of "Mean Diff from Pop" and "Usefulness Value" can be used to determine cluster descriptions. The cluster variance is the average "Mean Attr Variance" and helps determine within-cluster similarity.

Mean	Mean Attr Variance	Mean Diff from Pop	UValue		Mean	Mean Attr Variance	Mean Diff from Pop	UValue
1.00	0.000	0.500	0.231	**Married**	0.00	0.000	0.500	0.231
0.00	0.000	0.500	0.165	**Gender**	1.00	0.000	0.500	0.165
50500.0	0.375	0.013	0.664	**Income**	50000.0	0.500	0.013	0.664
39.00	0.346	0.019	0.452	**Age**	40.00	0.500	0.019	0.452
Cluster 1: Tuples 1, 2 Cluster Variance: 0.180					Cluster 2: Tuples 3, 4 Cluster Variance: 0.250			

Table 2. Agglomerative clustering using back-end usefulness

As one would guess, married and gender greatly influence the formation of these clusters, which can be defined as "married males" and "unmarried females". It is important to remember that clustering is a powerful preprocessing tool used in data mining. The results generated from a clustering algorithm are often used to determine the next step in mining the data. Various clustering algorithms may be executed on a set of data to determine various types of clusters. The goal is to provide the user with knowledge regarding the data. In this test, we can see that the clusters are well formed around "married" and "gender", since their "Mean Diff from Pop" is somewhat high and their variance is low. However, the usefulness values are also low for these attributes. This suggests that these attributes should not be used to describe the data, since the information would not be very useful to the user. However, the attribute with the highest usefulness has the lowest "Mean Diff from Pop". It makes no sense to describe these clusters using the attribute with the highest usefulness value, since the correlation between "income" and the formation of clusters is very low. This suggests that additional clustering may need to be performed. The next section shows the results of further clustering by applying the usefulness metric to the front-end of the clustering algorithm.

4 Front-end example

Applying the usefulness metric to the front-end of a clustering algorithm allows the algorithm to *seek out* useful clusters. We already know that married and gender will greatly influence the formation of clusters using the data in Table 1. At closer inspection, it can be seen that attributes income and age may also influence cluster formation. Which would be a more useful result? A second test on this data was conducted using the usefulness metric at the front-end of the algorithm. Equation 1, shown in Section 2, was used to weight the distance. The results are shown in Table 3.

Mean	Mean Attr Variance	Mean Diff from Pop	UValue		Mean	Mean Attr Variance	Mean Diff from Pop	UValue
0.50	0.500	0.000	0.066	**Married**	0.50	0.500	0.000	0.066
0.50	0.500	0.000	0.000	**Gender**	0.50	0.500	0.000	0.000
59000.0	0.050	0.438	0.804	**Income**	41500.0	0.075	0.438	0.804
50.50	0.096	0.423	0.585	**Age**	28.50	0.058	0.423	0.585
Cluster 1: Tuples 1, 3					Cluster 2: Tuples 2, 4			
Cluster Variance: 0.287					Cluster Variance: 0.283			

Table 3. Agglomerative clustering using front-end usefulness

Notice the differences between the clusters formed in this experiment and the previous experiment. Two completely different clusters were formed. In this experiment, the new clusters were greatly influenced by income and age. Not only do these attributes have a high "Mean Diff from Pop", they also have a higher usefulness value. We can see that the actionability and newness values play a contributing role in biasing the algorithm to form clusters on these attributes. The new clusters may be described as "older, high income" and "younger, low income". These new descriptions are more useful to the user. Of course, one must take into account the cluster variance to see if the correctness of the new clusters is seriously degraded. The new clusters do not have as high a within-cluster similarity as the first set of clusters, but the difference is small enough to argue that the new cluster descriptions should be used since they are considered more useful. Keep in mind the goal of clustering is often to find additional knowledge in order to help the user determine the next step in the data mining process.

   This small set of data was used to make it easy for the reader to see the results of applying the usefulness metric. However, it would be beneficial to see how these formulas work on a larger dataset. An additional test was conducted using the 1984 Congressional Voting Records Database as it appears on the UCI Machine Learning Repository (www.ics.uci.edu). This dataset contains 17 attributes and 435 tuples. The dataset was modified to numeric values and clusters were formed using the same agglomerative algorithm as discussed in section 2. Without the usefulness metric applied, two clusters were formed and the attributes with the three highest "Mean Diff from Pop" values were as follows: el-salvador-aid (.401), physician-fee-freeze (.393), voting-party (.382). As was expected, clusters formed with respect to voting party. If a user would like to determine voting patterns without respect to voting party, the usefulness metric can be applied.

The usefulness metric was applied to the back-end of the algorithm. The three attributes mentioned above were assigned 0 for actionability and newness. For this example we assumed a fictitious user was working on new crime legislation and was interested in finding out if clusters could be described using the crime attribute. The crime attribute was assigned 1 for actionability and newness. The remaining attributes were assigned .5 (default value) for actionability and 1 for newness. The attributes with the highest usefulness values, along with their "Mean Diff from Pop" for comparison were as follows: crime (.771/.336), aid-to-nicaraguan-contras (.617/.369), mx-missile (.611/.351). This set of attributes is quite different than the first set, whose usefulness values are .132, .130, and .126, respectively. Notice "Mean Diff from Pop" is not seriously degraded. A test was also conducted using the usefulness metric at the front-end of the algorithm but no significant changes resulted. This was to be expected, since the dataset reflected partisan voting and the accuracy using the more useful attributes was not seriously degraded when applying the usefulness metric at the back-end.

5   Conclusion and future considerations

This paper has shown how clustering algorithms can be modified to seek out more useful information without seriously degrading correctness. The goal of a clustering algorithm is to seek out the most accurate clusters; however, there are times when it would be beneficial to use the usefulness metric to define clusters with the understanding that accuracy may be slightly degraded. In data mining this is particularly understandable, since the usefulness of the information, which includes an accuracy component is generally more important than accuracy alone. The usefulness metric does not eliminate an objective metric, but rather balances it with subjective metrics.

Applying the usefulness metric relies on the user's ability to convey their knowledge regarding actionability and newness to the data miner. In this paper, these values were assigned individually or default values were used. It was discussed that newness values could be used based on previous clustering results. New ways must be developed in order to make assigning these values a painless process. It may be possible to obtain actionability values given various types of user information, such as, job descriptions and web usage patterns. It is important that effort is given to ease the burden of assigning actionability and newness values to all attributes.

Clustering is often used to gain knowledge about data before additional mining takes place. In this paper, the usefulness metric was applied to both the front-end and back-end of a clustering algorithm on datasets that did and did not support additional cluster formation. In both cases, the usefulness metric was successfully applied. The usefulness of information presented to users is becoming increasingly important. As new applications of data mining algorithms are developed, we must continue to look for new ways to meet the needs and demands of our users. The usefulness metric was developed for this purpose.

References

BERRY, M.J.A. and LINOFF, G. (1997): *Data Mining Techniques For Marketing, Sales, and Customer Support*. John Wiley and Sons, New York, NY.

FAYYAD U., PIATETSKY-SHAPIRO, G. and SMYTH, P. (1996): From Data Mining to Knowledge Discovery: An Overview. In: U. Fayyad, G. Piatetsky-Shapiro, P. Smyth, R. Uthurusamy (Eds.): *Advances in Knowledge Discovery and Data Mining*. AAAI Press, Menlo Park, CA, 1-36.

HAN, J. and KAMBER, M. (2001): *Data Mining Concepts and Techniques*. Morgan Kaufmann, San Diego, CA.

SILBERSCHATZ, A. and TUZHILIN, A. (1996): What Makes Patterns Interesting in Knowledge Discovery Systems. *IEEE Transactions on Knowledge and Data Engineering*. December. IEEE Computer Society, New York, NY.

ST.CLAIR, C., LIU, C. and PISSINOU, N. (1998): Attribute Weighting: A Method of Applying Domain Knowledge in the Decision Tree Process. In: G. Gardarin, J. French, N. Pissinou, K. Makki, L.Bouganim (Eds.): *Proceedings of the Seventh International Conference on Information and Knowledge Management*. ACM Press, New York, NY, 259-266.

ST.CLAIR, C. (2000): A Usefulness Metric and Its Application to Decision Tree Based Classification. *Ph.D Dissertation*. DePaul University, Chicago, IL.

UTHURUSAMY, R. (1996): Current Challenges and Future Directions. In: U. Fayyad, G. Piatetsky-Shapiro, P. Smyth, R. Uthurusamy (Eds.): *Advances in Knowledge Discovery and Data Mining*. AAAI Press, Menlo Park, CA, 561-572.

WEISS, S.M. and INDURKHYA, N. (1998): *Predictive Data Mining: A Practical Guide*. Morgan Kaufmann, San Francisco, CA.

Internet Thesaurus - Extracting Relevant Terms from WWW Pages using Weighted Threshold Function over a Cross-Reference Matrix

Raz Tamir

School of Computer Science and Engineering
The Hebrew University of Jerusalem
Jerusalem, Israel

Abstract. The "Internet Thesaurus" ("IT") concept aims to extract any phrase's meaning by scanning relevant WWW pages. Results can be used as an automatic query expansion, or even as an alternative term for better search results. IT algorithm runs Google search engine over a user defined phrase. The phrase meaning is extracted by analyzing WWW pages resulting from the search. Learning a weighted threshold function was applied over a novel "Cross Reference Matrix" ("CRM") approach. The Cross Reference concept is presented as a preferable way of proximity calculations, otherwise done by a Euclidian formula, when dealing with small but numerous texts such as WWW pages. Using weighted threshold function over CRM enables the user to give his own perspective over the expected results, forming a proximity measure depending on objective parameters (CRM) and subjective parameters (samples tagged by the user). This combination is ideal for creating a dynamic, personalized, fast and rather intuitive thesaurus.

1 Introduction

1.1 Internet Thesaurus ("IT")

The main concept behind IT is the ability to extract the sense of a given phrase, by scanning relevant WWW pages. IT gets a phrase (or a "seed term") as an input. The seed term is analyzed, and the output contains a few phrases related to the seed term, as reflected over the Internet. For example, using "Data Mining" as a seed term will result in various phrases like "Knowledge Discovery in Databases", "Machine Learning" etc. The motivation behind IT is to produce an on-line thesaurus, by using the Internet as a vast database of documents. Such a thesaurus can be used in various ways such as modifying user query strings in search engines, improving information retrieval.

The current work uses a probabilistic method (NC-Value measure, Frantzi and Ananiadou (1997)) for basic term extraction. Cross Reference Matrix (CRM) and Weighted Threshold function are then used to convey the relationship between potential terms, and identify the most important and meaningful ones, giving the best definition of the seed term. The basic strategy is:

1. Training (finding the best hypotheses for the current user):

1.1 Perform searches over few seed terms (current article used 4), known to the user (or chosen by him). For each seed term:

    1.1.1 Apply the NC-Value measure over all possible k-word strings (where k^3 1) of text to form an initial list of best potential terms.

    1.1.2 Let the user label each potential term as strongly related (to seed term), remotely related or not related.

    1.1.3 Form a CRM by multiple shallow searches over the potential terms.

    1.1.4 Calculate parameters chosen to represent the relationship between various terms.

1.2 Learn hypotheses, one for strongly related terms, one for remotely related and one for unrelated terms.

2. Analyzing new terms:

    2.1 Perform search over new seed term.

    2.2 Apply NC-Value measure over all possible k-words terms to form an initial list of best potential terms.

    2.3 Form a CRM by multiple shallow searches over the potential terms.

    2.4 Calculate parameters chosen to represent the relationship between various terms.

    2.5 Use hypotheses found in training stage (1.2) to grade all potential terms and select those best representing the seed term.

The training stage is needed only when user's perspective is desired. For most of the applications the algorithm can use pre-set parameters, and give an immediate analysis of potential terms.

1.2 Terms extraction methodologies

Sense extraction involves finding the "center of gravity" of a text, that is, extracting the essence of the text represented in a condensed form of terms and key phrases. Two common approaches were employed for this task: linguistic and probabilistic [Charniak, 1993]. In two researches [Yarowsky, 1995], [Pereira, Tishby and Lee, 1993] probabilistic methods were used for word clustering as a way of sense disambiguation. Others used a combination of probabilistic and linguistic methods for term extraction [Dias, Guillor and Lopes, 2000].

Traditionally, words extraction from texts was based on statistical methods such as Naive Bayes Methods and Hidden Markov Models, where others employed a part-of-speech-tagging in order to reveal key words [Brill, 1992] [Cutting, Kupiec, Pedersen and Sibun, 1992].

While most researches used large and rather homogeneous corpuses fewer dealt with term extraction from the Internet. In the past few years, along with the Internet's prosperity, researchers tried to implement known methods for the new media. Among these approaches are the employments of a combination of parsing and rule based learners [Soderland, 1997], statistical and relational approach [Craven and Slattery, to apear], usage of domain-specific thesaurus [Maynard and Ananiadou, 1998] and more.

Although linguistic methods bear a great potential, since they aim to give a real "understanding" of the sentence, they have a few major disadvantages:

- The corpus must be monolingual, in order to assure good accuracy.
- Linguistic algorithms tend to ignore a significant proportion of terms that do not match the a-priory defined syntax phrase structure (such as noun+adj, noun+prep+noun...)
- Languages such as those used for Internet communication are highly dynamic and constantly changing. They do not follow conventional linguistic rules, making it difficult to create appropriate linguistic rules.

On the other hand, the use of probabilistic methods for term extraction is based on frequency of appearance. Using pure frequency for grading a term's "information density" suffers from many problems such as:

- It is difficult to eliminate the appearance of all programming language terms (e.g. "times new roman"), without holding a database containing the knowledge of a variety of languages and their possible syntaxes.
- It is hard to recognize which part of a term is the "core" term that holds the vital information.
- Training needs a large and rather homogeneous corpus to properly adjust.

Despite its weaknesses, it seems that when analyzing the internet's dynamic, constantly changing, multi-lingual small "chunks" of texts, probabilistic methods are the preferable method.

2   Internet Thesaurus - from theory to practice

2.1   NC-value measure

Term extraction was based on the NC-Value method [Frentzi, 1997], which calculates the "Information Capacity" of a term by considering its various neighbors.

Calculation was done according to the formula:

$$[2.1]\ NC - Value(\alpha) = log_2 |\alpha| \bullet \left(f(\alpha) - \frac{1}{c(\alpha)} \sum_{i=1}^{c(\alpha)} f(b_i) \right)$$

Where:

α - a potential term being examined

$|\alpha|$ - number of words in α

$f(\alpha)$ - frequency of α appearance in the text

b_i - extracted potential terms that contains α as a part of it's string

$f(b_i)$ - appearance frequency of a term that contains α

$c(\alpha)$ - number of potential terms containing α

Most "promising" terms (those having the highest NC-Values) were compiled into the Cross Reference list.

2.2   Cross reference matrix)CRM(

Most probability-based methods (Bayesian, neural nets etc.) are based on a proximity calculation of an Eucledian nature between pairs of documents forming a cluster center of gravity. Eucledian calculation is performed over a vector of 1,0 where each position relates to a specific term, and 1 or 0 is placed according to the existence of the specific word in the text examined. Although the number of key words in a document is approximately constant, the total number of key words in a corpus is proportional to the total number of documents. This is the main reason for the rather poor performance of Eucledian calculation where text units are rather small (like in HTML pages containing only few KB) and numerous. In this case each vector contains only few 1's and proximity calculation renders rather similar small values for most of the text units.

Thus, a new definition of proximity is needed for such cases.

The matrix of cross-reference begins with the Cross Reference list of terms discussed earlier. Computation included performing a rather shallow search (while about 100 sites were scanned during initial seed term search, only 10 sites were scanned during the current stage) over each term and counting the number of appearance for any other term of the Cross Reference list. This procedure produces the following matrix (for example):

After building the CRM three factors were chosen in order to measure each term quality:

- *i*) Factor1 = number of times the current term was found while performing the search over the seed term.
- *ii*) Factor2 = number of other terms of the Cross Reference list found while searching the current term.
- *iii*) Factor3 = number of times the current term was found while searching other terms of the Cross Reference list.

All three factors were normalized by maximum values to give values varying between 0 and 1. The correct combination of these three factors was computed using a Weighted Threshold function.

2.3   Weighted threshold functions

Weighted Threshold functions were used as hypotheses "imitating" the unknown behavior of the user while tagging samples. Calculation employed the minimal disagreement principle, aiming to find the best hypothesis from possible hypotheses space, having the minimal number disagreements with a set of pre-tagged samples.

The basic threshold function consists of pairs of the three factors discussed in the previous chapter:

Found Searched	world science	fiction society	fiction conventions webring	book reading	fiction and fantasy	fantasy and science	fantasy book reading
world science	X	11	2	0	3	0	0
fiction society	7	X	1	0	4	0	0
fiction conventions webring	10	1	X	0	1	0	0
book reading	0	0	0	X	0	0	0
fiction and fantasy	0	0	0	0	X	0	0
fantasy and science	0	0	0	0	4	X	0
fantasy book reading	0	0	0	0	0	0	X

Table 1. In the above table, denoted T, the entry T[i,j] equals the number of times that the term labeling the i'th row was found while searching the term labeling the j'th column. Seed term was "Science Fiction"

$$[2.2]\ h(\alpha,\beta,\gamma) = \alpha \times Factor1 \times Factor2 + \beta \times Factor1 \times Factor3 + \gamma \times Factor2 \times Factor3$$

In order to give a positive prediction h(a,b,g) has to be bigger than a certain threshold for each a, b and g.

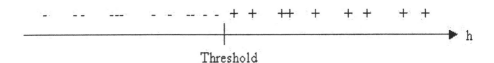

Threshold

Fig. 1. Threshold function hypothesis

Creating a hypothesis was done by training for a,b,g and threshold value over a sample data, tagged in advance by the user. The threshold value was changed until most of the positive tagged terms were graded higher and most of the negative tagged terms had lower grade. The quality of the a,b,g,threshold set was calculated by the prediction success as will be shown later. Sets of a,b,g,threshold were trained for three hypotheses, using three tagged sample sets. The user tagged each term according to the following questions (rules):

- Rule1: Is the current term strongly related to seed term?
- Rule2: Is the current term remotely related to seed term?
- Rule3: Is the current term not relevant when describing the seed term?

Finally, each question (rule) had its chosen set of a,b,g,threshold giving the best prediction over tagged data. The quality measure of a hypothesis, q(h), was set to the normalized number of correct labeled terms over sample data.

[2.3] $q(h(\alpha, \beta, \gamma)) = 1 - \frac{Minimal\ number\ of\ disagreements}{Total\ number\ of\ terms}$

Next all hypotheses were combined to give final grade for each potential term. Note that not only best hypotheses were used, but every hypothesis having a quality bigger than 0.5.

2.4   Grading potential terms

After constructing all hypotheses, the sets of a,b,g,threshold,quality were used to grade new potential terms. In order to give single grade for each potential term a few steps were taken. First, each hypothesis having a quality bigger than 0.5 was given a grade according to:

[2.4] $g(h(\alpha, \beta, \gamma)) = \begin{cases} 3 \bullet quality(h) & Rule1 \\ 2 \bullet quality(h) & Rule2 \\ 1 \bullet quality(h) & Rule3 \end{cases}$ Formula [2.4] gives high-

est weight (3) to terms found to be "very relevant" (rule 1), and lowest weight (1) to terms found to be "not relevant" (rule 3). Multiplying the weights by the quality can be viewed as a gain function where quality has a role similar to probability in a conventional gain function. Final grading, G, was by following formula:

[2.5] $G(potential\ \ term) = \frac{\sum_{h \in H} g(h)}{\sum_{h \in H} q(h)}$

Where H is the group of hypotheses having their quality bigger than 50%. For each potential term, G holds a grade varying from 1 to 3. Only potential terms having a grade bigger than 2 were chosen for the final output. Note that rule 3 (not relevant terms) acts as a counter balance for rule 1 (relevant terms).

Example: Suppose that during calculation a potential term was selected by two hypotheses, one belonging to rule 1 (relevant terms) and the other belonging to rule 3 (not relevant terms). If, for example, first hypothesis (relevant terms) labeled correctly 60% of sample data and second hypothesis (not relevant terms) labeled correctly 90%, final grade will be: $G(potential\ \ term) = \frac{3 \times 0.6 + 1 \times 0.9}{0.6 + 0.9}$, thus the algorithm will not select it as a relevant term since the result is smaller than 2.

3   Empirical results

3.1   Terms extraction

Four seed terms were fed into Google search engine, terms were chosen randomly with no intended connection between each other:

 i) Data Mining
 ii) Agnostic Learning
 iii) Palm Pilot
 iv) Bill Clinton

Each term underwent the following procedure:

 i) Retrieve the 100 (or less if there are not enough) first sites fetched by Google search engine. Save text as a long string of sentences.
 ii) Scan string and extract all possible terms from every sentence (all words pairs, triples etc.).
 iii) Use NC-Value calculation to grade each term. Select Cross Reference list as highest graded terms.
 iv) For each term in Cross Reference list:
   4.1 Perform a new search and retrieve 10 first sites fetched by search engine.
   4.2 Scan all sites for all other terms in Cross Reference list.
 v) Build Cross Reference Matrix and calculate three factors needed for the Weighted Threshold algorithm.

3.2   Labeling samples

In order to supply users opinion on the quality of each term in the CRM term list, three extra values were added stating if the term is relevant, remotely relevant or not related to seed term.

3.3   Testing hypothesis quality

Following table holds the results of running the Algorithm (section 3.1) over 6 new terms, not used as a part of the tagging sample.
Seed terms were randomly chosen representing different fields of interest.

4   Discussion

Neither existing dictionary nor conventional thesauruses are capable of correctly interpreting term such as "Global Hawk" (US unmanned air vehicle currently being developed), or "Blade Runner" (A science fiction movie). Thus, IT gives a solution for an otherwise unsolved problem of conveying the meaning of various terms.
It is interesting to view the changes in importance each term undergoes in the various stages of calculation:

Seed term	result1	grade1	result2	grade2	result3	grade3
Harry potter	potter books	2.66	potter and the chamber of secrets	2.61	potter movie	2.34
bed wetting	Children who wet the bed	2.64	cause of bed	2.49	treatments for bed	2.44
Blade runner	runner movie	2.58	runner fan club	2.49	runner partnership	2.42
global hawk	unmanned aerial	2.11	hawk air vehicle	2.0		
North pole	magnetic north	2.47	magnetic pole	2.35	pole expeditions	2.34
nuclear bomb	megaton bomb detonated	2.40	nuclear weapons	2.38	effect on the inhabitants of a city	2.36

Table 2. IT table created for various seed terms. Only 3 first terms are noted.

- Frequency calculation
- NC-Value calculation
- Weighted Threshold functions over CRM table

Following table holds the calculation stages of the seed term "North Pole". It is interesting to see how CRM table is able to give correct importance weights to different terms than NC-Value and frequency calculation.

CRM + Weighted Threshold Function	NC-Value	Frequency of Appearance	Relevancy Order
magnetic north	pole times	pole times	1.
magnetic pole	magnetic north	magnetic north	2.
pole expeditions	South pole	south pole	3.
geographic north	freddy goes to the north	magnetic pole	4.
pole itinerary	magnetic pole	freddy goes	5.

Table 3. Comparison between Frequency based, NC-Value and CRM calculation of relevant term for the "North Pole" seed term. The relevancy order states the grades order of the terms where 1 is the highest.

Terms as "pole times" and "freddy goes to the north" did not appear in final prediction although they had a good grading under frequency of appearance and NC-value criteria.

5   Concluding remarks

Combination of Weighted Threshold Algorithm over Cross Reference Matrix of NC-Valued terms has a good ability to convey a term meaning over a small corpus.
This method has the potential of extracting a term meaning over small data bases, disregarding the data format (e.g. HTML, Text, etc...). Cross Reference is a good measure for term proximity where each text unit (document) has but a few potential terms. Results are given in a table form, but can be transformed to conventional dictionary definitions, for more convenient use. The tagging process enables the user to give his perspectives on the algorithm, since the tagging is subjective, and varies from one person to another. Further more, one can choose tagging terms to suit one's own interests inserting a personalization factor into the algorithm. It is the author's notion that CRM method has the potential of conveying other properties of terms such as relationships like hierarchy relations, and forming clusters of terms. Results can also be used as an automatic query expansion, or even as an alternative term for better search results.

References

BRILL E.: A simple rule-based part of speech tagger. Proceedings of the Third Conference on Applied Natural Language Processing. *ACL, 152-155, 1992.*

CHARNIAK E., Statistical Language Learning. *MIT Press, Cambridge, 1993.*

CRAVEN M., SLATTERY S.: Relational learning with statistical predicate invention: Better models for hypertext. *Machine Learning, 43(1/2):97-119, 2001.*

CUTTING, D., KUPIEC, J., PEDERSEN, J. and SIBUN, P.: A Practical Part-of-Speech Tagger. *Proc. of the 3rd Conf. on Applied NLP, 133-140, 1992.*

DIAS G., GUILLOR S. & LOPES J.G.P. (2000b): Combining Linguistics with Statistics for Multiword Term Extraction: A Fruitful Association?. In: *"Proceedings of Recherche d'Informations Assiste par Ordinateur (RIAO2000)"*, College de France, Paris, France.

FRANTZI K. T. , ANANIADOU S.: Automatic term recognition using contextual cues. In: *Proceedings of 3rd DELOS Workshop* , Zurich, Switzerland 1997

MAYNARD D.G., ANANIADOU S.: Term sense disambiguation using a domain-specific thesaurus. In: *Proc. of 1st International Conference on Language Resources and Evaluation (LREC)*, Granada, Spain, 1998.

PEREIRA F.C., TISHBY N., and LEE L.: Distributional clustering of English words. In: *30th Annual Meeting of the Association for Computational Linguistics*, Columbus, Ohio, 183-190, 1993

SODERLAND S.: Learning to extract text-based information from the world wide web. In: *Proceedings of Knowledge Discovery and Data Mining, 1997.*

YAROWSKY D.: Unsupervised word sense disambiguation rivaling supervised methods. In: *Proceedings of the 33rd Annual Meeting of the Association for Computational Linguistics*, pages 189-196, Cambridge, MA, July 24-26 1995.

Reflections on a Supervised Approach to Independent Component Analysis

Cinzia Viroli

Dipartimento di Scienze statistiche
Università di Bologna, I-40126 Bologna, Italy

Abstract. This work focusses on a recent supervised approach to Independent Component Analysis, a linear transformation method that yields latent variables assumed to be non-gaussian and mutually independent. According to this approach the latent structure is identified by estimating the joint product density of independent components, using a technique that transforms the unsupervised learning problem into a supervised function approximation one. Like projection pursuit methodology, this procedure attempts to get interesting projections of the observed units, that seem to capture the latent clustered structure of the data.

1 Introduction

One of the aims of exploratory data analysis is the identification of the underlying structure, in order to detect interesting representations of multivariate data for purposes of classification or clustering; such representations are often sought among linear transformations of the observed data.

A recently developed method for discovering linear or non linear projections of the data onto a lower dimensional space is Independent Component Analysis (ICA). In this context, the latent variables are assumed to be nongaussian and mutually independent. In terms of exploratory data analysis, interesting non-gaussian distributional forms may be sub- or super-gaussian, bi-modal or multi-modal. In the particular context of classification we focus on multi-modal latent components, since they may indicate specific clusters and classes inherent in the data.

While many popular approaches to ICA are based on a suitable choice of a non-normality or dependence index, the aim of this paper is to test a different approach to ICA which has recently been proposed. According to this procedure, the latent structure is identified by viewing the density estimation task as a two class classification problem, after that a particular trick to transform the problem into a supervised form is applied. The built model can be interpreted as a generalized projection pursuit regression. The approach is tested on simple classification problems.

2 Independent Component Analysis

Denote by $x_1, x_2, ... x_p$ the observed variables, which are supposed to be modelled as linear combinations of q hidden variables $y_1, y_2, ..., y_q$:

$$x_i = a_{i1}y_1 + a_{i2}y_2 + ... + a_{iq}y_q \qquad \text{for all} \ \ i = 1, ..., p \qquad (1)$$

where the a_{ij} $(j = 1, ..., q)$ are some real coefficients. By definition, the y_i are *statistically mutually independent*. The basic ICA model can be put in the following compact formulation:

$$\mathbf{X} = \mathbf{AY}. \tag{2}$$

Since it describes how the observed data are generated by a mixing process of hidden components, the matrix $\mathbf{A}$ is often called *mixing matrix*. In the standard ICA model we have $p = q$ and thus the matrix $\mathbf{A}$ is square. In the model both the mixing matrix and the latent components are unknown and can be estimated under some precise restrictions. The fundamental assumption on which ICA rests is the independence of the latent components. As clearly shown in Hyvärinen *et al.* (2001), this condition implies that the research of a distributional form for the hidden projections moves onto the direction of non-gaussianity. In particular, the model is identifiable when at most one of the q independent components is gaussian.

The current algorithms for estimating independent components can be divided into procedures based on minimization or maximization of some relevant criterion functions (mutual information, kurtosis, negentropy...) and methods based on the stochastic gradient scheme which may be implemented by neural networks. Further details on these algorithms and their convergence properties can be found in Hyvärinen *et al.* (2001) and Hyvärinen and Oja (1997). All these procedures have the form of *unsupervised learning*, since they do not involve the use of some outcome variables to guide the learning process. An interesting alternative is represented by the introduction of a new dichotomous variable that allows to reinterpreted the unsupervised learning problem as a *supervised* function approximation one (Hastie *et al.*, 2001). The starting point is to consider the ICA model as the problem of marginalizing the joint density of the observed variables. If the y_i are *statistically mutually independent* their joint density function is factorizable:

$$h(\mathbf{y}) = \prod_{i=1}^{p} h_i(y_i). \tag{3}$$

According to the probabilistic result on the density of a transformation, the basic ICA model can be formulated in terms of density function estimation

$$g(\mathbf{x}) = \left| \det\left(\mathbf{A}^{-1}\right) \right| h(\mathbf{y}) = \left| \frac{1}{\det \mathbf{A}} \right| \prod_{i=1}^{p} h_i(y_i) = \prod_{i=1}^{p} h_i(y_i), \tag{4}$$

where the last equality is true when the mixing matrix $\mathbf{A}$ is an orthogonal matrix.

3   Unsupervised as supervised learning

Let $\mathbf{X}$ be the multivariate set of observed data, with joint probability density function $g(\mathbf{x})$. From equation (4) $g(\mathbf{x})$ has to be factorizable as the product of p unknown density functions. Let $g_0(\mathbf{x})$ be a specific known density function, used for reference. Suppose that the observed sample $\mathbf{X}$ has size N; then another sample of the same size N is drawn from $g_0(\mathbf{x})$ using Monte Carlo methods. The idea is to resample the same observed pattern $\mathbf{x}_n$ (with $n = 1, ..., N$) using the (different) probability of the reference density function $g_0(\mathbf{x})$. The two data sets $\{\mathbf{x}_1, \mathbf{x}_2, ..., \mathbf{x}_N\}$ and $\{\mathbf{x}_{N+1}, \mathbf{x}_{N+2}, ..., \mathbf{x}_{2N}\}$ are $i.i.d.$ random samples respectively from $g(\mathbf{x})$ and $g_0(\mathbf{x})$. These samples are pooled and a new random variable Y is created, assigning $Y = 1$ to those observations drawn from $g(\mathbf{x})$ and $Y = 0$ to those drawn from the reference density function $g_0(\mathbf{x})$. The conditional expectation of Y given $\mathbf{x}$ is:

$$\mu(\mathbf{x}) = E(Y|\mathbf{x}) = \frac{g(\mathbf{x})}{g(\mathbf{x}) + g_0(\mathbf{x})}. \tag{5}$$

This quantity can be estimated by supervised learning using the combined sample $(y_1, \mathbf{x}_1)$, $(y_2, \mathbf{x}_2)$ ..., $(y_{2N}, \mathbf{x}_{2N})$, where the variable Y can be reinterpreted as the outcome variable.

Moreover, the identity (5) can be solved for $g(\mathbf{x})$:

$$\hat{g}(\mathbf{x}) = g_0(\mathbf{x}) \frac{\hat{\mu}(\mathbf{x})}{1 - \hat{\mu}(\mathbf{x})}. \tag{6}$$

Applying the logarithm to the previous expression, the logit of $\mu(\mathbf{x})$ can be viewed as the difference:

$$\text{logit}\,(\mu(\mathbf{x})) = \log g(\mathbf{x}) - \log g_0(\mathbf{x}). \tag{7}$$

Thus, $\mu(\mathbf{x})$ provides information concerning departures of the data density $g(\mathbf{x})$ from the chosen reference density $g_0(\mathbf{x})$ and the logit $(\mu(\mathbf{x}))$ can be viewed as a "contrast" statistic. This expression offers a suggestion for choosing the form of the reference density function: a good choice for $g_0(\mathbf{x})$ is dictated by the types of departures that are considered most interesting. In the particular context of ICA the aim is the estimation of independent components and hence the *departure from dependence* is investigated. Since "independent components" means "non-gaussian components", this is equivalent to investigating the *departure from joint normality*. For this purpose a good choice for $g_0(\mathbf{x})$ could be the multivariate gaussian distribution.

Following the result in the equation (4), the aim is to factorize the expression (6) as a product:

$$\hat{g}(\mathbf{x}) = g_0(\mathbf{x}) \frac{\hat{\mu}(\mathbf{x})}{1 - \hat{\mu}(\mathbf{x})} = h_1(a_1^T \mathbf{x}) h_2(a_2^T \mathbf{x}) ... h_p(a_p^T \mathbf{x}), \tag{8}$$

where the components $a_1^T \mathbf{x}, a_2^T \mathbf{x}, ..., a_p^T \mathbf{x}$ are independent.

In order to factorize the reference function a change of variable is needed and it is easy to see that $g_0(a_1^T \mathbf{x}, ..., a_p^T \mathbf{x})$ is factorizable if $\{a_1, a_2, ..., a_p\}$ is a set of orthogonal vectors and $g_0(\mathbf{x})$ is a spherical multivariate gaussian distribution. This choice confirms all the previous implications of the (7). Secondly, in order to estimate the logit $(\mu(\mathbf{x}))$, Hastie *et al.* (2001) proposed an additive logistic regression:

$$\text{logit}\,(\mu(\mathbf{x})) = f_1(a_1^T\mathbf{x}) + f_2(a_2^T\mathbf{x}) + \dots + f_p(a_p^T\mathbf{x}). \qquad (9)$$

In this case:

$$\frac{\mu(\mathbf{x})}{1 - \mu(\mathbf{x})} = \exp\left\{f_1(a_1^T\mathbf{x})\right\} \cdot \exp\left\{f_2(a_2^T\mathbf{x})\right\} \dots \cdot \exp\left\{f_p(a_p^T\mathbf{x})\right\}. \qquad (10)$$

As the authors declared "*... while this procedure appears to work well on some simple examples, at the time of writing it is largely untested*". In the present work the logit $(\mu(\mathbf{x}))$ is modelled by a generalized projection pursuit regression. This choice is dictated by the intention to emphasize the analogies with exploratory projection pursuit. Moreover, the generalized projection pursuit regression is a more general and flexible approach than the generalized additive models, as explained in the following section.

4 Generalized Projection Pursuit Regression

Friedman, J.H. and Stuetzle, W. (1981) defined Projection Pursuit Regression as a model in which the response is related to a sum of smooth functions of linear combinations of the covariates:

$$E[Y|X_1, X_2, ..., X_p] = \beta_0 + \sum_{j=1}^{q} \beta_j f_j(\alpha_j^T\mathbf{x}). \qquad (11)$$

In order to be estimable, the model has to satisfy normalization and standardization conditions such as:

$$\sum_{k=1}^{p} \alpha_{kj}^2 = 1, \quad E(f_j) = 0, \quad E(f_j^2) = 1 \qquad \forall j = 1, ..., q.$$

We can generalize the projection pursuit model by allowing two extensions: the first one is that the distributional form of the response Y may come from the exponential family and secondly the relation between the response variable Y and its predictor is not necessarily the identity link but may be any monotonic differentiable function. Therefore Generalized Projection Pursuit Regression (GPPR) consists of three components:

- *random component*; the functional form of the response variable Y may be

$$f_Y(y; \theta, \phi) = \exp\left\{\frac{y\theta - b(\theta)}{\alpha(\phi)} + c(y, \phi)\right\},$$

where θ is the natural parameter and ϕ the scale parameter;

- *systematic component*; a weighted sum of smooth functions of linear combinations of covariates produces a predictor of Y

$$\eta(X) = \beta_0 + \sum_{j=1}^{q} \beta_j f_j(\alpha_j^T \mathbf{x});$$

- *link component*; the relation between the predictor $\eta(X)$ and the expected value μ of the response Y may be any monotonic differentiable function $g(E[Y|X]) = \eta(X)$.

5 Logistic Projection Pursuit Regression

As a particular case of the Generalized Projection Pursuit Model, Logistic Projection Pursuit Regression (LPP) models a binary response. In LPP model the response Y has a bernoulli distribution of parameter μ.

Since we have $0 < \mu < 1$ the link should map the interval $(0, 1)$ onto the whole real line. The link component is the logistic function:

$$g(\mu) = \log \left(\frac{\mu}{1 - \mu} \right) = \beta_0 + \sum_{j=1}^{q} \beta_j f_j(\alpha_j^T \mathbf{x}) = \eta(X).$$

Parameter and function estimation is obtained by using a modified version of a local scoring algorithm that combines iteratively reweighted least squares (IRLS) with a back-fitting procedure. Schematically the IRLS algorithm consists of looping until convergence the following two steps:

- calculate an adjusted dependent variable z with estimated variance w^{-1};
- regress z on the predictors with weights w.

The adjusted dependent variable is obtained by approximating $g(y)$ with a first-order Taylor series expansion about μ. In the logistic regression problem the adjusted responses z are:

$$z = \eta + \frac{y - \mu}{\mu(1 - \mu)} \quad \text{with weights} \ \ w = \mu(1 - \mu).$$

The algorithm used to estimate parameters and functions in the logistic projection pursuit regression is a modified version of Roosen and Hastie proposal (1993) and is based on the following steps:

- Initialize variables.
- Estimate all terms.
- Prune terms of least importance.
- Clean up.

In the initialization step, all the coefficients α_j are chosen randomly from the uniform distribution in $[-1, 1]$ and normalized. The smooth functions are set identically equal to zero. The parameters β_j are fixed equal to one. The initial choice of parameters and functions does not seem to have great influence on the convergence time.

In the second step, a total of $p \geq q$ terms is fitted and a backward selection procedure is then used to prune down to q terms. For each term the adjusted dependent variable z with weights w is calculated. Then the partial residuals r_i are obtained as difference between z_i and the previous terms (with $i = 1, ..., 2N$). Finally each term is updated with response r_i and weights w_i. The procedure is realized under the condition that the estimated vectors $\hat{\alpha}_j$ (with $j = 1, ..., p$) are orthonormal. This implies that it may be necessary to orthogonalize the resulting mixing matrix after each iteration, projecting the current estimated vector $\hat{\alpha}_j$ onto the orthogonal space generated from the previously estimated set $\{\hat{\alpha}_1, ..., \hat{\alpha}_{j-1}, \hat{\alpha}_{j+1}, ..., \hat{\alpha}_p\}$.

In the prune step, terms of least importance are dropped and then only q terms are updated using the backfitting procedure within local scoring. In LPP estimation we can consider the terms $\alpha_j^T \mathbf{x}$ as estimates of each independent component. To measure the importance of each term we can use the magnitude of the scale coefficient β_j or we can base on its t-statistics from the regression of y on $\{f_m(\nu_m)\}_{m=1}^{j}$. A further possibility is using the *negentropy*, a relevant concept of information theory. Let X be a random variables with probability density measured by $p(X)$. Let $p(X_G)$ the gaussian distribution with the same mean and variance-covariance matrix as $p(X)$. The negentropy is a particular relative entropy:

$$J(X) = \int p(x) \log \frac{p(x)}{p(x_G)} dx = H(X_G) - H(X),\qquad(12)$$

where $H(X)$ and $H(X_G)$ are the entropies of X and X_G respectively. The idea of using negentropy in this context is based on the following property: a gaussian variable has the largest entropy among all the random variables of equal variance. Hence, negentropy is always non-negative and it is zero if X has a gaussian distribution. This means that we can use negentropy to measure the departure from gaussianity. In practice this is obtained by dropping sequentially the estimated component with the lowest negentropy.

Finally, the clean up procedure consists of adjusting each estimated smooth function to have zero mean, changing the value of the coefficient β_0 accordingly.

6   Some applications to classification problems

The procedure has been applied to a simple simulated data set and to the Iris data set. The first example involves two latent variables, assumed to be a mixture of gaussians and a standard gaussian respectively:

$$f(y_1) = 0.4\mathcal{N}(-0.5, 0.2) + 0.6\mathcal{N}(0.5, 0.1) \quad \text{and} \quad f(y_2) = \mathcal{N}(0, 1).$$

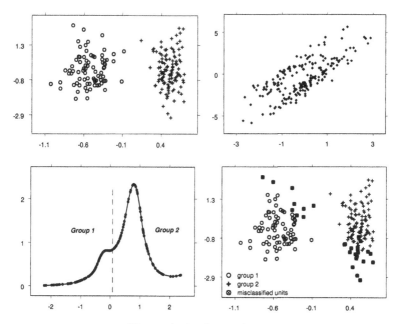

Fig. 1. A simple simulation.

The two independent variables are linearly mixed as follows:

$$\begin{bmatrix} x_1 \\ x_2 \end{bmatrix} = \begin{bmatrix} 1 & 1 \\ -1 & 2 \end{bmatrix} \begin{bmatrix} y_1 \\ y_2 \end{bmatrix}.$$

The first diagram in Figure 1 shows the joint distribution of the two latent variables. It's clear from this graph that there are two distinct groups. The second graph shows the joint distribution of the observed mixed variables, after some noise is added. In this second graph the discrimination between the two groups is not so clear. Note that, in this particular example, the application of principal component analysis does not allow to distinguish the two groups, since the first component lies in the direction of maximum variance and captures almost all the variability. The estimation by ICA gives two latent components but the second one is dropped because it is too much close to the normal distribution. The third graph shows the density distribution of the unique estimated component, that is clearly bimodal. It is possible to discriminate between the two groups by considering the minimum between the two modes. The last graph presents the estimated classification using the clustered latent structure: 28 units out of 200 are misclassified.

The application on the Iris dataset is also interesting. The unique nongaussian component presents three modes, as shown in Figure 2. In this case 26 units out of 150 are misclassified. The largest misclassification corresponds to

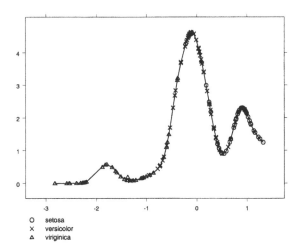

Fig. 2. ICA on IRIS dataset.

the distinction between the species *versicolor* and *virginica*: this is a problem usually encountered when this dataset is analyzed by linear discrimination.

7   Conclusions

This supervised approach to ICA allows to emphasize its relation with exploratory projection pursuit. In particular, under the constraint of orthogonality of the mixing matrix, it shows that independent component analysis is substantially equivalent to the aim of searching for interesting (and so non-gaussian) projection pursuit directions. In this spirit, the system of orthogonal coefficients of the mixing matrix can be properly reinterpreted as system of projection coefficients.

The procedure encounters some problems when the dimension of the observed variables is high. This is due to the fact that the observed data have to be resampled from a multivariate gaussian distribution by Monte Carlo methods. To better understand the nature of the problem let us consider a simple situation in which the observed data are generated from a uniform distribution in $[-3, 3]$ of dimensionality from 1 to 5 respectively. The marginal uniform random variables are supposed to be mutually independent and therefore the covariance matrix is diagonal. The simulated points are then resampled following the probabilities of a multivariate normal standard distribution. We compute the theoretical frequencies of the central interval $[\mu - \sigma, \mu + \sigma]$ in both distributions. The results are presented in the table (1). In this particular situation we see that with only 5 observed variables the probability of having an observed value near the mean is only equal to 0.064. In the simulation procedure the rare points in the central interval must be repeated lots of times in order to reflect the higher theoretical probabilities

Dimension	Normal	Uniform
1	0.683	0.577
2	0.466	0.333
3	0.318	0.192
4	0.217	0.111
5	0.148	0.064

Table 1. Areas of the central interval $[\mu - \sigma, \mu + \sigma]$ in the uniform and the standard normal distribution with different dimensionality.

of the multivariate normal distribution. The risk is not to observe any value "near" the mean, so that all simulated points lie onto the tails of the multivariate normal distribution. Therefore we don't evaluate departure from the entire body of the normal distribution but just from its tails. The seriouness of the problem depends on the number of the observed variables and especially on the *true* distribution underlying the observed data.

References

FRIEDMAN, J.H. and STUETZLE, W. (1981): Projection Pursuit Regression. *Journal of the American Statistical Association, 76, 817-823.*

GIROLAMI, M. CICHOCKI, A. and AMARI, S. (1998): A common Neural Network Model for Unsupervised Exploratory Data Analysis and Independent Component Analysis. *IEEE Transaction on Neural Netowoks.*

HASTIE, T. and TIBSHIRANI, R. (1990): *Generalized Additive Models.* Chapman and Hall.

HASTIE, T. TIBSHIRANI, R. and FRIEDMAN, J.H. (2001): *The Elements of Statistical Learning: Data Mining, Inference and Prediction.* Springer.

HYVÄRINEN, A. KARHUNEN, J. and OJA, E. (2001): *Independent Component Analysis.* John Wiley & Sons, INC.

HYVÄRINEN, A. and OJA, E. (1997): A Fast Fixed-Point Algorithm for Independent Component Analysis. *Neural Computation, 9, 1483-1492.*

ROOSEN, C.B. and HASTIE, T. (1993): Logistic Response Projection Pursuit. *AT&T Bell Labs Technical Report.*

Simulated Annealing and Tabu Search for Optimization of Neural Networks

Akio Yamazaki, Teresa B. Ludermir, and Marcilio C. P. de Souto

Center of Informatics, Federal University of Pernambuco
P.O.Box 7851, Cidade Universitaria, Recife-PE, Brazil, 50.732-970

Abstract. This paper shows results of using simulated annealing and tabu search for optimizing neural network architectures and weights. The algorithms generate networks with good generalization performance (mean classification error for the test set was 5.28% for simulated annealing and 2.93% for tabu search) and low complexity (mean number of connections used was 11.68 out of 36 for simulated annealing and 11.49 out of 36 for tabu search) for an odor recognition task in an artificial nose.

1 Introduction

Architecture design is a crucial issue for the successful application of Artificial Neural Networks (ANNs). This is because the architecture has significant impact on the networks information processing capabilities. Given a learning task, a neural network with only a few connections may not be able to perform the task at all due to its limited capability. In contrast, a network with a large number of connections may overfit noise in the training data and fail to have good generalization ability.

The design of the optimal architecture for a neural network can be formulated as a search problem in the architecture space, where each point represents an architecture. Given some cost measure, such as the training error and the network complexity (e.g., the number of weight connections), the cost of all architectures forms a discrete surface in the space. The design of the optimal architecture is equivalent to finding the lowest point on this surface.

A major problem with the design of neural architectures, when the weight connections and their respective values are not considered, is the noisy fitness evaluation (Yao and Liu (1997)). This happens when a network with a full set of weights is used to approximate the fitness of the solution, where the solution means a neural network without any weight information. For instance, different weight initializations and training parameters can produce different results for the same topology.

The problem described above (the design problem) can be minimized by designing neural network architectures and connection weights (with their respective values) simultaneously (Yao (1999)). In this case, each point in the search space is a fully specified neural network with complete weight information. Since there is an one-to-one mapping between a neural network and a point in the search space, fitness evaluation will be accurate.

One of the optimization methods that can be used to deal with the design problem is Simulated Annealing (SA), which was first presented by Kirkpatrick et al. (1983). They were inspired by the annealing (cooling) processes of crystals that reach the lowest energy, corresponding to the perfect crystal structure, if cooled sufficiently slowly.

This method has been widely and successfully used to solve global optimization problems in many fields, including training of ANNs (Chalup and Maire (1999)). However, SA has not been popular in simultaneous optimization of network weights and architectures. In fact, such a problem has been often handled by using Genetic Algorithms (GAs) (Yao (1999)), in spite of the simplicity of SA when compared to GAs.

Another technique that can be employed to deal with this problem is Tabu Search (TS), which was developed independently by Glover (1986) and Hansen (1986). This iterative search method is able to escape from local minima by using a flexible memory, which is designed to discourage cycles in the search trajectory (Pham and Karaboga (2000))(Sexton et al. (1998)).

The TS method has been often used in combinatorial optimization problems (Sexton et al. (1998))(Hertz et al. (1995))(Battiti and Tecchiolli (1995)), and there are few applications of TS for training feedforward neural networks (Sexton et al. (1998))(Battiti and Tecchiolli (1995))(Karaboga and Kalinli (1997)). As with SA, TS has not been popular in simultaneous optimization of neural network weights and architectures.

In this work, SA and TS are used for the optimization of architectures and weights of Multi-Layer Perceptron (MLP) networks (Rumelhart et al. (1986)). The networks were trained to classify three different vintages of a given wine (the data set was generated by an artificial nose). The results show that the algorithms are able to produce networks with good generalization performance (mean classification error for the test set was 5.28% for SA and 2.93% for TS) and low complexity (mean number of connections used was 11.68 out of 36 for SA and 11.49 out of 36 for TS) for the odor classification task.

The remainder of this paper is divided into five sections. Section 2 describes the odor classification problem. In Section 3, important details about the implementation of the SA method are given. Section 4 discusses the implementation details of the TS algorithm. The main contribution of this paper is presented in Section 5, where the results of the experiments are analyzed. Finally, in Section 6, some final remarks are presented.

2   Problem and data description

The two main components of an artificial nose are the sensor and the pattern recognition systems. Each odorant substance presented to the sensor system generates a pattern of resistance values that characterizes the odor. This pattern is often first pre-processed and then given to the pattern recognition system, which in its turn classifies the odorant stimulus (Gardner and

Hines (1997)). Sensor systems have been often built with polypyrrol-based gas sensors. Some advantages of using such kind of sensors are (Persaud and Travers (1997)): (1) rapid adsorption kinetics at environment temperature; (2) low power consumption, as no heating element is required; (3) resistance to poisoning; and (4) the possibility of building sensors tailored to particular classes of chemical compounds. ANNs have been widely applied as pattern recognition systems in artificial noses. Implementing the pattern recognition system with ANNs has advantages such as (Craven et al. (1996)): (1) the ability to handle non-linear signals from the sensor array; (2) adaptability; (3) fault and noise tolerance; and (4) inherent parallelism, resulting in high speed operation. The type of neural network most commonly used for odor classification in artificial noses has been the MLP, together with the back-propagation learning algorithm (Rumelhart et al. (1986)).

The aim is to classify odors from three different vintages (years 1995, 1996 and 1997) of the same wine (Almadem, Brazil). A prototype of an artificial nose was used to acquire the data. This prototype is composed of six distinct polypyrrol-based gas sensors, built by electrochemical deposition of polypyrrol using different types of dopants. Three disjoint data acquisitions were performed for every vintage of wine, by recording the resistance value of each sensor at every half second during five minutes. Therefore, this experiment yielded three data sets with equal numbers of patterns: 1800 patterns (600 ones from each vintage). A pattern is a vector of six elements representing the values of the resistances recorded by the sensor array.

In this work, the data for training and testing the network were divided as follows: 50% of the patterns from each vintage were assigned to the training set, 25% were assigned to the validation set, and 25% were reserved to test the network, as suggested by Proben1 (Prechelt (1994)). The patterns were normalized to the range [-1.0,+1.0], for all network processing units implemented hyperbolic tangent activation functions.

This data set was used in a previous work (Yamazaki and Ludermir (2001))(Yamazaki et al. (2001)), where two approaches were compared: MLP networks and TDNNs (Time Delay Neural Networks) (Lang and Hinton (1988)), with 2, 4, 8, 12, 16 and 20 hidden nodes. The results showed that the TDNN approach achieves better generalization performance (mean classification error of 4.32%) than that obtained by MLP networks (42.79%).

3   Implementation details of simulated annealing

The SA algorithm consists of a sequence of iterations. Each iteration consists of randomly changing the current solution to create a new solution in the neighborhood of the current solution. The neighborhood is defined by the choice of the generation mechanism. Once a new solution is created, the corresponding change in the cost function is computed to decide whether the new solution can be accepted as the current solution. If the change in the cost function is negative, the new solution is directly taken as the current solution.

Otherwise, it is accepted according to the Metropolis criterion (Metropolis et al. (1953)): if the difference between the cost function values of the current and new solutions is equal to or larger than zero, a random number in [0,1] is generated from an uniform distribution. If the random number is equal to or less than exp(-E/T), where E is the change in the cost function and T is the current temperature, then the new solution is accepted as the current solution. If not, the current solution is unchanged (Pham and Karaboga (2000)).

In this work, each MLP is specified by an array of connections, and each connection is specified by two parameters: (a) the connectivity bit, which is equal to 1 if the connection exists, and 0 otherwise; and (b) the connection weight, which is a real number. If the connectivity bit is 0, its associated weight is not considered, for the connection does not exist in the network.

The maximal network structure is an one-hidden-layer MLP with six input nodes (one for each sensor), four hidden nodes and three output nodes (one for each vintage of wine, for the output is represented by a 1-of-m code). Since the networks have all possible feedforward connections between adjacent layers - having no connection between non-adjacent layers -, the maximum number of connections is 36.

For each solution, the cost function used is the mean of two important parameters: (1) the classification error for the training set (percentage of incorrectly classified training patterns); and (2) the percentage of connections used by the network. Therefore, the algorithm tries to minimize both network performance and complexity. Only valid networks (i.e., networks with at least one unit in the hidden layer) were considered. If the solution created is an invalid network, a new neighbor solution is generated.

The generation mechanism acts as follows: first the connectivity bits for the current solution are changed according to a given probability, which in this work is set to 20%. This operation deletes some network connections and creates new ones. Then, a random number between -1.0 and +1.0 is added to each connection weight. These two steps can change both topology and connection weights to produce a new neighbor solution.

There are several cooling schedules in the literature (Osman (1991)). They are characterized by the different temperature updating schemes used. Examples of these schemes are the stepwise temperature reduction schemes, which are widely used (Pham and Karaboga (2000)). Stepwise schemes include very simple cooling strategies, such as the geometric cooling rule. According to this rule, the new temperature is equal to the current temperature multiplied by a temperature factor (smaller than 1 but close to 1) (Pham and Karaboga (2000)).

In this work, the cooling strategy chosen is the geometric cooling rule. The initial temperature is set to 1, and the temperature factor is set to 0.90. The temperature is decreased at each 10 iterations, and the maximum number of iterations allowed is 1000. The classification error on the validation set is measured after every tenth iteration.

The algorithm stops if: (1) the GL5 criterion defined in Proben1 (Prechelt (1994)) is met (based on the classification error for the validation set) after 300 iterations; or (2) the maximum number of 1000 iterations is achieved.

The GL5 criterion is a good way to avoid overfitting of the network to the particular training examples used, which would reduce the generalization performance. The generalization loss parameter (GL) at iteration t is the relative increase of the error on the validation set over the minimum-so-far (in percent). The GL5 criterion makes the training process stop as soon as the generalization loss exceeds 5% (Prechelt (1994)).

4   Implementation details of tabu search

In the TS algorithm, each iteration consists of evaluating the solutions in a neighborhood around the current solution. The best neighbor solution (in terms of the cost function) is accepted even if its cost is higher than the cost of the current solution. Therefore, the algorithm chooses the neighbor solution that produces the most improvement or the least deterioration in the cost function, and this provides the ability to escape from local minima. To keep from cycling, a tabu list is employed to store the most recently visited solutions, which are then classified as tabu (i.e., to be avoided) in later iterations. During this procedure, the best solution found so far is retained (Pham and Karaboga (2000))(Sexton et al. (1998))(Hertz et al. (1995)).

In this work, the representation of solutions and the cost function are the same used in the SA experiments. The generation mechanism for the neighbors is also the same. In each iteration, the mechanism produces 20 distinct neighbor solutions, and the algorithm chooses the best neighbor solution (in terms of the cost function) which is not in the tabu list.

The tabu list stores the 10 most recently visited solutions. Since the connection weights are real numbers, the likelihood of finding solutions that are identical is extremely small. Therefore, a proximity criterion is used to relax the strict comparison of weights, as implemented by Sexton et al. (1998) for the training of feedforward neural networks. According to this criterion, a new solution is considered equal to one of the tabu solutions in the list if each connectivity bit in the new solution is identical to the corresponding connectivity bit in the tabu solution and if each connection weight in the new solution is in the range [C+N,C-N], where C is the corresponding connection weight in the tabu solution, and the parameter N is a real number. In this work, N is set to 0.01.

The maximum number of iterations allowed is 100. The TS algorithm stops if: (1) the GL5 criterion defined in Proben1 (Prechelt (1994)) is met (based on the classification error for the validation set) after 30 iterations; or (2) the maximum number of 100 iterations is achieved.

5   Experiments and results

In this work, three different architectures were taken as initial topologies: one-hidden-layer MLP networks with 2, 3 and 4 hidden nodes, having all possible feedforward connections between adjacent layers. For each initial topology, 10 distinct random weight initializations were used, and the initial weights were taken from an uniform distribution between -1.0 and +1.0. For each weight initialization, 30 runs of the optimization method (SA or TS) were performed. The best 10 runs (the ones with lowest classification error for the validation set) and the worst 10 runs (the ones with highest classification error for the validation set) were excluded, and the 10 remaining runs were considered for the final results.

For the SA approach, the mean results for the three initial topologies are shown in Table 1. The results presented in this table show that the networks achieve good generalization performance (small classification errors on validation and test sets) and use fewer nodes and connections than the maximal architecture allowed, which has 36 connections. For this approach, the mean classification error for the test set was 5.28%, and the mean number of connections was 11.68 (out of 36).

Initial topology (hidden nodes)	Training set classif. error (%)	Validation set classif. error (%)	Test set classif. error (%)	Number of connections
2	5.200	5.645	5.187	11.750
3	4.665	5.072	4.653	11.770
4	5.960	6.466	6.007	11.510

Table 1. Results for simulated annealing.

For the TS implementation, the mean results for the three initial topologies are shown in Table 2. The mean classification error for the test set was 2.93%, and the mean number of connections was 11.49 (out of 36).

The initial topologies have also been trained with the backpropagation learning algorithm [Rumelhart et al., 1986]. In order to do so, the same 10 sets of initial weights considered for each topology were used in the backpropagation experiments. In all cases, the learning rate was set to 0.001, and the momentum term to 0.8. The training process was stopped if: (1) the GL5 criterion defined in Proben1 [Prechelt, 1994] was met (based on the sum squared error for the validation set); or (2) the maximum number of 1000 iterations was achieved. The results for the topologies with 2, 3 and 4 hidden nodes are

Initial topology (hidden nodes)	Training set classif. error (%)	Validation set classif. error (%)	Test set classif. error (%)	Number of connections
2	2.871	3.021	2.746	11.640
3	2.817	2.973	2.707	11.470
4	3.410	3.614	3.327	11.350

Table 2. Results for tabu search.

shown in Table 3. For this approach, the mean classification error for the test set was 48.80%.

Topology (hidden nodes)	Training set classif. error (%)	Validation set classif. error (%)	Test set classif. error (%)
2	50.841	50.578	50.711
3	42.707	43.452	42.978
4	52.900	53.022	52.696

Table 3. Results for backpropagation.

Comparing these results with those obtained with simulated annealing and tabu search, one can see that the maximal networks do not have to be used in order to achieve a good performance. Therefore, simulated annealing and tabu search have shown to be very efficient in finding minimal network architectures with better performance than the fully connected MLP trained by the backpropagation algorithm.

6   Final remarks

In this paper, results regarding the use of simulated annealing and tabu search for the optimization of neural network weights and architectures have been presented. It was shown that the algorithms are able to produce networks with low complexity (mean number of connections used was 11.68 out of 36 for simulated annealing and 11.49 out of 36 for tabu search) and better generalization performance (mean classification error for the test set was 5.28% for simulated annealing and 2.93% for tabu search) than MLP networks trained with the backpropagation algorithm (mean classification error of 48.80%) for the odor classification task. Thus, this work shows that low classification errors can be achieved without using all the connections in a standard one-hidden-layer fully connected MLP. This is very important in a wide range of applications, including hardware implementation of neural networks for artificial noses.

References

BATTITI, R. and TECCHIOLLI, G. (1995): Training neural nets with the reactive tabu search. *IEEE Transactions on Neural Networks, 6, 1185–1200.*

CHALUP, S. and MAIRE, F. (1999): A Study on Hill Climbing Algorithms for Neural Network Training. *Proceedings of the 1999 Congress on Evolutionary Computation, 3, 2014–2021.*

CRAVEN, M.A., GARDNER, J.W. and BARTLETT, P.N. (1996): Electronic noses - development and future prospects. *Trends in Analytical Chemistry, Vol. 5, n. 9.*

GARDNER, J.W. and HINES, E.L. (1997): Pattern Analysis Techniques. In: E. Kress-Rogers (Ed.): *Handbook of Biosensors and Electronic Noses: Medicine, Food and the Environment.* CRC Press, 633–652.

GLOVER, F. (1986): Future paths for integer programming and links to artificial intelligence. *Computers and Operation Research, 13, 533–549.*

HANSEN, P. (1986): The steepest ascent mildest descent heuristic for combinatorial programming. *Conf. on Numerical Methods in Combinatorial Optimisation, Capri, Italy.*

HERTZ, A., TAILLARD, E. and DE WERRA, D. (1995): A Tutorial on Tabu Search. *Proc. of Giornate di Lavoro AIRO'95 (Enterprise Systems: Management of Technological and Organizational Changes), Italy, 13–24.*

KARABOGA, D. and KALINLI, A. (1997): Training recurrent neural networks for dynamic system identification using parallel tabu search algorithm. *12th IEEE Int. Symp. on Intelligent Control, Istanbul, Turkey, 113–118.*

KIRKPATRICK, S., GELLAT JR., C.D. and VECCHI, M.P. (1983): Optimization by simulated annealing. *Science, 220, 671–680.*

LANG, K.J. and HINTON, G.E. (1988): The development of the time-delay neural network architecture for speech recognition. *Technical Report CMU-CS-88-152, Carnegie-Mellon University, Pittsburgh, PA.*

METROPOLIS, N., ROSENBLUTH, A.W., ROSENBLUTH, M.N., TELLER, A.H. and TELLER, E. (1953): Equation of state calculations by fast computing machines. *J. of Chem. Phys., Vol. 21, n. 6, 1087–1092.*

OSMAN, I.H. (1991): Metastrategy Simulated Annealing and Tabu Search Algorithms for Combinatorial Optimisation Problems. *PhD Thesis, University of London, Imperial College, UK.*

PERSAUD, K.C. and TRAVERS, P.J. (1997): Arrays of Broad Specificity Films for Sensing Volatile Chemicals. In: E. Kress-Rogers (Ed.): *Handbook of Biosensors and Electronic Noses: Medicine, Food and the Environment.* CRC Press, 563–592.

PHAM, D.T. and KARABOGA, D. (2000): Introduction. In: D.T. Pham and D. Karaboga (Eds.): *Intelligent Optimisation Techniques.* Springer-Verlag, 01–50.

PRECHELT, L. (1994): Proben1 - A Set of Neural Network Benchmark Problems and Benchmarking Rules. *Technical Report 21/94, Fakultat fur Informatik, Universitat Karlsruhe, Germany, September, 1994.*

RUMELHART, D.E., HINTON, G.E. and WILLIAMS, R.J. (1986): Learning internal representations by error propagation. In: D.E. RUMELHART and J.L. MC-CLELLAND (Eds.): *Parallel Distributed Processing Vol.1*. MIT Press, Cambridge, 318–362.

SEXTON, R.S., ALIDAEE, B., DORSEY, R.E. and JOHNSON, J.D. (1998): Global optimization for artificial neural networks: a tabu search application. *Eur. J. Operational Research, (106)2-3, 570–584*.

YAMAZAKI, A. and LUDERMIR, T.B. (2001): Classification of vintages of wine by an artificial nose with neural networks. *Proceedings of 8th International Conference on Neural Information Processing (ICONIP2001), Shanghai, China, Vol. 1, 184–187*.

YAMAZAKI, A., LUDERMIR, T.B. and DE SOUTO, M. (2001): Classification of vintages of wine by an artificial nose using time delay neural networks. *IEE Electronics Letters, 22nd November 2001, Vol. 37, n. 24, 1466–1467*.

YAO, X. (1999): Evolving Artificial Neural Networks. *Proceedings of the IEEE, 87(9), 1423–1447*.

YAO, X. and LIU, Y. (1997): A new evolutionary system for evolving artificial neural networks. *IEEE Transactions on Neural Networks, Vol. 8, n. 3, 694–713*.

Part IV

Finance, Marketing, and Management Science

Decentralizing Risk Management
in the Case of Quadratic Hedging

Julia Bondarenko[1], Nicole Branger[2], Angelika Esser[2], and Christian Schlag[2]

[1] Postdoctoral researcher in the Graduate Program "Finance and Monetary Economics",
Goethe University, Mertonstr. 17, D-60054 Frankfurt am Main, Germany
[2] School of Business and Economics
Goethe University, Mertonstr. 17, D-60054 Frankfurt am Main, Germany

Abstract. This paper deals with the problem of quadratic hedging with limited initial capital. We show (i) that the optimal amount of capital for the quadratic hedge of a portfolio of contingent claims is equal to the sum of optimal investments for the individual hedges of its components and (ii) that the optimal hedging strategies for individual claims add up to the optimal strategy for the total position. These results have the important implication for risk management that in the case of limited capital the quadratic hedge of a contingent claim can be decomposed into two problems: first, the claim is hedged as if the optimal amount of capital was available, and then an additional quadratic hedge is set up for a zero payoff where now the initial capital is given by the (negative) difference between available and optimal capital. Both this additional hedge and the increase in the expected squared hedging error arising from the capital restriction are independent of the original claim to be hedged.

1 Introduction and motivation

This paper deals with the problem of setting up a hedge for a derivative claim in an incomplete market under the additional constraint that not enough capital is available to install the globally optimal hedge. Furthermore, we discuss the implications of decentralizing the hedging decision in such a way that not the portfolio as a whole is hedged, but that a hedge is implemented for each individual claim.

Under the ideal conditions of a dynamically complete market and sufficient capital, the hedge portfolio can be chosen such that the risk of the claim is eliminated completely. If one of these conditions is not met, such a perfect hedge no longer exists. Considering the case of an incomplete market first, the manager of a derivative position has to choose the strategy which minimizes the remaining risk of the hedge. The actual choice of strategies depends on the criterion defining the term risk. If the hedging strategy is designed such that its terminal value is always enough to cover the stochastic liability generated by the claim, the strategy is called a *superhedge* (see El Karoui and Quenez (1995)). If on the other hand the loss function is the expected quadratic deviation of the terminal portfolio value from the payoff of the claim, the strategy is called a *quadratic hedge* or a *mean-variance hedge*. This type of hedging is discussed for example in Schweizer (1995, 1999).

Recently also the second problem of insufficient capital has been discussed in the literature. Föllmer and Leukert (1999) analyze what they call *quantile hedging*, i.e. they investigate strategies that are designed to maximize the probability of a successful hedge. A hedge is considered successful if it yields a terminal value at least as high as the liability to be covered. The authors discuss the Black-Scholes economy in detail and also show the basic structure of the solution for the case of an incomplete market, although they do not explicitly analyze the associated strategies in this case.

Our paper investigates quadratic hedging on an incomplete market with limited initial capital. The central result of our analysis is that the increase in expected mean squared hedging error (ESHE) due to the capital restriction is proportional to the squared difference between the given and the optimal amount of capital. The factor of proportionality is the ESHE when a payoff of zero should be hedged with an initial investment equal to minus one, which Gourieroux et al. (1998) call the *hedging numeraire*. To obtain this result we will first show that when a portfolio of claims should be hedged optimally in the mean square sense, the optimal initial investment for the portfolio is the sum of the optimal initial investments for the components. To put it differently, hedging can be decentralized in the sense that the components of the portfolio can be hedged individually with the optimal amount of capital, and the total capital invested is equal to the optimal investment for a single hedge of the total portfolio. Furthermore, the value processes of the hedging strategies for the individual claims with restricted capital will be shown to be additive as well, i.e. adding the terminal values of the individually optimal restricted hedges will yield the terminal value of the optimal restricted strategy of the total position. On the basis of these two results we then derive a theorem concerning the decomposition of the ESHE which basically says that the loss in hedging quality is entirely determined by the amount of reduction in capital, but independent of the type of claim.

An important consequence of our results is that quadratic hedging can be decentralized. For example, if the members of a group of risk managers have to hedge their positions individually, and the amount of capital available to the group as a whole is insufficient, the individual hedgers can nevertheless set up their portfolios *as if* enough capital was available. The only thing that has to be done in addition is to design a hedging strategy approaching a terminal payoff of zero as closely as possible with a negative initial investment equal to the difference between available and optimal total capital.

Note that (dis-)aggregation results like those derived in this paper are unlikely to hold for other objective functions. It is for example in the general case impossible to delegate quantile hedges, since the total amount of capital needed for individual hedges will not in general add up to the capital needed to hedge the total liability with a certain upper bound on the shortfall probability.

The remainder of the paper is organized as follows. In section 2 the basic framework of the analysis is presented, followed by the derivation of the central decomposition results for quadratic hedging strategies. Some numerical examples are provided in section 3 to illustrate the consequences of capital limitations. Conclusions and possible extensions are presented in section 4.

2   Decomposition results for quadratic hedges with limited initial capital

2.1   Basic framework

We consider a discrete time economy with a finite set of trading dates $t_0 \equiv 0, \ldots, t_N \equiv T$, and a finite discrete state space. Capital markets in the economy are assumed to be frictionless, i.e. there are no short-sale constraints and no divisibility restrictions. There are n assets, all of which are assumed to be non-redundant, and we assume that there exists an asset with a price process that is different from zero with probability one. This latter assumption is needed for the application of the methodology proposed by Gourieroux et al. (1998). There is at least one one-period subeconomy with the number of states exceeding the number of linearly independent assets, so that the capital market is dynamically incomplete.

Let $\mathcal{G}(0,T,0)$ denote the space of excess returns in T, i.e. the space of payoffs attainable at time T with an initial capital of zero at time $t_0 = 0$. In an analogous fashion $\mathcal{G}(0,T,c)$ denotes the set of time-T payoffs attainable with an initial capital of c at time 0. Finally the space of payoffs at time T which are attainable with an arbitrary initial capital at time $t_0 = 0$ is denoted by $\mathcal{G}(0,T)$.

2.2   Quadratic hedging with limited capital

Consider the following problem: There is a non-redundant European contingent claim paying off the random amount H at time T, and the initial capital for the associated hedging portfolio is given by some $c \in \mathbb{R}_+$. This amount will be invested in a trading strategy that is self-financing up to time t_{N-1}. We will briefly discuss the two cases when c is fixed and when it can be chosen optimally.

In the first situation the hedging strategy with an initial investment of c should be chosen such that the expectation of the squared hedging error is minimized under the physical probability measure P, i.e. the optimal strategy generates a terminal value $V^{H,c}$ which satisfies

$$V^{H,c} = \arg \min_{V \in \mathcal{G}(0,T,c)} E_P\left[(H - V)^2\right].$$

The optimal objective value is denoted by $J(H,c)$. It is straightforward to show that the condition for the terminal payoff $\hat{V}$ of some hedging strategy to be optimal is

$$E_P\big[(H - \tilde{V})\, Y\big] = 0 \qquad \forall\, Y \in \mathcal{G}(0,T,0). \tag{1}$$

To see this, consider the strategy $\tilde{V} := V^{H,c} + aY$ for some $a \in \mathbb{R}$ and $Y \in \mathcal{G}(0,T,0)$. Since the initial investment for Y is equal to zero, the total capital invested to obtain $\tilde{V}$ is equal to c, so $\tilde{V}$ is another candidate for the optimal hedge of H. The ESHE is given by $E_P\big[(H - V^{H,c} - aY)^2\big]$. Differentiating this expression with respect to a yields the first order condition for the optimal value a^*: $E_P\big[(H - V^{H,c} - aY)Y\big]|_{a=a^*} = 0$. Since $V^{H,c}$ is optimal, a^* must be equal to zero, yielding the optimality condition (1). Economically this means that there is no time-T payoff attainable with a zero initial investment that could further improve the quality of the hedge. Equation (1) is an orthogonality condition, saying that at the optimum the hedging error is orthogonal to the space $\mathcal{G}(0,T,0)$.

A similar argument can be made in the case when the initial capital available for the hedge is determined endogenously, i.e. c can be chosen such that the globally minimal ESHE is achieved. The problem thus becomes

$$\min_{V \in \mathcal{G}(0,T)} E_P\big[(H - V)^2\big].$$

The terminal value of the optimal portfolio is denoted by V^{H,c^*} where c^* is the associated optimal initial capital. The value of the objective function using the optimal strategy is represented by $J(H,c^*)$. The optimality condition for V^{H,c^*} is

$$E_P\big[(H - V^{H,c^*})\, Y\big] = 0 \qquad \forall\, Y \in \mathcal{G}(0,T), \tag{2}$$

which can be proved along the same lines as in the case of a fixed initial capital of c. Note that in contrast to (1), the orthogonality condition in (2) holds for any arbitrary attainable payoff Y. This ensures the global optimality of the strategy with terminal payoff V^{H,c^*}. We will use the properties of optimal strategies from equations (1) and (2) in the following analysis.

Our main result concerning quadratic hedging with limited initial capital is stated in a theorem at the end of this section. It says that the ESHE for a claim H with a given initial capital c can be decomposed into two terms. The first term represents the ESHE for H when the optimal capital c^* is used, whereas the second term corresponds to the ESHE for a zero payoff when an initial capital of $c - c^*$ is available. As a consequence the optimal strategy to hedge H with limited initial capital $c \le c^*$ thus consists of a first hedge using a capital of c^*, and a second strategy which hedges a payoff of zero with a negative initial capital equal to $c - c^*$.

To arrive at this result, we first have to show that terminal values of portfolio hedges are equal to the sum of the terminal values of the hedges of the component assets, and that the optimal capital c^* for the hedge of the total payoff H is indeed equal to the sum of optimal amounts of initial capital c_i^*.

We will first discuss the additivity of terminal values of mean square hedging strategies. Since we have assumed that all basis assets are non-redundant, the optimal portfolio strategy for each claim H_i is unique, so that according to the following proposition also the optimal hedging strategy for H will be unique.

Proposition 2 (Additivity of optimal strategies). *The terminal value of the optimal strategy for hedging a portfolio $H = \sum_{i=1}^{n} H_i$ with a fixed initial capital of $c = \sum_{i=1}^{n} c_i$ is equal to the sum of the terminal values of the optimal strategies for hedging each individual H_i with a fixed initial capital of c_i, i. e.*

$$V^{H,c} = V^{H_1,c_1} + \ldots + V^{H_n,c_n}.$$

Proof: For each i, V^{H_i,c_i} is the terminal value of the optimal hedging strategy for H_i, using fixed initial capital c_i. Therefore, the optimality condition (1) holds:

$$E_P\big[(H_i - V^{H_i,c_i})Y\big] = 0 \qquad \forall\, Y \in \mathcal{G}(0,T,0).$$

Adding this expression over all i yields

$$E_P\Big[\big(\sum_{i=1}^{n} H_i - \sum_{i=1}^{n} V^{H_i,c_i}\big)Y\Big] = 0 \qquad \forall\, Y \in \mathcal{G}(0,T,0).$$

This shows that $\sum_{i=1}^{n} V^{H_i,c_i}$ is indeed the terminal value of the optimal hedging strategy for the claim $H = \sum_{i=1}^{n} H_i$ with a fixed initial capital of $c = c_1 + \ldots + c_n$.   □

The statement in this proposition says that the distribution of the total amount c among the n hedge positions is irrelevant. Since it does not matter which claim is hedged with which amount of initial capital, the allocation of hedging capital can be decentralized. It suffices to give the total amount c to a group of n hedgers, each facing the problem of hedging a claim with terminal payoff H_i. Any distribution will yield the same terminal hedging result for the total position.

Note that these statements implicitly assume that for each of the hedges the available capital c_i has to be used in full, even if $c_i > c_i^*$. So in the more realistic case that money could be 'thrown away' if $c_i > c_i^*$, we would have to introduce the additional restriction that $c_i \leq c_i^*$ ($i = 1, \ldots, n$) for every possible distribution of the total capital $c = c_1 + \ldots + c_n$. Note further that the proposition does not say that the individual ESHE terms add up to the total ESHE of the portfolio payoff H. To get the ESHE for the portfolio we would, of course, have to consider cross terms between the hedging results for the individual claims.

Next we will show that the optimal initial capital c^* for the total payoff H is indeed equal to the sum of the optimal amounts of capital c_i^*. This is stated in

Proposition 3 (Additivity of optimal capital). *The optimal initial capital c^* for hedging a portfolio of claims with terminal payoff $H = H_1 + \ldots + H_n$ is equal to the sum of the optimal initial amounts of capital c_i^* for hedging the individual claims H_i $(i = 1, \ldots, n)$, i. e.*

$$c^* = c_1^* + \ldots + c_n^*.$$

Proof: For each i, V^{H_i, c_i^*} is the terminal value of the optimal hedging strategy for H_i, using the optimal initial capital c_i^*. Therefore, the optimality condition (2) holds:

$$E_P\big[(H_i - V^{H_i, c_i^*})Y\big] = 0 \qquad \forall\, Y \in \mathcal{G}(0, T)$$

This optimality condition is again additive:

$$E_P\big[(\sum_{i=1}^{n} H_i - \sum_{i=1}^{n} V^{H_i, c_i^*})Y\big] = 0 \qquad \forall\, Y \in \mathcal{G}(0, T)$$

Using proposition 2 for the special case $c_i = c_i^*$ $(i = 1 \ldots, n)$ we see that $V^{H_1, c_1^*} + \ldots + V^{H_n, c_n^*}$ is the terminal value of the optimal hedging strategy for the claim $H = H_1 + \ldots + H_n$, which therefore requires an initial capital of $c^* = c_1^* + \ldots + c_n^*$.   □

An important consequence of the result in this proposition is that the optimal amount of capital needed to set up a hedge for the total liability H will not increase if the n parts of the hedge are delegated to n portfolio managers. If each of the n managers is hedging the claim H_i with the optimal amount of capital c_i^*, the total capital needed is exactly equal to that needed for the global hedge of H. So delegation does not induce higher hedging costs. Reading it differently, the proposition implies that there is no gain in aggregating the individual payoffs into the total payoff H and then running just one hedge for H instead of hedging the individual H_i.

We can now state the main theorem:

Theorem 1 (Decomposition of ESHE). *The minimal ESHE $J(H, c)$ of a claim H with a given initial capital c equals the sum of*

i) the ESHE $J(H, c^*)$ for the claim H with the optimal initial capital c^* and
ii) the ESHE $J(0, c - c^*)$ for a payoff of zero with the remaining initial capital $c - c^*$, which is in turn equal to $(c - c^*)^2$ times the ESHE $J(0, -1)$ when hedging a payoff of zero with an initial investment equal to minus one.

Formally,

$$J(H, c) = J(H, c^*) + J(0, c - c^*) \tag{3}$$
$$= J(H, c^*) + (c - c^*)^2 J(0, -1) \tag{4}$$

Proof: Use the identities $c = c^* + (c - c^*)$ and $H = H + 0$ to decompose $J(H, c)$ as follows:

$$J(H, c) = E_P\left[(H - V^{H,c})^2\right]$$
$$= E_P\left[(H - V^{H,c^*})^2\right] + E_P\left[(0 - V^{0,c-c^*})^2\right]$$
$$+ 2 E_P\left[(H - V^{H,c^*})(0 - V^{0,c-c^*})\right]. \tag{5}$$

The second line follows from proposition 2 with the special choice $H_1 = H$, $H_2 = 0, c_1 = c^*, c_2 = c - c^*$ so that we can replace $V^{H,c}$ by $V^{H,c^*} + V^{0,c-c^*}$. Furthermore, since $-V^{0,c-c^*} \in \mathcal{G}(0,T)$, the last of the three terms in (5) equals zero, due to the optimality condition for V^{H,c^*} from equation (2). This yields equation (3). Now, for arbitrary x, $V^{0,-x} = xV^{0,-1}$, so that $E_P\left[(0 - V^{0,c-c^*})^2\right] = (c - c^*)^2 E_P\left[(0 - V^{0,-1})^2\right]$, yielding (4). $\square$

Summarizing the above discussion, propositions 2 and 3 together with theorem 1 suggest the following way to hedge a portfolio of claims $H_1, \ldots, H_n$: Let each of the n portfolio managers run the hedge for his or her claim H_i, using the optimal amount of capital c_i^*. Proposition 3 says that the total amount of capital $c_1^* + \ldots + c_n^*$ is then equal to the optimal amount of capital c^* needed to hedge H. ¿From proposition 2 we know that the total terminal value of these hedges will have minimal ESHE relative to the total payoff H. So delegation results in an optimal hedge for H in the ESHE sense using a capital of c^*. If the available amount c of capital is less than $c^* = \sum_{i=1}^n c_i^*$, a *single* additional hedge for a payoff of zero with initial capital $c - c^*$ has to be installed. Note that this represents a purchase of $c - c^*$ units of the hedge numeraire, each with a price of -1. The overall result of the two strategies is a hedge of H with initial capital c. Note that the additional hedge neither depends on the types of the individual claims nor on the total payoff H, but just on the amount of capital that is missing. This is important for the delegation of hedging, since it does not matter to the 'head' of the group what the positions of the individual hedgers are when the additional hedge has to be designed.

The theorem also shows that it can basically hurt to invest too much into the hedge portfolio, since the ESHE increases by the square of the difference between c and c^*. However, for practical purposes the only interesting case is of course a capital shortage $(c < c^*)$, since in the case of excess capital, one could always put the amount $c - c^*$ aside and run the hedge with the optimal initial investment of c^*.

3   Example

As we have shown in the previous section the hedge of a zero payoff with negative initial capital is one of the key things to look at when discussing quadratic hedging with limited initial capital. To gain some insight into the results of this hedge as a function of the parameters of the problem, we calculate $J(0, -1)$ for a discrete economy with two traded assets, a globally risk-free money market account and a stock. The uncertainty is represented by a trinomial tree for the price of the risky asset, so that the market is incomplete. The basic structure of the solution to the mean square hedging problem is given in Schweizer (1995). We use the methodology proposed by Gourieroux et al. (1998) to handle a non-zero interest rate.

$J(0, -1)$ depends on the expected excess return as well as on the volatility of the stock. Considering the dependence on the expected excess return first, it turns out that $J(0, -1)$ attains its maximum at a zero expected excess return, where the stock would not be used in the hedge of the zero payoff at all. Intuitively, this is due to the fact that we want to hedge a zero payoff with negative initial capital, so we need a hedge instrument that can create some drift away from the starting value of minus one. In the case of a positive excess return we would hold the stock long in our hedge. Otherwise when the expected return of the stock is less than the risk-free rate, we would sell the stock short to again create a positive drift in our hedge portfolio. When the expected return of the stock under the physical measure is exactly equal to the risk-free rate, neither of the two strategies can be employed, and including the stock would only increase the variance of the terminal value of the portfolio (remember that we are trying to hedge a constant payoff of zero). Therefore it will not be used, and the hedge would consist of investing minus one into the risk-free asset.

Considering the dependence on volatility, it turns out that the ESHE is increasing in volatility as one would intuitively expect. For very high levels of volatility the ESHE tends towards an upper bound. This is due to the fact that an extremely volatile stock is no longer a suitable hedging device for our problem. The variance of the terminal value of a strategy involving the stock would go up so much that it becomes necessary to reduce the share of the stock in the hedging portfolio further and further. In the limit the hedge portfolio will again only contain the risk-free asset, generating the same value of the ESHE as for the case of a zero expected excess return of the stock.

4   Conclusion

In this paper we have discussed quadratic hedging under the constraint of limited initial capital. Quadratic hedging means that a self-financing trading strategy is chosen to minimize the expected squared deviation of the portfolio payoff from the random payment of some contingent claim. This hedging technique is useful in incomplete markets, where we cannot exactly replicate the terminal payoff of some contingent claims by running self-financing portfolio strategies in the available basis assets. So far the combined problem of market incompleteness and capital limitations has not been adressed in the literature.

We derive two additivity results for quadratic hedging strategies. The optimal strategies for individual claims add up to the optimal strategy for the total position resulting from summing up the individual claims. Furthermore, when we add up the optimal amounts of initial capital for a number of claims, we exactly obtain the optimal initial capital for the total portfolio. These aggregation results can be combined to derive the main decomposition result in this paper: Quadratic hedging with limited initial capital can be decomposed into two separate steps. First, the claim (or portfolio) is hedged using the optimal amount of initial capital. Then a second hedge is run which starts with a negative initial capital equal to the difference between available and optimal capital. It is shown that the additional ESHE that arises from the capital restriction is entirely determined by the squared difference between available and optimal capital. Especially, it is independent of the original claim to be hedged. So, in the case of quadratic hedging, risk management can be decentralized.

Further research in the area of quadratic hedging could focus on the properties of optimal hedging strategies. As has become obvious from other computations not discussed in this paper, these optimal strategies exhibit a number of non-standard properties. For example, we have found that the number of units of the risky asset held in the hedge portfolio does not in general increase with the price of the risky asset when a hedge is run for a standard call option. Similarly, the number of units of the risky asset in the portfolio is not bounded from above by one, as it is in the case of a complete market. These and other issues, e.g. the path-dependence of the optimal strategies, deserve further attention.

A second point concerns the decentralization of the hedge. We have shown that when the objective is to minimize the ESHE, there is no difference between hedging the portfolio as a whole and hedging each individual component on its own. An interesting question would be to examine the impact of decentralization for some other hedging criteria like quantile hedging or expected shortfall hedging and to see by how much the hedging quality decreases and by how much the optimal initial capital changes.

References

EL KAROUI, N. and QUENEZ, M. C. (1995): Dynamic programming and pricing of contingent claims in an incomplete market. *SIAM Journal of Control Optimization, 33(1), 29–66.*

FÖLLMER, H. and LEUKERT, P. (1999): Quantile hedging. *Finance and Stochastics, 3, 251–273.*

GOURIEROUX, C.; LAURENT, J. P. and PHAM, H. (1998): Mean-variance hedging and numéraire. *Mathematical Finance, 8(3), 179–200.*

SCHWEIZER, M. (1995): Variance-optimal hedging in discrete time. *Mathematics of Operations Research, 20(1), 1–32.*

SCHWEIZER, M. (1999): A guided tour through quadratic hedging approaches. *Working Paper, Technische Universität Berlin.*

Multimedia Stimulus Presentation Methods for Conjoint Studies in Marketing Research

Michael Brusch and Daniel Baier

Institute of Business Administration and Economics,
Brandenburg University of Technology Cottbus, Postbox 101344,
D-03013 Cottbus, Germany

Abstract. With the increasing usage of multimedia in marketing research the possibilities have improved to realistically present new product concepts to potential buyers even before prototypical realizations are available. This usage of multimedia is expected to result in an improved quality of the collected data, e.g., preferential responses, and, consequently, to result in an improved predictive validity of the derived part worth estimates.

This paper examines the effects of different types of multimedia stimulus presentation methods using a conjoint study for comparison where new multimedia short message services (so-called MMS) of mobile phones are analyzed.

1 Introduction

The importance of multimedia as a marketing tool in various fields, among others in marketing research, is constantly increasing (see e.g., Zou (1999), Aunkofer (2000), Silberer and Zou (2002)). There, it can be used, e.g., to clarify innovative or (for the respondents) unknown objects of interest.

So, e.g., new product concept presentation methods have been developed which yield to improve the validity of stated preferences in conjoint analysis. One of these new methods is the incorporation of multimedia into the presentation (Ernst (2000), Ernst and Sattler (2000)).

In this paper first, we shortly discuss multimedia stimulus presentation, conjoint analysis as well as reliability and validity issues for marketing research. Then, in section 5, an empirical comparison of multimedia stimulus presentation methods is presented.

2 Multimedia stimulus presentation

In recent years the usage of multimedia has increased in marketing research, since it is assumed to bypass the known disadvantages of verbal descriptions of innovative new products. Stimulus presentations now utilize more multimedia elements, for example, pictures, video sequences, and acoustic elements (voices, noises, sounds) instead of written descriptions of the new product concept's attributes (see e.g., Baier (1999)). In this case, however, one assumes that not all qualities are to be represented exclusively by new elements; some qualities will still be described verbally.

The fundamental assumption of the model of cognition psychology implies that it is not the objectively observed, but rather the subjectively perceived cognitive reality that is responsible for behavior of individuals (Zimbardo and Gerrig (1999)). In the theoretical and empirical findings of imagery research (Ruge (1988), Kroeber-Riel (1993)), especially the dual coding approach (Paivio (1971), Paivio (1978)), fundamental differences have been found between the perception of verbal-textual descriptions and the perception of graphic and/or multimedia presentation forms. Humans require a much smaller cognitive expenditure to process picture information than text information (Scharf et al. (1996)). The close combination of perception and judgement during information processing brought about in multimedia presentation can have a positive influence on the validity of conjoint study results.

Therefore, the advantages expected from multimedia stimulus presentation methods are, e.g., a high participation motivation due to an interesting and less tiring stimulus presentation method, as well as a smaller cognitive load for the respondents through the easy and natural accessibility of the presented information (for a recent overview, see Brusch et al. (2002)).

3   Conjoint analysis

Conjoint analysis plays a meaningful role in marketing research to help to ascertain the preferences of customers and to derive the part worths of selected attributes and levels of new product concepts to the overall preference. This should yield a perfect database for designing products according to the wishes of the potential buyers and the producer's commercial interests (for an overview of application fields cf. e.g., Wittink et al. (1994), Baier (1999), Voeth (1999)). The validity of this ascertainment depends strongly on the presentation of the product concepts which are to be evaluated.

The first step in a conjoint study involves the collection of data. A sample of potential buyers (respondents) is asked to judge alternative product concepts (so-called stimuli) as a whole. These concepts are systematically varied, with respect to design attributes of research interest. Next, in the data analysis step of the conjoint study, the contribution of each product concept attribute and attribute-level to the whole preference (so-called part worths) is analytically determined using MONANOVA (monotone analysis of variance, see e.g., Kruskal (1965)):

Let be i an index for I respondents, j an index for $2J$ stimuli, k an index for K attributes, and l an index for L_k levels of the k-th attribute. With this notation, typical conjoint data are (binary) profile data $x_{111}, \ldots, x_{JKL_K}$ (where x_{jkl} indicates whether stimulus j has level l for attribute k (=1) or not (=0)) and response data $y_{11}, \ldots, y_{IJ}$ for the conjoint task (where y_{ij} describes the observed preference value for stimulus j obtained from respondent i on an ordinal scale) and $y_{i(J+1)}, \ldots, y_{i(2J)}$ for the holdout task (where y_{ij} describes the observed preference value for stimulus j obtained from respondent i in a second sorting task for controlling the data quality and validity). Model parameters are the respondents' part-worths $b_{111}, \ldots, b_{IKL_K}$, which are estimated in such a way that the stress function

$$S = \sqrt{\frac{\sum_{j=1}^{J}(f_i(y_{ij}) - \hat{y}_{ij})^2}{\sum_{j=1}^{J}(\hat{y}_{ij} - \bar{\hat{y}}_{ij})^2}} \quad \text{with} \quad \hat{y}_{ij} = \sum_{k=1}^{K}\sum_{j=1}^{J_k} x_{jkl}b_{ikl} \quad \forall i$$

is minimized (f_i is an arbitrary monotone ascending function).

4 Validity and reliability of previous empirical comparisons discussed in the literature

It is clear, that the type of stimulus presentation has an influence on the data quality and validity. So, numerous studies have compared the different types of product concept attribute presentations with regard to their reliability and validity (for an overview, see Ernst and Sattler (2000)). No clear statement can be made about the benefit of any of the traditional presentation methods (verbal, pictorial or real).

New results were brought by a first study, which compared two different multimedia stimulus presentation alternatives (Ernst (2000)). This study revealed better results for its "high multimedia" presentation than its "low multimedia" presentation in almost all types of validity criteria. However, Ernst's multimedia stimulus presentation methods were not largely different from each other. In addition, his "high multimedia" stimulus presentation method is outdated. Technology today allows for a much better production of multimedia elements.

Therefore, it is the purpose of this article, in opposition to the study by Ernst (2000), to compare multimedia stimulus presentation methods which are really different.

5 Empirical comparison of multimedia stimulus presentation methods

5.1 Design of the study

This study compares two multimedia stimulus presentation alternatives for conjoint studies, one using only a few multimedia elements ("less multimedia") and one using several multimedia elements ("more multimedia").

The new multimedia short message service (so-called MMS) was chosen as a product concept for this study since it could be judged with regard to static functions as well as dynamic functions. The results of a preliminary study determined the product concept attributes and the levels which were used in the conjoint study. The four attributes of the multimedia short message service and their levels in the study are shown in Table 1. We used a pricing model for our study that added surcharges for some attribute-levels.

In the interview, the individual product concept attributes and levels were first explained to the respondents. Then, the respondents were asked in a

Attributes	Attribute-levels			
Text	Up to 160 characters, not formatable	Up to 160 characters, formatable	Unlimited charac-ters, formatable	
Audio	Sending and receiv-ing of bell tones	Integration of sounds into the text	Sending of complete audiofiles	
Video	Sending of picture messages	Integration of pic-tures into the text	Sending of videos and animations	
Price	0.20 EUR	0.40 EUR	0.70 EUR	1.00 EUR

Table 1. Overview of attributes and levels used

conjoint task to sort sixteen stimuli of MMS in order of their individual preference. In the holdout task, sixteen additional stimuli of MMS were used to collect purchase intentions (with scales ranging from "definitely would buy" to "definitely would not buy"). The two sets of sixteen stimulus cards were generated systematically using orthogonal plans w.r.t. the attributes and levels in Table 1. The stimulus cards of the conjoint task and the holdout task had different product concept attribute-level combinations.

Within the "less multimedia" study, the attributes and their levels were explained to the respondents by means of text, pictures, and sound files. On the stimulus card and the cards shown in the holdout task, the attributes and their levels were presented using pictorial illustrations as well as written descriptions of the MMS stimuli. The holdout cards differed in their attribute-level combinations. They had the same design in the interviews for both studies.

"More multimedia" differed from "less multimedia" w.r.t. the description of the attributes and the attribute-levels. The respondents of "more multi-media" received the explanations of the attributes and their levels through texts, animations, and short videos instead of static pictures. A sample for a short video is shown in Figure 1.

This selection of the various degrees of multimedia was carried out according to the recommendations of Ernst (2000).

Two separate groups of 50 ("less multimedia") and 31 ("more multime-dia") respondents were chosen for the two studies as a between-subject design to test the influence of the two examined stimulus presentation types on the validity. In addition, the selection of independent partial random samples guaranteed that the respondents' faculty for supplying information is not overtaxed, and avoided the arrangement effects and/or learning effects which influence answer behavior and therefore can lead to distortions in the results (Huber et al. (1993), Agarwal and Green (1991)).

In order to achieve comparability between the two partial random sam-ples, the respondents were selected from a restricted homogenous population (students and employees of a German university). Due to the homogenity of the sample groups, it is difficult to generalize the results (for a more com-prehensive discussion compare, e.g., Sattler et al. (2001)). Furthermore, no

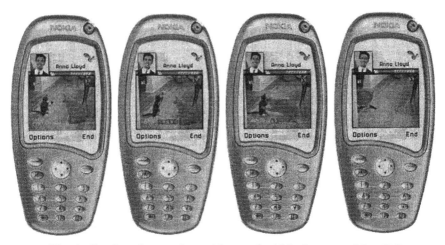

Fig. 1. Cuttings from a short video used within "more multimedia"

market potential estimate is possible with the achieved results, but that was not the goal of this comparison.

5.2   Results

The results are summarized in the following tables. Table 2 includes the differences in part worth estimates depending on the type of product presentation. The part worths were estimated using MONANOVA as described in section 3. The effects from additional pricing were substracted.

From the results the following statements are identifiable. Price is the most important attribute. The utility differences between the part worth estimates for the highest and lowest price levels dominate the other attributes. All attributes have the same tendency. The respondents of both presentation alternatives always most want the highest attribute-level for every attribute except for the price. The respondents want to be able to send messages with a number of unlimited characters, which have to be formatable and they want to send complete audiofiles. The respondents, furthermore, want the possibility to send videos and animations. The price should be low.

Table 3 shows the corresponding external validity values using the mean Spearman rank-order correlation and Kendall's τ as well as the first-choice hit rate for both stimulus presentation methods. The Spearman rank-order correlation and Kendall's τ compare the observed ordinal scale response data from the holdout task with the corresponding predicted preference values. The first-choice hit rate is the share of respondents where the stimulus with the highest predicted preference value is also the one with the highest observed preference value.

Attri-bute	Attribute level	"Less multimedia" Mean	*Std. dev.*	"More multimedia" Mean	*Std. dev.*
Text	Up to 160 characters, not formatable	0.028	*0.094*	0.033	*0.087*
	Up to 160 characters, formatable	0.116	*0.195*	0.206	*0.259*
	Unlimited characters, formatable	0.247	*0.267*	0.266	*0.245*
Audio	Sending and receiving of bell tones	0.026	*0.046*	0.048	*0.068*
	Integration of sounds into the text	0.027	*0.041*	0.070	*0.088*
	Sending of complete audiofiles	0.136	*0.116*	0.141	*0.145*
Video	Sending of picture messages	0.031	*0.060*	0.049	*0.075*
	Integration of pictures into the text	0.028	*0.043*	0.040	*0.057*
	Sending of videos and animations	0.149	*0.113*	0.139	*0.143*
Price	0.20 EUR	0.414	*0.272*	0.330	*0.222*
	0.40 EUR	0.339	*0.214*	0.241	*0.195*
	0.70 EUR	0.190	*0.119*	0.120	*0.118*
	1.00 EUR	0.004	*0.022*	0.020	*0.055*

Table 2. Estimation results for both multimedia stimulus presentation methods

Validity criteria	"Less multimedia" Mean	*std. dev.*	"More multimedia" Mean	*std. dev.*
Spearman rank order cor.	0.689	*0.281*	0.605	*0.335*
Kendall's τ	0.566	*0.255*	0.465	*0.281*
First-choice hit rate	48.0 %		25.8 %	

Table 3. The external validities for both multimedia stimulus presentation methods

The coefficients for the Spearman rank-order correlation and Kendall's τ did not show the expected result. The same is true for the first-choice hit rate. "Less multimedia" shows a higher external validity in all cases.

To find the reason for the differences in mean part worth estimates as well as the validity criteria we looked at the demographic structure for both presentation methods. No relevant differences could be identified. There was not even a noticeable increase in the average duration of the interviews. This cannot be the cause of the different validity values and/or the different mean part worth estimates. We believe one of the reasons to be the previously mentioned disadvantage, the possibility that the respondents would be distracted from the actual judgement task and become more interested in the multimedia aspects than the task at hand, for example a funny video sequence was shown. Another possibility is the complexity of the decision-making process for the respondents. Here the respondents had to deal with several different influences at the same time.

6   Conclusion and outlook

In our empirical comparison we could show that the validity of multimedia stimulus presentation depends on the various degrees of multimedia use. Nonetheless, multimedia stimulus presentation can improve the validity of conjoint study results compared to verbal presentations. A final decision as to which degree of multimedia is the best to use for stimulus presentation cannot yet be made. Cost and time aspects must also be considered.

Of course, further comparisons should be performed to examine the effect of various degrees of multimedia usage on the validity of the results. The sample sizes should be increased for more accurate results. More conclusive validity criteria should be used to more effectively show the differences between the presentation methods.

References

AGARWAL, M.K. and GREEN, P.E. (1991): Adaptive Conjoint Analysis versus Self Explicated Models: Some Empirical Results. *International Journal of Research in Marketing, 8, 141–146.*

AUNKOFER, R. (2000): *Zukunftskonzept Multimedia. Geschichtliche Entwicklungsstufen, Anwendungsfelder und Anwenderpräferenzen.* Eurotrans, Weiden.

BAIER, D. (1999): Methoden der Conjointanalyse in der Marktforschungs- und Marketingpraxis. In: Gaul, W., Schader, M. (Eds.): *Mathematische Methoden der Wirtschaftswissenschaften.* Physica, Heidelberg, 197-206.

BRUSCH, M., BAIER, D. and TREPPA, A. (2002): Conjoint Analysis and Stimulus Presentation - a Comparison of Alternative Methods. In: K. Jajuga, A. Sokołowski and H.H. Bock (Eds.): *Classification, Clustering, and Analysis.* Springer, Berlin, 203–210.

ERNST, O (2000): *Multimediale versus abstrakte Produktpräferenzformen bei der Adaptiven Conjoint-Analyse. Ein empirischer Validitätsvergleich.* Peter Lang, Frankfurt/Main.

ERNST, O. and SATTLER, H. (2000): Multimediale versus traditionelle Conjoint-Analysen. Ein empirischer Vergleich alternativer Produktpräsentationsformen. *Marketing ZFP, 2, 161–172.*

HUBER, J.C., WITTINK, D.R., FIEDLER, J.A. and MILLER, R. (1993): The Effectiveness of Alternative Preference Elicitation Procedures in Predicting Choice. *Journal of Marketing Research, 30, 105–114.*

KROEBER-RIEL, W. (1993): *Bildkommunikation. Imagerystrategien für die Werbung.* Vahlen, München.

KRUSKAL, J.B. (1965): Analysis of factorial experiments by estimating monotone transformations of the data. *Journal the Royal Statistical Society, Series B, 27, 251–263.*

PAIVIO, A. (1971): *Imagery and Verbal Processes.* Holt, Rinehart and Winston, New York a.o.

PAIVIO, A. (1978): A Dual Coding Approach to Perception and Cognition. In: Pick, A., Saltzman, E. (Eds.): *Modes of Perceiving and Processing Information.* Lawrence Erlbaum Associates, Hillsdale, 39–51.

RUGE, H.D. (1988): *Die Messung bildhafter Konsumerlebnisse.* Physica, Heidelberg.

SATTLER, H., HENSEL-BÖRNER, S. and KRÜGER, B. (2001): Die Abhängigkeit der Validität von demographischen Probanden-Charakteristika: Neue empirische Befunde. *Zeitschrift für Betriebswirtschaft, 7, 771–787.*

SCHARF, A., SCHUBERT, B. and VOLKMER, H.P. (1996): Conjointanalyse und Multimedia. *Planung und Analyse, 26–31.*

SILBERER, G. and ZOU, B. (2002): Multimedia in der Marktforschung, In: Böhler, H. (Eds.): *Marketing-Management und Unternehmensführung.* Schäffer-Poeschel, Stuttgart, 209–241.

VOETH, M. (1999): 25 Jahre conjointanalytische Forschung in Deutschland. *Zeitschrift für Betriebswirtschaft - Ergänzungsheft, 2, 153–176.*

WITTINK, D.R., VRIENS, M. and BURHENNE, W. (1994): Commercial Use of Conjoint Analysis in Europe: Results and Critical Reflections. *International Journal of Research in Marketing, 11, (1), 41–52.*

ZIMBARDO, P.G. and GERRIG, R.J. (1999): *Psychologie.* Springer, Berlin.

ZOU, B. (1999): *Multimedia in der Marktforschung.* Gabler, Wiesbaden.

Forecasting the Customer Development of a Publishing Company with Decision Trees

Andreas Hilbert and Alexander Spatz

Lehrstuhl für Mathematische Methoden der Wirtschaftswissenschaften,
Universität Augsburg, D-86135 Augsburg, Germany

Abstract. Many companies recognize that it is important to concentrate their marketing budget on customers with good prospects in future. This paper proposes a new approach which was applied to a company selling loose-leaf notebooks consisting of a basic volume and several updating volumes. In recent years the customers were valued with respect to their actual transaction volume. The validation has some drawbacks. Therefore, a new type of valuation described in this paper was introduced: now, the customers are valued due to their short term as well as their long term potential. The short term potential is the probability of ordering a basic volume. The number of updating volumes represents the long term potential.

1 Background of the analysis

In recent years the major attention of business companies is directed to the customer. Instead of a product-related point-of-view, the evaluation of the customer relationship is introduced. Being aware that a small part of the customers is often responsible for a large amount of the transaction volume the marketing budget should be concentrated on customers with good perspective (Bruhn et al. (2000)). Many business companies, however, recognize that the actual commission is not suitable for the prediction of future transactions (Tomczak and Rudolf-Sipötz (2001)). Therefore, the question how to predict the best customers in future is an important task for the companies.

In this study the potential of customers of a publishing company is analyzed. The company sells different products as loose-leaf notebooks. A loose-leaf notebook consists of a basic volume and several updating volumes. The company encounters a similar problem as many competitors with the same or a comparable strategy. The response rates of direct mails decline. This effect is even more dangerous due to shorter periods of subscriptions. Thus, there is especially one question of concern: which customers should be included in a selective advertising?

The purpose of the corresponding analysis is the identification of customers with either a high probability to order a basic volume or a time of subscription that is expected above average (or both). Hence, it seems functional to estimate an independent score value for both aspects. The probability to order a basic volume is more like a short term potential while the number of updating volumes is a long term potential. With these results the customer base can be assigned to four or more segments shown in Fig. 1.

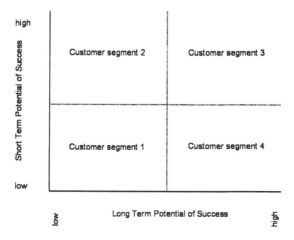

Fig. 1. Segmentation of the customer base

The intensity with which a customer receives direct mails depends on the customer segment he is assigned to:

- **Segment 1**: The customers in segment 1 have a low score for their short term potential as well as for their long term potential. Customers in this segment should not receive substantial advertising. The high effort necessary to attract these customers is not justified assuming there are no side effects as for instance up-buying.

- **Segment 2**: In this segment there are customers with a high short term potential. Their long term potential, however, is relatively low. Customers in this segment can be relatively easily attracted and thus, they should receive advertising. However, they are not critical for the long term success of the company.

- **Segment 3**: The best customers of the company are assigned to this segment. They have a high short term potential as well as a high long term potential. These customers and their number are crucial for the company's future.

- **Segment 4**: This segment consists of customers who order a basic volume only with a small probability. But their subscription time can be expected to be above average. In spite of their low short term potential this segment is of great importance for the company, because the updating volumes generate much of the earnings. For the company's future it is very important to attract many of those customers.

To separate the customer base into four or more segments a short term score and a long term score for all active, former and potential customers has to be built. The methods to achieve this are discussed in detail in the following paragraph.

2   The short term potential

In a short-term point-of-view the major objective of the company is the optimization of the response rates. In many companies the stock of addresses increases constantly. Meanwhile the companies notice decreasing response rates. Therefore, it is necessary to separate the customers with high response probability from those with low probability to increase the efficiency of a mail. To separate the buyers from the non-buyers different methods could be used, for example logistic regression, discriminant analysis, neural network or decision trees. The handling of missing values and nominal or ordinal scaled attributes is relatively uncomplicated using decision trees, compared to logistic regression or discriminant analysis. Furthermore, the results of a decision tree are provably easier to understand for the management than the results of all other methods, especially neural networks. Therefore, decision trees were used for the analysis. Other authors using decision tree algorithms in the framework of marketing are, for instance, Decker and Temme (2001) or Ittner et al. (2001). Thus, the decision tree approach seems to be suitable for the considered problem of customer evaluation.

Description of the data set
There are 38 attributes to separate the buyers from the non-buyers. Some of the attributes are related to the past commission of the customers and the number and time the customers received mails. Other attributes are personal ones, for instance the number of employees of the customer's company. The data set for each analyzed product is generated by the combination of several past direct mails. This combination is necessary due to the small number of customers who bought a product after such advertisements. In spite of this combination the relatively small number of buyers is a major drawback for the analysis. There are more than 40,000 persons analyzed for each product and only a few hundred buyers. The favoured partition of the data set in a training, evaluation and test data set leads to an even smaller number of buyers in each data set. Therefore, the data set is divided in a training and an evaluation data set without a test one. To analyze the single partitions SAS Enterprise Miner was used.

Problem of unbalanced data set
The above mentioned very unbalanced data situation is a huge problem for decision tree algorithms. Less than 1% of the persons bought a certain product and more than 99% did not buy it. It is almost impossible to create a purer node without creating another node with more impurity. To guarantee the ability to induce such a decision tree some strictly concave split criteria have to be used, for instance Gini index of diversity (Breimann et al. (1993)). In Fig. 2 two different types of split criteria are shown: one degrees linearly

and the other is strictly concave.

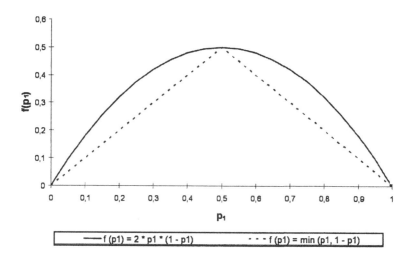

Fig. 2. Different types of split functions

The advantage of the strictly concave function can be shown in a small example: guess there is a node with 1% buyers split into two new nodes with the same size. In node 1 there are 0.5% buyers and in node 2 there are 1.5% buyers. Node 1 is now purer than the original node while node 2 has more impurity than the original one. The accuracy of the two nodes together measured by Gini index is better than the one of the original node. A linear split criterion would assess the original node as well as the new nodes in the same way. SAS Enterprise Miner uses a strictly concave function (Gini-Impurity) and therefore it is possible to induce a tree in spite of the unbalanced data set. The results of the decision tree do not depend on the splitting criterion. The same or nearly the same results occurred when using Entropy or CHAID algorithm.

Another possibility to induce a tree based upon unbalanced data sets is to apply oversampling methods, for instance the leave-k-out approach. Instead of considering all persons within the analysis, all buyers but only a small group of non-buyers are analyzed. Due to this modification the two groups have roughly the same size and no problems using decision tree algorithms arise. To ensure the stability of the results this approach was repeated many times and the individual classification rules were compared. The results, however, were very similar and corresponded to the one generated on the whole data set. In this case there are accordingly no hints for the necessity of oversampling methods, provided that strictly concave split criteria are used.

Pruning of the tree

The pruning of the decision tree is another problem to be solved. There are three standard methods in SAS Enterprise Miner to prune a decision tree. But each method has drawbacks. The proportion of correctly classified persons, for instance, cannot be used due to the unbalanced data set. The pruning of the decision tree, however, was not the major problem of the analysis. Due to the small number of buyers the pre-pruning rules stopped the induction of the tree in an early stage. A decision tree for one product is shown in Fig. 3. On the left hand side of each node the results based upon the training data set are shown, while on the right hand side the results based upon the evaluation data set are described.

Aggregation of the score values

A decision tree generates probabilities for each customer, whether he will order a certain product. The direct comparison of the probabilities for different products, however, is almost impossible. This is due to the different probabilities for buyers in the root of the tree, which are based upon the different products' success in the past. Thus, these absolut probabilities have to be normalized. Following the developed decision tree, customer j belongs to segment k_{ij}^* for product i. Then the normalized scores s_{ij} are defined by

$$s_{ij} = \frac{p_{ik_{ij}^*}}{q_i}.$$

$p_{ik_{ij}^*}$ is the order probability for product i in segment k_{ij}^* and q_i is the order probability for product i in the whole data set. Based upon these scores the comparison of the different products is possible.

Due to the disparity of the importance of the products for the company, it is not reasonable to build the score value for a customer by summarizing the scores of the products without regarding the different importance of the products. The score value over all products for a customer can be calculated with the following formula:

$$s_j = \sum_{i=1}^{n} g_i \cdot s_{ij}$$

n is the number of products and g_i is a well-drawn factor for the importance of product i. The value of g_i can be chosen proportional to profit contribution of the product or proportional to the strategic relevance of the product for the company or proportional to the growth rate of the product. But also a rating of the products by the management to estimate their relative importance is possible. This procedure has the advantage of implicitly containing all above mentioned factors. Additionally, the so generated results of the analysis are much better accepted by the management.

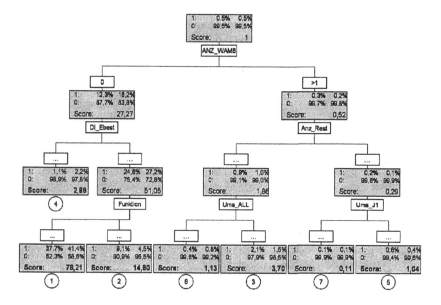

Fig. 3. A decision tree for one product

3 The long term potential

The order probability of a customer, however, is not the only criterion for the assessment of the customer. The length of subscription is another important factor for evaluating the customers. In contrast to the order probability, the perspective of the length of subscription is a long-term point-of-view.

Similar to the analysis of the short term potential an independent analysis for each product is desirable because the average subscription times distinguish between the products. But the model can be build only with those customers who have ordered the product and therefore the data set is extremely small. This leads to a compromise: in this part of the analysis all products are summarized to extend the data set.

Again two groups should be separated by a decision tree. Some tests with a metric dependent variable were also accomplished but the results were better when using a binary dependent variable. The threshold value for the decision whether a customer has an above average subscription time or not is four. Customers with four or less updating volumes are "bad" customers while those with more than four updating volumes are "good". This threshold value was chosen due to the price structure of the company: the fifth and the following updating volumes generate over-proportionally more earnings. In case the subscription of a customer is not finished yet and the customer has four or less updating volumes he is not included in the data set because it is impossible to decide whether the customer will have more than four updating volumes in the future or not. Furthermore, the change in subscription time over the last years has to be considered in the analysis. A customer with more than 4 updating volumes is currently an above average customer, but ten years ago, more than 4 updating volumes were normal. For this reason, the data set contains only customers whose subscription ended in the last two years.

Contrary to the data set of the short term potential analysis, in this case the data set is not so extremely unbalanced. The distribution between "bad" and "good" customers is about 3:1. The splitting criterion was again Gini impurity. An aggregation of scores is not necessary because there is only one model. The score value of a customer can be built by the probability to be a "good" customer itself or, for example, by dividing this probability through the probability in the root node. Then a score above one is a sign for a customer with above average probability to be a "good" customer.

4   Conclusion of the results

The results could be used to separate the customer base into different segments shown in chapter one of this paper. The segments with high potential in both dimensions get more intensive advertising than the segments with low potential. But the results could not only be used to separate the customer base into different segments. Another possible application for the results is the allocation of the advertising budget on individual basis. Instead of deciding segmentally whether a customer should receive a direct mail or not the decision is based on these individual scores. There are three possibilities to realize that.

- Only customers who exceed a minimum predefined score value on both axis receive a direct mail. The drawback of this rule is the skip of customers who are extremely highly rated on one axis but only on the average for the other: a customer who will buy a certain product for sure won't receive a direct mail because of his bad or even average long term potential.

- Instead of demanding a minimum score value on both axis, a higher score value on only one of the axis is necessary for a customer to receive a direct mail. But this rule contains also a major drawback. With this rule those customers are ignored who have relatively high scores on both axis but never an high score.

- The best rule to decide whether a customer should receive a direct mail is a combination of the previous rules. A customer receives a direct mail if he has either a relatively high score on both axis or an extreme high score on one of the axis. For further details see Spatz and Hilbert (2002).

In addition to this application, the results allow the company to consider the individual customers' needs. It would certainly be better to offer the customers of segment 2 classical books instead of loose-leaf notebooks because they obviously do not need current but basic information. If this is impossible a variation in the subscription mode might be adequate: instead of delivering the customers updating volumes every 3 months the customers should get for example an updating volume once a year. On the other hand, the customers of segment 4 seem to need current information but it is very difficult to attract them. It might be interesting to organize the direct mail for this customer according to the order probability for the products. The product with the highest order possibility should be the first and most emphasized one in the direct mail.

5   Summary

The results of this analysis enable the company to estimate the value of a customer based on his future potential and not only due to his present transaction volume. Furthermore, the analysis helps the company to decide which customers should receive a direct mail and above that, how those direct mails should be designed.

References

BREIMANN, L.; FRIEDMANN, J.H.; OLSHEN, R.A. and STONE, C.J. (1993): Classification And Regression Trees. Chapman & Hall, New York.

BRUHN, M.; GEORGI, D.; TREYER, M. and LEUMANN, S. (2000): Wertorientiertes Relationship Marketing: Vom Kundenwert zum Customer Lifetime Value. *Die Unternehmung, Vol. 54, 3/2000, 167–187.*

DECKER, R. and TEMME, T. (2001): CHAID als Instrument der Werbemittelgestaltung und Zielgruppenbestimmung im Marketing. In: H. Hippner, U. Küsters, M. Meyer and K. Wilde (Eds.): *Handbuch Data Mining im Marketing.* Vieweg, Braunschweig and Wiesbaden.

SPATZ, A. and HILBERT, A. (2002): Analyse des Kundenwertes für ein Unternehmen der Verlagsbranche. *Arbeitspapiere zur Mathematischen Wirtschaftsforschung, Universität Augsburg, Heft 182.*

ITTNER, A.; SIEBER, H. and TRAUTZSCH, S. (2001): Nichtlineare Entscheidungsbäume zur Optimierung von Direktmailingaktionen. In: H. Hippner, U. Küsters, M. Meyer and K. Wilde (Eds.): *Handbuch Data Mining im Marketing.* Vieweg, Braunschweig and Wiesbaden.

TOMCZAK, T. and RUDOLF-SIPöTZ, E. (2001): Bestimmungsfaktoren des Kundenwertes: Ergebnisse einer branchenübergreifenden Studie. In: B. Günter and S. Helm (Eds.): *Kundenwert: Grundlagen – Innovative Konzepte – Praktische Umsetzungen.* Gabler, Wiesbaden.

Estimation of Default Probabilities
in a Single-Factor Model

Steffi Höse and Stefan Huschens

Lehrstuhl für Quantitative Verfahren, insbesondere Statistik,
Fakultät Wirtschaftswissenschaften, Technische Universität Dresden,
Mommsenstraße 13, D-01062 Dresden, Germany

Abstract. The default probability is a central parameter of credit risk models and can be estimated by the relative default frequency in a portfolio. The distribution of this estimator is derived in the framework of a single-factor model. For a sample portfolio consisting of 15 rating categories with different default probabilities individual and simultaneous probability intervals are given.

1 Threshold model and the single-factor model

Within one period n obligors with the same default probability $p \in (0,1)$ are considered, where to each obligor belongs only one credit. The ability to pay of an obligor follows a stochastic process, where the standardized relative change in one period is described by a standard normal distributed random variable A_i, $i = 1, \ldots, n$. In a threshold model, the ith credit defaults if the rating variable A_i falls below a threshold at the end of the period. Since the default occurs with probability p, the threshold is given by $\Phi^{-1}(p)$, where Φ^{-1} denotes the inverse of the cumulative distribution function of the standard normal distribution. Default indicators for each credit i can be defined as

$$X_i := \mathbf{1}\left\{ A_i \leq \Phi^{-1}(p) \right\}, \quad i = 1, \ldots, n, \tag{1}$$

which are Bernoulli distributed random variables with default probability $p = P(X_i = 1)$. The dependency structure of the rating variables determines the correlation structure of the default indicators.

Assumption 1 *The rating variables A_i follow the model*

$$A_i = \sqrt{\varrho}\, Z + \sqrt{1 - \varrho}\, U_i, \quad i = 1, \ldots, n$$

with $0 < \varrho < 1$ and $Z, U_1, \ldots, U_n \overset{i.i.d.}{\sim} \mathcal{N}(0,1)$.

Assumption 1 is a single-factor model with standard normal distributed factors, which is used in the IRB-Approach of Basel II (Basel Committee on Banking Supervision (2001a, 2001b), Huschens and Vogl (2002)). Z can be interpreted as a common, systematic risk factor and the U_i as specific, idiosyncratic risk factors. The vector of rating variables is distributed as n-dimensional standard normal with correlations $Corr(A_i, A_j) = \varrho$ for $i \neq j$.

2   Distribution of the default frequency

The default probability can be estimated by the relative default frequency, defined as number of defaults relative to the total number of credits in the portfolio,

$$\hat{p} := \frac{\sum_{i=1}^{n} X_i}{n}. \tag{2}$$

If the rating variables A_i are stochastically independent, the number of defaults is binomially distributed on $\{0, 1, \ldots, n\}$, $n\hat{p} \sim \text{Bin}(n; p)$, and the relative default frequency $\hat{p}$ has a rescaled binomial distribution on $\{0, 1/n, \ldots, 1\}$. But under Assumption 1 the rating variables and the default indicators have a positive correlation. As a consequence, the estimator $\hat{p}$ is unbiased but not consistent for $n \to \infty$ and the law of large numbers does not hold, e. g. the variance of $\hat{p}$ has a positive limit for $n \to \infty$ (see Huschens and Locarek-Junge (2000)). Even in very large portfolios, the relative default frequency may deviate substantially from the default probability. These deviations are described by the probability distribution function of the relative default frequency derived in the following.

The conditional default probability for a fixed realization z of the systematic risk factor Z is given by

$$P(X_i = 1 | Z = z) = \Phi\left(\frac{\Phi^{-1}(p) - \sqrt{\varrho}z}{\sqrt{1 - \varrho}}\right) =: g(z; p, \varrho). \tag{3}$$

Note that $g(z; p, 0) = p$. Therefore, the total default probability p reads as

$$p = P(X_i = 1) = \int_{-\infty}^{\infty} P(X_i = 1 | Z = z) \, d\Phi(z).$$

Conditional on $Z = z$, the default events are stochastically independent. Hence, the number of defaults conditional on $Z = z$ is binomially distributed,

$$\sum_{i=1}^{n} X_i | Z = z \sim \text{Bin}(n; g(z; p, \varrho)).$$

Using the conditional independence, the distribution of the relative default frequency is for $h = 0, 1, \ldots, n$ given by

$$P\left(\hat{p} = \frac{h}{n}\right) = \int_{\mathbb{R}} P\left(\sum_{i=1}^{n} X_i = h \,|\, Z = z\right) d\Phi(z)$$

$$= \int_{\mathbb{R}} \binom{n}{h} g(z; p, \varrho)^h (1 - g(z; p, \varrho))^{n-h} \, d\Phi(z) \tag{4}$$

$$= \int_{(0,1)} \binom{n}{h} x^h (1 - x)^{n-h} dF(x; p, \varrho) \tag{5}$$

with

$$F(x; p, \varrho) := \Phi \left(\frac{\sqrt{1 - \varrho}\, \Phi^{-1}(x) - \Phi^{-1}(p)}{\sqrt{\varrho}} \right) \tag{6}$$

where (5) follows from (4) with the substitution $x = g(z; p, \varrho)$. Moreover, F is the asymptotical distribution of $\hat{p}$, which is approached when $n \to \infty$, see Höse and Huschens (2003), where the following theorem is proved.

Theorem 1 *Let $\hat{p}$ be defined by (1) and (2), and let F be defined by (6), then Assumption 1 is sufficient for*

$$\lim_{n \to \infty} P(\hat{p} \leq x) = F(x; p, \varrho), \quad x \in (0, 1).$$

The quartiles and the 0.5%- and 99.5%-quantiles of the asymptotical distribution of $\hat{p}$ are shown in Figure 1 for $\varrho = 0.1$. As one can see, the asymptotical

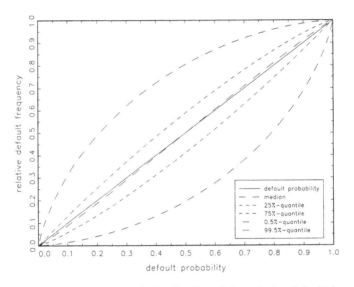

Fig. 1. Quantiles of asymptotical distribution of the relative default frequency.

distribution is positively (negatively) skewed for $p < 0.5$ $(p > 0.5)$ since the median is below (above) the default probability, respectively. The 0.5%- and 99.5%-quantiles are far away from the default probability p due to the considerably large variance of the estimator $\hat{p}$.

3   Portfolio with different default probabilities

In the following, a credit portfolio is considered with different rating grades $k = 1, \ldots, K$ and default probabilities $0 < p_1 < p_2 < \cdots < p_K < 1$. It is assumed that the credits and the corresponding rating variables $A_1, \ldots, A_n$

are ordered so that the first n_1 credits have grade 1, the next n_2 credits have grade 2 and so on. The total number of credits in the portfolio is

$$n = \sum_{k=1}^{K} n_k.$$

Assumption 1 is modified to allow different correlations.

Assumption 2 *The rating variables A_i follow the model*

$$A_i = \sqrt{\varrho_k}\, Z + \sqrt{1 - \varrho_k}\, U_i, \quad i \in \mathcal{I}_k, \quad 0 < \varrho_k < 1, \quad k = 1, \dots, K$$

with $Z, U_1, \dots, U_n \overset{i.i.d.}{\sim} \mathcal{N}(0,1)$ and index sets

$$\mathcal{I}_1 := \{1, \dots, n_1\}, \mathcal{I}_2 := \{n_1 + 1, \dots, n_1 + n_2\}, \dots, \mathcal{I}_K := \{n - n_K + 1, \dots, n\}.$$

Assumption 2 implies that the A_i are distributed as n-dimensional standard normal with correlations

$$Corr(A_i, A_{i'}) = \sqrt{\varrho_j \varrho_k}, \quad i \in \mathcal{I}_j, \quad i' \in \mathcal{I}_k, \quad i \neq i'.$$

The correlations ϱ_k may depend on p_k, see Basel Committee on Banking Supervision (2001c), Huschens and Vogl (2002). The default indicators for grade k are defined by

$$X_i := \mathbf{1}\{A_i \leq \Phi^{-1}(p_k)\}, \quad i \in \mathcal{I}_k,$$

and the relative default frequency in rating grade k is

$$\hat{p}_k := \frac{\sum_{i \in \mathcal{I}_k} X_i}{n_k}.$$

Note that the number of defaults $n_k \hat{p}_k$ is not binomially distributed because the X_i are not independent according to Assumption 2.

The further discussion uses the portfolio described in Fischer (2002) with $K = 15$ rating grades. Table 1 summarizes the default probabilities p_k, the proportions q_k, and the resulting numbers of credits $n_k = nq_k$ for the rating grades $k = 1, \dots, 15$. The portfolio structure given by the proportions q_k is a typical structure of a middle-sized German *Sparkasse*. The default probabilities p_k build a standard scale fixed by the DSGV (*Deutscher Sparkassen- und Giroverband*) for the use in several internal rating systems.
A portfolio with a total number of $n = 15\,000$ credits and the same correlation $\varrho_k = \varrho = 0.1$, $k = 1, \dots, 15$, are assumed. As an example, the distribution of $\hat{p}_{14}$ is shown in Figure 2 for rating grade 14. The probabilities of this distribution are computed by numerical integration of (4). They are plotted in the Figure 2 for $h = 0, 1, 2, \dots$ and connected by line segments.

k	1	2	3	4	5	6	7
$p_k \cdot 100$	0.07	0.12	0.17	0.26	0.39	0.59	0.88
$q_k \cdot 100$	0.1	1.5	4.9	11.6	15.3	9.7	8.5
n_k	15	225	735	1740	2295	1455	1275

k	8	9	10	11	12	13	14	15
$p_k \cdot 100$	1.32	1.98	2.96	4.44	6.67	10	15	20
$q_k \cdot 100$	13.9	7.2	8.6	3.7	6.1	3.0	1.5	4.4
n_k	2085	1080	1290	555	915	450	225	660

Table 1. A typical portfolio, see Fischer (2002).

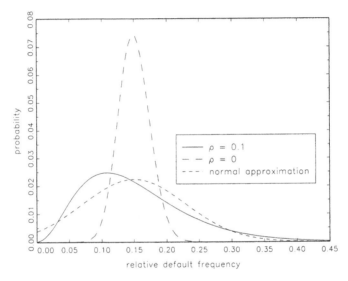

Fig. 2. Probability distribution of the relative default frequency for rating grade 14, $p_{14} = 15\%$ and $n_{14} = 225$.

This distribution deviates considerably from the rescaled binomial distribution of the relative default frequency, which results from independence and is plotted as a long-dashed curve. The rescaled binomial distribution is less skewed and underestimates the variance of $\hat{p}_{14}$. The third short-dashed curve shows a normal distribution with the same mean and variance as the exact distribution. For this continuous distribution the probabilities in the intervals $h/n \pm 1/(2n)$ for $h = 0, 1, \ldots$ are displayed. The deviation of the normal approximation from the highly skewed distribution of the relative default frequency persists even for a large number of credits in each rating grade. Thus, the normal approximation is not suitable (see Höse and Huschens (2003)).

Figure 3 shows the distribution of the relative default frequency for rating grade 6 and, as reference case, the rescaled binomial distribution. The third

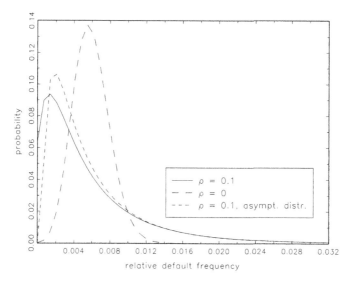

Fig. 3. Probability distribution of the relative default frequency for rating grade 6, $p_6 = 0.59\%$ and $n_6 = 1455$.

curve shows the asymptotical distribution of $\hat{p}_6$ given by (6). Despite the limited number of credits in this grade the asymptotical distribution agrees well with the exact distribution of $\hat{p}_6$ and is a better approximation than the rescaled binomial distribution.

In both figures the exact distribution of the relative default frequency is computed using (4). Alternatively, a simulation approach based on the model given by Assumption 1 or 2 can be used, cp. Bühler et al. (2002).

4   Probability intervals for the default frequency

The distribution function of $\hat{p}_k$ is

$$P(\hat{p}_k \leq x) = \int_{-\infty}^{\infty} P(\hat{p}_k \leq x | Z = z) d\Phi(z) \tag{7}$$

with

$$n_k \hat{p}_k | Z = z \sim \mathrm{Bin}(n_k, g(z; p_k, \varrho_k)),$$

where $g(z; p_k, \varrho_k)$, already given in (3), is the conditional probability of default given a realization z of the systematic factor Z.

For given probabilities $\alpha_1 > 0$, $\alpha_2 > 0$, $\alpha_1 + \alpha_2 < 1$ intervals $[p_k^L, p_k^U]$ for the relative default frequencies $\hat{p}_k$ with

$$P\left(\hat{p}_k \in [p_k^L, p_k^U]\right) \geq 1 - \alpha_1 - \alpha_2$$

can be computed from (7) by numerical integration. The lower and upper bounds p_k^L and p_k^U can be chosen so that the conditions

$$p_k^L, p_k^U \in \{0, 1/n_k, 2/n_k, \ldots, 1\},$$

$$P\left(\hat{p}_k < p_k^L\right) \le \alpha_1 < P\left(\hat{p}_k < p_k^L + \frac{1}{n_k}\right),$$

and

$$P(\hat{p}_k > p_k^U) \le \alpha_2 < P\left(\hat{p}_k > p_k^U - \frac{1}{n_k}\right)$$

are fulfilled.

Figure 4 gives for the portfolio of Table 1 the probability intervals $[p_k^L, p_k^U]$ for $\alpha_1 = \alpha_2 = 0.005$ and $\varrho_k = \varrho = 0.1$, $k = 1, \ldots, 15$. The 0.5%-quantiles p_k^L of

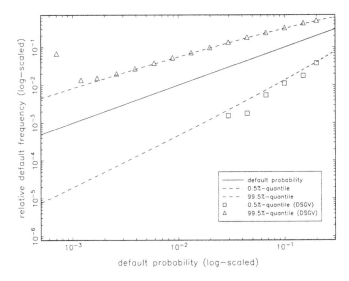

Fig. 4. Probability intervals for the distribution of the relative default frequency for all rating grades ($\varrho = 0.1$).

the distribution of $\hat{p}_k$ are denoted by squares and the 99.5%-quantiles p_k^U are denoted by triangles. The values $p_1^L = p_2^L = \ldots = p_9^L = 0$ do not appear in Figure 4 with log-scaled axes. For comparison, the 0.5%- and 99.5%-quantiles of the asymptotical distributions computed from (6) are plotted as dashed curves. This quantiles agree well the quantiles of the exact distribution. A large deviation only occurs in rating grade 1, where the number of credits is small ($n_1 = 15$).

The *simultaneous* probability for given intervals $[p_k^L, p_k^U]$, $k = 1, \ldots, K$, can be computed by numerical integration using the mixture

$$P\left(p_k^L \le \hat{p}_k \le p_k^U; k = 1, \ldots, K\right) = \int_{-\infty}^{\infty} \prod_{k=1}^{K} P\left(p_k^L \le \hat{p}_k \le p_k^U | Z = z\right) d\Phi(z),$$

because the random variables $\hat{p}_k$ are independent conditional on $Z = z$. The computation of the exact simultaneous probability for the 99%-intervals given in Figure 4 leads to a probability of 97.49%.

A common approach in simultaneous inference is to derive a lower bound for the simultaneous probability using the Bonferroni inequality,

$$P\left(p_k^L \le \hat{p}_k \le p_k^U; k = 1, \ldots, K\right) \ge 1 - \sum_{k=1}^{K} \left[1 - P\left(p_k^L \le \hat{p}_k \le p_k^U\right)\right],$$

which uses only the K given individual probabilities and holds for any dependency structure.

This gives for the sample portfolio with $P(p_k^L \le \hat{p}_k \le p_k^U) = 0.99$ the bound

$$P\left(p_k^L \le \hat{p}_k \le p_k^U; k = 1, \ldots, K\right) \ge 1 - 15 \cdot 0.01 = 0.85,$$

which is far from the exact probability.

5   Conclusions

In this contribution the estimation of credit default probabilities by relative default frequencies is investigated. The dependency structure of the default events is described by a statistical single-factor model. This framework is implicitly used within the Internal Ratings-Based Approach of Basel II (Basel Committee on Banking Supervision (2001a, 2001b)) for the calculation of the regulatory capital. Moreover, the estimation of default probabilities from dependent default events plays a key role for assessing the risk of credit portfolios.

Dependent default events influence statistical properties of the default frequency, which is a natural estimator of the default probability. It is found that the default frequency could deviate considerably from the default probability even for large, well-diversified credit portfolios. The distribution of the default frequency is positively skewed. Therefore, this distribution cannot be approximated by a normal distribution and the default frequency underestimates the default probability in most cases. The given probability intervals for the default frequency show that e. g. for a default probability of 1% the observed default frequency may range from 0.05% to 5% with an assumed correlation of 10% and a probability level of 99%. The length of the obtained intervals clearly shows that a reliable estimation of the default probability is not possible on the basis of dependent cross-sectional data. Consequently, backtesting solely based on actual default frequencies is almost impossible.

References

Basel Committee on Banking Supervision (2001a): *The New Basel Capital Accord*, Consultative Document. BIS, Basel.

Basel Committee on Banking Supervision (2001b): *The Internal Ratings-Based Approach: Supporting Document to the New Basel Capital Accord*, Consultative Document. BIS, Basel.

Basel Committee on Banking Supervision (2001c): *Potential Modifications to the Committee's Proposals*. BIS, Basel.

BÜHLER, W., ENGLE, C., KORN, O., and STAHL, G. (2002): Backtesting von Kreditrisikomodellen. In: A. Oehler (Ed.): *Kreditrisikomanagement – Kernbereiche, Aufsicht und Entwicklungstendenzen*. 2nd edition, Schäffer-Poeschel, Stuttgart, 181–217.

FISCHER, S. (2002): Erste Umsetzungsverfahren einer Sparkasse mit dem einheitlichen Rating-Verfahren. *Betriebswirtschaftliche Blätter, 05, 241–249*.

HÖSE, S. and HUSCHENS, S. (2003): Sind interne Ratingsysteme im Rahmen von Basel II evaluierbar? - Zur Schätzung von Ausfallwahrscheinlichkeiten durch Ausfallquoten. *Zeitschrift für Betriebswirtschaft*, accepted for publication.

HUSCHENS, S., LOCAREK-JUNGE, H. (2000): Konzeptionelle und statistische Grundlagen der portfolioorientierten Kreditrisikomessung. In: A. Oehler (Hrsg.): *Kreditrisikomanagement – Portfoliomodelle und Derivate*. Schäffer-Poeschel, Stuttgart, 27-49.

HUSCHENS, S. and VOGL, K. (2002): Kreditrisikomodellierung im IRB-Ansatz von Basel II. In: A. Oehler (Hrsg.): *Kreditrisikomanagement – Kernbereiche, Aufsicht und Entwicklungstendenzen*. 2nd edition, Schäffer-Poeschel, Stuttgart, 279-295.

Simultaneous Confidence Intervals for Default Probabilities

Steffi Höse and Stefan Huschens

Lehrstuhl für Quantitative Verfahren, insbesondere Statistik,
Fakultät Wirtschaftswissenschaften, Technische Universität Dresden,
Mommsenstraße 13, D-01062 Dresden, Germany

Abstract. A single-factor portfolio model for credit risk with K rating categories and different default probabilities p_k and correlations ρ_k for each rating category $k = 1, \ldots, K$ is considered. In this framework simultaneous confidence intervals for the default probabilities based on observed relative default frequencies are derived.

1 The credit portfolio model

A credit portfolio with n obligors is considered, where the obligors have different ratings $k = 1, \ldots, K$ and corresponding default probabilities with $0 < p_1 < p_2 < \cdots < p_K < 1$. Let the obligors be ordered so that the first n_1 have rating 1, the next n_2 have rating 2 and so on. The total number of obligors in the portfolio is

$$n = \sum_{k=1}^{K} n_k.$$

The ith obligor defaults if the rating variable A_i falls below a certain threshold at the end of the given time horizon. The variables A_i express the ability to pay and can be interpreted as standardized changes of the asset value.

Assumption 3 *The rating variables A_i follow the model*

$$A_i = \sqrt{\varrho_k}\, Z + \sqrt{1 - \varrho_k}\, U_i, \quad i \in \mathcal{I}_k, \quad 0 < \varrho_k < 1, \quad k = 1, \ldots, K$$

with

$$Z, U_1, \ldots, U_n \overset{i.i.d}{\sim} \mathcal{N}(0, 1)$$

and index sets

$$\mathcal{I}_1 := \{1, \ldots, n_1\}, \mathcal{I}_2 := \{n_1 + 1, \ldots, n_1 + n_2\}, \ldots, \mathcal{I}_K := \{n - n_K + 1, \ldots, n\}.$$

This assumption defines a single-factor model with standard normal distributed factors, which is used in the IRB-Approach of Basel II, see Basel Committee on Banking Supervision (2001a, 2001b). Z can be interpreted as a common, systematic risk factor and the U_i are specific, idiosyncratic risk factors.

Assumption 3 implies that $(A_1, \ldots, A_n)$ is distributed as n-dimensional standard normal with correlations

$$Corr(A_i, A_{i'}) = \sqrt{\varrho_j \varrho_k}, \quad i \in \mathcal{I}_j, \quad i' \in \mathcal{I}_k, \quad i \neq i'.$$

ρ_k is the correlation for two different obligors with the same rating k. The correlations ϱ_k may depend on p_k, see Basel Committee on Banking Supervision (2001a, 2001b), Huschens and Vogl (2002).

The default indicators are defined by

$$X_i := \mathbf{1}\{A_i \le \Phi^{-1}(p_k)\}, \quad i \in \mathcal{I}_k, \quad k = 1, \dots, K,$$

where Φ^{-1} denotes the inverse of the cumulative distribution function Φ of the standard normal distribution. The relative default frequency for rating k is

$$\hat{p}_k := \frac{\sum_{i \in \mathcal{I}_k} X_i}{n_k}.$$

Note that the $n_k \hat{p}_k$ are not binomial distributed because the X_i are correlated under Assumption 3.

2   Individual confidence intervals

By Assumption 3 the relative default frequency $\hat{p}_k$ does not converge to p_k for $n_k \to \infty$ in the sense of the law of large numbers but to a non-degenerate asymptotical distribution. The following theorem characterizes the asymptotical distribution of $\hat{p}$ and is proved in Höse and Huschens (2003).

Theorem 2 *The random variable*

$$Y_k := \frac{\sqrt{1 - \varrho_k}\, \Phi^{-1}(\hat{p}_k) - \Phi^{-1}(p_k)}{\sqrt{\varrho_k}} \tag{1}$$

converges for $n_k \to \infty$ in distribution to $Z \sim \mathcal{N}(0,1)$.

This theorem allows to construct one- and two-sided individual confidence intervals for each p_k based on $\hat{p}_k$.

Theorem 3 *Let $\alpha_2 > 0$, $\alpha_1 > 0$, $\alpha_2 + \alpha_1 < 1$. With*

$$L_{\alpha_1}(\hat{p}_k) := \Phi\left(\sqrt{1 - \varrho_k}\, \Phi^{-1}(\hat{p}_k) + \sqrt{\rho_k}\, \Phi^{-1}(\alpha_1)\right),$$

$$U_{\alpha_2}(\hat{p}_k) := \Phi\left(\sqrt{1 - \varrho_k}\, \Phi^{-1}(\hat{p}_k) - \sqrt{\rho_k}\, \Phi^{-1}(\alpha_2)\right),$$

$$I_k := [L_{\alpha_1}(\hat{p}_k), U_{\alpha_2}(\hat{p}_k)] \tag{2}$$

holds

$$\lim_{n_k \to \infty} P(p_k \le L_{\alpha_1}(\hat{p}_k)) = \alpha_1, \quad \lim_{n_k \to \infty} P(p_k \ge U_{\alpha_2}(\hat{p}_k)) = \alpha_2,$$

and

$$\lim_{n_k \to \infty} P(p_k \in I_k) = 1 - \alpha_1 - \alpha_2$$

for $k = 1, \dots, K$.

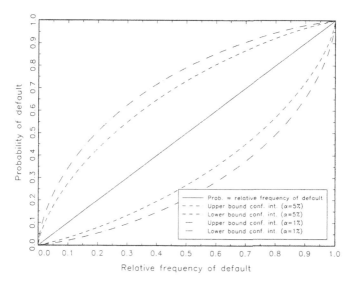

Fig. 1. Confidence intervals for default probabilities, $\varrho = 0.1$.

This theorem is proved in Höse and Huschens (2003). The intervals I_k are confidence intervals for p_k with asymptotical confidence level $1 - \alpha_1 - \alpha_2$. One-sided confidence intervals with asymptotical confidence level $1 - \alpha$ are given by $[0, L_{1-\alpha}(\hat{p}_k)] = [0, U_\alpha(\hat{p}_k)]$ and $[U_{1-\alpha}(\hat{p}_k), 1] = [L_\alpha(\hat{p}_k), 1]$.

Figure 1 shows confidence intervals of type (3) for $0 < p < 1$ with $\varrho = 0.1$, $\alpha_1 = \alpha_2$ and confidence levels $1 - \alpha_1 - \alpha_2 \in \{95\%, 99\%\}$. To show the effect of the correlation in Figure 2 the corresponding confidence intervals with $\rho = 0.05$ are given.

3   Simultaneous confidence intervals

In general, the construction of simultaneous confidence intervals is based on inequalities, e. g. the Bonferroni inequality, or on projections of multidimensional regions, see Miller (1980). The special dependency structure implied by Assumption 1 leads to another approach based on the asymptotical distribution of the relative frequencies. The following multivariate generalization of Theorem 2 allows to determine the simultaneous confidence level for K individual confidence intervals.

Theorem 4 *The random vector* $\mathbf{Y} = (Y_1, \ldots, Y_K)'$ *where each component is defined by (1) converges for* $n_1 \to \infty$, $\ldots$, $n_K \to \infty$ *in distribution to*

$$\mathbf{Z} = (Z, \ldots, Z)',$$

where $Z \sim \mathcal{N}(0,1)$.

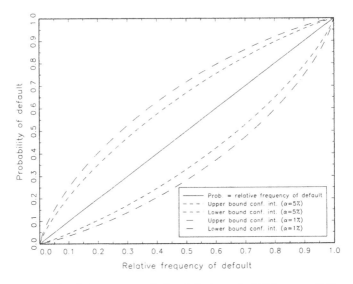

Fig. 2. Confidence intervals for default probabilities, $\varrho = 0.05$.

The proof is given in the appendix. Each component Y_k converges to a standard normal distribution, but the simultaneous asymptotical distribution is a highly degenerated distribution with realizations $(z, z, \ldots, z)' \in \mathbb{R}^K$. The immediate consequence of Theorem 4 is that the individual confidence intervals given in Theorem 2 are also simultaneous confidence intervals with the same confidence level.

Theorem 5 *Let $\alpha_1 > 0$, $\alpha_2 > 0$, $\alpha_1 + \alpha_2 < 1$ and I_k for $k = 1, \ldots, K$ be defined by (3). Then*

$$\lim_{n_1, \ldots, n_K \to \infty} P(p_k \in I_k; k = 1, \ldots, K) = 1 - \alpha_1 - \alpha_2.$$

The proof is given in the appendix.

Appendix

Proof of Theorem 4

1. Note first that

$$P(X_i = 1 | Z = z) = \Phi\left(\frac{\Phi^{-1}(p_k) - \sqrt{\varrho_k}\, z}{\sqrt{1 - \varrho_k}}\right) =: g(z; p_k, \varrho_k), \quad i \in \mathcal{I}_k$$

and that the X_i are independent conditionally on $Z = z$, see Höse and Huschens (2003). Thus, conditionally on $Z = z$,

$$\hat{p}_k \to g(z; p_k, \varrho_k), \quad \text{and} \quad Y_k \to z$$

in probability for $n_k \to \infty$. This implies

$$\lim_{n_k \to \infty} P(Y_k \le y_k \mid Z = z) = 1_{(-\infty, y_k]}(z).$$

2. The distribution of $\mathbf{Y}$ can be seen as a mixture of distributions, where the components of $\mathbf{Y}$ are independent conditionally on $Z = z$, which gives

$$P(\mathbf{Y} \le \mathbf{y}) = \int_{\mathbb{R}} \prod_{k=1}^{K} P(Y_k \le y_k | Z = z) d\Phi(z).$$

3. For each $\mathbf{y} \in \mathbb{R}^K$ holds

$$\lim_{n_1,\dots,n_K \to \infty} P(\mathbf{Y} \le \mathbf{y}) = \lim_{n_1,\dots,n_K \to \infty} P(Y_1 \le y_1, \dots, Y_K \le y_k)$$

$$= \lim_{n_1,\dots,n_K \to \infty} \int_{\mathbb{R}} \prod_{k=1}^{K} P(Y_k \le y_k | Z = z) d\Phi(z)$$

$$= \int_{\mathbb{R}} \prod_{k=1}^{K} \lim_{n_k \to \infty} P(Y_k \le y_k | Z = z) d\Phi(z)$$

$$= \int_{\mathbb{R}} \prod_{k=1}^{K} 1_{(-\infty, y_k]}(z) d\Phi(z)$$

$$= \Phi\left(\min_{k=1}^{K} y_k\right).$$

Noting that the distribution function of $\mathbf{Z}$ for $\mathbf{z} \in \mathbb{R}^K$ is

$$F_{\mathbf{Z}}(\mathbf{z}) = P(Z_1 \le z_1, \dots, Z_K \le z_k) = P\left(Z \le \min_{k=1}^{K} z_k\right) = \Phi\left(\min_{k=1}^{K} z_k\right)$$

completes the proof.

Proof of Theorem 5

For individual confidence intervals I_k given by (3) holds

$$P(p_k \in I_k; k = 1, \dots, K) = P\left(L_{\alpha_1}(\hat{p}_k) \le p_k \le U_{\alpha_2}(\hat{p}_k); k = 1, \dots, K\right)$$
$$= P\left(\Phi^{-1}(\alpha_2) \le Y_k \le \Phi^{-1}(1 - \alpha_1); k = 1, \dots, K\right)$$

and with Theorem 4 follows

$$\lim_{n_1,\dots,n_K \to \infty} P(p_k \in I_k; k = 1, \dots, K) = \Phi(\Phi^{-1}(1 - \alpha_1)) - \Phi(\Phi^{-1}(\alpha_2))$$
$$= 1 - \alpha_1 - \alpha_2.$$

References

Basel Committee on Banking Supervision (2001a): *The New Basel Capital Accord*, Consultative Document. BIS, Basel.

Basel Committee on Banking Supervision (2001b): *The Internal Ratings-Based Approach: Supporting Document to the New Basel Capital Accord*, Consultative Document. BIS, Basel.

Basel Committee on Banking Supervision (2001c): *Potential Modifications to the Committee's Proposals*. BIS, Basel.

HÖSE, S. and HUSCHENS, S. (2003): Sind interne Ratingsysteme im Rahmen von Basel II evaluierbar? - Zur Schätzung von Ausfallwahrscheinlichkeiten durch Ausfallquoten. *Zeitschrift für Betriebswirtschaft*, accepted for publication.

HUSCHENS, S. and VOGL, K. (2002): Kreditrisikomodellierung im IRB-Ansatz von Basel II. In: A. Oehler (Ed.): *Kreditrisikomanagement – Kernbereiche, Aufsicht und Entwicklungstendenzen*. 2nd edition, Schffer-Poeschel, Stuttgart, 279-295.

MILLER, R.G. (1980): *Simultaneous Statistical Inference*, 2nd ed. Springer, New York.

Model-Based Clustering With Hidden Markov Models and its Application to Financial Time-Series Data

Bernhard Knab[1], Alexander Schliep[2], Barthel Steckemetz[3], and Bernd Wichern[4]

[1] Bayer AG, D-51368 Leverkusen, Germany
[2] Department Computational Molecular Biology, Max-Planck-Institut für Molekulare Genetik, D-14195 Berlin, Germany
[3] Science Factory GmbH, D-50667 Köln, Germany
[4] ifb AG, D-50667 Köln, Germany

Abstract. We have developed a method to partition a set of data into clusters by use of Hidden Markov Models. Given a number of clusters, each of which is represented by one Hidden Markov Model, an iterative procedure finds the combination of cluster models and an assignment of data points to cluster models which maximizes the joint likelihood of the clustering. To reflect the partially non-Markovian nature of the data we also extend classical Hidden Markov Models to use a non-homogeneous Markov chain, where the non-homogeneity is dependent not on the time of the observation but rather on a quantity derived from previous observations.

We present the method and an evaluation on simulated time-series and large data sets of financial time-series from the Public Saving and Loan Banks in Germany.

1 Introduction

Grouping of data, or clustering, is a fundamental task in data analysis. Methods for clustering have been widely investigated (Everitt(1993)) and can be coarsely categorized into two classes: distance- and model-based approaches. The former base the decision whether to group two data points on their distance, the latter assign a data point to a cluster represented by a particular statistical model based on its likelihood under the model.

Model-based clustering is better suited for time-series data (MacDonald and Zucchini(1997)). Usually, there is no natural distance function between time-series. Several non-critical variances of signals — a delay, an overall slower rate, a premature cutoff — will be overly emphasized by, say, Euclidean distance. Hence, capturing the essential *qualitative* behavior of time-series is difficult.

Using stochastic models to represent clusters changes the question at hand from how close two given data points are to how likely one particular data point is under the model. One can expect a larger robustness with respect to noise virtue of the stochastic model. As it is straight-forward to generate artificial data given a model-based clustering, an analysis of the clustering quality based on the *predictive* performance of the inferred set of models becomes feasible.

Our approach of using Hidden Markov Models (HMMs) as clusters is motivated by the well known k-means algorithm (Everitt(1993)). Already Bock(1974) describes that an analogon of k-means can be used for model-based clustering. McLachlan and Basford(1988) implemented that for multivariate Gaussians. In the k-means algorithm the median represents a cluster and a clustering is computed by an iterative application of the following steps.

i) Assign each data point to its closest median, and
ii) Re-compute the median for each of the clusters.

When going over to HMMs as cluster representatives two modifications are necessary. The criterion for the re-assignment of data points to clusters is maximization of the likelihood of the data points. The re-computation of clusters is done by training the cluster models with the Baum-Welch re-estimation algorithm (Baum and Petrie(1966))(Baum et al.(1970)).

The savings and loan bank application we considered implied contractual constraints which violated the Markovian assumption inherent in *classical* HMMs. We accounted for these constraints by a model extension, which can be thought of as a HMM based on a non-homogeneous Markov chain. The non-homogeneity is not conditioned on the time of the observation but on a function summarizing and, hence, dependent on previous observations. This extension required only minor modifications to the relevant HMM algorithms. The clustering with the extended model provided a powerful modeling and analysis framework which improved the quality of the modeling substantially when compared with the methods previously used.

This paper is organized as follows: After establishing notation and necessary concepts in Sec. 2 we introduce the algorithm, analyze its computational complexity and discuss implementational questions in Sec. 3. The setting of the application problem and the data used in the experimental validation is subsequently described. This motivates the following extension to non-homogeneous HMMs introduced in Sec. 5. Experimental results and a discussion conclude the paper.

2   Definitions and notation

Hidden Markov Models (HMMs) can be viewed as probabilistic functions of a Markov chain (Burke and Rosenblatt(1958))(Petrie(1969)), where each state of the chain independently can produce emissions according to so-called emission probabilities or densities. We shall restrict ourselves to univariate emission probability densities. Extensions to multivariates or mixtures thereof as well as discrete emissions are routine.

Definition 2 (Hidden Markov Model). Let $O = (O_1, \ldots)$ be a sequence over an alphabet Σ. The following parameters fully determine a Hidden Markov Model λ: the states S_i, $1 \leq i \leq N$, the probability of starting in state S_i, π_i, the transition probability from state S_i to S_j, a_{ij}, and $b_i(\omega)$, the emission probability density of a symbol $\omega \in \Sigma$ in state S_i.

The obvious stochasticity constraints on the parameters apply. Rabiner(1989) gives a thorough introduction to HMMs. The problem we will address can be formally defined as follows.

Definition 3 (HMM Cluster Problem). Given n sequences O^i, not necessarily of equal length, with index set $\mathcal{I} = \{1, 2, \ldots, n\}$ and a fixed integer $K \ll n$. Compute a partition $\mathcal{C} = (C_1, C_2, \ldots, C_K)$ of $\mathcal{I}$ and HMMs $\lambda_1, \ldots, \lambda_K$ maximizing the objective function

$$f(\mathcal{C}) = \prod_{k=1}^{K} \prod_{i \in C_k} L(O^i | \lambda_k). \tag{1}$$

Here, $L(O^i | \lambda_k)$ denotes the likelihood function, that is, the probability density for generating sequence O^i by model λ_k: $L(O^i | \lambda_k) := P(O^i | \lambda_k)$.

It has been implicitly described before Smyth(2000) that the problem of computing a k-means clustering can be formulated as a joint likelihood maximization problem.

3   The clustering algorithm

Adapting the k-means algorithm, we propose the following maximum likelihood approach to solve a HMM Cluster Problem, given K initial HMMs $\lambda_1^0, \ldots, \lambda_K^0$.

i) **Iteration** $(t \in \{1, 2, \ldots\})$:
   (a) Generate a new partitioning of the sequences by assigning each sequence O^i to the model k for which the likelihood $L(O^i | \lambda_k^{t-1})$ is maximal.
   (b) Calculate new parameters $\lambda_1^t, \ldots, \lambda_K^t$ using the re-estimation algorithm for each model with their start parameters $\lambda_1^{t-1}, \ldots, \lambda_K^{t-1}$ and their assigned sequences.

ii) **Stop**, if the improvement of the objective function (1) is below a given threshold, ε, the grouping of the sequences does not change or a given iteration number is reached.

As there is a one-to-one correspondence between clusters and models we shall use the terms interchangeably in the following.

Convergence: The nested iteration scheme does indeed converge to a local maximum. This follows directly from the convergence of the Baum-Welch algorithm and the observation that re-assignment of sequences cannot decrease the likelihood. How to avoid the usual practical problems with local maximization is described later.

Implementation: The relevant data structures and algorithms are freely available in a portable C-library, the GHMM (Knab et al.(2002)), licensed under the Library GNU General Public License (LGPL).

Initialization: A suitable model topology, i.e. the number of states and the allowed transitions (the nonzero transition probabilities), and the number of initial models should be motivated by the application. Note that the topology remains unchanged during the training process.[1]

Since the clustering algorithm will only converge to a local maximum the choice of the model's start parameters will affect the maximum computed. The simplest approach is to set all parameter to random values subject to stochasticity constraints. This can easily lead to an unbalanced assignment of sequences to models, as random models might have near zero probabilities of producing any sequences in the set at all. Alternatively, one can initially train one HMM with all sequences, and subsequently use K copies of that model as the input for the clustering, after adding small random perturbations to the parameters of the K copies individually. Training enforces divergence of clusters in this case. Generally, one has to pay attention that in the first iteration step each sequence can be generated from at least one model — i.e., the likelihood of the set of sequences may not be zero. If there is only limited amount of training data available, pseudo-counts or Dirichlet priors (Sjolander et al.(1996)) can be used to dispatch with this over-fitting problem effectively.

4   Application to loan bank data

To evaluate the proposed clustering method, we use financial time-series data obtained from the public saving and loan banks in Germany for an ongoing co-operative research project (Knab et al.(1997)). The fundamental concept behind saving and loan banks is to combine a period of saving money, usually until some threshold D has been reached — the prerequisite for taking out a loan — which then has to be repaid in fixed installments. Contractual details vary widely, but manual inspection suggested a number of prototypical contract histories.

Each of the data points corresponds to an individual saving and loan contract. It consists of a time-series of feature vectors recorded in yearly intervals. Depending on the respective bank, there are as many as 3 million data points available.

There are about 40 individual quantities recorded in one feature vector. Out of those, we mainly consider the relative savings amount (RSA). The RSA quantifies the amount of money saved over the last period of twelve

---

[1] However, the trained model may contain transitions with low probability and therefore some states may hardly ever be reached. A pruning step can eliminate these states.

months relative, in percent, to the total volume of the loan. It is the most important feature of the time-series, since it is the dominant factor for the further development of the contract. Other recorded quantities, except demographical data etc., depend on it directly or indirectly. Modeling all 40 quantities can be easily accommodated in the HMM-Clustering framework.

In the RSA time-series data a number of typical patterns can be observed, which correspond to different types of behavior. This motivates a theoretical interest in classifying and clustering this data. From a practical point of view, the clustering process is highly relevant as it is the first step towards simulation of the whole collection of contracts. Simulation is used for liquidity forecasting and hence as the basis for executive decisions such as investment strategies or contract design.

The observed time-series exhibit global patterns that correspond to certain deterministic constraints imposed by the terms and regulations of loan banking (e.g. the threshold D which specifies the end of the saving period). A good model generates sequences also obeying those constraints. In the next section we demonstrate how this non-Markovian behavior can be accounted for in HMM modeling.

5 Model extensions

The basic idea of our Model extension is to allow transition probabilities to vary, similarly to time inhomogeneous Markov chains. However, in our case the transition probabilities do not depend on time but on the partial sequence observed so far. As an example we consider a sequence of savings which, when summed, exceed the threshold D. Usually the sequence will enter a state corresponding to amortizations instead of remaining in a saving phase state in the next time step.

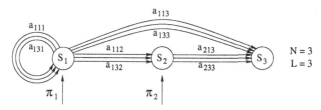

Fig. 1. Graph of an extended HMM with $L = 3$ conditional transition classes.

To accomplish this for generated sequences we extend the transition Matrix $A = (a_{i,j})$ to a set of matrices, cf. Fig. 1, $A \to (A_1, \ldots, A_L)$. Suppose the model is in state i at time t and we already observed the partial sequence $(O_1, \ldots, O_t)$. The function $l = f(O_1, \ldots, O_t)$ determines the current transi-

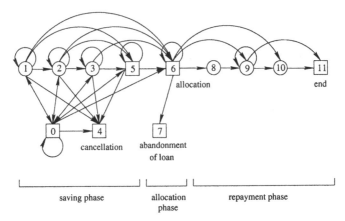

saving phase   allocation   repayment phase
phase

Fig. 2. Graph of an HMM for modeling the three phases of a loan banking contract.

tion matrix A_l. As a simple example we used the following step-function

$$f(O_1,\ldots,O_t) = \lceil L \sum_{\tau=1}^{t} O_\tau \rceil, \quad \text{where} \quad 0 \le \sum_{\tau=1}^{t} O_\tau \le 1.$$

Alternative choices for f have been developed by Wichern(2001). Knab(2000) shows how to modify the usual Baum-Welch reestimation formulas for this model extension.

6 Experimental results

We tested our training algorithm with data sets containing up to 50,000 time series from savings and loan bank data. In a first step we restricted our model to the saving period. Several different model topologies with varying number of states were examined, as well as variations on the number of HMMs and transition matrices (not shown). We achieved optimal and stable results with a simple left-right model with $N = 13$ states and self-transitions ($a_{ij} = 0$ if $j < i$). The number of HMM clusters was $K = 9$ and the number of transition matrices was $L = 6$. This model parameters are used for the results in this section.

The first quantity to be examined was the sum of the relative savings amount (SRSA) per sequence. Fig. 3 displays the SRSA of the real data and the prediction of three different models: the currently used k-means model (Bachem et al.(1997)), the naive HMM approach and our extended model of section 5. The SRSA of the real data is 0.0 until approximately 37 %, reaches a sharp maximum at 39 % and has a long tail until 80 %. Note that the contracts require a savings amount of at least 40 % including interest. The k-means prediction has a much too sharp maximum and consequently a much too small variance due to the fixed time lengths of the k-means prototypes. The

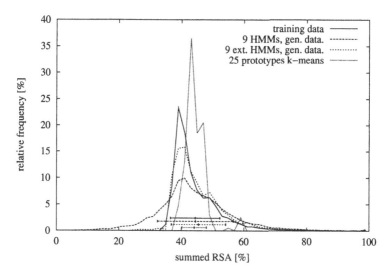

Fig. 3. Sum of relative savings amount (SRSA) for real data, generated data (HMMs and extended HMMs) and weighted k-means prototypes. The horizontal error bars show mean and standard deviation for the observed data.

naive HMM approach achieves the maximum with high accuracy, but results in a much too broad length distribution. This can be avoided when using our extended model, where both the maximum and the variance are met. The trained models are distinguishable from each other and reflect certain well known and typical structures of saving behavior (Knab(2000)).

A more complex model: further events in loan banking

Fig. 2 shows one of the model topologies we investigated with regard to its capability in modeling the complete course of loan bank contracts. The three periods saving, allocation, and repayment correspond to three distinct groups of model states. The square states represent important discrete events such as canceling the contract; unique numerical values are chosen as almost-sure emissions. Emission probabilities of those states are excluded from training.

Furthermore, the emission parameters of these special states are never changed during training.

Another view is given in Fig. 4. Here the capability of extending truncated real sequences is displayed. The predicted data were generated by two different models (of same size and topology) which were trained on two different sets of sequences. The training sets are: *pred1* containing all contracts for the year 1985 and *pred2* containing contracts regardless of the contract year. The truncated set consists of all contracts for the year 1986 and the sequences were truncated in 1992 and extended by the above mentioned models until a an end-state (e. g. a state with no outgoing transitions) was reached. Fig. 4

shows the yearly savings amount (YSA) and the yearly amortizations (YAM) summed over all sequences of the two generated sets (*pred1*, *pred2*) und of the real data (*real*, not truncated here). The YSA data is closely approximated by both predictions. For the YAM graph the prediction using the training set *pred1* is more accurate.

7 Conclusion and outlook

We presented a new algorithm for clustering data, which performed well for the task of generating statistical models for prediction of loan bank customer collectives. The generated clusters represent groups of customers with similar behavior. The prediction quality exceeds the previously used k-means based approach.

HMMs lend themselves to various extensions. Therefore, we were able to incorporate many other relevant loan-bank parameters into our current model, which still can then be estimated with *one* homogeneous statistical training algorithm, instead of requiring a collection of individual heuristics. We expect an even higher overall prediction accuracy and a further reduction of human intervention when applied to this and other application problems. Partial results are described elsewhere (Knab(2000))(Wichern(2001)). The clustering approach is general in its applicability: An analysis of gene expression time-series data from experimental genetics is forthcoming.

References

BACHEM, A. ET AL. (1997): Analyse großer Datenmengen und Clusteralgorithmen im Bausparwesen. In: C. Hipp, W. Eichhorn, W.-R., W.-R. Heilmann

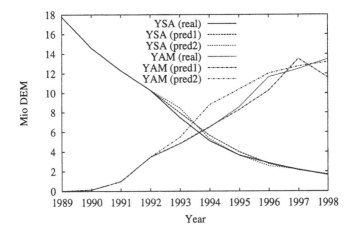

Fig. 4. Real and predicted yearly savings amount (YSA) and amortizations (YAM) for two different training scenarios. Prediction starts 1993.

(eds.), *Beiträge zum 7. Symposium Geld, Finanzwirtschaft, Banken und Versicherungen, Dezember 1996*, no. 257, 955–961.

BAUM, L. E., PETRIE, T. (1966): Statistical inference for probabilistic functions of finite Markov chains. *Ann. Math. Statist.*, *37*, 1554–1563.

BAUM, L. E., PETRIE, T., SOULES, G., WEISS, N. (1970): A maximization technique occurring in the statistical analysis of probabilistic functions of Markov chains. *Ann. Math. Statist.*, *41*, 164–171.

BOCK, H. H. (1974): Automatische Klassifikation. Theoretische und praktische Methoden zur Gruppierung und Strukturierung von Daten. Vandenhoeck & Ruprecht.

BURKE, C. J., ROSENBLATT, M. (1958): A Markovian function of a Markov chain. *Ann. math. stat.*, *29*, 1112–1120.

EVERITT, B. S. (1993): Cluster Analysis. Edward Arnold, London.

KNAB, B. (2000): Erweiterungen von Hidden-Markov-Modellen zur Analyse ökonomischer Zeitreihen. Ph.D. thesis.

KNAB, B., SCHLIEP, A., STECKEMETZ, B., WICHERN, B., GÄDKE, A., THORANSDOTTIR, D. (2002): The GNU Hidden Markov Model Library. Available from http://www.zpr.uni-koeln.de/ hmm.

KNAB, B., SCHRADER, R., WEBER, I., WEINBRECHT, K., WICHERN, B. (1997): Mesoskopisches Simulationsmodell zur Kollektivfortschreibung. Tech. Rep. ZPR97-295, Mathematisches Institut, Universität zu Köln.

MACDONALD, I. L., ZUCCHINI, W. (1997): Hidden Markov and other models for discrete-valued time series. Chapman & Hall, London.

MCLACHLAN, G., BASFORD, K. (1988): Mixture Models: Inference and Applications to Clustering. Marcel Dekker, Inc., New York, Basel.

PETRIE, T. (1969): Probabilistic functions of finite state Markov chains. *Ann. Math. Statist*, *40*, 97–115.

RABINER, L. R. (1989): A Tutorial on Hidden Markov Models and Selected Applications in Speech Recognition. *Proceedings of the IEEE*, *77*(2), 257–285.

SJOLANDER, K., KARPLUS, K., BROWN, M., HUGHEY, R., KROGH, A., MIAN, I. S., HAUSSLER, D. (1996): Dirichlet mixtures: a method for improved detection of weak but significant protein sequence homology. *Comput Appl Biosci*, *12*(4), 327–45.

SMYTH, P. (2000): A general probabilistic framework for clustering individuals. Tech. Rep. TR-00-09, University of California, Irvine.

WICHERN, B. (2001): Hidden-Markov-Modelle zur Analyse und Simulation von Finanzzeitreihen. Ph.D. thesis.

Acknowledgments: The research was conducted at the Center for Applied Computer Science at the University of Cologne (ZAIK) and partially (BK, BW) funded by the German Landesbausparkassen. We would like to thank Prof. Dr. R. Schrader (ZAIK) for his support.

Classification of Multivariate Data
With Missing Values Using
Expected Discriminant Scores

Wolfgang Kossa

Department of Finance,
University of Passau, D-94030 Passau, Germany

Abstract. A discriminant analysis used to classify multivariate data $y \in \mathbb{R}^k$ into classes $z \in 1 \ldots g$ is based on discriminant scores $d_z(y)$. An example of its application is the creditworthiness check where, as a rule, *missing values* (MV), i.e. incomplete feature vectors, are found. Therefore there is a necessity for an MV–admissible variant of the discriminant analysis, "MV–DA". Here, an algorithm is established which is based on *expected discriminant scores* under a conditional mixture distribution. It can be shown that the expected discriminant score $E[d_z(y)]$ is equal to the discriminant score of the expected feature vector $d_z(E[y])$ plus a correction term. In empirical tests the MV–DA classifies on a high level.

1 Introduction

A classification task can be described as estimating the unknown class membership of an object through the evaluation of a feature vector. For that purpose a relation function between the feature vector and its class membership is determined (Johnson and Wichern (1982), Anderson (1984)).

An example of its application is the creditworthiness check, i.e. the classification of credit applicants, with the classes of "good" and "bad" cases (Hand and Henley (1997), Thomas (1998)). Since the class membership of a credit applicant is unknown at the time of the credit application, it has to be estimated through the evaluation of a collected feature vector.

In order to determine the relation function between the feature vector and its class membership two sets of historical credit cases with known feature vectors and known class memberships are used. From the *training set* a relation function is derived whose goodness is estimated through an *ex post prediction* on the *test set*. As a quality criterion the *hit rate* is used, which represents the expected misclassification costs in the case of inversely proportional costs (Johnson and Wichern (1982), Thomas (1998)).

The case of incomplete feature vectors. When one considers credit cases in bulk business, as a rule incomplete feature vectors, i.e. feature vectors with *missing values* (MV), are found (Hand and Henley (1997)). Despite the *missing values*, incomplete feature vectors have existing entries, which can give some information about the relationship between the (rudimentary) feature vector and its class membership. There are technical reasons for *missing values*, e.g. bad readability, incorrect data processing, and so on. But there

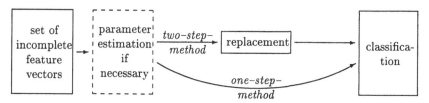

Fig. 1. One–step–method and two–step–method of classification.

are also problem–inherent reasons, e. g. an incompletely filled out application form or features which are not known of every applicant (e. g. previous account keeping), and so on.

If incomplete feature vectors were discarded, (i) some information from the training set would be lost and (ii) incomplete feature vectors from the test set could not be classified. Therefore incomplete feature vectors are *not* discarded. Two possibilities of analysis seem to be possible (cf. Figure 1). Using a *two–step–method* first of all a replacement of the *missing values* by estimated values takes place (if necessary after parameter estimation) and afterwards a classification of the possibly completed feature vectors is done. A disadvantage of this method is that falsification of the correct (but unknown) features occurs by replacement in general. An advantage is that standard methods of classification can be used. Using an *one–step–method* a classification method is applied (if necessary after parameter estimation) that is able to handle incomplete feature vectors without any preprocessing. An advantage of this method is that every feature vector is available unaltered. A crucial disadvantage is that suitable classification methods have to be established first.

2   Classification using expected discriminant scores

In the following, starting from the use of discriminant functions for continuous variables, one derives a simple two–step–method as well as an one–step–method. Both methods are based on the quadratic discriminant analysis (Anderson and Bahadur (1962), Anderson (1984)). While the two–step–method computes discriminant scores of expected feature vectors, the one–step–method computes expected discriminant scores. In particular the latter can be seen as an MV–admissible discriminant analysis.

The use of discriminant functions. If the probability density function of a feature vector y in class z ($z \in 1 \ldots g$) is modeled by the *class distribution* $f_z(y) = f(y \,|\, z)$, then, knowing the *prior probabilities*, $p(z)$, the *mixture distribution* $f(y) = \sum_{z=1}^{g} p(z) \cdot f(y \,|\, z)$ in the case of unknown class membership can be stated. If the *posterior probability* $p(z \,|\, y) = p(z) \cdot f(y \,|\, z) \cdot f(y)^{-1}$ is maximized at observed feature vector y with respect to class z under the assumption of class–specific normal distributions $\mathcal{N}(\mu_z, \Sigma_z)$, then the discriminant functions $d_z : \mathbb{R}^k \to \mathbb{R}$ of the quadratic discriminant analysis

$$d_z(y) = \ln p(z) - \frac{1}{2} \cdot \ln \det \Sigma_z - \frac{1}{2} \cdot (y - \mu_z)^T \cdot \Sigma_z^{-1} \cdot (y - \mu_z) \qquad (1)$$

follow (Anderson (1984), Fahrmeir et al. (1996)). An assignment of feature vector y to a class with maximal discriminant score (1) takes place, i.e. for the relation function $\varphi : \mathbb{R}^k \to \{1, \ldots, g\}$ it holds that $\varphi(y) \in \arg\max\{d_z(y) \mid z \in 1 \ldots g\}$. In order to be able to specify the discriminant function (1), the parameters μ_z, Σ_z have to be estimated using the training set. With incomplete feature vectors, the EM–algorithm can be used (Dempster et al. (1977)).

A two–step–method of classification. If an incomplete feature vector from the test set is to be classified, the representation

$$y = \begin{pmatrix} y_{\,o} \\ y_{\,m} \end{pmatrix} \qquad (2)$$

is used with observed features $y_{\,o}$ and missing features $y_{\,m}$, if necessary after suitable arrangement of the variables. Knowing $y_{\,o}$, the *conditional class distribution* $\overline{f}_z(y_{\,m}) = f(y_{\,m} \mid y_{\,o}, z)$ as well as the *conditional mixture distribution* $\overline{f}(y_{\,m}) = f(y_{\,m} \mid y_{\,o})$ follow. It holds that

$$\overline{f}(y_{\,m}) = \frac{\sum_z p(z) f(y_{\,o}, y_{\,m} \mid z)}{\sum_z p(z) f(y_{\,o} \mid z)} = \sum_{z=1}^{g} \underbrace{\frac{p(z) f(y_{\,o} \mid z)}{\sum_\zeta p(\zeta) f(y_{\,o} \mid \zeta)}}_{=: \overline{p}(z)} \cdot \underbrace{f(y_{\,m} \mid y_{\,o}, z)}_{\overline{f}_z(y_{\,m})}, \qquad (3)$$

so that the conditional mixture distribution (3) can be interpreted as a mixture distribution of the conditional class distributions $\overline{f}_z(y_{\,m})$ with *conditional prior probabilities*, $\overline{p}(z)$. Using (3) the expected value

$$\overline{\mathrm{E}}\,[y_{\,m}] = \sum_{z=1}^{g} \overline{p}(z) \cdot \mathrm{E}\,[y_{\,m} \mid y_{\,o}, z] \qquad (4)$$

follows, where under the assumption of normal distribution

$$\mathrm{E}\,[y_{\,m} \mid y_{\,o}, z] = \mu_{\,m,z} + \Sigma_{\,m,o,z} \cdot \Sigma_{\,o,o,z}^{-1} \cdot (y_{\,o} - \mu_{\,o,z}) =: \mu_z^{(m \mid o)} \qquad (5)$$

holds (Mardia et al. (1997)). Thereby the *missing values* in y define an arrangement of the parameters

$$\mu_z = \begin{pmatrix} \mu_{\,o,z} \\ \mu_{\,m,z} \end{pmatrix}, \quad \Sigma_z = \begin{pmatrix} \Sigma_{\,o,o,z} & \Sigma_{\,o,m,z} \\ \Sigma_{\,m,o,z} & \Sigma_{\,m,m,z} \end{pmatrix}. \qquad (6)$$

The two–step–method consisting of replacement of the *missing values* according to (4) and classification according to (1) is referred to "RepQDA".

An one–step–method of classification. If the incomplete feature vector y is not to be completed, but put in the discriminant function (1) without being preprocessed, it should be pointed out that with y_m the term $d_z(y) = d_z(y_m, y_o)$ is also random. Therefore the expected discriminant score

$$\overline{E}[d_z(y)] = \ln p(z) - \frac{1}{2} \cdot \ln \det \Sigma_z - \frac{1}{2} \cdot \overline{E}\left[(y - \mu_z)^T \Sigma_z^{-1} (y - \mu_z) \right]$$

$$= \ln p(z) - \frac{1}{2} \cdot \ln \det \Sigma_z - \frac{1}{2} \cdot \mathrm{tr}\left(\Sigma_z^{-1} \cdot \overline{E}\left[(y - \mu_z)(y - \mu_z)^T \right] \right) \quad (7)$$

is computed using the conditional mixture distribution (3). With

$$\overline{E}\left[(y - \mu_z)(y - \mu_z)^T \right] = \overline{\mathrm{Cov}}\left[y, y^T \right] + \overline{E}\left[y - \mu_z \right] \cdot \overline{E}\left[y - \mu_z \right]^T \quad (8)$$

it follows from (7) that

$$\overline{E}[d_z(y)] = d_z\left(\overline{E}[y] \right) - \frac{1}{2} \cdot \mathrm{tr}\left(\Sigma_z^{-1} \cdot \overline{\mathrm{Cov}}\left[y, y^T \right] \right), \quad (9)$$

i. e. the expected discriminant score is equal to the discriminant score of the expected feature vector plus a correction term.

The computation of both the expected value and the covariance in (9) uses the conditional mixture distribution (3). For the computation of $\overline{E}[y]$ one can use (4), for the computation of $\overline{\mathrm{Cov}}[y, y^T]$ it becomes clear that y_o is known, which is why

$$\overline{\mathrm{Cov}}\left[y, y^T \right] = \begin{array}{|c|c|} \hline 0 & 0 \\ \hline 0 & \overline{\mathrm{Cov}}\left[y_m, y_m^T \right] \\ \hline \end{array} \quad (10)$$

holds. Furthermore it holds that (Mardia et al (1997))

$$\Sigma_z^{-1} = \begin{array}{|c|c|} \hline \Sigma_{o,o,z}^{-1} & 0 \\ \hline 0 & 0 \\ \hline \end{array} + \begin{array}{|c|} \hline -\Sigma_{o,o,z}^{-1}\Sigma_{o,m,z} \\ \hline I \\ \hline \end{array} \cdot \left(\Sigma_z^{(m|o)} \right)^{-1} \cdot \begin{array}{|c|} \hline -\Sigma_{m,o,z}\Sigma_{o,o,z}^{-1} \,\, I \\ \hline \end{array} \quad (11)$$

with

$$\Sigma_z^{(m|o)} = \Sigma_{m,m,z} - \Sigma_{m,o,z} \cdot \Sigma_{o,o,z}^{-1} \cdot \Sigma_{o,m,z}, \quad (12)$$

so that starting at (9) and using (10) and (11), the equation

$$\mathrm{tr}\left(\Sigma_z^{-1} \cdot \overline{\mathrm{Cov}}\left[y, y^T \right] \right) = \mathrm{tr}\left(\left(\Sigma_z^{(m|o)} \right)^{-1} \cdot \overline{\mathrm{Cov}}\left[y_m, y_m^T \right] \right) \quad (13)$$

follows. If (13) is inserted in (9), then it follows that

$$\overline{E}[d_z(y)] = d_z(\overline{E}[y]) - \frac{1}{2} \cdot \mathrm{tr}\left(\left(\Sigma_z^{(m|o)} \right)^{-1} \cdot \overline{\mathrm{Cov}}\left[y_m, y_m^T \right] \right). \quad (14)$$

If there are two classes, $g = 2$, it holds that (Kossa (2002))

$$\overline{\mathrm{Cov}}\left[y_{\mathrm{m}}, y_{\mathrm{m}}^T\right] = \overline{p}(1) \cdot \Sigma_1^{(\mathrm{m|o})} + \overline{p}(2) \cdot \Sigma_2^{(\mathrm{m|o})}$$
$$+ \overline{p}(1) \cdot \overline{p}(2) \cdot \left(\mu_1^{(\mathrm{m|o})} - \mu_2^{(\mathrm{m|o})}\right)\left(\mu_1^{(\mathrm{m|o})} - \mu_2^{(\mathrm{m|o})}\right)^T. \quad (15)$$

After a parameter estimation of μ_z, Σ_z, e. g. by using the EM–algorithm, the one–step–method consisting of classification according to (14) by using (1), (4), (5), (12) and — if there are two classes — (15) is referred to "MV–DA", as it is an MV–admissible discriminant analysis.

3   Empirical results

In order to investigate the performance of the MV–DA in a classification task, empirical tests need to be carried out. For this purpose (i) feature vectors from a bank ("credit data") and (ii) artificially generated normally distributed data ("normal data") are used. *Missing values* are introduced artificially, and every data set is classified using the MV–DA as well as alternative methods.

Credit data. Starting from a bank's published categorical data (Fahrmeir et al. (1996)) five of originally 20 features are selected. Every feature is transformed by an univariate score evaluation and mapped into the interval $[-1, 1]$ by the *tanh*–function. In order to make available credit cases from each class in the same number, 300 good and 300 bad cases are used. In each class 150 feature vectors are used both in the training set and in the test set.

Normal data. The MV–DA (and also the EM–algorithm) assumes normal distribution. In order to investigate how the MV–DA classifies under ideal conditions, feature vectors are generated artificially using a simulation of normal distribution. Five features, analogous to the credit data, are used.

For each class a mean vector, a variance vector and a correlation matrix is set, whose concrete values are found in Kossa (2002). Thereby the class–specific distributions are specified and 300 feature vectors from each class are generated, analogous to the credit data.

Introduction of missing values. Credit data and normal data consist of complete feature vectors. In order to obtain incomplete feature vectors, 5 %, 10 %,…,75 % ("MV–rate") of the entries are deleted as Domma and Ingrassia (2001) e. g. also do. Both in the training set and in the test set the entries are deleted in the MCAR–sense (Little and Rubin (1987)).

In addition to the complete data sets 15 further data sets with incomplete feature vectors of different MV–rates are available. In empirical tests the hit rate can be investigated subject to the MV–rate.

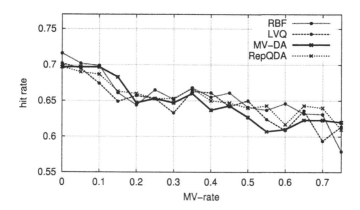

Fig. 2. Hit rates using the credit data.

Hit rates. For the purpose of classifying the credit data and normal data of different MV–rates the one–step–method MV–DA and the two–step–method *Rep*QDA are used. Furthermore, the MV–admissible neural network types LVQ (Kohonen (1986), Kohonen (1989)) and RBF (Leonard and Kramer (1991), Ahmad and Tresp (1993)) are used. Using the LVQ–network a *missing value* is replaced by the corresponding variable of *each* reference vector. Using the RBF–network the corresponding variable of the center of *each* basis function is used. Using the neural network methods some feature vectors are taken out of the test set and are used in a validation set in order to control the stop point of the iterative parameter estimation process.

The credit data generate the hit rates subject to the MV–rate in Figure 2. It can be seen that

- each method classifies at nearly the same level,
- the MV–DA classifies relatively high in the range $[0.05, 0.2]$ but relatively low in the range $[0.5, 0.6]$,
- the two–step–method *Rep*QDA classifies well for all MV–rates.

Since, concerning the credit data, every method classifies essentially at the same level, and since the generated hit rates are possibly data dependent, *no recommendation* can be made in favor of a certain method.

Knowing the (theoretical) distribution of the normal data, one should examine the hit rates subject to the MV–rate in Figure 3. It is observed, that

- the MV–DA classifies on a high level for all MV–rates,
- the RBF–network classifies well in the range $[0.3, 0.55]$,
- the LVQ–network classifies well in the range $[0.55, 0.75]$,

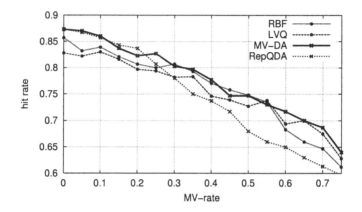

Fig. 3. Hit rates using the normal data.

- the distance between MV–DA and *Rep*QDA increases with an increasing MV–rate.

Therefore, concerning the normal data, it can be pointed out that using MV–admissible methods (MV–DA, RBF, LVQ) is of apparent benefit. Especially the MV–DA seems to be suitable. Under the ideal condition of normally distributed data, it generates the highest hit rates.

4 Summary and conclusion

The classification of credit applicants is an example of how it is necessary to be able to classify incomplete feature vectors. For this purpose the MV–admissible method of the MV–DA was introduced, which is based on the conventional quadratic discriminant analysis and computes expected discriminant scores. In order to investigate the performance of the MV–DA, empirical tests were carried out where the MV–DA proves to be useful.

First, the MV–DA has the advantage over neural network methods of being non–iterative (except the EM–algorithm for parameter estimation), so that advantages in running time result. Secondly, it is a deterministic method (with estimated parameters), so that a *unique, well defined* class assignment is ensured. The MV–DA can be implemented easily and promises, because of the deterministic outcome, a comparatively high degree of acceptance in the classification of credit applicants and therefore far reaching practical applicability.

References

AHMAD, S. and TRESP, V. (1993): Some Solutions to the Missing Feature Problem in Vision. In: S. J. Hanson, J. D. Cowan and C. L. Giles (Eds.): *Advances in Neural Information Processing Systems 5*. Morgan Kaufmann, 393–400.

ANDERSON, T. W. and BAHADUR, R. R. (1962): Classification into two multivariate normal distributions with different covariance matrices. *The Annals of Mathematical Statistics, 33, 420–431*.

ANDERSON, T. W. (1984): *An Introduction to Multivariate Statistical Analysis*. Wiley, New York.

DEMPSTER, A. P., LAIRD, N. M. and RUBIN, D. B. (1977): Maximum Likelihood from Incomplete Data via the EM Algorithm. *Journal of the Royal Statistical Society, B 39, 1–38*.

DOMMA, F. and INGRASSIA, S. (2001): Mixture Models for Maximum Likelihood Estimation from Incomplete Values. In: S. Borra, R. Rocci, M. Vichi and M. Schader (Eds.): *Advances in Classification and Data Analysis*. Springer, Berlin, 201–208.

FAHRMEIR, L., HAMERLE, A. and TUTZ, G. (1996): *Multivariate statistische Verfahren*. Walter de Gruyter, Berlin, New York.

HAND, D. J. and HENLEY, W. E. (1997): Statistical Classification Methods in Consumer Credit Scoring: a Review. *Journal of the Royal Statistical Society, A 160, 523–541*.

JOHNSON, R. A. and WICHERN, D. W. (1982): *Applied Multivariate Statistical Analysis*. Prentice–Hall, Englewood Cliffs.

KOHONEN, T. (1986): Learning Vector Quantization for Pattern Recognition. *Technical Report TKK–F–A601, Helsinki University of Technology*.

KOHONEN, T. (1989): *Self–Organization and Associative Memory*. Springer, Berlin.

KOSSA, W. (2002): *Klassifikation unvollständiger Datensätze am Beispiel des Konsumenten–Kreditgeschäfts*. Verlag Versicherungswirtschaft, Karlsruhe.

LEONARD, J. A. and KRAMER, M. A. (1991): Radial Basis Functions for Classifying Process Faults. *IEEE Control Systems, 11, 31–38*.

LITTLE, R. J. A. and RUBIN D. B. (1987): *Statistical Analysis with Missing Data*. Wiley, New York.

MARDIA, K. V., KENT, J. T. and BIBBY, J. M. (1997): *Multivariate Analysis*. Academic Press, London.

THOMAS, L. C. (1998): Methodologies for Classifying Applicants for Credit. In: D. J. Hand and S. D. Jacka (Eds.): *Statistics in Finance*. Arnold, London, 83–103.

Assessment of the Polish Manufacturing Sector Attractiveness: An End-User Approach

Dorota Kwiatkowska-Ciotucha[1] and Józef Dziechciarz[2]

[1] Department of Forecasting and Economic Analyzes,
Wrocław University of Economics, ul. Komandorska 118/120, 53-345 Wrocław,
Poland, e-mail: ciotucha@credit.ae.wroc.pl
[2] Department of Econometrics,
Wrocław University of Economics, ul. Komandorska 118/120, 53-345 Wrocław,
Poland, e-mail: jdzie@manager.ae.wroc.pl

Abstract. This is the presentation of the preliminary results of the larger project on the determination of the manufacturing branches attractiveness. For that purpose the hierarchical classification has been made. Additionally, the tendencies in branches position in the attractiveness hierarchy have been described. The attractiveness is defined depending on end-user of the classification. The theoretical framework for the study, and the economic background has been discussed on the XXV GfKl 2001 Conference in Munich (Kwiatkowska, et al. (2002)). The goal of this investigation is differences identification in the construction of the composite indicator Z depending on end-users' particular interest. This general framework may be used for any part of NACE Classification i.e. *unit (division), group* or *class*. In the present study the applicability of developed framework will be illustrated on the example of one of the *divisions* in the *section D* – Manufacturing.

1 Introduction

In recent years in Poland the demand for the information describing situation of the individual industries or branches (the branch is understood as *unit, group* or *class*) is rapidly growing. Comparative studies results find interest among various end-users. Individual end-user of the information applies specific assessment criteria for attractiveness or development potential of the branch. As the potential end-users of the results – four groups may be identified. First of them are *enterprises managers* who may need to evaluate their performance in comparison with other firms in the same branch or with firms in other branches. The second are *investors* seeking investment possibility. Further group are *bank managers* deciding on credit portfolio construction, evaluating loan applications etc. *Politicians* active in local governments is the next type of end-user. They have to decide which branches to promote in their region, which investments to attract, and which type of skills to teach in local schools and in retraining centers.

Present and future situation assessment of different branches in the Polish economy can be done by appraisal of enterprises' situation. Measuring the manufacturing branch attractiveness is a complex task, which in most cases requires application of the multivariate statistical analysis framework. As the evaluation criterion of manufacturing branches attractiveness a value of composite indicator can be used. The value of the composite indicator Z for each branch and each period can be calculated according to the following formula:

$$z_{jt} = \sum_{i=1}^{m} z_{ijt} \cdot w_i \qquad (1)$$

where:

z_{jt} – value of the composite indicator in period t for *branch* j,

z_{ijt} – value of the normalized i-th variable in period t for *branch* j,

w_i – weight ascribed to i-th variable, $w_i \in (0,1)$, $\sum w_i = 1$,

j – code of *branch* (NACE Classification),

i – index of component variable, $i = 1, \ldots, m$,

t – index of period, $t = 1, \ldots, n$.

Component variables Z_i should characterize different areas of enterprise's activities - on the other hand this description should cover all essential areas. The composite indicator has the nature of a stimulant (a variable whose higher value is desired or positively assessed), with values in range [0; 1]. On the ground of the composite indicator value an attempt to assess relative situation of individual branch with comparison to all other branches can be conducted. For this purpose – all branches can be sorted in according with the descending value of composite indicator Z.

2   The data

The Polish Central Statistical Office (GUS) collects the data describing the enterprise's condition on the quarterly and yearly basis. In order to assess branch condition - the situation of individual firms belonging to this branch are to be examined. To cover all aspects of the enterprises activity the following areas should be included into analysis: sale's tendency; liquidity; debt situation; efficiency and profitability. Corporate finance and managerial accounting literature gives a variety of measures describing the management quality (see Brigham and Gapenski (2000), Tyran (1992))). The following indicators have been chosen for the analysis - the nature of the variable (stimulant, destimulant, nominant) and suggested nominal values are stated:

- SALE'S TENDENCY ANALYSIS – X_1 **the dynamics of incomes from sale** *in fixed prices from January* 2002 – *chain base index* – *analogous period previous year* = 100%, stimulant;
- LIQUIDITY ANALYSIS – X_2 **current ratio** (*current assets / current liabilities*), nominant with recommended value range [1.2–2.0]; X_3 **quick ratio** (*current assets − inventories / current liabilities*), nominant with recommended value range [1.0–1.5]; X_4 **finished goods inventory utilization ratio** in days (*finished goods inventory / sales * 360*), destimulant; X_5 **cash (financial means) cycle ratio** in days (*inventory*

turnover + receivable turnover − accounts-payable turnover), destimulant;

- DEBT ANALYSIS − X_6 **debt ratio** (*total debt / total assets*), nominant
  with recommended value range [0.57–0.67]; X_7 **debt-equity ratio** (*total
  debt / equity*), nominant with recommended value range [1.0–3.0]; X_8
  long-term debt ratio (*long-term debt / equity*), nominant (0.5);
- EFFICIENCY ANALYSIS − X_9 **cost ratio** (*prime cost of sales / sales*),
  destimulant or destimulant with threshold value 1; X_{10} **fixed assets
  utilization ratio** (*sales / fixed assets*), stimulant; X_{11} **productivity
  on one employee** (*sales / average number of employees*), stimulant;
- PROFITABILITY ANALYSIS − X_{12} **profit margin on sales** (*net income / sales*), stimulant or stimulant with threshold value 0; X_{13} **return
  on assets** (*net income / total assets*), stimulant or stimulant with veto
  threshold value 0; X_{14} **return on equity** (*net income / equity*), stimulant or stimulant with veto threshold value 0.

3   Composite indicators' differentiation

The composite indicators, which are built for particular groups of end-user
should take into consideration these users specific needs. Differentiation of
composite indicators for different end-users can be result of differences in:

- component variables selection,
- component variables weighting,
- component variables normalization – the use of the appropriate formula
  depends on their nature – stimulant, destimulant or nominant.

The multivariate statistical analysis literature widely discusses both component variable selection as well as the proposals for the component variables
weighting. But the results of earlier research pointed out (see Kwiatkowska
and Załuska (2001)) that the way of component variables' weighting has little
impact on manufacturing branches ordering. Additionally, because of variety
of end-users – the composite indicator construction should be as simple as
possible. Having this in mind – following simple weighting procedures are proposed: all variables have the same importance – the weights for all variables
are the same; the second solution gives all analysis areas the same importance
– the weights for all areas are the same; in the third procedure – component
variables weighting is done in accordance with end-user suggestions.

Another important differentiation factor is the way of component variables normalization. Most commonly used transformation formula resulting
in [0; 1] range of the normalized values is ratio transformation where as the
scaling factor (value) – the maximal value (for the stimulant) or minimal
value (for the destimulant) is used. The extreme values are taken from the
analyzed dataset. Unfortunately – in the situation when outliers are present
in analyzed data or if extreme values in the dataset vary substantially from
the rest of the values in this dataset, such a transformation results in very low

variation of the normalized values. In the dataset used for the Polish manufacturing branches attractiveness analysis, described phenomena occurred quite often. To deal with this problem, as an alternative solution ninth decile for stimulants and the first decile for the destimulants were chosen as the scaling factor. Table 1 shows the normalization formulas. To meet different

The nature of the variable	Normalisation formula
Stimulant with values from R_+	$z_{ijt} = \begin{cases} \dfrac{x_{ijt}}{d_9(x_{it}^k)} & \text{for } x_{ijt} < d_9(x_{it}^k) \\ 1 & \text{for } x_{ijt} \geqslant d_9(x_{it}^k) \end{cases}$
Nominant with recommended value range $[x_{i,min}; x_{i,max}]$ from R_+	$z_{ijt} = \begin{cases} 1 & \text{for } x_{i,min} \leqslant x_{ijt} \leqslant x_{i,max} \\ \dfrac{x_{ijt}}{x_{i,min}} & \text{for } x_{ijt} < x_{i,min} \\ \dfrac{x_{i,max}}{x_{ijt}} & \text{for } x_{ijt} > x_{i,max} \end{cases}$
Nominant with recommended value x_i from R_+	$z_{ijt} = \begin{cases} 1 & \text{for } x_{ijt} = x_i \\ \dfrac{x_{ijt}}{x_i} & \text{for } x_{ijt} < x_i \\ \dfrac{x_i}{x_{ijt}} & \text{for } x_{ijt} > x_i \end{cases}$
Destimulant with values from R_+	$z_{ijt} = \begin{cases} \dfrac{d_1(x_{it}^k)}{x_{ijt}} & \text{for } x_{ijt} > d_1(x_{it}^k) \\ 1 & \text{for } x_{ijt} \leqslant d_1(x_{it}^k) \end{cases}$

x_{ijt} – value of the variable X_i in j-th *division*, *group* or *class* in period t,
z_{ijt} – value of the normalised i-th variable in the period t,
$d_9(x_{it}^k)$ – ninth decile of the variable X_i in the period t for the k-th level,
$d_1(x_{it}^k)$ – first decile of the variable X_i in the period t for the k-th level,
$k = 1, 2, 3$ for *divisions*, *groups* and *classes* levels,
$x_{i,min}$ – the value of lower limit of the recommended value range,
$x_{i,max}$ – the value of upper limit of the recommended value range,
i – variable's number,
j – code of *division*, *group* or *class* (NACE Classification),
t – period's number

Table 1. The normalisation formulas

needs of end-user the appropriate normalization procedures may be used. In particular the differentiation of normalization procedures may be formulated as follow:

- in the case of stimulant (destimulant): taking (or not) veto threshold into consideration; using maximal (minimal) value as a scaling factor, or using decile as a scaling factor;
- in the case of nominant – normalization with recommended value or with recommended value range.

As an illustration – profitability ratios may be discussed. *Managers, local politicians* and *bankers* would consider them as a stimulant without veto threshold. *Investors* – would consider profitability ratios as a stimulant with veto threshold value 0 (or sometimes long term bank interest rate).

One have to add that the choice of scaling factor (extreme values or deciles) is determined rather by data characteristics than the users needs.

The biggest impact of end-user needs on normalization procedures choice one may observe in the case of nominant. Particular users differently assess recommended range of values. Some users may prefer values close to lower boundary, the other close to upper limit. As an example – variable X_2 current ratio – which is nominant with, recommended value range [1.2–2.0]; may be shown. From *manager's* point of view the most desirable values are situated near lower limit of recommended range of values. In contrast – *investors* and *bank managers* prefer values near upper limit of recommended range of values. On the other hand – for local *politicians* only the fact that values are inside limits of recommended range of values is important. Following this discussion – one may propose appropriate normalization formulas depending on who will be user of the analysis results. For *firms' managers* the variable may be considered as the nominant with recommended value equal 1.2; for *bank managers* and for *investors* – nominant with recommended value equal 2.0; for local *politicians* – nominant with recommended value range [1.2–2.0].

4   The illustrative example

The illustrative application of the proposed framework has been undertaken on relatively homogeneous group of 26 *classes* from the *division* 15 (Food Industry) of *section D* Manufacturing. The data source was the official statistics (aggregated Balance Sheets from enterprises) covering period 1996-2000.

The composite indicator Z had been built in accordance with the formula (1) described in the section 1 of this paper. The used data covered indicators listed in section 2. For each of four end-users group identified in the section 1, six variants of composite indicator Z had been calculated. The differentiation between first two variants was based on the scaling factor – the extreme values versus deciles. In both variants all variables had the same weights. Further variation came from weights differentiation variant 3 – analogous with variant 1 had equal weights for each activity area. Variant 4 – analogous with variant 2 also had equal weights for each activity area. All fifteen variables were taken into account in variants 1, 2, 3, and 4.

Variant 5 – was analogous with variant 2, variant 6 – analogous with variant 4. In variants 5 and 6, not all variables were used. The choice of variables was based on the individual needs of end-user groups. The variable selection had been discussed with representatives of end-users.

Twenty-six *classes* of *division* 15 had been sorted in descending way according to values of individual variants of composite indicator Z. The ordering results for all pairs of rankings obtained for each variant of composite indicator Z, and for each year from the period 1996-2000 were compared. The similarity of obtained orderings was examined in two ways:

- by comparing the pair of orderings of all the analyzed classes – for this purpose, Spearman's coefficient of rank correlation was applied:

$$\rho_{rs} = 1 - \frac{6 \sum_j d^2_{jrs}}{c(c^2 - 1)},$$

- by comparing the locations, which have been occupied by a given class in a pair of rankings – for that the differences between the locations occupied by a specific class in individual ranking were calculated and then the arithmetic mean for absolute values of those differences were calculated – for the whole scope of *classes*:

$$d_{rs} = \frac{1}{c} \sum_j |d_{jrs}|^2.$$

where:
ρ_{rs} – value of Spearman's rank correlation coefficient between ranking r and s,
d_{jrs} – difference between the location occupied by class j in ranking r and s,
d_{rs} – arithmetic mean of absolute values of d_{jrs},
c – number of the analyzed *classes*; $c = 26$.

The goal of the ranking comparison may be formulated as follow: it is desirable that for the same end-user type, regardless of the way the composite indicator Z was constructed – the inference on branch attractiveness is similar (or identical); on the other hand the picture from the different end-user group point of view should differ depending on the way the composite indicator Z was constructed.

According to the formulated assessment criteria it has been found out that:

- The were no significant differences in branch attractiveness assessment from the one end-user group point of view – average differences of the branch place in rankings obtained on two variants of indicator Z were between 1.1 and 2. The average value of the Spearman's correlation coefficient was 0.95.
- For the different end-users groups – in the rankings done for the same variant of the composite indicator Z – differences in branch placements were higher. Differences of the branch place in rankings were between 0.3–3.2. The average value of the Spearman's correlation coefficient was 0.90.

The latter comparison had been done for the variant 4 of the composite indicator Z. Additionally it has been found out, that the difference in the assessment results done from the point of view of manager and local politician were insignificant. The same result was visible in each from the five analyzed years (1996-2000). Average differences of the branch place in rankings obtained were between 0.3 and 0.8. The average value of the Spearman's correlation coefficient was over 0.99. It may indicate, that for the further investigations those two types of end-user (manager and local politician) may be considered jointly. The highest differences were observed between bank managers and investors. Average differences of the branch place in rankings were between 2.2 and 3.2. The average value of the Spearman's correlation coefficient was 0.86.

As an example – the comparison of the orderings results obtained according to the values of variant 4 of composite indicator Z, from the bank manager's and investor's point of view (for the year 2000) is shown in the table 2.

Performed analysis confirms necessity of the composite indicator structure differentiation with accordance to specific end-users preferences.

Code of the class	Class description	Class's place according to variant 4 ordering (banker)	Class's place according to variant 4 ordering (politician)	Place's differences (higher banker's assessment)	Place's differences (higher politician's assessment)
15.11	Production and preserving of meat	10	9		1
15.12	Production and preserving of poultry meat	14	15	1	
15.13	Production of meat and poultry meat products	9	8		1
15.20	Processing & preserving of fish & fish products	16	14		2
15.31	Processing and preserving of potatoes	19	20	1	
15.32	Manufacturing of fruit and vegetable juice	25	19		6
15.33	Processing & preserving of fruit & vegetables	22	22		
15.43	Manufacturing of margarine & similar edible fats	26	26		
15.51	Operation of dairies and cheese making	7	11	4	
15.52	Manufact. of ice cream	23	21		2
15.71	Manufacturing of prep. feeds for farm animals	6	5		1
15.81	Manufacturing of bread; manufacture of fresh pastry goods and cakes	4	7	3	
15.82	Manufacturing of rusk and biscuits; preserved pastry goods and cakes	17	24	7	
15.83	Manufacturing of sugar	15	6		9
15.84	Manufacturing of cocoa; chocolate & sugar conf.	18	17		1
15.85	Manufacturing of macaroni, noodles, couscous & similar farinac. prods	20	18		2
15.86	Process. of tea & coffee	1	1		
15.87	Manufacturing of condiments and seasonings	3	3		
15.88	Manufacturing of homogenized food preparations & dietetic food	13	2		11

Table 2. Places of classes of division 15 (*Food Industry*) in orderings obtained according to the values of variant 4 of composite indicator Z – year 2000

15.89	Manufacturing of other food products	2	4	2	
15.91	Manufacturing of distilled potable alcoholic beverages	5	10	5	
15.92	Production of ethyl alcohol fr. ferment. materials	12	12		
15.93	Manufacturing of wines	24	25	1	
15.94	Manufacturing of cider & other fruit wines	8	13	5	
15.96	Manufacturing of beer	11	16	5	
15.98	Production of mineral waters & soft drinks	21	23	2	

Table 2. Continued

References

BRIGHAM E.F. and GAPENSKI L.C. (2000): *Financial Management.* The Dryden Press, Chicago.

GNANADESIKAN R. (1997): *Methods for Statistical Data Analysis of Multivariate Observation.* 2nd ed., Wiley, New York.

KWIATKOWSKA-CIOTUCHA D. and ZALUSKA U. (2001): The Composite Indicators as an Assessment Criterion of Manufacturing Branches in Polish Economy. *Arqumenta Oeconomica, 1, 145-153.*

KWIATKOWSKA-CIOTUCHA D., ZALUSKA U., DZIECHCIARZ J. (2002): Manufacturing Branches in Poland – A Classification Attempt. In: O. Opitz and M. Schweiger (Eds.): *Explanatory Data Analysis in Empirical Research.* Springer, Heidelberg, 479-487.

TYRAN M.R. (1992): *The Vest-Pocket Guide to Business Ratio.* Prentice-Hall, New York.

Developing a Layout of a Supermarket Through Asymmetric Multidimensional Scaling and Cluster Analysis of Purchase Data

Akinori Okada[1] and Tadashi Imaizumi[2]

[1] Department of Industrial Relations, School of Social Relations,
Rikkyo (St. Paul's) University, 3-34-1 Nishi Ikebukuro,
Toshima-ku Tokyo, 171-8501 Japan
[2] Tama University, Hijirigaoka, Tama city Tokyo, 206-0022 Japan

Abstract. A layout of a supermarket, which increases the jointly purchasing items of different categories, was developed based on purchase data of more than 14,000 customers for half a year at a supermarket. Similarities among 24 categories of items sold at the supermarket were defined, for each of 12 conditions (the age of the customers, the place they live, and the day they purchased), by using (a) the proportion of the jointly purchasing items of any two categories and (b) the amount of items of categories purchased. Because differences among conditions were not significant, one layout was derived based on the similarities for all (unconditional) purchases.

1   Introduction

Items sold at a supermarket ranges over a lot of categories. This characterizes the supermarket, and differentiates it from traditional stores which sells items of only one category, for example, meat, fish or vegetable. Customers of a supermarket can purchase items of more than one category. Items of a category might be very frequently purchased when items of another category were purchased, but they might be rarely purchased when items of another different category were purchased.

Thus, it seems interesting to investigate a layout of a supermarket which promote jointly purchasing items of different categories. If the relationships of joint purchase is symmetric, a layout which simply locates items having higher possibility of joint purchase as close as possible, seems enough to promote customers to purchase items of different categories jointly.

But the possibility of purchasing items of a category when items of another category were purchased is not necessarily equal to the possibility of purchasing items of the latter category when items of the former category were purchased. The relationships of jointly purchasing two different categories are asymmetric. The idea here is to use the asymmetry of the relationships for investigating a layout of a supermarket. The purpose of the present paper is to develop a layout of a supermarket which promotes customers purchasing items earlier, which have higher possibilities of purchasing other items, and purchasing items later, which have lower possibilities of purchasing other items. In developing a layout it is necessary to know the direction of asymmetry of joint purchases. The asymmetric multidimensional scaling (MDS) and cluster analysis are utilized in the analysis.

2   The data

The purchase data at a supermarket in a small town in Kyushu (the west most island of four major islands consisting Japan) were collected for six months from April through October 2000. More than 14,000 customers, whose attributes (age and address) are known to the supermarket, purchased at the supermarket during the six months.

Then 4,488 customers were selected, who were within the upper 25% in one of three requirements; (a) the frequency of purchasing at the supermarket, (b) the amount of money purchased, and (c) the number of items purchased during the six months. The purchase data of these 4,488 customers were analyzed. The reason to analyze the data only from the selected customers is that it seems preferable to develop a layout of the supermarket for steadily customers of the supermarket. Items sold at the supermarket are classified into 25 categories. In the present study 24 categories were dealt with. The category of items to be used as gifts were eliminated, because the peculiarity of the category looks very different from that of the other categories. The 24 categories are shown in Table 1. The emboldened word(s) in Table 1 are used to represent each category in Figures 1, 2, and 3.

1 **Cosmetic**	13 Dried vegetable and **sea vegetable**
2 **Commodity**	14 **Noodle**
3 **Toiletry**	15 **Rice**
4 **Kitchen** item	16 **Munchy**
5 **Meat**	17 **Bread**
6 **Ham** and sausage	18 **Tofu**
7 **Raw fish**	19 **Fish sausage**
8 **Salted** and dried **fish**	20 **Egg**
9 **Vegetable** and fruit	21 **Frozen foods**
10 **Condiment**	22 **Dairy**
11 **Canned** and bottled **drink**	23 **Ice cream**
12 **Canned** and bottled **food**	24 **Cooked food**

Table 1. Twenty four categories.

The relationships of the joint purchase of items of different categories might be influenced by the age of customers, the place they live, and the day of the week of the purchase. Twelve conditions: (a) Age; (1) younger than 30 years old, (2) 30-39, (3) 40-49, (4) 50-59, (5) 60-69, (6) older than 69, (b) Place; (7) same zone of the supermarket, (8) same town, (9) farther areas, and (c) Day of the week; (10) weekdays, (11) Tuesday (bargain sale day), (12) weekend and holiday, were set. For each of 12 conditions, a 24×24 matrix, whose

(j, k) element represents the proportion of purchasing items of the category corresponding to column k when items of the category corresponding to row j were purchased, was derived. Each matrix was normalized to take account of the amount of purchase of each category, i.e., each row and column of the matrix was multiplied by the square root of the number of items of the corresponding category purchased (cf. DeSarbo, Manrai, and Burke (1990)). In addition to these 12 matrices, the matrix of the normalized proportion of joint purchase for all (unconditional) purchases was derived. The part of the normalized unconditional matrix is shown in Table 2, because the original matrix is too large to be shown.

Category	1	2	3	$\cdots$	14	15	$\cdots$	24
1 Cosmetic	1010.3	69.3	1276.8	$\cdots$	617.8	73.1	$\cdots$	1223.0
2 Commodity	64.1	1444.3	1012.9	$\cdots$	682.6	91.5	$\cdots$	1400.0
3 Toiletry	229.6	196.8	8284.7	$\cdots$	216.8	4587.2	$\cdots$	3533.8
$\vdots$				$\ddots$				$\vdots$
14 Noodle	112.4	134.2	1876.1	$\cdots$	11352.7	248.7	$\cdots$	4676.0
15 Rice	43.9	59.4	724.7	$\cdots$	821.8	1697.2	$\cdots$	1402.5
$\vdots$				$\ddots$				$\vdots$
24 Cooked food	147.0	181.8	2362.2	$\cdots$	3090.1	280.5	$\cdots$	23587.7

Table 2. The part of the normalized joint purchase matrix (unconditional).

3   The analysis

The set of 12 normalized proportion of joint purchase matrices or $24 \times 24 \times 12$ two-mode three-way asymmetric similarities was analyzed by the two-mode three-way asymmetric MDS (Okada and Imaizumi (1997)) in five- through unidimensional spaces. The smallest stress obtained by the analysis in five-through unidimensional spaces were 0.222, 0.243, 0.251, 0.252, and 0.296 respectively. These figures suggest adopting the two-dimensional result as the solution. In the asymmetry weight configuration of the two-dimensional result, all conditions, except for age <30, are very close to a line emitting from the origin. It seems that the model with the constraint on the asymmetry weight is appropriate to the data; the asymmetry weight for condition i on dimension t is multiplicatively decomposed into two terms, i.e., the asymmetry weight for condition i and the asymmetry weight on dimension t (Okada and Imaizumi (2000)). Two dimensional result of the analysis based on the model with the constraint yielded the smallest stress 0.267. The figure is slightly larger than that of the result obtained by the analysis based on the model without the constraint. The two-dimensional result based on the model with the constraint was adopted as the solution.

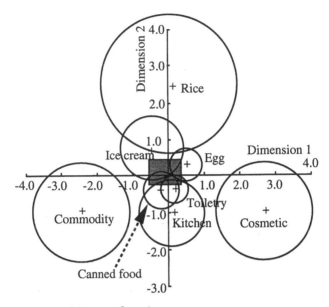

Fig. 1. The common object confiuration.
Five categories are represented as a point and a circle, and the other 19 categories
(points and cicles) are in the grey rectangular area.

The common object configuration which represents joint purchase relationships among 24 categories are shown in Figure 1. Each category is represented as a point and a circle centered at that point. Figure 1 shows that 24
categories are classified into two groups; those having the larger radius and
are located at the peripheral area of the configuration, and those having the
smaller radius and are very closely located each other at the central area.
In the present application of the asymmetric MDS, the larger radius means
that the corresponding category yields the larger tendency of purchasing the
items of other categories when the items of the corresponding category was
purchased.

Table 3 shows the asymmetry weight configuration. Because all 12 conditions,
except for age <30, have similar asymmetry weights, differences among conditions seem small. Thus the matrix of the normalized proportion of joint
purchase for all (unconditional) purchases in Table 2 was analyzed by the
asymmetric cluster analysis without the self-clustering (Okada (2000)) after
the transposition. The reason for the transposition was that the asymmetric
cluster analysis in the present study intended to construct clusters when a
category, yielding the larger tendency of purchasing the other categories, absorbed another category, yielding the smaller tendency. The analysis resulted
in the dendrogram of Figure 2. While the algorithm of the present analysis
corresponds to the mean method, the obtained dendrogram shows a complete chain. The later a category absorbs the existing cluster, the larger the

tendency of purchasing items of other categories the category yields. Categories having the larger radius are absorbed later at the clustering, which is validated by the correlation coefficient of -0.65 between the radius and the normalized proportion of joint purchase when a category was absorbed.

Condition	Dimension1	Dimension 2
1 Age <30	0.202	0.112
2 Age 30-39	1.622	0.900
3 Age 40-49	1.479	0.820
4 Age 50-59	1.479	0.820
5 Age 60-69	1.479	0.820
6 Age >69	1.479	0.820
7 Same zone	1.484	0.823
8 Same town	1.493	0.828
9 Farther areas	1.532	0.849
10 Weekdays	1.487	0.824
11 Tuesday	1.515	0.840
12 Weekend and holiday	1.495	0.829

Table 3. Asymmetry weight configuration.

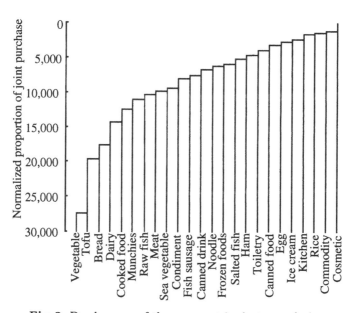

Fig. 2. Dendrogram of the asymmetric cluster analysis.

4   The result

The result obtained by using the asymmetric MDS tells that there are two groups of categories; one consists of categories yielding the larger tendency of purchasing items of the other categories, and the other consists of categories of yielding the smaller tendency of purchasing items of the other categories. The dendrogram obtained by using the asymmetric cluster analysis is consistent with the two groups, i.e., categories differ in the tendency of purchasing items of the other categories when a category was purchased.

A layout of 24 categories at the supermarket was developed which increases the normalized proportion of jointly purchasing items of two different categories. The result of the asymmetric MDS shows two groups of categories, thus we limited the development of the layout which has two shops; one shop for categories having the larger radius or absorbed at the later stages of the clustering, and the other shop for categories having the smaller radius or absorbed at the earlier stages of the clustering. Because differences among 12 conditions were small except for one condition (age <30), one layout was developed. A layout was derived by simplifying Figure 1 so that the layout has two shops. Figure 3 shows the resulting layout. One shop for categories having the larger radius is located in the peripheral area, and another shop for categories having the smaller radius is located at the center. Coordinates of categories at the former shop are given by the common object configuration shown in Figure 1, and those at the latter shop are given by their averaged coordinates of the common object configuration.

In Figure 3, five categories, featured by extremely larger radius than that the other categories have, are located in the peripheral area, and the other 19 categories and a casher are located at the center. A customer, for example comes downward, may purchase the rice category and, goes to the casher at the center. The possibility of purchasing items of the 19 categories after the

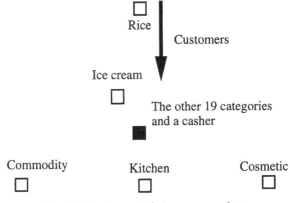

Fig. 3. The layout of the supermarket.

rice category was purchased is larger than that obtained when the customer purchased items of one of the 19 categories first and then purchase the rice category. In the former case, a customer travels the distance from the rice category to the center in order to go to the casher after one's first purchase. In the latter case a customer travels the twice of the distance in order to go to the casher after one's first purchase.

5   Discussion

A layout of a supermarket was developed based on the results obtained by the asymmetric MDS and cluster analysis. The distances among categories in the layout are not exactly but approximately monotonically decreasingly related with the observed similarities among the categories. An index was derived to evaluate the goodness of the layout using the similarities among categories. A similarity from categories j to k is defined by the proportion of purchasing items of category k when items of category j was purchased multiplied by the square root of the number of items of category j and that of category k purchased.

Let the similarity from categories j to k is larger than that from categories k to j. And suppose the customer, who wants to purchase items of a category located at the peripheral area, comes into the supermarket from the direction where the category is located. When category j is located at the peripheral area, the opportunity of purchasing items of category j first is larger than that when category j is located at the center. Purchasing items of category j leads to purchasing items of category k for the customer more than purchasing items of category k leads to purchasing items of category j, because the similarity from categories j to k is assumed to be larger than that from categories k to j. Purchasing items of category j first and then purchasing items of category k corresponds to the similarity from categories j to k which is larger than the similarity from categories k to j. Thus it seems possible to evaluate the goodness of a layout by the sum of similarities among categories.

The sum of all off diagonal elements of the original similarities of Table 2 can be regarded to show the goodness of the layout where we do not know which category is located to be purchased first more easily. When category j is moved to the peripheral area and category k is in the center, the (k, j) element of the table is replaced by the (j, k) element. If the (j, k) element is larger than the (k, j) element, the sum or the index will become larger. The index is 2,292,320 for the original data of Table 2. When the rice category is located at the peripheral area and the other 23 categories are in the center, it increased to 2,321,743. The layout of Figure 3 has the value of the index 2,429,532. Thus, the index given by the present layout increased in magnitude, suggesting the larger benefit of jointly purchasing for the supermarket than that of the original layout has.

In developing the layout we paid attention only to the radius or to the difference of two conjugate similarities, and did not consider which of the two categories induced the purchase of items of another category. If the actual order of purchases of items are known, we can utilize the order to develop the layout. The present layout also has several points to be considered; (a) it might be unpractical, because facilities for electricity and water supply are neglected, (b) it relies only on the joint purchase of items of two categories, or it ignores the possibility of the joint purchase of items of more than two categories, and (c) it cannot cope with the random purchase.

References

DESARBO, W.S., MANRAI, A.K., and BURKE, R.R. (1990): A Nonspatial Methodology for the Analysis of Two-Way Proximity Data Incorporating the Distance-Density Hypothesis. *Psychometrika, 55, 229-253.*

OKADA. A. (2000): An Asymmetric Cluster Analysis Study of Car Switching Data. In: W. Gaul, O. Opitz, and M. Schader (Eds.): *Data Analysis: Scientific Modeling and Practical Application.* Springer, Berlin, 495-504.

OKADA, A. and IMAIZUMI, T. (1997): Asymmetric Multidimensional Scaling of Two-Mode Three-Way Proximities. *Journal of Classification, 14, 195-224.*

OKADA, A. and IMAIZUMI, T. (2000): Two-Mode Three-Way Asymmetric Multidimensional Scaling with Constraints on Asymmetry. In: R. Decker and W. Gaul (Eds.): *Classification and Information Processing at the Turn of the Millennium: Scientific Modeling and Practical Application.* Springer, Berlin, 52-59.

Market Segmentation Method From the Bayesian Viewpoint

Kazuo Shigemasu[1], Takuya Ohmori[1], and Takahiro Hoshino[1]

Graduate school of Arts and Sciences,
The University of Tokyo, Tokyo, Japan

Abstract. The model of consumers' choice behavior was built from the entirely Bayesian perspective. The consumer i's choice probability of the k-th alternative $p(k|i)$ was extended by introducing the latent variables. The model is hierarchical and two additional latent variables (latent assignment variable to the latent class and latent utility variable) were introduced so that the analysis(Gibbs Sampler) should be easier and the psychological reality of the variables should be attained. The simulation study showed that the model and the analysis were appropriate.

1 Introduction

The objective of this paper is to develop a model of consumers' choice and propose a numerical procedure to analyze data based on this model. The necessary model is to describe the probability that a certain consumer "i" chooses a certain goods "k", namely; $P(k|i)$. Suppose that we have some observation about the i-th consumer, which is denoted by the $(p \times 1)$ vector x_i, and also about the attributes of the k-th goods(which is called "alternative" hereafter), denoted by the $(q \times 1)$ vector y_k.

Considering that there exist individual differences in the choice behavior, the model should take into account the individual differences but still keep the number of parameters small enough to have their stable estimates.

A good compromise is to introduce the latent classes. That is, we assume that the individual consumers are classified into one of latent classes, and the individuals in the same latent class obey essentially the same choice behavior. This can be understood as a good example of "theorem of the extension of the conversation"(Lindley,1985,p39). That is,

$$P(k|i) = \sum_{l}^{L} P(k|l)P(l|i), \qquad (1)$$

where l is the number of latent classes. Theorem of the extension of the conversation means that we introduce additional variables to make the evaluation of $P(k|i)$ easier, and more precise.

The proposed model explained in the next section follows the simple and sound probability law as Eq.1. Additional feature of the proposed model is the introduction of latent variables, which have psychometric tradition such as Law of Paired Comparison or Law of Comparative Judgment(See, e.g. Bock and Jones,1968).

The idea of Latent Class Analysis (Lazarsfeld and Henry, 1968) has been used for years for marketing research (see. e.g. Wedel and Kamakura,2000, Magidson and Vermunt, 2001, for the review of literature). A particular type of the models that is related to the proposed model in this paper is called "concomitant variable latent-class model"(Dayton and Maready, 1987). Bandeen-Roche, Miglioretti, Zeger & Rathouz(1997) proposed the ML estimation of the Dayton & Mitchell's model with some modification to the link function. Formall(1992) also proposed a logistic latent class model which make use of the covariates measuring each latent class and each category.

The proposed model is different from the previous studies in that

- The model is established in fully Bayesian way. For example, the probability of membership is given by Bayes Theorem, and need not a particular statistical model such as multinomial logit model.
- The model integrates the information about the consumer and the alternative in a coherent way
- The posterior distributions of all relevant unknown quantities(parameter, latent variables, probabilities and the like) are given numerically and accurately so that exact statistical inference should be possible.

2   Model

The model basically has the two parts; $P(l|i)$ and $P(k|l)$.

The probability $P(l|i)$ is evaluated by the following Bayes formula,

$$P(l|i) = \frac{\prod_j^J \pi_{jl}^{x_{ij}}(1 - \pi_{jl})^{1-x_{ij}}\alpha_l}{\sum_l^L \prod_j^J \pi_{jl}^{x_{ij}}(1 - \pi_{jl})^{1-x_{ij}}\alpha_l} \tag{2}$$

Assuming that the background information is given by the dummy variable x_{ij} where the α_l is the prior probability $P(l)$, and $\alpha_L(= 1 - \sum_l^{L-1}\alpha_l)$. The model for the probability $P(l|i)$ is sometimes called latent class model and this probability is expressed by a function of the parameters of $\alpha_l(l = 1, \cdots, L), \pi_{jl}(j = 1, \cdots, p; l = 1, \cdots, L)$, and the observation $x_{ij}(i = 1, \cdots, n; j = 1, \cdots, p)$.

The result of latent class assignment is denoted by z_{il}, which takes the value of 1 if the $i - th$ individual belongs to the $l - th$ class, and 0 otherwise. Of course, this variable is unobservable, but the reason why this latent dummy variable is introduced will be given when we derive the full conditional distributions.

On the other hand, the model for $P(k|i, l)$ is to depict the selection process of the alternative k among the K alternatives. One of popular models with the attribute vector y_{ik} given is multinomial logit model, but in this paper we model this probability by introducing another latent variables u_{ik}, which represents the latent preference(or utility) for the alternative k of the individual i.

Then if the consumer i chooses the k-th alternative, it is natural to regard the corresponding u_{ik} is bigger than the preferences for other alternatives $u_{ik'}(k' \neq k)$, That is $P(k|i) = P(k = argmax_{k'}(u_{ik'}))$.

We further assume the regression model for the latent variable u_{ik};

$$u_{ik} = y_k^t \beta_l + \epsilon_{ik}, \tag{3}$$

where ϵ_{ij} is identical and independent distributed as $N(0, \sigma^2)$.

Note that the structural parameter β_l is common for all individuals who belong to the latent class l.

Finally, the model for $P(k|i)$ is given as follows;

$$P(k|l) = P(u_{ik} = max_{k'}(u_{ik'}|y, \beta)) \tag{4}$$

The actual observation of the choice process is denoted by r_{ik}, which is 1 if i chooses k and 0 otherwise.

3 Modeling of the choice behavior by joint density as a hierarchical model

In this section, the model building is explained step by step as a hierarchical model. All unknown quantities and the vectors contained in this model are listed as follows;

$$\alpha_l;\ l = 1, \ldots, L; \alpha(L \times 1)$$
$$\pi_{jl};\ j = 1, \ldots, p; l = 1, \ldots, L; \pi_l(p \times 1); \pi(pL \times 1)$$
$$\beta_{jl};\ j = 1, \cdots, q; l = 1, \ldots, L; \beta_l(q\times); \beta(qL \times 1)$$
$$x_{ij}(dummy);\ i = 1, \ldots, n; j = 1, \ldots, p; x_i(p \times 1); x(np \times 1)$$
$$y_{kj};\ k = 1, \ldots, K; j = 1, \ldots, q; y_k(q \times 1); Y(K \times q)$$
$$u_{ik};\ i = 1, \ldots, n; k = 1, \ldots, K; u_i(K \times 1); u(nK \times 1)$$
$$z_{il}(dummy):\ i = 1, \ldots, n; l = 1, \ldots, L, z_i(L \times 1); z(nL \times 1), and$$
$$r_{ik}(dummy);\ i = 1, \ldots, n; k = 1, \ldots, K; r_i(K \times 1); r(nK \times 1)$$

(1)Prior Specification We need prior distributions for parameters(α, β, π and σ^2), because they are never characterized by data generation model.
(2) Data generation model of x_{ij}

$$p(x_i|\pi, \alpha) = \sum_l^L \prod_j^p \pi_{jl}^{x_{ij}}(1 - \pi_{jl})^{1-x_{ij}}\alpha_l \tag{5}$$

(3) Data generation model of latent variable z_{il}

$$p(z_{il}|x, \alpha, \beta, \pi) \tag{6}$$
$$= \prod_l p(z_{il}|x, \alpha, \beta, \pi)^{z_{il}} \tag{7}$$
$$= \prod_l \left(\frac{\prod \pi_{jl}^{x_{ij}}(1 - \pi_{jl})^{1-x_{ij}}\alpha_l}{\sum_l \prod \pi_{ij}^{x_{ij}}(1 - \pi_{jl})^{1-x_{ij}}\alpha_l}\right)^{z_{il}} \tag{8}$$

(4) Data generation model of latent variable u_{ik}

Assuming that $z_{il} = 1$, the utility vector u_i is distributed as $N_K(Y\beta_l, I_K)$,

$$p(u_i|z, x.y, \alpha, \beta, \pi) \tag{9}$$

$$= p(u_i|z_i, y_i, \beta) \tag{10}$$

$$= \prod_l^L p(u_i|z_i, y_i, \beta_l)^{z_{il}} \tag{11}$$

$$\propto \prod_l^L (\exp(-\frac{1}{2\sigma^2}(u_i - Y\beta_l)^t(u_i - Y\beta_l)))^{z_{il}} \tag{12}$$

(5) Data generation Model of r_{ik}.

First note that whether $r_{ik} = 1$ or 0 depends only on the values of u_i when they are given.

Note $P(r_{ik}|u_i) = 1$ when $r_{ik} = 1$ and $u_{ik} > u_{ik'}$ for all $k' \neq k$, and $r_{ik} = 0$, otherwise. Also, $P(r_{ik}|u_i) = 0$ for the profile u_i which is not consistent with the observed value. Let us denote the subspace of u_i which is consistent with the observed data r; $U_i \subset U$.

4   Prior distributions

Now, we have to specify the prior form for the parameters. We employ the following prior distributions.

For, α, we assume the Dirichlet distribution, with the degrees of freedom(ν_1 $\nu_2, \cdots, \nu_L$).

For π_{jl}, we assume the beta distribution with the degrees of freedom(ϕ_{jl}, $n_0 - \phi_{jl}$).

For β, we assume that the β_l are exchangeable among L classes. That is β_l is distributed as the multivariate normal with the mean vector 0 and the covariance matrix $\lambda^{-1}I$; $N_q(0, \lambda^{-1}I)$. For σ^2, we assume the inverse χ^2 distribution with the degrees of freedom μ_{σ^2} and scale parameter τ.

5 Posterior distribution of parameters with Y, x and r given

The joint posterior distribution of all quantities are defined only for $U_i, i = 1, \cdots, n$, which is as follows;

$$
\begin{aligned}
p(\alpha, \beta, \pi, u, z | Y, x, r) \propto\ & \alpha_1^{\nu_1} \cdots \alpha_L^{\nu_L} \times \exp\{-\frac{\lambda}{2}\beta_l^t \beta_l\} \\
& \times \pi_{11}^{\phi_{11}} \pi_{12}^{\phi_{12}} \cdots \pi_{pL}^{\phi_{pL}} (1 - \pi_{11})^{n_0 - \phi_{11}} \cdots (1 - \pi_{pL})^{n_0 - \phi_{pL}} \\
& \prod_j \prod_l \pi_{jl}^{z_{.l}x_{.j}} (1 - \pi_{jl})^{z_{.l} - z_{.l}x_{.j}} \alpha_l^{z_{.l}} \\
& \times \prod_i^n \prod_l (\exp\{-\frac{\sigma^2}{2}(u_i - Y\beta_l)^t(u_i - Y\beta_l)\})^{z_{il}}, \quad (13)
\end{aligned}
$$

$$
\text{where } z_{.l} = \sum_i z_{il} = n_{.l}, \text{ and } (z_{.l}x_{.j}) = \sum_{i=1}^n z_{il} x_{ij}
$$

6 Full conditional distribution

Gibbs Sampler is used to derive the posterior distribution, which needs the full conditional distributions. It is desirable for the full conditional distributions to produce random samples, easily.

We derive full conditional distributions for the parameters. That is , the following distributions are the posterior distribution of the parameters with all other quantities given.

Note that by assuming the z_{il} as realized values, the full conditional distributions needed for Gibbs Sampler belong to the standard distributions

Also note that by observing r, the distribution of u_i is truncated by U_i.

$$
\alpha \sim Dirichlet(\nu_l + z_{.l}) \quad (14)
$$

This conditional posterior distribution enjoys the natural interpretation, because the ν_l is the hypothetical prior observation of the l'th class and $n_{.l}$ is the hypothetical observations.

$$
\pi_{jl} \sim Beta(\phi_{jl} + (z_{.l}x_{.j}), n_0 + n_l - \phi_{jl} - (z_{.l}x_{.j})) \quad (15)
$$

Note that $(z_{.l}x_{.j})$ is the number of consumers who belong to the l'th class and have the attribute j.

$$
\beta_l \sim N_k((\lambda I + Y^t Y)^{-1} Y^t u_{.l}, (\lambda I + n_0(Y^t Y))^{-1}) \text{ where } u_{.l} = \frac{1}{n_l}\sum u_i \quad (16)
$$

The posterior distributions of β_l is that of Ridge-type regression model

Finaly, z_{il} is distributed as the multinomial distribution with the posterior conditional probability $P^*(l|i)$ which is given as follows;

$$
P^*(l|i) = \frac{\prod_j^J \pi_{jl}^{x_{ij}}(1 - \pi_{jl})^{1 - x_{ij}} \alpha_l \exp\{-\frac{\sigma^2}{2}(u_i - Y\beta_l)^t(u_i - Y\beta_l)\}}{\sum_l \prod_j^J \pi_{jl}^{x_{ij}}(1 - \pi_{jl})^{1 - x_{ij}} \alpha_l \exp\{-\frac{\sigma^2}{2}(u_i - Y\beta_l)^t(u_i - Y\beta_l)\}}
$$

$$(17)$$

The equation 17 is particularly interesting that the latent assignment of z_{il} depends not only the attribute x_i, but also the prediction performance.

7 Numerical algorithm

We use the following numerical algorithm to obtain the posterior distribution of relevant parameters. First, the hyperparameters(ϕ_{jl}'s and λ) should be determined.

  i) Prepare the starting values for α, β and π.
 ii) Calculate $P^*(l|i)$ using the current values of the other parameters and u.
iii) Based on the probability $P^*(l|i)$ and the uniform random number, determine the latent class to which the individual i belongs, and hence determine z_{il} .
 iv) Generate $u_{ik}, k = 1, \cdots, K$, using the current value of β.
  v) Repeat generating u_{ik}, until the generated u_{ik}'s conform to the data r_{ik}. The limit of iteration is specified(e.g. $t = 100$). If the suitable u_i is not found within this limit, stop iteration and the corresponding u_i remains unspecified and treated as missing values.
 vi) Using the simulated data u_{ik}'s, calculate the posterior distribution β with the other parameters and observations given, and generate β. Generate β based on the full conditional distribution.
vii) Generate α and π based on full conditional distributions.
viii) Go back to step 2.

8 Numerical example

We generated the simulated data, assuming $L = 3, p = 3, q = 3, K = 4$. The hyperparameters ($\phi'_{jl}s$ and λ) are set to be equal to one, so that the particular values do not influence too much estimation of parameters.

Table 1 shows the result of estimation, comparing the true values and their estimates. Fig. 1,2 and 3 show the simulated posterior distributions of $\pi_{11}, \beta_{11}, \alpha_1$. Fig. 4 and 5 show the trace of simulated runs, showing 5000 runs, discarding the first 500 runs as gwarm-inh process.

9 Further extension

The model proposed in this paper has a hierarchical structure and two latent variables. This model is so flexible that this can be extended easily to cope with the response data(e.g. "pick any" data, ranking data). The response data limit the range of the latent variable u_i. The "pick any" data are consistent with the u_i if the selected alternatives have higher values then the rest The ranking data are consistent with the u_i if the elements have the same order as the ranking data.

Also, the model can be extended to cope with the attribute vector y_k which consist of various kinds of quantitative and qualitative data. Basically, the latent class model only requires the calculation of the Bayes formula. The latent class in the model is introduced for the purpose of predictions of the choice result(r_{ik}'s). The model choice in terms of the Bayes factor can be applied to determine which number of latent classes(L) is the most appropriate. That is, $P(r, x|L)$ can be calculated numerically(e.g. by Reversible Jump Method), which optimizes L.

N=200	TRUE	ESTIMATE	S.D.
$\alpha 1$	0.5	0.5235	0.0223
$\alpha 2$	0.3	0.2932	0.0192
$\alpha 3$	0.2	0.1833	0.0188
$\beta 11$	1	1.0302	0.0692
$\beta 12$	0.5	0.5290	0.0538
$\beta 13$	-0.5	-0.5703	0.0543
$\beta 21$	-0.5	-0.5144	0.0238
$\beta 22$	1	1.0870	0.0687
$\beta 23$	0.5	0.4361	0.0238
$\beta 31$	0.5	0.4841	0.0236
$\beta 32$	-0.5	-0.6159	0.0538
$\beta 33$	1	1.1342	0.0685
$\pi 11$	0.8	0.7938	0.0396
$\pi 12$	0.4	0.3952	0.0370
$\pi 13$	0.4	0.4447	0.0347
$\pi 21$	0.4	0.3791	0.0368
$\pi 22$	0.8	0.8286	0.0402
$\pi 23$	0.4	0.4202	0.0367
$\pi 31$	0.4	0.4050	0.0330
$\pi 32$	0.4	0.4044	0.0368
$\pi 33$	0.8	0.7957	0.0401

Table 1. Estimates of parameters

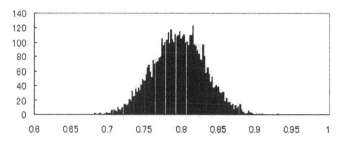

Fig. 1. Distribution of π 11

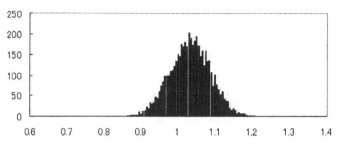

Fig. 2. Distribution of β 11

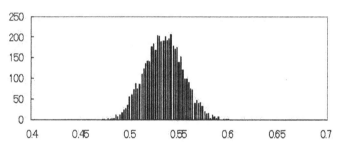

Fig. 3. Distribution of α 1

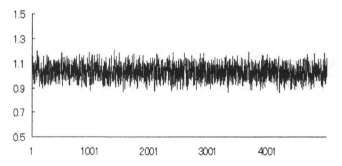

Fig. 4. The behavior of random sample sequences of β 11

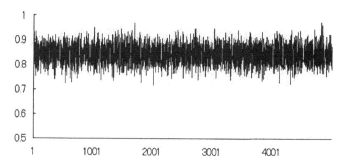

Fig. 5. The behavior of random sample sequences of π 11

References

BANDEEN-ROCHE, K., MIGLIORETTI, D.L., ZEGER, S.L. & RATHOUZ, P.J. (1997), Latent Variable Regression for Multiple Discrete Outcomes, *Journal of the American Statistical Association*, **92**, 1375–1386.

BOCK,R.D. and L.V.JONES(1968): *The Measurement and Prediction of Judgment and Choice*. Books on Demand.

DAYTON, C.M., & MACREADY, G.B. (1988), Concomitant-Variable Latent Class Models, *Journal of the American Statistical Association*, **83**, 173–178.

Formann, A.K. (1992), Linear Logistic Latent Class Analysis for Polytomous Data, *Journal of the American Statistical Association*, **87**, 476–486.

LAZARSFELD, P.F., & HENRY, N.W. (1968), *Latent Structure Analysis*. New York: Houghton-Mifflin.

LINDLEY,D.V.(1985): *Making Decisions(Second Edition)*. Wiley.

MAGIDSON,J. and J. K. VERMUNT(2001): Latent Class Factor and Cluster Models, BiPlots, and Related Graphical Displays. *Sociological Methodology 2001 Volume 31, 223–264*.

WEDEL, M. and W.KAMAKURA(2000): *Market Segmentation*. Kuwer Academic Pablishers.

Support Vector Machines for Credit Scoring: Comparing to and Combining With Some Traditional Classification Methods

Ralf Stecking and Klaus B. Schebesch

Institut für Konjunktur- und Strukturforschung,
Universität Bremen, D-28359 Bremen, Germany

Abstract. Credit scoring is being used in order to assign credit applicants to good and bad risk classes. This paper investigates the credit scoring performance of a nonstandard neural network technique: support vector machines (SVM). Using empirical data, the results of the SVM are compared with more traditional methods including linear discriminant analysis and logistic regression. Furthermore, a two-step approach is being tested: first SVM selects the most informative cases, and subsequently, these are used as inputs to linear discriminant analysis and logistic regression. Extensive experiments show that SVM outperforms the more traditional, computationally less demanding methods.

1 Introduction

Credit scoring is the formal process of determining how likely applicants are to default with their repayments (Hand and Henley (1997)). Based on experience with previous credit-granting, credit scoring methods aim at assigning credit applicants to good and bad risk classes.

Recently, support vector machines (SVM) attracted considerable interest by being well suited for treating a very general situation of data classification without prior function (separation) hypothesis. Using empirical data, the results of the SVM are compared and combined with more traditional methods including linear discriminant analysis and logistic regression.

2 Classification: Theory and applications of SVM

In classification problems patterns are generically represented as a set of N cases $\{x_i, y_i\}_{i=1}^{N}$, with input data $x_i \in \mathcal{R}^m$ and the associated class membership $y_i \in Y$. Usually, the number of distinct classes is small, e.g. $Y = \{-1, 1\}$ for "negative" (e.g. "rejection") and "positive" (e.g. "acceptance") cases.

Support vector machines (SVM) and related concepts (Vapnik (1998), Cristianini and Shawe-Taylor (2000)) enable classification of arbitrarily complex cases by shaping arbitrarily complex decision sets. SVM identify special data points from the decision sets - the support vectors - which attempt to describe the boundaries between decision sets in a parsimonious way. Overfitting is avoided by "capacity control" which implicitly penalizes the number of support vectors of the data models.

Without imposing any a priori distributional assumptions on the data except stationarity, SVM with adequate capacity control achieve a certain quality for out-of-sample performance: if support vectors are few related to the total number of cases, then misclassification rate measured in-sample is not expected to rise considerably on some out-of-sample data set (for details cf. Vapnik (1998)).

SVM starts from the notion of a linear separator for binary classes, which is associated with clear notions of model capacity and parsimony. Hard linear separation divides the input set by a hyperplane $wx + b$ into two subsets, which correspond to "negative" and "positive" cases. Parameters $w \in \mathcal{R}^m$ and $b \in \mathcal{R}$ are unknown in advance and wx denotes the dot product. Then, the following inequalities should hold for all cases $i = 1, \ldots, N$

$$\left. \begin{array}{l} wx_i + b \geq +1 \text{ if } y_i = +1 \\ wx_i + b \leq -1 \text{ if } y_i = -1 \end{array} \right\} \quad \text{or} \quad y_i(wx_i + b) - 1 \geq 0.$$

The distances of the parallel "tight" hyperplanes $wx+b = 1$ and $wx+b = -1$ from the separating hyperplane are $|1-b|/||w||$ and $|-1-b|/||w||$ respectively, with their sum $r = 2/||w||$ denoting the "margin" to be maximized (Burgess (1998)). This amounts to minimizing $||w||$, respectively the more convenient $\frac{1}{2}||w||^2$ or $\frac{1}{2}ww$, which leads to the quadratic optimization problem

$$\min_{w,b} \frac{1}{2}ww \quad \text{s.t.} \quad y_i(x_iw + b) - 1 \geq 0, \quad i = 1, \ldots, N$$

solved uniquely by w^* and b^*. The classification rule for new (out-of-sample) data x is then given by the sign of $w^*x + b^*$.

In order to allow for a certain amount of misclassification by hard margins, a soft margin linear SVM compensates inequality violation by introducing "slacks" $\zeta_i \geq 0$. The optimization problem then reads cet. par.:

$$\min_{w,b,\zeta} \frac{1}{N}\sum_{i=1}^{N}\zeta_i + \frac{1}{2}ww \quad \text{s.t.} \quad y_i(x_iw + b) \geq 1 - \zeta_i, \quad \zeta_i \geq 0, \quad i = 1, \ldots, N.$$

Arbitrary non-linear separation SVM lift the non-linear separation problem of the inputs to soft margin linear separation into a (possible infinite dimensional) feature space $\mathcal{F}$. Some (unknown) map $\phi : \mathcal{R}^m \to \mathcal{F}$ will now "encode" the inputs in feature space, which formally leads to

$$\min_{w,b,\zeta} C\sum_{i=1}^{N}\zeta_i + \frac{1}{2}ww \quad \text{s.t.} \quad y_i(\phi(x_i)w + b) \geq 1 - \zeta_i, \quad \zeta_i \geq 0, \quad i = 1, \ldots, N,$$

with $w \in \mathcal{R}^{dim(\mathcal{F})}$ now being a conform (possibly infinite dimensional) vector. A user-supplied constant $C \geq 0$ to penalizes the slack variables in feature space and thereby controls the capacity of the model. This linear separation problem in feature space has the augmented Lagrange

$$L(w, b, \zeta; \alpha, \mu) = C\sum_{i=1}^{N}\zeta_i + \frac{1}{2}ww - \sum_{i=1}^{N}\alpha_i(y_i(\phi(x_i)w + b) + \zeta_i - 1) - \sum_{i=1}^{N}\mu_i\zeta_i.$$

with dual multipliers $\alpha, \mu \in \mathcal{R}^N$ and $\alpha_i, \mu_i \geq 0$, for all $i = 1, \ldots, N$. The optimality condition for $L(w, b, \zeta; \alpha, \mu) \to MIN$ read in part

$$\partial L/\partial w_k = 0 \rightsquigarrow w_k = \sum_{i=1}^{N}\alpha_i y_i \phi_k(x_i), \quad k = 1, \ldots, dim(\mathcal{F}) \qquad \text{(c1)}$$

$$\partial L/\partial b = 0 \rightsquigarrow \sum_{i=1}^{N}\alpha_i y_i = 0 \qquad \text{(c2)}$$

$$\partial L/\partial \zeta_i = 0 \rightsquigarrow C - \alpha_i - \mu_i = 0 \rightsquigarrow C \geq \alpha_i \geq 0, \quad i = 1, \ldots, N \quad \text{(c3)}.$$

Using (c1) we read $w = \sum_{i=1}^{N}\alpha_i y_i \phi(x_i)$ and rearrange terms to simplify L into

$$L'(b, \zeta; \alpha, \mu) = C\sum_{i=1}^{N}\zeta_i \underbrace{- \sum_{i=1}^{N}\alpha_i\zeta_i - \sum_{i=1}^{N}\mu_i\zeta_i}_{=0} + \underbrace{b\sum_{i=1}^{N}\alpha_i y_i}_{=0} -$$

$$\underbrace{-\frac{1}{2}\sum_{i=1}^{N}\sum_{j=1}^{N}\alpha_i\alpha_j y_i y_j \phi(x_i)\phi(x_j)}_{\equiv \frac{1}{2}ww-ww} + \sum_{i=1}^{N}\alpha_i.$$

In the optimum, the first underbraced term vanishes because of condition (c3), and the second term vanishes owing to condition (c2). Thus, the feature space and the map ϕ may be defined implicitly by the more accessible kernel functions $k(u, v) \equiv \phi(u)\phi(v)$, with u, v points from input space. Examples of kernels are polynomial dot products $(uv)^d$, $d \geq 1$, radial basis functions (RBF) $\exp(-||u - v||^2/s)$, $s > 0$, and others (Vapnik (1998), Schölkopf et al. (1998)) for general $k(u, v)$ inducing dot products. From L', c2 and c3 the dual optimization problem using kernels is

$$\max_{\alpha} \sum_{i=1}^{N}\alpha_i - \frac{1}{2}\sum_{i=1}^{N}\sum_{j\neq i}\alpha_i\alpha_j y_i y_j k(x_i, x_j) \quad \text{s.t.} \quad \begin{cases} \sum_{i=1}^{N}y_i\alpha_i = 0, \\ C \geq \alpha_i \geq 0, \quad i = 1, \ldots, N. \end{cases}$$

A dual variable α_i is positive if the ith constraint in the primal is strictly fulfilled. Owing to the simplicity of the primal restriction system $\alpha_i > 0$ means data point x_i is on the boundary of a decision set and hence is a support vector. After solving the optimization problem for α^*, the optimal offset b^* can be readily calculated from any binding constraint. The classification rule for new data x is now given by the sign of $\sum_{i=1}^{N}\alpha_i^* y_i k(x, x_i) + b^*$.

Suitable capacity control and prior or adaptive kernel selection can be vital for model performance. In case of RBF-kernels the latter resumes to selecting an appropriate width $s > 0$. Owing to their flexible localization properties and to the fact that $k(x, x) = 1$ for all x, RBF kernels seem least "pathological" and well suited as prior in case of credit scoring applications. In the context of SVM with RBF-kernels multiple cross-validation to set C and s seems to result in most faithful estimation of generalization error (Duan et al. (2001)). Furthermore, prior knowledge can be easily introduced into RBF-kernels, e.g. by restricting the domain of the dot products (Zien et al. (2000)). For the computation of credit class assignments we therefore use SVM with RBF-kernels.

3 Credit scoring: Experimental design

Credit scoring data

The data set used is provided by a German building and loan association. It consists of 658 cases (credit applicants) and 17 variables.

- **One** target variable (credit worthiness, $1 =$ "defaulting", $-1 =$ "non defaulting"). The number of defaulting and non defaulting applicants is of nearly equal size (323 "defaulting" against 335 "non defaulting"). The target population, of which this sample is taken, consists of 17158 credit applicants. The true rate of defaulting applicants out of all applicants amounts to 6.7%.
- **Seven** metric predicting variables. For standardization purpose from each of them the mean is subtracted and subsequently divided by its standard deviation.
- **Nine** categorical predicting variables. One of them is dichotomous. The others consist of three to seven categories. Each of them was recoded into $c - 1$ dummy variables (where c is the number of categories and a dummy is a variable containing only zero and one). Thus, 41–dimensional input patterns are presented to the data models.

Credit scoring models

To compare the results of the SVM to more traditional methods and to model combinations the following experimental design was chosen. The whole data set is divided into ten equally sized intervals at random. Subsequently, each interval is being used as an out–of–sample validation set for the model that was generated using the remaining nine intervals as a training set. By repeating this ten fold the whole data set is being used as an out–of–sample validation set. The following models are compared in the sequel:

i) Support vector machine (SVM),
ii) Linear discriminant analysis (LDA),

iii) Logistic regression (LR),

iv) Linear discriminant analysis using support vectors (SV–LDA) and

v) Logistic regression using support vectors (SV–LR).

Linear discriminant analysis and logistic regression are two of the most common approaches to the classification step in credit scoring (Hand and Henley (1997), Mays (2001), Thomas (2000)). They are used as a benchmark for the SVM. Furthermore, two combined approaches are being tested: SV–LDA and SV–LR.

The classification rule of the SVM (see dual problem above) is given by the sign of $S = \sum_{i=1}^{N} y_i \alpha_i^* k(x, x_i) + b^*$, with $y_i = \{-1, 1\}$ for non defaulting and defaulting credit applicants. As mentioned above $\alpha_i^* > 0$ are the dual variables indicating that the training pattern x_i is a support vector. To avoid overfitting, the α_i are bound by some constant C. The chosen kernel is the radial basis function (RBF) defined as $k(x, x_i) = \exp\left(-\|x - x_i\|^2 / 2\sigma^2\right)$. Consequently, just two hyperparameters need to be chosen: the kernel width σ and the penalty C. There are several ad hoc rules for initializing the width σ, usually depending on some sort of distance function between the training patterns (Brown et al. (1999)). For final adjustment K–fold cross validation is known to be most effective in determining σ and C. Starting with "infinite C" (the hard margin case), for different σ tenfold cross validation is used. Subsequently σ is held constant and variations of C are being tested (starting with C slightly smaller than the largest α_i) using tenfold cross validation once again. Finally, this alternating multistep process has lead to $\sigma = 0.05$ and to $C = 5$.

The model of the LDA is given by a linear combination of the predicting variables $\hat{y} = \sum_{j=1}^{K} b_0 + b_j x_j$, where x_j is the j-th predicting variable and b_j is the linear coefficient, respectively. With proper adjustments the classification rule is given by the sign of $\hat{y}$. It can be shown that determining the vector of linear coefficients b is equivalent to solving an Eigenvalue problem (Backhaus et al. (2000)).

Logistic regression is defined as $\ln(p/(1-p)) = \sum_{j=1}^{K} \beta_0 + \beta_j x_j$, where p is the probability that y assumes the label "default". Determining the linear coefficients β is done by maximizing a likelihood function. Probability p can be seen as a *latent default probability* given the predicting variables x. So logistic regression replaces discrete class membership with the latent class probability. Usually a critical value of $p = 50\%$ decides whether a credit applicant is "defaulting" or "non defaulting".

Using support vectors as inputs for LDA and LR

Usually, support vectors are a small subset of the training data. Besides determining the margin of the separating hyperplane in feature space support vectors represent the most informative patterns (Evgeniou et al. (2002)). For out–of–sample classification only the support vectors need to be stored. Non support vectors can be discarded without any loss of information. Therefore, by building an SVM, the whole data set is divided into two groups:

- support vectors as *critical* examples on the boundary between "defaulting" and "non defaulting" credit applicants, and
- non support vectors as *typical* examples, the classification of which is trivial.

First, in a combined approach the capacity of the SVM to select the most critical and therefore most informative training examples is used as input filtering. Subsequently, these cases are used as inputs for LDA and LR. SV–LDA and SV–LR are then estimated in the standard way via LDA and LR, using the support vectors identified by the SVM. One could expect this to be an enhancement for the more traditional and simple methods used by practitioners.

4   Results

Tenfold cross validation results

Table 1 shows the credit scoring results for each model after tenfold cross validation. The second column ("good rejected") is the number of non defaulting applicants that were taken for "bad" by mistake. The third column ("bad accepted") is the number of defaulting applicants that were taken for "good", respectively. Column 4 and 5 ("bad rejected" and "good accepted") are the ones that were classified correctly. Column 2 and 5 sum up to the number of non defaulting credit applicants (355), column 3 and 4 to the number of defaulting credit applicants (323).

	Tenfold Cross Validation				
Model	Good rejected	Bad accepted	Bad rejected	Good accepted	Error Rate
SVM	80	91	232	255	26.0 %
LDA	98	84	239	237	27.7 %
LR	93	88	235	242	27.5 %
SV–LDA	96	92	231	239	28.6 %
SV–LR	96	91	232	239	28.4 %

Table 1. Credit scoring model error and error rate.

Finally, the last column is the error rate. It is the total number of misclassified ("good rejected" and "bad accepted") relative to the total number of applicants. The error rate of the SVM e. g. is $(80 + 91)/658 = 26,0\%$. It is the lowest error rate. Both traditional methods (LDA and LR) yield higher error rates. Contrary to expectations there was no overall success of the combined approach although inspection suggests that there exist many cases with combined approaches superior to the solutions of the simpler models.

Table 1 shows no overwhelming superiority of SVM in terms of error rate, but for this problem class, even small improvements might vastly reduce misclassification costs.

The observed inferior performance of the combined approaches is one of three possible outcomes, namely superior, intermediate and inferior performance related to the basic models. In the present case we suspect the support vectors to shape a subset which, submitted to simpler models, does not contain the mass information needed by these models to properly separate the full data set (good and bad credit applicants). In case of intermediate performance (as would be expected by practitioners) mass information of the full data set biases the classification function of the simpler models away from the true boundary (between good and bad applicants). Superior performance of the combined approach indicates a badly parametrized SVM.

Cost of misclassification

To derive an estimation of the real cost of misclassification one has to consider at least two aspects: the prior probability of default and the unequal costs of the two types of misclassification. Fortunately, there are detailed informations about the target data from which our sample is taken. Out of 17158 applicants to whom credit was granted, 1149 defaulted, the empirical "bad" rate being about 6.7%. In order to introduce costs of misclassification it is assumed, that a "bad accepted" produces much higher costs than a "good rejected", because there is a chance to lose the whole amount of credit while accepting a "bad" and only losing the interest payments while rejecting a "good". According to the building and loan association a relation of costs between "bad accepted" and "good rejected" of 5 : 1 is adequate.

	Tenfold Cross Validation (Weighted)				
Model	Good rejected	Bad accepted	Bad rejected	Good accepted	Cost
SVM	3823	324	825	12186	5442
LDA	4683	299	850	11326	6177
LR	4444	313	836	11565	6009
SV–LDA	4588	327	822	11421	6224
SV–LR	4588	324	825	11421	6206

Table 2. (Weighted) Credit scoring model error and cost of misclassification.

In table 2 the unbalanced proportion of defaulting applicants is considered as well as the asymmetric costs of misclassification. Table 2 exhibits the weighted results from table 1. Column 2 and 5 (the non defaulting applicants) were weighted with $16009/355 = 47.79$. Column 3 and 4 (the defaulting applicants) were weighted with $1149/323 = 3.56$. The 3823 "rejected good" from table 2 thus correspond to 80 ("good rejected" from table 1) multiplied with the weight of 47.79. The total costs of misclassification are now computed by:

$$\text{Cost} = \text{Good rejected} + 5 * \text{Bad accepted}$$

The costs are shown in the last column of table 2. It is evident that SVM again is the most attractive model with the lowest costs. Both traditional models LDA and LR yield higher costs. The combined approaches SV–LDA and SV–LR again are the worst models with the highest costs of misclassification.

5   Conclusion and outlook

This paper shows that SVM is well suited for credit scoring. SVM yields lower error rates and lower costs of misclassification than the more traditional methods LDA and LR. The combined approach however did not succeed in the reported results, however instances were observed in which model combinations are indeed superior to the respective traditional model. Further research is needed. Perhaps other kernel functions than RBF or modified RBF are still better for the purpose of input filtering.

Future research will also include adjustment of the SVM to non standard situations, e.g. to consider that the target population does not have the same proportion of credit worthiness as the sampling population and that different types of misclassification lead to different costs. Algorithms for the SVM in non standard situations can be found in Lin et al. (2002).

Furthermore it might be useful to derive class probabilities from the discrete class membership resulting from the SVM. Subsequently, these "probabilities of default" may establish the substructure of a more sophisticated scoring system. The derivation of posterior probabilities from discrete SVM output is treated in Kwok (1999).

References

BACKHAUS, K., ERICHSON, B., PLINKE, W. and WEIBER, R. (2000): *Multivariate Analysemethoden, 9. Auflage.* Springer, Berlin.

BROWN, P.S., GRUNDY, W.N., LIN, D., CRISTIANINI, N., SUGNET, C., ARES, M., HAUSSLER, D. (1999): Support Vector Machine Classification of Microarray Gene Expression Data. *UCSC-CRL-99-09, Department of Computer Science, University of California, Santa Cruz.*

BURGESS, C. (1998): A Tutorial on Support Vector Machines for Pattern Recognition. *Data Mining and Knowledge Discovery, 2, 121–167.*

CRISTIANINI, N. and SHAWE-TAYLOR, J. (2000): *Support Vector Machines.* Cambridge University Press, Cambridge.

DUAN, K., KEERTHI, S.S. and POO, A.N.R. (2000): An Empirical Evaluation of Simple Performance Measures for Tuning SVM Hyperparameters. *Dept. Mechan. Engineering, National University of Singapore.* http://guppy.mpe.nus.edu.sg/~mpessk/publications

EVGENIOU, T., POGGIO, T., PONTIL, M., VERRI, A. (2002): Regularization and statistical learning theory for data analysis. *Computational Statistics & Data Analysis, 38, 421-432.*

HAND, D.J. and HENLEY, W.E. (1997): Statistical Classification Methods in Consumer Credit Scoring: a Review. *Journal of the Royal Statistical Society A, 160 Part 3, 523-541.*

KWOK, J.T. (1999): Moderating the Outputs of Support Vector Machine Classifiers. *IEEE Transactions on Neural Networks, 10, 5, 1018-1031.*

LIN, Y., LEE, Y. and WAHBA, G. (2002): Support Vector Machines for Classification in Nonstandard Situations. *Machine Learning, 46, 1-3, 191-202.*

MAYS, E. (Ed.) (2001): *Handbook of Credit Scoring.* Glenlake Publishing, Chicago.

SCHÖLKOPF, B., SMOLA, A., MÜLLER, K.-R., BURGESS, C. and VAPNIK, V. (1998): Support Vector Methods in Learning and Feature Extraction. http://citeseer.uj.nec.com/36943.html

THOMAS, L.C. (2000): A survey of credit and behavioural scoring: forecasting financial risk of lending to consumers. *International Journal of Forecasting, 16, 149-172.*

VAPNIK, V. (1998): *Statistical Learning Theory.* Wiley, New York.

ZIEN, A., RÄTSCH, G., MIKA, S., SCHÖLKOPF, B., LENGAUER, T. and MÜLLER, K.-R. (2000): Engineering Support Vector Machine Kernels That Recognize Translation Invariant Sites. *Bioinformatics 16, 9, 799-807.*

Part V

Biology, Archaeology, and Medicine

Classification of Amino-Acid Sequences Using State-Space Models

Marcus Brunnert, Tillmann Krahnke, and Wolfgang Urfer

Fachbereich Statistik,
Universität Dortmund, D-44221 Dortmund, Germany

Abstract. The secondary structure classification of amino-acid sequences can be carried out by a statistical analysis of sequence and structure data using state-space models. Aiming at this classification, a modified filter algorithm programmed in S is applied to data of three proteins. The structures of Ubiquitin, Raf and RalGEF are similar according to results of experimental methods (Wittinghofer and Waldmann, 2000). The application leads to correct classifications of Raf and RalGEF even when using relatively simple estimation methods for the parameters of the state-space models. Considering the experimental results, the secondary structure data of these two proteins used for estimating the state-space models yield a correct classification of the underlying amino-acid sequences. Furthermore, it has been shown that the assumed initial distributions strongly influence the classification results referring to two proteins.

1 Introduction

In molecular biology the analysis of proteins according to their structure and function is essential to understand any organism. Proteins are built as long linear chains of several chemical components. Among these are the 20 amino-acids. The structure of a protein can be described by the principal concept of the primary structure (amino-acid sequence), the secondary structure (α–helix or β–sheet structures) and the tertiary structure (folded secondary structure). In this context, the classification of proteins into different secondary and tertiary structures enables the molecular biologist to draw conclusions about the function of the protein.

Two approaches commonly used for the empirical classification are the *hidden Markov models* (HMMs) and *discrete state–space models* (Bienkowska et al. (2000), Stultz et al. (1993) and White et al. (1994)). These statistical approaches are also important tools in many other molecular biological problems like the protein fold recognition problem (Bienkowska et al. (2000)) or DNA sequence analysis (Urfer (2001)). Here, we model the secondary structure aiming at discrete state-space models by using the structural information from the RCSB-databank. The advantage of this secondary structure modelling is that very rare secondary structures can be considered in discrete state-space models. There is only a single structure needed to build the model instead of training sets (He et al., 2002). In order to apply for example the Viterbi-, forward- or backward-algorithm (Krogh et al., 1994) the parameters in an HMM have to be estimated first from training sets. This makes it more difficult in HMMs to consider very rare protein structures.

In the project we describe here, the discrete state–space model was applied to a secondary structure classification. The statistical model is described in Section 2, followed by the description of the likelihood computation used as a classification criterion in Section 3. The following Section 4 contains the stochastic modelling of six proteins that belong to the Ubiquitin-like folded family (SCOP-databank- http://scop.mrc-lmb.cam.ac.uk/scop/ Murzin et al. (1995)). Empirical results of an application to these proteins are presented in Section 5. The software package S-plus (MathSoft (2000)) was used to implement the modified filter algorithm. Finally, Section 6 discusses the statistical method and the results of the application.

2   State-space model

Considering the primary sequence of amino–acid residues, the correspondence between the amino–acids on the primary sequence and the amino-acids on the secondary structure can be thought of as a Markov chain. As a result of this, the stochastic output of an observable amino-acid y_t at the residue position $t=1,2,3...$ depends on the unobservable current state x_t at this residue position. The state describes the underlying secondary structure at this residue position. Additionaly, the current state depends on the realized past state x_{t-1}. Assuming these stochastic characteristics hold true, a discrete state–space model can be defined as follows:

$$y_t = Hx_t \tag{1}$$

$$x_{t+1} = \Phi x_t \tag{2}$$

In contrast to a Gaussian state–space model, the output variables y_t and the state variables x_t, $t=1,2,3...$, of this categorical state-space model are only discrete random variables taking values in finite sets. Moreover, the output probability matrix H and the state transition matrix Φ are only arrays of conditional probability distributions. Each column of the matrices is conditioned on a specific state. Let denote a state–space by $S=\{1,2,...,n\}$, where $x_t \in S$ and an output set $A=\{1,2,...,m\}$, where $y_t \in A$. The elements of the $(m \times n)$–output probability matrix H are

$$H(k,j) = P(y_t = k|x_t = j), k = 1, 2, \ldots, m, j = 1, 2, \ldots, n \tag{3}$$

and the elements of the $(n \times n)$-state transition matrix are

$$\Phi(i,j) = P(x_{t+1} = i|x_t = j), i, j = 1, 2, \ldots, n. \tag{4}$$

The distribution of one state x_t to a residue t is denoted by

$$x_t = \begin{pmatrix} P(x_t = 1) \\ P(x_t = 2) \\ \vdots \\ P(x_t = n) \end{pmatrix} \tag{5}$$

and the output probability distribution at residue position t is denoted by

$$y_t = \begin{pmatrix} P(y_t = 1) \\ P(y_t = 2) \\ \vdots \\ P(y_t = m) \end{pmatrix}. \tag{6}$$

The sequence $(x_t)_{t=1,2,3,\dots}$ can be interpreted as a Markov chain of order 1. The sequence $(y_t)_{t=1,2,3,\dots}$ can be interpreted as a semi–Markov process, where the transition from y_t to y_{t+1} depends only on x_t and not on y_t. Since $(x_t)_{t\in S}$ is not observable, the stochastic processes $((x_t)_{t=1,2,3,\dots}, (y_t)_{t=1,2,3,\dots})$ can be interpreted as a hidden Markov model (Rabiner (1989)). Summing up, a state–space model for a specific protein structure with an initial state distribution x_1 is completely described by five parameters: $\mathcal{M} = (m, n, \Phi, H, x_1)$.

3 Statistical analysis

For the secondary structure classification problem here, a categorical filter has to be applied. Aiming at the filtering of a primary sequence, the model parameters have to be known or they have to be estimated according to data on the protein structure. A re-estimation method for these parameters using the EM–algorithm (Dempster et al. (1977)) is described in Sousa et al. (2001). The following filtering algorithm is adapted from White et al. (1994):

Input	:	Model $\mathcal{M} = (m, n, \Phi, H, x_1)$	
		and $Y_d = (y_1, y_2, \dots, y_d)$.	
Initialization	:	$x_1^- = x_1$	(7)
Recursion for $1 \leq t \leq d$:			
State update	:	$y_t^- = H x_1^-$	(8)
		$\nu_t = H[y_t = k]^T * x_t^-$	(9)
		$l = \sum_{j=1}^{n} \nu_t(j)$	(10)
		$x_t^+ = \dfrac{\nu_t}{l}$	(11)
State propagate	:	$x_{t+1}^- = \Phi x_t^+.$	(12)
Termination $t=d$.			

The notation $*$ denotes the Hadamard (elementwise) product of two matrices. In addition, $H[y_t = k]$ is the vector of the kth row of the $(m \times n)$-output probability matrix H, while y_t is the vector of the conditional distribution of the current observation $y_t = k$, $k \in A$, at the sequence position t, given all past observations $Y_{t-1} = (y_1, y_2, \ldots, y_{t-1})$, i.e.,

$$
y_t^- = \begin{pmatrix} P(y_t = 1|Y_{t-1}) \\ P(y_t = 2|Y_{t-1}) \\ \vdots \\ P(y_t = m|Y_{t-1}) \end{pmatrix}.
\tag{13}
$$

For the current state x_t, the vector x_t^- is analogously defined as

$$
x_t^- = \begin{pmatrix} P(x_t = 1|Y_{t-1}) \\ P(x_t = 2|Y_{t-1}) \\ \vdots \\ P(x_t = n|Y_{t-1}) \end{pmatrix}.
\tag{14}
$$

The conditional distribution of the current state x_t, given all past and present observations is denoted by:

$$
x_t^+ = \begin{pmatrix} P(x_t = 1|Y_t) \\ P(x_t = 2|Y_t) \\ \vdots \\ P(x_t = m|Y_t) \end{pmatrix}.
\tag{15}
$$

The classification of a protein structure can be connected with the search for the most probable model for a primary sequence. Given a primary sequence Y_d and a model $\mathcal{M}$, the computation of the probability that the sequence Y_d is generated by the model $\mathcal{M}$ enables the search for the most probable model. For that reason, the computation of the likelihood $L(Y_d \mid \mathcal{M}_l)$ due to several models $\mathcal{M}_1, \ldots, \mathcal{M}_q$ enables the classification of the primary sequence to q protein structures. Here, the likelihood $L(Y_d \mid \mathcal{M}_l)$ is as follows:

$$
L(Y_d \mid \mathcal{M}_l) = P(Y_d \mid \mathcal{M}_l) = P(y_1) \prod_{t=2}^{d} P(y_t \mid Y_{t-1})
\tag{16}
$$

Considering the output of the filtering algorithm in Section 3, the log-likelihood can be calculated recursively as follows:

$$
\log L(0) = 0 \text{ and} \tag{17}
$$
$$
\log L(t) = \log L(t-1) + \log P(y_t \mid y_{t-1}), \textit{ for } t=1,\ldots,d. \tag{18}
$$

Next, this log-likelihood calculation was applied to classify an amino-acid into structural hypothesis $\{\mathcal{M}_l\}_{l=1}^{q}$. In this context a classification criterion up to a sequence position t is denoted by the difference,

$$
u_t^{(l)} = \log L(Y_t|\mathcal{M}_{reference}) - \log L(Y_t|\mathcal{M}_l), l = 1,\ldots,q, t = 1,\ldots,d, \tag{19}
$$

where $\mathcal{M}_{reference}$ is the reference state-space model according to the amino-acid sequence to be analysed.

4   Modelling the secondary structure with state-space models

The protein structure is built in an hierarchical fashion using the three basic modelling structures: α-helix, β-strand and an "other" or random structure that is neither an α-helix nor a β-strand. These basic structures are put together to larger secondary structures called *plexes*. Two basic structures are linked together at "junctions". These junctions are silent states with no output. For simplicity, only one plex is used here: the β-sheet containing two β-strands and one additional state. This additional state contains only one residue (amino-acid) and therefore no basic modelling is needed.

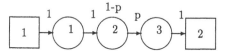

Fig. 1. Schematic modelling of the α-helix.

As we consider here a minimal length of an α-helix of three residues, the transition matrices referring to Figure 1 are given

$$\phi_{ss} = \begin{pmatrix} 0 & 0 & 0 \\ 1 & 1-p & 0 \\ 0 & p & 0 \end{pmatrix}, \phi_{sj} = \begin{pmatrix} 1 & 0 \\ 0 & 0 \\ 0 & 0 \end{pmatrix}, \phi_{js} = \begin{pmatrix} 0 & 0 & 0 \\ 0 & 0 & 1 \end{pmatrix} \text{ and } \phi_{jj} = \begin{pmatrix} 0 & 0 \\ 0 & 0 \end{pmatrix},$$

where ϕ_{ss}, ϕ_{sj}, ϕ_{js} and ϕ_{jj} denote the state-to-state transition matrix, the junction-to-state transition matrix, the state-to-junction matrix and the junction-to-junction matrix. Note, that the sum of some columns is 0 with respect to forbidden transitions.

Considering Figure 2, we get the following transition matrices for a β-strand,

$$\phi_{ss} = \begin{pmatrix} 1-p & 0 \\ p & 0 \end{pmatrix}, \phi_{sj} = \begin{pmatrix} 1 & 0 \\ 0 & 0 \end{pmatrix}, \phi_{js} = \begin{pmatrix} 0 & 0 \\ 0 & 1 \end{pmatrix} \text{ and } \phi_{jj} = \begin{pmatrix} 0 & 0 \\ 0 & 0 \end{pmatrix}.$$

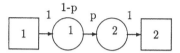

Fig. 2. Schematic modelling of the β-strand.

The stochastic modelling of the random structure is shown in Figure 3. The transition matrices for a random structure with a minimal length of 1 is given by,

$$\phi_{jj} = \begin{pmatrix} 0 & 0 \\ 0 & 0 \end{pmatrix}, \phi_{sj} = \begin{pmatrix} 1 & 0 \end{pmatrix}, \phi_{js} = \begin{pmatrix} 0 \\ p \end{pmatrix} \text{ and } \phi_{ss} = \begin{pmatrix} 1-p \end{pmatrix}.$$

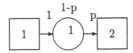

Fig. 3. Schematic modelling of the random structure.

The next hierarchical level in the state modelling describes combinations of basic structures. The plex described here, links two β-strands at an additional state. Contrary to a junction state, the additional state is not silent and yields an output. Connecting the two basic structures β-strand by an additional

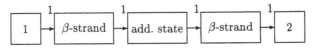

Fig. 4. Schematic modelling of the β-sheet plex.

state (cf. Figure 4) with one output yields the following transition matrices,

$$\phi_{ss} = \begin{pmatrix} 0\,0\,0 \\ 1\,0\,0 \\ 0\,1\,0 \end{pmatrix}, \phi_{sj} = \begin{pmatrix} 1\,0 \\ 0\,0 \\ 0\,0 \end{pmatrix}, \phi_{js} = \begin{pmatrix} 0\,0\,1 \\ 0\,0\,0 \end{pmatrix} \text{ and } \phi_{jj} = \begin{pmatrix} 0\,0 \\ 0\,0 \end{pmatrix}.$$

Now, the basic structures and plexes have to be put together to models for protein structures according to the application in Section 5. The corresponding transition probabilities are presented here for each state transition. Considering uniform transition probabilities for admissible (or allowed) basic structure transitions, one obtains the transition matrix,

$$\hat{\Phi}_1 = \begin{pmatrix} 0\,0 & 1/3\,0 & 0\,0\,0 & 0\,1/3 \\ 1\,0.6\,0 & 0 & 0\,0\,0 & 0\,0 \\ 0\,0.4\,0 & 0 & 0\,0\,0 & 0\,0 \\ 0\,0 & 1/3\,0.6\,0\,0\,0 & 0\,1/3 \\ 0\,0 & 0 & 0.4\,0\,0\,0 & 0\,0 \\ 0\,0 & 0 & 0 & 1\,0\,0 & 0\,0 \\ 0\,0 & 0 & 0 & 0\,1\,1/2\,0\,0 \\ 0\,0 & 0 & 0 & 0\,0\,1/2\,0\,0 \\ 0\,0 & 1/3\,0 & 0\,0\,0 & 1\,1/3 \end{pmatrix}$$

for the states referring to Raf, RalGEF, Rfl, Rgl and $P_i(3)$-kinase. The uncertainty of transitions within basic structures are assumed by $p=0.4$. Supplementary to the nine modelled states of these state-space models referring to these proteins, the state-space-model referring to Ubiquitin has to consider an extra state according to the RCSB-databank. For that reason, the transition matrix for the structure model of Ubiquitin is defined analogously to Φ_1 with respect to an extra column.

5   Application

In an application, a modified filtering algorithm is applied to the primary and secondary structure data of domains of the Ubiquitin-like folded proteins RalGEF, Raf, Rlf, Rgl, $P_i(3)$-kinase and Ubiquitin (sequence and structure data from the RCSB protein data bank; id no(s). 1lxdB, 1guaB, 1rlf, 1ef5, 1he8B, 1ubi). The state update in the filtering algorithm is modified according to the admissible transitions in the secondary structure (see Figures 1-4). For example, an inadmissible state transition in the α-helix structure (see Figure 1) is the transition from state 1 to state 3. Formally, the state update (8) to (11) of the last section is modified as follows:

$$\nu_t^{admissible} = x_t^- e_j, \tag{20}$$

$$l = \sum_{j=1}^{n} \nu_t^{admissible}(j), \text{ and} \tag{21}$$

$$x_t^+ = \frac{\nu_t^{admissible}}{l}, \text{ where} \tag{22}$$

e_j is the $(n \times 1)$-unit vector and j is the state number according to the highest probability in x_t^-. This modified filtering algorithm has been implemented in S-plus. Two different distributions for the initial states were assumed, on the one hand the uniform distribution and on the other hand the one point distribution.

Three methods for the estimation of the output probability matrices according to each of the models have been applied. These are:

1. Computation of relative frequencies of the occurrence of amino-acids given a state.

2. Consideration of pseudocounts using Laplace's rule (Durbin et al., 1998).

3. Consideration of pseudocounts using the following estimator (Durbin et al., 1998):

$$\widehat{H(k,j)} = \frac{c_{k,j} + 20p_{k,j}}{\sum_{k'} c_{k',j} + 20}, where \tag{23}$$

$c_{k,j}$ is the number of occurrences of amino-acid k given state j. The output probability $p_{k,j}$ referring to amino acid k given state j is estimated by using the relative frequency of the occurence of amino acid k given state j according to the data of all six proteins.

Figure (5) demonstrates the course of $u_t^{(l)}$ for the Raf sequence, starting with the first observed residue $t=1$. The H matrix was estimated by method 2. A positive classification criterion indicates a less probable structure than the reference structure. If we consider the positive values in this figure belonging to the false structure models, the Raf sequence is classified correctly in its modelled secondary structure (reference state-space model). After filtering the whole sequence, the estimation methods (1-3) according to the emission probabilities do not influence the resulting lowest logarithmic likelihood

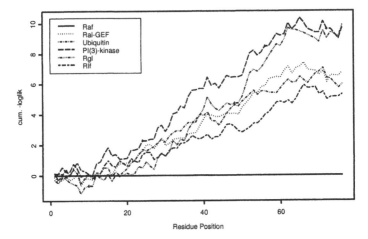

Fig. 5. Differences of negative log-likelihoods referring to the Raf-sequence.

(Figures concerning method 1 and 3 are not shown). A graphical analysis analogous to the last figures for all six models with a fixed initial state for all six models has been carried out by using the one point distribution for the initial states (Figures not shown). In this graphical analysis the classification of the Raf sequence and the Ral sequence has been influenced by the choice of the initial state. The Ubiquitin sequence classification was not influenced by the choice of an initial distribution.

6   Discussion

In this paper a modified filter algorithm was applied to sequence and structure protein data in order to classify six amino-acid sequences each consisting of about 100 residues according to their secondary structures. The application demonstrated that the choice of the initial distribution influenced the classification results. Further applications of this filtering algorithm should consider this kind of influence in order to avoid false classification. In this context, the iterative applications of this filtering algorithm is of interest and will be investigated in further analyses. The estimations of the H matrices were done by a simple computation of relative frequencies. The transitions concerning the state transitions from basic to plex structures was modelled by using an uniform distribution. Therefore, only low information about these transitions was considered. For that reason, the estimation methods can be improved by the application of the EM-algorithm. Nevertheless, the results for the Raf and the RalGEF sequence demonstrated that the state-space modelling is appropriate for the secondary structure classification even for a small number of observation and simple estimation methods. An application to whole protein sequence or structure families will aim at a further validation of this classification model. In Bienkowska et al. (2000) the state-space modelling has been applied successfully to 188 protein structures by comparing these results with HMM approaches.

References

BIENKOWSKA, J.R., YU, L., ZARAKHOVICH, S., ROGERS, R.G and SMITH, T.F. (2000): Protein fold recognition by total alignment probability. *Proteins: Structure, Function and Genetics, 40, 451-462.*

DEMPSTER, A.P., LAIRD, N.M. and RUBIN, D.B. (1977): Maximum likelihood from incomplete data via the EM algorithm. *Journal of the Royal Statistical Society, Series B, 39, 1-38.*

DURBIN, R., EDDY, S., KROGH, A. and MITCHISON, G. (1998): *Biological sequence analysis.* Cambridge University Press, Cambridge.

HE, H., MCALLISTER, G., SMITH, T.F. (2002): Triage Protein Fold Prediction. *Proteins: Structure, Function, and Genetics, 48, 654-663.*

KROGH, A., BROWN, M., MIAN, I.S., SJÖLANDER, K. and HAUSSLER, D. (1994): Hidden Markov Models in Computational Biology-Applications to Protein Modeling, *Journal of Molecular Biology,* 235, 1501-1531.

MATHSOFT (2000): *S-PLUS 2000.* Mathsoft Inc., Seattle, WA.

MURZIN, A.G., BRENNER, S.E., HUBBARD, T., CHOTHIA, C. (1995): SCOP: A Structural Classification of Protein Databases for the Investigation of Sequences and Structures. *Journal of Molecular Biology,* 247(4), 536-540.

RABINER, L.R. (1989): A tutorial on hidden Markov models. *Journal of Basic Engineering, 82, 35-45.*

SOUSA, L., SANTOS, M., TURKMAN, M.A.A. and URFER, W. (2001): Bayesian Analysis of Protein Sequence Data. *Technical Report 48/2001, SFB 475, University of Dortmund.*

STULTZ, C.M., WHITE, J.V. and SMITH, T.F. (1993): Structural analysis based on state-space modeling. *Protein Science, 2, 305-314.*

URFER, W. (2001): Statistical tools for extracting information from DNA sequence data. *In: Mathematical Statistics with Applications in Biometry: Festschrift in Honour of Siegfried Schach. J. Kunert and G. Trenkler (eds.), Eul Verlag, Köln, 103-112.*

WHITE, J.V., STULTZ, C.M. and SMITH, T.F. (1994): Protein classification by stochastic modeling and optimal filtering of amino-acid sequencing. *Mathematical Biosciences, 119, 35-75.*

WITTINGHOFER, A. and WALDMANN, H. (2000): Ras-A Molecular Switch Involved in Tumor Formation. *Angewandte Chemie, 39/23, 4193-4214.*

Acknowledgement: The authors are grateful to the Deutsche Forschungsgemeinschaft (SFB 475, "Reduction of complexity for multivariate data structures").

Quantitative Study of Images in Archaeology: I. Textual Coding

Sergio Camiz[1] and Elena Rova[2]

[1] Dipartimento di Matematica "Guido Castelnuovo" - Universitá di Roma "La Sapienza". E-mail: sergio.camiz@uniroma1.it.
[2] Dipartimento di Scienze dell'Antichitá e del Vicino Oriente - Universitá "Ca' Foscari", Venezia. E-mail: erova@unive.it.

Abstract. For the analysis of a corpus of Mesopotamian seals, aiming at studying them on the image structure point of view, the problem of a suitable coding is discussed. For the analysis of the image composition a textual coding was developed. In this way, both the iconographical elements and attitudes and the subpattern composing the image, can be treated, through textual exploratory techniques. The results of a textual correspondence analysis are discussed.

1 Introduction

Archaeologists[1] are often faced with the problem of studying large assemblages of finds bearing rather stereotyped figurative decorations. These objects -which may be pottery vessels, terracottas, stone or metal reliefs, seals, etc.- were produced by specialised craftsmen, often in large amounts. Their decoration was based on simple icons, which where combined in different ways -often involving fixed repeated sequences, thus providing a larger variety of different images. Unlike simple decoration patterns consisting of a single icon repeated all over the available space, such images are characterised by a hierarchical iconographical structure, so that the spatial relations among composing elements (dimensions, closeness, order, etc.) represent significant features of the resulting image.

Unlike major artworks, that may be profitably studied separately, the study of objects of the type described above requires a global approach, since every specimen's full meaning may be explained only in the framework of the whole assemblage to which it belongs, so that in this context its individual features must to be evaluated. On account of the large amount of items involved, and of the limited (though sometimes significant) number of elements used -in different associations- in their decoration, an exploratory analysis approach appears especially promising.

In order to discuss this problem, we focus on a corpus of 1247 images from Near Eastern cylinder seals of the late IV millennium B.C. (Rova (1994)). The study of its coding and of the consequent data analysis tools has been the object of a long-lasting research project carried out by the authors. Their large number and the wide variety of the images made them especially suitable for

---

[1] This work has been carried out thanks to research grants no. CNRC00D101.001 and CNRC00D101.003 of Consiglio Nazionale delle Ricerche.

our present purposes. The images appeared to have been obtained through the combination of more or less fixed elements (human beings, animals and objects) and attitudes into some basic compositional patterns.

Several different approaches were tested for the analysis of the engraved images, on the basis of their iconographic contents. These are relevant for the study and the classification of the seals, since, as Rova (1994) shows, they reflect the seals' different functions or uses and the social status of their owners. Such a study should take into account at least three different levels: i) the elements that appear in the image and their attributes; ii) the small, sometimes repeated subpatterns that compose the image; and iii) the relations among subpatterns in the image composition. The analysis methods ranged from the classical coding of presence/absence of iconographic elements, to a formalised text describing the image in full details, according to pre-defined criteria, to symbolic strings describing the syntax of the image, i.e. its iconographic structure (for complete references, see Camiz and Rova (2001)).

In this paper, we deal with the problems of the textual coding technique used to describe the seals images, sketching the different ways of coding experienced. We found that the main distinctive features of the analysed assemblage clearly emerged in every case, thus confirming both the general validity and the robustness of the used techniques. Nevertheless, the differences turned out not to be totally irrelevant, since different methods especially suited particular groups of images characterised by different structural features. This may be of particular interest for the study of different corpora, since it will allow to select *a priori* the most suitable techniques on the basis of the specific characteristics of the corpus, in order to quickly obtain the best and clearest results.

Lastly, we shall show an example of the results obtained through Textual Correspondence Analysis (*TCA*, Lebart and Salem (1988, 1994)) applied to the textual coding of the images. Here, the first factor subspaces obtained through *TCA* show the main distinctions that the used coding puts in evidence. For clarity purposes, the analyses will be performed on a limited sample of 100 images belonging to the aforementioned corpus of seals. Their results may thus be compared with those obtained with a different coding of the same images presented in another paper (Camiz, et al., in this volume).

2 The study of images

The problem of studying images through quantitative methods concerns primarily the study of a suitable coding susceptible to be properly analysed, since choices made at this stage of the work will heavily influence the results of any analysis, or, even worse, bias them. In this respect, it is clear that, for instance, the identification of the iconographic elements, their positions, and their mutual relations, involves a certain degree of arbitrariness, which should be part of the scholar's responsibility. It must be pointed out that, in our approach to the problem, coding is not intended as a universal descriptive tool, as aimed at, e.g., in the work of the group of French archaeologists working with Jean-Claude Gardin (Gardin et al. (1976); Gardin (1978); for ancient Near Eastern seals see, in particular, Digard et al. (1975)). Instead, our coding is especially tailored to suit the specific corpus under study, based on *a priori* hypotheses on the iconographic element signification: e.g., we call *king-priest* a man wearing a long gown, naked in the upper part of the body, his hair bound in a chignon, rather than describing each of these single features separately. Of course, the problem is not limited to the archaeological framework: every scholar, during his/her investigation, selects for his/her purposes a particular subset of a population of reference (the *sample*) and, for each sampled unit, he/she selects a particular subset of the information available, namely the *characters*, considered useful for his/her purposes. In our case, the selection was made keeping in mind the archaeologist's point of view, by no means different from that of other scholars, even if interested in the same subject.

In order to undertake a study of a set of images of the type dealt with here, one must consider that these images have a hierarchical structure. In fact, three different levels of image description deserve being considered:

1) The lowest is the mere presence of distinct icons, i.e. iconographic elements, like *human beings, animals, objects,* or *symbols,* which can appear in different attitudes, like *sitting, passing by, with open arms,* etc.

2) The second level is the presence of small sets of elements, i.e. small fixed subpatterns, such as *woman with open arms sitting on a bench* ; *king-priest passing right with asymmetric arms with bow and arrow* ; or *caprid passing left plus curved ladder* ; etc. These may occur repeatedly on the same image and/or in different seals images, and contribute to the image composition.

3) The highest level is the image syntax, that is the overall composition resulting from the combination of sub-patterns, such as *image composed by three sub-patterns on one row, each one composed by two elements* ; *image composed by three main subpatterns on one row, the first two further subdivided into two sub-sub-patterns, the last one formed by a single element* , or *image composed by two sub-patterns, each one subdivided into three* , etc.

In principle, each different level may require a specific coding, that must have specific characteristics, in order to suit the description needs (in particular, for the analysis of the third level, see Camiz et al., in this same volume). Whereas it is important to stress that only the integrated study of the three levels can provide a complete picture of the studied corpus, in this paper we will not take into account the problems of coding unification nor those of a unified analysis. As well, we will not consider any external character, such as origin, date, type of sealing, etc., whose handling does not show any particular difficulty, albeit its importance is primary in the archaeological studies (for an application to Near Eastern seals, see Rova (1994)).

For each of these levels, it is necessary to take into account, while coding, a specific point of view:

1) For the first level, it is important to identify a set of elements/attitudes whose presence or frequency in each image should be taken into account. So, a classical data table crossing images with characters, each identifying a specific element/attitude, may be used. The definition of some of the iconographic elements involves a certain degree of interpretation, since they are defined both by formal features and by function inferred from the image context. A purely descriptive codification, as advocated by Suter (1999: 49-51), in which figures and objects are identified in terms of their postures, gestures and formal features alone, could be adopted, but it would result in an too large number of elements, many of which would not be useful for the specific analysis aims (see, e.g., the type of coding proposed for seal images by Digard et al. (1975)). For the definition of positions, more strict formal criteria can be used, so that a cross-check for the identification of the iconographic elements may derive. If one wants to keep track, in his/her study, of the elements taxonomy, a hierarchy of characters can be used: a specific element, say a *female craftsman*, may be taken into account at the same time as *human being, female*, and *craftsman* by simply coding the presence of all three characters in the image. As well, specific *animals* may be coded in addition, as *lion, caprid, snake*, etc., and the same may be done for objects. As concerns the attitudes, one can consider general characters as *passing, rampant, sitting*, etc., and variants of them, like: *with parallel arms, with open arms, with parallel paws, with turned head*, etc. This is the classical coding, whose limitations are evident, since no information concerning the subpatterns or the general image structure can be derived from the coded data, unless specifically previewed. For the analysis of such data table, *Correspondence Analysis* is suitable and a classification usually follows, based on the distance among items on the factor spaces considered of interest.

2) For the second level, the said classical coding is not sufficient. At this level, the subpatterns are the structures which deserve the highest interest, but it is not possible to code each of them as a specific character, since too many different characters should be taken into account, and the small differences among them could not be correctly identified. We considered then that a textual coding could be suitable and we built for each image a specific text, fully describing its content. The advantage of such a coding advantage is its ability to describe the relations among elements and/or attitudes and to represent at the same time the subpatterns, simply through a subtext sufficiently. To analyse textual coding, *Textual Correspondence Analysis* is suitable, and the classification follows the same principles as in the previous case.

3) For the third level, that we shall discuss in another paper (Camiz et al., in this same volume), we decided to use a totally different coding, based on symbolic sequences, able to define the organisation of the elements composing the subpatterns. These are delimited by couples of parentheses, and the relations among subpatterns that compose the overall image are

represented by special symbols. For this study, a specific distance measure must be defined, to be used with a specific multidimensional scaling and classification techniques.

3   The textual coding

After a first stage, where we adopted the first level coding, we therefore turned to the textual coding, since, once very strict rules are defined for the construction of a formalised text describing the image content, the information transferred in this way is sufficiently complete to understand the content of the image. Unlike the classical use of textual analysis, where differences in style are considered important, in our case special care was devoted to constantly use the same form for the description of the same element or attitude. So, all terms were not inflected according to grammatical rules, otherwise losing the 1-1 correspondence between descriptors and described objects. Several advantages can be attributed to such coding: with a good practice, it may be easier to proceed to this coding than to the previous one; instead, with particular care, the previous one may be included in, or at least automatically extracted from the latter, via a computer program. Furthermore, the text may be inspected not only for the identification of the occurrences of a single form, corresponding to an element or an attitude, but as well for either *repeated segments*, i.e. sequences of forms that appear exactly in the same way in different texts, or *nearly-segments*, i.e. sequences of forms differing from each other only for one or two forms (Bécue and Haeusler (1995)). Segments and nearly-segments are very important for our descriptive task, since there are objects and/or attitudes that may be described only through *polyforms*, i.e. sequences of forms having a unique meaning; in addition, the association among elements and attitudes is as well described through polyforms, i.e. segments. Segments are thus able to discribe image sub-patterns involving two or more elements may, or at least nearly-segments, when minor differences among them are not important.

The texts were built according to a set of fixed rules. Starting from the top left of the image, continuing rightwards and from the top to the bottom, each icon was described by means of a sequence of lexical forms, defining, in this order, the iconographical element, its position, the position of arms and/or paws (according to the same criteria used in the classical coding) and its orientation (*right*, or *left*). Additional lexical forms were added to record specific attitudes (e.g. the presence of animals with turned head). Different elements were connected through relation markers (*and, plus, on, above, intertwined with, inside, above-below/alongside*), while different sub-patterns were divided through punctuation marks: *comma, semicolon, period*.

We soon became aware, however, that the effectiveness of textual analysis (especially as far as repeated segments were concerned) was reduced by a number of problems, connected with the chosen coding rules, the analysis procedure and major software limitations. For this reason, these were repeatedly altered in some details, in order to obtain more satisfactory results.

As for the changes in coding rules, let us consider this seal image:

This was coded according to three-different texts:

Coding 1) *vessel type_3 on vessel type_3 upside_down, woman craftsman sittingp left parallel arms on bench; vessel type_3 on vessel type_3 upside_down, man craftsman sitting left parallel arms on bench; vessel type_3 on vessel type_3 upside_down, woman craftsman sitting left parallel arms on bench.*

Coding 2) *vessel type_3 on vessel type_3 upside_down, woman craftsman sitting parallel_arms left on bench; vessel type_3 on vessel type_3 upside_down, man craftsman sitting parallel_arms left on bench; vessel type_3 on vessel type_3 upside_down, woman craftsman sitting parallel_arms left on bench.*

Coding 3) *vessel_3 on vessel_3 upside_down, w_craftsman sitting_parallel_a left on bench; vessel_3 on vessel_3 upside_down, m_craftsman sitting_parallel_a left on bench; vessel_3 on vessel_3 upside_down, w_craftsman sitting_paral-lel_a left on bench.*

There are reasons for this successive adjustment: the first one was the exact description of the seal content, based on the previous classical coding: care was taken for every element, body, and arms/paws position to correspond to a single lexical form. Some lexical forms corresponding to the more general categories used in the first coding were also added, but this was not systematically done, to avoid texts to become too long. Therefore, a subjective choice was made between what was considered more interesting (for instance, *man* and *woman, hybrid*) and what could be omitted (for instance, *human being, animal, object*). This involved a lower degree of control by the researcher on the interplay between these different types of variables. The second and third coding were specifically developed from the first one for the analysis of repeated segments.

As an example, let us consider the position of the lexical forms defining the orientation: originally located between the element and its position (*woman craftsman sitting left with open arms*), they were transferred to the end of the sequence (*woman craftsman sitting with open arms left*) in order not to interrupt the continuity between the element and its position.

Later it was decided to join some lexical forms through an underscore, so that a single form could identify the element completely (i.e. *woman craftsman* became *woman_craftsman*, etc.). As a result, in the final coding every icon is normally described by a maximum of three lexical forms, describing the element, its attitude (including both body and arms/paws positions), and its orientation. No lexical forms describing general element or attitude categories (like *woman, sitting*, etc.) are present any more. Even if this implied a certain loss of information, on the whole this coding is more objective and consistent than the previous one.

Some polyforms were progressively tied through underscores, in order to transform them into forms. In this way, some lexical forms, that had very limited or confusing meaning or interest when left alone, were correctly tied to the main element. It is the case of the forms *type_1, type_2*, etc., used to distinguish among different types of *vessels, standards*, etc., that otherwise could be confusing. Other polyforms were abbreviated, only due to program results readability.

On the other hand, some polyforms were joined to single longer lexical forms (e.g. *woman craftsman sitting with open arms left* became *woman_craftsman sitting with_open_arms left*, and *w_craftsman sitting_with_open_arms left*): in order to be treated as forms. by the software. In this way, most elements could be described with just three forms, as *caprid passing right*. This helped to have balanced segments.

4   The textual analysis

In Figure 1 the 100 seals are plotted on the plane spanned by the first two factors of Textual Correspondence Analysis on presence / absence of forms corresponding to coding 3). On this plane around 11% of total inertia is explained. On the first axis the opposition may be seen between schematic and complex naturalistic seals: a sequence can be detected, starting from *rows of spiders*, of *pots*, of *sitting women crafting pottery*, of *women passing carrying standards*, through complex naturalistic *sacred, craftsmanship, war, and hunting* scenes ending with *animal scenes* and particular compositions with *hybrids, snakes*, etc. The most representative seals of each group are shown in Figure 2.

On the second axis, the opposition between *humans* and *animals* is outlined and the following axes distinguish specific themes: the third axis opposes *humans naturalistic* and *schematic images*, and the same distinction concerns the *animals* on the fourth. On this one, a distinction is set in evidence between simple *rows of animals, rows of animals alternating with objects (ladders, pottery)*, and compositions with *hybrids* and particular animals, such *snakes, lions*, and *birds of prey* in very elaborated schemes.

5   Conclusion

The textual coding proved effective in approaching sufficiently well the first level traditional coding, although some special care must be taken in the coding procedure, in order to avoid redundant information. In Camiz and Rova (2001) the comparison among the different coding and different analysis techniques shows that in any case the main classes of images appear sufficiently

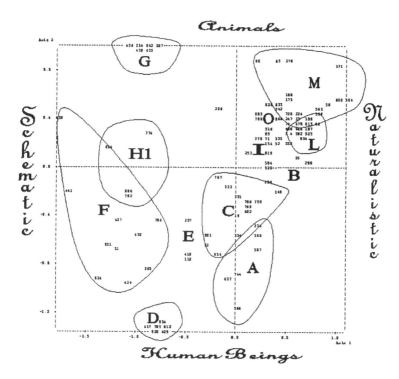

Fig. 1. - Qualitative Textual Correspondence analysis of lexical forms. Seal projected on the plane 1-2. A: war scenes; B: hunting scenes; C: naturalistic sacred scenes; D: schematic sacred scenes (rows of women carrying standards); E: naturalistic storage craftsmanship scenes; F: schematic craft scenes (sitting women manufacturing pottery); G: spiders; H1: schematic pottery; I: scenes with humans, animals, and pottery; L: animals alternating with ladders; M: hybrids and special animals; O: animals on rows.

well described. This proves the robustness of the method. As well, the flexibility of the proposed coding must be stressed, since, starting from a good coding, it is very easy to obtain global modifications, such as merging a couple of contiguous forms into a single one, or selecting particular forms to analyse. In this way, subsequent analyses may be performed in order to enlighten various aspects of the image iconography and composition which leads to results that can help in better understanding the corpus variability. In addition, the use of repeated segments, or quasi-segments, allows to extend the study to the second level of the image description, i.e. the subpatterns. Although some attempts were already performed on the reduced corpus, the whole corpus analysis will be able to ensure the true capacity of this procedure.

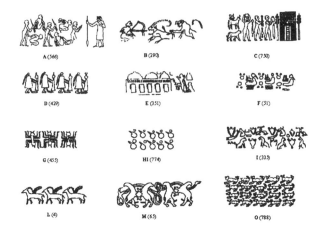

Fig. 2. - The most representative seals of the groups described in Figure 1.

References

BÉCUE, M. and HAEUSLER, L. (1995): Vers une post-codification automatique. In S. Bolasco, L. Lebart and A. Salem (Eds.) *JADT 1995 - III Giornate Internazionali di Analisi Statistica dei Dati Testuali*, CISU, Roma, 1, 35-42.

CAMIZ, S. and ROVA, E. (2001): Exploratory Analyses of Structured Images: a Test on Different Coding Procedures and Analysis Methods. *Archeologia e calcolatori*, 12, 7-46.

CAMIZ, S., ROVA, E., and TULLI, V. (1998): Exploratory Analysis of Images Engraved on Ancient Near-Eastern Seals based on a Distance among Strings. *Statistica*, 58(4), 669-689.

DIGARD, F. *et al.* (1975): *Répertoire analytique des cylindres orientaux publiés dans les sources bibliographiques éparses* (3 vols.). Editions du Centre National de la Recherche Scientifique, Paris.

GARDIN, J.C., CHEVALIER, J., CHRISTOPHE, J., and SALOMÉ, M.R. (1976): *Code pour l'analyse des formes de poteries*, CNRS, Paris.

GARDIN, J.C. (1978): *Code pour l'analyse des ornements*. Paris.

LEBART, L. and SALEM, A. (1988): *Analyse statistique des données textuelles*. Dunod, Paris.

LEBART, L. and SALEM, A. (1994): *Statistique textuelle*. Dunod, Paris.

ROVA, E. (1994): *Ricerche sui sigilli a cilindro vicino-orientali del periodo di Uruk / Jemdet Nasr*. Istituto per l'Oriente "C. Nallino", Roma, Orientis Antiqui Collectio, 20.

SUTER, C.E. (1999): Review of Rova 1994. *Journal of Near Eastern Studies*, 58, 47-53.

Quantitative Study of Images in Archaeology: II. Symbolic Coding

Sergio Camiz[1], Elena Rova[2], and Vanda Tulli[3]

[1] Dipartimento di Matematica "Guido Castelnuovo" - Università di Roma "La Sapienza". E-mail: sergio.camiz@uniroma1.it.

[2] Dipartimento di Scienze dell'Antichitá e del Vicino Oriente - Universitá "Ca' Foscari", Venezia. E-mail: erova@unive.it.

[3] Dipartimento di Metodi Quantitativi per l'Economia - Universitá di Milano Bicocca. E-mail: vanda.tulli@unimib.it

Abstract. For the analysis of a corpus of Mesopotamian seals, aiming at studying them on the image structure point of view, the problem of a suitable coding is discussed. For the analysis of the image syntactical composition a special coding was developed, based on hierarchical sequences of symbols, whose differences are measured through a particular Levenshtein distance. The results of principal coordinates analysis on these distances are discussed.

1 Introduction

Ancient[1] Near Eastern cylinder seals, originating in the Uruk/Jamdat Nasr period (IV Millennium B.C.) are little stone cylinders, round which a drawing was engraved, giving, once rolled on plastic clay, a wide variety of images as for iconography as well as for composition and style. This variety is obtained by associating a limited number of stereotyped iconographic elements in fairly simple and repetitious compositional patterns. The authors studied a corpus of 1247 images seals, aiming at describing their iconographic structure, adopting different coding techniques (Rova (1994); Camiz and Rova (2001); Camiz et al. (1998)).

This variety of the Uruk seal images suggested to use them to study in detail the problems of coding images in a suitable way, able to describe both the elements composing the image and the syntactical structure that ties the elements among them. In order to describe an image thoroughly, several levels of description should be considered, from the simplest quoting of presence of single elements or attitudes, to the occurrence of fixed sets of elements, that compose as a whole small subpatterns, and finally to the overall image composition, i.e. the syntactical structure connecting subpatterns. Note that pattern recognition techniques seem not suitable to our purposes, since their ability to correctly identify the items composing the image, and especially to distinguish the different levels involved, seems questionable. In particular, our definition of specific iconographic elements (e.g. different categories of human beings) is at times left to the archaeologist's personal evaluation.

---

[1] This work has been carried out thanks to research grants no. CNRC00D101.001 and CNRC00D101.003 of Consiglio Nazionale delle Ricerche.

788   602

Fig. 1. - Two seals images: one with a repeated element on multiple rows and a complex non periodical image.

This was discussed in a previous paper (Camiz and Rova, in this volume), where the textual coding is used to study the first two levels. In this paper, we focus on the third level, that is the study of the image composition, and describe the special coding that we developed to describe the image structure. We shall then show the results of *Principal Coordinates Analysis* applied to the distance among images, as calculated by a *distance among hierarchical strings*, developed on purpose, based on Levenshtein (1966) ideas.

2 The image structure coding

For the analysis of the third level, the information concerning the kind of elements involved in the subpatterns was ignored, since the nature of both elements and attitudes appearing in the images belongs to the lower levels of description. Therefore, for this study, the image structure is described through a string of symbols which represent the structure skeleton, that is the presence of generic elements, together with their spatial relationship with other elements. We decided to maintain in the coding only the distinction among main and secondary elements and a precise definition of elements orientation, since these have a bearing on the general image composition. A couple of parentheses encloses those sets of symbols that compose a subpattern. This allows to distinguish among *terminal* elements, i.e. the elements corresponding to the said symbols, and *non-terminal* ones, namely those corresponding to a set of symbols enclosed by a couple of parentheses, i.e. the subpatterns. With the use of parentheses, *hierarchical strings* result, since one may consider the content of each encapsulated couple of parentheses as belonging to a lower level. In Table 1 the set of used symbols, with their meaning, is shown. Here, the symbol *"on/under and by"* refers to the case in which an object lies aside another and partially covered by a part of it. It must be reminded that the relation symbols and the parentheses correspond exactly to the connective forms and the punctuation marks used in the textual coding. For this reason, once the latter is achieved and the structural items to consider are selected, it is likely that an automatic coding can be developed to extract from texts the structural information of interest.

Elements		Relationships	
D	Main element right oriented	.	adjacent to
S	Main element left oriented	+	joined with, touching, attribute
X	Main element not oriented	*	interlaced with
F	Main element doubly oriented, main right	/	on
J	Main element doubly oriented, main left	∧	on / under and by
d	Secondary element right oriented	∩	into
s	Secondary element left oriented	|	above
x	Secondary element not oriented		Subpattern
f	Secondary element doubly oriented, main right	(	beginning
j	Secondary element doubly oriented, main left	)	end

Table 1. - The symbols used in pattern description strings.

Several rules concerning the precedence of connections, use of parentheses, etc. were considered in the construction of strings, in order to avoid ambiguities and to reach an acceptable degree of uniformity in the description of seal images structure throughout the whole corpus. In particular, the image is described from left to right and from the top to the bottom. In Figure 1 two seals are shown whose descriptive strings are respectively:

(788):(S.S.S.S.S)/(S.S.S.S.S)/(S.S.S.S.S)/(S.S.S.S.S).

(602):((x+S).(X).(D).(((s.s)/(x))/(S)).(S+x))∩(X)

They will be used as an example throughout the description of the method for the computation of distances among images.

3   Distance among strings

In order to compare couples of strings, a distance measure was chosen according to Levenshtein (1966) and Lu and Fu (1978), based on the *insertion, deletion,* or *substitution* of symbols. Let S be an alphabet composed by all used symbols representing both image elements and relations. Let S^* be the set of all possible meaningful strings generated by S. Three unary operations may be defined in S^*:

1) *deletion* of a symbol σ: this operation maps a string $s1$ to a string $s2$, where σ, appearing at least once in $s1$, is removed in $s2$ from that position.

2) *insertion* of a symbol σ: this operation maps a string $s1$ to a string $s2$, such that σ appears once in $s2$ in a place where it was not present in $s1$.

3) *substitution* of symbol σ with symbol τ: this operation maps the string $s1$ to a string $s2$, such that τ appears once in $s2$ where σ was present in $s1$.

An *unweighed Levenshtein distance* between $s1$ and $s2$ is defined as the minimum number of operations necessary to map $s1$ to $s2$.

Since the archaeologist requested that differences among strings should be considered as having different weight, according to the different items involved, a system of weights was introduced, so that we defined the *weighted Levenshtein distance* as the weight of minimum weight sequence of operations, necessary to map $s1$ to $s2$; it is clear that the weight of a sequence is the sum of the weights of all the operations composing the sequence.

The definition of the weights system is a delicate problem, since it has a strong influence on the results, both from the archaeological and from the metric point of view. Although the unweighed measure is trivially proved to

$ins(D) = del(D) = 10$	$sost(D,S) = sost(S,D) = 12$	$sost(X,s) = sost(s,X) = 17$	$sost(s,f) = sost(f,s) = 12$
$ins(S) = del(S) = 10$	$sost(D,X) = sost(X,D) = 12$	$sost(X,x) = sost(x,X) = 5$	$sost(s,j) = sost(j,s) = 8$
$ins(X) = del(X) = 10$	$sost(D,F) = sost(F,D) = 10$	$sost(X,f) = sost(f,X) = 17$	$sost(x,f) = sost(f,x) = 10$
$ins(F) = del(F) = 10$	$sost(D,J) = sost(J,D) = 14$	$sost(X,j) = sost(j,X) = 17$	$sost(x,j) = sost(j,x) = 10$
$ins(J) = del(J) = 10$	$sost(D,d) = sost(d,D) = 5$	$sost(F,J) = sost(J,F) = 12$	$sost(f,j) = sost(j,f) = 10$
$ins(d) = del(d) = 5$	$sost(D,s) = sost(s,D) = 17$	$sost(F,d) = sost(d,F) = 15$	$sost(.,+) = sost(+,.) = 12$
$ins(s) = del(s) = 5$	$sost(D,x) = sost(x,D) = 17$	$sost(F,s) = sost(s,F) = 19$	$sost(.,*) = sost(*,.) = 14$
$ins(x) = del(x) = 5$	$sost(D,f) = sost(f,D) = 15$	$sost(F,x) = sost(x,F) = 17$	$sost(.,/) = sost(/,.) = 30$
$ins(f) = del(f) = 5$	$sost(D,j) = sost(j,D) = 19$	$sost(F,f) = sost(f,F) = 5$	$sost(.,\wedge) = sost(\wedge,.) = 24$
$ins(j) = del(j) = 5$	$sost(S,X) = sost(X,S) = 12$	$sost(F,j) = sost(j,F) = 17$	$sost(.,\cap) = sost(\cap,.) = 26$
$ins(.) = del(.) = 15$	$sost(S,F) = sost(F,S) = 14$	$sost(J,d) = sost(d,J) = 19$	$sost(+,/) = sost(/,+) = 30$
$ins(+) = del(+) = 16$	$sost(S,J) = sost(J,S) = 10$	$sost(J,s) = sost(s,J) = 19$	$sost(+,\wedge) = sost(\wedge,+) = 24$
$ins(*) = del(*) = 17$	$sost(S,d) = sost(d,S) = 17$	$sost(J,x) = sost(x,J) = 17$	$sost(+,\cap) = sost(\cap,+) = 26$
$ins(/) = del(/) = 25$	$sost(S,s) = sost(s,S) = 5$	$sost(J,f) = sost(f,J) = 17$	$sost(*,/) = sost(/,*) = 30$
$ins(\wedge) = del(\wedge) = 21$	$sost(S,x) = sost(x,S) = 17$	$sost(J,j) = sost(j,J) = 5$	$sost(*,\wedge) = sost(\wedge,*) = 24$
$ins(\cap) = del(\cap) = 23$	$sost(S,f) = sost(f,S) = 19$	$sost(d,s) = sost(s,d) = 10$	$sost(*,\cap) = sost(\cap,*) = 26$
$ins(()) = del(()) = 0$	$sost(S,j) = sost(j,S) = 15$	$sost(d,x) = sost(x,d) = 10$	$sost(/,\cap) = sost(\cap,/) = 30$
$ins/del(nonterminal) = 35$	$sost(X,F) = sost(F,X) = 12$	$sost(d,f) = sost(f,d) = 8$	$sost(\wedge,\cap) = sost(\cap,\wedge) = 28$
$ins/del(terminal) = 25$	$sost(X,J) = sost(J,X) = 12$	$sost(d,j) = sost(j,d) = 12$	
	$sost(X,d) = sost(d,X) = 17$	$sost(s,x) = sost(x,s) = 10$	

Table 2. The weights used in computing the distances between strings.

be a distance (dealing with one step transformations at a time, in triangular inequality the equality holds if the second string is in the shortest sequence of operations mapping the first string to the third), in weighted case, it depends on the chosen set C of weights. In particular:

1) weights should be all positive;

2) weights of deletion and insertion of the same item must be equal;

3) substitution weights must be symmetric;

4) triangular inequality should be checked for all triplets of symbols.

In addition:

5) weights must be coherent with the application aims: namely, they must be chosen according to the relevance on the structure of the corresponding operation. So, greater weights should be attributed to operations having greater importance on structure variation, according to the archaeologist's evaluation. In particular, insertion and deletion of main elements are more important than those of secondary ones and substitution of a main (secondary) element with a different main (secondary) element affects the general image structure less than substitution of a main with a secondary element (or *vice versa*). For the same reason, insertion and deletion of non-terminal elements are more important than those of terminal ones. In the same way, relations (., +, *) which do not significantly alter the *normal* single row image pattern have in general a lower weight than relations (/, ^, ∩, —), which greatly affect the image appearance. Finally, substitution of relations should be weighted according to their mutual degree of similarity.

6) weights must be coherent among each other: if different structures may be represented in different ways or the variation between two strings may be described in different ways, the corresponding weights should be equal.

The weights used in the analysis are shown in Table 2. They are but one example, since they may be chosen by the archaeologist according to his needs, provided that the rules stated above are observed. In this way he is free to tailor the weights according to the specific problem under study.

$(S.S.S.S.S)/(S.S.S.S.S)/(S.S.S.S.S)/(S.S.S.S.S)$ $((x + S).(X).(D).(((s.s)/(x))/(S)).(S + x)) \cap (X)$
First string factorization   *Second string factorization*
1)$(S.S.S.S.S)$ 6)$(x + S)$
2)$(S.S.S.S.S)$ 7)(X)
3)$(S.S.S.S.S)$ 8)(D)
4)$(S.S.S.S.S)$ 9)$(s.s)$
                                                       10)(x)
5)$1/2/3/4$ 11)(S)

                                                       12)$(S + x)$
                                                       13)(X)
                                                       14)$9/10$
                                                       15)$14/11$
                                                       16)$6.7.8.15.12$
                                                       17)$16 \cap 13$

Table 3. - Example of factorization of the two strings corresponding to seals 788 and 602.

In order to take the hierarchical structure of strings into account, our weighted distance was slightly modified: from the inner level of couple of parentheses appearing in a string, each substring, starting with a left parenthesis and ending with corresponding right one, was substituted by a new symbol (i.e., a number identifying the substring); this procedure results in a *string factorization*, that leads to the identification of the whole string with the lastly introduced symbol. Consequently, the new alphabet S' is built, obtained by adding the new symbols (numbers) to S.

As an example, in Table 3 the factorization of the strings describing the two seals in Figure 1 is shown: the new alphabet is $S' = S \cup \{1, 2, ..., 17\}$ and the said two strings correspond to symbols 5 and 17 respectively.

One may distinguish between *simple factors*, composed by the original symbols of S, and *composed factors*, obtained through composition of factors corresponding to new alphabet symbols with the alphabet relations.

In the example, 1, corresponding to *(S.S.S.S.S)*, is a simple factor, whereas $14 = 9/10$ is a composed one, corresponding to a subpattern formed by the simple factor $9 = $ *(S.S)* on the simple one $10 = $ *(x)*.

Given two factorized strings, identified by the symbols (numbers) *n1* and *n2*, their distance is the weight of subst(*n1*, *n2*). This weight depends on the sum of the weights of all operations necessary to map each decomposition factor of the first string to a corresponding one of the second.

Eventually, in the example, the distance between the two strings is the weight of subst(5,17).

In order to evaluate such a weight, starting from the original system of weights C a set of weights C' is built, corresponding to the enlarged alphabet S', according to the following set of operations, each operation followed by a C' updating:

1) deletion weights of all simple factors of first string are computed, as Levenshtein distance between the factor and an empty string, considering only the weights set C initially defined; so, C is updated to C'.

In the example: *del(1)* = *del(2)* = *del(3)* = *del(4)* = *del(S)* + *del(.)* + *del(S)* + *del(.)* + *del(S)* + *del(.)* + *del (S)* + *del(.)* + *del (S)* = 10 + 15 + 10 + 15 + 10 + 15 + 10 + 15 +10 = 110.

2) deletion weights of composed factors of first string are computed in a similar way, taking into account C'.

In the example: $del\ (5) = del(1) + del(/) + del(2) + del(/) + del(3) + del(/) + del(4) = = 110 + 25 + 110 + 25 + 110 + 25 + 110 = 515.$

3) Insertion weights of simple factors of second string are computed, as Levenshtein distance between the factor and an empty string, based on C and so updating C'.

In the example: $ins(6) = ins(x) + ins(+) + ins(S) = 5 + 16 + 10 = 31$
$ins(7) = ins(X) = 10\ ins(8) = ins(D) = 10$
$ins(9) = ins(s) + ins(.) + ins(s) = 5 + 15 + 5 = 25$
$ins(10) = ins(x) = 5\ ins(11) = ins(S) = 10$
$ins(12) = ins(S) + ins(+) + ins(x) = 10 + 16 + 5 = 31$
$ins(13) = ins(X) = 10$

4) insertion weights of composed factors of second string are computed in a similar way, taking into account C'.

In the example: $ins(14) = ins(9) + ins(/) + ins(10) = 25 + 25 + 5 = 55$
$ins(15) = ins(14) + ins(/) + ins(11) = 55 + 25 + 10 = 90$
$ins(16) = ins(6) + ins(.) + ins(7) + ins(.) + ins(8) + ins(.) + ins(15)$
$+ ins(.) + ins(12) = 31 + 15 + 10 +$
$15 + 10 + 15 + 90 + 15 + 31 = 232.$
$ins(17) = ins(16) + ins(\cap) + ins(13) = 232 + 23 + 10 = 265.$

5) substitution weights of simple factors of first string with simple factors of second one are evaluated, by computing Levenshtein distance between the two factors, considering only the weights set C. The substitution may be done in different ways, that may be viewed as a path through an ordered graph, connecting the two factors. The source and the sink of this graph are the two factors, each edge consists of an insertion, a deletion of a symbol of the current alphabet, or a substitution with another, and each node results from such operation.

6) substitution weights are computed of a) simple factors of first string with composed factors of second, b) composed factors of first string with simple factors of second, and c) composed factors of first string with composed factors of second one in a similar way, considering C'.

In the example, $dist\_Lev(788,602) = sost\ (5,\ 17)$ can be computed in different ways, according to any path on the following oriented graph, as previously explained:

In the figure, paths in bold have all minimum weight, so that any of them may be chosen. It results $sost(5, 17) = 704$, since one may consider the following path:

$$sost(1, 16) = 292 giving 16/2/3/4\ + del(/) = 25 giving 162/3/4$$
$$+ del(2) = 110 giving 16/3/4\qquad + del(/) = 25 giving 163/4$$
$$+ del(3) = 110 giving 16/4\qquad + sost(/, \cap) = 30 giving 16 \cap 4$$
$$+ sost(4, 13) = 112 giving 16 \cap 13 = sost(5, 17) = 704$$

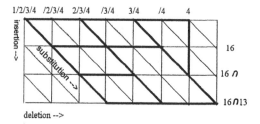

Fig. 2. - Grid graph showing paths to compute the cost of sost (5, 17). Boldface paths are all minimum weight.

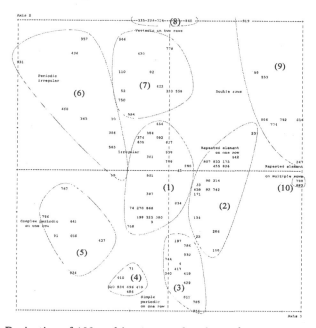

Fig. 3. - Projection of 100 seal images on the plane of axes 1 and 2 of PCoA.

Clearly, the weights of both $sost(1,16)$ and $sost(4,13)$ were computed as described in step 5) along the found minimum weight paths in the corresponding graph.

4   The Principal Coordinates Analysis results

We show here some results of the Principal Coordinates Analysis of the distance matrix built on a set of 100 images taken from the said corpus. They are the same used for the Textual Correspondence Analysis, whose results are shown in Camiz and Rova, in this same volume.

In Figure 3, the scatter of seals on the plane spanned by the first two axes is shown. On the first axis, a clear opposition is found between images showing highly structured one-row compositions, characterized by repeated sequences of several elements (periodical images), and seals where an animal is repeated many times on several rows. On the top of second axis, there are seals showing complex sequences on two rows and irregular compositions, opposed on the bottom to images with simple repeated sequences of animals and human beings alternating with objects, all on one row. Looking at the plane of the first two axes, homogeneous groups may be distinguished: in the figure they are grouped according to an automatic partition in 10 groups, obtained considering the Euclidean distance on the first three axes of *PCoA* with minimum variance method. In Figure 4 are represented the images of some *typical* seals, chosen among the 4 closest to each group centroid. In group 1, the closest to the axes center, most of the complex irregular scenes appear (Figure 4: 351). Group 2, to the right of it, contains all repeated sequences of single animals and objects on one row, beside some irregular seals (455). Simple repeated sequences of two alternating elements on one row are found in both groups 3 (429) and 4 (496), at the negative end of axis 2, while more complex periodic images with repeated subpatterns involving more than two elements, are typical of group 5 (51), at the negative end of both axes. In the upper left quadrant, more irregular repeated patterns are found in group 6 (450), whereas non-repetitive complex patterns appear in group 7 (602). Repeated sequences of elements on two rows (728) are found in group 8, at the positive end of axis 2. Finally, group 9 in the upper right quadrant is composed by two and three rows homogeneous sequences of animals and objects (774), and in group 10 there are two seals with multiple rows of repeated animals (788) set at the positive end of first axis.

5   Conclusion

The results obtained through the described method proved to be effective in separating different types of structure skeletons of the analyzed images. It is clear that these results are closely related to the system of weights taken into account, actually an archeologist's responsibility. Preliminary experimentations with different sets of weights showed that a variation of 10-20% in the weights assignment does not modify noticeably the results, provided that the weights order is not affected, so that the distinction between the main patterns of image composition was not obscured. A problem unsolved by the current method concerns the proper alignment of the two strings before the computation of distances. This seems to have a high importance in order to correctly consider the presence of common subpatterns in the compared images, in particular if they are repeated. In addition, the archaeologist suggests to give a special weight to the common structure (or substructure) once that the differences among elements (main, secondary, orientation, etc.) are ignored. For this reasons, we are currently trying to overcome these problems through a new procedure based on a more complex algorithm, closer to the actual archeologist's reasoning when comparing images with different composition. Since this will highly affect the results of the study, we consider that

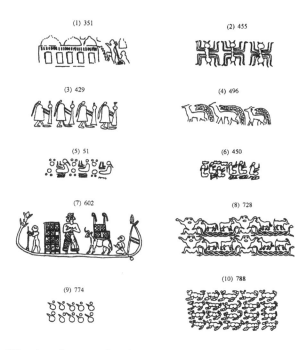

(1) 351

(2) 455

(3) 429

(4) 496

(5) 51

(6) 450

(7) 602

(8) 728

(10) 788

(9) 774

Fig. 4. - Images of seals typical of classification groups.

a better discussion of the weights system should follow this improvement of the method. At that stage, a further experimentation is forecasted, with very different weighting systems, to check to what extent the different structural elements are put in evidence by the different systems.

In our opinion, both textual and symbolic coding, as well as the weights system, are strongly tied to the corpus under study and they can be hardly generalized to other material. However, at this stage of the study, it is interesting to point out that a clear correspondence seems to exist between the image structure and its composing elements, as it can be understood by comparing the present results with those obtained on the image iconography, as given in Camiz and Rova, in this volume: very complex single row patterns mostly represent sacred or official scenes, whereas small repeated sub-patterns on one or two rows often represent craft scenes, the simplest highly repetitive patterns on one or multiple rows representing animals or objects. This should be checked through a simultaneous analysis of both coding techniques, textual and symbolic. Since in our opinion the textual coding is the best way to describe the seals image, an automatic procedure, able to extract automatically the sequences of symbols from the texts, should be attempted, since it would dramatically speed up the coding phase.

References

CAMIZ, S. and E. ROVA (2001): Exploratory Analyses of Structured Images: A Test on Different Coding Procedures and Analysis Methods. *Archeologia e Calcolatori*, 12, 7-46.

CAMIZ, S., E. ROVA, and V. TULLI (1998). Exploratory Analysis of Images Engraved on Ancient Near-Eastern Seals based on a Distance among Strings. *Statistica*, 58(4), 669-689.

LEVENSHTEIN, A. (1966): Binary Codes capable of correcting Deletions, Insertions, and Reversals. *Sov. Phy. Dokl.*, 10, 707-710.

LU, S.Y. and K.S. FU (1978): A Sentence-to-Sentence Clustering Procedure for Pattern Analysis. *IEEE Transactions on Systems, Man, and Cybernetics*, SMC-8, 5, 381-389.

ROVA, E. (1994): *Ricerche sui sigilli a cilindro vicino-orientali del periodo di Uruk / Jemdet Nasr*. Roma, Istituto per l'Oriente "C. Nallino", Orientis Antiqui Collectio, 20.

Power Functions in Multiple Sampling Plans Using DNA Computation

Carles Capdevila, M. Angels Colomer, Josep Conde, Josep Miret, and Alba Zaragoza

Departament de Matemàtica,
Universitat de Lleida, S-25001, Spain

Abstract. Recently the massive parallelism together with the Watson–Crick complementarity of DNA has provided the possibility of approaching some hard computations using DNA computing. In this paper we present an alternative method, which is more efficient computationally, to get the power function of a multiple sampling plan by means of biomolecular computation techniques. In this way, we propose an encoding of the conforming and defective units using strands of DNA for generating samples of a required size that simulate a binomial distribution, which can be used to calculate the power function.

1 Introduction

Recent studies have shown the possibility of solving some computationally intractable problems by using biochemical processes. One of the first works in this context was Adleman's experiment, in which biochemical techniques were used to make several computations. More precisely, Adleman (1994) solved the Hamiltonian path problem by using some operations with strands of DNA (Deoxyribonucleic Acid). This work became the base of a new research field called DNA computing.

These techniques are used in this paper as an alternative methodology in order to obtain the power functions in sampling attributes plans, which are frequently used in industrial processes to accept or reject certain lots of products. In each sampling plan it is useful to know the plan capacity of detecting quality levels which do not reach the required ones. Therefore, it is necessary to know the corresponding power function.

On the other hand, the multiple sampling attributes plans allow us to have a similar power function as the simple sampling plans, but reducing the average of the sample size, which is an especially interesting point for destructive sampling, even though the computation complexity of the power function increases at the same time as the sampling plan multiplicity does.

Therefore, in this paper we study the computation of the power function of multiple sampling plans by means of biomolecular computation techniques. In this way, we have encoded the conforming and defective units using strands of DNA, from which we can generate samples of a required size. Gel electrophoresis techniques have been used to choose the samples and the Watson–Crick complementary chains have been used to identify the number of defective units.

2 Overview of DNA computing

DNA itself carries genetic information of cellular organisms encoded. It is comprised of subunits called nucleotides that are joined into *polymer chains,* commonly referred to as DNA *strands.* There are four sorts of nucleotides in DNA which depend on the base attached to it. These bases are *adenine, cytosine, guanine* and *thymine* denoted by A, C, G and T. Nucleotides are linked together to form DNA strands via reaction between the 5' phosphate of one nucleotide and the 3' hydroxyl of another. This way of linking induces a natural orientation in any strand. Usually single strands are pair forming double strands (see Figure 1) which have a helix structure discovered by

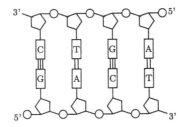

Fig. 1. Structure of a DNA double–strand

Watson and Crick (1953). This pairwise is due to hydrogen bonding between A, T and C, G called *complementary bases.*

2.1 Biological operations

Every model of computation using DNA is based on a sequence of operations that can be applied to a set of strands in a test tube. The ones needed in our work are the following:

- *Synthesis.* This operation allows us to generate prefixed short strands.
- *Amplification.* Strands can be duplicated via a process called *polymerase chain reaction* (PCR).
- *Annealing.* It consists in fusing simple strands into double strands by complementary bases pairing.
- *Denaturing.* It consists in dissolving double strands into simple strands.
- *Gel electrophoresis.* It consists in sorting strands by size.

Notice that we can represent a simple strand of DNA by means of a string x over the alphabet $\{A, C, G, T\}$. Furthemore, we will denote by $\uparrow x$ a simple strand with its orientation, that is to say, adding the character 5' at the begining of the string x and the character 3' at the end, in order to give the orientation $5' \longrightarrow 3'$ to the strand. With these notations, we will denote by $\downarrow x$ the Watson-Crick complementary strand and by $\updownarrow x$ the double strand.

Below we describe some more biological operations with DNA using previous notation (see Păun et al. (1998) or Pisanti (1998)):

- *Union.* Given two sets of strands S_1 and S_2, the mixture **union**(S_1, S_2) of both dissolutions is formed.
- *Merge.* Given two sets of strands S_1 and S_2, a set **merge**(S_1, S_2) is formed, consisting of strands we get linking strands of S_1 with strands of S_2 using enzymes called *ligases* (see Figure 2).
- *Cut.* Given a set of strands S and a string x, it produces the set **cut**(S, x) consisting of all strands that we get cutting the strands of S according to the pattern x (see Figure 2).

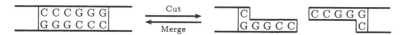

Fig. 2. Cut and merge operations

- *String-extract.* Given a set of strands S and a string x, by means of complementarity, two sets $+$**sextract**(S, x) and $-$**sextract**(S, x) are produced. The first set consists of all strands in S which contain $\updownarrow x$ as a substrand and the second one consists of those strands which do not contain $\updownarrow x$.
- *Length-extract.* Given a set of strands S and an integer n, by means of gel electrophoresis, two sets $+$**lextract**(S, n) and $-$**lextract**(S, n) are produced. The first one consists of all strands in S with length equal to n and the second one with length different from n.
- *Tag.* Given a string x and a set of strands S of the form $\updownarrow z \uparrow y$, where $\updownarrow z$ is an arbitrary double strand and $\uparrow y$ is a fixed simple strand, a set **righttag**(S, x) is produced, consisting of strands of the form $\updownarrow zyx$. Similarly, when the strand $\updownarrow x$ is appended to the left of the strands of S the set we get will be denoted by **lefttag**(S, x).

3   Multiple sampling attributes plans

In the reception of primary materials or final product it is useful to evaluate whether the product has the suitable quality. Much of this acceptance inspection is done using *sampling plans*, which are a statiscal tool for assessing product quality.

In order to carry out this control process, products are grouped together into lots, the lot size being the number of units that comprise the lot. So, to evaluate the lot quality it is necessary to determine the proportion of defective units in the lot. In this sense, a sampling attributes plan consists in contrasting the following hypothesis test: $H_0 : p \leq p_0$, where p is the proportion of defective units in the whole population and p_0 is the acceptable quality of the lot.

Sampling plans can be *simple* or *multiple*: in the first case we decide the acceptance of a lot using a unique sample, while in the second case it can be necessary to consider more than one sample. A simple sampling plan is defined by means of two parameters (n, c), where n is the sample size and c is the maximum natural of defective units that can be the sample to accept the lot. In order to define a multiple sampling plan of multiplicity $m > 1$, first let us consider for all $1 \leq i \leq m$ the following notations:

n_i the size of the i-th sample.

c_i maximum number of defective units allowed among the first i samples to accept the lot.

r_i minimum number of defective units among the first i samples to reject the lot.

X_i binomial variable $B(n_i, p)$ which expresses the number of defective units found in the i-th sample.

Then a multiple sampling plan of multiplicity m can be given as follows: $\{(n_1, c_1, r_1), (n_2, c_2, r_2), \ldots, (n_m, c_m, r_m)\}$, where $r_i > c_i + 1$, $1 \leq i \leq m - 1$, and $r_m = c_m + 1$. The scheme to decide whether a lot is accepted or rejected is as follows (see Farnum (1994)):

(1) Take a random sample of size n_1 from the lot:
  - If $X_1 \leq c_1$, then accept the lot;
  - If $X_1 \geq r_1$, then reject the lot;
  - If $c_1 < X_1 < r_1$, then (2);
(2) Take a random sample of size n_2 from the lot:
  - If $X_1 + X_2 \leq c_2$, then accept the lot;
  - If $X_1 + X_2 \geq r_2$, then reject the lot;
  - If $c_2 < X_1 + X_2 < r_2$, then (3);

$\ldots$

(m) Take a random sample of size n_m from the lot:
  - If $X_1 + \cdots + X_m \leq c_m$, then accept the lot;
  - If $X_1 + \cdots + X_m \geq r_m$, then reject the lot.

3.1 Power functions

In the design of a sampling attributes plan the following conditions (see Dernam and Ross (1997)) should be considered:

- *Acceptance quality level* (AQL): Maximum allowable proportion of defective units in a lot.
- *Rejection quality level* (RQL): Minimum acceptable proportion of defective units in a lot.

Moreover, we will denote by α the probability of rejection of a lot with quality level AQL and by β the probability of acceptance of a lot with quality level RQL. From these conditions we can find the size of the samples and the acceptance region, so that if we take $p_0 = AQL$ then the risk of rejection of a conforming lot is α and if we take $p_0 = RQL$ then the risk of acceptance of a non–conforming lot is β.

When we carry out a sampling plan we take the decision to accept or reject the lot, but we can take a wrong decision too. So, it is important to quantify the risk of error, which depends on the quality of the lot. Therefore, we need to know a function, called *power function*, that gives the risk. More precisely, the power function Ψ associated a multiple sampling plan $\{(n_1, c_1, r_1), (n_2, c_2, r_2), \ldots, (n_m, c_m, r_m)\}$ is given by the probability of rejecting a lot in terms of its quality. Notice that, taking into account the former considerations, the power function Ψ goes through the points (AQL, α) and $(RQL, 1 - \beta)$. In Figure 3 we can see a graphic of a power function. In

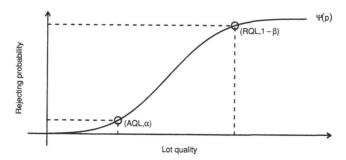

Fig. 3. Power function

this context, the image of the quality p of a lot under the power function Ψ can be computed by the following expression:

$$\Psi(p) = 1 - P(Y_1 \leq c_1) - \sum_{k=2}^{m} P\left(\bigcap_{j=1}^{k-1}\{c_j < Y_j < r_j\} \cap \{Y_k \leq c_k\}\right)$$

where $Y_j = X_1 + \cdots + X_j$ and $X_i \sim B(n_i, p)$. Observe that, in practice, this expression is computationally hard to evaluate since the probabilities that appear in it correspond to products of conditional probabilities. In fact, for each term in the expression we need to compute the products $\prod_{i=1}^{k} P(X_i = a_i)$, where $c_j \leq \sum_{i=1}^{j} a_i \leq r_j$, $1 \leq j \leq k - 1$, and $\sum_{i=1}^{k} a_i \leq r_k$. So, the number of these products depends on the differences $r_j - c_j$ and it increases exponentially with m. From now on, to avoid these combinatorical computations, we will give an alternative method to calculate the power function using DNA computing.

4   Evaluating multiple sampling attributes plans using DNA computation

In this section we present a method based on DNA computation to evaluate, given a multiple sampling plan and the quality of a lot, the probability of rejection of the lot. In this approach there exist some advantages as the massive parallelism of reaction of the DNA strands and the Watson-Crick complementarity to construct just those sequences we are interested in. However, some drawbacks also appear: the length of time that several basic operations take to be carried out.

4.1   Representing units of the samples

For our work we will encode several elements x that we need. The codification of each element x will consist of a central part representing a double strand and denoted by $\updownarrow x_c$, and one or two parts representing simple strands and denoted by $\uparrow x_l$ and $\downarrow x_r$ that we attach at the ends of $\updownarrow x_c$. Then we will write $x = \uparrow x_l \updownarrow x_c \downarrow x_r$, where x_l, x_c and x_r are strings over the alphabet $\{A, C, G, T\}$. In order to carry out the experiment, these strings should have at least a length of 18 for x_c and 6 for x_l and x_r. More precisely, we will encode the following kinds of units (see Figures 4 and 5):

Fig. 4. Defective, neuter and conforming units

- Conforming units or *successes* (s): they will be encoded by $\uparrow s_l \updownarrow s_c \downarrow s_r$, with $s_l = s_r$.
- Defective units or *failures* (f): they will be encoded by $\uparrow f_l \updownarrow f_c \downarrow f_r$, with $f_l = f_r$.
- Elements (u) that allow us to link strings that encode defective units with conforming units: they will be called *neuter units* and encoded by $\uparrow u_l \updownarrow u_c \downarrow u_r$, where $u_l = f_r$ and $u_r = s_l$.

Fig. 5. Ending elements

- Elements (y) that avoid linking strings that encode defective units among themselves: they will be encoded by $\updownarrow y_c \downarrow y_r$, where $y_r = f_l$.
- Elements (z) that avoid linking strings that encode conforming units among themselves: they will be encoded by $\uparrow z_l \updownarrow z_c$, where $z_l = s_r$.

4.2 Algorithm to obtain accepted and rejected samples

The encoding presented in the previous subsection enables us to use biological operations with DNA strands to perform certain operations on strings that represent the conforming and defective units of a lot.

In fact, the idea of the following algorithm is to obtain strands representing samples that simulate a binomial distribution $B(n,p)$, where n is the size sample and p is the probability of a unit being a defective unit. To do this we merge strands representing units of the sample. Notice that, because of the encoding of the units, our strands should be of the form $f \ldots fus \ldots s$ as we show in Figure 6. Then we only need to choose those with size n, that is

Fig. 6. Strand encoding a sample

to say, those strands of length $l(n + 1)$, where l is the length of the strings that represent successes, failures and neuters. The remaining strands will be separated into units and linked again repeating the same process until there are no neuters left.

Algorithm "GeneratingSamples"
Input: The size n of the sample, the set S_{sf} of strands that encode successes (s) and failures (f) with ratios p and $1 - p$, respectively, and the set S_u of strands that encode neuters (u) with ratio $1/n$ with respect to all the successes and failures.
Output: The set Ω_n of strands that encode samples of size n.

$\Omega_n := \emptyset$
while $(S_u \neq \emptyset)$ **do**
    # we obtain strands of the form $f \cdots fus \cdots s$ using ligase
    $L \longleftarrow$ **merge**(S_{sf}, S_u)
    # we obtain strands of the form $f \cdots fus \cdots s$ of lenght $l(n + 1)$
    $L_+ \longleftarrow$ **+lextract**$(L, l(n + 1))$ **and** $L_- \longleftarrow$ **−lextract**$(L, l(n + 1))$
    $S_{sfu} \longleftarrow$ **cut**(**cut**$(L_-, s), f)$
        $S_{sf} \longleftarrow$ **−sextract**(S_{sfu}, u) **and** $S_u \longleftarrow$ **+sextract**(S_{sfu}, u)
    $\Omega_n \longleftarrow$ **union**(Ω_n, L_+)
endwhile

Now we give an algorithm (that calls the previous one) to determine the number of accepting and rejecting samples of a multiple sampling plan using DNA operations. The idea of the algorithm is as follows:

- We generate using the first algorithm strands encoding samples of size n_1. We separate those samples with a number of defective units equal or less than c_1 from those whose number is equal or greater than r_1. For those undecided by the first step of the sampling plan, we generate samples of size n_2.
- We link each n_2-sample with a n_1-sample cutting this one by its neuter (see Figure 7).

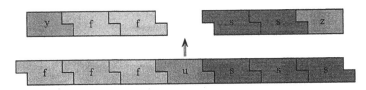

Fig. 7. Linking samples

- Once again, we separate accepted samples from rejected samples at the second step of the plan and so on until the m-th step.

Algorithm "SamplingPlans"
Input: A multiple sampling plan $\{(n_1, c_1, r_1), \ldots, (n_m, c_m, r_m)\}$, the sets S_{sf}^i, $1 \leq i \leq m$, of strands that encode successes (s) and failures (f) with ratios p and $1 - p$, respectively, and the sets S_u^i that encode neuters (u) with ratios $1/n_i$ with respect to all the successes and the failures.
Output: The set A of strands that are accepted by the sampling plan and the set R of strands that are rejected.

$A := \emptyset; R := \emptyset; D_- := \emptyset$
$j := 1; i := 1$
while $(i \leq m$ and $j = 1)$ **do**
    # we obtain strands that encode samples of size n_i
    $G \longleftarrow$ GeneratingStrings(S_{sf}^i, S_u^i, n_i)
    # we obtain strands that encode samples of size $n_1 + \cdots + n_i$
    $C \longleftarrow$ **merge**(D_-, G)
    # we separate those samples with a number of failures $\leq c_i$
    # f_{c_i} is the string that represent $c_i + 1$ failures
    $C_- \longleftarrow -$**sextract**(C, f_{c_i}) **and** $C_+ \longleftarrow +$**sextract**(C, f_{c_i})
    # we separate those samples with a number of failures $\geq r_i$
    # f_{r_i} is the string that represent $r_i + 1$ failures
    $D_- \longleftarrow -$**sextract**(C_+, f_{r_i}) **and** $D_+ \longleftarrow +$**sextract**(C_+, f_{r_i})

$A \longleftarrow \textbf{union}(A, C_-)$
$R \longleftarrow \textbf{union}(R, D_+)$
if $D_- = \emptyset$ **then** $j := 0$
if i=1 **then** $D_- \longleftarrow \textbf{lefttag}(\textbf{righttag}(D_-, y), z)$
  # we cut those samples with a number d of failures $c_i < d < r_i$
  $D_- \longleftarrow -\textbf{sextract}(\textbf{cut}(D_-, u), u)$
  $i := i + 1$
endwhile

Now, we can obtain the image of a given lot quality p under the power function Ψ as the ratio of the amount of rejected strands with respect to the amount of the accepted and rejected strands.

In order to give a first valuation of this method, we have implemented two algorithms to estimate the power function in multiple sampling attributes plans, one using the method presented here simulating biological operations and the other simulating binomial distributions. The empirical results obtained in both methods are very close. As an example, we give in Table 1 the values $\Psi_{bio}(p)$ and $\Psi_{bin}(p)$ obtained under the power function using the biological and the binomial methods, respectively, for the sampling plan S_7 of multiplicity $m = 7$ given by $\{(20, 0, 5), (20, 3, 8), (20, 6, 10), (20, 8, 13), (20, 11, 15), (20, 14, 17), (20, 18, 19)\}$ and proposed by the Military-Standard 105D.

p	0.50	0.30	0.25	0.20	0.18	0.15	0.13	0.10	0.08	0.05	0.03
Ψ_{bio}	1.00	0.9988	0.9905	0.9324	0.8683	0.6611	0.4672	0.1628	0.0531	0.0046	0.0002
Ψ_{bin}	1.00	0.9985	0.9906	0.9352	0.8709	0.6656	0.4559	0.1554	0.0506	0.0050	0.0018

Table 1. Values of the power function of the sampling plan S_7.

References

ADLEMAN, L. (1994): Molecular computation of solutions to combinatorial problems. *Science, 266, 1021-1024.*

DERMAN, C. and ROSS, S. (1997): *Statistical Aspects of quality control.* Academic Press.

FARNUM, N. (1994): *Statistical Quality Control and Improvement.* Duxburry Press.

PǍUN, G., ROZENBERG, G. and SALOMAA, A. (1998): *DNA Computation.* EATCS Series, Springer.

PISANTI, N. (1998): A survey on DNA computing. *Bulletin of the EATCS 64, 171-187.*

WATSON, J.D., CRICK, F.H.C. (1953): Molecular structure of nucleic acids: A structure for deoxyribose nucleic acid. *Nature 171, 737-738.*

Methodological Issues in the Baffling Relationship Between Hepatitis C Virus and Non Hodgkin's Lymphomas*

Stefano De Cantis[1], Daria Mendola[2], and Emilio Iannitto[3]

[1] Dip. Metodi Quantitativi per le Scienze Umane,
Università di Palermo, I-90128 Palermo, Italy
[2] Dip. Scienze Statistiche e Matematiche "Silvio Vianelli",
Università di Palermo, I-90128 Palermo, Italy
[3] Cattedra di Ematologia,
Policlinico Universitario "Paolo Giaccone", I-90128 Palermo, Italy

Abstract. The association between Hepatitis C Virus infection and B-cell Non-Hodgkin's Lymphoma has been the matter of several studies: they showed disagreeing results with a marked regional variability. In this paper we present a review of the literature, highlighting methodological issues and main statistically critical aspects. Review suggests that studies were often not methodologically well approached. Moreover, we present main results from an original case-control study conducted in Italy, in an area of high endemicity of Hepatitis C Virus infection. In particular, we put attention in selection of a properly matching control group and in the role of age as a confounding variable.

1 Introduction

Several studies suggest a possible involvement of chronic Hepatitis C Virus (HCV) infection in the development of B-cell Non-Hodgkin's Lymphoma (B-NHL). The postulated mechanism for this association (clonal B-cell proliferation in response to a lymphotrophic virus) is biologically plausible.

Since 1997 (year in which Silvestri et al. published the first and unique review on this matter) around thirty papers and a hundred of abstracts appeared in the major international journals of hematology, hepatology and gastroenterology. A significant association between HCV and NHL was mostly reported by studies conducted in Countries with high HCV endemicity (Italy, Japan, Spain, Romania, Hungary, Turkey), while those studies conducted in areas with low HCV endemicity (UK, Germany, France, Canada) failed to confirm such a figure. Whether these conflicting results are due to biologic differences in lymphoproliferative responses to HCV, virologic differences in genotypes and subtypes, or merely reflect a cohort or period effect or an inadequate power to detect the association in areas of low prevalence, remains to be explored. Therefore, we believe that these disagreeing results clearly suggest, from a statistical point of view, that the association between HCV and NHL

---

* Although this paper is due to the common work of the Authors, sections 3 and 4 are attributable to S. De Cantis, sections 1 and 5 to E. Iannitto, section 2 to D. Mendola.

has not been methodologically well approached. After a brief review covering designs and methods more frequently used in literature, we present the results of an original case-control study conducted in Italy, in an area of high HCV endemicity.

2   Designs and methods to assess relationship between HCV and B-NHL: a brief review

From a statistical and epidemiological point of view, empirical studies can be classified according to the different perspectives they adopt in verifying the putative association between HCV and NHL. We distinguished them in:
- *hematological perspective*: estimating in B-NHL population (cases) HCV prevalence and comparing it to that of a *healthy* (not-affected by B-NHL) population (controls); main target is to assess HCV prevalence rate in case and control populations;
- *gastroenterological perspective*: estimating in HCV infected population (cases) the B-NHL prevalence and comparing it to that of a *healthy* (not-infected by HCV) population (controls); main target is to assess B-NHL prevalence rate in case and control populations;
- *biological perspective*: in vitro studies focusing on virological, immunological, molecular and biological aspects of HCV infection in subjects affected by NHL. Main target is to identify data to ascertain the biological role of HCV in the development of NHL.

The relationship between HCV and B-NHL can depend on many cofactors that interact on association putting it in evidence or hiding or distorting it. Possible factors to be evaluated in their effects on the relationship are all potential risk factors for HCV (e.g. blood transfusions, age –as cohort and generation effect–, injecting-drugs abuse, background endemicity, genotype and subtypes of the C virus) and factors characterizing NHL disease (e.g. its peculiar age structure, histo-pathological characteristics, sex).

Table 1 concisely reports more recent literature results on the study of this association conducted in the hematological perspective, in the sense previously specified. These studies differ greatly from each other in many aspects that can be synthesized as follows:
- *prevalence of HCV* infection: detection of association is clearly influenced by the background HCV prevalence in the community, which differs markedly in different geographical areas (2-10% in Italy, 1-10% in Japan and around 0% in United Kingdom);
- choice of the *study population*: new cases in a time interval (incidence analysis), all cases at a fixed date (prevalence analysis), cohort studies, case-control studies;
- choice of the *control population*: it is often selected from general population on the basis of available large scale epidemiological studies. These Controls generally do not match for exposure to environmental risk factors. Sometimes a self-selected population is assumed as controls. It happened, for example,

with blood donors in Cavanna et al. (1995), De Rosa et al. (1997), Kuniyoshi et al. (2001), and others. Alternatively, in some studies, controls are hospitalized patients with diseases presumably not correlated with lymphoma or HCV (like in Collier et al.(1999), Hausfater et al. (2001), Pioltelli et al. (2000), and so on);

- *sampling methods*: with randomization (e.g. Poisson, selected pseudo-sample, systematic sample), or, sometimes, with not well declared enrolment rules;
- *time of HCV test*: at diagnosis, before/after treatment or at some point during the clinic history of patients;
- *statistical analysis*: in most studies we can find Fisher's exact test or a X^2 test on the 2 × 2 contingency table (HCV pos/neg × NHL/Controls). Alternatively (or in addition) they often present comparisons between proportions of HCV positive patients (crude rates) in both populations, using tests of significance of their difference;
- accounting for *confounding variables*: almost few studies take account of possible intervening variables (see Tab.1).

Comparing all these studies, we can observe some statistical weakness of adopted designs and methods of analysis. In particular, we note that the retrospective nature of some of the studies, with inclusion of both incident and prevalent cases, the comparisons with control groups at different risk for HCV infection and the lack of a proper age and sex matching are to be considered as the main biases. Moreover, although in some studies we can see a matching for age, sex or other influencing variables, the final comparisons between proportions of HCV in controls and B-NHL patients is always performed on the global table of association, while neglecting the "not negligible" role of these factors. But, as it is well explained in Breslow and Day (1980), if the exposure to risk factor increases the rate of disease for one part of the population and decreases it for another, then the role of this factor is *"not negligible"*. This implies the impossibility to compare crude rates and move toward using only specific rates which will be compared singularly and not in an aggregated manner. Finally, we think that in Countries with a low HCV endemicity, where HCV rates are very small in the general population, the comparison by the difference of the proportions is meaningless and may also lead to erroneous results, so one should rather resort to their ratio.

Analogous considerations can be drawn for the studies (according to a gastroenterological perspective) reported in Table 2. On the basis of the considerations above, we think that regional variation of some confounding variables (such as endemicity of HCV or ethnic characteristics and environmental risk factors) is so high that it is not proper to conduct studies on aggregated data, often coming from national or international databases.

We think that performing studies conducted on small areas with an accurately chosen/matched control population would be a more suitable approach. Moreover, once one has realized that there are important intervening variables, it is necessary to investigate if their role on the association between

References	Country	HCV prevalence in B-NHL patients (%)	Controls, HCV prevalence in Controls (%)	Statistical analysis; matching or adjusting for
Brind et al. (1996)	UK	0/63 (0)	–	–
Cavanna et al. (1995)*	Italy	38/150 (25)	Blood Donors, 53/3108 (2)	Fisher or X^2; age, sex
Collier et al. (1999)	Canada	0/100 (0)	Nonhemat mal, 0/100 (0)	– –
Cucuianu et al. (1999)*	Romania	35/68 (51)	Gen loc pop, 46/943 (5)	Fisher or X^2; –
De Rosa et al. (1997)*	Italy	21/93 (23)	Blood Donors, 298/1568 (2)	Fisher or X^2; –
Gasztonyi et al. (2000)*	Hungary	10/42 (24)	–	–
Germanidis et al. (1999)	France	4/201 (2)	Hodgkin's dis, 1/94 (1)	Comp. Prop.; –
Hausfater et al. (2001)	France	30/164 (2)	Internal med pats, 3/694 (0.4)	Fisher or X^2; –
Kuniyoshi et al. (2001)	Japan	20/348 (8)	Blood Donors, 10593/1513358 (0.7)	M-H, Fisher or X^2; sex, age
Iannitto et al. (2002a)	Italy	24/134 (18)	Gen loc pop, 75/721 (10)	M-H, B-D Stand meth, RR; sex, age
Izumi et al. (1996)*	Japan	12/54 (22)	Blood Donors, – (1)	– –
King et al. (1998)	USA	1/73(1)	Hodgkin's disease, 0/20 (0)	– –
Luppi et al. (1998)*	Italy	35/157 (22)	Gen loc pop, – (2)	Fisher or X^2; –
Mazzaro et al. (1996)*	Italy	57/199 (29)	Gen lo pop, 1 99/6917 (3)	Fisher or X^2; –
McColl et al. (1997)	Scotland	0/72 (0)	–	–
Pioltelli et al. (2000)	Italy	48/300 (16)	Int and surg dis, 51/600 (9)	RR; sex, age
Rabkin et al. (2002)	USA	0/95 (0)	Non mal dis, 0/95 (0)	RR; sex, age, race
Shariff et al. (1999)	Canada	2/88 (2)	T-NHL, 11/1085 (1)	Comp. Prop.; –
Silvestri et al. (1996)*	Italy	28/311 (9)	Gen loc pop, – (3)	RR, Fisher or X^2; –
Silvestri et al. (1997)*	Italy	42/470 (9)	HCV+ subjects, – (3)	RR, Fisher or X^2; –
Thalen et al. (1997)	Netherlands	0/115 (0)	–	–
Vallisa et al. (1999)*	Italy	65/175 (37)	Hospital inpatients, 17/175 (10)	Fisher or X^2; –
Zignego et al. (1997)*	Italy	37/150 (25)	Healthy pop, 0/70 (0)	Fisher or X^2; –
Zucca et al. (2000)	Switzerland	17/180 (9)	Blood Donors, 51/5424 (1)	Comp. Prop., X^2; –
Zuckerman et al. (1997)*	USA	26/120 (22)	Internal med pats, 7/154 (5)	Fisher or X^2; –

* studies that confirmed the association between HCV and NHL

Legend:

Nonhemat mal = Not hematological malignancies;
Gen loc pop = General (healthy) local population;
Int and surg dis = Internal and surgical disease;
Non mal dis = Non malignant disease;
T-NHL = T-cell Non Hodgkin's lymphoma;
Internal med pats = Internal medicine patients;

Fisher or X^2 = Fisher's or Pearson's X^2 test;
M-H = Mantel-Haenszel common odds ratio;
B-D = Breslow and Day Test;
Stand meth = Standardization methods;
RR = Relative risk;
Comp. Prop. = test on proportions difference.

Table 1. Studies on HCV prevalence in subsets of B-NHL patients (hematological perspective)

References	Country	B-NHL prevalence in HCV patients(%)	Controls, B-NHL prevalence in Controls (%)	Statistical analyses; matching for
Ferri et al. (1996)	Italy	14/500 (2.8)	NA, NA	NA; NA
Ohsawa et al. (1999)	Japan	4/2162 (0.19)	gen pop, NA (0.09)	Risk estimation; sex, age, calendar year
Sànchez et al. (1995)	Spain	3/148 (2)	NA, NA	NA; NA

Table 2. Studies on B-NHL prevalence in subsets of HCV patients (gastroenten-terological perspective)

HCV and NHL could be considered "negligible" or not (according to the Breslow-Day definition).

3   An original case-control study

In light of the reported literature, and on the basis of previously presented considerations, we designed a case-control study (in the hematological perspective) to analyze association between Hepatitis C Virus and B-cell Non Hodgkin's Lymphoma, trying to overcome some of the limitations found in similar studies. We compared the prevalence of HCV infection in a sample of consecutive unselected Sicilian B-NHL patients to that of a *healthy* (not affected by lymphoma) population from the same geographical area.

We believe that if a relationship between HCV and lymphoproliferative disorders does exist, it could be more evident and easy to study in an area with a high prevalence of HCV infection such as Sicily (in the South of Italy). Moreover people with cancer are often referred to highly specialized centers far away from where they live. As a consequence, for the sake of comparison, control groups properly matching for age, ethnic and geographical origin should be used (Iannitto et al. (2002b)). In order to do this, we set up a study aimed at determining the prevalence of HCV infection in patients with B-NHL in which Controls were matched for ethnicity and age and randomly chosen from the general population.

Study population: A Poisson sample of 134 consecutive unselected B-NHL patients seen at the Haematology and Bone Marrow Unit of Palermo University Hospital between January 1st 1997 and December 31st 2000 has been evaluated. All patients were born and lived in Palermo or in other nearby western provinces of Sicily. They all were HIV negative, heterosexuals, with no history of intravenous drug abuse. There were 84 men and 50 women and the mean age was 60.8 years (SD 13.9; range 17-87 years). To avoid potential risk factors for HCV infection (e.g. hospitalization and therapy), antibodies against HCV were detected at diagnosis. For more clinical details and pathological features of B-NHL patients see Iannitto et al. (2002).

Control population: The control population was drawn with a systematic 1:4 sampling from the population census of Camporeale, a small town of approximately 4000 inhabitants nearby Palermo. A total of 721 subjects were enrolled. There were 316 men and 405 women; the mean age was 40.4 years (SD 18.0; range 10-90 years). Control group is homogeneous to study population according to ethnical characteristics and geographical origin; this should assure a homogeneity in exposure to main environmental risk factors. None of the subjects in this group showed, at the moment of screening, clinical evidence of lymphoproliferative disease. For more details see Di Stefano et al. (2002).

Statistical methods: We highlighted the possible confounding effect of age in assessing the relationship between HCV and B-NHL in De Cantis and Iannitto (2001). The comparison between Controls and B-NHL patients by means of direct standardization methods and the decomposition of difference between two crude prevalence rates showed that the age effect encompasses a large part of this difference with both rate effect and interaction effect playing a secondary but *not negligible role*. In this paper we analyzed with more details the association structure between the two diseases in different age strata using categorical data methods. Cochran's and Mantel-Haenszel statistics were used to test for independence between a dichotomous factor (Study and Control Population) and a dichotomous response (HCV positiveness and negativeness), conditional upon covariate patterns defined by the layers of age variable (Landis et al. (1999)). The Mantel-Haenszel common odds ratio (Kuritz and Landis (1988)) was also computed, along with Breslow-Day and Tarone's statistics (Breslow and Day (1980), Tarone (1985)) for testing the homogeneity of odds ratios among age classes .

4   Results

HCV antibodies were detected in the sera of 24 patients affected by B-NHL, resulting a crude prevalence rate of 17.9%. Among Controls, 75 out of 721 were HCV positive (10.4%). Two groups differ significantly both for age distribution and age-specific HCV prevalence rates, as reported in Table 3. Ignoring confounding effect of age, both odds ratio and relative risk crude estimates are significantly different from unity. On the other side, the Mantel-Haenszel common odds ratio estimate (OR_{MH}), controlling for different age strata, does not differ significantly from unity (OR_{MH} =0.749; $CI_{95\%}$: (0.448; 1.253)). Last result confirms that correction by age makes not significant the association between HCV and B-NHL. Moreover age-specific relative risks differ greatly: Breslow-Day's test and the Tarone's test for homogeneity of odds ratios among the age strata give a low p-value (0.008). Note that the risk of being HCV positive is higher for the younger B-NHL patients rather than for Controls. In particular, putting a cut off at age 50, the relative risk between under and over 50 years for B-NHL patients was 0.615 ($CI_{95\%}$: (0.193; 1.957)), ten times ($P < 0.001$) greater than for Controls (0.062). This suggests that the effect of the age variable in the association between Hepatitis C virus and B-cell Non Hodgkin lymphoma is not negligi-

Stratum	Study Population		Control Population		Risk Estimates	
age in years	cases	HCV+	cases	HCV+	OR	RR
10-40	11	1	387	4	9.575	8.795
40-50	20	3	110	8	2.250	2.063
50-60	29	6	79	17	0.951	0.961
60+	74	14	145	46	0.497	0.592
Total	134	24	721	75	**1.879**	**1.722**
					$CI_{95\%}$: $(1.137, 3.105)$	$CI_{95\%}$: $(1.130, 2.623)$

Test for homogeneity of Odds Ratios among strata:
Breslow-day test: p-value < 0.008
Tarone's test:p-value < 0.008
Mantel-Haenszel common Odds Ratio estimate
(controlling for age strata): 0.749 $CI_{95\%}$: $(0.448, 1.253)$

Table 3. Analysis of association and risk estimates (Odds Ratio and Relative Risk) to be HCV+ between Controls and B-NHL patients for age strata

ble and it makes not interpretable: a) the difference between crude prevalence rates and even b) the difference between direct standardized prevalence rates.

5   Some final remarks

In our study, the crude prevalence rate of HCV infection in B-NHL patients was higher (17.9%) than that of the control population (10.4%). However, when adjusting the result by age, this difference becomes not significant and it means that it was in large part due to the confounding effect of age. We noted a difference in the shape of the HCV prevalence rate curve of B-NHL from that of Controls, with a higher than expected HCV prevalence rate in younger lymphoma patients and lower in the older age group. Also the relative risk of being HCV positive for B-NHL patients compared to Controls is significantly higher in the under 50 age class. The issue of the presence of B-NHL in young HCV positive subjects deserves particular attention: from the biological point of view the duration of HCV persistence in the organism should be shorter than that in old subjects, taking for granted a similar age of infection. Thus, the risk should be high in elderly subjects in whom the infection has lasted for decades. In these patients, instead, the two processes (HCV infection and B-NHL) appear to progress in an autonomous fashion. It could be speculated that a seroconversion later in life (Rabkin et al. (2002)), a distinct way of infection or infection caused by HCV genotype with high lymphotropism may account for a higher risk of developing a B-NHL. Alternatively, it could be hypothesized that other co-factors, till now unknown, must be present at the time of HCV infection or that a particular individual susceptibility to develop lymphoid malignancies may play a role. Hence, if a causative role could be played by HCV virus in the multistep path of the lymphoma development, it should be confined to some selected fraction of subjects.

Finally, we were not able to confirm, even in a high HCV endemic area (such as Sicily), a higher prevalence of HCV infection in B-NHL patients. This study suggests that HCV would play a different role in the different age groups with respect to the development of B-cells lymphoma. If this is the case, the young patients with B-NHL could be the main focus in this research area.

References

ALTER, HJ.(1995): To C or not to C : these are the question. *Blood, 85, 1681–1695.*
BELLANTANI, S., TIRIBELLI, C., SACCOCCIO, G. et al. (1994): Prevalence of chronic liver disease in the general population of Northern Italy: the Dionysos study. *Hepatology, 20, 6, 1442–1449.*
BRESLOW, NE. and DAY, NE. (1980): *Statistical Methods in Cancer Research I. The analysis of Case-Control Studies.* IARC, Lyon.
BRIND, AM., WATSON JP. BURT A. et al. (1996): Non-Hodgkin's lymphoma and hepatitis C virus infection. *Leuk Lymphoma, 21 (1-2), 127–130.*
CAVANNA, L., SBOLLI, G., TANZI E. et al. (1995): High prevalence of antibodies to hepatitis C virus in patients with lymphoproliferative disorders. *Haematologica, 80, 486–487.*
COLLIER, JD., ZANKE, B., MOORE, M. et al. (1999): No association between hepatitis C and B-cell lymphoma. *Hepatology, 29, 1259–12615.*
CUCUIANU, A., PATIU, M. and DUMA, M. (1999): Hepatitis B and C virus infection in Romanian non Hodgkin's lymphoma patients. Br J Haematology, 107, 353–356.
DE CANTIS, S. and IANNITTO, E. (2001): The confounding effect of age in the association between HCV and NHL. In: Ist. Statistica, Universitá di Palermo (Ed.): *Book of Short Papers CLADAG2001.* 213–216.
DE ROSA, G., GOBBO, ML. and DE RENZO, A. (1977): High prevalence of hepatitis C virus infection in patients with B-cell lymphoproliferative disorders in Italy. *Am J Hematol., 55, 77–82.*
DE VITA, S., SACCO, C., SANSONNO, S. et al. (1997): Characterization of overt B-cell lymphomas in patients with hepatitis C virus infection. *Blood, 90, 2, 776–782.*
DE VITA, S., SANSONNO, D., DOLCETTI, R. et al. (1995): Hepatitis C virus within a malignant lymphoma lesion in the course of type II mixed cryoglobulinemia. *Blood, 86, 1887–1892.*
DI STEFANO, R., STROFFOLINI, T., FERRARO, D. ET AL.(2002): Endemic hepatitis C virus infection in Sicilian town: further evidence for iatrogenic transmission. *J. Med. Virol., in press.*
FERRI, C., LA CIVITA, L., MONTI, M. et al. (1996): Chronic hepatitis C and B-cell non-Hodgkin's lymphoma. *Quart J Med, 89, 117–122.*
FERRI, C., MONTI, M., LA CIVITA, L. et al. (1993): Infection of blood mononuclear cells by Hepatitis C virus in mixed cryoglobulinemia.*Blood, 82, 12, 3701–3704.*
GASZTONYI, B., PAR, A., SZOMOR, A. et al. (2000): Hepatitis C virus infection associated with B-cell Non-Hodgkin's lymphoma in Hungarian patients. *Brit J of Haematology, 110, 493–499.*
GERMANIDIS, G., HAIOUN, C., POURQUIER, J. et al. (1999): Hepatitis C virus infection in patients with overt B-cell non-Hodgkin's lymphoma in a French center. *Blood, 93, 1778–1779.*

HAUSFATER, P., CACOUB, P., STERKERS, Y. et al. (2001): Hepatitis C virus infection and lymphoproliferative disease: prospective study on 1576 patients in France. *Am J Hematol, 67,168-171.*

IANNITTO, E., BARBERA, V., CIRRINCIONE, S. et al. (2002a): The baffling relationship between HCV and Non Hodgkin's Lymphomas. Unexpected higher prevalence of HCV infection in young age classes of Non Hodgkin's lymphomas in a geographical area of high HCV endemicity. *Blood.* (in press)

IANNITTO, E., DE CANTIS, S., CIRRINCIONE, S. et al. (2002b): Are blood donors an adequate control group to ascertain the HCV prevalence in non-Hodgkin's lymphoma patients? *J Gastroent Hepatol.* (in press)

IVANOVSKI M., SILVESTRI F., POZZATO G. et al. (1998): Somatic hypermutation, clonal diversity, and preferential expression of the Vh 51p1/VLkv325 immunoglobulin gene combination in hepatitis C virus-associated immunocytomas. *Blood, 91, 7, 2433-2442.*

IZUMI, T., SASAKI, R., MIURA, Y. et al. (1996): B-cell malignancies and hepatitis C virus infection *Leuk Res, 20, 445* .

KING, PD., WILKES, JD., DIAZ-ARIAS AA. et al. (1998): Hepatitis C virus infection in non-Hodgkin's lymphoma *Clin Lab Haematol, 20, 107-110.*

KUNIYOSHI, M., NAKAMUTA, M., SAKAI, H. et al. (2001): Prevalence of hepatitis B or C virus infections in patients with non-Hodgkin's lymphoma *J Gastroent Hepatol, 16, 215-219.*

KURITZ, SJ. and LANDIS, JR. (1988): Attributable risk estimation from matched case-control data. *Biometrics, 44, 355-367* .

LANDIS, JR., SHARP, TJ., KURITZ, SJ. et al. (1998): Mantel-Haenszel methods. In: P. Armitage and T. Colton (Eds.): *Encyclopedia of Biostatistics.* Wiley & Sons, New York

LUPPI, M., FERRARI MG., BONACCORSI ET AL. (1998): Hepatitis C virus infection in subsets of neoplastic lymphoproliferations not associated with cryoglobulinemia *Leukemia, 10, 351-355.*

MAZZARO C., ZAGONEL, V., MONFARDINI, S. et al. (1996): Hepatitis C virus and non Hodgkin's lymphomas *Br J Haematol, 94, 544-550.*

McCOLL, MD., SINGER, IO., TAIT, RC. et al. (1997): The role of Hepatitis C virus in the aetiology of non Hodgkin's lymphoma – a regional association? *Leuk Lymphoma, 26,127-130.*

OHSAWA, M., SHINGU, N., HIDEAKI, M. et al. (1999): Risk of non-Hodgkin's lymphoma in patients with hepatitis c virus infection. *Intr J Cancer, 80, 237-239.*

PIOLTELLI, P., GARGANTINI, L., CASSI, E. et al. (2000): Hepatitis C virus in non Hodgkin's lymphoma. A reappraisal after a prospective case-control study of 300 patients. *Am J Hematol, 64,95-100.*

RABKIN, CS., TESS, BH., CHRISTIANSON, RE. et al. (2002): Prospective study of Hepatitis C viral infection as a risk factor for subsequent B-cell neoplasia. *Blood, 99,11,4240 -4242.*

SANCHEZ, IP., REDONDO JR., MONFORTE AG. et al. (1995): B-lymphoproliferative disorders in patients with hepatitis C virus infection. *Haematologica, 13, 418-424.*

SANSONNO, D., DE VITA, S., CORNACCHIULO, V. et al. (1996): Detection and distribution of hepatitis C virus-related proteins in lymph nodes of patients with type II mixed cryoglobulinemia and neoplastic or non-neoplastic lymphoproliferation. *Blood, 88, 12, 4638-4645.*

SANSONNO, D., LOTESORIERE, C., CORNACCHIULO, V. et al. (1998): Hepatitis C virus infection involves CD34+ hematopoietic progenitor cells in Hepatitis C virus chronic carriers. *Blood, 92, 9, 3328-3337.*

SHARIFF, S., YOSHIDA, EM., GASCOYNE, RD. et al. (1999): Hepatitis C infection and B-cell non Hodgkin's lymphoma in British Columbia: a cross-sectional analysis. *Annals of Oncology, 10, 961-964.*

SILVESTRI, F., BARILLARI, G., FANIN, R. et al. (1997): The genotype of the hepatitis C virus in patients with HCV-related B-cell non Hodgkin's lymphoma. *Leukemia, 11, 2157-2161.*

SILVESTRI, F., PIPAN, C., BARILLARI, G. et al. (1996): Prevalence of hepatitis C virus infection in patients with lymphoproliferative disorders. *Blood, 87, 10, 4296-4301.*

TARONE, RE. (1985): On heterogeneity tests based on efficient scores. *Biometrika, 72, 91-95.*

THALEN, DJ., RAEMAEKERS, J., GALAMA, J. et al. (1997): Absence of hepatitis C virus infection in non Hodgkin's lymphoma. *British Journal of Haematology, 96, 880-881.*

VALLISA, D., BERTE', R., ROCCA, A. et al. (1999): Association between hepatitis C virus and non Hodgkin's lymphoma, and effects of viral infection on histologic subtype and clinical course. *Am J Med, 106, 556-560.*

ZIGNEGO, AL., GIANNINI, C., GENTILINI, P. (1997): Could HGV infection be implicated in lymphomagenesis? *British Journal of Haematology, 98, 778-782.*

ZUCCA, E., ROGGERO, E., MAGGI-SOLCA, N. et al. (2000): Prevalence of Helicobacter pylori and hepatitis C virus infections among non Hodgkin's lymphoma patients in Southern Switzerland. *Haematologica, 85, 147-153.*

ZUCKERMAN, E., ZUCKERMAN, T., LEVINE, AM. et al. (1997): Hepatitis C virus infection in patients with B-cell non Hodgkin's lymphoma. *Annals Inter Med, 127, 423-428.*

Class Discovery in Gene Expression Data: Characterizing Splits by Support Vector Machines

Florian Markowetz and Anja von Heydebreck

Max-Planck-Institute for Molecular Genetics
Computational Molecular Biology
Ihnestrasse 63-73, D-14195 Berlin, Germany
{florian.markowetz, anja.heydebreck}@molgen.mpg.de

Abstract. We present a variation of the class discovery method for microarray data described by Heydebreck et al. (2001). The objective is to discover biologically relevant structures in the gene expression profiles of different tissue samples in an unsupervised fashion. Our method searches for binary partitions in the set of samples that show clear separation. Mathematically, each class distinction is characterized according to the size of margin achieved by a support vector machine (SVM) separating the two classes. In three data sets from cancer gene expression studies the SVM margin approach succeeds in detecting relationships between the tissue samples. The known biological classes (cancer subtypes) exhibit an exceptionally large value of the SVM margin.

1 Introduction

In microarray experiments different tissue samples are characterized by profiles of gene expression levels. The aim of our work is to find class distinctions among a set of tissue samples which show a clear separation with respect to a subset of genes. In (Heydebreck et al. (2001)) this class discovery problem is approached by a method called ISIS (for "identifying splits with clear separation"). It consists of two steps: First, based on the classification method *Diagonal Linear Discriminant Analysis* a score function (the so called *DLD score*) is proposed to quantify the degree of separability of a given binary class distinction of the set of samples. This score function is defined on the graph of all bipartitions of the set of samples. In the second step all bipartitions are declared as interesting which represent local maxima in this graph, i. e. for which the score does not increase if the class label of a single sample is changed. Since an exhaustive search over all bipartitions is in general not feasible, Heydebreck et al. (2001) propose a fast heuristic to find candidate partitions as starting points for a search of local maxima.

In this paper we will contrast the DLD score with a measure of separability based on *Support Vector Machines*. This results in a variation of the original ISIS algorithm called SVM-ISIS. We show that SVM-ISIS detects the known tumor subtypes present in three example data sets in an unsupervised fashion.

2   Methods

2.1   Microarray gene expression data

Microarrays allow to quantitate the expression of thousands of genes in parallel and thus to observe gene expression variation in a variety of human tumours (Chipping forecast (1999)). Mathematically, the result of a gene expression study is a matrix $X = (x_{gj})$, whose columns correspond to tissue samples ($j = 1, \ldots, n$) and whose rows correspond to genes ($g = 1, \ldots, k$). Using this matrix, each tissue sample is interpreted as a point in $\mathbb{R}^k$.

2.2   The graph of bipartitions

Two subsets $M, \overline{M}$ of the set of samples $\{1, \ldots, n\}$ define a *bipartition* or *split* $\mathcal{B} = \{M, \overline{M}\}$ of this set if $M \cap \overline{M} = \emptyset$ and $M \cup \overline{M} = \{1, \ldots, n\}$. Let Γ be the graph whose vertex set is the set of all bipartitions of $\{1, \ldots, n\}$. Two different vertices are joined by an edge (are neighbors) iff they differ only by the class assignment of a single sample.

We will now define a score $S(\mathcal{B})$ on the vertex set of Γ that measures how clearly the two classes representing a given bipartition are separated by gene expression levels.

2.3   The SVM margin score

Given a bipartition $\mathcal{B} = \{M, \overline{M}\}$ we separate the samples in M from the samples in $\overline{M}$ by a Support Vector Machine with linear kernel, i. e. by a hyperplane yielding a maximal margin of separation (Figure 1).
A hyperplane $\mathcal{H} = \{\, x \mid \langle w, x \rangle + b = 0 \,\}$ is defined by its normal vector w and offset b. It can be shown that the maximal margin hyperplane is constructed by solving the following constrained optimisation problem (Vapnik (1998)). For $i = 1, \ldots, n$

$$minimize\ \ \frac{1}{2}\|w\|^2$$

$$subject\ to\ \ y_i(\langle w, x_i \rangle + b) - 1 \geq 0,$$

where $x_i \in \mathbb{R}^k$ are the data points (with k the number of genes) and $y_i = +1$ if $i \in M$ and $y_i = -1$ if $i \in \overline{M}$. The margin $\gamma(\mathcal{H})$ of the separating hyperplane depends on the normal vector w by $\gamma(\mathcal{H}) = 2/\|w\|$.

With this background we define the *SVM margin score* $S(\mathcal{B})$ of a bipartition $\mathcal{B} = \{M, \overline{M}\}$ as the margin achieved by a Support Vector Machine separating the samples in M from the samples in $\overline{M}$.

Our goal is to find bipartitions of the set of samples with high SVM score. Since the total number of bipartitions of n samples equals 2^n, we can not compute the score function for all of them. Instead, we use the same heuristic as described in Heydebreck et al. (2001). Here we will give a short summary.

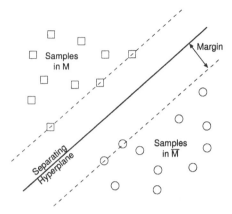

Fig. 1. The margin of separation. The two subsets of samples are separated by a hyperplane. The distance between the hyperplane and the nearest sample is the margin. In Support Vector Machines, the separating hyperplane is chosen such that the margin is maximized. The points on the dashed lines are called *support vectors*, because they alone determine the separating hyperplane.

2.4   Finding candidate partitions

We begin with the data matrix $X = (x_{gj})$ with $j = 1, \ldots, n$ and $g = 1, \ldots, k$. From this we compute average expression profiles of clusters of genes obtained by a hierarchical clustering. This yields a new data matrix $Y = (y_{ij})$, the rows of which are the cluster average profiles.

For every gene cluster i and every sample $j^* = 1, \ldots n$, the value y_{ij^*} defines a bipartition given by the subsets $M^- = \{\, j \mid y_{ij} \le y_{ij^*} \,\}$ and $M^- = \{\, j \mid y_{ij} > y_{ij^*} \,\}$. Whenever both M^- and M^+ have at least two elements, we compute the two-sample t-statistic. We argue that a large value of t provides evidence for an interesting bipartition defined by the cut point y_{ij^*}, with a strong separation of the two classes by the expression levels of the genes belonging to cluser i. We order the splits by the value of the t-statistic and take the 50 top-scoring partitions as candidates for the further search.

2.5   Feature selection

In highdimensional data sets, classification often benefits from a selection of a subset of variables which show the strongest correlation with the class distinction of interest. We measured this correlation by the two-sample t-statistic $t_g(\mathcal{B})$ for each gene g:

$$t_g(\mathcal{B}) = \frac{\mu_{gM} - \mu_{g\overline{M}}}{\sqrt{(m-1)\sigma_{gM}^2 + (\overline{m}-1)\sigma_{g\overline{M}}^2}} \times \sqrt{\frac{m\overline{m}(n-2)}{n}},$$

where $m = \|M\|$ and $\overline{m} = n - m$. For each split $\mathcal{B}$ we selected the 50 genes with highest absolute value of $t_g(\mathcal{B})$.

2.6   Local search for maxima

From each bipartition $\mathcal{B}$ obtained by this procedure, we proceed along a path in Γ to a local maximum of the SVM score in a greedy manner: Starting at $\mathcal{B}$, we choose in each step the neighboring vertex with the highest SVM score until a local maximum is reached. The resulting high-scoring bipartitions can then be graphically displayed as in Figures 2–5.

3   Example data sets

The performance of the SVM score was tested on three different data sets: leukemia, lymphoma/leukemia and a melanoma data set. We will shortly describe the datasets and sum up the important features in Table 1.

Dataset	# samples total	# genes used (total)	classes: # samples
Leukemia Golub *et al.* (1999)	72	4,000 (6,817)	AML: 25 B-cell ALL: 38 T-cell ALL: 9
Lymphoma / leukemia Alizadeh *et al.* (2000)	62	4,026 (17,856)	CLL: 11 FL: 9 DLBCL-G: 21 DLBCL-A: 21
Melanoma Bittner *et al.* (2000)	31	3,613 (6,971)	cluster: 19 remaining: 12

Table 1. Overview of example data sets. Listed are the names of the data sets with reference, the total number of samples, the number of genes used in our computations compared to the total number of genes on the chips and in the last column the name of the subclasses with number of samples therein.

Leukemia: described by Golub et. al. (1999). For a set of 72 acute leukemia mRNA samples, expression levels of 6,817 genes were measured with Affymetrix oligonucleotide arrays. Subclasses are *acute myeloid leukemia* (AML, 25 samples) and *acute lymphoblastic leukemia* (ALL, 47 samples), which is further split into the subtypes B-cell ALL (38 samples) and T-cell ALL (9 samples). Our analysis is based on 4,000 genes with highest median expression levels over the samples.

Lymphoma/Leukemia: (Alizadeh et. al. (2000)) Expression profiles of 62 lymphoma and leukemia samples were produced with a "Lymphochip" containing 17,856 cDNA clones. A subset of 4,026 clones was selected by the authors for being "well measured" across the samples. The samples represent the following types of lymphoid malignancies: *chronic lymphocytic leukemia* (CLL, 11 samples); *follicular lymphoma* (FL, 9 samples) and *diffuse large B-cell lymphoma* (DLBCL, 42 samples), which is further subdivided into *germinal center B-cell like DLBCL* (DLBCL-G, 21 samples) and *activated B-cell like DLBCL* (DLBCL-A, 21 samples).

Melanoma: described by Bittner et. al. (2000). 31 RNA samples of cutaneous melanoma were investigated by hybridization to a cDNA array representing 6,971 genes. We used the data from 3,613 clones selected by the authors for being "strongly detected" across the samples. By multidimensional scaling and different cluster algorithms, the authors identified a cluster of 19 samples separated from the remaining 12 samples.

4 Results

4.1 Significance of the SVM score

To investigate the significance of the SVM margin score in characterizing phenotypical class distinctions, we compared its outcome on the biological partitions in the three data sets to the outcome on 10,000 random partitions of the data. The results are shown in Table 2.

For each tumor subtype present in the data set, its SVM margin score, the distance to the next local maximum and the SVM margin at this local maximum is shown. The numbers in the brackets show the percentage of random splits with equal or less distance to the next local maximum or a higher SVM score.

Dataset	Class	distance to local max.	SVM margin	SVM margin at local max.
Leukemia	AML	3 (58.7%)	1.6 (0%)	2.2 (0%)
	T-cell ALL	0 (0.4%)	2.6 (0%)	2.6 (0%)
	B-cell ALL	1 (14.8%)	1.9 (0%)	2.8 (0%)
Lymphoma/	CLL	2 (13.5%)	2.0 (0%)	2.8 (0.1%)
leukemia	FL	0 (0.2%)	2.4 (0%)	2.4 (0.3%)
	DLBCL-G	3 (24.6%)	1.7 (0%)	2.0 (4.7%)
	DLBCL-A	5 (49%)	1.7 (0%)	2.9 (0.1%)
Melanoma	cluster of 19 samples	1 (8.8%)	1.2 (0%)	2.0 (10.2%)

Table 2. Significance of the SVM score. The SVM score of the biological partitions in the example data sets is compared to the performance on 10,000 random partitions. In brackets: percentage of random partitions with a smaller or equal distance to the next local maximum or a higher SVM score.

One can see that proximity to a local maximum is not rare in the random splits, while the scores of all cancer subtypes are very high compared to the sampled random splits. This indicates that a high score is much more significant as a small distance to a local maximum alone. The same was observed for the DLD-score in (Heydebreck er al. (2001)).

4.2   Output of SVM-ISIS

The rows of the matrices in Figures 2–5 show the top scoring bipartitions found by SVM-ISIS. They are ordered by their SVM margin score which is displayed to the right of each row. The columns are arranged according to cancer subtypes with no particular order within these types.

Leukemia dataset. [Figure 2] All three classes are recovered individually: AML in row 4 (3 errors) and row 10 (2 errors), T-cell ALL in row 2 (without error) and B-cell ALL in row 1 (1 error).

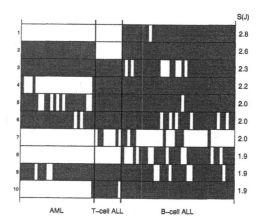

Fig. 2. Partitions of leukemia samples.

Melanoma dataset. [Figure 3] The class distinction identified by Bittner et al. (2000) as biologically meaningful is found in row 3 of the table of partitions with one error.

Lymphoma/leukemia dataset. [Figure 4, Figure 5] First, we tried SVM-ISIS on the dataset by selecting the 50 genes with highest t-statistic for each split. This does not achieve satisfying results: only the split between CLL+FL and DLBCL is found (see in Figure 4: rows 1,2 and 3 with few misclassifications), but none of the classes is detected individually.

In this situation we tried the performance of SVMs on high-dimensional data. Figure 5 shows the results of SVM-ISIS on the data set without feature selection. Row 4 detects CLL and row 8 FL. Even if germinal center B-cell like DLBCL is still not clearly separated from activated B-cell like DLBCL, this is an serious improvement to Figure 4. In the other two data sets doing witut feature selection for each split did not improve the results.

5   Discussion

We have introduced the SVM margin as a criterion to characterize the cancer subtypes represented in three gene expression data sets. Applying this crite-

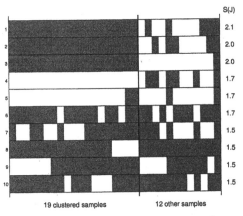

Fig. 3. Partitions of melanoma samples

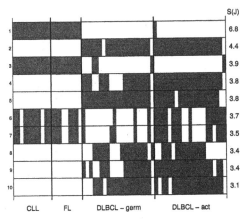

Fig. 4. Partitions of lymphoma/leukemia samples on 50 selected genes

rion, we recovered these subtypes in an unsupervised fashion without using prior knowledge.

The behavior of classification methods on high-dimensional data sets, such as microarray data, is far from being understood. There is the danger of overfitting to training data, if the variance of the parameter estimates determining the classification rule is high. Our results provide empirical evidence that linear SVMs are not very prone to overfitting at least on the microarray data sets studied: The true biological class distinctions are clearly among those with the biggest SVM margin, or, in other words, it is practically impossible for a random bipartition to achieve a similarly large, but meaningless margin.

Further steps in the analysis could be to identify the genes that are differentially expressed across the samples, or to examine the geometry of the separating hyperplane: which samples are support vectors, which violate the margin or are misclassified? By this one can see whether in some samples

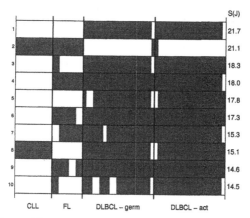

Fig. 5. Partitions of lymphoma/leukemia samples without feature selection

the class assignment is unclear. The stability of the class distinction may be assessed by observing the change in the SVM margin due to reassignments of single samples. Thus, our method provides an auspicious beginning for a more detailed analysis of the data.

References

ALIZADEH et al. (2000): Distinct types of diffuse large B-cell lymphoma identified by gene expression profiling. *Nature, 403, 503-511.*

BITTNER et al. (2000): Molecular classification of cutaneous malignant melanoma by gene expression profiling. *Nature, 406, 536-540.*

CHIPPING FORECAST (1999): The chipping forecast. *Special supplement to Nature Genetics, volume 21.*

DUDOIT, S., FRIDLYAND, J., and SPEED, T. (2002): Comparison of discrimination methods for the classification of tumors using gene expression data. *Journal of the American Statistical Association, 97, 77-87.*

GOLUB et al. (1999): Molecular classification of cancer: Class discovery and class prediction by gene expression monitoring. *Science, 286, 531-537.*

VON HEYDEBRECK,A., HUBER,W., POUSTKA,A. and VINGRON,M. (2001): Identifying splits with clear separation: a new class discovery method for gene expression data. *Bioinformatics, Vol. 17 Suppl.1, S107–S114.*

VAPNIK, V. (1998): *Statistical Learning Theory* Wiley, New York.

Efficient Clustering Methods for Tumor Classification With Microarrays

Jörg Rahnenführer[1]

Max-Planck-Institut für Informatik,
Stuhlsatzenhausweg 85, D-66123 Saarbrücken, Germany

Abstract. Microarray experiments yield expression measurements of thousands of genes simultaneously. One important application is the classification of cancer tumor types. For this task, we present a comparison of hierarchical clustering algorithms, PAM, fanny, k-means and SOM's on two real microarray data sets. Several distance measures are used to build dissimilarity matrices from the data. We introduce the new resampling approach bootstrap-scaling (BOSC) to simulate different amounts of noise in the data. Based on the simulation results, the k-means algorithm and the Manhattan distance give the best results.

1 Introduction

Microarrays measure the abundance of thousands of gene transcripts in two different samples relative to each other (Schena et al. (1995), Shalon et al. (1996)). The interpretation of such data presents an enormous biological and statistical challenge. One major focus with clinical relevance has been on the classification of cancer tissue samples, see e.g. Golub et al. (1999), Bittner et al. (2000) and Ross et al. (2000). Here, the two primary goals are class prediction and class discovery. The first aims at finding fast and reliable methods to distinguish different classes of cancer, which is crucial for the following treatment to maximize efficiency and minimize toxicity. The second aims at finding new classes of cancer by molecular markers.

The statistical methods to address these problems are discriminant analysis and cluster analysis. Discriminant analysis is supervised learning, where class memberships of all objects are known. Cluster analysis is unsupervised learning, where no class labels are known. Objects are then grouped by some measure of similarity, see Gnanadesikan and Kettenring (1989) for an overview. For discriminant analysis, Dudoit et al. (2001) compared three standard algorithms. For cluster analysis, comparisons have been done only for gene clustering, but not for sample clustering. The present paper therefore provides a comparison of hierarchical clustering, PAM (Partitioning around medoids) and fanny (a fuzzy method), each with Euclidean, Manhattan and correlation distance, as well as k-means and SOM's (Self organizing maps).

Yeung et al. (2001b) introduce the figure of merit (FOM) for validation of gene expression clusters. FOM is an estimate of the predictive power of a cluster algorithm. On three microarray data sets, they compare CAST (Cluster Affinity Search Technique, Ben-Dor and Yakhini (1999)), k-means (MacQueen, 1967) and a new heuristic iterative partition algorithm. It turns out that the optimal choice differs between data sets, yet CAST and k-means produce relatively high quality clusters. Bittner et al. (2000) add normal noise with mean 0 to the log-ratios of expression values and re-cluster the results. This distributional assumption seems to be inadequate for typically heavy-tailed microarray data, see Kerr et al. (2000), who propose ANOVA models to estimate relative gene expression and account for other sources of variation in the data. Yeung et al. (2001a) present model-based approaches by adapting different Gaussian mixture models to microarray data. On two data sets with known class labels, they demonstrate superiority of their approach to CAST. A prominent new approach to detect clusters in gene expression data is "Gene shaving", introduced by Hastie et al. (2000). The goal is to find several small (possibly overlapping) groups of genes with small between-gene variance and large between-sample variance. The method is applied successfully for predicting patient survival. Both supervised and unsupervised versions are introduced.

In this paper, as a new objective quality measure for a cluster algorithm, the 'critical stretch factor" (csf) is introduced. Cluster midpoints are calculated and gene values move towards or away from these midpoints. The specific stretch factor that causes a predetermined cluster quality loss is called critical stretch factor. To model data characteristics as precisely as possible, replicates of the original data are drawn by resampling an expression value from the same gene and the same sample (tumor) class only. The use of other resampling procedures, for example based on ANOVA models, will be considered elsewhere. In the present simulation study, cancer data sets with known class labels are used. Thus, external cluster indices as objective criteria for cluster validity are available. Comparisons of algorithms are made with fixed numbers of clusters. The optimal number of clusters is not addressed, for a proposal see Tibshirani et al. (2001), who introduce the gap statistic.

2 Cluster algorithms

All cluster algorithms are run in the statistical programming language R (Hornik (2001)). The algorithms under consideration are hierarchical clustering, k-means, PAM, Fanny and SOM's. Whereas k-means and SOM's take the original data directly as input, the other algorithms allow the choice of a dissimilarity matrix d, that assigns to each pair of objects i_1 and i_2 a value $d(i_1, i_2)$ as their distance. Here, three distance measures are considered: (a) The Euclidean distance between two vectors is the square root of the sum of the squared differences over all coordinates. (b) The Manhattan distance is the sum of the absolute (unsquared) differences over all coordinates. It is well established in robust statistics. (c) The correlation distance is $1\text{-}corr(i_1, i_2)$, where $corr(i_1, i_2)$ is the Pearson correlation of the objects i_1 and i_2.

Average linkage **hierarchical clustering** was the first algorithm used in microarray research to cluster genes (Eisen et al. (1998)). First, each object is assigned to its own cluster. Then, iteratively, the two most similar clusters are joined, representing a new node of the clustering tree. Here, the node is computed as average of all objects of the joined clusters. Then, the similarity matrix is updated with this new node replacing the two joined clusters. This process is repeated until only a single cluster remains. The procedure provides a hierarchy of clusterings, with the number of clusters ranging from 1 to the number of objects n.

K-means is a partitioning algorithm with a prefixed number k of clusters. It tries to minimize the sum of the variances within the k clusters. First introduced by MacQueen (1967), it is widely applied. The algorithm chooses a random sample of k different objects as initial cluster midpoints. Then it alternates between two steps until convergence. 1. Assign each object to its closest of the k midpoints with respect to Euclidean distance. 2. Calculate k new midpoints as the averages of all points assigned to the old midpoints, respectively. Since k-means is a randomized algorithm, two runs usually produce different results. We apply k-means 10 times to the same data set and choose the result with minimal sum of within-cluster-variances.

PAM (Partitioning around medoids) is a partitioning algorithm, and can be seen as a generalization of k-means (Kaufman and Rousseeuw (1990), chapter 2, Struyff et al. (1997)). For an arbitrary dissimilarity matrix d it tries to minimize the objective $\sum_{i=1}^{n} \min_{j=1,...,k} d(i, m_j)$, where the sum is taken over all objects $i = 1, \ldots, n$, and $m_1, \ldots, m_k$ are k cluster midpoints. PAM consists of two steps. In the BUILD phase, initial 'medoids' are constructed: m_1 is the object with the smallest $\sum_{i=1}^{n} d(i, m_1)$ and m_2 to m_k are chosen iteratively such that the objective decreases as much as possible. In the SWAP phase, the following step is repeated until convergence: Consider all pairs of objects (i, j) with $i \in \{m_1, \ldots, m_k\}$ and $j \notin \{m_1, \ldots, m_k\}$ and make the $i \leftrightarrow j$ swap (if any) which decreases the objective most.

Fanny is a fuzzy clustering method (Kaufman and Rousseeuw (1990), chapter 4). For each object i and each cluster v, a membership value u_{iv} indicates how strongly the object belongs to the cluster. The membership values have to be non-negative, and for a fixed object i, the sum over all clusters j is 1. In this way objects are distributed over clusters. Fanny tries to minimize the objective $\sum_{v=1}^{k} [(\sum_{i,j=1}^{n} u_{iv}^2 u_{jv}^2 d(i,j))/(2 \sum_{j=1}^{n} u_{jv}^2)]$ with respect to the membership values u_{ij}. Fanny uses an iterative algorithm to treat the constrained minimization problem by means of Lagrange multipliers. In contrast to other fuzzy methods fanny does not need to calculate averages. Thus a dissimilarity matrix is sufficient input for the algorithm.

SOM's (Self organizing maps) (Kohonen (1984)) are similar to k-means, but with additional constraints. Tamayo et al. (1999) first introduced them to gene clustering. SOM's define a mapping from the input space onto a one- or two-dimensional array of k total nodes. Every node i is associated with a vector m_i in the input space. Iteratively, input vectors v are (randomly) chosen and compared with the prototypes m_i. The closest prototype is moved most towards v, other prototypes are moved less. The magnitude of this shift is determined by a learning rate τ that decreases with the distance of m_i to v and with the iteration number. The algorithm terminates when the process converges or when a fixed number of iterations is reached.

3   Data sets and cluster validity

Two publicly available microarray cancer data sets were analyzed, the Leukemia data set of Golub et al. (1999) and the NCI60 cancer data set of Ross et al. (2000). The **Leukemia data set** (http://www.genome.wi.mit.edu/MPR) consists of 3 different cancer classes, including 25 acute myeloid leukemia (AML) and 47 acute lymphoblastic leukemia (ALL) cases, the latter subdivided into 9 T-cell ALL and 38 B-cell ALL. Gene expression values were measured with Affymetrix high-density oligonucleotide arrays. The same preprocessing steps regarding thresholds and filtering as in the paper were applied. Expression values below 100 and values above 16000 were set to these thresholds. Then genes with $\max / \min \leq 5$ or $(\max - \min) \leq 500$ were excluded, leaving 3571 of 6817 genes. Here, per gene the terms max and min refer to most extreme values across samples. Logarithm with base 10 was applied to eliminate skewness. The **NCI60 data set** (http://genome-www.stanford.edu/nci60) consists of 9 different classes of cancer with 63 total cases, particularly 9 breast, 6 central nervous system, 7 colon, 8 leukemia, 8 melanoma, 9 lung, 6 ovarian, 2 prostate and 8 renal cancers. Here, 9307 gene expression values were measured with cDNA microarrays. The red-fluorescent cDNA targets were prepared from 60 cell lines of the National Cancer Institut's anti-cancer drug program, the green-fluorescent reference targets were a mixture of 12 of those cell lines. The authors excluded genes with more than 2 missing values. Due to this filtering 5244 genes were used in the final analysis. Logarithm with base 2 was applied to the red/green ratios of single genes. Finally, 3.3% missing values were imputed based on a k-nearest neighbor algorithm (here with $k = 5$) with correlation distance.

External cluster indices use given class labels that represent 'correct' *a priori* known group memberships to check the **validity** of a clustering result. These labels are compared with the results of the clustering algorithm. In the absence of such labels, internal indices are used, which measure similarity of objects within clusters and/or dissimilarity between clusters. Most clustering algorithms are especially shaped to optimize internal cluster indices, among those k-means, PAM and fanny. The goal in cluster analysis is to detect consistent groups in data when cluster labels are not known. For both data sets under consideration, true labels are known, which provides objective quality measures and makes the choice of arbitrary internal indices superfluous. Here, the **number of misclassifications** mc was used as external cluster index. It is calculated as follows. Iteratively, search for cluster i and a priori group j with the most common objects, identify them with each other, and then eliminate them from the assignment process. Continue until no more clusters or no more a priori groups are available. The index mc is the difference of the number of all samples and of the number of samples that were assigned during this process. If all clusters represent original groups, mc is 0. Alternatively, the generalized **Rand index** (Rand (1971)), was calculated. The Rand index is a probabilistic measure and did yield similar results, which will be reported elsewhere.

4   BOSC (Bootstrap-scaling) modeling approach

In this chapter, a new method for comparing cluster algorithms is presented. To find the most suitable algorithms to cluster microarray samples, real data sets are used as a basis for realistic models. Purely theoretic probabilistic models are not well worked out yet. Due to the complex structure of microarray data, presently no specific broadly accepted model for cluster structure is available. In microarray experiments, heavy tails of the data distributions make the normal distribution assumption unsuitable. Comparing k-means type algorithms, Rahnenführer (2002) showed that robustifications of the standard k-means algorithm greatly improve the ability to discriminate cancer tumor types based on microarray data. This effect was not observed, when simply Gaussian noise was added to the data. Thus, in the present simulation study replicates were obtained from the original data by drawing gene expression values randomly with replacement from the same gene and the same cancer type. To quantify the noise, expression values are moved on a virtual line to the empirical mean of their cluster.

Definition 4. BOSC (Bootstrap-scaling):
Let $n, p, k, B \in I\!N_{\geq 0}$. Let $(M_{ij})_{i=1..p, j=1..n}$ be a data (gene expression) matrix of dimension $p \times n$ (for p genes and n samples) and $(l_1, \ldots, l_n) \in (1, \ldots, k)^n$ an n-dimensional label vector that assigns every sample to one of k classes (tumor types).

i) For $b \in (1, \ldots, B)$:
Create replicate M_{ij}^b by randomly drawing from all values $M_{i_0 j_0}$ of the original data matrix that fulfill $i_0 = i$ and $j_0 \in \{j : l_j = l_{j_0}\}$.

ii) For $s \in (s_1, \ldots, s_S)$ with $0 < s_1 < s_2 < \ldots < s_S < \infty$:
Define the modified (stretched) replicate $M_{ij}^b(s)$ as

$$M_{ij}^b(s) := (1 - s) \left(\frac{1}{\#\{j_0 : l_j = l_{j_0}\}} \sum_{\{j_0 : l_j = l_{j_0}\}} M_{i j_0} \right) + s\, M_{ij}^b.$$

This means that for fixed stretch factors s new samples are chosen as linear combinations of their cluster prototype and the replicate M_{ij}^b. The value s is called *stretch factor*. For $s = 0$, samples collapse to their prototype, for $s = 1$, they remain unchanged. With growing s, they drift apart more and more, making a distinction between clusters increasingly difficult.

Definition 5. Critical stretch factor (csf):
Let $0 < s_1 < s_2 < \ldots < s_S < \infty$ be a series of stretch factors and $s \rightarrow f(s)$ a cluster validity function, that assigns to each stretch factor s the average value of an external index evaluation according to the BOSC approach. The minimal stretch factor s_i, $i \in \{1, \ldots, S\}$, for which $f(s_i)$ crosses a prefixed bound c is called *critical stretch factor (csf)*.

Several modifications and generalizations are possible: The resampling procedure can be a more sophisticated bootstrap or ANOVA type approach. The midpoints for the correct classes can be chosen as spatial medians instead of means. The critical stretch factor can be replaced by an overall quality measure of the external index function, such as the area under that function. Single object cluster validity can be obtained, for example, by measuring how often an object is clustered with members of its own *a priori* group. And the model for the correct cluster structure could be more complex, for example by representing a class by more than one prototype and then moving an object on the line with the closest of the prototypes of its class.

5   Simulations, results and conclusions

Two versions of k-means were implemented, one with a single run and one with 10 repetitions, keeping the best result. The latter leads to better local optimums of the objective function by eliminating bad starting points. SOM's were applied to the data with default parameters of the contributed R package *GeneSOM* (Kohonen et al.(1995)). The starting positions of the nodes were chosen as a random sample of the objects, and 100.000 (leukemia) respectively 200.000 (NCI60) iteration steps were carried out. To reduce background noise and save computing time, only the 100 (leukemia) respectively 200 (NCI60) genes with the biggest variances across all samples were used. BOSC was implemented with stretch factors 0.1, 0.2, ..., 3.0. For every stretch factor and every algorithm, final results are averages of 100 clustering results.

In Figure 1 and 2, the average numbers of misclassifications are plotted for all algorithms. In the first three plots, line types indicate dissimilarity measures, *solid* for Euclidean, *dashed* for correlation and *dotted* for Manhattan distance. In the bottom right picture, results for k-means are plotted by solid lines, thin for 1 and thick for 10 repetitions, SOM results are plotted as circles. Horizontal dashed lines are drawn at 5 respectively 10 misclassifications. The stretch factor at which this line first is crossed, is the *critical stretch factor*. For **small stretch factors**, k-means with repeated runs is the most successful algorithm. K-means$_1$ (with 1 run only) often gives low quality results, even for extremely small stretch factors. For the leukemia data, hierarchical clustering with correlation distance and PAM with Manhattan distance also yield superior results. Fanny and k-means$_1$ never give reasonable values. SOM's work well for the leukemia data, but fail for the NCI60 data set. Applying the algorithms to the original data without a resampling step in most cases leads to slightly lower *csf*s (data not shown). The basic regime to use

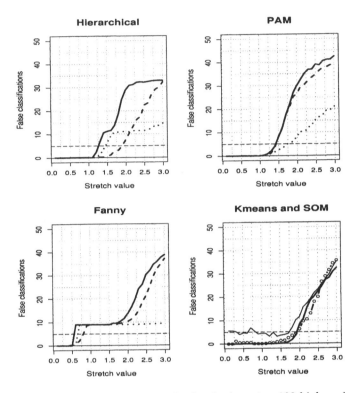

Fig. 1. Number of misclassifications, Leukemia data, top 100 high-variance genes

only high-variance genes also increases clustering quality, but it is unclear if the variance is a good measure for this purpose. The identification of statistically more appropriate and successful ways to preselect good genes is an additional challenge. Both data sets consist of rather well separated classes, such that the choice of a cluster algorithm becomes crucial only for noisy data. Thus, we also have to look at **large stretch factors**. In this case, the Manhattan distance proves to be the most appropriate distance, followed by correlation and Euclidean distance, almost independent of algorithm and data set.

Although PAM with Euclidean distance has the same objective function as k-means, it produces significantly inferior results. The reason must be either in the BUILD phase or in the STEP phase of PAM. Fixed starting points in the BUILD phase should be replaced by random starting points, or the STEP phase of PAM might be less efficient than the alternation used by k-means. If this is the case, then a robustification of the k-means algorithm should yield even better results, since we know that PAM also performs better with the more robust Manhattan distance. SOM's also can be compared to k-means,

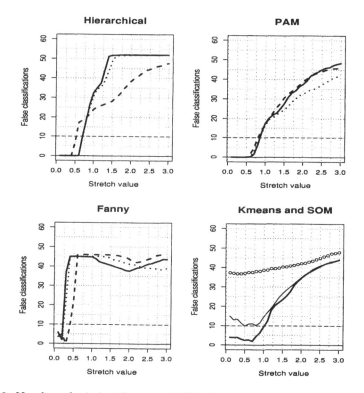

Fig. 2. Number of misclassifications, NCI60 data set, top 200 high-variance genes

since again, in theory, the objective functions are similar. The SOM approach is powerful, but also dangerous, since a SOM heavily depends on parameter adjustment. For example, for the NCI60 data even 200.000 iterations were not sufficient to produce good results.

To summarize, the ability to distinguish cancer tumor types based on gene expression measurements extremely varies between cluster algorithms. But no single winning approach can be identified. K-means and PAM with Manhattan distance perform best, thus a combination, for example a robustification of the k-means algorithm, seems to be most promising.

References

BEN-DOR, A., YAKHINI, Z. (1999): Clustering gene expression patterns, *Proc. 3rd Intern. Conf. on Comput. Biol. (Recomb 99)*, 33-42.
BITTNER, M., MELTZER, P., CHEN, Y., JIANG, Y., SEFTOR, E., HENDRIX, M., RADMACHER, M., SIMON, R., YAKHINI, Z., BEN-DOR, A., SAMPAS, N., DOUGHERTY, E., WANG, E., MARINCOLA, F., GOODEN, C., LUEDERS, J., GLATFELTER, A., POLLOCK, P., CARPTEN, J., GILLANDERS,

E., LEJA, D., DIETRICH, K., BEAUDRY, C., BERENS, M., ALBERTS, D. and SONDAK, V. (2000): Molecular classification of cutaneous malignant melanoma by gene expression profiling, *Nature 406, 536-540.*

DUDOIT, S., FRIDLYAND, J. and SPEED, T.P. (2001): Comparison of Discrimination Methods for the Classification of Tumors Using Gene Expression Data, to appear in *J. Amer. Stat. Assoc. 97, 77-87.*

EISEN, M. B., SPELLMAN, P.T., BROWN, P.O. and BOTSTEIN, D. (1998): Cluster analysis and display of genome-wide expression patterns, *Proc. Natl. Acad. Sci. 95, p.14863-14868.*

GNANADESIKAN, R. and KETTENRING, J. (1989): Discriminant analysis and clustering, *Statistical Science, 4, 34-69.*

GOLUB, T.R., SLONIM, D.K., TAMAYO, P., HUARD, C., GAASENBEEk, M., MESIROV, J.P., COLLER, H., LOH, M.L., DOWNING, J.R., CALIGIURI, M.A., BLOOMFIELD, C.D. and LANDER, E.S. (1999): Molecular classification of cancer: class discovery and class prediction by gene expression monitoring, *Science 286, 531-537.*

HASTIE, T., TIBSHIRANI, R., EISEN, M.B., ALIZADEH, A., LEVY, R., STAUDT, L., CHAN, W.C., BOTSTEIN, D. and BROWN, P. (2000), 'Gene shaving' as a method for identifying distinct sets of genes with similar expression patterns, *Genome Biology, 1(2): research0003.1-0003.21.*

HORNIK, K (2001): *The R FAQ,* http://www.r-project.org/.

KAUFMAN, L. and ROUSSEEUW, P.J. (1990): *Finding groups in data: An introduction to cluster analysis,* Wiley, New York.

KERR, M.K., MARTIN, M. and CHURCHILL, G.A. (2000): Analysis of Variance for Gene Expression Microarray Data, *J. Comp. Biology, 7, 819-837.*

KOHONEN, K. (1984): *Self organization and associative memory,* Springer.

KOHONEN, HYNNINEN, KANGAS, and LAAKSONEN (1995): *SOM-PAK, the Self-Organizing Map Program Package (version 3.1),* http://www.cis.hut.fi/research/papers/som_tr96.ps.Z.

MACQUEEN, J. (1967): Some methods for classification and analysis of multivariate observations, *Proc. 5th Berkeley Sympos. on Math. Stat. and Prob..*

RAHNENFÜHRER, J. (2002): Data Compression and Statistical Inference - Clustering of Gene Expression Microarray Experiments, to appear in *Proc. of MSRI Workshop: Nonlinear Estimation and Classification,* Berkeley.

RAND, W.M. (1971): Objective criteria for the evaluation of clustering methods, *J. Amer. Stat. Assoc., 66, 846-850.*

ROSS, D.T., SCHERF, U., EISEN, M.B., PEROU, C.M., REES, C., SPELLMAN, P., IYER, V., JEFFREY, S.S., VAN DE RIJN, M., WALTHAM, M., PERGAMENSCHIKOV, A., LEE, J.C., LASHKARI, D., SHALON, D., MYERS, T.G., WEINSTEIN, J.N., BOTSTEIN, D. and BROWN, P.O. (2000): Systematic variation in gene expression patterns in human cancer cell lines, *Nature Genet., 24,* 227-235.

SCHENA, M., SHALON, D., DAVIS, R.W. and BROWN, P.O. (1995): Quantitative monitoring of gene expression patterns with a DNA microarray, *Science, 210, 467-470.*

SHALON, D., SMITH, S.J. and BROWN, P.O. (1996): A DNA microarray system for analyzing complex DNA samples using two-color fluorescent probe hybridization, *Genome Res., 6, 639-645.*

STRUYF, A., HUBERT, M. and ROUSSEEUW, P.J. (1997): Integrating robust clustering techniques in S-PLUS, *Comput. Stat. Data Anal., 26, No.1, 17-37.*

TAMAYO, P., SLONIM, D., MESIROV, J., ZHU, Q., KITARREWAN, S., DMITROVSKY, E., LANDER, E.S. and GOLUB, T.R. (1999): Interpreting patterns of gene expression with self-organizing maps: methods and application to hematopoietic differentiation, *Proc. Natl. Acad. Sci. 96, 2907-2912.*

TIBSHIRANI, R., WALTHER, G., HASTIE, T. (2001): Estimating the number of clusters in a dataset via the gap statistic, *J. Royal Stat. Soc. B, 63, 2, 411-423.*

YEUNG, K.Y., FRALEY, C., MURUA, A., RAFTERY, A.E. and RUZZO, W.L. (2001): Model-Based Clustering and Data Transformations for Gene Expression Data, *Bioinformatics, 17, No.10, 977-987.*

YEUNG, K.Y., HAYNOR, D.R., RUZZO, W.L. (2001): Validating Clustering for Gene Expression Data, *Bioinformatics, 17, No.4, 309-318.*

Acknowledgments: This work was supported by the German Research Foundation (DFG) (JR, RA 870/2-1) and through a consultancy on NIH grant RO1HD037 804-04 (Claudia Kappen).

A Method to Classify Microarray Data

Marco Scarnó[1], Donatella Sforzini[1], Alessandra Ulivieri[2], and Sergio Nasi[2]

[1] CASPUR, Consorzio interuniversitario Applicazioni di SuperCalcolo,
Università di Roma *La Sapienza*, P.le A. Moro 5, 00185 Roma, Italy
[2] Istituto di Biologia e Patologia Molecolari CNR,
Università di Roma *La Sapienza*, P.le A. Moro 5, 00185 Roma, Italy

Abstract. DNA microarrays are a technology that is used for monitoring the expression of thousands of genes simultaneously. Microarray data create new opportunities for biomedical sciences but also pose serious challenges for statistical analysis, due to their complexity. Inference of biological meaning from gene expression profiling involves the classification of genes whose expression is correlated to a given functional condition. To test the value of Correspondence Analysis for microarray data classification, we compared gene expression profiles of cells in the presence or absence of a dominant negative Myc mutant. As compared to other microarray analysis methods, this procedures allows the projection of a complex data set into an easily visualized, low dimensional space, in which association between variables (genes) and observations (experiments) can be more easily evaluated. Correspondence Analyisis is a powerful technique for gene-expression data analysis, particularly when combined with other classification techniques.

1 Introduction

The use of microarrays to monitor gene expression is growing exponentially. Major areas of application are the elucidation of cell signalling pathways, the study of brain function, and clinical problems such as transcriptional profiles of tumors. Data processing and analysis still remain a bottleneck: advances in this area have the potential of greatly accelerating biological research, with a powerful impact in clinical diagnostics. Statistical approaches are useful for data validation as well as for grouping genes into functional classes, contributing to a deeper understanding of gene regulation. Several statistical algorithms can be used for comparison between experiments, based on the evaluation of a distance metric between gene expression profiles. The most popular approach involves clustering algorithms, in which similar objects are placed in the same cluster. An alternative are projection algorithms, such as Correspondence Analysis, a method introduced by Benzécri and co-workers for contingency tables (Benzécri (1973)): by these techniques similar objects are placed in the proximity of each other in a projection space. Microarray data are viewed as a *statistical table*, in which relationships between rows (genes), columns (hybridization experiments), or between rows and columns are found and evaluated.

2 Data processing

To test the method, we analyzed data from several microarray hybridization experiments (work in preparation) aimed at elucidating cell regulation by

Myc, whose activity plays a key role in cell proliferation and differentiation and is commonly altered in a wide range of tumors. Myc is a transcription factor that binds to DNA and controls the expression of a large number of target genes: identifying and classifying these genes is thought to be important for understanding the pathways that control the behaviour of normal and tumor cells. In these experiments, the expression profile of 8799 rat genes was compared at different time points (0, 90 and 240 minutes) following serum stimulation of cells in the presence or absence of Omomyc, a mutant protein that interfers with Myc biological activity (Soucek et al. (2002)). In these experiments oligonucleotide arrays (GeneChips) from Affymetrix were used. Such chips represent about half of the studies currently performed with DNA microarrays and are believed to pose less problems for data normalization than other systems utilizing two fluors. Fluorescence intensity data from hybridization experiments were processed with the GeneChip software (from the same company) which involves a Perfect Match/Mismatch probe strategy analyzing a set of probes for the detection of a single transcript.

A probe set for a given gene sequence usually consists of 20 probe pairs, arranged in 40 probe cells: each probe cell is a small square within the microarray, containing a single stranded DNA oligonucleotide, usually 25 bases long. For each probe designed to perfectly match the target sequence, a partner probe is present that is identical except for a single base mismatch at the central position. These probe pairs, called the Perfect Match (PM) and the Mismatch (MM) probes, allow the quantification and subtraction of signals caused by non-specific cross-hybridization. The difference in hybridization signals between the partners, as well as their intensity ratios, serve as indicators of specific target abundance.

Data comparison of different samples is performed in two steps: the first one is an absolute analysis and the second a comparative one, in which a single condition or sample is taken as reference. In particular, absolute analysis calculates a variety of metrics on the fluorescence intensities measured by the scanner. Some utilize intensity data from the entire probe array for background and noise calculations. Others compare the intensities of PM with control MM probe cells for each probe set, which are then used by a decision matrix to determine whether a transcript is Present (P), Marginal (M) or Absent (A). Several values, such as average fluorescence intensity for each probe cell and number of positive and negative probe pairs for each probe set, are taken into account in absolute analysis, and used to compute indexes (i.e. Positive Fraction and Pos./Neg. Ratio) that describe the performance of each probe set. Other indexes are Log Average Ratio and Average Difference, calculated using probe cell intensities directly. The aim of comparative analysis is to identify differences in gene expression profile between experimental and reference arrays for every probe set. The absolute analysis of one hybridization experiment is taken as the source of reference data and a second experiment as the source of experimental data to be compared to the reference. Additional calculations allow to compare gene expression levels. At the end, data from a single microarray hybridization could be represented in a table, as shown in Table 1.

Probe set	PairsinAvg	LogAvg	AbsCall	MaxIncDecRatio	AvgDiffChange	FoldChange
AFFXRatBetaActin3At	20	3.92	P	0.20	6630	1.1
AFFXRat5SrRnaAt	19	1.58	A	0.90	-7118	-7
AFFXRatb1/X12957At	18	0.96	M	0.10	-26	-1
CAI070295GAt	16	4.39	P	0.81	-4452	-4.1
U93306	15	1.90	P	0.56	253	3.8
.	.	.	.	.	.	.

Table 1. Data table from Affimetrix GeneChips. Genes are indicated in the first column; the meaning of other indexes is summarized in the text.

The last column, Fold Change, is the most relevant for comparative analysis since it represents an indicator of the relative change of expression of each gene represented on the probe array. Fold change depends on several factors such as average level of gene expression, array type and noise of the experiment. In particular Fold change has the form:

$$FoldChange = \frac{\overline{Diff_{\exp}} - \overline{Diff_{base}}}{\max\left[\min\left(\overline{Diff_{\exp}}, \overline{Diff_{base}}\right), Q_m * Q_c\right]} +$$

$$+ \left\{ \begin{array}{l} +1 \text{ if } \overline{Diff_{\exp}} >= \overline{Diff_{base}} \\ -1 \text{ if } \overline{Diff_{\exp}} < \overline{Diff_{base}} \end{array} \right\}$$

where:

Q_m is a constant equal to 2.1 or 2.8 according to different type of arrays used; Q_c is the maximum value between Q_{exp}, the noise of the experiments, and Q_{base}, the noise of the baseline;

$$\overline{Diff_{\exp}} = \frac{\sum (PM - MM)}{\text{Pairs in Avg}}$$

is the Average Difference calculated on the experiment and $\overline{Diff_{base}}$ is the same indicator calculated on the reference.

Fold change is a positive number if gene expression (transcript abundance) is increased, and a negative number if it is decreased with respect to the reference sample. True differences in gene expression can be hidden by the potential presence of a large number of random and systematic errors in a microarray experiment. Other difficulties are the consequence of the small number of experiments relative to the large number of variables. Only differences in expression that exceed a threshold defined by the presence of noise can be considered statistically significant. By data filtering, only data above the threshold (usually set at a Fold change value of 3 for data obtained with Affymetrix chips) are kept for further analysis. For comparison of different hybridizations, data are displayed in a table in which rows represent genes and columns hybridization experiments: the value of each cell is the Fold change of a single gene in a single experiment. Six experimental conditions were taken into account in our experiments, as defined by the presence (+) or absence (-) of the Omomyc mutant at three time points: 0, 90 and 240 min. Since the GeneChips contained 8799 gene sequences, the data table was a *8799 x 6* matrix.

3 Microarray data analysis

Data analysis methods are aimed at defining groups of genes with similar expression profiles in a given set of conditions. One of the most widely used techniques is hierarchical clustering based on pairwise average linkage. Usually this method evaluates the distances between rows (genes) by an Euclidean distance metric. The hierarchical tree (dendrogram) that is formed can be graphically displayed (Figure 1); by convention each gene is represented by a single column, each experimental condition is represented by a single row (Eisen et al. (1998)).

Fig. 1. Tree of associations obtained using Cluster Analysis (Eisen et al. (1998)). Different colors are used to explain the meaning of each cluster, separate clusters are indicated by colored bars and by identical coloring of the corresponding region of the dendogram.

Hierarchical clustering is well suited for analyzing associations between genes, for instance in time course studies. On the other hand, Correspondence Analysis appears to provide a more direct way for revealing the association between genes and experiments, as also reported by other authors (Fallenberg et al. (2001)). Easily evaluating such associations may be of great value in the analysis of clinical samples, where it is important to find out which genes better characterize a given pathological condition.

4   Correspondence analysis (CA)

The underlying idea is to study the relationship between rows and columns (genes and hybridizations, in the case of microarrays experiments), by embedding them in the same virtual space. Rows (genes) and columns (experiments) are *independent* when row values do not change in correspondence to different column values. Therefore, a *perfect independence* condition holds when all genes display the same expression value (e.g. the same Fold change) in all hybridizations. Vice versa, a *perfect dependence* condition is present when each gene has an expression value different from zero in only one hybridization. Obviously these are extreme cases, but CA can measure the *distance* between the *perfect independence* condition and the real case and evaluate the influence of each column to the determination of each row, or vice versa. Moreover, the original data can be reconstructed at a desired level of *information loss*, making it possible to *drop* the part of information supposedly due to experimental errors. Correspondence Analysis takes as input a data set of positive values, a condition not strictly necessary but that simplifies the technique. The original data matrix is normalized and the normalized matrix is decomposed by means of algebraic approaches (see Fallenberg et al. (2001) for a detailed description).

Let $\mathbf{X}$ denote the original data matrix, composed by n rows (genes) and m columns (hybridizations). Such matrix has to be normalized according to row and column profiles $\mathbf{R}_p$ and $\mathbf{C}_p$ (i.e. the total of each row and column values) where $\mathbf{R}_p$ is a n-dimensional vector and $\mathbf{C}_p$ a m-dimensional vector.

The product $\mathbf{R}_p\mathbf{C}_p'$ is again a $n \times m$ matrix. Let $\mathbf{Z}$ denote the normalization of $\mathbf{X}$:

$$\mathbf{Z} = \mathbf{X}\left(\mathbf{R}_p\mathbf{C}_p'\right)^{-\frac{1}{2}}.$$

$\mathbf{Z}$ is also an $n \times m$ matrix that can be decomposed into a product of three matrices: $\mathbf{Z} = \mathbf{U}\mathbf{\Sigma}\mathbf{V}'$, by using the Singular Value Decomposition. $\mathbf{U}$ and $\mathbf{V}$ are two matrices of dimension $n \times n$ and $m \times m$, respectively, composed by eigenvectors. $\mathbf{\Sigma}$ is a $n \times m$ *diagonal* matrix of s diagonal elements (where s = min (n,m)) named the singular values of $\mathbf{\Sigma}$ (we indicate with σ_j the j-th element of this matrix, in the hypothesis that $\sigma_1 > \sigma_2 > \ldots \sigma_s$).

Chosen a dimension k, such that $k \leq s$, it is possible to consider the first k eigenvectors of $\mathbf{V}$, the k singular values of $\mathbf{\Sigma}$ and the first k eigenvectors $\mathbf{U}$.

The matrix $\mathbf{Z}_{n,m} = \mathbf{U}_{n,k}\mathbf{\Sigma}_{k,k}\mathbf{V}_{m,k}'$ is again an $n \times m$ matrix, but its values differ from the original matrix. It is possible to measure the amount of total information that is kept upon the reduction into k dimensions by considering the % inertia (I):

$$\%I = 100 \cdot \frac{\sum_{i=1}^{k} \sigma_i^2}{\sum_{i=1}^{s} \sigma_i^2}$$

Chosen an appropriate k (most frequently $k = 2$ or 3) it is possible to project rows and columns into a k dimensional *compromise space*, in which distances between each couple of rows or columns can be easily determined. In microarray data analysis, it is important to be able to find associations between rows (genes) and columns (hybridizations). It is well known, however, that the Euclidean distance between their projections is not very meaningful.

We can consider each row or column projection as a vector r_i or c_j, where i=1,..,n and j=1,..,m originating from the centroid of the data, and take into account the angle α between such vectors (see Figure 2) The scalar product of such vectors can be taken as a measure of association between rows and columns. More in detail we can consider $d_{ij} = < r_i, c_j > = \cos \alpha \, \|r_i\| * \|c_j\|$ and compute all scalar products for each row-projection by varying the index j: we will associate r_i to the column-projection that has the biggest value of d_{ij}.

If there are more than one columns-projections having the same angle α for a single r_i, the vector r_i will be associated to the column-projection with the biggest norm. This seems reasonable because the column-projection with the biggest norm gives the highest contribution to the total inertia of the column point and can be considered as an *attractor*.

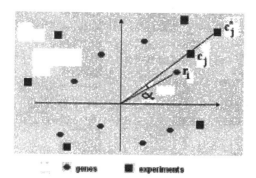

Fig. 2. Example of rows and columns projections into the compromise space. In this case r_i will be associated to the column indicated by its projection c_j*; this is due to the high contribution of this column to the scalar product with r_i

As already mentioned, CA algorithms require a data matrix of positive values. Fold change values (columns) of microarrays experiments, however, can take negative values when gene expression is repressed relative to the control. To avoid this problem, the original negative columns are split into two parts made only of positive values and representing, respectively, activated and repressed genes. That is, from COLj we construct COLj(-) and COLj(+) using:

$$if COL_{ij} < 0 \Rightarrow COL_{ij}^{(-)} = abs\,(COL_{ij})\ \ and\ COL_{ij}^{(+)} = 0$$

$$if COL_{ij} >= 0 \Rightarrow COL_{ij}^{(-)} = 0\ and\ COL_{ij}^{(+)} = (COL_{ij})$$

5   Experimental results and conclusion

Results of correspondence analysis on our microarray data are shown in Figure 3, in which genes and six experimental conditions (as already explained at the end of pharagraph 2) are plotted together in a plane (k=2); this projection explains a percentange of Inertia equal to 80In the upper part of the figure there are all the genes (8799) regarding our microarray, in the bottom part 4 there are the genes (1473) obtained by data filtering with a Fold change threshold equal to 3.

The relationship between genes and experiments can be easily visualized by calculating the scalar product mentioned before. It is also possible to spot genes whose expression is strongly linked to a single experimental condition, or genes that can be associated to more than one condition. We also analyzed the same data with a hierarchical Clustering algorithm (Cluster and Tree-View sofware, (Eisen et al. (1998)), and the results were compared to those of CA. Table 2 shows a comparison of the two techniques results. In particular we have choosen 292 genes as respressed in the presence of Omomyc after 90 minutes of serum treatment from tree association.

According to correspondence analysis, 234 genes (80% of the total selected) were best characterized by the property of being repressed at 90 min, whereas the remaining 20% was attributed to different categories.

Overall, a similar composition of clusters was obtained with both methods, but the interpretation of the meaning of the clusters was more straightforward with CA. Concerning the possibility to evaluate the difference between our method and the most common clustering techniques, cross validation can be taken as a more stringent criterion for gene classification.

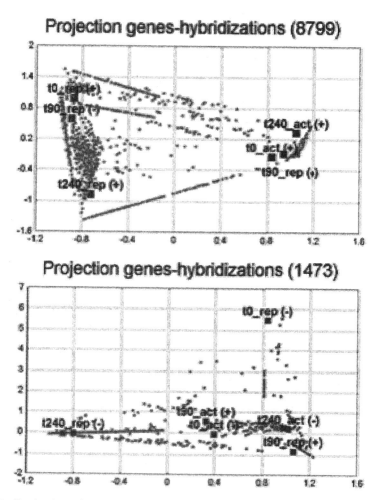

Fig. 3. Projection of hybridizations and genes into the *compromise space*. All the 8799 genes present in the macroarray are shown in the upper part of the figure. Only the genes (1473) filtered by a Fold Change threshold of 3 are shown in the bottom part. Six experimental conditions were taken into account in the experiments, as defined by the presence (+) or absence (-) of the Omomyc mutant at three time points (t): 0, 90 and 240 min; *Act* and *rep* indicate, respectively, activated and repressed genes subsets

688   Scarnó et al.

Omomyc (Presence (+); Absence (-))	Time (min.)	Activated (A)	Repressed (R)	Total
+	0	4	7	11
-	90	5	6	11
+	90	16	234	250
-	240	2	14	16
+	240	3	1	4
Total	.	30	262	292

Table 2. A comparison between results obtained from CA and Cluster + TreeView Software; 234 genes identified by CA belongs also to the cluster of genes identified by TreeView Software

References

BENZÉCRI, J.P. (1973): *L'Analyse des Donnes*. Dunod, Paris.
EISEN, M. B., SPELLMAN, P. T., BROWN, P. O. & BOTSTEIN, D. (1998): *Cluster analysis and display of genome-wide expression patterns*. Proc. Natl. Acad. Sci. **95**, 14863-14868, USA
FELLENBERG, K., HAUSER N. C., BENEDIKT B., NEUTZER A., HOHEISEL, J. D & VINGRON M. (2001): *Correspondence Analysis applied to microarray data*. Proc. Natl. Acad. Sci. **98**, 10781-10786, USA
GREENACRE, M. J. (1984): *Theory and Applications of Correspondence Analysis*. Academic, London.
SOUCEK L., JUCKER R., PANACCHIA L., RICORDY R., TATÒ F. & NASI S. (2002): *Omomyc, a potential Myc dominant negative, enhances Myc-induced apoptosis*. Cancer Research **62**, 3507-3510.

Index

13-Term Henderson Smoothing Filter, 13

Additive Interaction Terms, 22
Agnostic Learning, 492
Algorithm, 209
ALS, 226
Alternating Least Squares, 226
Amenta, P., 100, 201
Anthropology, 348
Archaeology, 624, 633
archaeometry, 74
Aria, M., 369
Association Rules, 421
Asymmetric Correlation Measure, 447
Atkinson, A., 3

B2B, 421
Baier, D., 430, 530
Baragona, R., 133
Bartel, H.-G., 74
Battaglia, F., 133
Bayesian Dynamic Linear Models, 358
Bayesian Hierarchical Models, 165
Bayesian Inference, 313
Bayesian Neural Networks, 378
Becker, C., 279
Bee Dagum, E., 13
Berghoff, S., 118
Bernoulli Trials With Dependance, 261
Bezerra, B.L.D., 395
Biebler, K.-E., 127
Binary Variables, 127
Biplot, 30
Bock, H.H., 143
Boley, D., 57
Bondarenko, J., 521
Boolean Symbolic Objects, 218
Bootstrap-Scaling, 670
Bouchard, G., 155
Box-Cox Transformation, 3
Bozza, S., 165, 378
Branger, N., 521
bronzes from Luristan, 74

Brunnert, M., 615
Brusch, M., 530

Calò, D.G., 83
Camiz, S., 624, 633
Cancer Studies, 662
Canonical Variate Analysis, 30
Capdevila, C., 643
Categorical Predictor Variables, 30
Cerioli, A., 3, 49
Ceulemans, E., 173, 296
Change-Points, 261
Changed Segments, 261
Chavez-Demoulin, V.C., 387
Chiogna, M., 182
Choice Models, 595
Class Discovery, 662
Classification, 3, 173, 270, 296, 570
Classification And Regression Trees, 321
Classification Error, 92
Classification Of Pitch Deviation, 118
Classification Tree, 65
Cluster, 680
Cluster Algorithms, 670
Cluster Analysis, 3, 39, 49, 133, 587
cluster analysis, 74
Clusterhomogeneity, 270
Clustering, 127, 483, 561
Clustering Of Vocal Performance Quality, 118
Clusterwise Regression, 155
Colomer, M.A., 643
Comparative Analysis, 578
Composite IndicatorLinear Ordering, 578
Computer Intensive Data Analysis, 305
Conde, J., 643
Confidence Intervals, 555
Confounding Effect, 652
Conjoint Analysis, 530
Connected Shapes, 244
Consensus Tree, 65
Constructivism, 235

Consumer Behavior, 412, 421, 595
Convex Hulls, 244
Corbellini, A., 49
Correspondance Analysis, 680
Correspondence Analysis, 329
Credit Risk Models, 546, 555
Credit Scoring, 604
Creditworthiness, 570
Critchley, F., 191
Cross Reference Matrix, 492
Cubic Smoothing Spline, 13
Customer Relationship Management, 538

D'Ambra, L., 201
D'Enza, A.I., 288
Data Analysis, 226, 405
Data Clustering, 501
Data Mining, 447, 483, 538
data preparation, 74
Datamining, 387
De Cantis, S., 652
de Carvalho, F. de A. T., 395
de Souto, M.C.P., 510
Decision Tree, 447, 538
Default Probabilities, 546
Demicheli, L., 438
Dendrogram, 191
Density Estimation, 39
Digital Libraries, 412
Dimensionallty Reduction Methods, 201
Discriminant Analysis, 109, 127, 321
Discrimination, 92, 570
Discriminative Clustering, 456
Dissimilarity Measures, 670
Distributed Systems, 412
Divisive Partitioning, 57
DNA Computing, 643
DNA Sequences, 261
Dolata, J., 74
Durand, J.-F., 22
Dziechciarz, J., 578

E-Commerce, 430
E-Learning, 430
EM Algorithm, 133, 155, 252
Esser, A., 521
Estimation, 546

Etschberger, S., 209
Evaluation, 421
evaluation of objekts, 74
Evolutionary, 209
Evolutionary Monte Carlo, 378
Exploratory Data Analysis, 118
Extreme Value Theory, 387

Factorial Symbolic Data Analysis, 244
Filter Algorithm, 615
Finacnial Data, 561
Forward Search, 3
Frequentist Probability, 235
Friesen, K., 405
Fritzke, B., 252
Functional Data, 49

Gaetan, C., 182
Galimberti, G., 83
Gardner, S., 30
Gating Network, 155
Gaussian Kernel, 13
Gaussian Mixture Model, 155
Gene Expression, 670
Gene Expression Data, 662
Generalized Additive Model, 387
Generalized Least Squares, 83
Generative Topographic Mapping, 501
Genetic, 209
Genetic Algorithms, 133
Genetic Algotithms, 378
Genome Analysis, 337
Geyer-Schulz, A., 412, 421
Giordani, P., 218
GIS, 438
Göcks, M., 430
Goodness Of Fit, 235
Graphical Models, 279
Graphical Representations, 288
Güttner, J., 118

Hader, S., 39
Hahsler, M., 412, 421
Hamprecht, F. A., 39
Hansohm, J., 226
Hasse-Becker, P., 118
Hennig, C., 235
Hermes, B., 438
Hidden Markov Models, 561

Hierarchical Classes Analysis, 173, 296
Hierarchical Clustering, 191
High Dimensional Data, 57
Hilbert, A., 209, 447, 538
Höse, S., 546, 555
Horizontal Ordering, 191
Hoshino, T., 595
Huschens, S., 546, 555
Hybrid Learning, 464

Iannitto, E., 652
Image Data, 624, 633
Imaizumi, T., 587
Incomplete Data, 329
Independant Component Analysis, 501
Influential Cases, 109
Information Filtering, 395
Information Metric, 456
Information Retrieval, 438, 473
Ingrassia, S., 49
IPF Procedure, 329
Irpino, A., 244
Iswanto, B. H., 252

Jäger, B., 127
Jarvis, S.A., 387

k-Tangent Algorithm, 143
Kalian Filter, 358
Kaski, S., 456
Knab, B., 561
Kossa, W., 570
Krahnke, T., 615
Krauth, J., 261
Kriging, 358
Krolak-Schwerdt, S., 270
Kuhnt, S., 279
Kullback-Leibler Information, 143
Kwiatkowska-Ciotucha, D., 578

Latent Budget, 369
Latent Factor Models, 305
Lauro, C., 244
Lauro, C.N., 288
Lavalle, C., 438
LBG-U Algorithm, 252
Learner Records, 405
Learning Metrics, 456
Learning Systems, 405

Ligges, U., 118
Linear Discriminant Analysis, 604
Linear Factor Discriminant, 100
Linear Model, 155
Littau, D., 57
Localised Mixture of Experts, 155
Locally Weighted Regression, 13
Logfiles, 387
Logistic Regression, 604
Lombardi, L., 296
Lombardo, R., 22, 201
Longitudinal Data, 83
Louw, N., 109
Luati, A., 13
Ludermir, T. B., 464
Ludermir, T.B., 510
Luebke, K., 305

Mantovan, P., 313, 378
Manufacturing Branches Attractive-
    ness, 578
Market Segmentation, 595
Marketing, 538
Marketing Research, 530
Markowetz, M., 662
Masked Outliers, 3
Matching Function, 395
MCMC, 165, 378
MCMC inference, 182
MCMC Methods, 358
MDS, 209, 587
Mean Difference, 321
Mendola, D., 652
Methods Of Classification, 348
Microarray, 670
Microarray Data, 337
Microarrays, 680
Miglio, R., 65
Miret, J., 643
Missing Values, 570
Mixture Density Estimation, 252
Mixture Model, 155
Mixture Models, 133
Mixture of Experts, 155
Modal Symbolic Objects, 395
Monari, P., 321
Montanari, A., 321
Mooijaart, A., 369
Mucha, H.-J., 74

Multicollinear Data, 92
Multidimensional, 209
Multimedia, 430, 530
Multivariate Analysis, 226
Multivariate B-spline, 22
Multiway Data Analysis, 173, 296

Nasi, S., 680
Neumann, A., 412
Neural Network, 369, 510
Neural Networks, 464, 570
Nonparametric Classification, 127
Normalized Gaussian Network, 155

O'Hagan, A., 165
Ohmori, T., 595
Okada, A., 587
Optimal Scaling, 226
Optimization, 92
Ordinary Least Squares, 201
Osteoarchaeology, 348
Outliers, 279

Pärna, K., 329
Palumbo, F., 288
Parafac, 218
Parallel Coordinates, 288
Partition, 65
Pastore, A., 313
Perera, R., 387
Phenotypic Variability, 348
Pillati, M., 83
PLS Regression, 100
PLS via Spline Regression, 22
Pouwels, B., 92
Power Functions, 643
Prediction Oriented Projections, 305
Predictive Power, 305
PRESS Criterion, 22
Principal Component Analysis, 218
Principal Components, 321
Protein Structure, 615
Prudêncio, R. B. C., 464
Purchase Data, 587

Quadratic Hedging, 521
Quasi-Independence, 329

Radial Basis Function Networks, 83

Rahnenführer, J., 670
Rapp, R., 473
Rating Variables, 546, 555
Real-Time Prediction, 313
Recommender Services, 412, 421
Recommender Systems, 395
Redundancy PLS, 100
references, 74
Regression Trees, 83
Repeat-Buying, 421
Reversals, 30
Riani, M., 3
Risk Management, 521
Robin, S., 337
Robustness, 3
Roehrl, A.S.A., 387
Röver, C., 92
Roux, N., 30
Rova, E., 624, 633

Sabatier, R., 100
Sampling Plans, 643
Scaling, 209
Scarnó, M., 680
Schebesch, K. B., 604
Schiavo, R.A., 378
Schlag, C., 521
Schliep, A., 561
Schmiedl, S.W., 387
Schmitz, H., 405
Second-Order Integration Effect, 652
Self-Managed Learning, 405
Sensitivity Analysis, 279
Sensorial Data, 369
Separability, 165
Sequencing, 337
Sforzini, D., 680
Shigemasu, K., 595
Shrinkage Regression Methods, 201
Siciliano, R., 369
Simulated Annealing, 305, 378, 510
Simulation Study, 670
Single-Factor Portfolio Model, 546, 555
Sinkkonen, J., 456
Smoothing Splines, 387
Sołtysiak, A., 348
Soffritti, G., 65
Sondergaard, M.P., 387
Space-Time Models, 165

Spatz, A., 538
St.Clair, C., 483
State Space Models, 313
State-Space Model, 615
State-space models, 182
Steckemetz, B., 561
Stecking, R., 604
Steel, S., 109
Stempfhuber, M., 438
Structural Zeros, 329
Subjectivist Probability, 235
Support Vector Machines, 604, 662
Switching Regression, 155
Symbolic Analysis, 49
Symbolic Coding, 633
Symbolic Objects, 288

Tabu Search, 510
Tamir, R., 492
Textual Coding, 624
Thede, A., 412, 421
Theis, W., 92
Thesaurus, 492
Threshold Function, 492
Tonellato, S.F., 358
Transvariation, 321
Tree Topology, 65
Tucker3, 218
Tulli, V., 633

Tumor Classification, 670
Two- and Three-modally Data Analysis, 270
Two-Way Clustering, 143

Ulivieri, A., 680
Unsupervised Clustering, 57
Unsupervised Learning, 501
Urfer, W., 615
Usefulness Metric, 483
User Interface, 438

Van Mechelen, I., 173, 296
Variable Selection, 109
Vector Quantization, 456
Verde, R., 244
Viroli, C., 501
Visualization, 209, 244
Vivien, M., 100
Vocal Time Series, 118
von Heydebreck, A., 662

Weihs, C., 118, 305
Wichern, B., 561
Wodny, M., 127

Yamazaki, A., 510

Zaragoza, A., 643
Ziggurat Decomposition, 191

Printing: Strauss GmbH, Mörlenbach
Binding: Schäffer, Grünstadt